Better Homes and Gardens®

New Complete Guide to

HOME REPAIR

& IMPROVEMENT

Better Homes and Gardens® Books
Des Moines, Iowa

Better Homes and Gardens® Books
An imprint of Meredith® Books

New Complete Guide to Home Repair and Improvement
Editor: Benjamin W. Allen
Research, Writing, and Illustrations for the updated edition: Charlie Wing
Contributing Editors: Steven Cooper, Steven Mumford, William L. Nolan, James Sanders
Associate Art Director: Tom Wegner
Copy Chief: Angela K. Renkoski
Contributing Copy Editor: Kim Catanzarite
Contributing Proofreader: Sharon L. Emmons
Contributing Illustrator: Harijs Priekulis
Electronic Production Coordinator: Paula Forest
Editorial and Design Assistants: Judy Bailey, Susan McBroom, Jennifer Norris, Karen Schirm
Production Director: Douglas M. Johnston
Production Manager: Pam Kvitne
Prepress Coordinator: Marjorie J. Schenkelberg

Meredith® Books
Editor in Chief: James D. Blume
Design Director: Matt Strelecki
Managing Editor: Gregory H. Kayko
Editor, Shelter Books: Denise Caringer
Director, New Product Development: Ray Wolf

Vice President, General Manager: Jamie L. Martin

Better Homes and Gardens® **Magazine**
Editor in Chief: Jean LemMon
Executive Building Editor: Joan McCloskey

Meredith Publishing Group
President, Publishing Group: Christopher M. Little
Vice President and Publishing Director: John P. Loughlin

Meredith Corporation
Chairman of the Board: Jack D. Rehm
President and Chief Executive Officer: William T. Kerr

Chairman of the Executive Committee: E.T. Meredith III

Cover photograph: Tony Kubat Photography

All of us at Better Homes and Gardens® Books are dedicated to providing you with the information and ideas you need to enhance your home. We welcome your comments and suggestions about this book. Write to us at: Better Homes and Gardens® Books, Do-It-Yourself Editorial Department, LN-112, 1716 Locust St., Des Moines, IA 50309–3023.

Note to the Reader: Due to differing conditions, tools, and individual skills, Meredith Corporation assumes no responsibility for any damages, injuries suffered, or losses incurred as a result of following the information published in this book. Before beginning any project, review the instructions carefully, and if any doubts or questions remain, consult local experts or authorities. Because codes and regulations vary greatly, you always should check with authorities to ensure that your project complies with all applicable local codes and regulations. Always read and observe all of the safety precautions provided by any tool or equipment manufacturer, and follow all accepted safety procedures.

HOW TO USE THIS BOOK

The *New Complete Guide to Home Repair and Improvement* has all the information you need to keep your house running smoothly, presented in an easily accessible way.

A general table of contents listed on pages 6 and 7 shows you how the book is divided into four broad sections—"Inside Your Home," "Outside Your Home," "Your Home's Systems," and "Basics You Should Know." This general table of contents allows you to quickly assess areas of the book that might be helpful at the beginning of any home repair or improvement project.

If you want to know more about a specific project, you can go straight to the more detailed table of contents that describes each section. Each of the four sections begins with a page-by-page listing that helps you find exactly what you want to know about a particular subject without hunting through unrelated material.

If you're not sure where to look for information, turn to the index at the end of the book.

Highlighted features about tools, materials, hints, and special techniques are placed throughout the book so you can immediately

see the information when following the steps of a project.

Each project is clearly laid out in a step-by-step fashion so you can easily follow the process and know at a glance what's involved in each project. We also highlight the estimated time commitment, skill level required, and tools you'll need, letting you know what you're getting into before you start.

We've also included page references to related information, enabling you to quickly assess the implications of each project you do.

Special Features

MATERIAL MATTERS PROS AND CONS

When there's a question about the best material to use for a job, we show you the choices you face and the pros and cons of each material.

TOOL TALK SPECIAL INSTRUCTIONS

If you'll need to use special tools not commonly found in a homeowner's toolbox, we tell you about them in Tool Talk.

HELPFUL HINTS TIPS

Tricks of the trade can make all the difference in helping you do a job quickly and well. Helpful Hints gives you tips on how to make the job easier.

TIMELY TECHNIQUES GETTING RESULTS

When a project requires a special technique, Timely Techniques calls your attention to the fine details so you get the results you want.

YOU'LL NEED...

Each project includes a feature called You'll Need... that lists the skills, time, and tools needed to complete the project. This information helps you quickly see the extent of the project so you can decide if you're ready to tackle it.

BEFORE YOU START

ZONING, BUILDING CODES, AND PERMITS

Your first step is to check the zoning regulations, building codes, and permits that regulate all home improvement projects. All three types of regulations are based on national models, but can vary substantially depending on where you live.

Zoning

Zoning regulations determine the type of construction you can do on your property. Some homeowners may resent a local government telling them what they can or can't do. But you should be aware that zoning regulations are there to protect everyone's property rights. For instance, zoning regulations may prohibit your neighbor from building an unsightly wall right on the edge of your property.

Codes

Building codes determine how your home improvement work should be done. These regulations are based on a national standard that sets a minimum level that must be met during construction. Any do-it-yourselfer with an eye to quality and long-term results will want to meet or exceed the building codes, so they usually don't cause you to spend more money than you want to. Building codes vary substantially from region to region based on differing conditions. For example, construction techniques required for earthquake-prone areas are different than other areas, and construction in areas that are consistently wet may require weather-resistant materials in outdoor applications. Whenever you're undertaking home improvements, make sure you know what and how your local building codes apply to your project.

Permits and Inspections

Permits are required by some local governments before you begin home improvements, so get your permits in order before you begin the work.

Often you'll be required to have your work inspected by the local building department. Keep in mind the inspectors are helping you get the job done right. Be open and friendly with them so they are your allies and don't become an obstacle to completing the project.

What to Do

Finding out about the regulations you need to follow is easy. Just call the building departments of your city or county. These departments are almost always listed in the government section of your local phone book.

The consequences of ignoring these regulations can be harsh: You may be required to have the work professionally checked, or you may be required to tear out the work. Also, insurance companies may balk at paying a claim for damage done to your house if you have not followed the regulations.

MINIMIZING THE MESS OF HOME IMPROVEMENT

All do-it-yourselfers start with the beautiful final results in mind, but all must recognize there will be a point in any home improvement project where you must create some mess. It may just be spattered paint from a roller, or it may be the dust and debris of a major renovation. In all cases it's a good idea to think of how to minimize the trash before the triumph of a completed project.

If your project creates a lot of sawdust or will produce plaster dust, use plastic sheets and duct tape to seal off the area so the dust doesn't spread to the rest of the house. Also, remove furniture from nearby areas or, at the very least, cover it with a drop cloth. If your project involves the exterior of a house, protect prized plants with drop cloths or put up barriers so you don't accidentally damage the plants.

If your project will produce lots of trash, plan a way to get the trash out of the house and into a dumpster outside. Also, lay down plastic sheets or cardboard to protect the floors so you don't damage them when removing the trash. Although considering a way to get trash out of the house may only apply to big projects, just thinking about how to store the trash you create will make cleanup easier after even the smallest jobs.

If you don't own a large shop vacuum, rent or borrow one to help with the cleanup afterward.

STAYING SAFE

Although home improvement projects can give you a sense of accomplishment and provide economic savings, they also can be dangerous. Many projects call for sharp tools or power tools that can cause injuries, or they place you in a precarious position, such as up on a ladder. Let common sense be your guide. If you're unsure how to minimize the danger, read more about the project you have in mind, or talk to local authorities or experts.

If you're using a power tool, read the instruction manual and follow the manufacturer's safety cautions.

Materials you cut will splinter, and particles may be thrown as you work. Err on the side of protection and wear protective eye gear if you think the work may produce small projectiles. Also wear protective clothing, such as long sleeves, long pants, and gloves to protect your skin, unless the extra clothing hinders your handling of tools.

Don't overexert yourself when handling heavy objects. Get a helper to lift heavy objects.

If you're working with electricity, learn how to shut off the power at the breaker box and how to test to make sure the electricity is off. Let everyone in the house know you're working on the electricity and put a sign on the box so no one turns the power back on in the middle of your project.

When working on a ladder, don't lean away from the center of the ladder. Keep your body weight between the sides of the ladder. It may take longer to get off the ladder and move it to reach farther, but it is well worth your time. Falls are one of the most common causes of injuries in the home.

WHEN YOU WORK WITH PROFESSIONALS

This book is designed for avid do-it-yourselfers. If you are the kind of homeowner who wants to help only with planning a project and doing the finishing touches after the majority of the work is done, be realistic about your do-it-yourself abilities. Read the instructions for projects in this book and decide if you can do the job. If you decide you need a professional, read the tips below.

Hiring a Contractor

If you hire a contractor for a larger home improvement project, use the following tips to help you choose one wisely.
■ Get the names of several contractors by asking friends for recommendations.
■ Get rough estimates from all contractors who interest you. It will help you narrow the field of candidates and judge how candid they are about money matters.
■ Get at least three bids. Give a contractor about three weeks to produce the bid. Read the bids closely. Review any bid markedly

different from the others, low or high, with healthy skepticism.
■ When accepting bids, find out how long the contractor has been in business—the longer the better. Ask who finances the contractor's company (usually it's a bank). Call and ask the bank about the contractor's solvency. You don't want a contractor to go bankrupt in the middle of your project. Determine if the contractor carries insurance. Every contractor's insurance should, at a minimum, cover property damage, liability, and workers' compensation.

Contracts

Once you've chosen a bid, you need to negotiate a contract. Contracts should contain these elements:
■ **Description of the work.** The description should include all work to be done and specify the type of materials and finishes. A good contract also addresses sticky points—such as weather-related delays or change orders—so everyone knows how they will be handled.

■ **Price.** Fixed-price contracts should specify the total cost of the job. Cost-plus contracts should specify the cost of materials and labor costs.
■ **Pay schedule.** This part of a contract spells out when you will pay the contractor.
■ **Dates.** A schedule of when work begins and ends should be specified.
■ **Right of recision.** This provision gives the homeowner the right to back out of a contract within 72 hours of signing.
■ **Certificate of insurance.** This section guarantees that the contractor has appropriate insurance and names the insurance agent.
■ **Warranty.** Look for a guarantee that the labor and materials are free from defects, preferably up to a year.
■ **An arbitration clause.** You and the contractor agree on and name a method for resolving disputes, such as binding arbitration.
■ **Release of liens.** This provision assures homeowners they won't be slapped with any liens, or charges to pay debts, that might be filed against the contractor.

CONTENTS

Inside Your Home

For a more detailed content listing of this section, see pages 8–9.

Outside Your Home

For a more detailed content listing of this section, see pages 118–119.

Your Home's Systems

For a more detailed content listing of this section, see pages 230–231.

Basics You Should Know

For a more detailed content listing of this section, see pages 422–423.

8

Inside Your Home

FLOORS AND STAIRS

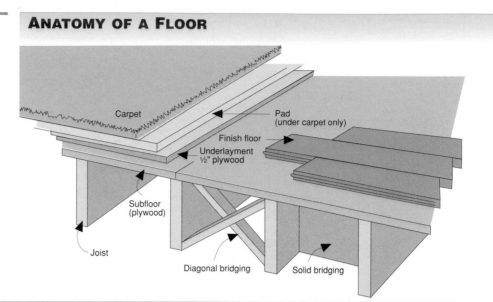

Carpet

Pad (under carpet only)

Finish floor

Underlayment ½" plywood

Subfloor (plywood)

Joist

Diagonal bridging

Solid bridging

Fixing Floors

SILENCING SQUEAKS FROM ABOVE

Most finished wood floors will develop squeaks at sometime or another. The section view above shows a typical floor. The joists stretch from exterior wall to exterior wall; bridging stiffens the joists to prevent sagging; and the subfloor adds rigidity.

Temperature and humidity changes cause the various floor parts to shrink and swell at different rates. The result: Squeaks develop where loose boards rub against each other or against loose nails.

If joists below the squeaks are concealed, you'll have to repair the squeaks from above, as shown at right. If the joists are exposed, use the techniques on the page 11. If squeaks persist, look for more loose areas in the floor.

YOU'LL NEED...
SKILLS: Basic carpentry skills.
TIME: 10 or 15 minutes per squeak.
TOOLS: Drill, hammer, nail set.

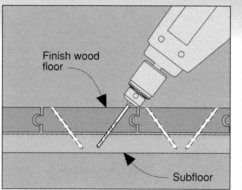

Finish wood floor

Subfloor

1. To quiet a loose finish board from above, nail it to the subfloor. Drill pilot holes so the wood won't split, angling them as shown.

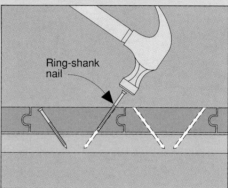

Ring-shank nail

2. Drive in ring-shank or cement-coated flooring nails. Use these nails because smooth nails might work loose, causing the squeak to reoccur.

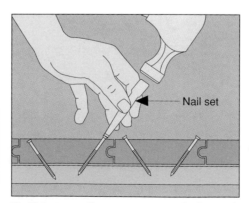

Nail set

3. Using a nail set, countersink the nail heads about ⅛ inch below the surface of the floor.

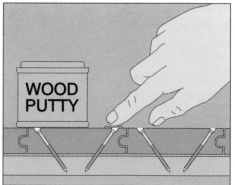

WOOD PUTTY

4. Fill the nail holes with wood putty. Mound the putty slightly, let dry, and sand flush.

SILENCING SQUEAKS FROM BELOW

You can treat squeaks easily from below if you have access. Watch while someone walks on the noisy spot. If the subfloor moves, use the methods shown at right. No movement may mean the finish floor is loose and needs to be pulled down with screws, as shown below.

YOU'LL NEED...

SKILLS: Basic carpentry skills.
TIME: 10 to 15 minutes per squeak.
TOOLS: Hammer.

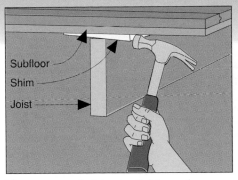

Use a tapered shim to tighten a loose subfloor board. Dip the tip of the shim in glue and tap it between the joist and subfloor until it's snug.

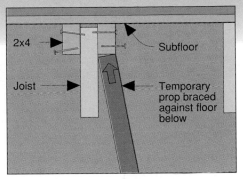

To tighten a series of boards, force a 2×4 up against the subfloor using a temporary prop. Nail the 2×4 to the joist. Repeat on the other side.

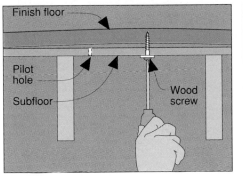

Pull down loose finish boards using 1¼-inch roundhead screws. Drill pilot holes and use washers so screws won't pull through subfloor.

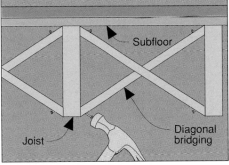

If the bridging isn't tight between joists, drive in new, larger nails at an angle. If squeaks persist, add steel bridging as shown at right.

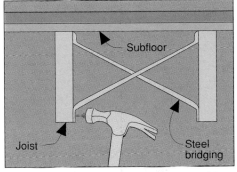

To quiet squeaks between joists, add steel bridging. Push it tight up against the subfloor, then nail it to the bottom inside of joists.

LIFTING A SAGGING FLOOR

If a floor has a major sag in it, you may have to add a supporting jack post under it. Break out a section of the basement floor and pour a 24×24×8-inch concrete pad for the post to sit on (see pages 180–184). Let the concrete cure for a week.

Place the jack post on the pad and a 4×4 pressure-treated beam long enough to span several joists on top of the jack. Screw the jack up until the beam is snug against the joists, then raise one-quarter turn more. Wait a week and make another quarter turn, continuing this process until the sag is gone. Don't lift faster, or you may cause structural damage.

YOU'LL NEED...

SKILLS: Intermediate masonry skills.
TIME: 2 to 4 hours, plus curing time.
TOOLS: Sledgehammer, cold chisel, masonry trowel, string.

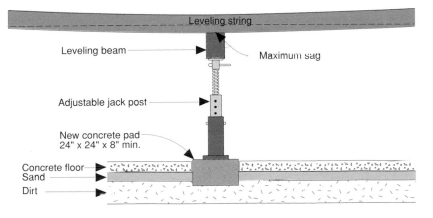

Fixing Floors (continued)

PATCHING WOOD FLOORS

Replacing a section of a finished floor that is interlocked with tongues and grooves is as easy as splitting off the bottom edge of a groove and slipping a new board into place.

Use the technique shown below for short sections of boards. If the floorboard is very long and most of the board is in good condition, cut out the damaged section of the flooring with a circular saw set to a depth exactly equal to the thickness of the finished flooring. Then pry out the damaged section.

YOU'LL NEED...

SKILLS: Basic carpentry skills.
TIME: 45 to 60 minutes per area.
TOOLS: Drill, hammer, chisel, pry bar, nail set, circular saw.

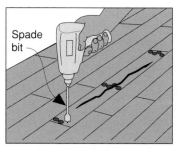

1. Using a spade bit, bore holes across the ends and middle of the board(s).

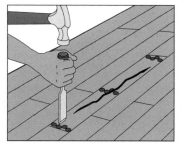

2. Use a wood chisel to split the board lengthwise between the holes.

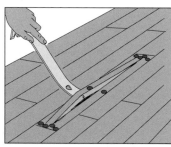

3. Slip a pry bar into a split and carefully remove the damaged board.

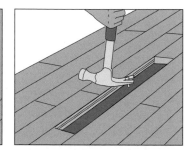

4. Using a claw hammer, pull out any old nails that remain in the subfloor.

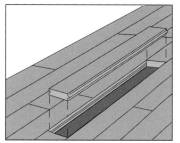

5. Carefully cut the new boards for a tight fit. Slip the groove of each new piece into the tongue of the adjacent board.

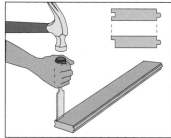

6. When you get to the last board, turn it over and chisel away the lower part of its groove. Note how the boards will interlock.

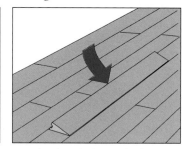

7. Blind-nail through the tongue all but the last piece, as if installing a new floor (see page 19).

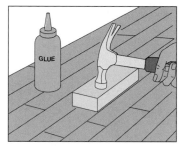

8. Apply glue to the subfloor, tongue, and half-groove of the last piece, then tap it into place. Use a hammer block to protect the wood surface.

TIMELY TECHNIQUES   REMOVING SCRATCHES

Remove surface cuts or scratches (left) with steel wool and a solvent, such as mineral spirits. Rub with the grain, rinse, and refinish.

For deeper cuts (right), sand with the grain and work in wood filler with a brush. Let the filler set overnight, sand with the grain, and refinish.

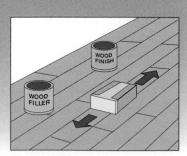

REFINISHING WOOD FLOORS

Refinishing a wood floor is a job that takes care and patience. You'll need to rent an upright drum sander and a disc edge sander. Ask the rental dealer to demonstrate the machines. Some companies rent upright versions of random orbital sanders, also called jitterbug sanders, that don't work as fast as drum sanders, but are less likely to damage the floor if you're inexperienced.

Do this work on a day when you can open doors and windows to let out the dust. Wear a respirator to protect your lungs from the fine dust and be sure to seal off adjoining rooms with dampened sheets.

YOU'LL NEED...

SKILLS: Basic carpentry skills.
TIME: 6 to 8 hours over 2 days for a 10×12-foot room.
TOOLS: Hammer, nail set, drum-type or jitterbug sander, disc-type edge sander, vacuum, tack cloth, putty knife, paint brush or wax applicator.

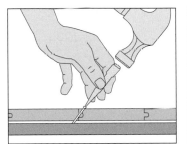

1. After you have removed all room furnishings, pry off baseboard shoe moldings. Set popped nails below the floor surface.

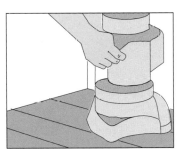

2. Rock the sander back at the beginning and end of each pass. Otherwise, the drum will make a depression wherever you start or stop.

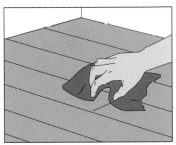

3. Use care with the edge sander. Its circular cuts differ from those made by a drum sander, so don't use it for open areas.

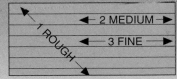

4. After each sanding pass (see below), vacuum the floor thoroughly. Use a tack cloth after each vacuuming to pick up remaining dust.

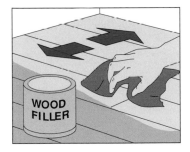

5. Apply paste wood filler with the grain. When the filler begins to set, wipe across the grain with an old rag to remove excess. Let dry overnight.

6. Apply two to four coats of polyurethane finish with a brush or a wax applicator, sanding with fine sandpaper between coats. Use a tack cloth to pick up all dust between coats. Do not wax polyurethane finishes.

TIMELY TECHNIQUES   SANDING TECHNIQUES

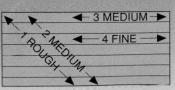

A. Three sandpaper cuts—with the grain—will smooth most floors. You may need several passes with each cut.

B. Getting nowhere sanding with the grain? Try one diagonal pass, but never sand directly across the grain.

C. Badly cupped or warped old floors may require four cuts. Always be sure to overlap each pass.

Fixing Floors (continued)

PATCHING TILE FLOORING

Most resilient floor tiles lift out easily once you apply some heat to soften the adhesive underneath them. Use a heat lamp or an electric iron, working carefully to make sure that you do not mar adjacent tiles.

If you cannot raise a corner, use a chisel, working out from the center to the edges. Once the tile is removed, you must scrape or sand off all old adhesive from the floor so the new tile will lie flat.

Different types of tile require different adhesives. To avoid confusion, ask the salesperson from whom you make the purchase to recommend a suitable adhesive.

To make the new tile look less conspicuous, rub off the gloss with fine steel wool.

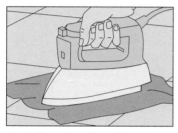

1. Soften the tile with a medium-hot iron. Don't overlap onto adjacent tiles.

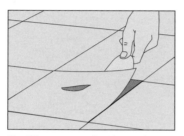

2. Slip a putty knife under a corner. Do not pry against surrounding tiles.

3. Scrape away as much of the adhesive as possible. Sand off any remainder.

4. Be sure the new tile will fit and lie flat. If not, mark as shown.

5. If the new tile is too large, use a sharp knife and a straightedge to cut it.

6. Apply adhesive with a serrated spreader, if required, or simply brush on.

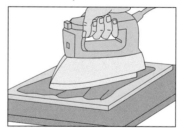

7. Use the iron to soften the new tile. Protect the tile's surface with a cloth.

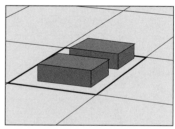

8. Drop—do not slide—the new tile into position. Weight down for 24 hours.

HELPFUL HINTS

SOLVING OTHER TILE PROBLEMS

■ Heat often is the answer for tiles that have come partially unglued. Exceptions to this are asphalt and vinyl asbestos tiles, which you will have to remove by chipping from the center out with a chisel. Work an iron (protected by a pressing cloth) back and forth until you can peel up the curled corner, then remove as much adhesive from the tile as possible. The

more adhesive you can remove, the better the repair you can make.
■ If the tile has cooled, be sure to heat it again, then apply a thin, even coat of adhesive to the tile. Stand on the corner of the tile to press it into place. Wipe off any excess adhesive with a damp cloth, then weight down the tile with a heavy object.
■ Scouring—plus some careful

scraping with a sharp knife—also will remove shallow burns. For scratches, see the techniques explained in the Helpful Hints on page 15.
■ Often, you can remove stains by rubbing them with a mild detergent solution. If that doesn't work, try a white appliance wax. As a last resort, scour stains with very fine steel wool and a household cleanser.

PATCHING SHEET FLOORING

Most sheet flooring is glued to the floor with a bed of adhesive. Some newer types of flooring, designed especially for do-it-yourself installation, require adhesive only at seams and edges. Some require no adhesive at all (see page 29).

If the entire floor has been laid in adhesive, you usually can work a putty knife underneath and peel up the damaged piece. You may need to apply heat. To make the patch less conspicuous, take time to carefully match its pattern to the floor's. To patch the newer types of flooring, cut out the damaged section and cement a patch as you would the seam of a new floor.

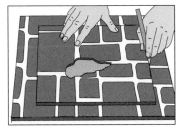

1. Use a framing square to mark and cut around the damaged area. Cut with a utility knife.

2. Lay the cutout on a piece of matching material and trace around it. Accuracy is essential for a good fit.

3. Guide your cuts with the square. Use a scrap of plywood to prevent scoring the surface underneath.

4. Clean the underlayment well, then test the patch for fit. If it is a bit too large, slightly sand the edges.

5. Apply adhesive to the new tile with a serrated spreader. Align one edge, matching the pattern, and lower the new section into place.

6. Wipe off adhesive that might have oozed up around the edges, then weight down the patch evenly for at least 24 hours.

HELPFUL HINTS   SOLVING OTHER SHEET FLOORING PROBLEMS

■ Many resilient floorings tend to heal themselves. In fact, if you fill shallow scratches with floor wax, they probably will disappear in time. For deeper cuts, try compressing the edges by dragging a worn coin along them.
■ If the material has torn all the way through, lift the edges of the wound, scrape away any old adhesive, apply fresh adhesive, and stick them down again. For the repair to lie flat, you may need to sand one edge.

■ If a blister develops in your flooring, flatten it by making a clean cut through its center. Alternating edges, press down on one edge of the cut, work adhesive underneath the other edge, and apply weight.
■ Filling small holes in vinyl flooring is a tougher assignment, but one that can be done. The best and quickest way is to fill the void with a special seam-welding product offered by the manufacturer of the flooring. This

product dissolves the vinyl then sets up again to complete the repair.
■ Another solution is to scrape flakes from a piece of scrap flooring and grind them into a powder. Mix the powder with clear lacquer or nail polish to make a putty-like paste. Work the paste into the hole, packing it well and mounding slightly to compensate for shrinkage. After the paste dries, sand the repair and wax according to the manufacturer's directions.

Fixing Floors (continued)

CLEANING CARPETS

Keeping carpets fresh requires commitment. Once a week—more often in high traffic areas—use an upright or canister vacuum cleaner with a power (beater) nozzle. This keeps dirt from settling to the bottom and grinding at the fibers. Once a year, shampoo or steam-clean your carpets depending on how deep the dirt is embedded.

Shampoo comes as either a concentrated liquid detergent you mix with water or an aerosol spray foam. Remember that shampoo is a surface cleaner only. Either remove all of the furniture or allow two days, doing half the carpet each day. Whip the detergent into a foam by vigorously scrubbing the carpet, let the foam dry, then vacuum the dried detergent and loosened dirt. Do not soak the carpet or it may shrink, the colors may run, and mildew may grow.

Steam-cleaning machines actually spray a hot water/detergent mix deep into the pile, then immediately vacuum up both the solution and dislodged dirt before the carpet becomes soaked. Steaming is much more effective than shampooing. Hardware, home centers, and carpet stores usually have steamers for rent.

Oriental and antique rugs require professional cleaning to make sure they don't run or shrink.

CLEANING UP SPILLS ON CARPETS

When a spill occurs, speed is of the essence to avoid permanent staining. Remove as much of the spill as possible with a large spoon, spatula, putty knife, or large knife.

Consult the table at right to select a cleaning agent. Apply the first cleaning agent listed for the type of stain. Do not pour the agent directly onto the spill area. Instead, pour it onto a sponge and blot—don't rub—the stained area. Remove as much liquid as possible by pressing a paper towel into the stain.

Repeat the pour-into-sponge, blot, and dry sequence with each of the remaining cleaning agents listed in the table. After all agents have been applied and removed, rinse the area with clean, fresh water. Dry the area by stepping on a pile of paper towels stacked on the wet area.

If the stain type is not listed, try trichloroethane (T), a dry cleaning solution available at many stores, followed by detergent (D).

CARPET STAIN FIRST AID

Spill	Treatment
Blood	W – D
Butter	T – D
Catsup	D – A
Chocolate	D – A
Coffee	D – V
Crayon	T – D
Egg	D – A – V
Fruit juice	D – A – V
Furniture polish	T – D
Grease, oil	T – D
Ice cream	D – A – V
Lipstick	T – D – A – V
Mayonnaise	T – D
Paint, oil	T
Paint, latex	D
Shoe polish	T – D – A – V
Tea	D – V – T
Urine	V – A – V – D
Wax	Scrape – T
Wine	D – V

A = ammonia   D = detergent
T = trichloroethane   V = vinegar
W = water

PATCHING A DAMAGED CARPET AREA

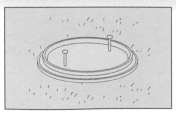

1. Nail a clean can lid or other template over the damaged area. Leave the heads of the nails projecting.

2. Using the lid as a guide, cut carpet with sharp utility knife. Repeat Steps 1 and 2 for the matching patch.

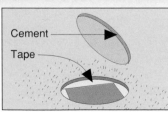

Cement
Tape

3. Vacuum up loose fibers. Slip double-faced tape halfway under carpet edges. Apply seam cement to edges.

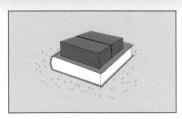

4. Press the patch into place. Weight the patch overnight with a book or board and a heavy object.

Fixing Stairs

The staircases in your home have many parts—all of them interlocked with sophisticated joinery that is usually concealed from view.

The basics are simple: A pair of stringers slopes from one level to the next. The composite illustration at right shows both "open-" and "closed-stringer" staircases.

The stringers support a series of steps, called treads. A simple staircase—such as one that leads to a basement or deck—consists of little more than stringers and treads.

Complications begin when risers are added to fill the vertical gaps between the treads. Finally, a balustrade—which consists of a handrail, balusters, and newel post—provides safety along the side(s) of an open staircase.

You can treat most of the ills that afflict staircases using the techniques shown on page 18. If you want to build a basic, open-riser staircase, see page 188.

ANATOMY OF A STAIRCASE

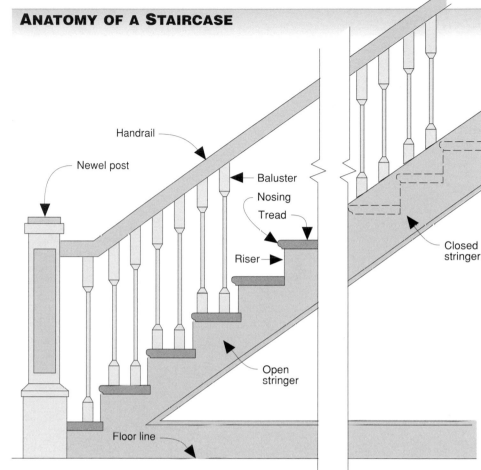

Handrail
Newel post
Baluster
Nosing
Tread
Riser
Closed stringer
Open stringer
Floor line

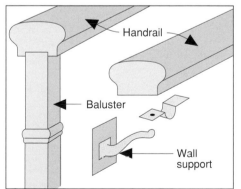

Handrail
Baluster
Wall support

Some balusters fit into holes in the handrail and treads. Others are toenailed and glued. Brackets support wall-mounted rails.

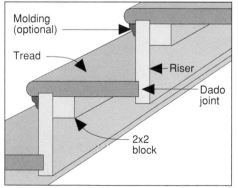
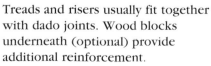

Molding (optional)
Tread
Riser
Dado joint
2x2 block

Treads and risers usually fit together with dado joints. Wood blocks underneath (optional) provide additional reinforcement.

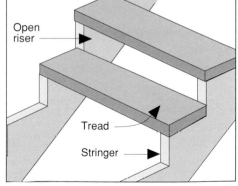

Open riser
Tread
Stringer

Treads on open-riser staircases usually are simply nailed to the stringers. Note that this type of staircase also has open stringers.

Fixing Stairs (continued)

SILENCING SQUEAKS FROM ABOVE

Most staircase squeaks result from a tread rubbing against the top or bottom of a riser or a stringer. To locate the problem, rock back and forth on each tread. If the tread moves, it's time for you to take corrective action.

Work from below if you have access to the underside of the staircase. Otherwise, you'll have to attack the situation from above. A few well-placed nails, screws, or hardwood wedges should solve the squeaking problems.

YOU'LL NEED...
SKILLS: Basic carpentry skills.
TIME: 10 to 15 minutes per tread.
TOOLS: Drill, hammer, utility knife.

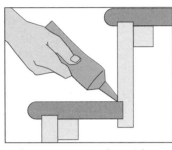

Lubricating squeaks with powdered graphite may quiet them, but only temporarily.

For a permanent fix, drill pilot holes at opposing angles and drive in ring-shank flooring nails.

You can also coat wedges with glue, tap into place, and let dry. Cut off wedge ends with a utility knife.

For uncarpeted stairs, you can tighten joints with molding. Apply glue and nail into both risers and treads.

SILENCING SQUEAKS FROM BELOW

YOU'LL NEED...
SKILLS: Basic carpentry skills.
TIME: 10 to 15 minutes per squeaky tread.
TOOLS: Drill, hammer, screwdriver, utility knife.

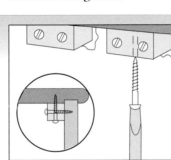

Use hardwood blocks to tighten joints between treads and risers. Glue and screw to both surfaces.

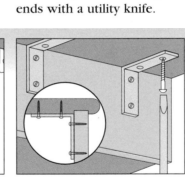

If the entire tread is loose, use two or three metal angle brackets to tighten it down to the riser.

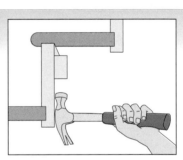

If old wedges are loose, remove them and replace with new ones.

TIGHTENING RAILS AND BALUSTERS

Wobbly handrails call for detective work. Are the rails working loose from the balusters, or are the balusters parting company with the treads? If the rail is pulling away from a newel post, adapt these techniques. Loose newel posts require a pro's help.

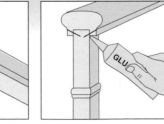

Drill a pilot hole at an angle through the baluster into the rail or tread. Countersink a wood screw in the hole.

Work glue into the joint and drive nails through the railing's side. Again, drill pilot holes for the nails.

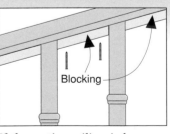

If the entire railing is loose, add blocking as shown. Cut angles for a snug fit, glue, and nail.

Laying New Floor Materials

LAYING A FLOATING PREFINISHED FLOOR

Prefinished plank flooring is as easy to install as hardwood flooring and offers the same appearance. The "planks" consist of medium-density fiberboard (MDF) sandwiched between plastic laminate. The top laminate looks like random-grain wood, but its plastic composition makes it scratch- and stain-resistant.

Precision-milled tongue-and-groove edges make precise installation a snap. The whole assembly is glued together at the edges and floats on a thin, closed-cell polyethylene foam pad.

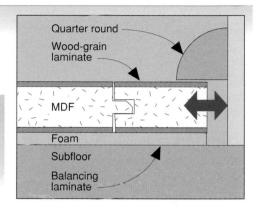

YOU'LL NEED...

SKILLS: Basic carpentry skills.
TIME: 6 to 8 hours for a small room.
TOOLS: Circular saw, hammer, pry bar, coping saw, offset saw.

1. Make sure subfloor is clean, dry, and level. Lay down 8-mil polyethylene if subfloor is bare concrete.

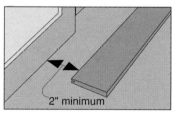

2. Plan layout with flooring dealer. Width of the last row must be at least 2 inches. If not, ripsaw the first row.

3. Unroll first strip of foam in direction planks will run. Do not overlap foam edges or adhere foam to floor.

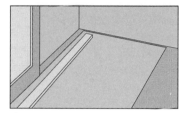

4. If you're not starting against a wall or wall is uneven, nail a straightedge to floor to align first row.

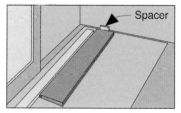

5. Lay first strip with ¼-inch spacer between grooved end and wall. Fill end grooves with glue. Wipe up excess.

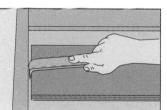

6. Cut last piece in first row with ¼-inch space at end. Use pry bar to push planks tight. Save leftover plank.

7. Cut first plank of second row 12 inches shorter; cut grooved end. Fill all grooves with glue; tap into place.

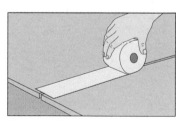

8. After first pad is covered, unroll next pad, butt edges, and tape. Continue gluing planks to the last row.

9. Undercut door casings with an offset handsaw. Use a piece of scrap flooring as a depth gauge

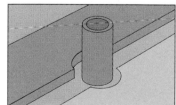

10. Cut planking with a coping saw to fit around pipes, making holes ¼ inch larger than pipes.

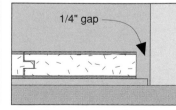

11. Ripsaw tongued edge of last plank ¼ inch narrower than remaining gap. Glue groove and pry into place.

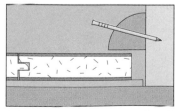

12. Remove spacers and nail shoe molding to wall (do not nail to floor). Wash floor with clean, warm water.

Laying New Floor Materials (continued)

MATERIAL MATTERS

■ Wood flooring comes in strips, planks, and blocks. Strip flooring, by far the most common, typically measures 2¼ inches wide. Plank flooring is wider—3 to 8 inches—and often is installed in a combination of several different widths. Block (or parquet) flooring consists of strips glued together into squares or rectangles. You can purchase flooring

CHOOSING WOOD FLOORING

types as finished or unfinished material. Prefinished flooring costs more, and you must install it with extreme care to avoid marring the surface. Unfinished flooring, on the other hand, takes less care during installation but must be sanded (page 13) to smooth minor surface irregularities, then finished.

■ Flooring grades vary depending on the kind of wood. Clear typically is

the best, followed by select, No. 1 common, No. 2 common, and 1½-foot shorts, which are the remnants from the other grades.

■ Before you lay flooring, it is important to let the wood acclimate to the moisture conditions in your house. Have it delivered at least 72 hours in advance and spread it out in the room where it is to be laid.

LAYING A WOOD BLOCK FLOOR

Wood block flooring is easy to install. You don't have to use nails; modern adhesives work well. On concrete, it's best to lay down a layer of polyethylene film, sleepers, and a subfloor (see page 21) before laying the tiles.

YOU'LL NEED...

SKILLS: Basic carpentry skills.
TIME: 3 to 4 hours for a 12×15-foot room if subfloor is prepared.
TOOLS: Framing square, tape measure, chalk line, power nailer.

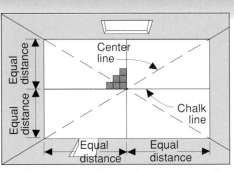

1. Plan the installation by squaring off the room with chalk lines and checking what will happen at borders, as shown on page 28.

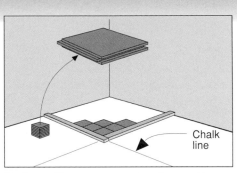

2. Get off to a square start by tacking down a pair of 1×2s along the chalk lines. Tongue-and-groove edges keep the later courses true.

TOOL TALK

USING A POWER NAILER

Most wood flooring interlocks with tongues and grooves. To fasten it, nail at a 45-degree angle through the tongue. Set the nail so the groove of the next board will fit over the tongue of the one you've just nailed.

A power nailer—available from flooring or rental dealers—speeds the job and saves your back. Using a heavy hammer, simply hit the piston drive mechanism to set each nail.

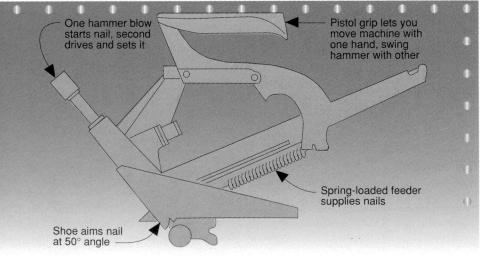

One hammer blow starts nail, second drives and sets it

Pistol grip lets you move machine with one hand, swing hammer with other

Spring-loaded feeder supplies nails

Shoe aims nail at 50° angle

LAYING STRIP AND PLANK FLOORING

You can lay strip and plank flooring across existing floorboards. Sweep the floor well, set popped nails, and remove baseboard moldings. Level bad dips by pulling up the old flooring, nailing shims to the joists, and renailing the old boards. Minor floor problems can be smoothed by laying down building paper. If nailing to plywood, finished flooring should be perpendicular to joists. Leave a ⅜-inch gap between the flooring and walls. Molding will cover the gap when you're done.

YOU'LL NEED...

SKILLS: Intermediate carpentry skills.
TIME: 2 to 3 hours for a 12×15-foot room if subfloor is prepared.
TOOLS: Square, hammer, pry bar, power nailer, compass, sabersaw, nail set.

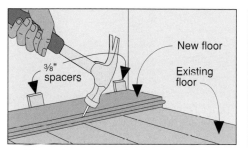

1. Place the grooved edge of the first board ⅜ inch from the wall. Blind-nail through the tongue every 12 inches.

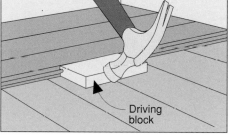

2. To keep the courses parallel, tap boards together before nailing. Use a wood scrap to protect the flooring.

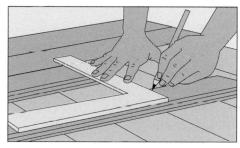

3. Measure before cutting the last piece in each course. Don't cut off the edge with the tongue or the groove that you'll need.

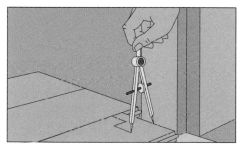

4. To fit around irregularities, scribe with a compass (see page 432) and cut with a sabersaw.

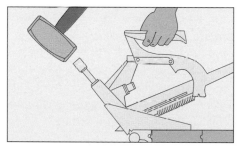

5. Fit to the tongue of the previous row, then nail with the power nailer (see page 20).

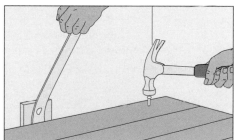

6. Protecting the wall with a wood scrap, push the last courses tight with a pry bar. Face nail the last course.

LAYING WOOD FLOORING OVER CONCRETE

Strip and plank flooring can't be attached directly to concrete. Seal the concrete against moisture (see page 114). Lay a polyethylene vapor barrier over concrete. Fasten down 2×4 sleepers every 16 inches with masonry nails (see pages 457–458). Lay rigid foam insulation between sleepers. Then nail the subfloor to sleepers and the flooring to subfloor.

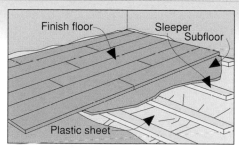

Laying strip or plank flooring over concrete requires a vapor barrier, sleepers, and a subfloor.

YOU'LL NEED...

SKILLS: Intermediate carpentry skills.
TIME: 1 to 2 hours additional time to add vapor barrier, sleepers, and subfloor for a 12×15-foot room.
TOOLS: Hammer, nail set, power nailer. If you rent a power nailer, watch a demonstration of how to use it, and wear ear and eye protection

Laying New Floor Materials (continued)

MATERIAL MATTERS   CHOOSING AND BUYING CARPETING

Carpeting offers more colors, patterns, and textures than anything else you can put underfoot. Compare the fibers to determine the one that best fits your needs (see below) and ask your carpet dealer about the density of the fiber or pile. The more fibers per square inch, the longer the carpet life.

Most carpeting sold is tufted or "jute-backed," meaning the yarn is pulled through a woven backing and an additional backing is added for strength and stability. Most backing is made from polypropylene, although some is still made from jute.

Carpeting is sold by the square yard in widths of 9, 12, and 15 feet. To compute square yards, measure the room (in feet) at the widest and longest points. Multiply the two numbers and divide by 9. Take the measurements to a carpet salesperson, who can figure the exact yardage requirements.

Don't skip padding. A good pad prolongs a carpet's life, makes it more comfortable, and insulates against noise and cold. Choose between felt and sponge-rubber pads, but don't use felt in high-humidity areas or rubber over radiant-heated floors.

Integral-pad carpeting is bonded to its own cushioned backing. It's skid-proof, mildew-proof, and ravel-proof, which means you can lay it directly over a concrete basement floor. Installation is easy (see page 25). Indoor/outdoor carpeting also can be laid without a pad.

Carpeting also comes in tiles, again in a wide range of colors and fibers. Most carpet tiles have a self-stick backing that does not require adhesive. Some, however, require a flooring adhesive. Lay them as you would resilient tiles (see page 28).

COMPARING CARPET FIBERS

Fiber	Properties	Relative Cost
Wool	The traditional standard against which other fibers are compared; durable, resilient, and abrasion-resistant; needs mothproofing; fairly easy to clean	Expensive
Acrylic	Closest to wool of all synthetic fibers; resists abrasion, mildew, insects, and crushing; wide choice of colors; some tendency to pill (form fuzz balls); sheds dirt	Moderate
Nylon	Strongest synthetic fiber; very durable and resistant to abrasion, mildew, and moths; should be treated for static electricity; hides dirt	Wide price range
Polyester	Bright, clear colors; cool to the touch; resists mildew and moisture; can be used anywhere; susceptible to oil-based stains; resists soiling	Moderate
Polypropylene olefin	A key fiber in most indoor/outdoor carpeting; extremely durable, moisture-resistant, and nonabsorbent; lower-priced versions tend to crush; most stain-resistant of all	Wide price range

TOOL TALK   TOOLS FOR LAYING CARPETING

No matter what the job, things go more smoothly with the right tools. Carpet laying is no exception. You'll have some of the basic tools: a utility knife, tape measure, hacksaw, straightedge, chalk line, and awl.

With integral-pad carpeting (see page 25), you can get by without all the rented gear. But if you plan to stretch the carpeting, you'll need to rent several other items.

Strip cutters make quick work of cutting tackless strip, which fits around the perimeter of a room. A staple hammer fastens padding to wood floors. (Use pad adhesive if the floor is concrete.) Join pieces of carpeting using seam tape and a seaming iron. A knee kicker and a power stretcher help you pull the carpeting taut. A carpet trimmer cuts neatly along walls.

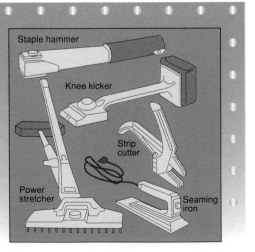

Staple hammer

Knee kicker

Strip cutter

Power stretcher

Seaming iron

LAYING TUFTED OR JUTE-BACK CARPETING

Before you start, unroll the carpet and padding goods in a separate room to make sure you have the amount of carpet you ordered and it is free of defects.

Prepare the room by removing all furniture and baseboard shoe moldings. Plane down all high spots in the floor and fill wide cracks or dips with floor leveling compound. For badly worn floors, you should install underlayment (see page 27). Then you can install the tackless strip, carpet pad, and the carpet, using the techniques shown below and on the next page.

YOU'LL NEED...

SKILLS: Basic to intermediate skills.
TIME: 5 hours for a 12×15-foot room, if it doesn't have complex corners.
TOOLS: Hammer, plane, putty knife, carpeting tools (see page 22).

Installing Tackless Strip And Padding

Tackless strip creates a framework over which carpeting is stretched and held in position. When laying out the strip, make sure the pins face the adjacent wall or opening. Position ½ inch from the wall and nail in place.

When abutting a floor covering other than carpeting, nail a metal threshold strip with gripper pins to the floor. Where one carpet section adjoins another, do not use tackless strip. Later, you will seam the two carpet pieces together.

Lay the carpet padding within the framework and cut it to size with a utility knife. Make sure the side with the slick membrane faces up. Staple the padding in place, paying special attention to seam lines and edges. If the floor is concrete, roll back one section of padding at a time and spread pad adhesive. Lay the padding back in place.

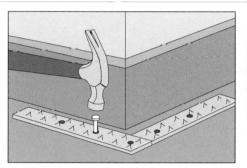

1. With pins facing the wall, nail the tackless strip to the floor. Use adhesive on concrete floors.

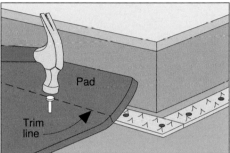

2. Nail padding to wood floors. Glue it to concrete floors. Make sure padding does not overlap the tackless strip.

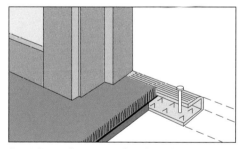

3. When abutting a hard surface floor, use a metal threshold. Hammer the lip flat using a protective board.

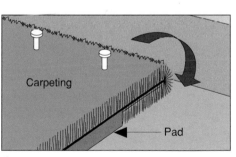

4. Another way to finish an edge is to fold the carpeting under itself. Be sure to stop the padding short.

TIMELY TECHNIQUES

You once needed a heavy-duty needle, thread, and lots of patience to join two pieces of carpeting. Now most pros bond a special heat-setting tape to the backing, as shown at right.

Trim the carpet edges straight and butt them carefully. Fold back both and

CARPET-SEAMING TECHNIQUES

lay tape along the floor where the seam will fall. Move the heated iron slowly along the tape. As the adhesive melts, press the edges of the carpeting into it with your other hand.

Weight down the seam for a few minutes after joining the carpeting.

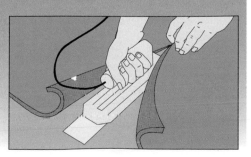

Laying New Floor Materials (continued)

TIMELY TECHNIQUES   STRETCHING AND TRIMMING TECHNIQUES

Stretch the carpet in the following order as shown in Step 1 below. 1. Use a knee kicker and stretch it to the wall opposite the doorway. 2. Kick the goods to the wall adjacent. 3. Make a power-stretch into the adjacent corner. 4. Knee kick to the adjacent wall. 5. Stretch the carpeting diagonally into the opposite corner. Trimming comes last. Start anywhere you want, and work your way around the edge of the room, using either a utility knife or a carpet trimmer. Replace the shoe molding by nailing it to the baseboard, not the floor through the carpeting.

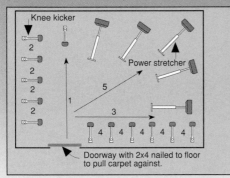

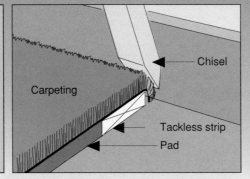

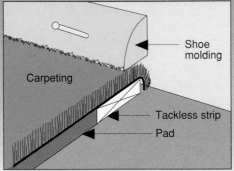

1. Knee kickers and power stretchers force the carpeting onto the tackless strip's pins. (See above for how-to.)

2. Trim off excess carpet, leaving ¼ inch. Tuck edge between strips and baseboard with a masonry chisel.

3. Finish by replacing shoe moldings. Nail them to the baseboard, not the floor (see page 40).

CARPETING A STAIRWAY

To carpet stairs, you can use a strip left over from carpeting an adjoining room or purchase a runner. If you opt to use a carpeting strip, use tackless strips to anchor it. Make sure the pile of the carpet runs down the stairs (that is, it feels smoother when you run your hand in the downstairs direction).

If you decide to use a runner, the best way to secure it is with rods. To do so, lay padding in one strip from top to bottom. Tack it temporarily at the top. Tack the runner face down to the bottom tread next to the second riser, then stretch the runner under the nosing at the top of the first riser and tack it in place. Pull the runner up the stairs. Starting at the bottom, stretch the carpeting over the lowest step, and tack it temporarily at the back of the first tread. You'll have a double layer of carpet on the first tread and no carpet on the first riser.

Screw an eye or rod bracket to each side of the tread, ½ inch from the carpet edge, and slip a rod over the carpeting and through the eye. Proceed to the next step. At the top, tack the end just under the nosing.

> ### YOU'LL NEED...
> **SKILLS:** Basic carpeting skills.
> **TIME:** 2 hours.
> **TOOLS:** Hammer, drill, knee kicker (see page 22).

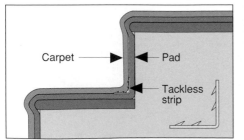

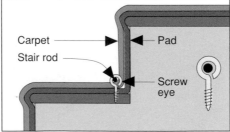

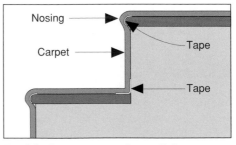

You can use special tackless strips to secure carpeting strips. Lay the pad first, then the strips.

Stair rods are work to install, but are easy to maintain because they are entirely above the carpeting.

Double-face tape works well for padless installations. Stick it to each nosing as well as to tread-riser joints.

LAYING INTEGRAL-PAD CARPETING

Integral-pad carpeting is bonded to its own cushioned backing, thus eliminating the need to use a carpet pad. It's ideal for applying directly on concrete floors. In small spaces, such as baths and closets, you can cut the carpeting to fit and lay it without carpet tape. Edges have a tendency to curl in time, however, so it's best to anchor big pieces with double-faced tape.

Prepare the room as you would for any other type of carpeting (see page 23). Clean the floor well before you begin because tape won't adhere properly to a dirty surface.

YOU'LL NEED...

SKILLS: Basic carpeting skills.
TIME: 2 to 3 hours for a 12×15-foot room.
TOOLS: Tape measure, utility knife, seam roller or kitchen rolling pin, hammer, nail set.

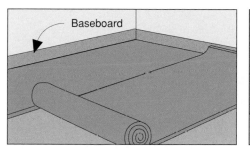

1. Dry-fit the carpeting. Make sure piles fall in the same direction. Allow about 1 inch extra all around.

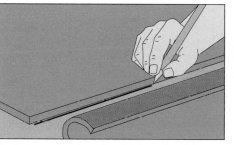

2. Join any seams by folding back one piece and drawing a line on the floor along the other piece.

3. Center double-faced tape on the line and stick it to the floor. Check the seam before you peel off the tape's paper.

4. Press one piece of carpeting into place and apply seam adhesive along its edge to cement the backings together.

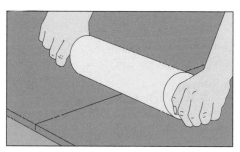

5. Use a rolling pin to press the carpeting firmly against the tape. Brush the pile lightly for an invisible seam.

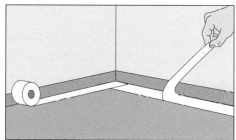

6. Fold back the carpeting from the walls and make a tape border. Smooth the tape well before removing paper.

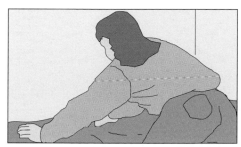

7. Pull carpeting taut, then drop onto tape. Smooth edges with your hands so the tape adhesive gets a good grip.

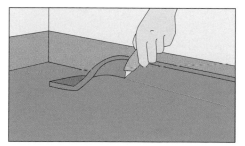

8. Trim off excess with a utility knife and tamp edges down. The pile will hide minor irregularities.

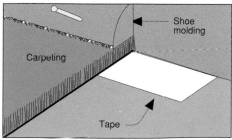

9. Finish by installing or replacing the base shoe molding. Nail molding to the baseboard, not the floor (see page 40).

Laying New Floor Materials (continued)

MATERIAL MATTERS   CHOOSING AND BUYING RESILIENT FLOORING

Resilient flooring—softer underfoot than any other flooring except carpeting—is available in the form of tiles or sheet goods.

Tiles have been a popular do-it-yourself item since World War II, although they have changed considerably in size (from 9 to 12 inches square), appearance (from dull, streaked greens and beiges to vivid colors and patterns), and composition (from asphalt and nasty asbestos to varying blends of vinyl).

Sheet goods have been around awhile also. Because they come in rolls up to 12 feet wide, installation is more difficult. Installation kits for do-it-yourselfers are available, but be aware that a cutting mistake can ruin an entire roll, not just a single tile. (See page 29 for sheet good installation.)

Choosing tiles or sheet vinyl depends to some extent on the use your new floor will get (see chart below).

Cushioned vinyl is soft underfoot, has a minimum of dirt-catching seams, and does a decent soundproofing job. Tiles are less expensive, easier to install (see page 28), and much more resistant to dents from items such as chair legs. Also, you should consider if you want a smooth or textured surface. Smooth floors mop up easily, show dirt more readily, and inevitably collect a few permanent scuffs and dents.

Before you buy, be sure you are clear about the installation directions. Most resilient floorings can be installed on any grade. A few, however, should not be laid on concrete in contact with the ground, and most should not be applied over existing resilient flooring. If an old wood floor is in good condition and has a subfloor underneath it, you can lay resilient materials directly over it. Otherwise, you'll have to put down underlayment first (see page 27).

Because all but a few of today's tiles are 1-foot square, determining how many you will need requires only simple computations. Estimating the amount of sheet flooring needed is trickier, especially if there's a pattern involved and you have a seam somewhere. It's best to make an accurate plan of the room on graph paper and take it to a flooring dealer.

SAFETY

If you need to remove tiles to lay a new floor, be aware that many older tiles contain asbestos. Some states require a licensed asbestos remover to take them out. Ask your flooring dealer to see how to test old tiles for asbestos and if you need to hire a licensed firm to remove them.

COMPARING RESILIENT FLOORINGS

Material	Properties	Relative Cost
Sheet vinyl	Solid vinyl; several grades available; should be laid by a professional; vulnerable to burns, but quite durable otherwise	Moderate
Cushioned sheet vinyl	Several grades available—from moderately durable to very durable; resistant to abrasion and discoloration; durability ranges from that of vinyl asbestos tile to about one-half as durable; vulnerable to burns; usually contains a vinyl foam layer	Wide price range
Roto sheet vinyl	Design is printed on a cellulose felt or mineral fiber backing, then coated with a thin film of vinyl; easy to lay loose or with tape; mineral-backed grade can be used from basement to bedroom; cellulose-backed can be used only above grade level; less durable than other types listed; vulnerable to burns and tears; usually contains vinyl foam layer	Wide price range
Solid vinyl tile	Basically the same composition and characteristics as sheet vinyl; vulnerable to cigarette burns	Moderate

INSTALLING UNDERLAYMENT

To smooth badly worn wood floors, you should cover them with underlayment before installing resilient tiles or sheet goods. Make sure that the material you choose is suitable for use as underlayment (it must have no voids, such as knot holes, for example). Use ¼-inch or thicker hardboard or plywood labeled for use as underlayment.

Acclimate the material to the temperature and humidity of the room in which you plan to lay it by standing it on edge for at least two days in the room where you intend to install it.

To secure the underlayment, you will need lots of ring-shank flooring nails. Drive in one every 4 inches around the perimeter and every 8 inches across the sheets into joists. Stagger the sheet joints, and space them about 1/32 inch apart—the thickness of a dime—to allow for expansion without buckling.

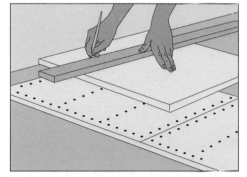

1. Begin at the center of the room and arrange 4×4 or 4×8 panels so that four corners never meet at a point.

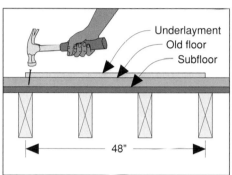

2. Tap with a hammer or drill from below to locate a joist. Center the first panel's edge over it and nail through the subfloor with ring-shank nails.

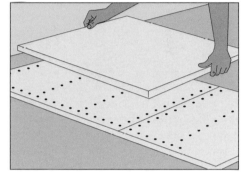

3. Along the edges of the room, slide a sheet of material against the wall, overlapping and squaring it with the previously nailed panel.

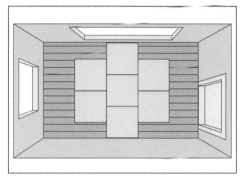

4. With a scrap of underlayment or a straightedge as a guide, draw a line along the length of the edge piece. Cut the sheet along the line.

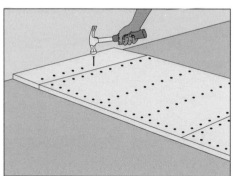

5. Nail the edge piece into place. Don't worry if it doesn't fit exactly. The base molding and shoe will cover a gap of at least an inch.

Laying New Floor Materials (*continued*)

LAYING RESILIENT TILES

Most tiles come with instructions. Pay attention to the preparation of the floor. (For wood floors, see page 27; for concrete, see pages 21 and 114.) Start with a dry run to ensure you'll end up with even margins. If borders measure less than half a tile, shift the layout by half the width of a tile. Put the first tile down with one corner at the center point.

Peel off the paper backing, place the tile carefully, and kneel on it. If the tile you choose does not have an adhesive backing, buy a brush-on adhesive recommended by the manufacturer.

YOU'LL NEED...

SKILLS: Basic skills.
TIME: 4 hours for a 12×15-foot room.
TOOLS: Tape measure, framing square, chalk line, utility knife.

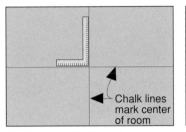

1. Snap chalk lines between the midpoints of the walls. Adjust, if necessary, so the lines make a right angle.

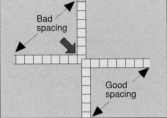

2. Dry-lay tiles in an L from center. Check border tiles. If necessary, shift the L half a tile, and snap new lines.

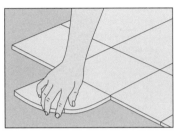

3. Apply tiles, starting with the L corner and building a pyramid. Be certain to keep tiles square with chalk lines.

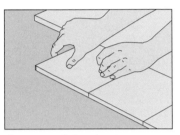

4. Don't slide tiles into position. Butt edges against adjacent tiles, lay in place, and press firmly.

5. At borders, lay a tile on top of the last full one in the row. Put another against the wall and mark overlap.

6. Corners are easy to cut. Mark from one of the walls, just as you would for a border tile.

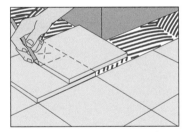

7. Shift the tiles to the other wall (but don't turn them) and mark again. Put an X on the section to be cut out.

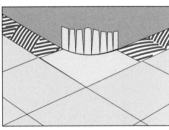

8. For odd shapes, make a template of cardboard first; cut with scissors, and transfer pattern to the tile.

9. You can cut most tiles with a utility knife. If you have difficulty, place in a warm oven.

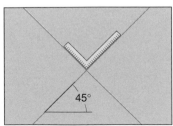

10. For a diagonal pattern, locate the center of the room and snap chalk lines at 45-degree angles to the wall.

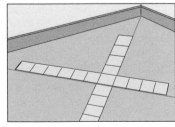

11. Dry-lay tiles along the lines and adjust for good border spacing. At the walls, you'll need to cut triangles.

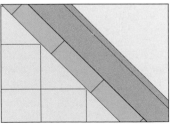

12. For an interesting look, border the diagonal field with a row of conventionally laid tiles.

LAYING CUSHIONED SHEET FLOORING

Techniques shown here are for sheet flooring designed for loose-laying. Roll out the sheet material in a space larger than the one you will be flooring, then transfer your measurements from the room to the material. In that workspace, orient one edge of the material to the longest wall of the room to be floored, then make all your measurements from this starting edge. Allow 2 inches extra at the other edges to compensate for errors and corners that are not square. For larger rooms, you'll need to make the seam cuts as shown before rolling out the material in the room to be floored.

YOU'LL NEED...

SKILLS: Basic skills.
TIME: 4 to 6 hours for a 12×15-foot room, depending on complexity.
TOOLS: Tape measure, chalk line, utility knife, square, straightedge, compass, brush, rolling pin, screwdriver.

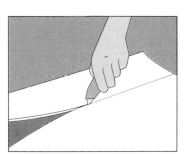

1. You can cut sheet material with heavy shears. Or, protect the underlying floor and use a utility knife.

2. The starting edge of the material must be square. If not, snap a chalk line on the rolled-out vinyl and cut.

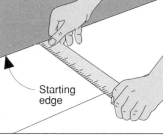

3. Check measurements before cutting. For complex rooms, make a template or a scale plan on graph paper.

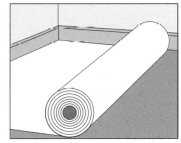

4. To move material, roll it up with the starting edge outside. Place it against the starting wall and loose-lay.

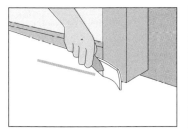

5. You may have to trim off some margins here and there to unroll the material. Cut other margins to fit later.

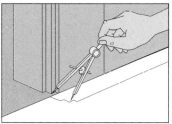

6. Make contour cuts after the material is loose-laid. Mark them with a compass or a scriber (see page 432).

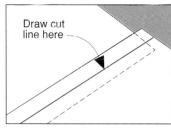

7. To seam two pieces, overlap them, matching the pattern, and draw a line in the middle of the overlap.

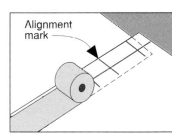

8. Make cross marks to help you align the pieces later. Tape the pieces together and continue measuring.

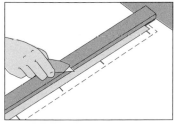

9. Using a very sharp utility knife, cut through tape and both layers of flooring in a single pass. Remove tape.

10. Butt the edges perfectly. Roll them back, apply a wide swath of adhesive, and press edges into it.

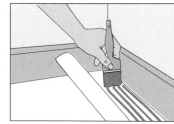

11. Secure the perimeter by brushing on adhesive, then pressing on flooring. Further secure with base shoe.

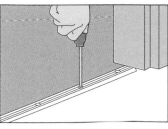

12. At doorways, protect edges with threshold strips. Screw directly into the floor, not through the material.

Laying New Floor Materials (continued)

MATERIAL MATTERS   CHOOSING AND BUYING CERAMIC FLOOR TILE

Hard-surface flooring—ceramic, mosaic, slate, and quarry tile—are easy to maintain, but sometimes difficult to install, depending on the material.

Floor tiles are heavier than wall tiles, and the two can't be interchanged.

Floor tiles with smooth glazes are easier to maintain than textured tiles, but are slippery when wet.

COMPARING HARD-SURFACE FLOORING

Material	Description	Installation
Glazed ceramic tile	Sizes range from 1 to 12 inches square; most common size is 4¼ inches square by ⁵⁄₁₆ inch thick; wide selection of colors, glazes, patterns, and shapes	Moderately easy
Ceramic mosaic tile	Available in 1- and 2-inch squares and 1×2-inch rectangles, ¼ inch thick; mounted to sheets of paper or mesh; very popular with do-it-yourselfers	Easy
Pregrouted tile	Individual or mosaic-sized units also are bonded to big sheets, but with flexible, pregrouted joints; quick installation, but relatively expensive; limited selection	Easiest
Quarry and paver tile	Made from natural clays in large sizes, 6- to 12-inch squares, and 4×8-inch rectangles; normally ½ inch thick; earthen colors in reds, browns, and buffs	Fairly difficult
Special tile	Usually ½ inch thick; widest selection of colors, glazes, patterns, designs, and shapes	Difficult

PREPARING FOR CERAMIC TILES

Because ceramic tiles are brittle, they can be laid only over a surface that is absolutely smooth and rigid.

Over wood floors, you should lay down 1/2-inch exterior plywood or concrete board underlayment to prevent movement that could crack grout between tiles (see page 27).

Concrete makes a good tile base, but check the floor carefully with a straightedge to find low spots, then fill with latex or vinyl cement and sand smooth. Clean the floor thoroughly to ensure a good bond. Dry-set mortar does a good job of bonding tiles to concrete, but do not use it over underlayment.

Lay out the job so you'll have full tiles at doorways. This will ensure that the first thing a person sees when entering the room is a full tile.

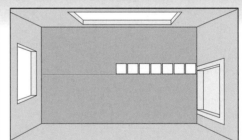

1. Snap a chalk line from the door to the opposite wall. This line must be perpendicular to the door.

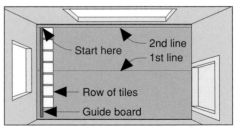

2. Dry-lay a row of tiles along the line, starting at the door. If the tiles aren't self-spacing, be sure to use spacers.

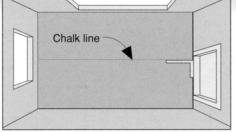

3. Nail a guide board perpendicular to the chalk line where the last full tile will be placed. Dry-lay along the board.

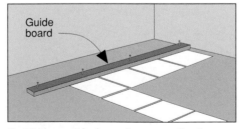

4. Adjust row for even borders. Snap a second chalk line from where border begins. Start laying tiles on second line.

LAYING CERAMIC TILES

Ask your tile dealer to recommend the adhesive, grout, and serrated trowel for the tile you have chosen. Floor tiles have no spacer lugs, so you'll need to make your own spacers. Lay the tiles as shown and grout them as you would wall tiles (see page 45).

YOU'LL NEED...

SKILLS: Basic skills.
TIME: 4 to 5 hours to lay tile in a 12×15-foot room; 1 to 2 hours on a second day for grouting.
TOOLS: Tape measure, chalk line, straightedge, hammer, serrated trowel, tile cutter, tile nippers.

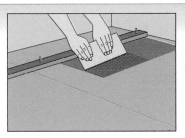

1. With a serrated trowel, spread about 2 square feet of adhesive.

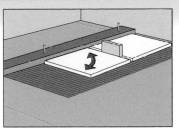

2. Twist tiles into position and tap until level, using a board to protect the tile. Check with a level.

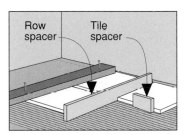

3. Use spacers of wood or tile scraps or plastic ones available from tile dealers.

4. Mark border tiles as with resilient tiles (see page 28). Trim with tile cutter.

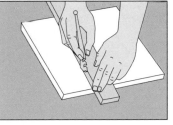

5. You also can trim ceramic tiles with a straightedge and glass cutter.

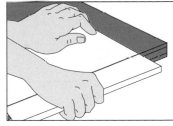

6. Place scored tile at edge of a board and snap. Smooth the edge with a file.

LAYING MOSAIC TILES

Mosaic tiles come mounted on paper-faced sheets or backed by nonremovable mesh. Mosaics install quickly. Square up the room with guide boards (see page 30) and begin laying from a corner. Use spacers between sheets for uniform gaps.

YOU'LL NEED...

SKILLS: Basic skills.
TIME: 4 to 5 hours to lay tile in a 12×15-foot room; 1 to 2 hours on a second day for grouting.
TOOLS: Tape measure, chalk line, straightedge, hammer, serrated trowel, tile cutter, and tile nippers.

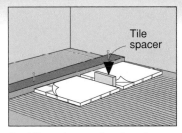

1. Align sheets, lay in place, and twist slightly. Peel paper back to check that individual tiles align.

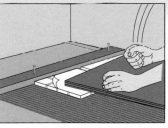

2. Tamp sheets into place and level by pounding on a piece of plywood. Wipe up excess adhesive.

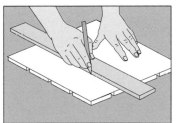

3. Mark border cuts on paper. Cut between tiles with a utility knife.

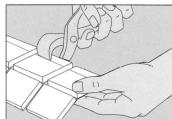

4. Cut tile with nippers. For a hole, cut tile in half, then nibble notches in each half.

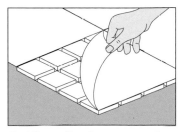

5. After adhesive sets, soak paper backing with warm water and remove.

6. Pack grout into joints with a squeegee. (See page 45 for more about grouting.)

INTERIOR WALLS

The illustration at right shows a typical wood-frame wall. These walls begin with a sole plate nailed to the subfloor. The plate supports vertical studs, which in turn are nailed to a top plate.

Around all openings, the studs are doubled for extra rigidity and topped with a header, usually two 2×4s or 2×6s nailed together and installed on edge. Some walls also include horizontal fire blocking, usually at the 4-foot level.

The material on the surface of the wall, the only element that you actually see, might be drywall, plaster, or paneling.

ANATOMY OF A WALL

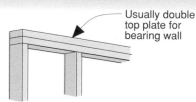

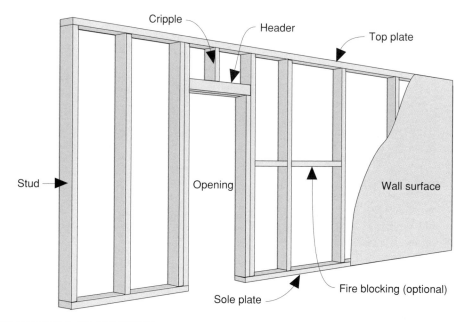

IDENTIFYING A BEARING WALL

All walls fall into one of two structural categories—bearing walls, which support a load above, and nonbearing walls, which support only themselves. If you removed or made a big opening in a bearing wall, you could literally bring down the house.

To determine whether a wall is bearing or not, you will have to do some sleuthing in the basement or attic—wherever there are exposed joists or rafters. If joists run parallel to the wall in question, you can be sure it's not a bearing wall. If, however, they are perpendicular to the wall—as shown at right—you can be fairly certain that the wall is bearing a load.

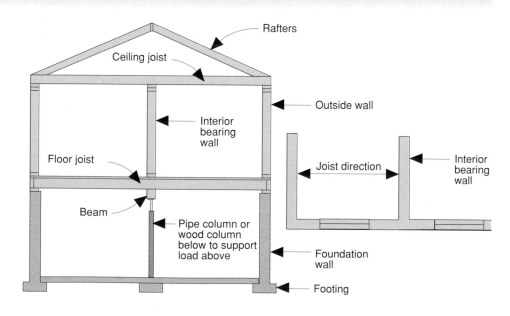

ANATOMY OF A PLASTER WALL

Most plaster walls begin with the same framing used for drywall construction. Beyond the frame, however, plaster entails a lot more work. The studs must be covered with lath—formerly made of narrow strips of wood, but more recently made with a heavy mesh called expanded metal lath or strips of drywall known as rock lath (not shown). The lath then is covered by three layers of plaster.

The scratch coat of plaster grips the lath. The brown coat smooths out the surface. Finally, a finish coat is applied to produce a texture from rough to glassy smooth.

If your home has solid stone, brick, or block walls, the same three coats of plaster might be applied directly to the masonry.

Due to their high cost, plaster walls have all but disappeared from modern-day homes.

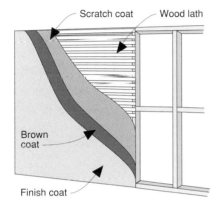

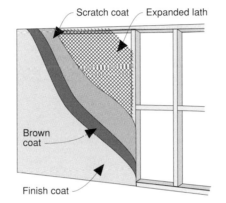

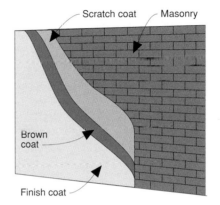

FINDING STUDS IN A WALL

Most studs are spaced at regular intervals. After you've found one, you can plot others by measuring.

Shown at right are four common ways to find that first stud. Begin your search toward the wall's center, not at the ends, where spacing might be irregular. Also, ignore the studs on either side of a door or window opening. Electronic stud finders can help and are available at most hardware stores.

Once you've found one stud, measure 16 inches—the most common spacing—in one direction or the other. If you cannot find a second stud, try 24 inches, a spacing used in some newer houses.

YOU'LL NEED...

SKILLS: Basic skills.
TIME: 10 minutes or less.
TOOLS: Drill, coat hanger, or electronic stud finder.

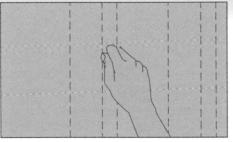

Often, you can "sound out" a wall by rapping along it with your knuckles. A solid thunk indicates a stud.

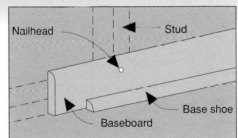

If rapping doesn't tell you anything, look for nails in the baseboard. They're usually driven into the studs.

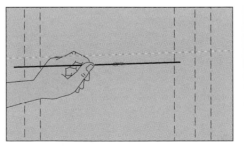

You can also drill a small, angled hole and probe with a straightened wire coat hanger to find the stud.

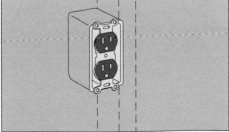

Take the face plate off an electrical receptacle. Wall boxes usually are nailed to the side of a stud.

Solving Wall Problems

HANGING LIGHT OBJECTS

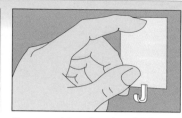

Ordinary, nailed picture hooks hold items up to about 20 pounds.

Gummed hooks should be used only on very light-weight objects.

YOU'LL NEED...

SKILLS: Basic skills.
TIME: 10 to 15 minutes, depending on the hanger type.
TOOLS: Drill, hammer, screwdriver.

HANGING MEDIUM-WEIGHT OBJECTS

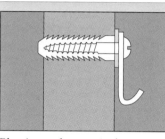

Plastic anchors grip by expanding as you drive screws into them. Drill the right-sized hole for a snug fit.

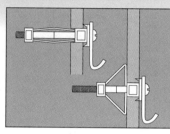

Hollow-wall anchors open behind the wall surface for an installation that cannot pull loose.

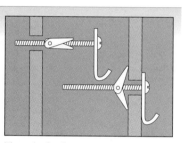

Toggle bolts screw into wings that pop open inside the wall. Assemble with the fixture before inserting.

HANGING HEAVY OBJECTS

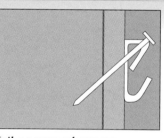

Nail or screw hangers directly to studs to provide excellent security for mirrors or large, heavy pictures.

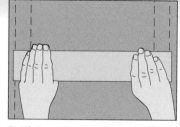

Bridging studs with a 1×4 gains strength and freedom from stud spacings. Nail or screw hanger to bridging.

ATTACHING TO MASONRY WALLS

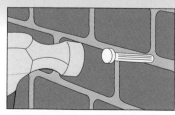

Drive hardened masonry nails into concrete block or mortar joints. Wear safety goggles when doing this.

Drill a hole with a masonry bit and tap a plastic or lead anchor into it. These expand as you drive screws in.

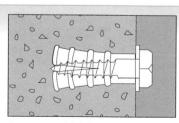

For more holding power, use a lead expansion shield and lag screw. The screw cuts its own threads.

REPAIRING DRYWALL

Drywall—also known as plasterboard and gypsum board—consists of big sheets of pressed gypsum that are faced with heavy paper on both sides. After the sheets have been nailed, screwed, or glued to the studs, the joints between the sheets are covered with a perforated paper or fiberglass mesh tape. Joints are smoothed over with joint compound, often referred to as mud, to create a continuous, smooth surface.

Drywall repairs are easy once you get the knack of working with the material, especially the joint compound. (See pages 54–56 for more about working with drywall.)

Filling Dents

YOU'LL NEED...
SKILLS: Basic skills.
TIME: 10 to 20 minutes depending on the size of the repair.
TOOLS: Drywall taping knife, sponge, hammer.

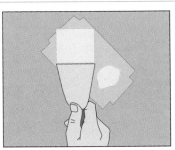

1. Pack with joint compound and smooth. If the patch shrinks after drying, apply a second coat.

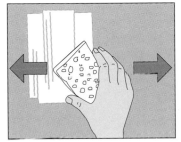

2. Sand surface very lightly—or smooth by wiping with a damp sponge.

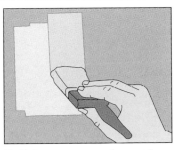

3. Joint compound must be primed before you paint. Some paints self-prime.

Mending Split Tape

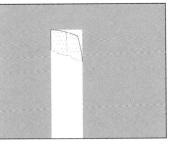

1. Use a sharp knife to make a clean break at the edges, then carefully pull away the loose tape.

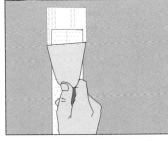

2. Apply joint compound, position new tape, then smooth bubbles with light, vertical strokes of the knife.

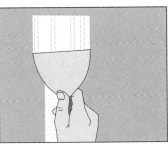

3. Apply compound over tape right away. Let dry, then coat again, feather out the edges, and sand.

Setting Popped Nails

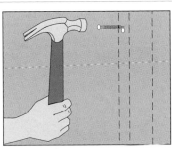

1. Drive in ring-shank nails or screw in drywall screws above and below the popped nail.

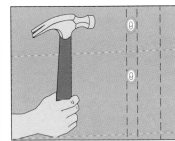

2. If using nails, "dimple" the nails below the surface. Fill the dimples or screw holes with compound.

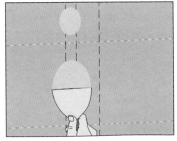

3. Apply a second coat of compound, feathered at the edges. Wait a day, then sand, prime, and paint.

Solving Wall Problems (continued)

REPAIRING DRYWALL (continued)
Patching Small Holes

YOU'LL NEED...

SKILLS: Basic skills.
TIME: 20 to 30 minutes of actual work, plus drying time.
TOOLS: Putty knife, sponge, sanding block, pencil or stick.

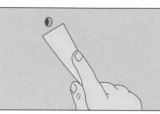

For very small holes, apply joint compound to the void with a putty knife. After drying, sand smooth.

1. For larger holes, cut pegboard slightly larger than the hole, but which you can get through the hole.

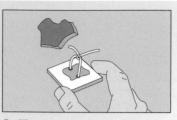

2. Tie wire to it, smear compound on hardboard, and slip into wall. Patch will cling to the back of the wall.

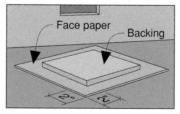

3. Tie wire to a pencil and twist tight. After patch dries, cut the wire off and fill the recess with compound.

4. Fill with two or three thin coats of compound, lightly sand, and sponge to blend repair.

Patching Large Holes

YOU'LL NEED...

SKILLS: Basic skills.
TIME: 30 minutes of actual work, plus drying time.
TOOLS: Broadknife, sponge, keyhole saw, hammer, utility knife.

1. For holes up to 8 inches, mark a rectangle and cut it out with a keyhole saw.

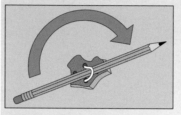

Face paper   Backing

2"   2"

2. Cut a drywall rectangle 2 inches larger than the hole. Remove 2-inch perimeter, but leaving facing paper.

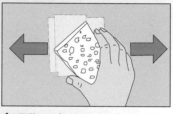

3. Spread compound around the damaged area. Also, butter its inside edges to serve as an adhesive.

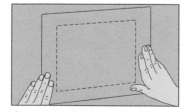

4. Insert patch, smooth down, and hold in place for a few minutes. Blend in by feathering with compound.

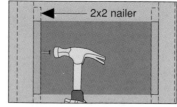

2x2 nailer

5. For larger holes, cut area to centers of adjoining studs. Toenail 2×2s to top and bottom to use as nailers.

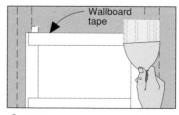

Wallboard tape

6. Nail or screw in patch, tape, and smooth. You'll need three coats of compound for a good job.

REPAIRING PLASTER WALLS

If your home has plaster walls, you can resign yourself to patching before every paint job. Harmless cracks will return with regularity no matter how often you fill them. Watch, though, for loose or crumbly cracks, holes, and bulges; these may mean you have a leak. If you have a leak, fix it before doing any work on the walls (see page 38).

Too much or too little water in the original mix also weakens plaster. It's easier to use premixed materials for small repairs.

Drywall joint compound works easily into all but the finest cracks, smooths bumpy surfaces, and fills fairly deep holes in a couple of applications. Surfacing compound, available in powder, paste, or aerosol form, fills hairline cracks, holes left by picture hooks, and other small blemishes.

Patching plaster must be mixed with water, but it is stronger than surfacing or joint compound. Use it for broad cracks or big holes.

Spackling Hairline Cracks

YOU'LL NEED...

SKILLS: Basic skills.
TIME: 20 to 30 minutes.
TOOLS: Hammer, chisel, putty knife, paintbrush.

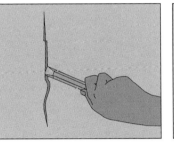

1. Widen the crack to about ⅛ inch with a chisel and blow out any loose plaster.

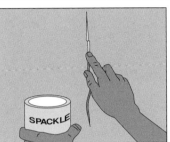

2. Wipe crack with a dab of surfacing compound, pressing it into the fissure.

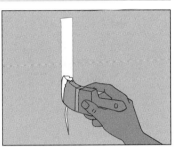

3. Seal patches with primer before painting, or the patch may "bleed" through.

Patching Large Cracks

YOU'LL NEED...

SKILLS: Basic skills.
TIME: 1 hour of work, but allow for two overnight periods of drying.
TOOLS: Hammer, chisel, putty knife, broadknife, old toothbrush, sandpaper.

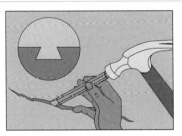

1. Undercut wide cracks, making them broader at the bottom than the surface to lock in the filler material.

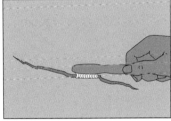

2. Clean the debris and crumbly material out of the crack with an old toothbrush.

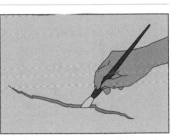

3. If you are using plaster for the repair, thoroughly wet the crack before patching to ensure a good bond.

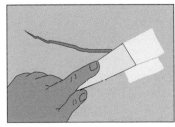

4. Pack plaster into the crack with a putty knife or a wide-blade taping knife.

5. Let dry 24 hours, then level off the repair with a second application.

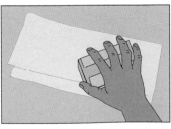

6. After the second coat has dried, sand smooth, then seal with primer before painting.

Solving Wall Problems (continued)

REPAIRING PLASTER WALLS (continued)
Patching Holes

Before you attack a big hole or bulge, find out what caused the plaster to fail in the first place. Water stains and damp plaster are sure tip-offs—but since leakage usually attacks walls from behind, you may have to do some probing to find the real source of trouble. Fix the cause first, then repair the plaster. (See pages 113-115 to learn about tracking down and repairing leaks.)

Always cut back to sound plaster; you won't get a solid bond with crumbling edges. If there's no lath behind the hole, make a backing as shown on page 36.

Fill medium-size holes with patching plaster and larger ones with ready-mix—the same material used for plastering new walls. Do not use surfacing or joint compound because they shrink too much.

Use the techniques shown here for holes up to about 1 foot across. For larger areas, piece in drywall and blend it in with tape and compound (see pages 36 and 56).

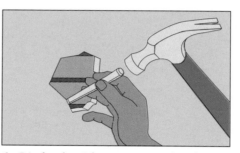

1. Dig back with a masonry chisel until you encounter solid plaster. Brush out remaining debris.

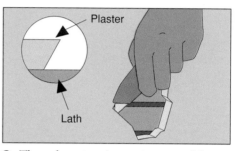

Plaster

Lath

2. Though not as important as with cracks, undercutting edges makes a stronger repair.

3. If there is wood lath behind the hole, staple expanded-metal lath to the wood lath for a better grip.

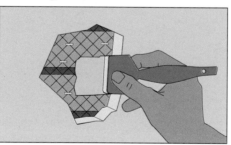

4. Thoroughly dampen the edges and backing. Dry surfaces absorb water and weaken the plaster.

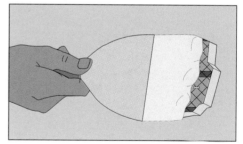

5. Fill the edges with ready-mix first, then work toward the center. Apply three coats with time to dry between.

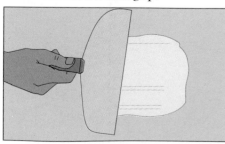

6. For a slick finish, run a wet brush across the patch, followed by the edge of the broadknife.

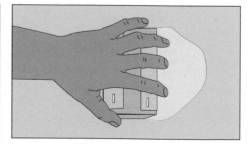

7. Sand after 24 hours, but don't prime or paint until the plaster is hard. High humidity slows the cure.

REPAIRING PANELING

If you scratch or mar paneling, you usually can make a cosmetic repair in a few minutes with paste wax or a crayonlike touch-up stick. Don't try to spot-sand and refinish prefinished paneling; you risk doing more harm than good.

If a panel has suffered serious damage, you'll have to replace an entire 4×8-foot section. Finding a match among the myriad styles and finishes offered by manufacturers may be your biggest challenge.

If your paneling was glued directly to drywall, you may have to replace the drywall before putting your patch in place. If there's electrical wiring anywhere in the wall you're working on, shut off the power to the circuit before doing any cutting, sawing, or nailing.

> ### YOU'LL NEED...
> **SKILLS:** Basic skills.
> **TIME:** 1 hour.
> **TOOLS:** Hammer, pry bar, putty knife, pliers, caulking gun.

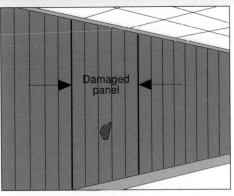

1. Identify and mark the edges of the panel that is damaged.

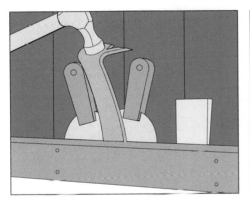

2. Pry off the baseboard and top molding by inserting a putty knife, then a pry bar. Pull nails with pliers.

3. Pull the panel off the wall. Start at the bottom, where there's usually no adhesive. Pull nails as they pop.

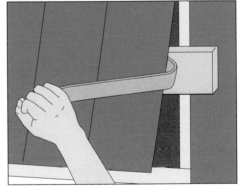

4. Continue prying the panel away from bottom to top. Use a wood block to protect adjacent panels.

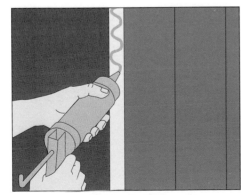

5. Remove all old adhesive with a scraper or chisel. Apply panel adhesive to studs with a caulking gun.

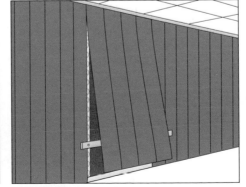

6. Nail the panel loosely at the top and wedge out, as shown, until the adhesive gets tacky.

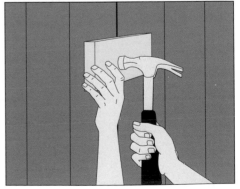

7. Press the panel into place, tapping it against the studs, as shown, and nail edges with color-matched brads.

Solving Wall Problems *(continued)*

REPAIRING BASEBOARDS

Like most other trim work, fitting a new baseboard is trickier than you might imagine. So don't be overly dismayed if you miscut a miter on your first effort; it takes a bit of concentration to keep track of which way those angles should go.

Baseboard moldings, sometimes called base moldings, come in a wide variety of sizes and styles. Take along a piece of the old molding when you shop for a replacement. In an older home, you may discover the baseboard actually consists of several different moldings fastened together. If so, you may be able to make a convincing-from-a-distance facsimile with modern-day millwork.

Base shoe molding not only protects the baseboard from scuffing, it is also flexible enough to rise and fall with uneven flooring. So instead of scribing and painstakingly fitting your new baseboard to the floor, you might prefer to hide any gaps with a base shoe.

Finally, to save yourself some frustration when cutting miters, bring your miter box close to the job and set it up beside the angle you are cutting. This lets you orient the angle in the miter box to the one needed for the baseboard.

ANATOMY OF A BASEBOARD

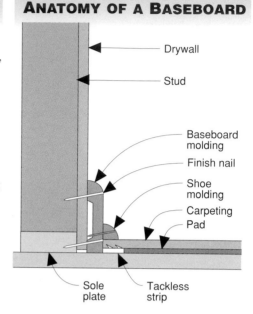

- Drywall
- Stud
- Baseboard molding
- Finish nail
- Shoe molding
- Carpeting
- Pad
- Sole plate
- Tackless strip

REPLACING A DAMAGED BASEBOARD

YOU'LL NEED...

SKILLS: Intermediate carpentry skills.
TIME: 30 to 45 minutes, not including finishing.
TOOLS: Hammer, nail set, putty knife, pry bar, miter box, backsaw.

To save a base shoe without breaking it, drive its finish nails all the way through with a nail set.

Pry off the baseboard and top molding by inserting a putty knife, then a pry bar. Pull nails with pliers.

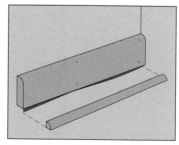

Measure carefully. Add 1/16 inch to the length and spring the molding into place so it fits tightly.

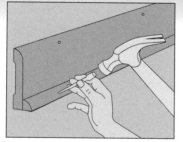

You can cut baseboards with an inexpensive miter box and a backsaw.

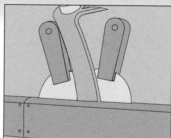

Drill pilot holes and drive the finish nails into the studs and sole plate. Glue the outside corners.

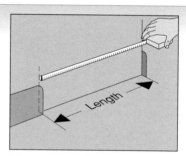

Base shoe will cover floor irregularities. Drill pilot holes and nail to baseboard or floor, but not to both.

REPLACING CERAMIC TILES

The drawings here show how to replace a single ceramic tile. If you have a leak behind a tile wall, you'll have to remove all the affected tiles and replace the wall behind the tiles. Adapt the same technique to larger areas, but apply adhesive to the wall, not the tiles (see page 44).

When replacing a section of tiles, plan the opening so it straddles two studs. Then it's it easier to patch the wall behind the tiles. Use water-resistant drywall or cement backerboard for your wall patch. Don't bother salvaging old tiles; most will break anyway.

YOU'LL NEED...
SKILLS: Basic tiling skills.
TIME: 45 to 60 minutes for a few tiles, more if repairing the wall.
TOOLS: Hammer, small chisel or grout scraper, sponge.

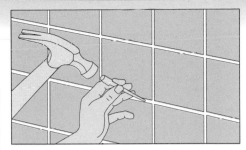

1. Isolate the bad tiles by chipping away the grout around them with a grout scraper or chisel. Smash them one at a time, knocking out the pieces.

2. Scrape all old adhesive from the wall. Spread the back of each new tile with a thin, even coat of tile adhesive.

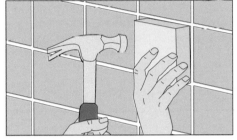

3. Press the tile into place, adjusting the grout spacing, then tap in place with a wood block and hammer.

4. Wipe excess adhesive from the surface. Clean out the grout spaces and grout (see page 45).

SEALING AROUND A TUB

Bathtubs have their ups and downs—caused by filling and emptying hundreds of pounds of water. Grout, a rigid mortar compound, cannot withstand this flexing. The result: Cracks develop where the tub meets the walls.

Fill these troublemakers with silicone caulking compound designed for tubs or tiles. While you're at it, seal off openings where fixtures come through the wall. (See pages 145–146 for more about working with caulking materials).

YOU'LL NEED...
SKILLS: Basic skills.
TIME: 30 minutes.
TOOLS: Grout scraper, caulking gun.

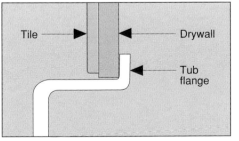

Tile → ← Drywall

← Tub flange

1. Remove old grout with a grout scraper or chisel. You'll find a narrow space between the bottom of the wall and the top of the tub.

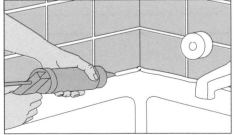

2. Run an even bead of tub or tile caulk along the joint. Use either the cartridge-type, shown here, or smaller squeeze tubes. Smooth with a finger.

3. To seal under a spout, unscrew it first; with faucets, you should remove the decorative covers before caulking.

Putting Up New Walls

MATERIAL MATTERS: CHOOSING AND BUYING CERAMIC TILE

Ceramic tiles are relatively brittle, but once you have cemented them to a solid backing and grouted the joints with special mortar, you have an exceptionally sturdy wall.

In shopping for ceramic tile, you will find an enormous range of colors, shapes, sizes, and textures. Specialty items can cost two to three times as much as standard tiles. Ceramic wall tiles differ from floor tiles in that they are thinner and slicker.

To piece together a smooth tile installation, you will need two types of tiles (see diagram below). Field tiles, typically 4¼- and 6-inch squares, cover most of the surface, and trim tiles round off edges and get around corners. Don't get carried away with a low per-square-foot price for field tiles until you have determined what the trim tiles will cost. Sold by the lineal foot, these can add quite a bit to the final bill.

Smaller mosaic tiles (see page 31) come bonded to pieces of 1×1- or 1×2-foot paper or fabric mesh; they go up a little faster, but require more grouting.

Pre-grouted tile sheets are made up of 4¼-inch tiles with flexible synthetic grouting; you cement the sheets to the wall, then seal edges with caulking. These are the easiest to put up, but there is a limited selection of colors and styles to choose from.

You can choose from a number of mastic-like tile adhesives that have been developed especially for do-it-yourselfers. Ask your dealer to recommend one.

FIGURING TILE NEEDS

To compute how many field tiles you will need for an installation, make a scale drawing of each wall on graph paper, count the squares, and add about 5 percent for waste.

In a shower stall, the tiles should run to a height of at least 6 inches above the showerhead. Other bathroom walls usually are tiled to the 4-foot level; kitchen walls, to the bottoms of the wall cabinets.

Estimate trim tiles, such as bullnoses, caps, and coves, by the lineal foot. Order mitered corners, angles, and other specialty items by the piece.

Choose an organic, or "Type I," adhesive for tub, shower, and other wet locations and a "Type II" adhesive for lightly wetted surfaces, such as a kitchen walls. One gallon covers about 50 square feet.

Dry-mix grout usually comes in 5-pound bags. One bag will grout 100 square feet of 4¼-inch tiles or about 15 square feet of mosaics.

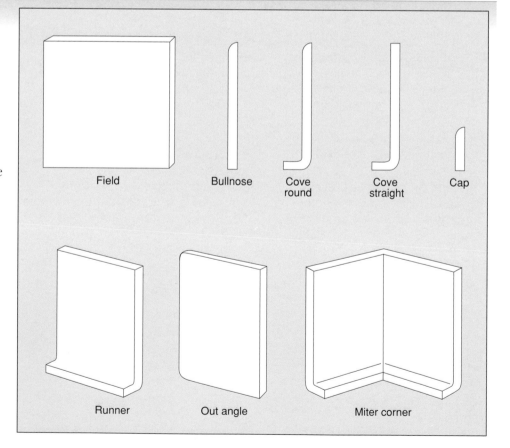

Field   Bullnose   Cove round   Cove straight   Cap

Runner   Out angle   Miter corner

TOOL TALK

A tile cutter cuts quick, accurate straight lines. Ask your dealer for a demonstration—and expect to ruin a few tiles before you get the hang of it. Nippers nibble out curved cuts. A good job can take a long time, so first set all the tiles that do not have to be cut, then rent the cutter and nippers you will need for trimming around the edges.

The serrated edges on the notched trowel let you spread adhesive to just the right thickness; a notched spreader gets into tight spots.

A rubber float facilitates grouting, but you also can get by with an ordinary window washer's squeegee.

TOOLS FOR TILE WORK

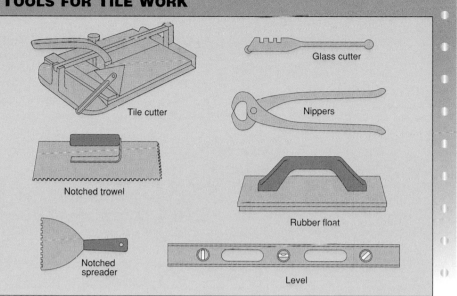

Tile cutter

Glass cutter

Nippers

Notched trowel

Rubber float

Notched spreader

Level

PREPARING WALLS

For decorative tiling you can apply ceramic tiles to any drywall, plaster, or plywood surface that is smooth and sound. But in areas of high moisture, walls should be covered with cement backerboard or waterproof drywall. Strip off wallpaper or scrape away loose paint on existing walls. Sand the sheen off glossy finishes.

Pay attention to the point where tile will meet the top of a tub or shower base. Chip away all old material here and leave a ¼-inch space; this will be caulked after tiling (see page 41). Don't bother taping and smoothing joints in a new wall. Application of the adhesive will seal these spots.

Take care in laying out the job. The drawings below show how to establish guidelines to start in the center of a wall. This method results in equal-sized tiles at each corner. If that is not important to you, start in a corner. But check it for plumb first; you probably will have to trim some tiles to compensate.

YOU'LL NEED...

SKILLS: Moderate tiling tiles.
TIME: 3 to 4 hours to tile a 10×6-foot area and 1 to 2 hours for grouting on a second day.
TOOLS: Scraping and cleaning tools, tape measure, level, plumb bob.

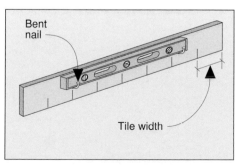

1. Create a layout tool by fastening a level to a board. Mark off tile widths, including ¹⁄₁₆-inch spaces for grouting.

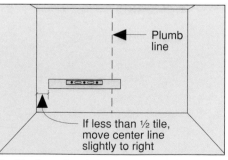

2. Mark a plumb line at the wall's midpoint. Use the guide to determine the edges. Shift the field, if necessary.

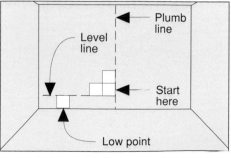

3. Find the wall's lowest point. Mark a level line one tile width above it. Begin setting full tiles above this line.

Putting Up New Walls (continued)

INSTALLING CERAMIC TILE

Ceramic tiles are the longest lasting, most water-resistant, and easiest cleaning wall surface. Although not difficult, setting tiles calls for slow and exacting work.

Field tiles, which cover most of a wall, go up quickly. Set all of them before turning to the tedious tasks of trimming and fitting around edges, pipes, and fixtures.

Establish the guidelines as shown on page 43. If the tiles are the heavier type with edge lugs, tack up a 1×2 along the bottom to support the tiles as the adhesive cures.

When you start, apply adhesive in 2-square-foot sections; you can increase the coverage after you get better at setting tiles. Open a window for adequate ventilation, especially in confined areas, such as a shower stall, as the adhesive odor can be overpowering.

After all the field tiles are up (leaving space for soap dishes or other accessories), you can begin filling in the corners with cut tiles. Expect slow going at first while you master the knack of cutting tiles.

Grouting—the final stage—goes quickly. Some tiles require special grout; check with your dealer. With conventional grout, you can speed the curing process by misting with water for several days. After two weeks, coat it with a sealer designed to ward off dirt and mildew.

(See page 30 for more about floor tiles and page 218 for outdoor tiles.)

YOU'LL NEED...

SKILLS: Moderate tiling skills.
TIME: 8 to 10 hours to set tile for a simple shower; 1 to 2 hours for grouting on a second day.
TOOLS: Level, notched trowel, tile cutter, tile nippers, glass cutter, file, compass, old toothbrush, rubber float, sponge.

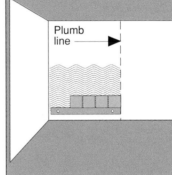

1. Spread adhesive with a notched trowel, combing in beaded lines; areas between lines should be nearly bare.

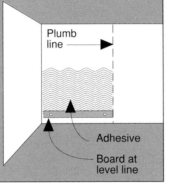

2. Set the first full tiles. Use a slight twist, but don't slide them. Keep about ¹⁄₁₆ inch between tiles for grout.

3. After you check that a tile is square and properly spaced, press it firmly into the adhesive.

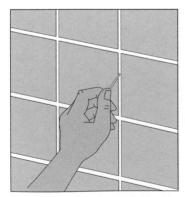

4. If adhesive oozes from under the tile, you are applying too much. Use a toothpick to remove excess.

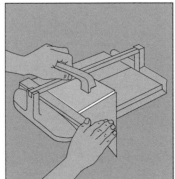

5. To cut tiles, bear down on tile cutter and score a single line. Snap with a flick of the handle.

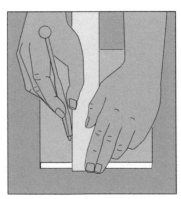

6. If you're using a glass cutter, don't go back over the score or you'll get a crumbly break.

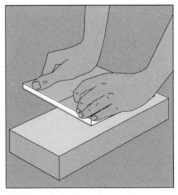

7. Place the score over an edge, hold the tile firmly, and snap downward.

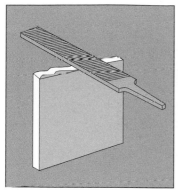

8. Smooth cut edges and enlarge notches with an ordinary wood file.

9. Make curved cuts with nippers. To avoid breaking the tile, start at the edge and bite off tiny chunks.

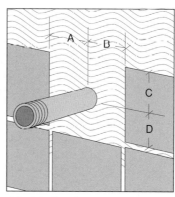

10. To fit tiles around pipes, crack the glaze with a file and drill with a masonry bit, or piece it, as shown at right.

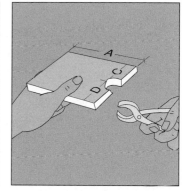

11. After measuring, cut the tile in two and nibble out semicircular notches from each piece.

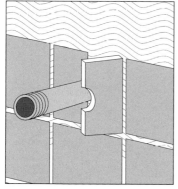

12. Smooth the notches with a file and fit around the pipe. After grouting, seal with silicone caulk.

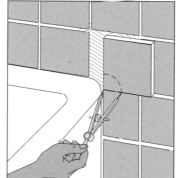

13. Scribe tiles to fixtures using a felt-tip pen held in a compass. Let the steel tip follow the contour.

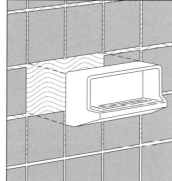

14. Install soap dishes and other accessories last. Cement in place with two-part epoxy putty.

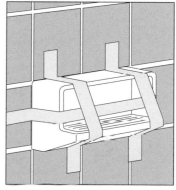

15. Use masking tape to hold accessories until the putty hardens. Don't apply pressure for a week.

16. After adhesive sets overnight, apply grout with diagonal passes of a rubber float. Pack all of the joints.

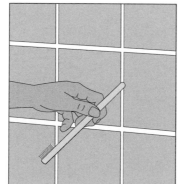

17. After 10 minutes, tool and pack the joints with the handle of a toothbrush.

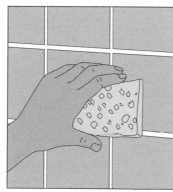

18. Wash grout off the surface with a wet sponge. Scrub, but be careful not to damage joints.

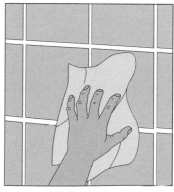

19. Polish the tiles with a soft cloth. Do not use the shower or tub for about two weeks.

Putting Up New Walls (continued)

MATERIAL MATTERS CHOOSING AND BUYING PANELING

The secret to paneling's easy installation is the vertical grooves scored down every panel's face. Although these grooves seem randomly spaced, you will find one every 16 and 24 inches—the most typical wall stud spacings. The grooves hide nails and disguise panel joints.

The lightweight sheets are installed with nails and panel adhesives that bond to studs, furring strips, drywall, or almost any existing wall.

When you shop for paneling, you'll find dozens of styles, textures, and wood tones from which to choose— but all can be divided into three general categories.

Plywood panels faced with genuine wood veneer provide the most natural look; often, no two panels have exactly the same pattern. But these panels can be expensive.

The less expensive, embossed, simulated-wood-grain plywoods have

come a long way from the flimsy, obvious fakes you may remember. In fact, many look convincingly like wood, except that the pattern repeats every so often along the wall.

Solid-board paneling still offers the greatest design versatility, but it usually is the most expensive. You can nail up the boards vertically, horizontally, diagonally, even in herringbone patterns. Solid-board paneling comes with plain or interlocking edges.

COMPARING PANELING MATERIALS

Material	Features	Relative Cost
Plywood	Three-ply construction, usually with a tough, prefinished face; normally $5/32$ inch thick, but you can buy $1/8$- and $3/16$-inch sizes; easy to install	Moderate to expensive
Hardboard	Compressed wood fibers with durable vinyl or paper overlays; good resistance to moisture; comes in $1/8$ or $1/4$ inch thicknesses; installation is almost the same as for plywood	Low to moderate
Solid boards	Includes everything from rosewood to barn siding; edges may be plain, tongue-and-grooved, or shiplapped; thicknesses range from $3/8$ to $3/4$ inch; installation is slower and requires more advanced carpentry skills than applying sheet goods	Moderate to very expensive

FIGURING YOUR PANELING NEEDS

Successful paneling calls for more head work than hand work. First, assess what you expect the paneling to do. If you simply want to dress up drab or deteriorating walls, you probably can cement most materials directly to the old surfaces. The walls must be even, however, because mole hills sometimes turn into mountains under paneling.

Before you panel a basement wall, or any uneven surface, you'll need to put up furring strips (see page 47). If you want to panel a new partition, install insulation and

drywall first; paneling simply is not designed to retard noise or fire.

Draw up the job on graph paper. Make elevation drawings of each wall individually, accurately locating all windows, doors, offsets, pipes, and electrical outlets. By counting squares, you easily can calculate how many 4×8 paneling sheets you will need. Tailor 4×8-square graph-paper cutouts to these detailed plans and you will have a cutting diagram for each panel. But be sure to double-check all measurements before picking up a saw.

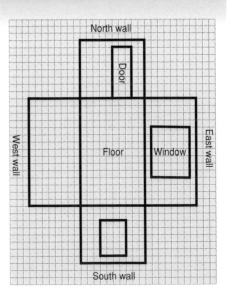

INSTALLING FURRING STRIPS TO PANEL A CONCRETE WALL

How flat are your walls? Select a straight 2×4 and hold it on edge against the surface. If you see gaps under the 2×4, you need to even the wall with furring before paneling. You might build a 2×4-stud framework instead (see pages 50–51) to allow space for pipes, insulation, and electrical outlets.

Before you begin, make sure your foundation walls have been sealed properly against moisture (see pages 113–115).

Use 1×2s or 1×3s for furring. You also will need panel adhesive and wood shingles for shimming.

Use 16-inch center-to-center spacing. This lets you put up standard 4-foot-wide materials without a lot of trimming.

To learn about insulating basement walls, turn to page 397.

To learn about insulating basement walls, turn to page 397.

YOU'LL NEED...

SKILLS: Basic carpentry skills.
TIME: 4 to 8 hours for an 8×24-foot area of wall.
TOOLS: Tape measure, hammer, level, chalk line, caulking gun.

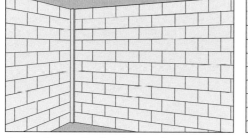

1. On flat walls, begin by gluing up a strip at one corner. With all verticals, leave ½-inch space at the bottom.

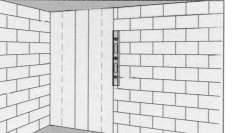

2. Set the first panel in place, plumb it, and trim the corner edge, if necessary. Draw a line for the first joint.

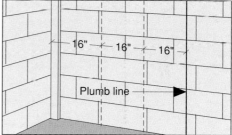

3. Take all measurements from that joint line. Remember to maintain the correct center-to-center spacing.

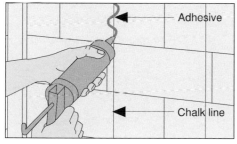

4. Lay beads of adhesive on the lines, press strips against them, remove the strips, and reapply after 10 minutes.

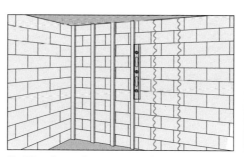

5. Plumb each strip carefully before permanently fixing it to the wall. Double-check the 16-inch spacings.

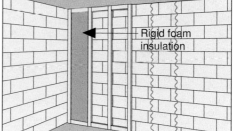

6. Glue horizontal strips on the top and bottom between the vertical strips Install insulation now if you wish.

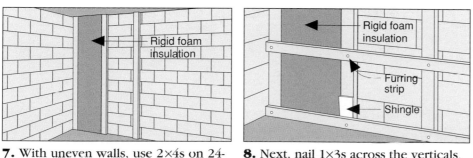

7. With uneven walls, use 2×4s on 24-inch centers for vertical furring. If you plan to insulate, do it before next step.

8. Next, nail 1×3s across the verticals. Insert shingle wedges behind these horizontals wherever you need to shim.

9. Fill in spaces between horizontals with short lengths of furring. Shim low spots here, too, if necessary.

Putting Up New Walls (continued)

INSTALLING PANELING

Once you have done the preparation work, which can be considerable, paneling with plywood or hardboard goes quickly and easily.

You should not expect paneling to bridge wide spans without buckling, so apply it to a firm backing. Paneling often accentuates wall irregularities. If you nail sheets directly to studs, you could end up with an undulating wall as the lumber shrinks, swells, and warps. Install drywall first (see pages 54-56), then apply your paneling to the drywall with adhesive.

Or even up irregular and masonry walls with furring (see page 47). Make sure that all panels will be well supported along their edges and every 16 to 24 inches vertically and horizontally.

If a nonmasonry wall is true, just find and mark the stud locations.

Figure out where the panels will join and spray-paint wide black swaths down the backing or furring strips. These stripes will provide reference points as you work. And if a panel shrinks later, the gap will not be conspicuous.

Acclimate panels by stacking them several days in advance in the room where they will be installed.

Measure the exact ceiling height at several different points. When cutting the panels, allow for ½-inch clearance between the paneling and the floor. This makes it easier to fit the panels into place and compensates for settlement.

Cut plywood or hardboard paneling with a fine-tooth power or handsaw. Cut paneling face up with a hand or table saw and face down with a portable circular or saber saw. To avoid costly mistakes, make a cutting diagram (see page 46), then check each measurement before you cut. Support long cuts with sawhorses with 2×4s spaced directly on each side of the cut; otherwise, the thin paneling might snap.

YOU'LL NEED...

SKILLS: Basic carpentry skills and a helper to handle the paneling.
TIME: 45 to 60 minutes for an 8×24-foot wall.
TOOLS: Tape measure, hammer, putty knife, pry bar, fine-tooth saw (hand or power), keyhole saw, caulking gun.

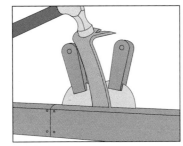

1. Pry off baseboard molding (see page 39) and remove covers from receptacles.

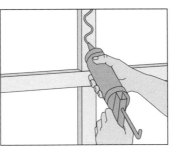

2. Apply adhesive—one panel at a time—to furring strips or at 16-inch intervals.

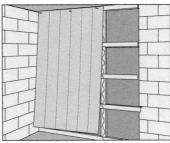

3. Position panel in place and secure it by partially nailing it along the top.

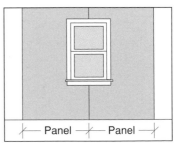

4. Wedge the bottom of the panel away from the wall until the adhesive gets tacky.

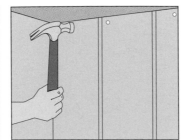

5. Press the panel to the wall and embed by tapping with a cloth-padded block.

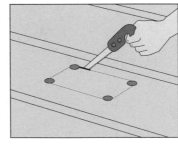

6. Drive the top nails home and space four more along the bottom edge.

7. For an electrical box, rub box edges with chalk, press panel against it, and cut out.

8. Around large openings, piece panels together instead of making one big cutout.

INSTALLING MOLDINGS

Finish your paneling project by trimming with millwork or prefinished moldings that are designed to match the paneling.

You can make most cuts with an inexpensive miter box and a backsaw. You may need a coping saw for fitting "coped" joints in curved moldings. The tricky part of trim work is accurately measuring mitered or coped joints and getting the miters angled in the proper directions. (See pages 40 and 498 for help in mastering these techniques.)

Secure the moldings with special color-matched nails. If you use regular casing nails, conceal them with touch-up stick putty available from paneling dealers or try the technique shown below.

YOU'LL NEED...

SKILLS: Basic carpentry skills.

TIME: 2 to 4 hours for a 12×15-foot room.

TOOLS: Tape measure, hammer, nail set, miter box, backsaw, coping saw, utility knife.

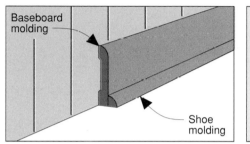

Baseboard molding protects finished paneling from scuffing and hides gaps along the floor line.

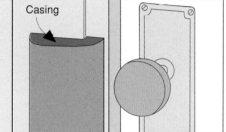

Casing trims around door and window frames. Most prefinished moldings look like those illustrated here.

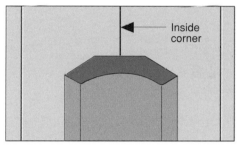

You may not need inside-corner moldings, depending on how neatly the paneling butts together in corners.

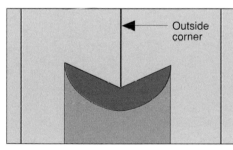

Outside-corner molding hides and protects panel edges. Be sure to nail it to both surfaces.

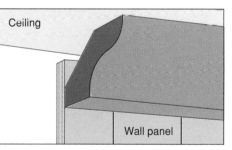

Crown or cove molding conceals any gaps between the top of the wall and the ceiling.

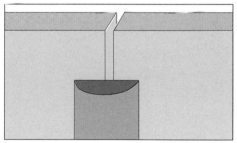

Seam molding, or batten, hides joints between panels. You do not usually need it with grooved paneling styles.

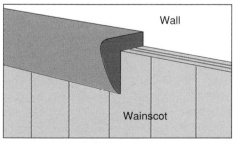

Use cap molding for wainscoting and other installations where the panel stops short of the ceiling.

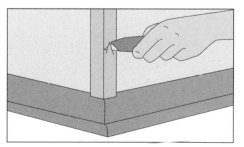

To completely hide nails, cut with a sharp knife to lift slivers of wood, then drive and countersink the nails.

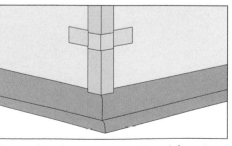

Press the slivers down using dabs of glue, tape until dry, then smooth by sanding lightly with fine sandpaper.

Putting Up New Walls (continued)

FRAMING A PARTITION

With framing, appearances do not count much. What does matter is that you keep everything plumb, square, and structurally sound.

Start by planning how you'll tie a new wall into your home's structure. How do the ceiling joists run in relation to your proposed wall? In a basement with exposed joists, it's easy to determine; for closed-ceiling situations, see pages 32 and 59.

If the new wall will cross the joists, simply pinpoint exactly where you want the wall and nail the top plate to the joists at those points. If,

however, it will run parallel to the joists, you may have to shift the wall's location a few inches so you can nail directly to a joist.

Fasten a new wall to masonry with adhesive and/or expansion shields and lag screws. If attaching to a hollow framed wall, you may be lucky enough to find a stud. If not, secure the new wall's first and last studs with toggle bolts.

The drawings here and on page 51 show two different framing techniques. Preassembly (below) makes sense for short walls on relatively level floors. You build the

entire partition flat on the floor, making it 1½ inches shorter than the ceiling height, then lift into place on top of the sole plate.

Toenailing studs (see page 51) works better when you have to deal with uneven floors or ceilings. But it takes some practice before you can toenail studs to the plates squarely.

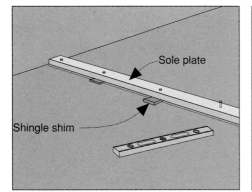

1. Lay out the wall with chalk lines, then level a 2×4 sole plate with shingle shims and nail or screw to the floor.

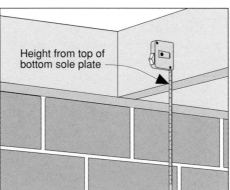

2. Measure the ceiling height at several points. Make your partition height fit the shortest floor-to-ceiling dimension.

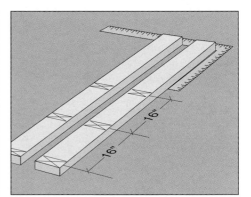

3. Cut the top and bottom plates, lay side by side, and mark stud spacings, as shown. Begin ¾ inch from one end.

4. Cut the studs, allowing for the thickness of the top, bottom, and sole plates. Assemble with 16d nails.

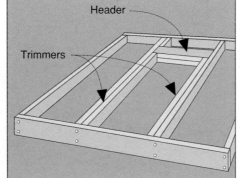

5. If the wall includes a doorway, add trimmers and header. Cut out the sole plate after positioning the wall.

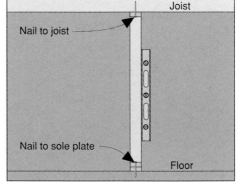

6. Lift the partition into place on the sole plate. Plumb carefully, then nail the top and bottom plates in place.

Toenailing Studs into Installed Plates

Installing the top and bottom plates first, then cutting the studs one at a time, results in a tight-fitting wall without shimming. You will face two problems—getting the top plate in place and toenailing.

Attaching the top plate is a four-handed job that requires you to hold a heavy length of lumber against the ceiling, then nail up through it into the joist. Make this job easier by starting the nails first, then wedge the plate against the ceiling with another length of lumber while you nail it in place. Or use the metal-track technique, shown on page 52. Either way, wear goggles and keep your mouth closed while you hammer; you'll probably create a shower of dust with each blow.

To minimize the frustration of toenailing, cut each stud about ⅛ inch longer than necessary and tap it into place for a force fit. You also can make a 14½-inch-long spacing block, which is the space between studs; lay it against the plate and nail, as shown at right.

YOU'LL NEED...

SKILLS: Basic carpentry skills.
TIME: 2 to 3 hours for a simple wall.
TOOLS: Tape measure, hammer, saw.

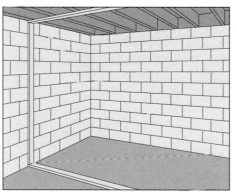

1. Using this method, you secure the top and bottom plates and end studs first, then toenail the wall's other studs.

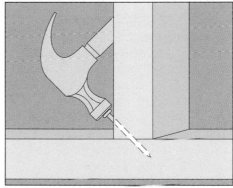

2. To toenail, drive an 8d common nail at a 45-degree angle, as shown. Expect to see the stud move from its mark.

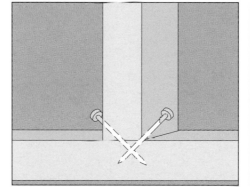

3. Now drive a second 8d nail from the other side and knock the stud back into its original position.

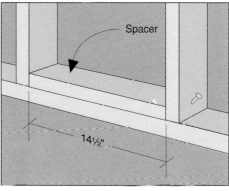

4. Until you get the hang of toenailing, use a spacer to temporarily brace each stud against the previous one.

Two Ways to Turn a Corner

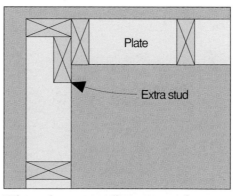

Plate

Extra stud

Where the new wall meets another, you have to provide nailing surfaces for all drywall or paneling edges. Fit in an extra stud, as shown.

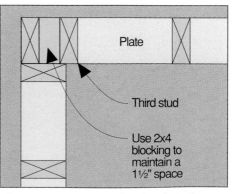

Plate

Third stud

Use 2x4 blocking to maintain a 1½" space

Alternatively, locate the third stud about 1½ inches from the one at the end of the new wall.

Putting up New Walls (continued)

FRAMING WITH METAL

A metal-stud partition seems flimsy only until you lock it together with ⅝-inch drywall screws and self-tapping sheet-metal screws. In doing so, you have a system with as much lateral strength as a wood-frame wall. It will probably be a lot straighter, too, because metal doesn't warp the way wood does.

The only disadvantage of metal framing is that it does not have as much compressive strength as wood. So, you can't use it for bearing walls or load it with heavy shelving.

You'll appreciate the convenience of metal when you install the tracks, which serve as top and bottom plates. Instead of hefting a heavy 2×4 up a ladder, then trying to nail it to the ceiling from an upside-down position, you simply position the lightweight track on the ceiling and secure it by screwing in a few drywall screws with an electric drill.

Once the tracks are in place, snip studs to length, slip them into position and twist, as illustrated below. Make sure all the studs are located on 16-inch centers, secure the studs with sheet-metal screws, then begin drywalling.

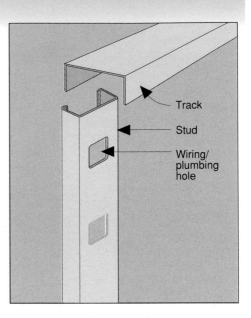

Track

Stud

Wiring/ plumbing hole

> ### YOU'LL NEED...
> **SKILLS:** Basic sheet metal skills.
> **TIME:** 2 to 4 hours to build a partition wall.
> **TOOLS:** Tin snips, drill, plumb bob, chalk line.

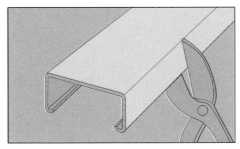

1. Cut studs or runners to required lengths using tin snips or a circular saw with an abrasive, metal-cutting blade.

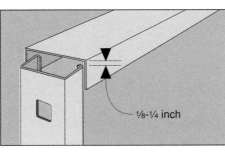

⅛-¼ inch

2. For an easier fit, cut the studs ⅛ to ¼ inch shorter than the height between the ceiling and floor runners. The studs bear no vertical weight.

3. Attach the ceiling runner to the joists with drywall screws. If new partition runs parallel to joists, install wood blocking between the joists first.

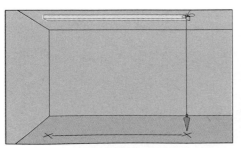

4. Drop a plumb bob from the ceiling runner to the floor below to establish the position of the floor runner. Snap a chalk line between two end points.

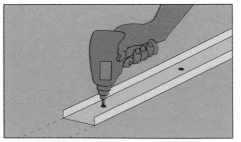

5. Attach the floor runner with drywall screws. Use powder-actuated fasteners for a concrete floor. Mark stud locations on top and bottom runners.

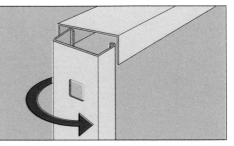

6. Insert stud into runners and twist into place. Orient all studs the same way for easier drywall, plumbing, and wiring installation.

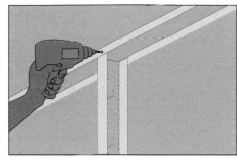

7. Attach studs to ceiling and floor runners with 7/16-inch pan or wafer-head sheet-metal screws.

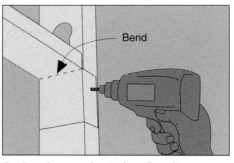

8. Cut door and window headers 8 inches longer than space, then bend 4-inch tabs at both ends. Install with tabs pointing either up or down.

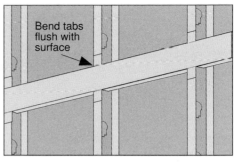

9. As a supporting beam for cabinets or other wall-mounted items, attach a runner across studs. Runners must be notched where they cross studs.

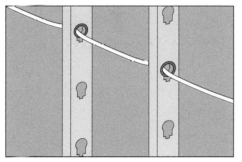

10. Insert plastic grommets or pieces of pipe insulation into the prepunched stud holes through which you can then pass wiring or plumbing.

11. Attach drywall to the metal studs using drywall screws. Space the screws 12 to 16 inches on-center. Work toward the open sides of the studs.

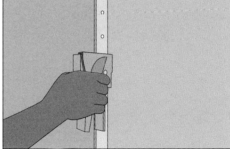

12. Install metal corner beading and trim at outside corners and panel edges using either drywall screws or stainless steel staples.

MIXING WOOD AND METAL FRAMING MEMBERS

If you need wood studs to support heavy loads, you can still substitute metal runners for the top and bottom sole plates of a wall.

You will find metal runners sized the same as their wooden ancestors: 1½×3½ inches for "2×4s" and 1½×2½ inches for "2×3s."

Simply install the runners, then cut a wood stud, slip it between the tracks, and twist. Check to see if any of the studs are bowed. If any are, align all the bows so that the wall looks even, then secure the studs with drywall screws.

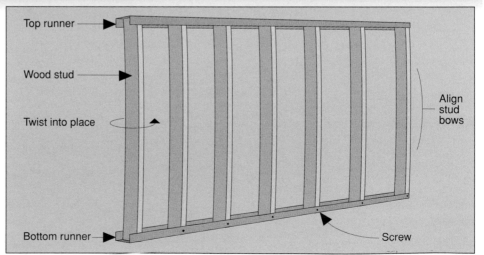

Putting Up New Walls (continued)

INSTALLING DRYWALL

Drywall is a cross between plywood and plaster. Like plywood, it comes in layered, uniformly sized sheets; like plaster, it is dense, noise-retarding, noncombustible, and fragile once you break through its paper face.

Its fragility makes drywall easy to work with. You can cut it with a utility knife and straightedge, as shown below, or use a keyhole saw, as illustrated on page 55. Power tools kick up too much dust.

Although you can chop a hole through drywall with almost any pointed implement, do not dismiss it as a weak covering material. Nailed, glued, or screwed to studs, it becomes an integral part of the wall's structure. Use it as a base for paint, paper, plaster, ceramic tile, or paneling; laminate double layers for superior fire or sound control.

Drywall typically comes in 4×8-foot sheets that are ⅜, ½, or ⅝ inch thick, but you can order other lengths ranging from 6 to 16 feet. Check your building code before you buy. Most specify ½-inch drywall for home construction, but some call for ⅝-inch material. A few even call for "Type X," which has a core that is even more fire- and sound-resistant. Use ⅜-inch drywall only for double-layer applications or over an existing wall.

Nail up ⅜- and ½-inch panels with 1⅝-inch ring-shank drywall nails; for ⅝-inch panels, use 1⅞-inch nails. If you are attaching to metal studs, you will need to drive in drywall screws with a drill. Some professionals prefer to use screws for wood-stud applications as well; although more expensive, they can't pop loose as nails sometimes do. For metal studs use ⅞-inch screws to fasten ½-inch drywall; use 1-inch screws for ⅝-inch material. For wood studs, you should use 1¼-inch screws, regardless of the drywall thickness.

For a really strong installation, you can use both nails and drywall adhesive. For each 1,000 square feet of drywall, you will need about eight tubes of adhesive.

Cutting Drywall

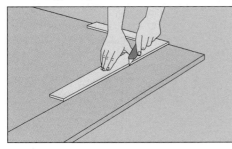

1. Make a chalk line and cut across panels with a metal straightedge and sharp utility knife. Score completely through one paper face.

2. Stand the sheet on edge, apply firm pressure, and snap the board downward. This breaks through the gypsum core along the scored line.

3. Slice through the paper backing with the knife and smooth rough edges with a medium-tooth wood file. Keep your utility knife sharp.

Nailing or Screwing Drywall

YOU'LL NEED...

SKILLS: Basic skills.
TIME: 10 to 15 minutes per sheet, excluding time for custom cuts.
TOOLS: Hammer, variable-speed drill or screw gun.

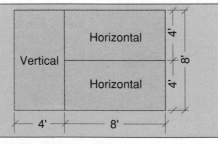

Install panels parallel or perpendicular to the studs, whichever arrangement will result in fewer joints.

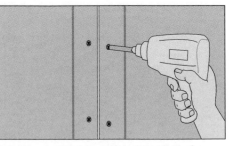

Locate screws or nails every 8 inches. Dimple nails or screws below the surface, but don't break the paper.

Making Openings In Drywall

YOU'LL NEED...
SKILLS: Basic skills.
TIME: 10 to 15 minutes per hole.
TOOLS: Tape measure, drill, keyhole saw.

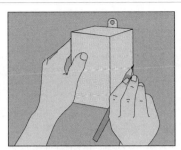

1. Measure and mark carefully. For receptacles, trace an outline around a spare electrical box.

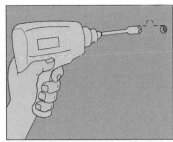

2. Bore holes at each corner or poke the end of a keyhole or drywall saw through the drywall.

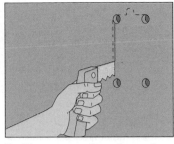

3. Most saws slice through drywall easily. Protect your floors; gypsum dust is difficult to clean up.

Fitting Around Pipes

YOU'LL NEED...
SKILLS: Basic skills.
TIME: 20 to 30 minutes for a set of pipes.
TOOLS: Tape measure, drill, keyhole saw, hammer.

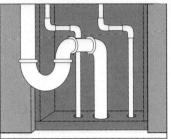

1. Do not disconnect plumbing fixtures. Attach drywall to the studs flanking the pipes.

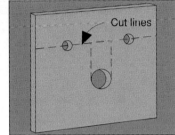

2. Cut a piece to width, mark the locations of the pipes, bore holes, and cut between holes.

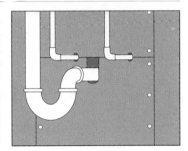

3. Finally, piece your puzzle back together and nail or screw to the studs.

LAMINATING DRYWALL

To improve a wall's sound and fire resistance, glue one layer of ½- or ⅜-inch drywall to another. You can use this same process to bond a new drywall layer to an existing wall.

For either job, you will need drywall adhesive and joint compound, plus some 8d common nails to tack the top layer until the adhesive sets.

Find all wall studs and mark their locations on the floor and ceiling. Laminate the second panel to the first, as shown below. Partially drive a few nails through the top layer into each stud to temporarily hold the panels in place. After the adhesive sets, pull the nails carefully or dimple them into the drywall and cover the heads with joint compound when you tape the joints.

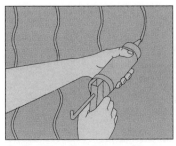

1. Apply adhesive to the wall surface according to label directions.

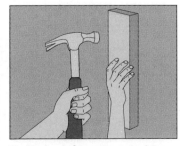

2. Embed the new panel in the adhesive by tapping with a hammer and block of wood.

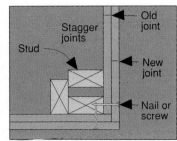

3. Stagger panel joints as shown. At the outside corners, alternate overlaps.

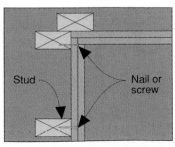

4. At inside corners, nail only the overlapping board of the first layer.

Putting Up New Walls (continued)

TAPING DRYWALL

The trickiest part of a drywall project comes when you finish off the joints, which are covered with tape and drywall compound, then sanded.

You'll need 5 gallons of joint compound and 500 feet of paper "tape" for each 1,000 square feet of surface. Invest, too, in a pair of 4- and 10-inch-wide finishing knives. Budget plenty of time for the first coat. Get the tape up smoothly and you'll be spared headaches later.

YOU'LL NEED...
SKILLS: Basic to intermediate skills.
TIME: 4 hours for an 8×24-foot wall.
TOOLS: 4- and 10-inch taping knives, sponge, sanding block.

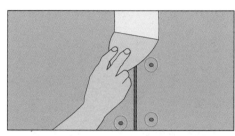

1. With a 4-inch knife, apply a uniform swath of compound to the tapered trough between the panels.

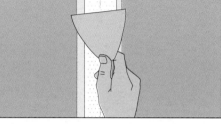

2. Immediately, unroll the tape and embed it in the compound by pressing down with knife. Smooth out wrinkles.

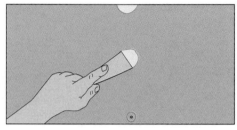

3. Fill nail dimples and other blemishes at this time. Pack in a dab of compound, then level the surface.

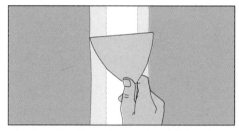

4. Give the "bedding" coat 24 hours to dry, then apply compound again, feathering out edges about 6 inches.

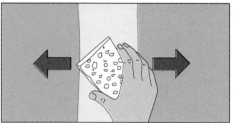

5. After second coat dries, sand it smooth, being careful not to sand any exposed paper tape.

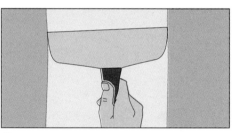

6. Apply a skim coat with a 10-inch knife, spreading edges to about 12 inches. Sand smooth after drying.

Taping Corners

Inside and outside corners call for slightly different taping techniques. Reinforce outside corners with strips of lightweight perforated metal angle. Use ordinary joint tape for inside corners, but cut it to length first, then crease it vertically down the middle before applying.

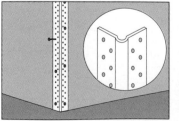

1. Nail metal "corner bead" through drywall to framing every 5 inches.

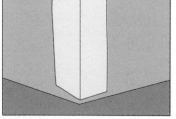

2. Apply two coats of compound, feathering it out about 4 inches on each wall.

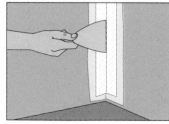

3. For inside corners, fold tape down the middle before embedding it in compound.

4. Apply later coats to one wall, let dry, then do the other wall.

REMOVING A PARTITION

Armed with a wrecking bar and general destructive tendencies tempered with restraint, you can knock out an average wall in a few hours. The hard work is removing the debris and patching the remaining walls where they met the wall that was removed.

Before you begin, make absolutely sure that the wall you want to remove is not a load-bearing wall (see page 32). If you have doubts, consult an experienced contractor. Also, find out in advance if the wall contains wiring, plumbing, or heating lines. These can be relocated later, but you will want to shut off the systems while you work.

Remove furnishings or cover them with heavy drop cloths; plaster and gypsum dust make a terrible mess to vacuum up. Protect yourself with hard hat, goggles, heavy shirt, and face mask.

YOU'LL NEED...

SKILLS: Basic demolition skills.
TIME: 2 to 4 hours if there is no plumbing or electric wiring in wall.
TOOLS: Hammer, putty knife, pry bar, wrecking bar, sledgehammer.

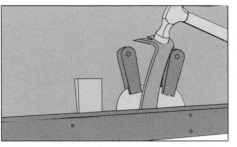

1. Door casings, baseboards, and other trim go first (see page 40). You might want to salvage these for patching use.

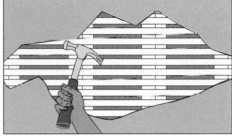

2. Forget about recycling plaster, lath, or drywall. Just whack it, then peel it off with a wrecking bar.

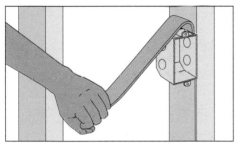

3. Once the wall is stripped to its studs, remove wiring. Toss out all old cable, but save the boxes and fittings.

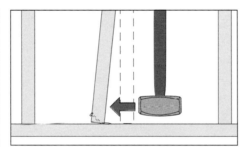

4. Knock the stud bottoms out with a sledgehammer, then twist the studs away from the top plate.

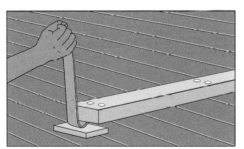

5. Take care when you pry off the plates and end studs. You may be able to reuse most of the framing lumber.

EXPOSING BRICK WALLS

Before you remove plaster from a masonry wall, chip away a small area and decide if the brick or stone is worth saving.

If you like what you see, prepare for a dusty task. The plaster may have been applied directly to the masonry or it may be clinging to a lath- and furring-strip framework. Attack first with a sledgehammer and a wrecking bar, being careful not to damage the brick surface that you want to save. Wire-brush the surface to get rid of solid residue, then go over it with a mild solution of muriatic acid. Rinse well.

After you have finished, seal the wall with polyurethane. Otherwise, more dust will periodically work its way out of the mortar joints.

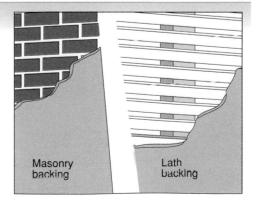

Masonry backing

Lath backing

Putting Up New Walls (continued)

CONTROLLING NOISE

Most wood-stud walls make poor sound insulators. They leak noise through cracks, around electrical receptacles, under baseboards, and so on. Their drumlike construction also transmits sound waves through the studs themselves.

Acoustic caulking under the plates and at the tops and bottoms of drywall panels stops airborne noise. So, too, will foam gaskets under electrical cover plates. Insulation between the studs soaks up sound that might penetrate wall cavities.

Special metal resilient channels "decouple," or separate, the wall's surfaces, cutting off acoustic pathways through the studs. Another layer of drywall on the decoupled side further muffles sound.

ANATOMY OF A QUIET WALL

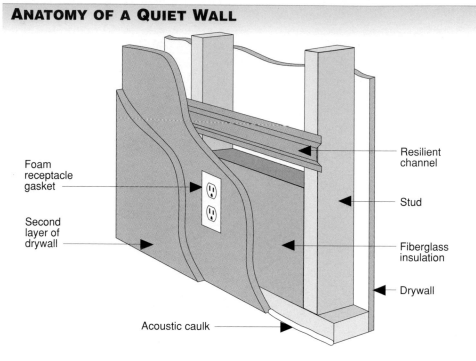

Foam receptacle gasket

Second layer of drywall

Acoustic caulk

Resilient channel

Stud

Fiberglass insulation

Drywall

QUIET AN EXISTING WALL

If you need a soundproof room, line its walls and ceiling with lead-core drywall, which was developed for recording studios and X-ray facilities. Expect to pay dearly for this acoustic privacy. Otherwise, follow the series of less expensive steps outlined below and stop when you get the din to an acceptable level.

Consider the origin of the noise. If the noise comes from a single place (for example, an appliance), try to muffle the sound at its source. Use carpeting, heavy draperies, and acoustical or cork tiles to help cut clatter within a room. Don't expect these solutions to block transmission from one space to another.

Remove baseboards and molding and seal all cracks along the walls with nonhardening acoustic sealant. Be thorough—miss just one crack and your work may be in vain.

> ### YOU'LL NEED...
> **SKILLS:** Basic carpentry skills.
> **TIME:** Varies, depending on measures taken.
> **TOOLS:** Caulking gun.

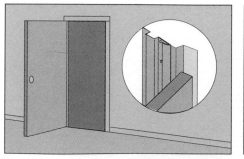

Replace hollow-core doors with solid types, then weather-strip around the entire perimeter (see pages 388–389).

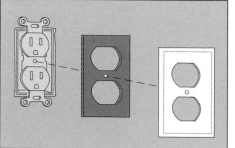

Remove cover plates from electrical receptacles and switches and install foam gaskets.

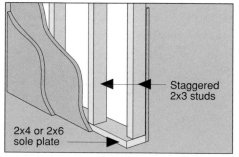

Staggered 2x3 studs

2x4 or 2x6 sole plate

As a last resort, rebuild the wall with staggered studs and double layers of drywall, as shown.

CEILINGS

Combine the framing for a floor with the covering materials used for walls, and you get the anatomy of a typical home ceiling, shown here.

The ceiling begins with the same joists that support the subfloor above. Furring strips can be added to the bottom edges of the joists to level them. Or, if the lumber is level to begin with, drywall or plaster lath can be attached directly to the joists. Finally, the ceiling is finished with plaster or joint tape and joint compound.

There are several obvious exceptions to this construction cutaway, however. Sloping top-floor ceilings, for example, usually are attached directly to the roof framing. In properly built homes, insulation is placed between the ceiling and roof (see pages 392–393). You also may encounter lightweight ceiling tiles suspended below the joists of an old ceiling (see page 65). Open-beam ceilings consist of nothing more than the finished underside of the roof decking.

ANATOMY OF A CEILING

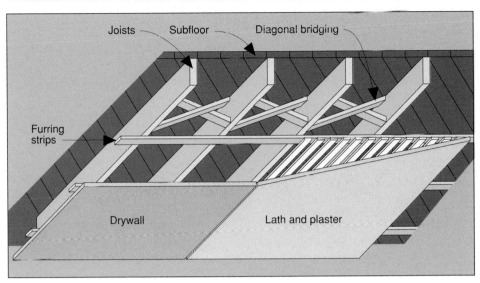

Joists   Subfloor   Diagonal bridging

Furring strips

Drywall   Lath and plaster

Solving Ceiling Problems

CHECKING OUT COMMON CEILING PROBLEMS		
Problem	**Cause**	**Cure**
Cracks	Settlement and vibrations; these conditions bedevil plaster ceilings especially, but also affect drywall joints	Pack cracks with surfacing or joint compound (see pages 36–37)
Popped nails	Improperly nailed drywall ceilings will pull away from the joists or furring strips	Shore up ceiling with a prop (see page 61), then drive in ring-shank or drywall screws (see page 35)
Peeling tape	Excessive humidity or improper installation	In high humidity areas, improve the ventilation (see pages 403–407), then retape (see page 35)

Solving Ceiling Problems (continued)

REPAIRING LARGE HOLES

Plaster and drywall ceilings are more difficult to patch than walls. First of all, you have to tackle the repair from an uncomfortable position. Second, the patch must cling to the ceiling structure more securely than with a wall.

Don't try to replaster a ceiling yourself. Hire a professional or piece-in a drywall patch.

If you choose to drywall, use self-tapping drywall screws; they hold better than nails and are easy to drive. Protect yourself against dust and debris with goggles, a dust mask, and a hard hat.

For a smooth repair, measure the exact thickness of your existing ceiling and buy drywall of the same size or shim thinner material.

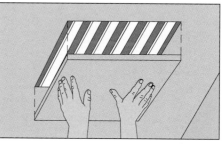

> **YOU'LL NEED...**
> **SKILLS:** Basic drywalling skills.
> **TIME:** 1 to 2 hours for a 1-foot square patch.
> **TOOLS:** Hammer, chisel, keyhole saw, drill, screwdriver, drywall taping knifes.

Fixing Plaster Ceilings

Small holes and cracks can be filled with surfacing or drywall joint compound (see page 37). But patching is easier for larger holes. The patching technique shown here works well for repairs when the lath above is in good condition. If the lath is as much of a problem as the ceiling plaster, you will want to consider redoing the whole ceiling or turning the job over to a pro.

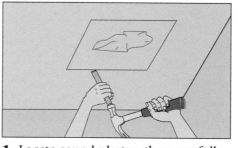

1. Locate sound plaster, then carefully square off a section and chip it out with a hammer and cold chisel.

2. Cut a drywall patch to size. Butter edges with compound, press in place, and drive screws into lath above.

Fixing Drywall Ceilings

The technique above can be used to mend a drywall ceiling also. But because the drywall's backing is as regular as its face, you will get an even smoother repair with the technique shown at right.

Mark a square off around the hole, then drill holes at the corners and cut out the section with a keyhole saw. Cut a piece of ½-inch plywood about 2 inches longer and narrower than the opening. Make sure the plywood will clear the joists on either side. Slip it into place and secure it and the new drywall patch with screws, as shown.

Taper the join as you would any drywall joint (see page 56). But when you apply the second and third coats of joint compound, feather them out more than you would on a wall.

Finally, prime and paint the entire ceiling with flat white or another light color paint. Flat paint shows surface irregularities less than gloss or semigloss paint.

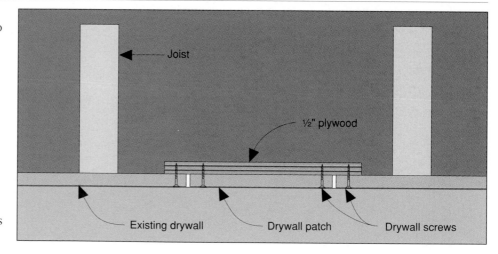

Joist

½" plywood

Existing drywall   Drywall patch   Drywall screws

RAISING A SAGGING CEILING

A plaster ceiling is locked into place as the plaster is forced between the lath and spreads out, forming what are called keys on the back side of the lath. Often keys break off, and the plaster ceiling sags. More rarely, the lath itself may start to pull away from the joists.

For minor sags, try anchoring the plaster with screws and plaster washers. Make a T-shaped brace about ½ inch taller than the ceiling height. Wedge it in place to raise the sag. Drill pilot holes to make sure you hit a lath board. Drive in the screws with washers, spacing them about 4 inches apart. Wherever you encounter a joist, drive in longer screws for additional support. Cover the screws and washers with drywall compound, (see page 56).

For serious sags in a ceiling, you may have to replace the entire ceiling, a job for a contractor.

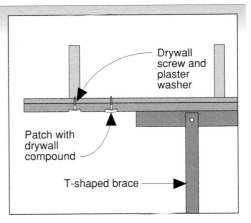

Drywall screw and plaster washer

Patch with drywall compound

T-shaped brace

REPLACING A DAMAGED CEILING TILE

The biggest challenge you may face when replacing a ceiling tile is finding one that matches. If you're lucky, whoever installed the ceiling tile will have saved a few extra tiles for such an occasion.

The trick to replacing a tile is cutting off the top lip of the grooved edge of the new tile (see Step 2). Once you've trimmed off the top lip of the groove, you can place the tongue edge in the grooves of the adjacent tile and pivot the patch tile into place.

YOU'LL NEED...

SKILLS: Basic skills.
TIME: 30 to 45 minutes per tile.
TOOLS: Utility knife, straightedge, chisel or putty knife.

1. Cut away the damaged area first so you can get a grip on the tile. Work in a knife and slice the edges free.

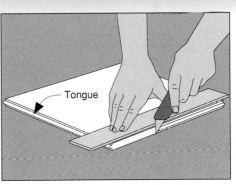

Tongue

2. Trim the appropriate edges from a new tile, guiding the cuts with a metal straightedge. Check for a snug fit.

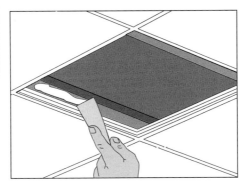

3. Clear away all old adhesive or staples from furring strips and the other tiles, then apply fresh adhesive.

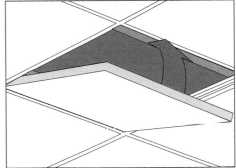

4. Fit the tongue edge in first, then press the tile into position and hold for a few minutes until the adhesive grabs.

Putting Up New Ceiling Materials

DRYWALLING A CEILING

The hardest part of this project is lifting heavy drywall panels into place. A nifty tool is the simple brace shown in Step 3. For big ceiling jobs, rent a jack designed for lifting drywall up to ceilings.

To determine if you need to install furring strips, stretch level, diagonal strings ½ inch below the old ceiling. If the surface deviates more than ¼ inch, install 1×3 furring strips.

YOU'LL NEED...

SKILLS: Basic drywalling skills.
TIME: 8 hours for a 12×15-foot room.
TOOLS: Ladder, string, wire, hammer or drill, drywall finishing tools.

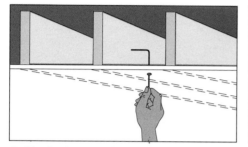

1. To find joists above old ceiling, drill a hole, insert a bent wire, and rotate. Check by tapping with a hammer.

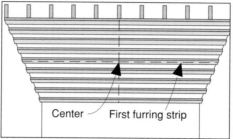

Center — First furring strip

2. Measure carefully to find the ceiling's exact center, then nail furring strips across the joists 16 inches apart.

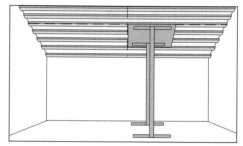

3. Start at the center and work toward the edges. Use braces to hold the panels while you drive nails or screws.

MATERIAL MATTERS   CHOOSING AND BUYING CEILING TILES

Compared to drywall, ceiling tiles and panels are a breeze. Instead of awkward, 4×8-foot sheets, you work with lightweight materials and modular installation techniques. Once the new ceiling is up, there is no need to mess with joint compound or paint.

Before choosing a style, consider the available headroom. If you have space to drop the new surface 3 inches—especially if you want to cover pipes, wiring, and ducts—consider a suspended grid system (see page 65).

If a dropped ceiling would cut the room's overall height to less than 7½ feet, you should apply interlocking tiles to the old ceiling or to a network of furring strips (see pages 63-64). You can cement or staple tiles directly to a sound ceiling. If there are exposed joists, put up furring first.

Some ceiling tiles have acoustical properties that help reduce the noise level within a room. Don't expect them to muffle sound transmission completely from one space to another.

Compute the square footage by multiplying the length of the room by its width. Then figure in several extra tiles to allow for cutting and waste.

COMPARING CEILING TILES AND PANELS

Material	Properties/Costs	Sizes/Applications
Wood-fiber	The oldest and least expensive type; some are treated for fire resistance	1×1-, 1×2-, and 2×4-foot tiles; cement to existing plaster or staple to drywall or furring
Mineral-fiber	Most expensive and durable; noncombustible	1×1-, and 2×2-foot tiles; 2×4-foot panels for suspended systems
Fiberglass	Medium priced; some fire-resistant and quieting; thick panels provide thermal insulation	2×2-, 2×4-, and 2×8-foot panels for grid systems; also 4-foot-wide panels in lengths up to 16 feet
Polystyrene	Lowest cost; may not be legal under some local building codes	1×1- and 2×2-foot tiles; 2×4-foot panels for suspended systems

ATTACHING TILES TO AN OLD CEILING

YOU'LL NEED...

SKILLS: Basic skills.
TIME: 6 to 8 hours for a 12×15-foot room, if you do not need to add furring strips.
TOOLS: Tape measure, chalk line, utility knife, caulking gun or staple gun.

1. Draw the room to scale, then lay a tracing-paper grid over it. Shift until the border tiles are equal.

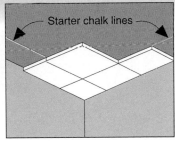

2. With a chalk line, transfer grid to the ceiling, marking starter lines. Cut the border tiles according to that line.

3. Begin in a corner. Apply tile adhesive according to instructions or staple as explained below.

ATTACHING TILES TO FURRING STRIPS

Even up an irregular ceiling or exposed joists with wood furring strips (shimmed) spaced to suit the size of the tiles you have chosen.

One tile company offers a metal furring system that is similar to a suspended-ceiling grid, except that all supporting elements are hidden

from view. This method requires a minimum 2-inch drop from the existing ceiling level.

YOU'LL NEED...

SKILLS: Basic skills.
TIME: 12 hours for a 12×15-foot room.
TOOLS: Tape measure, chalk line, hammer, utility knife, caulking gun or stapler.

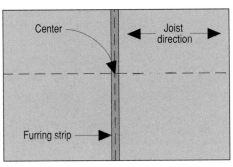

1. Locate the room's center and put the first strip there. Furring always should run perpendicular to the joists.

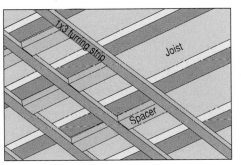

2. Space subsequent strips with their centers one tile's width apart. Nail spacers where two tiles will interlock.

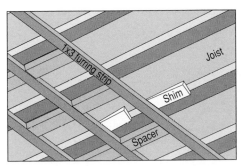

3. Shim small irregularities. For a very bumpy ceiling, use the double-furring technique shown on page 64

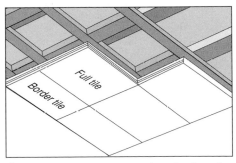

4. Begin in a corner, cutting the border tiles. Chalk lines on the furring will help you align the first full row of tiles.

5. Drive two staples atop each other into each exposed tile corner. The first staple flares the legs of the second.

Putting Up New Ceiling Materials (continued)

HELPFUL HINTS

■ Heating ducts, wiring, beams, and plumbing lines sometimes need hiding when you finish a room. If the obstruction is small, you may be able to tuck it against the joists and add double-furring, as shown at right. If not, you will need to box in the obstruction. Use lightweight materials, such as 1×2s, 1×3s, or 2×2s, for framing. You even can use ½- or ¼-inch plywood or hardboard materials.

CONCEALING OBSTRUCTIONS

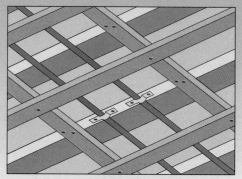

Double-furring often lowers a ceiling just enough to get below electrical conduit and plumbing supply lines.

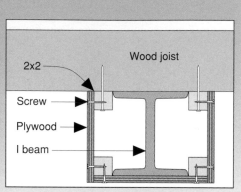

To cover a support beam, nail 2×2s along either side, then build a three-sided plywood box, as shown.

Installing Recessed Lighting

For even, unobtrusive lighting, buy incandescent fixtures that fit into the ceiling-tile grid. Route the electrical wires to where you'll install the lights (see pages 244–253) before you build the furring network.

Install each fixture as you come to it while using the tiling instructions on page 63.

YOU'LL NEED...

SKILLS: Basic electrical skills.
TIME: 30 minutes per light.
TOOLS: Screwdriver, wire strippers.

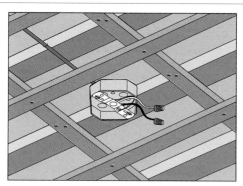

1. Often, you can tap power from an existing ceiling box. First, make sure the circuit is not loaded heavily.

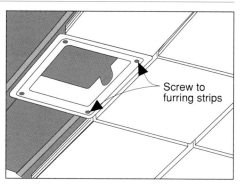

2. Align the fixture's frame with the tiles on either side, then drive screws into the furring at all four corners.

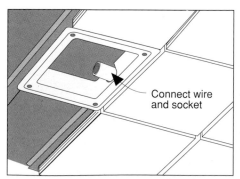

3. Shut off the power and make the electrical connections. Many lamps come with their own junction boxes.

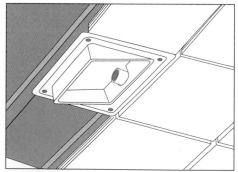

4. Assemble the reflector system. Read the manufacturer's instructions before installing any fixture.

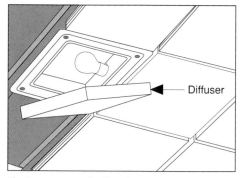

5. Screw in a bulb (do not exceed the wattage specified) and snap the plastic diffuser panel into place.

INSTALLING A SUSPENDED CEILING

The secret to installing a suspended ceiling lies in the components—lightweight steel or aluminum channels that you hang from wires and snap together into a grid. Then you finish by simply setting ceiling panels into place.

Most ceiling tile dealers will have planning guides to help you plan the room layout and the materials you will need. Here are the main structural items:

■ Main tees run perpendicular to the joists and are suspended from wires. They come in 10-foot lengths, which you can cut or splice.

■ Wall angles extend around the room's edges at ceiling's height.

■ Cross tees clip to the main tees at each panel intersection.

One joy of installing a suspended ceiling is that you need to do little or no preparation work. Just mark the locations of any concealed joists and establish a height for your new suspended ceiling.

YOU'LL NEED...

SKILLS: Basic skills.
TIME: 8 to 10 hours for a 12×15-foot room.
TOOLS: Tape measure, string or mason line, level or line level, hammer, drill, pliers.

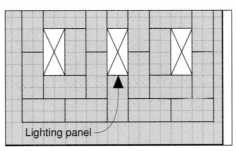

1. Make measurements on a scaled layout to plot sizes for the border panels and locations of light fixtures.

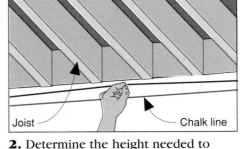

2. Determine the height needed to clear obstacles above the grid, then snap level chalk lines along the walls.

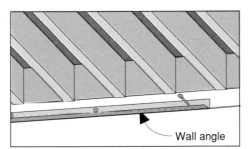

3. Attach the wall angles, aligning bottom edges with the chalk line. Use adhesive if fastening to concrete.

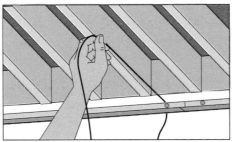

4. To guide in hanging main tees, stretch taut, level strings across the room at several points along the angles.

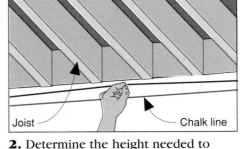

5. Measure the width of one border tile out from the wall. Drive screw eyes into every other joist at 4-foot intervals.

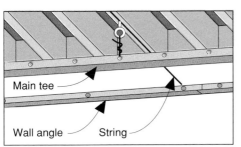

6. Loop wire through eyes and holes in the main tees, level the tees, then twist the wire tight.

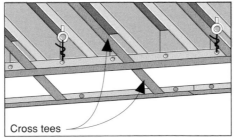

7. Install the cross tees. Cut them to length wherever necessary and rest their ends on the main tees.

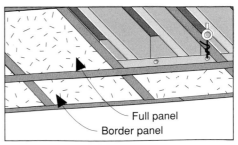

8. Trim border panels with a knife and straightedge, set in place, then fill in the rest of the grid with uncut panels.

Putting Up New Ceiling Materials (continued)

INSTALLING A SUSPENDED CEILING (continued)
Installing Lighting

Suspended ceilings lend themselves to a variety of lighting solutions: surface-mounted fixtures, recessed incandescent fixtures, recessed fluorescent units sized to fit the grid, or even a luminous ceiling.

For incandescent fixtures, cut a 2×4 long enough to straddle two main tees, attach a junction box to it, and rest the 2×4 on top of the main tees. Make your electrical connections. Then cut a hole in the ceiling panel for the junction box.

One type of fluorescent fixture substitutes for a ceiling panel. Simply drop the unit into place and make the electric hookup. Another type stands on brackets above the grid, as shown below.

Remember that fixtures add weight—so be sure to add extra hanger wires to carry the load.

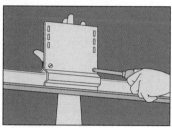

1. Install light fixtures before panels. With this type, mounting brackets clamp to the main tees.

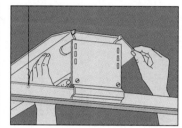

2. A tab-and-slot system lets you adjust the distance between a fixture's tubes and its plastic diffuser panel.

3. Make the electrical connections. Then fit the fixture's reflector panels in place and install the fluorescent tubes.

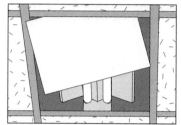

4. For the diffusers, you can select clear, translucent white, or egg-crate styles. They rest on the grid like any other panel.

Installing a Luminous Ceiling

The moment you flip the switch for a luminous ceiling system, you bathe the entire room in even, glare-free light that instantly dispels any down-in-the-basement feeling.

Begin the installation by painting all surfaces above the new ceiling with a couple coats of flat white paint. Next, affix rows of ordinary fluorescent fixtures end to end across the joists. Space them 24 inches apart and about 10 inches from all walls. Connect the lights to each other and to a single- or multiple-switch-controlled ceiling box. Then install the ceiling grid (see page 65) just below the lighting fixtures. Use diffusers for all the ceiling panels. (See page 274 for more about fluorescent fixtures).

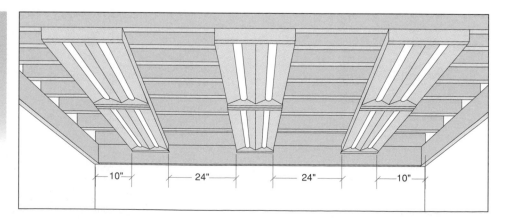

WINDOWS

Wind eye—the original meaning of the word window—pretty well describes the dual function of these home components. Not only do windows provide light and views of the outside world, they also control the flow of air throughout the interior spaces of your home.

Not all windows are operable (that is, able to be opened). Most windows, however, include one or more movable sashes. Keeping these—and their related shades, blinds, and draperies—in good working order is the main focus of this chapter.

There are a few projects you will not find here. These include replacing broken glass panes, repairing and installing screens and storm windows, and putting in an entirely new window or sliding glass door. All these outside jobs are covered on pages 142-169.

Windows also play a vital role in the way your home gains and loses heat. To learn about sealing windows with weather stripping, see pages 386–388.

Getting to Know Your Windows

There is more to a window than meets the eye, especially with the older double-hung type shown at right. Concealed behind the frame's side jambs are heavy sash weights. Connected via a rope-and-pulley system, the weights counterbalance the sashes, making them easier to open, and hold them in any vertical position you wish.

A series of stops fitted to the jambs provides channels in which the sashes slide. Check the top view and note that, although the outside blind stop is more or less permanently affixed, the parting stop and inside stop can be pried loose if you want to remove the sashes.

In newer double-hung windows the weight-and-pulley mechanisms are replaced with a pair of spring lift devices (see pages 69-70).

With both types of windows, the lower sash comes to rest behind a flat stool. Its outside counterpart, the sill, slopes so water can run off. Trim—called casing at the sides and top and an apron below—covers gaps between the jambs and the wall material.

ANATOMY OF A DOUBLE-HUNG WINDOW

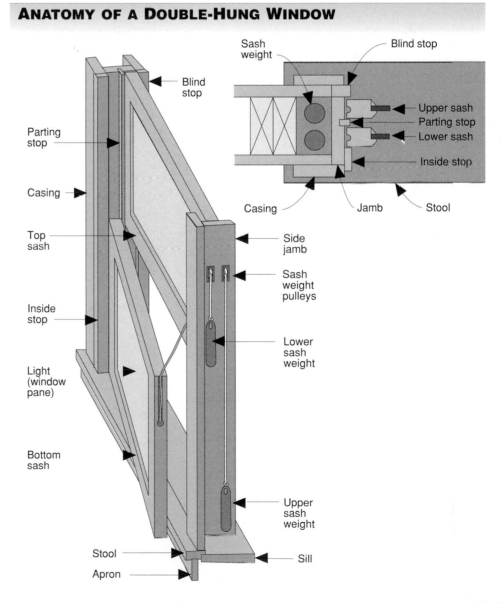

Getting to Know Your Windows (continued)

ANATOMY OF A CASEMENT WINDOW

Casement windows open and close like a door. In the version at right, muntins separate the panes. With most double-glazed casements, though, the muntins—often referred to as grills—snap to the inside of the window to facilitate cleaning, or are absent altogether.

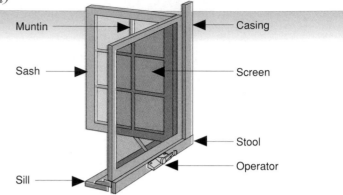

Muntin

Casing

Sash

Screen

Stool

Operator

Sill

ANATOMY OF A SLIDING WINDOW

As with double-hung sashes, sliding sashes open up only 50 percent of the total window area for ventilation. Some sliding windows have one fixed and one sliding sash, as shown here; with others, both sashes slide along continuous tracks. Sliding windows can be made with wood, metal, or plastic.

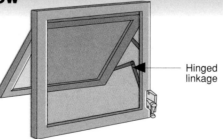

Sliding sash

Fixed sash

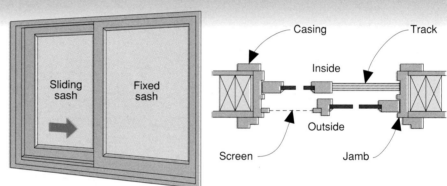

Casing

Track

Inside

Outside

Screen

Jamb

ANATOMY OF AN AWNING WINDOW

An awning window works in the same fashion as a casement window, but the sash tilts outward. Some awnings slide downward as they tilt, so that you can open them to a nearly horizontal position for maximum cooling airflow.

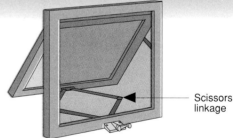

Hinged linkage

Scissors linkage

ANATOMY OF A JALOUSIE WINDOW

Turning the crank of a jalousie window pivots a series of glass slats. The frames consist of short metal channels at either end of the slats. The glass-to-glass joints tend to leak air, so jalousies usually are used only in breezeways, porches, and other unheated zones.

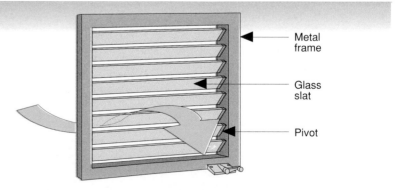

Metal frame

Glass slat

Pivot

Solving Window Problems

REPAIRING DOUBLE-HUNG WINDOWS

When a window binds or refuses to budge, don't try to force it. Instead, take a look around the sash, both inside and out. Chances are, you will find that paint has sealed the window shut or that a stop molding has warped. Both difficulties usually respond to the gentle prying techniques shown below.

With double-hung windows, the culprit could be a faulty spring lift or a broken or jammed sash cord. Replacing these involves dismantling the window (see page 70).

> ### YOU'LL NEED...
> **SKILLS:** Basic skills.
> **TIME:** 30 minutes depending on the cause of the problem.
> **TOOLS:** Utility knife, pry bar, hammer.

Freeing a Balky Sash

To break a paint seal, run a sharp utility knife several times between the sash and stop.

As an alternative, pry from the outside edges with a pry bar and protective block. Work inward from edges until the sash pops free.

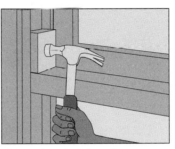

If a sash is binding between its stops, try separating the stops slightly by tapping along their length with a hammer and wooden block.

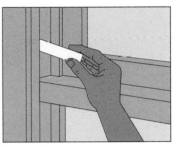

Once you get the window moving, lightly sand its jambs, then lubricate with paste wax, paraffin wax or a candle, or bar soap.

HELPFUL HINTS

Tube-type lifting devices house a spring-driven twist rod that helps lift the sash. To improve sash movement, you can adjust the spring devices as

ADJUSTING SPRING LIFTS

shown below. But before tampering with these, check to be sure the window has not been painted shut. If it has, follow the procedures above.

If the device doesn't seem to be working at all, it is probably broken, and you'll need to replace it using the instructions shown on page 70.

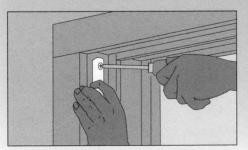

Grip the tube before you remove the screw holding it to the jamb, or the spring will unwind in a hurry.

If the window sails up too easily, hold the screw and let the spring turn a couple of revolutions.

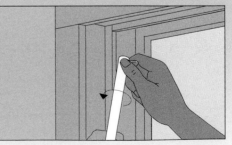

If the window is hard to raise, tighten the spring by turning it clockwise. You may need to adjust both lifts.

Solving Window Problems (continued)

REPAIRING DOUBLE-HUNG WINDOWS *(continued)*
Replacing Sash Cords

YOU'LL NEED...

SKILLS: Basic carpentry skills.
TIME: 1 to 2 hours if there are no surprises.
TOOLS: Putty knife, utility knife, screwdriver, hammer.

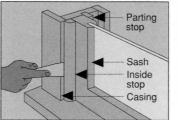

1. Using a putty knife, pry carefully at several points to remove the sash.

2. Lift the sash and swing it clear from the frame. The cords will still be connected.

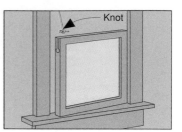

3. Hang on to the cord when you unhook it, then slip a nail through the knot.

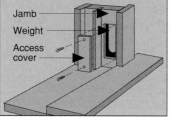

4. If there is no access cover at the base of the jamb to get to the weight, you may have to pry off the jamb.

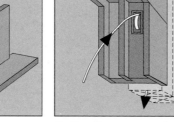

5. Feeding new sash cords over pulleys can be tricky, so bend them first. Replace the cords on both sides.

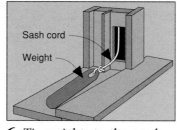

6. Tie weights to the cords and return to windows. Knot the other ends and fit cords into grooves in the sashes.

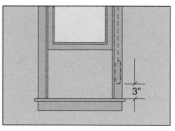

7. Weights should hang 3 inches above the channel bottoms when the lower sash is raised fully.

8. To replace the cords on an upper sash, you have to remove the lower one, then one of the parting stops.

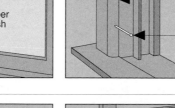

9. When you replace stops, partially drive in longer nails, then raise and lower the sash to check positioning.

Replacing Spring Lifts

YOU'LL NEED...

SKILLS: Basic carpentry skills.
TIME: 1 hour.
TOOLS: Putty knife, hammer, screwdriver.

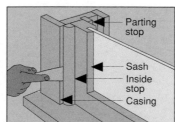

1. Remove the inside stop on one side of the sash. This should make room enough to remove the sash.

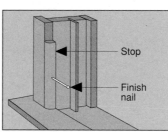

2. Remove the screw that secures the tube, let the spring unwind, then pull out the sash.

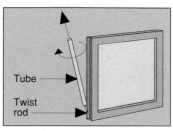

3. Remove and replace the twist rod/tube unit. Reinstall sash and adjust tube (see page 69).

REPAIRING CASEMENT WINDOWS

Accumulations of paint, grease, or dirt cause most casement window difficulties. If your casement is malfunctioning, check all sash and frame edges. A few minutes with a wire brush or scraper may remove the debris that is causing the rub.

If not, partially close the sash and check its fit. Wood casements sometimes suffer the same problems that bedevil doors. Solve these problems by adapting the door-fitting and planing techniques illustrated on pages 80 and 81.

Finally, examine the unit's mechanical components. All you probably will need is a lubricant to set things right.

> **YOU'LL NEED...**
> **SKILLS:** Basic skills.
> **TIME:** 20 to 30 minutes per window.
> **TOOLS:** Screwdriver, wire brush.

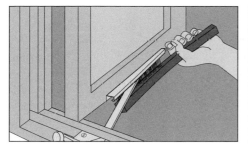

If the sash is difficult to close, try cleaning the sliding arm mechanism with a wire brush.

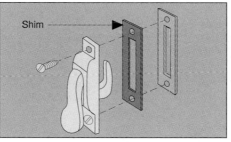

Tighten loose latch screws. If a handle won't pull its sash snug, shim under it or add weather stripping.

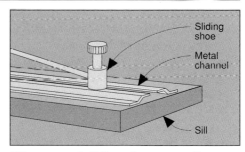

If a wood sash has warped, counter-warp it with wood strips. Leave the strips in place for a couple weeks.

Servicing Operators

Most casement operators are sliding- or scissor-arm mechanisms that may or may not be driven by a geared cranking device.

If a sash is not working smoothly, check the arm. Look for bent metal, loose screws, rust, or paint that might be interfering with the action.

Also, check out the cranking system. Sometimes you can free jammed gears with a wire coat hanger. If the gears are badly worn or stripped, you may have to replace the entire assembly.

> **YOU'LL NEED...**
> **SKILLS:** Basic skills.
> **TIME:** 20 to 30 minutes per mechanism.
> **TOOLS:** Screwdriver.

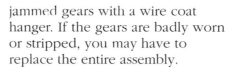

Sill-mounted sliding shoes trap dirt. Unscrew the channel, clean it and the sill, then lubricate with paste wax.

To keep cranks turning freely, apply a light oil or graphite. With some, you may need to take off the handle first.

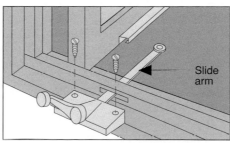

To dismantle an operator, disconnect the slide arm from the sash, then unscrew it from the frame.

If the gears are encrusted with old grease, soak in a solvent, then repack with a multipurpose lubricant.

Solving Window Problems (continued)

REPAIRING SLIDING WINDOWS

To keep sliding sashes moving, clear paint or dirt from their tracks and lubricate with silicon lubricant. If a slider jams, binds, or jumps loose, something may be lodged in the track or the track may be bent.

If all seems clear, lift out the sash and check its grooved edges. Clean and wax these, too, if necessary.

Bigger windows roll on sets of nylon wheels called sheaves, which are self-lubricating and rarely need attention. If a sheave is mangled, remove the assembly and replace it.

To remove a sliding sash, partially open the window, then lift it up and pull its lower edge toward you.

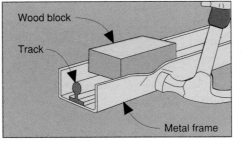

To straighten a bent track, cut a wood block to fit snugly in the channel and carefully tap the track against it.

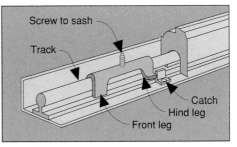

"Catch-and-dog" window latches can get bent. Adjust them so that the dog's "hind leg" hits against the catch.

REPAIRING AWNING WINDOWS

Awning windows are repaired like casements (see page 71).

Keep operators moving freely. A stiff arm assembly could pull screws loose or even force apart the sash joints. Clean off rust with steel wool and lubricate with paraffin wax or graphite; never use oil because it attracts dust.

1. To remove an awning sash, open it as far as you can, then disconnect the operator's side or scissors arm.

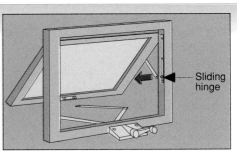

2. Tilt the sash to a horizontal position, disengage its sliding hinges, and pull the window free from its frame.

REPAIRING JALOUSIE WINDOWS

Jalousie window mechanisms depend on a series of gears and levers that may be concealed in the jambs. This makes jalousies relatively difficult to repair. Often you must dismantle the entire window to get at the vertical arms. If your unit jams, try freeing it with graphite or another non-oil lubricant, as shown at far right.

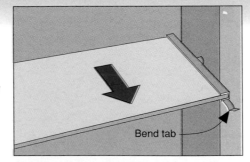

Simple tab-like clips hold jalousie slats in place. To remove one, just bend open the tab and slide out the pane.

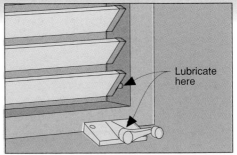

Don't force a mechanism. Lubricate the crank shaft and pivot points, then work the handle back and forth.

REPAIRING WINDOW SHADES

A window shade has a hollow roller with a coiled spring inside. Drawing down the shade puts tension on the spring; a ratchet and flat pin at one end hold this tension until you release it. A stationary pin at the other end turns freely in its bracket.

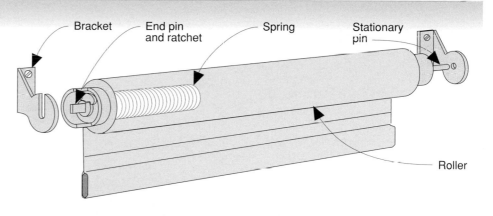

Bracket — End pin and ratchet — Spring — Stationary pin — Roller

---

HELPFUL HINTS — TROUBLESHOOTING WINDOW SHADES

Problem	Cause	Solution
Goes up with a bang	Too much tension on the spring	Take down the shade, unroll a few inches, and replace it in its bracket
Goes up too slowly	Not enough tension on the spring	Increase tension by rerolling
Will not catch	Bent or worn brackets; ratchet not holding	Straighten brackets; if ratchet, replace roller
Binds	Not enough clearance from brackets	Bend brackets apart or shorten the stationary pin
Falls	Excess clearance at brackets; broken spring	Relocate brackets; if spring is shot, replace roller

---

Replacing Shade Cloth

If you take down an old shade and unroll it, you will see that its shade material has been stapled to the roller. Take off the old material. Then, square off the edge of the new material. Carefully align this edge with the guideline on the roller before you drive in the new staples.

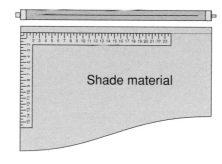

Shade material

YOU'LL NEED...

SKILLS: Basic skills.
TIME: 20 to 30 minutes per window.
TOOLS: Framing square, scissors or utility knife, staple gun.

Measuring and Cutting Shades

Cutting shades is easy. For inside mounting, measure jamb to jamb and subtract ⅛ inch for clearance. For outside mounting, simply cut to length desired. Add 8 to 12 inches to the height. Remove the material, saw the roller to length, reinsert the stationary pin, cut the material to size, and replace it.

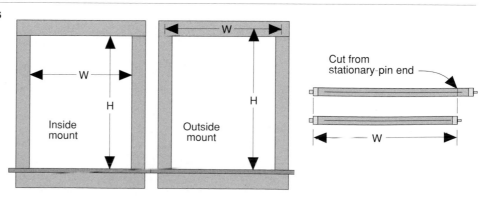

Inside mount — W, H
Outside mount — W, H
Cut from stationary-pin end — W

Solving Window Problems (continued)

REPAIRING VENETIAN BLINDS

Inside the head box of a venetian blind, a tilt tube supports a pair of tape ladders on which the blind's slats rest. To open or close the slats, you pull one end of a tilt cord wrapped around the pulley of a worm gear. This gear rotates the tube and changes the pitch of the slats. A lift cord, strung over a series of pulleys and down through the slats to the base piece, raises and lowers the entire slat assembly.

When the tilting mechanism balks, look for cord threads or dirt in the worm gear. If the blind refuses to go up or down, the lift cord has either broken, frayed, or jammed. If so, replace both cords and check the tape ladders as well.

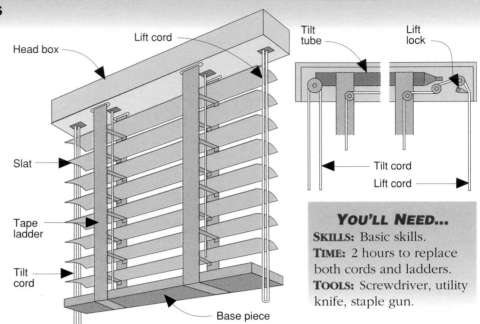

YOU'LL NEED...

SKILLS: Basic skills.
TIME: 2 hours to replace both cords and ladders.
TOOLS: Screwdriver, utility knife, staple gun.

Replacing Tape Ladders and Cords

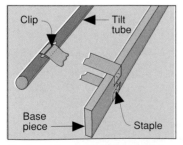

1. Remove clamps holding tapes to base. On wood blinds, the tapes are stapled.

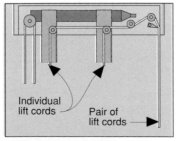

2. Snip off lift cord at either side and remove by pulling, as if raising the blind.

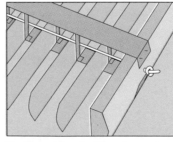

3. Slide slats from ladders. If replacing only the cords, leave the slats in position.

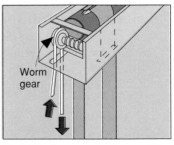

4. In head box, find clips holding tapes to tilt tube. Remove clips to free tapes.

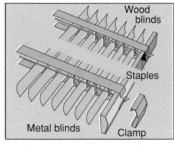

5. Attach new tapes to tilt tube and base piece, then extend ladders and slide other slats into place.

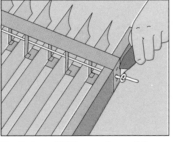

6. Thread lift cords from base piece on each side up, over the pulleys, and back down through lift lock.

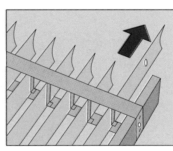

7. Note that ladders' rungs are offset from each other. Weave lift cord on alternate sides of the rungs.

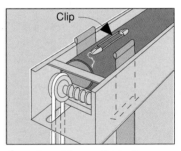

8. Snip the tassels from old tilt cord, thread new cord over worm gear pulley, and replace tassels.

CONTROLLING HEAT GAINS AND LOSSES

Stand in front of an undraped window on a chilly evening, and it seems to radiate cold. Actually, you are feeling heat loss from your body.

Try the same spot on a sunny day. Regardless of the temperature outside, the area will feel warmer than its surroundings; you are gaining heat. If you learn to control window heat gain and loss, you can reduce your home's heating and cooling bills substantially.

Make sure your windows are snugly weather stripped (see pages 386–387). Air leaks around sashes or frames will negate whatever gain-loss strategy you might attempt.

Analyze your windows' insulation value, or R-value. A single pane of glass has an R-value of 1. A second layer—either storm windows or insulating glass—doubles that R-value and halves the heat loss. A third layer of glass—triple-glazing—reduces heat loss even further. A well-insulated window pulls sunlight into a room, then traps its heat—often gaining far more than it loses.

Window treatments—drapes, shades, and blinds—further reduce both heat loss and gain. Opening draperies, blinds, or shades on a sunny winter day takes a big load off your home's heating system. Conversely, closing window treatments on hot days reflects solar rays, making less work for your air-conditioning system.

Look for substantial heat gains at south-facing windows first, then at eastern and western exposures. Beef up the insulation value of north-facing windows. The chart below compares the effectiveness of different gain-loss tactics you can use.

Double-glazing uses the air space, which is a good insulator, to block heat loss through glass, which is a poor insulator.

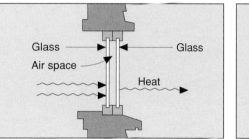

Glass ——▶ ◀—— Glass
Air space
Heat

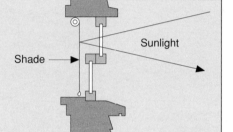

Sunlight
Shade ——▶

Shades cut heat gains by reflecting solar rays. On the exterior, eaves, awnings, and well-placed trees do an even better job.

MATERIAL MATTERS   WINDOW TREATMENTS COMPARED

Treatment	Description	Summer Reflective Efficiency	Winter Insulating Efficiency
Venetian blinds	White slats	Effective when closed and clean	Virtually none
Draperies	Tightly woven white fabric	Same as venetian blinds	Fairly effective if tight-fitting
Shades	White shade cloth	Same as venetian blinds	Virtually none
Double-glazing	Insulating glass or single-glazing plus storm—either inside or out	Not very effective	Cuts heat loss by 50%
Triple-glazing and Low-E glazing	Insulating glass plus storm (inside or out) or coated glass	Low-E fairly reflective	Cuts heat loss by 70%
Thermal shades	Quilted, fiber-filled material sealed tightly to window frame	Very effective	Cuts heat loss by 80% or more

Solving Window Problems (continued)

INSTALLING INTERIOR STORM SASHES

Fitting a storm sash on the inner side of an existing window cuts heat loss in half without the expense of buying exterior storm windows.

However, an inside sash must be removed for ventilation. Also, if it's made of clear acrylic, it scratches easily. Wash acrylic with mild liquid detergent and lots of water or a manufacturer-specified cleaner.

You can install kit sashes, as shown below. Or, you can make your own from ⅛-inch acrylic held in place with wood picture-frame molding. Use self-adhesive weather stripping around edges and fasten to window casings with screws so you can remove the pane easily.

For more about working with acrylic, see page 516. If you're considering exterior storm windows, turn to page 165.

For more about working with acrylic, see page 516. If you're considering exterior storm windows, turn to page 165.

> **YOU'LL NEED...**
> **SKILLS:** Basic skills.
> **TIME:** 2 to 3 hours per window.
> **TOOLS:** Tape measure, framing square, hacksaw, utility knife.

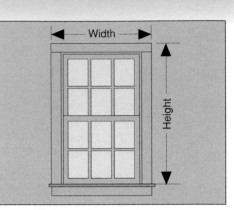

1. Measure to the outside of casings, then subtract enough to allow for trim at the sides, top, and sill, if any.

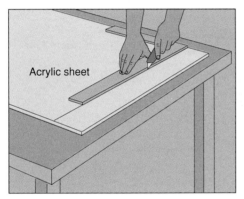

2. To trim acrylic, draw a sharp knife along straightedge several times, place the score on a table edge, and snap.

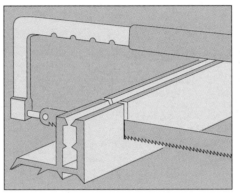

3. Cut the sill trim with a hacksaw. When you measure, be sure to allow for the strips at the sides.

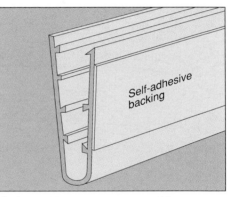

4. Most trims snap open and have adhesive backings. Apply trim around the pane's perimeter.

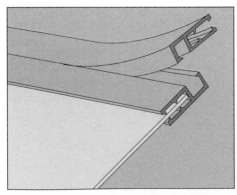

5. Special joiner strips splice together several acrylic sheets for large windows or patio doors.

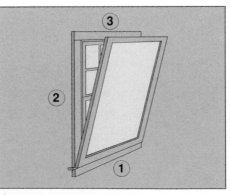

6. After assembly, lift unit into place, secure the sill trim, then the sides and top. Make sure there are no air gaps.

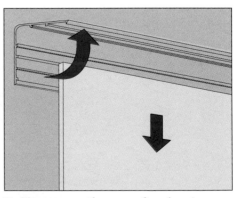

7. To remove the pane for cleaning or ventilation, snap open the side and top trim and lift out the plastic.

USING WINDOW TREATMENTS IN COLD CLIMATES

On average, windows comprise only 10 percent of the wall area of a house and only 3 percent of its total surface area. Yet windows account for as much as 40 percent of a house's heat loss. The reason is the R-values of windows.

R-value measures resistance to heat flow. The R-value of a single layer of glass is about 1; that of a double-glazed window is about 2. By contrast, the R-value of a 6-inch insulated wood-frame wall is about 20. Because heat loss is proportional to 1/R, a single-pane window loses 20 times as much heat per square foot as a normal wall.

The table at right shows the approximate R-values of various windows and window-treatment options. Which option has the quickest payback period in fuel savings depends on the cost of installing the treatment, fuel prices, and the severity of your climate.

A home energy audit—free from many gas and electric utility companies and many state energy agencies—shows you the savings and payback period.

WINDOW TREATMENT R-VALUES	
Window/Treatment	**R-value**
Single (SG)	0.9
Double (DG), ½-inch airspace	1.9
DG with Heat Mirror	4.0
DG with Low-E	3.2
DG with quilted shade	4.4
DG with insulated shutters	5–7

EVALUATING WINDOW TREATMENTS

Effective window treatment involves more than simply hanging drapes. The temperature difference between indoors and outdoors creates a convection current between the glass and the insulation with two results.

First, the cold air generated in the airspace flows out at the bottom, reducing the R-value of the treatment. Second, moisture in the air condenses on the cold glass. The condensate may run down onto the sill right away, or it may accumulate as frost to later melt and run down. Either way, the condensate may damage the sill.

The key to window insulation is a vapor-impervious construction and tight air seals at the sides and bottom. Both of the do-it-yourself treatments shown below and on the next page work well.

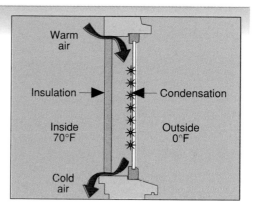

Installing Quilted Panels

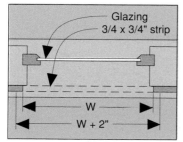

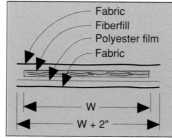

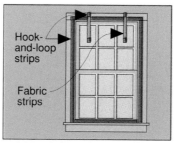

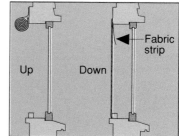

1. Nail a ¾×¾-inch wood strip to the sill between the interior window casings, creating a continuous, flush surface for sealing the fabric panel edges.

2. To make fabric panel, cut fiberfill, polyester film, and face fabric to widths shown. Cut fiberfill 1 inch shorter and film and fabric 1 inch longer than height. Stitch layers together along edges and ¾-inch in from edge.

3. Stitch one half of ¾-inch adhesive hook-and-loop strips to edges of the fabric panel; apply other half to casings and sill strip. Staple ¾×9-inch fabric strips to top casing at points one-quarter of the way in from casings.

4. Line up panel; press into hook-and-loop strips. When perfect, staple top edge to upper casing. Attach hook-and-loop dots to ends of ¾×9-inch strips and to points on upper casing to hold panel up when it's rolled up.

Solving Window Problems (continued)

INSTALLING INTERIOR SHUTTERS

Interior window shutters date back to pre-Colonial days. In New England states, solid-wood interior shutters provided a measure of protection against both intruders and frigid winter nights. The shutters described below—high in R-value, simple to construct, inexpensive, and decorative—make an ideal family project.

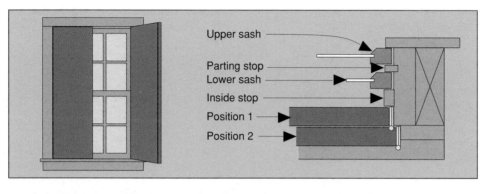

Shutters fit inside either the window jambs (Position 1) or the casings (Position 2). Check your windows to see which arrangement provides the tightest fit. You'll need at least ¾ inch of flat edge in either case. For the shutters, you can use a material such as Thermoply—a ⅛-inch thick, dense cardboard with foil/foil or foil/white plastic facings. Ask for this or a substitute material at your lumberyard.

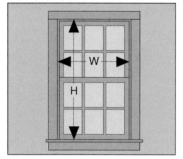

1. Measure height and width between casings or jambs. Deduct ⅜ inch from both for your final dimensions.

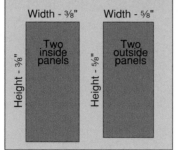

2. Cut two panels to your final dimensions and two additional panels ¼ inch smaller in both dimensions.

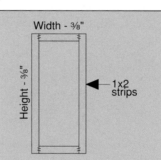

3. Cut two sets of 1×2 strips to form frames. Butt and staple the joints loosely together.

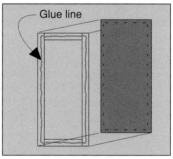

4. Glue the large panels— white face up—onto the frames. Align the edges and fasten with ½-inch staples.

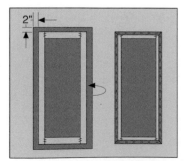

5. Stretch decorative fabric around shutter unit; staple, leaving 1-inch wood border. Glue smaller panel to wood.

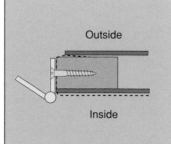

6. Screw loose-pin hinges to the shutter edges. Do not mortise (recess) the hinges into the frames.

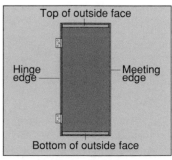

7. Support shutters on sill on scraps of panel while you screw the hinges to either the jamb or edge of casing.

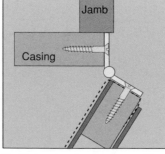

8. Weather-strip shutter's vertical and inside bottom edges. Install wood strip on sill to seal bottom edge.

INTERIOR DOORS

ANATOMY OF A PANEL DOOR

Almost every modern wood panel door has a vertical stile and horizontal rail framework. This construction helps counteract the wood's tendency to shrink, swell, and warp with humidity changes. With a panel door (right), you can see the framing. Spaces between frame members are paneled with wood, louvered slats, or glass.

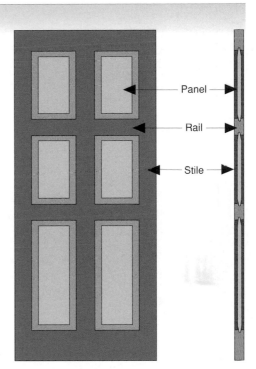

Panel

Rail

Stile

ANATOMY OF A FLUSH DOOR

Flush doors hide their framing beneath two or three layers of veneer. Alternating the veneer's directions minimizes warping. A solid-core flush door has a dense center of hardwood blocks or particleboard; a hollow-core door uses lighter material in the interior, such as corrugated cardboard or rigid foam insulation.

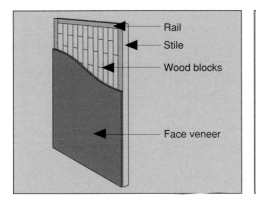

Rail
Stile
Wood blocks
Face veneer

Rail
Stile
Corrugated cardboard
Rail
Face veneer

ANATOMY OF A BYPASS DOOR

Bypass doors come in pairs and, as the name implies, slide past each other to open or close. Panel or flush, solid- or hollow-core, they roll along an overhead track and are guided by metal or nylon floor guides screwed to the floor.

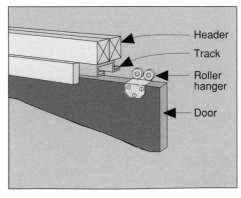

Header
Track
Roller hanger
Door

ANATOMY OF A BIFOLD DOOR

Bifold doors are hinged together at their center. One half of the door pivots on fixed pins; the other half slides along a header track—secured to the head jamb—as the center hinge opens or closes.

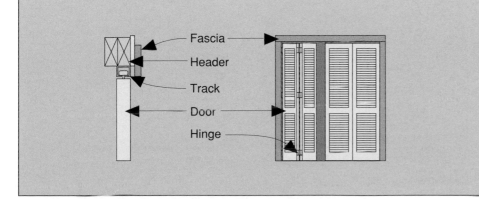

Fascia
Header
Track
Door
Hinge

Solving Door Problems

REPAIRING A HINGED DOOR

When a hinged door sticks, don't be too quick to take it down to plane its edges. Many difficulties call more for analysis than for work—and they're better dealt with by making minor adjustments in place.

Most problems result from one or more of the following causes: improperly aligned or loose hinges, an improperly aligned strike plate, warping of the door itself, or a frame that is out-of-square.

YOU'LL NEED...

SKILLS: Basic carpentry skills.
TIME: 30 to 90 minutes depending on if you have to plane the door.
TOOLS: Hammer, nail set, chisel, block or smooth plane, screwdriver.

TIMELY TECHNIQUES

If a door sticks or refuses to fit into its frame, check for the items listed above. If those don't seem to be the problem, close the door as best you can and sight carefully around its perimeter. Look for an uneven gap along the hinge jamb; this means the hinges need attention. If the door seems too big for its frame—or out of square with it— mark the tight spots, then sand or plane those spots.

WHERE'S THE RUB?

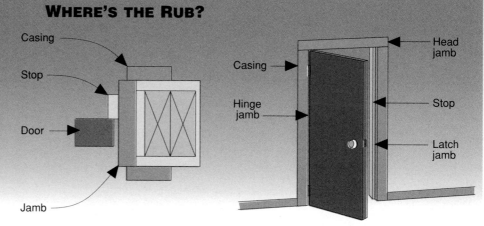

Freeing a Binding Door

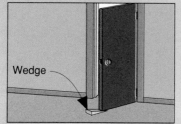

1. Loose hinge screws can cause sags. To tighten, wedge door open under the latch edge.

2. Remove screws and plug their holes with glue-coated scrap wood or dowel. Drive new screws into dowels.

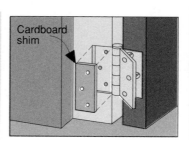

If the bottom edge binds, shim out the bottom hinge; shim out the top hinge for a top bind.

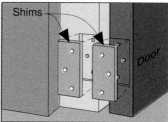

For doors that don't bind but are difficult to close, insert shims under each of the hinge leaves.

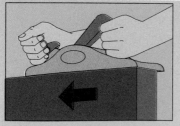

1. If you need to plane the top, usually you won't have to remove it from its hinges.

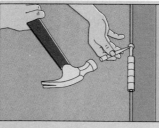

2. To trim bottom or edges, mark high spots, then tap out hinge pins—bottom first.

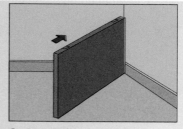

3. Brace the door for planing. Work from the edges toward the middle.

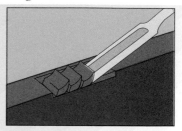

4. If you plane the hinge side a lot, you may have to reset the hinges (see page 83).

Correcting Strike Problems

When a door will not latch, or if it rattles when latched, look at the strike plate attached to the jamb. Minor adjustments here probably will solve the problem.

Take a close look at what happens when you try to close the door. Is the latch engaging the strike plate? If not, determine if the latch is too far from the strike or if it is hitting the strike but missing the hole. Scratches on the strike plate often provide a good clue as to how far it is out of alignment.

A door that does not fit snugly against its stop molding almost certainly will rattle. To silence it, move the strike plate or reposition the stop (see warping, below).

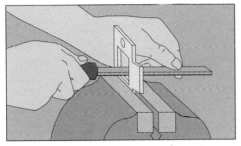

If the strike plate is off only ⅛ inch or so, file the opening in the plate. You may need to chisel away some wood.

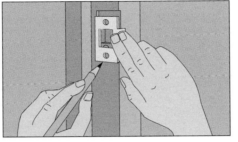

For bigger shifts, relocate the strike. You will need to extend the mortise. (For cutting mortises, see page 83.)

Use thick cardboard to shim a strike that is too far away to engage the latch. Resetting hinges can cause this.

Fixing a Warped Door

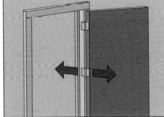

On the latch side, pry off the stop, close the door, and renail the stop snugly.

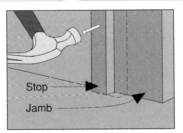

On the hinge edge, add a hinge in the middle to force the door into line.

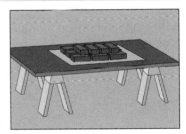

Try straightening a warped door by weighting it for several days.

Silencing Squeaky Hinges

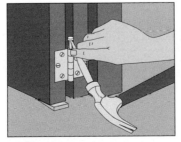

If oiling does not quiet a rusty hinge, dismantle and clean one hinge at a time.

Clean pins with steel wool. Poke out the pin holes with a wire-brush pipe cleaner.

Coat moving parts with graphite. Don't drive in pins tight; leave space for prying.

Solving Door Problems (continued)

REPAIRING A HINGED DOOR (continued)
Lubricating Balky Latches

YOU'LL NEED...
SKILLS: Basic skills.
TIME: 10 to 15 minutes per latch.
TOOLS: Screwdriver.

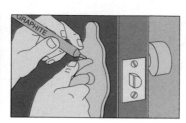

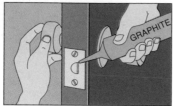

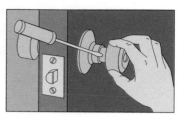

Turn handle to retract the latch, then puff powdered graphite into the works.

Lubricate a thumb-operated latch lever by puffing graphite into the lock body.

If lubricating won't free a latch, you may have to replace it (see page 87).

REPAIRING BYPASS DOORS

Compared to swinging doors, bypass units rarely malfunction When they do, a few turns of a screwdriver usually will fix them. Maintenance is minimal because most roll on self-lubricating nylon wheels.

If a bypass jams or jumps its track, suspect alignment problems. Check first to see that the door has not warped. You may be able to compensate for minor warping by shifting the guides slightly; otherwise, you might as well replace the door. Correct other alignment difficulties as shown below.

Some bypass doors, such as sliding glass patio types, roll on wheels along a bottom track. Adjust and maintain these as you would a sliding window (see page 72).

YOU'LL NEED...
SKILLS: Basic skills.
TIME: 15 to 20 minutes per door.
TOOLS: Screwdriver.

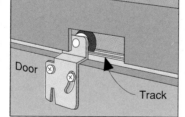

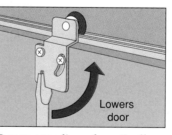

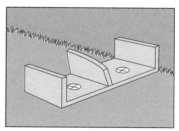

To remove a bypass door, lift it and tilt out slightly. Be careful—the door is heavy.

With some, you can free the door only when its wheels are at a key opening.

Doors are aligned vertically by raising or lowering the wheels overhead.

Fix or replace floor guides that are broken, bent, or out of line.

HELPFUL HINTS

To correct misaligned bifold doors, use a wrench to raise or lower the doors. A screw-and-slot on the lower pivot bracket helps you get them plumb. Do not lubricate the top assembly guides, as most of them are self-lubricating.

REPAIRING BIFOLD DOORS

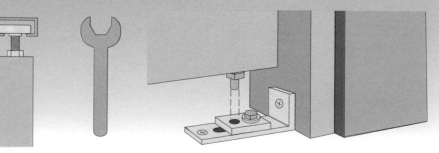

Installing New Doors

HANGING A DOOR

Replacing a door or hanging a new one in an existing opening is a satisfying carpentry project, provided you keep things square, measure and cut carefully, and visually check your work at every step.

Most doors measure 80 inches high. If you have to alter the size of one, allow ⅛ inch for clearance at top and sides and at least ⅜ inch at the bottom—more if it must clear carpeting. Never cut more than ¾ inch from either end to avoid weakening the door's rail.

Once you have hung a door, install stops on the jamb so the door cannot swing against its hinges. To mark for stops, close the door and draw a line on the jambs along the door's inside edge.

YOU'LL NEED...

SKILLS: Basic carpentry skills, including use of a finish saw.
TIME: 2 hours if the jamb is already in place.
TOOLS: Hammer, saw, smooth plane, chisel, drill, screwdriver.

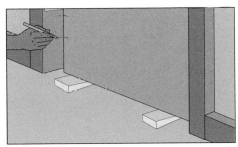

1. Check squareness of frame. Measure its height on both sides, then trim door to fit. See above for clearances.

2. Measure the width. If you only have to plane, work from the door's edge toward the center of the door.

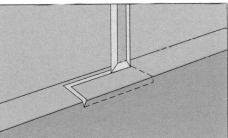

Shim

3. Unless the frame has stops, you'll need help to position the door in its opening. Use shims at all edges.

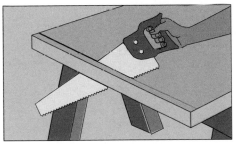

4. Measure for hinge locations and mark on door and jamb. Solid-core doors should have three hinges.

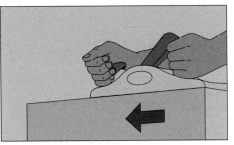

5. Position the top hinge no less than 6 inches from the top; the bottom hinge, at least 9 inches from the floor.

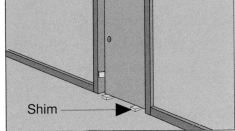

6. Begin a mortise by scoring around marked edges. Do not cut deeper than the thickness of the hinge leaf.

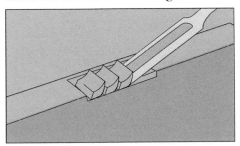

7. Make parallel cuts across the grain, holding the chisel as shown. (See page 413 for more about mortises.)

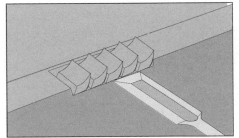

8. Knock out chips from the side. Then lay in the hinge leaf. You may need to shave away more wood.

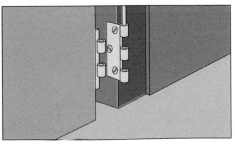

9. Screw the hinge leaves to the mortises, set door in place, and insert pins. (To install latch, see page 87.)

Installing New Doors (continued)

CUTTING IN A DOORWAY

Plot a location that will not require moving heating or plumbing lines. You may encounter wiring, but it is fairly easy to relocate. Size the opening to accurately fit the new door and frame. Most doors require ½-inch clearance all around. (See page 85 for prehung doors.)

Use a hammer and chisel to break open a plaster wall. Cut wood lath with a saw; use snips on metal lath; a saber or keyhole saw on drywall.

Note that these instructions apply only to interior walls. (See pages 168-169 for openings in exterior walls. Pages 32–41 tell how walls are constructed and how to finish off the surface around a new doorway.)

(See page 85 for prehung doors.)

> **YOU'LL NEED...**
> **SKILLS:** Moderate carpentry skills.
> **TIME:** 4 to 6 hours.
> **TOOLS:** Hammer, chisel, sabersaw, keyhole saw, handsaw.

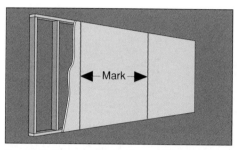

1. Mark the stud locations. Open up the wall to the ceiling and nearest stud on either side of the new opening.

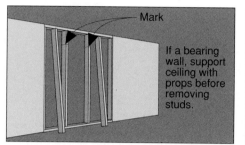

2. Before removing studs, measure down from the ceiling for the door's height. Make cuts along this line.

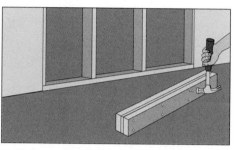

3. Build a header by nailing ½-inch plywood between two 2×4s or 2×6s. Nail it to adjacent studs and cripples.

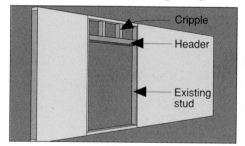

4. Locate one side of the opening against an existing stud. Leave an extra 3 inches (two 2×4s) for trimmers.

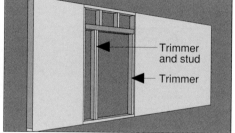

5. Cut trimmers for both sides of the opening. They support the header and make the doorway more rigid.

6. Cut out the sole plate last. You may have to patch holes in floor or install a saddle (see page 162).

CLOSING UP A DOORWAY

> **YOU'LL NEED...**
> **SKILLS:** Basic carpentry skills and moderate wall-finishing skills.
> **TIME:** 3 to 4 hours.
> **TOOLS:** Pry bar, hacksaw, handsaw, hammer.

1. Pry off moldings on sides of door. Slip a hacksaw blade between the frame and studs to cut nails.

2. Remove the frame in one piece and reuse it if possible. If the assembly sticks, tap lightly to free it.

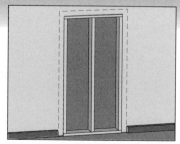

3. Nail 2×4s to top, sides, and bottom of opening, then toenail a stud in the center. Apply drywall (see page 54).

INSTALLING A PREHUNG DOOR

Building a custom door saves money, but takes time and expertise. Prehung units cost more, but you get everything you need—door, hinges, jamb, stop and casing moldings, and even a latch if you want it—all in one accurately made component.

Before you buy a prehung door, measure the thickness of the wall; plaster and drywall surfaces call for different jamb widths. The procedure shown here applies to prehung door assemblies that have a removable casing on one side. With another type, split-jamb doors, the casings are attached permanently on both sides, but side and head jambs are split down the middle. You install half the unit into one side of the wall, then install the other half from the opposite side (see page 86).

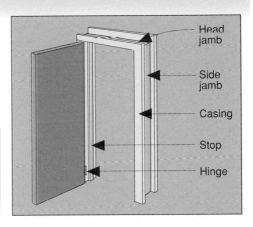

Head jamb
Side jamb
Casing
Stop
Hinge

YOU'LL NEED...

SKILLS: Moderate carpentry skills.
TIME: 2 hours.
TOOLS: Hammer, level, framing square, handsaw.

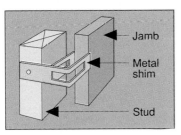

Jamb
Metal shim
Stud

1. Align unit in its opening with wood shingle shims—or use the metal versions included with some doors.

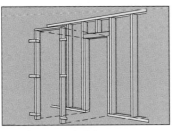

2. Clip metal shims onto jambs after the door, jamb, and one casing are in place.

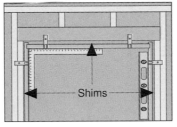

Shims

3. Make sure the head jamb is square and the side jambs are plumb. Shim wherever necessary before nailing.

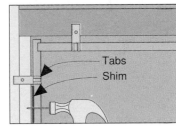

Tabs
Shim

4. Drive in finish nails through jambs and shims, then break off the shim's tabs. Install casing molding.

MATERIAL MATTERS   CHOOSING AND BUYING HINGES

Most full-size doors hang on butt hinges. If you are replacing a butt hinge, replace its mate, too. Measure the old hinge, noting first its height, then its width when open. For some hinge types, you also will need to know whether it is a right- or left-hand door (see below).

Generally, it is best to purchase loose-pin hinges, as they permit you to remove the door more easily than fixed-pin hinges.

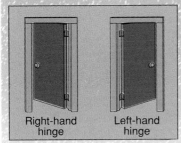

Right-hand hinge   Left-hand hinge

A hinge's "hand" refers to the side of the door that it is on. To check this, stand opposite the door's swing.

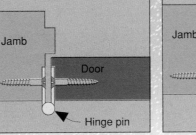

Jamb
Door
Hinge pin

The common full-mortise hinge is cut into both the jamb and door edge. It makes a neat installation.

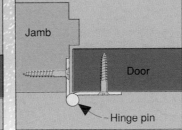

Jamb
Door
Hinge pin

A half-mortise hinge is cut only into the jamb. For extra strength, you can fasten the hinge to the door with bolts.

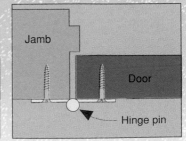

Jamb
Door
Hinge pin

Surface-mounted hinges are not cut into either the door or jamb. The door must be flush with the casing.

Installing New Doors (continued)

INSTALLING A SPLIT-JAMB PREHUNG DOOR

Most prehung interior doors come fully assembled, with jambs and casings in place, hinges and strike plate mortised, door hung, and a hole for the lockset drilled. With a split-jamb door, the side and top jambs consist of two tongue-and-groove halves that slide together to accommodate variations in wall thickness. The door is held in place mainly by finish nails driven through the casings into the door's framing.

This works fine for lightweight hollow-core doors. For heavier solid-wood panel doors and even heavier solid-core doors, however, nailing the casings alone is not enough. For these doors, specify solid jambs of a width to match wall thickness.

A rough opening for a door frame is usually 1 inch higher and 2 inches wider than the door, but check with your supplier for exact dimensions.

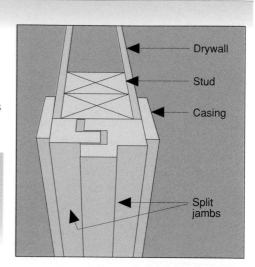

Drywall
Stud
Casing
Split jambs

YOU'LL NEED...
SKILLS: Moderate carpentry skills.
TIME: 1 to 2 hours.
TOOLS: Handsaw, hammer, level, nail set, screwdriver, chisel.

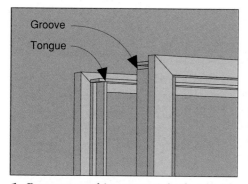

Groove
Tongue

1. Remove packing materials that hold the two jamb pieces together. Separate the jamb pieces, leaving the door closed inside the stop jambs.

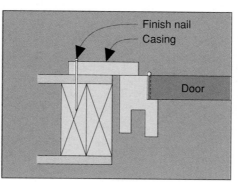

Finish nail
Casing
Door

2. Place door in opening with casing against wall. With door centered, drive an 8d finish nail through top outside edge of casing into stud.

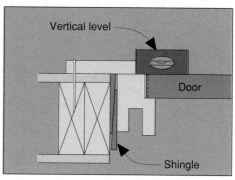

Vertical level
Door
Shingle

3. With a level held vertically against the inside edge of the side casing, shim the jamb at the hinge locations to plumb the casing.

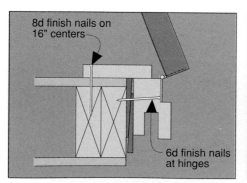

8d finish nails on 16" centers
6d finish nails at hinges

4. Drive 8d finish nails in hinge-side casing at hinges and every 16 inches in between. Drive 6d finish nails through jamb—not stop—and shims into stud.

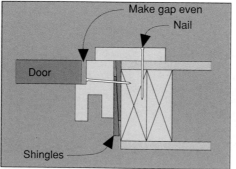
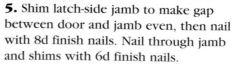

Make gap even
Nail
Door
Shingles

5. Shim latch-side jamb to make gap between door and jamb even, then nail with 8d finish nails. Nail through jamb and shims with 6d finish nails.

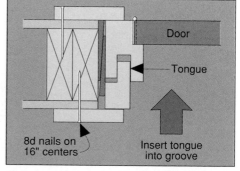

Door
Tongue
8d nails on 16" centers
Insert tongue into groove

6. Insert the second jamb half so that the tongues fit into the grooves. Nail around the casings with 8d finish nails every 16 inches.

INSTALLING A KNOB SET

Interior knob and-latch sets differ little in overall design, although there are many different styles and quality levels. Most modern doors have the cylinder-type knob-and-latch set shown here or a slight variation called the tubular lock.

Mortise knob sets no longer are used on interior doors, but you can replace one easily with a cylinder unit (see below). Ornamental escutcheons hide the holes left by the old unit.

Measure the door's thickness before buying a knob set. Some units fit both $1\frac{3}{8}$- and $1\frac{3}{4}$-inch-thick doors; others fit only one size.

YOU'LL NEED...

SKILLS: Basic carpentry skills.
TIME: 1 to 2 hours.
TOOLS: Drill, hole saw, screwdriver, hammer, chisel.

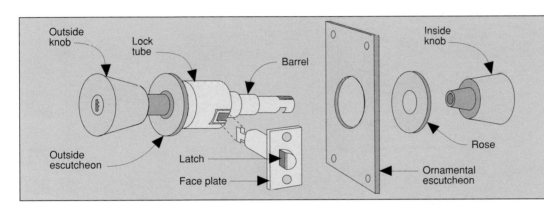

Outside knob · Lock tube · Barrel · Inside knob · Outside escutcheon · Latch · Face plate · Rose · Ornamental escutcheon

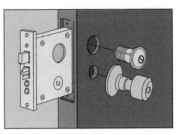

1. To remove an old mortise latch, take off the knobs, then unscrew and pull out the latch assembly.

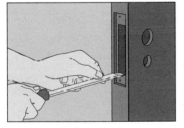

2. Rework the mortise to size with a file or chisel. On new doors, locate knob 36 inches from the floor assembly.

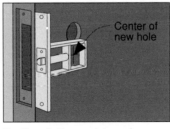

Center of new hole

3. Carefully position the new latch assembly and mark where you must bore a hole through the door.

4. To avoid splintering, bore halfway through from one side with hole saw; halfway through from other side.

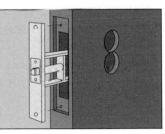

5. Slip in the latch assembly and fasten top and bottom to edge of doors with screws.

6. Install escutcheons; slip in outside knob assembly. Most latches can be set for left- or right-hand operation.

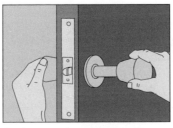

7. Secure the inside rose, then the knob. Before tightening, check to be sure the latch works freely.

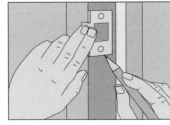

8. Close the door, carefully locate the strike plate, then open and mark its position on the jamb with a pencil.

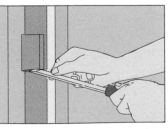

9. You probably will need to enlarge the original mortise. (See page 83 for more information about mortises.)

STORAGE

HELPFUL HINTS

With proper storage planning, you may be able to clear your existing clutter and anticipate future crunches as well.

Begin by asking yourself if you really need more places to put things or just better organization of what you have. Often, the simple space-engineering ideas on the next three pages can do wonders for the capacity of a closet or other storage area. And remember that you can rotate seasonal gear. Try letting such things as the charcoal grill and snow shovel trade places.

STORING STRATEGY

When deciding where to locate new storage units, plan to keep everyday items at or near their points of use and once-a-year specials in more remote spots. Survey your entire home, measuring all potential sites, then plot them on a graph-paper floor plan. The overview below points out the most likely spots to check.

Finally, select the type of storage you need. Open shelves (see pages 92–93) are relatively inexpensive and easy to install, but they invite dust. Cabinets (see pages 94–98) provide more protection for stored items and are available in sizes to fit almost any space. New closets (see page 99) offer permanent and unobtrusive storage. An impressive array of ready-made storage units (see page 100) also is available. Wire closet organizers (see page 101) provide another solution because of their modular characteristics.

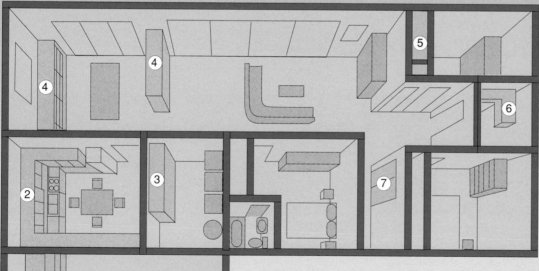

1. Run a bank of shelves the length of one garage wall.

2. Plan as much kitchen shelf space as you can. If possible, include a utility closet as part of your kitchen storage.

3. If your home is blessed with a mud room, stash family coats, boots, umbrellas, and other everyday outerwear there.

4. Shelves or cabinets can span a wall or serve as a room divider and offer more storage per area than furniture.

5. For a linen closet, consider borrowing space from a closet. Don't keep linens in a bathroom; they will absorb humidity.

6. High, wall-mounted cabinets can help you solve a bathroom storage problem. Consider using the space above the toilet.

7. Reserve part of an entry closet for guests' coats. Hooks on the inside of doors hold hats, handbags, and whatnot.

Organizing Existing Storage

Tailoring storage spaces to your exact needs makes everything easier to get at and increases the capacity of a closet or cabinet by as much as one-third. This means that modifying three closets could give you the space of four.

Study the drawings on this and the next two pages, inventory the things around your home that you want to make places for, then adapt the designs to suit your needs.

Tables on the following pages give typical sizes for many household items. Plan spacings carefully. For example, be sure to allow for the thickness of shelves and dividers. Don't over-engineer, however, because you'll need a few inches of free space for getting the contents in and out and enough flexibility to accommodate changes later on—or even the likes of the next homeowner if you move.

GETTING MORE INTO A SHALLOW CLOSET

Shallow bedroom closets—typically 24 inches deep by 5 to 8 feet wide—offer lots of room for improvement. With most, you get a single pole, plus a shelf above it, and a pair of sliding bypass doors.

Start your analysis of a closet's efficiency by examining the doors. Do you find yourself opening one, then rolling them both to the other side (and maybe back again) every morning? If so, consider replacing these bypass panels with a set of bifold units (see page 79).

Study how space is used inside. Chances are you'll notice that a few dresses, robes, and coats fill most of the vertical space between the rod and the floor, while the bulk of your clothing hangs down only a little more than half-way. Group garments by size and you will discover a sizable empty space under the shorter items.

Both of the designs shown below put the space inside shallow closets to better use. The closet at left, which works with either bypass or bifold doors, includes a drawer case, taking pressure off storage elsewhere. The closet at right features two rods on one side to accommodate shorter clothes, creating more hanging space. It would require bifold doors so you can access the center drawer case.

In adapting these designs, keep in mind that the spaces allowed for hanging clothes are minimums. A table of typical clothing sizes appears on page 90.

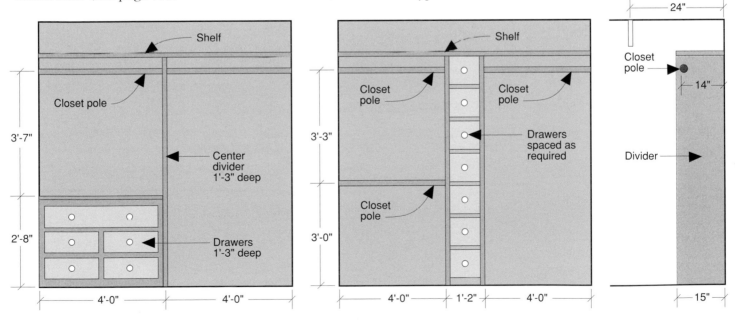

Organizing Existing Storage (continued)

GETTING MORE INTO A WALK-IN CLOSET

Walk-in closets, although usually larger than their shallow cousins, actually provide less storage per square foot. Subtract the minimal 2-foot-wide access corridor and you can see why. If a walk-in closet measures just 4 to 5 feet deep and access isn't a problem, you might be wiser to convert it into two shallow closets located back to back.

Otherwise, you can install closet poles along the longer wall(s). If you double-tier poles for short items, you can gain one-half again as much hanging space.

Shelves—either at the back or along one wall—can hold your folded clothes. Spacing them about 7 inches minimizes rummaging.

Don't neglect shelf possibilities above the closet poles. Although you may have to stretch or use a step stool to reach them, boxes stored here are good for holding seasonal or seldom-worn clothing. If you install a second shelf about 12 inches above the existing one, you won't have to stack the boxes on top of each other.

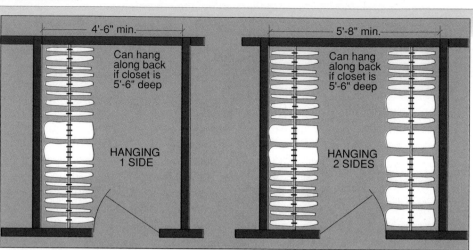

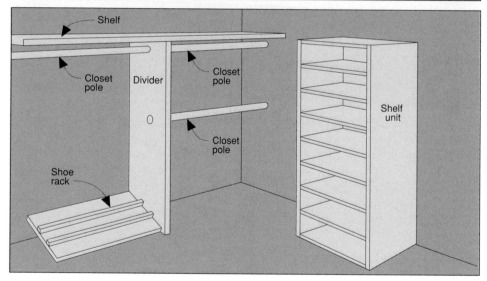

HELPFUL HINTS   CLOTHES DIMENSIONS YOU NEED TO KNOW

Familiarize yourself with a few basic measurements before you take on a closet reorganization. A wooden coat hanger with a heavily padded jacket on it occupies a space about 20 inches deep. Closet poles normally are hung 12 to 14 inches from the wall. In an extra-tight situation, you could cut this distance to 10 inches and still be able to hang the jacket. The table shown at right lists dimensions of other typical items in a clothes closet.

Women's Items		Men's Items		Accessories	
Long dresses	69"	Topcoats	50"	Garment bags	57"
Robes	52"	Pants, unfolded	44"	Shoe bags	36"
Coats	52"	Travel suit bags	41"	Umbrellas	36"
Travel dress bags	48"	Suits	38"	Canes	36"
Dresses	45"	Shirts	28"		
Skirts	35"	Ties	27"		
Suits	29"	Pants, folded	22"		
Blouses	28"				

GETTING MORE INTO A LINEN CLOSET

The trouble with tall stacks of folded sheets or towels is that you have to be a magician to remove the lower ones without rumpling the rest or toppling adjacent stacks as well. The solution: compartmentalize.

The drawing at right shows one scheme to put foldables in their places. Bulky blankets go up top, then bath towels, sheets, hand towels, washcloths, and so on. Drawers and a cabinet provide concealed storage below.

Plan your divisions according to the things you have, leaving a few inches of clearance for getting them in and out.

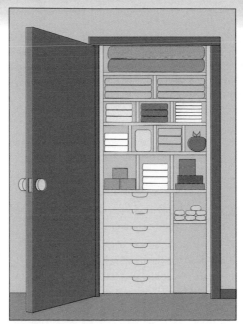

LINEN CLOSET ITEMS
(Maximum Requirements)

Blankets	27"×22"
Fitted sheets	18"×11"
Flat sheets	14"×15"
Bath towels	14"×13"
Dish towels	10"×16"
Bath mats	10"×9"
Pillowcases	7"×15"
Washcloths	7"×7"
Hand towels	6"×10"

GETTING MORE INTO A CLEANING CLOSET

Here again, compartments help organize the jumble of awkward shapes that utility storage must handle. The closet at right garages an upright vacuum, provides shelves for an assortment of cleaning products, and secures a mop and broom so they won't fall out every time you open the door. Note, also, how a slanting compartment near the bottom of the closet cuts the clutter of stored paper bags.

For even more storage, look to the inside of the closet door. Lipped shelves and/or a cloth caddy for vacuum attachments put this bonus space to good use. If space in a cleaning or linen closet is really tight, consider outfitting it with perforated metal or plastic-coated metal shelving rather than wood shelving. You will gain storage space and improve air circulation as well.

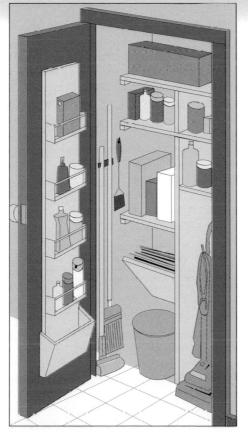

CLEANING EQUIPMENT

Canister vacuum	14"×17"
Floor polisher	12"×45"
Upright vacuum	14"×48"
Carpet sweeper	16"×54"
Broom	10"× up to 60"
Whisk broom	6"×10"
Dust pan	11"×9"
Push broom	14"× up to 54"
Dry mop	14"×66"
Wet mop	12"×48"
Scrub bucket	11"×12"
Cleansers	8-10"× up to 14"

Adding New Storage

The answer to a storage shortage may be as simple as a few coat hooks at the front entry or as complex as an entire wall of custom built-in cabinets in the living room. Most solutions fall somewhere in the middle, with open shelving leading the list. If you select the right hardware (below) and master a few basics (page 93), you will never again be floored by a shelf project.

Another alternative is to use prefabricated kitchen cabinets (see pages 94–97). Available in a wide variety of styles and finishes, they make sense for almost any room.

As a last resort, consider building a new closet or closets (see page 99). Before you begin a project like that, however, consider the almost-instant alternatives offered by prefabricated or kit storage units that you can buy (see page 100).

MATERIAL MATTERS

The success of a shelving project rests upon its support system. So ask yourself these questions before making a choice. What weight and spans must the hardware hold (see page 93)? Do you want fixed or adjustable brackets? How will you attach the shelves to the wall (see pages 34 and 93)? Do you really need hardware at all, or could you use cleats (see table at right)?

Once you have answered the mechanical questions, consider appearance. Styles range from strictly utilitarian to hardwood wall furniture. You will discover that price is a factor, too—sometimes the hardware can cost more than the shelving material.

The chart at right illustrates the eight most commonly used support systems, but there are dozens of variations. With standards and brackets, for example, you can choose painted or plated finishes, different bracket shapes and locking mechanisms, and even specialty items, such as angled supports that serve as magazine racks.

While you are thinking about hardware, give some thought to buying prefinished shelving as well. Though considerably more expensive than ordinary lumber or plywood, it saves a lot of tedious finishing work.

CHOOSING SHELF HARDWARE

Rigid pressed-steel angle brackets hold medium loads. Always mount them with the longer of the two legs against the wall.

Brackets clip into uprights, allowing vertical adjustment of the shelves. Choose 8-, 10-, or 12-inch brackets. Properly installed, this system supports surprisingly heavy loads.

Cleats are the simplest way to attach shelves inside closets or cabinets; use one at each end. For long spans, attach a strip to the unit's back to support the rear of the shelf.

Pin-type clips pop into predrilled holes. Relatively inexpensive, they'll support heavy loads on ¾-inch thick boards up to about 30 inches long.

End-mounted standards with clips also provide for vertically adjustable shelves. For a flush installation, you can dado the standards into the cabinet's sides.

Tension poles wedge between the floor and ceiling in situations where you can't or don't want to make holes in the walls. They're relatively expensive.

Folding brackets allow you to drop a shelf out of the way when you're not using it.

Light-duty wire brackets are accessories for perforated hardboard. Measure the shelf board's thickness before you buy; ¼- and ⅛-inch sizes require different devices.

PUTTING UP SHELF STRIPS

Bracket shelving appears to put a lot of weight on the few small fasteners that secure the strips. But those fasteners do not actually bear the load—they simply clamp the strips to the wall. The strength of a bracket shelving system actually depends more on the fasteners' holding power than it does on their size.

Use plastic anchors for light duty installations only. Wood screws driven directly into studs hold much better, however, you must adjust the spacing to the wall framing. Hollow-wall fasteners, such as expansion and toggle bolts (see page 464), let you put strips exactly where you want and have good holding power.

Equipped with the proper fasteners and a power screwdriver, drill, and level, you can hang the strips quickly. It is best to plumb the strips so they will be perfectly vertical. But if your walls are out of square, you may have to measure from floor or ceiling to make the spacing aesthetically acceptable.

YOU'LL NEED...
SKILLS: Basic carpentry skills.
TIME: 30 to 60 minutes.
TOOLS: Level, drill, screwdriver, hammer.

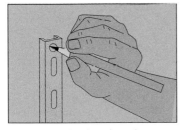

1. Note whether bracket strip has a top and bottom. Mark and drill for the top hole only.

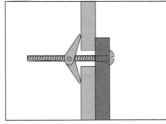

2. Insert a bolt, but don't tighten it until you've plumbed the strip. Drill lower holes and install bolts.

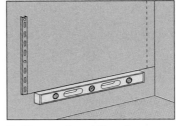

3. Draw a level line from the strip's top or bottom to locate the position of the last strip.

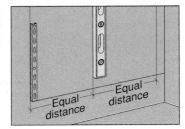

4. Position the intermediate strips at equal distances; the number depends on span length and weight load.

HELPFUL HINTS

Plot shelf spacings carefully, using graph paper and the dimensions at right, to minimize surprises later. The span table gives the maximum distance you should allow between supports, assuming the shelf will be holding a full load of books, which are the heaviest items you're likely to put on shelves.

You can save space and cut down on dusting by tailoring vertical spacings to accommodate your possessions exactly. Leave an extra inch or two so you can tip out a book or compact disk. Allow more leeway if you decide on fixed shelves.

Before determining your final shelving layout, consult the lower table at right for the spacing required between shelves for several often-shelved items.

FIGURING SHELF SPACINGS AND SPANS

SHELVING SPANS

Material	Max. Span	Material	Max. Span
¾-inch plywood	36"	2×10 or 2×12 lumber	48"-56"
¾-inch particleboard	28"	½-inch acrylic	22"
1×12 lumber	24"	⅜-inch glass	18"

SHELF SPACING GUIDE

Item	Height	Item	Height
Paperback books	8"	Compact disks	5"
Hardback books	11"	Cassette tapes	5"
Oversize hardbacks	15"	Video tapes	8"
Catalog-format books	16"	Circular slide carousels	9¾"

Adding New Storage (continued)

MATERIAL MATTERS · CHOOSING AND BUYING KITCHEN CABINETS

There is a broad range of options when it comes to buying kitchen cabinets. You can order stock cabinets knocked down (unassembled), unfinished, or prefinished and ready for installation.

Judge cabinet construction by taking a close look at how joints are fitted and the way the insides and backs have been finished. Check hardware, too. Quality cabinets have doors that swing freely and latch securely and drawers that roll on metal tracks. Look, too, for a NKCA (National Kitchen Cabinet Association) certification label. This group sets minimum standards for the cabinet industry.

COMPARING CABINET MATERIALS

Cabinet Material	Features	Relative Cost
Particleboard	Better units have wood or plastic veneers, but some have lacquered or photographed finishes that work well, too	Low to moderate
Hardboard	Often used for doors, backs, and sides on wooden frames	Moderate
Hardwood	Usually veneered plywood with hardwood frames; sturdy construction, easy-care finishes	Moderate to high
Steel	Baked enamel finishes; some are noisy, prone to rusting; not much demand for them	Low to high

TIMELY TECHNIQUES · MEASURING FOR NEW CABINETS

Standardized dimensions and modular designs greatly simplify the job of tailoring cabinets to your kitchen. Just measure the space available, order a series of units that comes close to fitting it, then make up the difference with fillers between the cabinets.

Plot your kitchen area on graph paper, making both a floor plan and an elevation drawing. Be sure to include door swings, heating vents, window casings, pipes, electrical outlets and switches, appliance sizes, and other limiting factors.

Visit a cabinet dealer for more ideas, then plan your layout using information at right. Height measurements shown accommodate the reach of an average-height person and are accepted as standards throughout the kitchen and appliance industries.

Don't forget that kitchen cabinets also can be used in other rooms for your storage needs.

Base cabinets usually are 36 inches high by 24 inches deep. Wall cabinets measure 12 to 30 inches high and 12 inches deep.

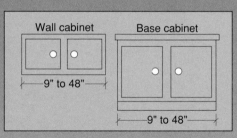

Manufacturers offer plenty of choices when it comes to cabinet widths—from 9 to 48 inches wide.

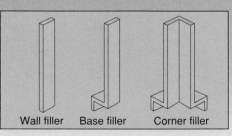

Filler strips fit between cabinets or cabinets and walls, letting you adjust a bank of cabinets to the space available. Ripsaw to the width required.

DESIGNING A KITCHEN LAYOUT

Rather than planning the layout for a new or remodeled kitchen yourself, you can avail yourself of free design services offered by home centers, lumberyards, and kitchen centers. Investigate more than one center, too, because each may handle different cabinet brand names.

Measure your kitchen (or bath), including lengths of walls, widths and locations of doors and windows, location of existing plumbing, and heights of window sills and the ceiling. Also, you'll want to note the dimension of existing appliances (or fixtures in the bath) that you will have to accommodate in the plan.

Plot these dimensions on graph paper and take the sketch to a home center. You'll see samples of many cabinet styles, ranging from unfinished pine to hardwoods and ultra-modern European designs. After selecting a product line that suites your taste and budget, sit down with the designer.

The designer will key your sketch dimensions into a computer-aided design (CAD) program. Working from the list of cabinet sizes available in your chosen line, they can plug cabinets into the layout. When they're done, the design for your kitchen will appear.

Changing cabinet widths, heights, or even styles is as simple as a few computer key strokes. At any point in the room, the designer can specify a point from which to view the kitchen, and your design will instantly appear, in three dimensions and in color. Move around the room and see how it looks. When you are satisfied with the design, the designer will print the plan, the view(s), and a list of cabinets and their prices. With one more key stroke, the cabinets are ordered and on their way to your home.

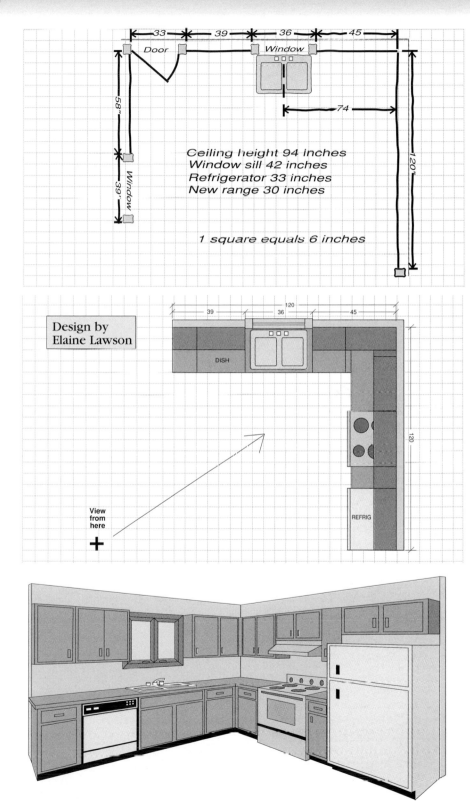

Ceiling height 94 inches
Window sill 42 inches
Refrigerator 33 inches
New range 30 inches

1 square equals 6 inches

Design by
Elaine Lawson

DISH

REFRIG

View from here

Adding New Storage (continued)

INSTALLING KITCHEN BASE CABINETS

A built-in look with prefabricated cabinets might seem to call for tricky carpentry. Not so! The cabinet manufacturer has done most of the work, providing you with perfectly square modules that you can interlock with screws or dowels. Assembly consists of leveling and plumbing each cabinet, then fastening it to the wall and its neighboring units.

Use the screws specified by the manufacturer, and drive in screws through frames rather than the thinner back and side panels.

If a baseboard, door, or window casing gets in the way, remove it carefully, trim to fit after the cabinets are in place, and reinstall.

Cap off base cabinets with a countertop from a home center or a kitchen supplier. Most dealers will cut one to size and even make a cutout for the sink if you supply a pattern. Measure carefully, because countertop mistakes are costly. You can make your own countertop by veneering exterior-grade plywood with plastic laminate (see page 515).

Install the countertop by screwing angle brackets to the counter's underside and to the cabinet frame.

To hang heavy wall cabinets without help, build a temporary, movable support you can set on the counter or floor. Rest a unit on the support, shim behind the cabinet to plumb it, then screw through the cabinet frame and shim into the wall studs. Finish off the job by installing filler strips or molding to cover any gaps between the cabinets and walls or floor.

YOU'LL NEED...

SKILLS: Intermediate carpentry skills.
TIME: 4 hours for a 12-foot run of base cabinetry.
TOOLS: Stud finder, tape measure, level, chalk line, drill, screwdriver, clamps, hammer, chisel.

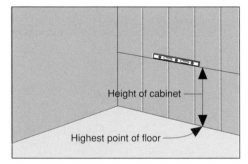

1. Mark the locations of the wall studs (see page 33). Then mark a level line at the height of the base cabinets at the highest point of the room's floor.

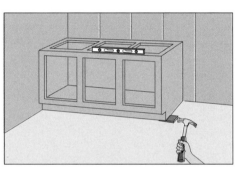

2. Set a cabinet in place and level it to your line by tapping shims under low points. Level from front to back as well as from side to side.

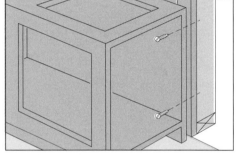

3. Drill pilot holes and drive screws through the cabinet framing into the studs. A screwdriver attachment on an electric drill speeds this job along.

4. Once a unit has been leveled and secured, chisel away any shims that protrude. You're ready to install the next cabinet.

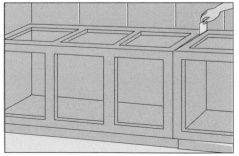

5. Sometimes a thin shim between cabinets will compensate for minor irregularities. Face edges must butt tightly, though.

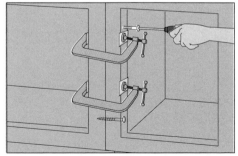

6. Fasten units together by clamping face frames together, drilling pilot holes, and driving in screws as shown. Countersink screws about ¼ inch.

INSTALLING KITCHEN WALL CABINETS

The biggest problem with hanging wall cabinets is lifting their weight to the required height. You may be strong, but you'll find it invaluable to have a helper hold the cabinets in place while you drill and fasten them to the wall studs. Remove the doors and any shelves before hoisting the cabinets into place to lighten the load.

If you can't find a willing helper, cut a 55-inch-long 2×4 and wedge it between the floor and the front bottom edge of the cabinet to hold it up temporarily. Also, it's easier to work on wall cabinets if you hang them before installing any base cabinets beneath them.

YOU'LL NEED...

SKILLS: Intermediate carpentry skills.
TIME: 3 to 4 hours for a straight run of cabinets; more if corner cabinets are complicated.
TOOLS: Hammer, screwdriver, drill, stud finder, level, clamps, chalk line, measuring tape, handsaw, miter box.

1. Find stud locations with a stud finder. Snap vertical chalk lines to indicate either the stud centers or the stud edges.

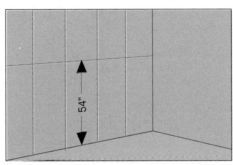

2. Measure up 54 inches—the standard height of wall cabinets—from the floor at both ends of the wall and snap a horizontal chalk line.

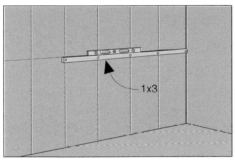

3. Starting in the corner with the highest floor point, nail up a temporary straight 1×3 so it's level; it may not match chalk line if floor is not level.

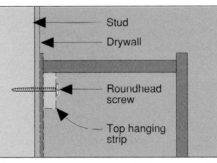

4. Place a corner or end cabinet on the 1×3; check level. Drill 3/16-inch pilot holes and drive in 2½-inch roundhead screws in top hanging strip into studs.

5. Position the next cabinet on the ledger snug to the first. Drill pilot holes and fasten the top hanging strip with 2½-inch roundhead screws.

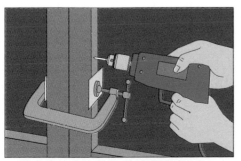

6. Clamp together face frames of adjacent cabinets. Drill counterbored holes through one face frame. Fasten frames with 2½-inch drywall screws.

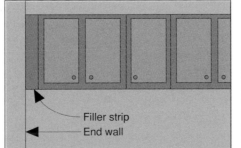

7. At the wall juncture, fit a filler strip to the remaining gap. Screw the filler strip to the face frame of the last cabinet as in the previous step.

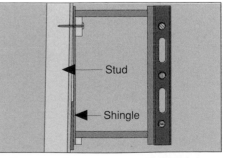

8. Remove the temporary 1×3 strip. Using a level, plumb the cabinet fronts by shimming between the wall and the bottom hanging strip at stud locations.

Adding New Storage (continued)

INSTALLING KITCHEN WALL CABINETS *(continued)*

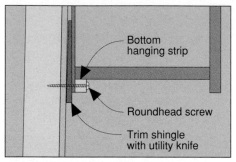

9. Drill ³⁄₁₆-inch pilot holes and fasten the bottom hanging strip with 2½-inch roundhead screws into the studs. Trim the shims with a utility knife.

10. Apply trim molding to cover gaps between the backs of the cabinets and the wall. Stain or paint the trim to match the cabinets.

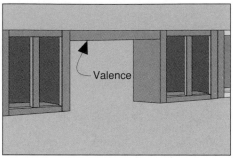

11. Cut a valence board to fit any gap over the sink. Drill countersunk pilot holes and screw through adjacent face frames into the valence.

INSTALLING CEILING-HUNG CABINETS ABOVE PENINSULAS OR ISLANDS

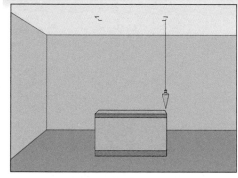

1. Using a plumb bob, mark on the ceiling the four corners of the peninsula or island cabinet below.

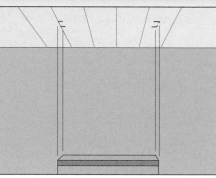

2. Using either a stud finder or the location of a ceiling fixture box, mark the centerlines of the ceiling joists.

3. Using a chalk line, outline the perimeter of the peninsula or island hanging cabinet(s) on the ceiling.

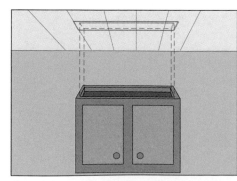

4. Measure the inside dimensions of the cabinet top cavity and transfer the cavity outline to the ceiling.

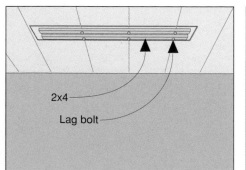

5. Cut a frame of 2×4s to fit inside the cavity outline. Fasten the 2×4s to the ceiling joists with lag bolts.

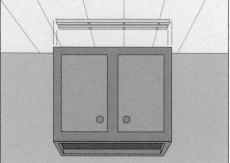

6. Fasten cabinet to the 2×4s through the top cabinet frame using drywall screws. Countersink and fill screws.

BUILDING A CLOSET

Before you leap into a closet-building project, determine if you're making the best use of existing facilities. The techniques on pages 88-91 might help create enough space in your existing closets.

Give some thought to how much closet space you need. The charts on pages 90-91 show dimensions for shallow and walk-in closets.

If possible, locate a new closet near the point of use for the items you'll be keeping in it. Too often, however, rooms that lack storage don't have floor space to spare,

either. Instead of further cramping a bedroom, for example, you might want to build a new closet in underused areas of the basement, attic, or garage (see page 88).

A new closet may solve other problems. A closet by the front door, for example, might provide much-needed separation between the entry and the living room.

Innovative closet ideas abound. Familiarize yourself with the two basic designs below, then adapt one to your needs. The conventionally framed unit on the left goes together

just as your existing closets did. The closet made from panels on the right provides more storage per square inch of floor space because it does not require framing.

YOU'LL NEED...

SKILLS: Moderate carpentry skills.
TIME: 1 to 2 days for framing and drywalling; additional day for finishing.
TOOLS: Hammer, circular saw or handsaw, utility knife, drywall taping knifes.

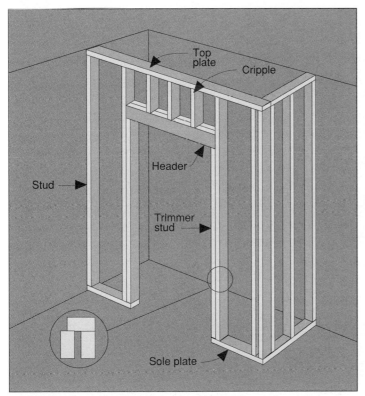

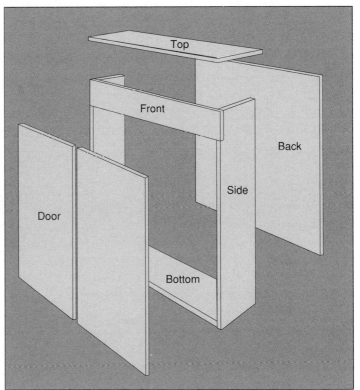

The framed closet above fits nicely into a corner. Learn the basics of partitions (see page 50) and you can put together the framing in a single day. For the studs, choose 2×4s or 2×3s. You'll need a pair of 2×4s or 2×6s for the header. Cover the unit with drywall (see pages 54–55) or sheathe with paneling (see page 48). Finish off with shelves, rods, and a door.

The closet above is made with ¾-inch plywood panels like a huge box (see page 508). Medium-density overlay plywood (see page 504) lends itself to a smooth, painted look. Once you have applied the finish, set the unit directly on the floor in the desired location. Or, you could rest it on a rectangular 2×4 base set back 3 inches from the front of the unit to serve as a toe kick.

Adding New Storage (continued)

BUYING STORAGE UNITS

Why spend several evenings cutting and joining the lumber for a simple bookcase, when you can purchase a similar unfinished or finished piece for little more than it would cost to buy the materials?

You don't have to settle for a utilitarian look, either. You can dress up unfinished or drab units with paint, stain, or fabric coverings. (See pages 571–581 for wood finishing or page 565 for metal finishing.)

Shown below are common types of modular, knocked-down (unassembled), and assembled (but unfinished) units you can buy at home centers, lumberyards, paint stores, or department stores.

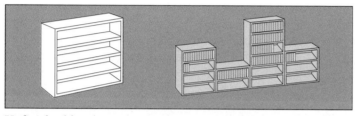

Unfinished bookcases come in modular sizes ideal for lining up or stacking anywhere you need open-shelf storage. Get steel bookcases from office suppliers. The better quality wood units have rabbeted backs and dadoed shelves; surfaces should need only light sanding before finishing.

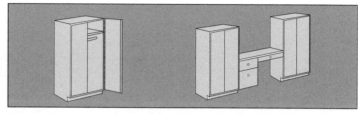

Wardrobes may be wood, metal, or hardboard. They come knocked-down or assembled. For an entire wall of storage, flank a desk with a pair of units. Better wood and hardboard versions have hardwood frames. Avoid flimsy construction and metal cabinets with sharp edges.

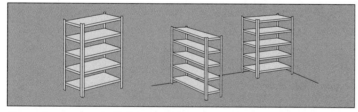

Open-frame steel shelving stands on its own, making it handy for use as a divider as well a wall unit. Shelves run as deep as 24 inches. Look for units with sturdy posts and nut-and-bolt locking systems to minimize swaying. Big units may need cross-bracing or anchoring to a wall.

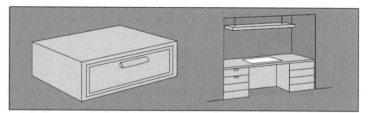

Drawer cases stack to any height. Some have open sides for built-in situations. For a desk, lay a hollow-core door across two stacks. Note this compact study desk. Good drawer cases have rabbeted fronts and move easily on metal or hardwood guides. (See page 509 for more about drawers.)

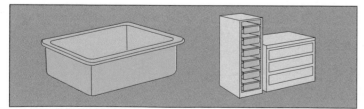

Plastic trays and bins make inexpensive drawers. Construct a case for them by building a plywood box with cleats inside to support the tray lips. Clear acrylic trays allow you to see contents at a glance. Rubberized types, which are available in a variety of colors, hold heavier loads.

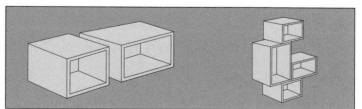

Cubes and boxes stack any which way for modular storage. Choose wood, plastic laminate, or solid or egg-crate plastic versions. Some interlock with each other. Well-made wood cubes have reinforced corners all around. If made of particleboard, be sure they're surfaced with plastic laminate.

WIRE-FRAME CLOSET ORGANIZERS

Because of their popularity, wire-frame closet organization systems now are available in most home centers or hardware stores. The systems typically consist of shelves, baskets, brackets, and supports—all made of heavy gauge steel with a protective epoxy coating.

Some special wall fasteners require only measuring and marking locations, drilling ¼-inch holes, inserting the fastener, and tapping gently on the actuating pin. Other fasteners install by simply screwing

them into the predrilled hole.

The only tools required for installation are a tape measure, hammer, level, drill with a ¼-inch bit, and sometimes a screwdriver. You also may need a hacksaw if you need to cut a shelf to size.

There is no limit to the variety of storage solutions you can create with these modular systems. The illustrations below show just a few options. Your nearest home center may have guides to help you plan your installation.

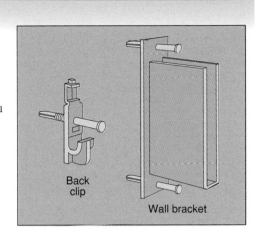

Back clip

Wall bracket

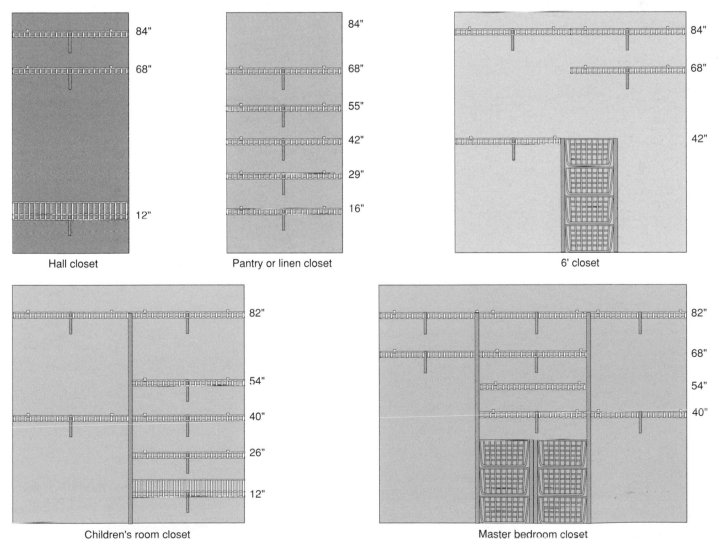

Hall closet

Pantry or linen closet

6' closet

Children's room closet

Master bedroom closet

FIREPLACES

As you can see in the illustrations below, there is a lot more to a good fireplace than just a cheery glow. Efficient modern-day fireplaces keep logs burning for hours at a time—and send all but a few whiffs of smoke up the chimney. Most of the action takes place in the firebox. Its splayed sides help funnel air across the hearth to the base of the fire. The firebox's sloping rear wall then deflects heat back into the room.

Just above the firebox, the throat pulls the smoke up the chimney. Below the throat, there usually is a damper that controls the draft. The lintel, the firebox's top front edge, also directs smoke up the chimney.

Above the damper-throat assembly, a smoke chamber stops cold air from coming down the chimney and diverts it back up the flue. Were it not for the smoke chamber, outside air could drop straight into the fire and push the smoke directly back into the room.

An ash door in the hearth lets you push debris into the ash pit. A cleanout door in this pit, usually in the basement, means you don't have to haul dusty ashes through the house. In some fireplaces, a vent in the ash pit helps create a better draft.

ANATOMY OF A FIREPLACE

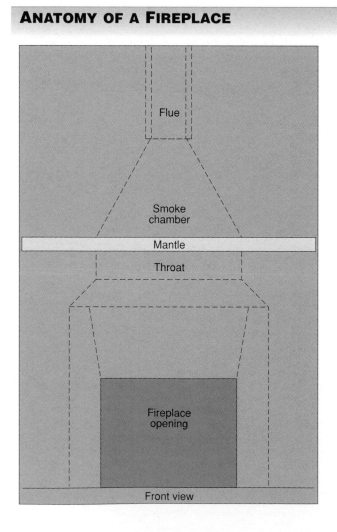

Flue

Smoke chamber

Mantle

Throat

Fireplace opening

Front view

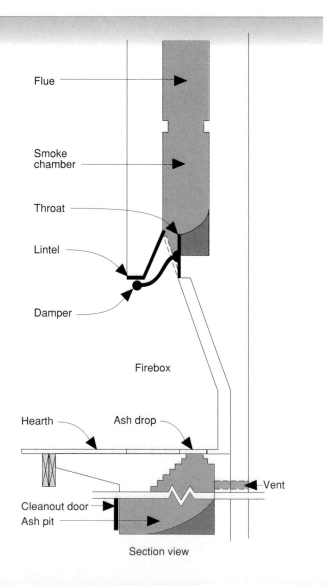

Flue

Smoke chamber

Throat

Lintel

Damper

Firebox

Hearth

Ash drop

Vent

Cleanout door

Ash pit

Section view

HELPFUL HINTS

Because of modern building codes, today's fireplaces need little attention. Chimney fires still happen, however, often because someone neglected a

MAINTAINING A FIREPLACE

quick inspection before lighting the first logs of the season. Each fall, look over your chimney from basement to attic to roof. If you see any major

settlement-related cracks, call in a masonry contractor. The chart below outlines other important items that you should check out.

CHECK THESE EVERY FALL

Flue	Open the damper and peer up the flue. If you cannot see light, check the flue with a mirror and flashlight to determine what is causing the blockage. Clean the flue every few years (see page 132). Repair any masonry cracks (see pages 149–150).
Damper	A damper must seal tightly or you will lose heated house air through it. If yours will not close securely, feel around its edges; sometimes small bits of mortar lodge there. Ensure that the hinges and handle work smoothly so you can make necessary draft adjustments.
Firebox	For safety, most fireboxes are lined with high-temperature firebricks. Check to see if any have broken or come loose. If so, repair them, as shown on page 104. Clean soot off masonry with a mild solution of muriatic acid and water; wear rubber gloves.
Ash pit	Usually ash pits need attention only every other year. If the ashes seem soggy and hard to remove, suspect leakage. If there are outside cleanout doors, seal gaps that might admit cold air.

BUILDING A FIRE THAT LIGHTS AND LASTS

When you cannot get a good blaze going in your fireplace, don't be too quick to blame the fireplace or the fuel. A fire consumes a surprising amount of air, and in a tightly weather-stripped house, you might not have enough air to create a strong updraft.

Test for this by opening the damper, wetting a finger, and sticking it into the firebox. If you feel air coming from above, there is a downdraft that will either kill your fire or smoke up the house.

To increase the amount of inside air available, shut off any exhaust fans that might be running; even a small bathroom fan evacuates a lot of air. Crack open a window near the fireplace. As last resorts, try the remedies shown on page 104.

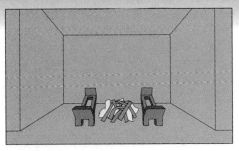

1. For a fast start, crumple paper between the andirons, then crisscross kindling on top.

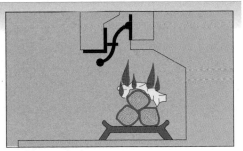

2. Before lighting, set a match to some crumpled paper laid on top. This warms the flue for a positive draft.

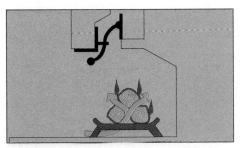

3. You need at least three logs for a fire. Note how the draft rises around them and feeds on their inner surfaces.

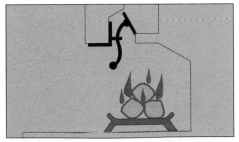

4. After your fire is burning well, close down the damper a bit. With it partially closed, you won't lose as much heat.

Solving Fireplace Problems

REPLACING BRICKS

Breaks or cracks in the lining of a firebox pose a fire hazard, so make needed repairs without delay. If bricks are broken or loose, replace them (below). Measure the old ones first; sizes vary. Make sure you use fireclay bricks; you also will need fireclay mortar, which is mixed from fireclay cement rather than ordinary cement.

If just the mortar joints have deteriorated, restore them with the repointing techniques illustrated on page 132; again, use fireclay mortar.

YOU'LL NEED...
SKILLS: Basic masonry skills.
TIME: 2 to 4 hours depending on how many bricks are removed.
TOOLS: Hammer, bricklayer's chisel, vacuum, brush, trowel, joint strike.

1. Chop out loose or broken bricks by chipping away mortar with a heavy hammer and bricklayer's chisel.

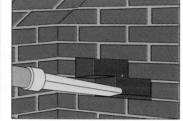

2. Remove remaining loose mortar, then clear debris from the cavity with a brush and vacuum cleaner.

3. Dampen the cavity before applying mortar. Dry bricks draw water from the mortar and weaken the bond.

4. Prepare a 1:3 mix of fireclay cement and sand; add water to make a paste. Butter surrounding bricks.

5. Butter the bricks before you slip them into place. If the fit is tight, tap with the handle of your trowel.

6. Scrape away excess mortar, let repair set for 10 minutes, then shape the joints with a joint strike.

HELPFUL HINTS

If your fireplace lets smoke into the room, make sure it is getting enough air (see page 103). If those strategies don't clear the air, try the more drastic remedies shown here or consult a professional chimney sweep or mason.

If you're up to the task, you can loose-lay firebricks to adjust the firebox's size and proportions. If that works, mortar them as shown above.

Check out the situation on the roof, too. For a proper draw, a chimney must extend at least 2 feet higher than nearby structures.

CURING A FAULTY DRAW

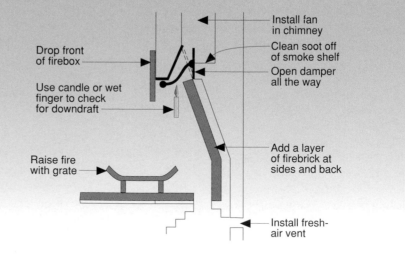

Drop front of firebox

Use candle or wet finger to check for downdraft

Raise fire with grate

Install fan in chimney

Clean soot off of smoke shelf

Open damper all the way

Add a layer of firebrick at sides and back

Install fresh-air vent

TRACKING DOWN FLUE PROBLEMS

The chimney in your home may include several flues—one for each fireplace, plus one for a furnace or water heater.

This makes a defective flue doubly dangerous. It could set the house on fire, but it also could poison the air with deadly, odorless carbon monoxide fumes.

To protect against these hazards, modern chimneys are lined with flue tiles that rarely leak. If yours is an older home with a fireplace that has not been used for several years, don't put it back into action until a professional has examined the flue.

Flue problems usually involve loose joints between tiles or downdrafts that pull smoke from one flue to another at the roof. For either problem, call in a professional chimney contractor.

You can test for leaks yourself. Open doors and windows and build a fire. After it gets going, cover the top of the flue with wet burlap and dump wet leaves on the fire. Smoke leaks will be readily apparent.

If you have a leaky flue, you will see smoke oozing from the chimney's exterior mortar joints. Also check in the attic for smoke leaks.

If a fireplace smokes when there's no fire in it, suspect either a flue-to-flue leak or a downdraft problem.

Staggering the heights of flues can eliminate downdrafts from one flue to the other. This is a job for a mason.

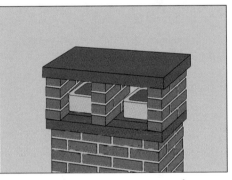

Another solution is to increase the chimney's height, separating the flues, and capping them with a hood.

INSTALLING GAS LOGS AND STARTERS

If you don't like dealing with the mess of starting or cleaning up after a wood fire—or if wood is scarce in your area—consider warming your hearth with a set of ceramic logs fired by natural or LP gas. Install gas-log sets only in a wood-burning fireplace, and operate them only with the damper open.

A gas log lighter starts wood logs quickly without need for kindling. Touch a match under the fire basket, wait until the wood is thoroughly ignited, then shut off the starter and let the logs burn normally.

In either case, you will need to route a gas line to the firebox. Installation is fairly simple, but you may want to use a plumber for the job. If you run the gas line yourself, use pipe tape, or the sealer specified by the manufacturer of the unit, at all pipe joints. When you fill the line, check all of the joints for leaks. Do this by mixing a solution of household detergent and water and dabbing some on each joint. Bubbles will form at the joint if you have a leak. (See pages 328–335 for more about gas systems.)

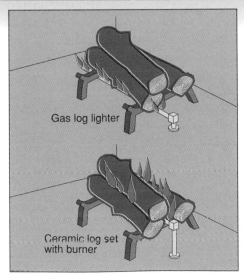

Gas log lighter

Ceramic log set with burner

Installing a New Fireplace

Thinking about treating yourself to the warmth and crackling aroma of a new fireplace? If so, you have lots of choices and decisions to make.

Unless you are building a new home, you probably will rule out an all-masonry type fireplace right away. Pouring deep footings or making structural alterations is too expensive compared to the cost of installing prefabricated units that come in kits.

What's more, many prefabricated units burn more efficiently than all-masonry fireplaces. Some fireplaces that were built before energy became a major expense lose as much as 90 percent of their heat output up the chimney. Worse yet, they rob heated air from your home for combustion, which means that your furnace might actually work harder to heat rooms not warmed by the fireplace.

CHOOSING AND BUYING A PREFAB FIREPLACE

When shopping for a prefabricated unit, you first must decide if you prefer a built-in or freestanding unit.

Built-ins, which can be fairly difficult to install, look like traditional fireplaces. Freestanding units come in many shapes, sizes, colors, and styles, and most have a contemporary look.

Both types vent through insulated metal chimneys that you can run up through walls, ceilings, and roofs. Not only are these metal flues easy to assemble, but some also feature a "positive draft" that guarantees a smokeless fire.

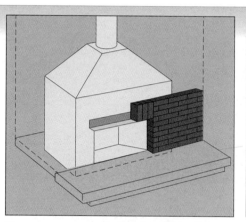

You can veneer prefabricated built-in units with masonry or, in some cases, build conventional wood-framed walls around them.

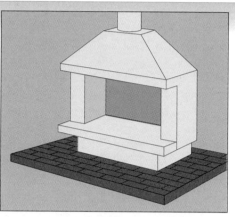

Freestanding fireplaces usually occupy less space and offer more design flexibility. Just set one in place and hook up a chimney.

SELECTING ENERGY SAVERS

If you plan to use your new fireplace as a source of heat, shop for efficiency.

Heat-circulating fireplaces include built-in ducting to direct warmed air back into the room or into adjacent rooms. Add electric blowers and you have a wood-burning furnace.

Fresh-air-feed fireplaces don't rob heat from your home while they burn. Instead, they pull in combustion air from outside via a dampered duct. They also distribute a lot of heat.

For the most efficient solid-fuel heat source, check out the airtight stove shown on page 369.

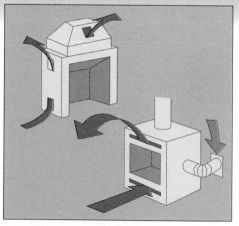

Both heat-circulating (left) and fresh-air-feed fireplaces create convection currents that supplement the firebox's radiant heat.

The old-fashioned Franklin stove is still a thrifty design. Closing the doors greatly improves its heating efficiency.

INSTALLING A FREESTANDING UNIT

Lightweight construction and easily assembled components make installing a freestanding fireplace a feasible project for any do-it-yourselfer willing to tackle the tricky task of getting a chimney through the roof (see page 109).

If the fireplace requires a noncombustible base, construct this first. You can pour a thin concrete slab, mortar bricks or tiles together, or fill a wooden, tin-bottomed frame with loose gravel.

Be sure to check building codes before you buy any prefabricated chimney—not all makes are widely approved. You may need a building permit, too.

YOU'LL NEED...

SKILLS: Moderate carpentry and sheet metal skills.
TIME: 2 to 3 days.
TOOLS: Basic tools and a plumb bob, keyhole saw, saber or reciprocating saw, tin snips, riveter.

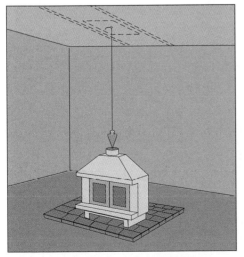

1. Decide how the chimney will vent. With a room upstairs, you can box it in or route it through a closet.

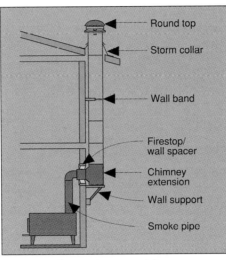

2. As an alternative, consider an outside-wall installation. Watch roof clearances, though (see page 109).

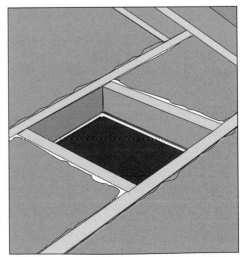

3. Check building codes and the manufacturer's data for minimum clearances from combustible surfaces.

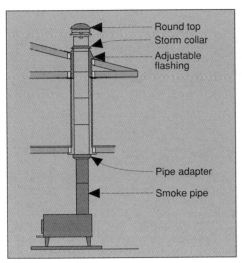

4. Drop a plumb line to determine where to cut the ceiling. If necessary, shift the unit to pass between joists.

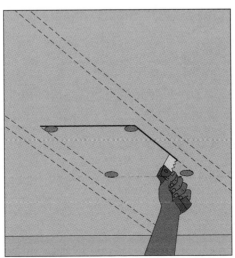

5. To make the ceiling opening, bore holes at each corner, then cut with a keyhole saw or saber saw.

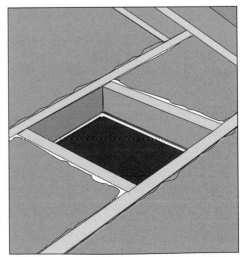

6. Toenail headers between the joists and install a fire-stop or chimney support. (For roof work, see page 109.)

Installing a New Fireplace (continued)

INSTALLING A BUILT-IN FIREPLACE

Face a prefabricated fireplace assembly with bricks or stone, and no one need ever know you didn't build the whole thing yourself. You will have to master a few masonry techniques, of course.

Or, choose a double-wall unit designed for "zero clearance" from combustible materials. These can be enclosed with wood-stud walls.

Either way, first locate the fireplace and install a chimney (see pages 107 and 109), then construct the enclosure.

(see pages 107 and 109)

YOU'LL NEED...

SKILLS: Moderate carpentry and metal working skills.

TIME: 1 to 2 days.

TOOLS: Basic tools, saber or reciprocating saw, tin snips, and masonry tools.

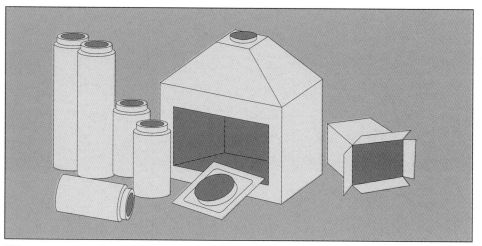

When you unpack your fireplace, read the instructions carefully. Follow your local building code to the letter.

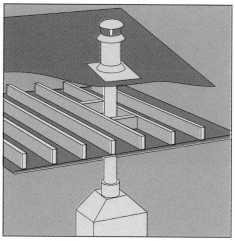

You have options when topping off a prefabricated unit. The housing style here is called a contemporary cap.

If you don't like the appearance of metal pipe, conceal it inside a simulated brick housing.

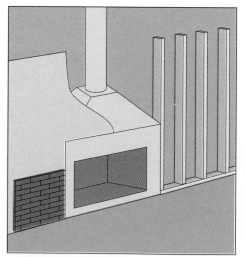

To create a masonry look indoors, cover the framing with plywood and mortar up an artificial brick facing.

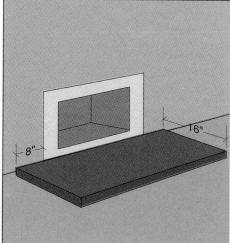

Most codes specify a noncombustible hearth 16 inches wider than the fireplace opening and 16 inches deep.

INSTALLING A PREFABRICATED CHIMNEY

A prefabricated metal chimney gets through the roof at a fraction of the cost of masonry, and you need only a minimal distance between the chimney and combustible materials.

Before you order, measure the height from the firebox to the top of the chimney—including enough to reach a point at least 2 feet higher than any portion of the roof within 10 feet horizontally from the top of the chimney.

Besides the pipe sections, you'll need special flashing to seal against roof leaks, sheet-metal fire-stop spacers for each floor or ceiling the chimney penetrates, a terminal cap or chimney housing, and, if you're venting a freestanding unit, a chimney base support.

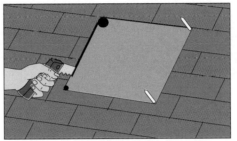

1. Mark under roof sheathing for the opening, then drive four long nails up through the sheathing and roofing.

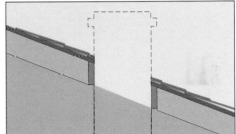

2. Slice away shingles with a utility knife, then cut through the sheathing with a keyhole or saber saw.

3. Frame in the opening with the same size material as rafters to allow for attaching a fire-stop or a support box.

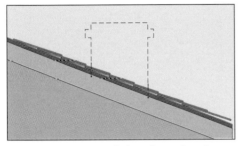

4. Slip the fire-stop up into the opening and nail or screw through the flanges into the frame.

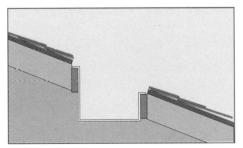

5. For freestanding units, insert the chimney support box in the opening, make flaps of its edges, nail to headers.

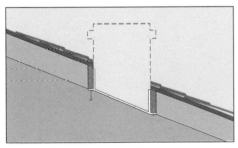

6. Another type of chimney support sits on top of the rafters and pivots to match the slope of the roof.

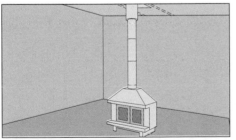

7. Stack flue sections atop the firebox, snapping, twisting, or screwing them together until you penetrate the roof.

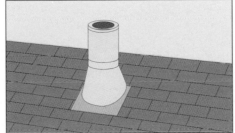

8. Slip flashing over pipe and under the roofing on the upper side. Seal lower edge with roofing cement.

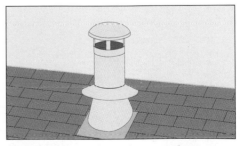

9. Install the terminal cap and storm collar, and you're ready for your first fire. Check pipe joints for smoke leaks.

Installing a New Fireplace (continued)

VENTING GAS STOVES DIRECTLY OUTSIDE

At first, the idea of venting stoves and fireplaces through a side wall seems preposterous. What about the standard rule that masonry chimneys should extend above the roof peak?

The answer lies in the efficiency of modern gas appliances—and now gas versions of fireplaces and stoves. These versions emit only carbon dioxide and water vapor, and these exit the flue at below-boiling temperatures. All this makes side-wall venting possible, if you follow the guidelines shown at right.

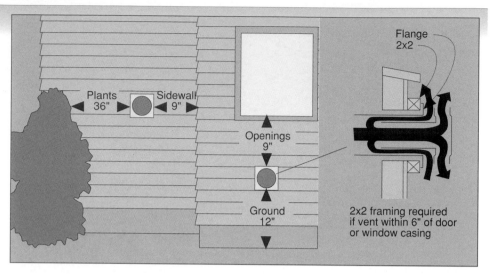

SELECTING GAS STOVES

You can purchase gas-fired versions of many wood-burning stove styles. Artificial logs inside the firebox produce the illusion of burning logs. These new stoves come in a variety of finishes, from unfinished black cast iron to elegant green, blue, and red enamels.

For real lounge-chair types, there are even models that can be turned on and off via infrared remote controls units!

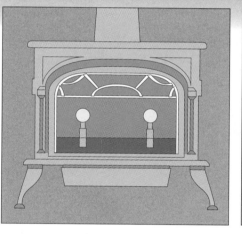
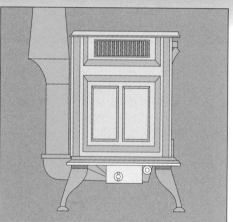

UNDERSTANDING MOUNTING CLEARANCES

Even though they don't burn wood or coal, gas-fired stoves still get plenty hot. Minimum clearance distances that must be maintained between stove back, sides, and top are specified by the National Fire Protection Association. Typical clearances are shown at right, but check with your dealer for specifics for the stove you're considering.

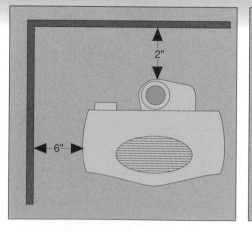
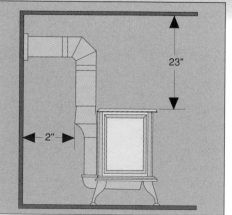

VENTING GAS FIREPLACES AND UNDERSTANDING MINIMUM CLEARANCES

Gas fireplaces are, in reality, gas stoves made to look like old-fashioned fireplaces. They also can be vented directly out a sidewall. Examples are shown at right.

Gas fireplace units also have minimum required clearances to combustible surfaces. Again, the clearances shown below are suited to particular units; check with your gas fireplace dealer for specifics for the units you are considering.

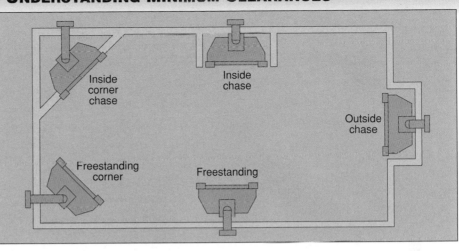

Understanding Minimum Clearances for Freestanding Installations

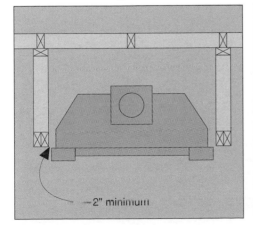

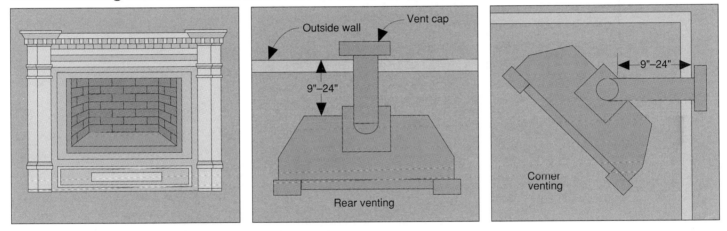

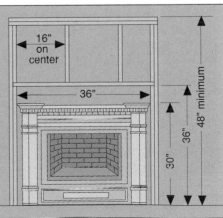

Understanding Minimum Clearances for Recessed Installations

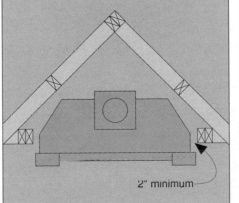

BASEMENTS AND FOUNDATIONS

The foundation of your house has several tough assignments. First, it has to support the weight of the entire house. Second, it acts as a retaining wall and must have enough strength to hold back the earth around its edges. Finally, it may shelter a basement—the main subject of this chapter.

Basement/foundation walls begin with a concrete footing designed to spread the thousands-of-pounds-per-square-foot loads. The footing also supports the thinner slab used for most basement floors. The footings may or may not be protected by drain tiles laid in sand or gravel to remove water.

The walls may be made of concrete block, poured concrete, brick, stone, or even treated wood. Regardless of the material, the walls' exterior should be waterproofed before the soil is replaced.

On top, the walls support a wood sill plate upon which joists are laid for the subfloor and finish floor above. (See page 10 for more about floors and page 142 for sill plates.)

This section digs into basements and foundations from the inside out—beginning indoors where you're likely to notice basement problems, then moving to the exterior side if interior remedies fail.

If your house has only a crawlspace underneath it, the house either sits atop shorter supporting walls or it is held up by a series of piers. (See pages 394 and 402 for more about crawlspace problems.)

Alternatively, your house may have no space under it at all. If this is the case, the structure rests on a concrete slab similar to those used for patios (see pages 172 and 178-184)—but much thicker, of course.

ANATOMY OF A BASEMENT

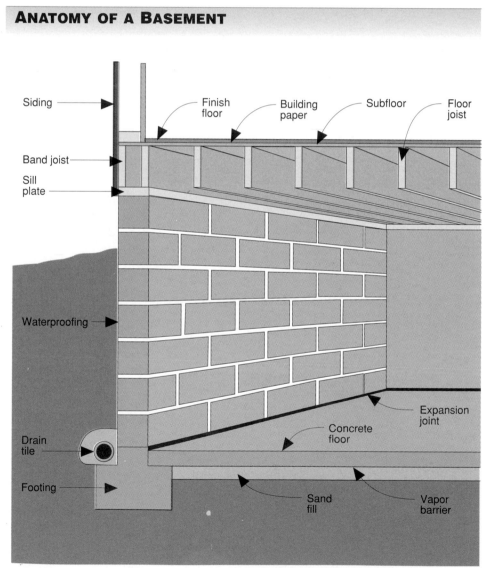

Siding

Finish floor

Building paper

Subfloor

Floor joist

Band joist

Sill plate

Waterproofing

Drain tile

Footing

Expansion joint

Concrete floor

Sand fill

Vapor barrier

Solving Basement Problems

Basements suffer from a special ill that doesn't afflict other spaces inside your home—moisture. Differences between the temperature below ground (50 to 60°F in summer) and that of the air upstairs or outside often create the potential for a slight mustiness, especially in muggy summer weather.

However, if the floor or walls in your basement chronically sweat—or worse yet, if puddles of water collect on the floor—it is time to take action. A wet basement not only wastes potential space for living or storage, it eventually could decay your home's floor joists and sills.

The chart below explains the four sources of below-ground moisture problems. Simple tests help you distinguish one from the other and direct you to their remedies. In tracking down the origin of the water, don't neglect the possibility that it might be a combination of factors—condensation coupled with seepage, for example.

If you are planning to finish the basement walls and floor, you will want to dry them out permanently before you begin any interior construction work. That may require more costly exterior waterproofing methods (see pages 116–117). Don't worry about mild condensation; putting up insulation and a vapor barrier (see page 397) usually will eliminate that problem. If you are not sure that this will work in your situation, apply two coats of exterior sealant on the inside of the walls.

To learn about finishing basement walls, see pages 47–55; for floors, check out pages 19 and 24–27; for ceilings, turn to pages 59–66.

HELPFUL HINTS — WHERE'S THE WATER COMING FROM?

Problem	Symptom/Test	Cause	Solution
Condensation	Damp walls, dripping pipes, rusty hardware, mildew—all are forms or indications of condensation.	Excess humidity in the air, usually from an internal source, or a significant difference in temperature between the wall and the inside air.	Install a dehumidifier, improve ventilation, or insulate the foundation walls.
Seepage	General dampness on the floor or a particular wall, especially near floor level. Tape polyethylene to the wall. If moisture condenses behind it, seepage is the culprit.	Surface water is forcing its way through the foundation or an expansion joint. Source may be poor roof drainage, a window well, or a clogged drain tile.	Improve surface drainage. An interior sealer may work on minor seepage. If not, waterproof the foundation from outside.
Leaks	Localized wetness, oozing, or trickling from a foundation wall or floor. Check the damp area carefully, paying attention to mortar joints between blocks.	Cracks resulting from normal settling or faulty roof drainage, a grade that slopes toward the wall, or a clogged drain tile.	Plug a single hole from inside. Otherwise, dig down and work from outside. Waterproof entire foundation wall and install drain tile. Slope grade away from wall.
Subterranean water	A barely noticeable film of water on the floor could be a sign. Lay down a sheet of polyethylene for several days; if moisture is penetrating, it will dampen the concrete underneath.	Usually a high water table is forcing up water from below under high pressure, turning your basement into a well. This may happen only during rainy periods.	Drain tiles installed around the perimeter of the foundation or floor may help, but only if connected to a lower spot or a storm sewer. You may need a sump pump.

Solving Basement Problems (continued)

WRAPPING PIPES

Exposed cold water lines sweat or collect moisture even under ideal humidity conditions. Insulating them solves this problem. While you're at it, wrap the hot water pipes with insulation also—you'll save energy that is normally wasted in cold weather.

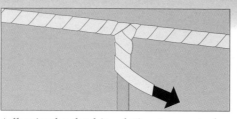

Adhesive-backed insulating tape winds around pipes. Cover all fittings, too—but leave valve handles exposed.

Slit-sleeve insulation makes a thick jacket for longer pipe runs. More about installing these on page 396.

SEALING INTERIOR WALLS

Waterproofing compounds designed for basement walls and other masonry surfaces effectively stop the kind of seepage that makes walls feel clammy to the touch. Don't expect them to solve a severe moisture problem.

If you can see a film of water on the wall, it probably is coming in under pressure—and that same force will push any sealer aside. In this case, you need to seal from outside, as shown on pages 116 and 117.

Waterproofing formulations come in powder or liquid form. The powder type include cement and must be mixed with water. These products should be applied to a damp surface. The liquid types are ready to use after stirring, but the wall must be dry for them to adhere.

Both types of sealants require that you first clean away all dirt, grease, or powder. Wash with household cleaner and wire brush; remove grease with a liquid degreaser.

If a wall has visible holes or cracks, plug them as illustrated on page 115, then let the repairs thoroughly cure before applying a sealer. Prepare yourself for some hard work when you apply these heavy coatings.

YOU'LL NEED...

SKILLS: Basic painting skills.
TIME: 4 to 6 hours for actual waterproofing after wall preparation.
TOOLS: Hose and sprayer, stiff brush, roller.

1. Avoid an arduous job. Make sure you purchase premixed compound.

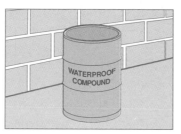

2. Prepare walls for cement-base sealer by wetting with a fine mist from a hose.

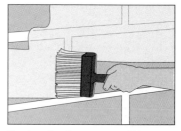

3. Apply these paste-like sealers with a stiff brush. Fill every pore in the blocks.

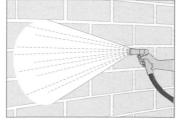

4. Pack the mortar joints. The first coat will require lots of time and compound.

5. Prevent too-rapid drying of cement-based coatings. Keep the base coat moist for several days.

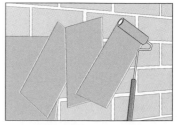

6. For a tight seal, you will need two applications. The second goes on more easily, but cover completely.

7. You can paint over the waterproofing. Wait until it's thoroughly cured, based on manufacturer's label.

PLUGGING HOLES AND CRACKS

Before patching a break in a basement wall, watch it over a period of months. Most cracks come from normal settling and soon stabilize. However, they also could be a sign of a major structural problem. If so, you will need professional help.

Determine if water is leaking through the crack. If so, fill it with a quick-hardening plugging cement or epoxy. Patch dry spots with a mortar of one part cement, two parts sand, and just enough water to make a doughy consistency. Add the water slowly and stir it in well.

If a new leak springs up near your repair, it could mean that there is water backing up against the exterior of the foundation—a case for the more drastic solutions shown on pages 116–117.

YOU'LL NEED...

SKILLS: Moderate masonry skills.
TIME: 20 to 30 minutes per crack, depending on their size.
TOOLS: Cold chisel, regular or mason's hammer, trowel, putty knife.

1. Use a cold chisel to enlarge hole; undercut edges so the plug can't pop loose.

2. Mix plugging cement and work it into a tapered, stopper shape.

3. The moment cement stiffens, pop it in like a cork; hold it for several minutes.

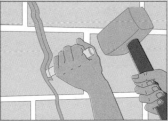

1. Cut cracks back to sound material and bevel edges. Then moisten cracks well.

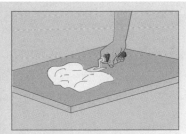

2. Turn the mortar with a trowel several times, then pack the crack. Work the mortar into the crack with the tip of the trowel.

3. After the mortar begins to harden, pack the crack full, then shave off excess with a wet trowel or a putty knife.

REPAIRING WINDOW WELLS

Water stains or seepage in the wall under a basement window usually indicate that the window well is flooding due to poor drainage. Sometimes a faulty downspout or clogged gutter turns out to be the culprit, so check your roof drainage first (see pages 134–135).

If the well doesn't seem to be getting more water than it can handle, clean out any debris and flush with a hose to see if it's draining properly. The drawings at right show the construction you will likely encounter.

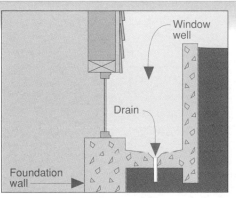

With concrete wells, try inserting a hose in the drain and blowing out any obstructions. If the drain is clear, waterproof as shown at right.

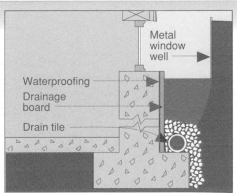

With a gravel well, remove the fill and waterproof the foundation's outside wall. Also install fiberglass drainage board next to the wall.

Solving Foundation Problems

Think of the earth around your house as a gigantic sponge. Water that the sponge cannot absorb flows downhill until it meets resistance—a foundation wall, for instance. There, a reservoir fills up, the pressure increases, and the wall turns into a natural dam.

Just as you can't repair a dam from its downstream side, neither can you stop severe seepage from inside your basement. You have to divert the flow or totally waterproof the wall—both outside projects that entail a lot of excavation.

Beware of waterproofing "specialists" who promise to do the job without digging. They inject a chemical into the ground under pressure, much the same way exterminators eradicate termites (see pages 152–153). The processes use different chemicals, of course, and they differ in effectiveness; soil injection works well against termites, but it may not work for waterproofing a foundation wall or floor.

Before you tear up your yard, ask your water department about the water table level. If it's only slightly below your basement floor, you might be better off installing a sump pump, as shown on page 117.

IMPROVING DRAINAGE

A good drainage system catches water and sends it elsewhere before it reaches your foundation. One often-overlooked solution is to use shallow-rooted shrubs and trees, which can drink up a surprising quantity of water. Check with a nursery for the best species to plant and their optimum locations.

Make sure downspouts and gutters are not dumping water alongside the foundation walls. Spouts should empty onto splash blocks, connect to underground pipes, or drain into a catch basin or dry well, such as the one shown on page 135.

Most of the systems illustrated here use perforated or solid tiles to collect and carry away water. They all depend upon gravity and must discharge water to a lower area.

If you install drainage tiles, you may as well waterproof the foundation wall, too (see page 117). This way the time, money, and inconvenience of all that excavating pay off with twice the protection.

YOU'LL NEED...
SKILLS: Excavation skills.
TIME: All cases shown take at least a few hours and possibly more.
TOOLS: Shovel, hammer, level.

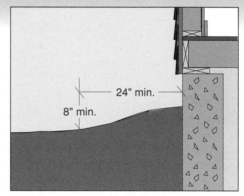

A grade that slopes away from the house will divert water away from the foundation. Build up the earth at least 8 inches and slope it away as shown.

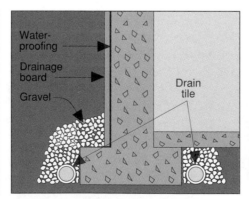

In severe cases, excavate to the footing, lay drain tiles, apply waterproofing and drainage board, and backfill (see page 117).

If water is coming up through the basement floor, install tiles inside the footing, as well. This means breaking up, then patching, the basement floor.

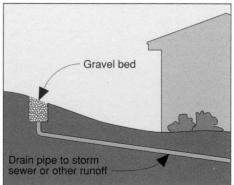

If water is flowing from a higher elevation, use a "curtain drain"—an upslope, gravel trench that spans the width of your lot, with a drain outlet.

WATERPROOFING A FOUNDATION

If sealing basement walls and regrading the soil around the foundation fail to stem your water problem, resign yourself to some arduous ditch digging. If the leaks are only near the top of the walls, you may get by with sealing only partway down. Otherwise, unless you have access to and know how to use large excavating equipment, this is probably a job for a contractor. Narrowing down the leaks to one or two walls can save you a lot—of work and money.

If you're up to the task, here's what you (or a contractor) will have to do: Excavate to the footings. Install a drain tile at the base of the footing. Scrub the wall clean and coat it with a waterproofing compound. Place fiberglass drainage board against the wall. Cover the drain tile with gravel and coarse sand. Place filter fabric over the drainage board and the gravel to prevent soil from clogging the board and tile. Backfill with soil, making sure the ground slopes away from the foundation wall.

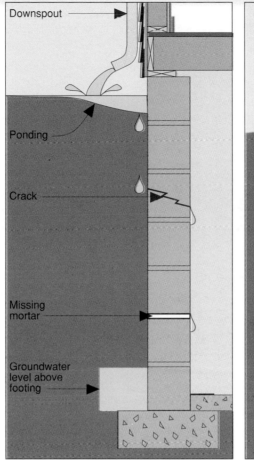

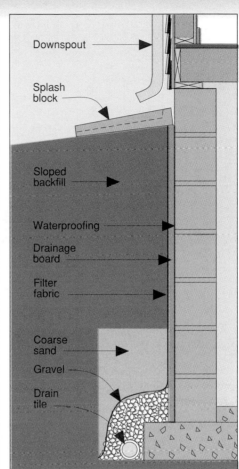

INSTALLING A SUMP PUMP

If subterranean water is welling up from below your basement, you may have to pump it out. Installing a sump pump probably is another job for a contractor. You must make a hole in the basement floor at its lowest point, dig a sump pit, then install a pump and drainage line.

As water rises in the sump pit, it lifts a float, activating the pump, which expels the water through a drainage line. A check valve prevents backflow. Make sure the system will handle the largest flow you might receive. Also install a backup battery system in case of a power failure.

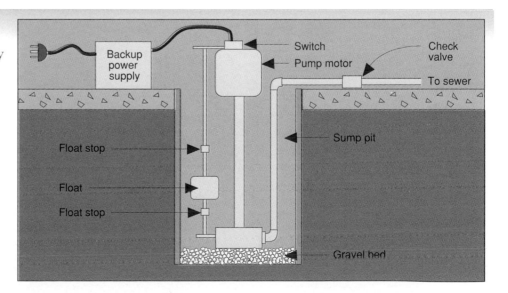

OUTSIDE YOUR HOME

ROOFS

A pitched roof sheds water much the same way a duck's feathers do. Courses of roofing material—most often some variation of the shingle—lay one atop the other and overlap, like a bird's feathers. Shingles on a roof are layered at least two deep, with exposed portions that are slightly smaller than half the total area of the shingle. At the top, an extra layer straddles the ridge.

Valleys, the places at which two slopes meet, direct runoff into gutters, which in turn direct the water down through downspouts. For additional protection against leakage, metal or composition flashings are placed under the shingles at the roof's most vulnerable points—typically valleys, dormers, vents, and chimneys, or anything else that penetrates the roof's surface.

Beneath the roofing material lies a house's most complex structure, designed to tie the wall structures together and hold not only the weight of the shingles—unlike feathers, shingles are heavy—but other loads, such as snow and ice in colder climates. Rafters, rising from the top plate of the wall to the ridge board, define the roof's pitch. Collar ties in the attic help keep the rafters from spreading; headers box in any openings.

Deck sheathing, usually plywood, goes on top of the rafters to give the structure rigidity. A layer of building felt seals the sheathing against moisture. Rafter ends are trimmed at the eaves with a fascia board and along the edges with rake boards. Then, the shingles can go on.

ANATOMY OF A ROOF

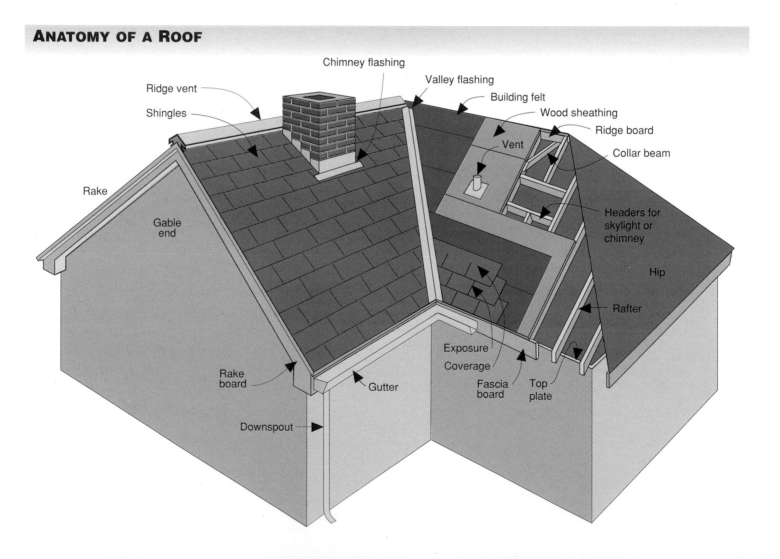

Chimney flashing

Valley flashing

Ridge vent

Building felt

Shingles

Wood sheathing

Ridge board

Vent

Collar beam

Rake

Headers for skylight or chimney

Gable end

Hip

Rafter

Exposure

Coverage

Rake board

Gutter

Fascia board

Top plate

Downspout

MATERIAL MATTERS   GETTING TO KNOW YOUR ROOF

You may already know what's up on your roof—but do you know how long it will last and how to maintain it?

The chart below lists the most commonly used materials. Consult it when selecting a new roof, too. Note that the first five categories are all of the water-shedding-type materials that work well on the pitched roofs explained on page 120. But they will not protect a flat or only slightly sloping surface from standing water. Such surfaces require a watertight membrane system (see page 128) and often a contractor's help.

COMPARING ROOF MATERIAL

Material	Features	Maintenance	Life Span
Asphalt shingles	By far the most popular, they are made of roofing felt saturated with asphalt and coated with mineral granules; newer ones have a fiberglass base for improved weather- and fire-resistance	Very little at first, but over the years, shingles curl, crack, and lose their surface coatings; most cement themselves down in the hot sun; repairs are fairly easy (see page 125)	15 to 30 years under temperate weather conditions; better quality shingles carry 25-year guarantees
Wood shingles and shakes	Shingles have a uniform, machine-sawn appearance; shakes, a rustic, hand-split look; both have a poor fire rating unless specially treated; both are expensive	Unsealed types sometimes tend to rot, warp, and split—and soon weather to a soft gray; like asphalt shingles, they are not difficult to repair or replace (see page 124)	20 years or more for shingles; up to 50 years for shakes if maintained properly
Slate or clay tiles	Both are heavy, expensive, and absolutely fireproof; tiles are more common in the Southwest, and slate in the East, where the quarries are located	An occasional cracked or chipped tile can be a tricky repair project (see page 127); slate is somewhat easier to repair (see page 126)	Life of the house, provided repairs are made before underlayment is damaged
Roll roofing or selvage	Same material as asphalt shingles, but comes in the form of wide strips that are lapped horizontally across the roof's surface	Lightweight, single-layer installations fail frequently—but repairs are easy (see page 129)	5 to 15 years; ask if company will come back for patching
Metal roofing	Older types include terne—a tin/steel alloy—and copper; modern styles include corrugated or ribbed aluminum and galvanized-steel panels. Aluminum, steel, and terne often are painted	All must be flashed and fastened with the same type of metal, or electrolytic action will cause deterioration; may need periodic painting (see page 127)	35 years for aluminum and steel; copper and terne are even more durable
Built-up roofing	Used on flat or low-pitched roofs, built-up roofs must be absolutely waterproof; fabricated on the job by laminating layers of felt with asphalt or coal tar, then topping with gravel	Leaks due to a poor job will plague you through the life of the roof; fortunately, repairs are not very difficult (see page 129)	5 to 20 years; generally, the more layers, the longer life you can expect it to have

TOOL TALK　　CHOOSING AND USING EXTENSION LADDERS

For strength and rigidity, select a Type I- or Type II-class ladder (see page 536). The ladder should be long enough to extend 3 feet above the highest eaves on your house. Add another 1 foot to this distance to make up for the propping angle. Remember, too, that the extended height of a ladder will be about 3 feet less than the total of its sections.

Set up a ladder, as shown below, and observe these precautions:

■ If you have never scaled an extension ladder, ask someone to steady it from below when you make your first few climbs. You will soon gain confidence.

■ Watch out for power lines: Metal, and even wet, wooden ladders can conduct electricity.

■ Never allow more than one person on a ladder at a time.

■ Don't use ladders on windy days.

■ Never paint a wooden ladder. You could be hiding future defects.

■ Store ladders indoors, away from moisture and "second-story" burglars.

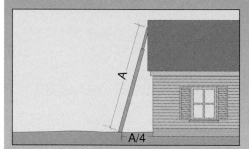

To set up a ladder, place its feet firmly against the foundation. Do not extend it now; wait until it's vertical.

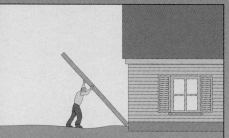

"Walk" the ladder up, hand over hand, keeping your arms straight. It will seem to get lighter as it rises.

To extend the ladder, brace a rail with your foot, lift from the house, and pull the rope. Make sure both locks catch.

Position the ladder so that the distance from the base to the wall is about one-fourth of its extended length.

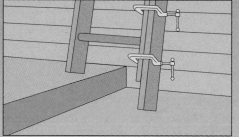

Place both feet on firm ground. Don't try to shim with bricks or boards; instead, extend one leg as shown.

Use two hands when climbing. Instead of loading yourself with tools, put them in a bucket and hoist them with a rope.

Keep your hips between the rails and don't overreach; erect ladders aren't difficult to move.

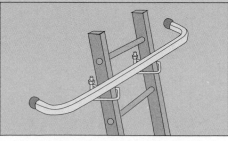

A brace improves a ladder's stability, protects siding, spans obstacles, and keeps the ladder away from the house.

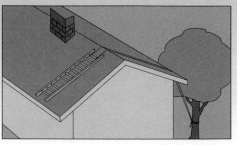

For roof work, hook a stabilizer over the ridge. Or, secure the ladder with ropes tied to a tree on the other side.

GIVING YOUR ROOF A CHECKUP

To keep a tight roof overhead, you should examine it every spring and fall. You need not haul out that awkward extension ladder and risk life and limb getting on the roof to do so. Just scan it from all sides through binoculars, paying special attention to the problem areas illustrated below.

If you do decide to climb up for a closer look, exercise caution. Also bear in mind that the sun does more damage than the wind and rain combined, so you may want to focus most of your effort on the sunny side of the house.

If a number of shingles are broken, blistered, or balding and most seem to have lost their luster, prepare yourself for a reroofing job (see pages 138–139).

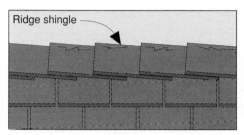

Ridge shingles often fail first. Look for cracks and wind damage. A leak here can show up anywhere inside.

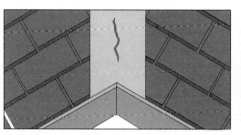

Valleys are another place where deterioration causes problems. If there's flashing, make sure it's sound.

Check other flashing too. It should be tight, rust-free, and sealed with pliable caulking or roofing cement.

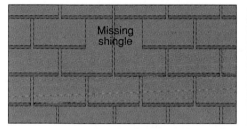

Loose, curled, or missing shingles leak moisture that weakens sheathing and harms walls and ceilings.

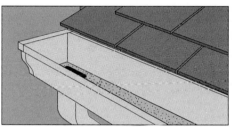

A large accumulation of granules in the gutter means your roof is losing its coating. Expect problems soon.

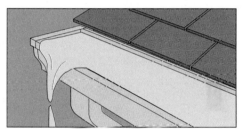

Watch during a heavy rain to see if gutters are free-flowing. Flooding can work up under lower shingle courses.

PINPOINTING LEAKS

Water that gets through your roof may follow a meandering, brooklike course—along sheathing, a rafter, even electrical cable—before it shows up as a drip or damp spot on a ceiling or wall.

You may be able to trace the trickle to its source from the attic. Look for water stains on framing and sheathing, bearing in mind that a leak will originate higher than the area where it first appeared.

On a sunny day, a leak may appear as a pinhole of light in the attic. If you find one of these, drive a nail through it, as shown at right, marking the spot on the roof itself; it also will guide the water to a bucket until you can make the repair.

If your attic is finished, you will have to do your sleuthing on the roof, examining the critical points shown above. Wait for a dry, mild day, wear sneakers or other rubber-soled shoes, and don't walk on the roof any more than necessary.

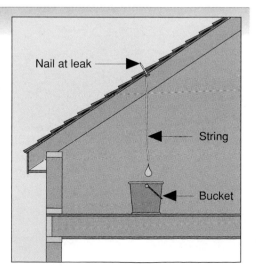

Solving Roof Problems

If you are queasy about moving around on high places—especially if your roof is steeply pitched—hire a professional for even small jobs.

If you conquer your fears, you will find most repairs are relatively simple. The biggest challenges often are figuring out how to hoist up your tools and materials and how to get around on the roof itself.

On gentle slopes, wear shoes with rubber soles. Attack steep pitches by hooking or tying an extension ladder over the ridge of the roof (see page 122). Or, construct a "chicken ladder" by nailing 1×2 cleats across a 1×10-inch board. Both of these

devices distribute your weight more evenly across materials not meant to be walked on; neither relies on relatively insubstantial gutters.

With any type of roof, don't walk on it any more than necessary. And you shouldn't go up at all during hot or cold weather extremes. Try to repair asphalt shingles on medium-warm days (40°–80°F); asphalt roofing turns brittle in cold weather and is too soft to handle when hot.

Wood shingles and shakes are not temperature sensitive, but they are affected by humidity. Soaking them makes them much more pliable; dry shingles may split when you drive

nails in them. Wet wood shingles can be very slippery, however.

Only a few supplies are required for repair work—roofing cement, butyl caulk, galvanized roofing nails, and a few of the shingles, slates, or sections of roll goods that match your present roofing.

Patch cracks, minor splits, and holes with roofing cement. Drive home popped nails and seal them or the shingles that cover them. Make sure all shingles lie flat. If any are even slightly curled, fasten them down with dabs of cement. Don't be stingy with roofing cement or caulking around flashing.

REPAIRING WOOD SHINGLES

As wood shingles age they gradually weather to a darker color than new replacement shingles. Consequently, new shingles you use to repair your roof may stand out dramatically for several years before their color matches the older shingles. If your repair is in a quite visible area of the roof, try to repair the existing shingles as shown below so that

your repair job doesn't noticeably stand out.

If you must buy new shingles, make sure to buy the best. Shingles are rated in grades from one to four, with one being the best. Grade one shingles, sometimes identified by the color blue, are composed entirely from heartwood. Heartwood contains oils and tannic acid that

make the wood resistant to insects and to fungi and will last far longer than shingles made from sapwood.

When replacing shingles, be sure to match the spacing between the existing shingles. Butting the replacement shingle against the old shingles may create a tight joint that traps moisture, which will encourage rot and decay.

YOU'LL NEED...

SKILLS: Basic carpentry skills.
TIME: 30 to 60 minutes per shingle, depending on roof accessibility.
TOOLS: Hammer, pry bar, nail set, caulking gun.

Mend splits by drilling pilot holes and nailing, then seal the gap and nailheads with roofing cement. Some cements can be applied like caulk.

For holes, drive a sheet of aluminum flashing material under the shingle. Be sure it extends beyond the leak.

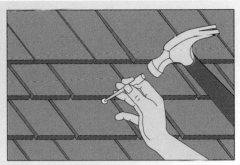

1. After removing a broken shingle, place the flat end of a pry bar over the old nailheads and strike with hammer to drive the nailheads flush.

2. With a block of wood and hammer, drive up the butt of the new shingle until it is flush with the row and the nail heads are covered.

3. Drive two shingle nails into the new shingle at 45 degrees close to the butt of the shingle above. Drive nailheads flush with a nail set; seal with caulk.

REPAIRING ASPHALT SHINGLES

Buy roofing cement in caulking tubes to seal minor cracks and holes and glue down curled shingles. If you have a larger job, buy the roofing cement in larger containers.

If the damage is extensive, replace the shingle, as shown below. When working with asphalt shingles, wait for a warm day when the shingles will be flexible and therefore easier to work with.

YOU'LL NEED...

SKILLS: Basic roofing skills.
TIME: 30 minutes.
TOOLS: Hammer, pry bar, putty knife, flat shovel, caulking gun.

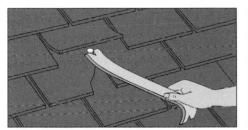

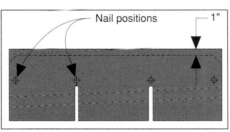

Nail positions — 1"

1. Loosen nails in the shingle above by slipping a flat shovel underneath. Pull the nails with a pry bar and remove the bad shingle.

2. Remove 1 inch from the top edge of the new shingle and slip it into place under the shingle above. Note the positions of the four nails.

3. Try to drive in new nails through the holes left by the old ones. If you cannot, carefully seal the old openings with roofing cement.

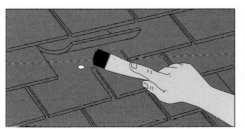

4. Coat the nailheads with roofing cement, then firmly press the upper course back into place. Weight it down, if necessary.

5. You also can back up a damaged shingle with a piece of metal flashing. Secure the flashing with roofing cement and nails under the shingle.

Solving Roof Problems *(continued)*

REPAIRING SLATE SHINGLES

Slate roofs last for decades if they are installed and maintained properly. In addition to a regular inspection a couple times each year, inspect a slate roof after particularly violent and windy storms.

Because walking on a slate roof may damage the slate tiles, the easiest, safest method of inspection is to stand back away from your home and use a pair of binoculars to look for damage to the tiles or for missing tiles.

Although a hacksaw can be used for less extensive repairs, it can take time to saw through the nails holding a tile in place. Consider renting or buying a slate ripper. Slate rippers slip up under tiles, hook onto the nails holding the tiles in place, and allow you to pull out the nails quickly.

Caution: Slate tiles can be extremely slippery, especially if they are damp or wet. Use care when working on a slate roof.

> ### YOU'LL NEED...
> **SKILLS:** Moderate carpentry skills.
> **TIME:** 1 hour, depending on extent of the damage.
> **TOOLS:** Hacksaw or slate ripper, glass cutter, drill, hammer, nail set, tin snips, pliers.

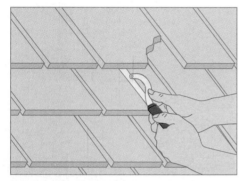

1. Slip a hacksaw blade under the broken slate and cut the nails concealed under the course above.

2. To cut slate, score both sides deeply with a glass cutter. Align the score over an edge and snap downward.

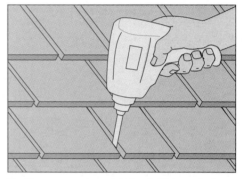

3. Use a masonry bit to drill two holes about ¾ inch above the bottom edge of the course above.

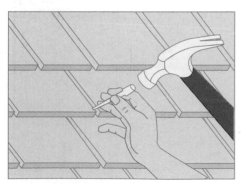

4. Drive in galvanized roofing nails through the holes you just drilled. Set the nails just flush using a nail set.

5. Cut a piece of galvanized steel flashing. Slightly cup it to provide tension and slip it under the slate above and over the nails.

REPAIRING METAL ROOFS

Master a few simple soldering skills (see page 522), and you easily can mend any roofing metal, except aluminum. Each, however, calls for a slightly different approach.

Solder terne with rosin flux, then coat the repair with red-lead primer and paint to match the rest of your roof. Terned stainless steel does not need to be primed or painted.

Galvanized steel also requires rosin flux. It also does not need priming or painting until its zinc coating begins to wear. Then, prime with zinc-oxide or a specially formulated zinc-enriched finish paint.

To solder copper, you must use acid flux. Copper roofs do not require paint.

Aluminum cannot be soldered. Seal cracks with caulk and patch bigger damage with fiberglass cloth (see illustrations below). Again, you need not paint aluminum.

Remember that when dissimilar metals come in contact, you risk an electrolytic reaction that greatly accelerates corrosion. This means that terne roofs must be patched with terne, copper with copper, and so forth. Don't let any different metal, even a TV mast, directly touch your roofing.

Minor holes in aluminum can be cleaned, degreased, lightly sanded, then sealed with a polysulfide caulk.

1. For larger holes, clean and sand the area, then spread roofing cement with a putty knife.

2. Press a layer of fiberglass cloth—available at auto parts stores—into cement, then coat with more cement.

REPAIRING SPANISH TILE

Spanish ceramic clay tiles weigh as much as 15 pounds each. And to make it more difficult, they must be maneuvered on a fragile, slippery surface that may shift underfoot. For your own safety, hire a contractor who specializes in tile roofs for replacement and major repair jobs. If you do venture onto a tile roof, always spread your weight over at least two tiles.

You can seal small cracks and flashing with roofing cement. Bigger gaps, and especially cap tiles along the ridge, should be mortared by a professional contractor.

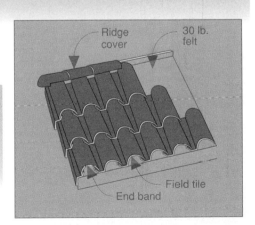

Solving Roof Problems (continued)

PATCHING ELASTOMER MEMBRANE ROOFING

The modern way to waterproof large flat roofs is to cap them with gigantic elastomer membrane sheets fabricated from rolls of ethylene propylene diene monomer (EPDM) or other rubber materials. The rolls come in standard sizes—100 feet long by 10, 15, or 20 feet wide.

You probably will have to hire a roofer licensed by the EPDM manufacturer to install or repair such a roof. But, if you can obtain the materials shown below, the drawings show how to patch a leak.

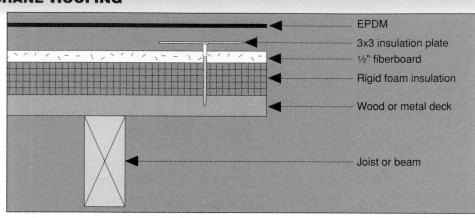

— EPDM
— 3x3 insulation plate
— ½" fiberboard
— Rigid foam insulation
— Wood or metal deck
— Joist or beam

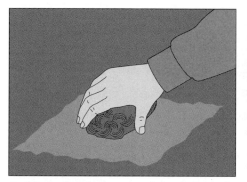

1. Wash the deck around the leak with mild detergent and water. Rinse with fresh water, then wash with "splice wash" to prepare the surface.

2. Using a stiff brush, apply "splice adhesive," which resembles contact cement, to the prepared area of roof.

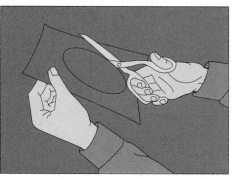

3. Cut a round patch of EPDM rubber 4 inches larger in diameter than the damaged area.

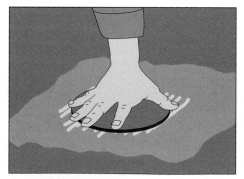

4. Apply splice adhesive to the patch and let adhesive dry to touch. When dry, place the patch carefully, and press into place.

5. Roll the adhered patch with a 2-inch steel roller. If you cannot find a 2-inch roller, rent a linoleum roller or use a piece of steel pipe.

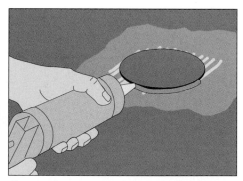

6. Wait 30 minutes to let the adhesive volatiles escape. Then, using a caulking gun, apply lap sealant to seal the edges of the patch.

REPAIRING ROLL AND BUILT-UP ROOFING

Mineral-surfaced roll roofing and built-up asphalt roofing differ considerably in cost and durability—but you can patch them using the same techniques. Repairs on membrane roofs are best left to roofing contractors.

Roll and built-up roofing usually are applied to nearly flat roofs, so you can work on them easily. But don't walk on them any more than you have to.

Watch when you repair blisters. After you've excised one, look inside for traces of moisture. The presence of moisture means water has seeped under the roofing—usually from a defective flashing nearby (see page 130)—or possibly from a hole or a crack in the membrane farther away from the blister.

Asphalt-aluminum roof paint can add a few years to the life of deteriorated flashings or roofing. Apply the mastic-like fibered type to fill small holes and cracks, especially in flashings. For bigger expanses, brush on the non-fibered version.

YOU'LL NEED...

SKILLS: Basic skills.
TIME: 1 hour for a small patch.
TOOLS: Whisk broom, putty knife, utility knife, hammer.

1. If your roof is topped with gravel or crushed stones, carefully brush them away from the damaged area with a whisk broom.

2. Clean out small cracks, pack them with roofing cement, then feather out more cement for about 3 inches on either side.

3. Slice open blisters, work cement inside, then fasten the blister edges down by driving in roofing nails along each side of the incision.

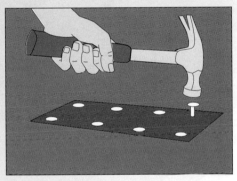

4. Top off all repairs with a building-paper patch that is much larger than the damaged area. Cement it, nail, and apply more cement. Replace gravel.

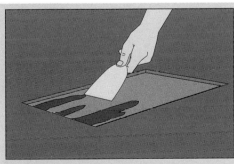

1. Replace extensively blistered or buckling sections. Cut out the old roofing with a utility knife and scrape away the old cement.

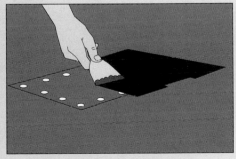

2. Trim a new piece of roofing for a snug fit, then nail and cement it in place. Apply enough cement to lap all sides by 3 inches.

3. Press a second, larger patch into the cement; nail and seal it, too. Double-patching makes a strong, watertight, long-lasting repair. Replace gravel.

Solving Roof Problems (continued)

REPAIRING AND REPLACING FLASHING

Think of flashing as a special-purpose shingle. Like a shingle, flashing overlaps and interweaves with other roofing materials to shed water like a duck's feathers do.

Most flashing, however, is made of thin-gauge metal that can be easily bent and formed to fit angled joints where two or more surfaces come together. Because these intersections are more vulnerable to leakage, flashing deserves even closer scrutiny than the rest of your roof.

Look for flashing that has pulled away from adjoining surfaces and for roofing cement or caulk that has dried and cracked. Holes can be almost microscopic; when in doubt, apply new cement or caulk.

Badly rusted, cracked, or corroded flashing around chimneys, dormers, and plumbing vents will last for a few more years if you trowel on a coat of fibered asphalt-aluminum roof paint. If there is widespread deterioration or valley-flashing failure, you should call in a roofer or sheet-metal specialist to replace these sections entirely (unless you feel confident in doing it yourself).

Often, flashing shields around vents and chimneys fail first. You can replace these yourself if you're handy at snipping and shaping lightweight materials. (See pages 520–525 for more about working with metals.)

For durability at a reasonable price, choose aluminum flashing—but first note the caution about mixing dissimilar metals on page 127. Vent flashing comes as a single molded piece of metal or plastic that you simply fit over the pipe and cover with roofing on the uphill side, as shown below. Fabricate other types from rolls, strips, and sheets, as illustrated on page 131.

YOU'LL NEED...

SKILLS: Basic sheet-metal skills.
TIME: 30 minutes for a simple plumbing vent.
TOOLS: Hammer, tin snips, pliers, nail set.

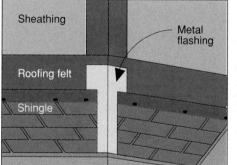

Because it is visible, open-valley flashing is easy to inspect. Cement down shingles that are even slightly curled or loose.

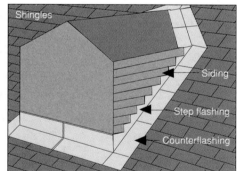

Closed-valley flashing hides beneath the roofing. In some cases, shingles are so interlaced on top that it is impossible to check the flashing.

Dormer flashing tucks up under lap siding on the dormer or is capped with counterflashing, as illustrated on the chimney on page 131.

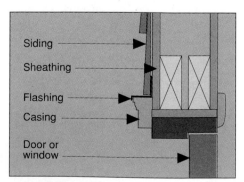

Over windows and doors, drip cap flashing keeps water from seeping under the frames. Check them periodically for damage.

Don't bother repairing a faulty vent flashing. Just install a new neoprene and aluminum replacement. You'll need to replace only a few shingles.

FLASHING A CHIMNEY

Most chimneys have a two-part flashing system to ride out minor structural shifting. Base flashing fits under shingles along the sides of the chimney (called step flashing there) and "up roof" from the chimney; it lays on top of the shingles below the chimney. Counterflashing is applied over the base flashing and serves as a cap to keep water out. Its top edge, bent into an L shape, is mortared into the chimney's mortar joints to hold it securely in place.

Replacing chimney flashing is a task that calls for time and patience. You can use copper, aluminum, or galvanized steel flashing (use copper for the counterflashing for a more durable seal). Flashing material is available in sheet roll form that you can cut with tin snips; often step flashing is available in prebent forms.

You should build an A-frame cricket on the up-roof side of the chimney so water will not settle there and deteriorate the flashing.

Counter-flashing

Base flashing

YOU'LL NEED...

SKILLS: Moderate sheet-metal skills.
TIME: 4 to 6 hours.
TOOLS: Tin snips, putty knife, hammer, cold chisel, trowel, joint strike, ladder, rope.

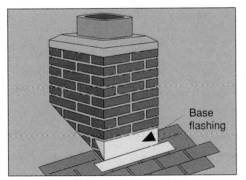

Base flashing

1. Apply asphalt primer to bricks and install base flashing to the front, overlapping roof shingles 4 inches.

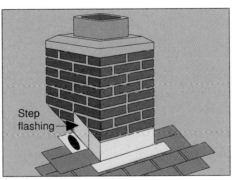

Step flashing

2. Nail step flashing over plastic cement. Bed overlapping roof shingles in additional plastic cement.

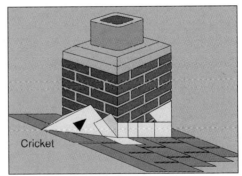

Cricket

3. Install a plywood cricket on the up-roof side and shingle to its edge. Bed the rear corner flashings in cement.

4. Bed the rear base flashing that covers the cricket in plastic cement. Nail the flashing to the deck only.

5. Set the counterflashing on the front and sides into raked-out mortar joints. Refill joints with new mortar.

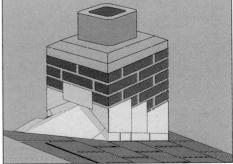

6. Make and install counterflashing suitable to the situation on the up-roof corners and side of the chimney.

Solving Roof Problems (continued)

REPAIRING AND CLEANING FIREPLACE CHIMNEYS

Chimneys have two enemies: heat and water. The crackling fire you enjoy on winter evenings subjects masonry to temperature extremes that can chip out mortar, especially at the top where the flue penetrates the cap (see the cutaway at right).

Your chimney may differ from the illustration shown here. Some are all brick; a few use firebrick instead of a ceramic tile flue liner. Many also include a cap to keep out rain, nesting birds, and downdrafts.

Regardless of your chimney's construction, it pays to inspect it every fall. Inspect every surface you can see, including in the attic, looking for cracks and deteriorated mortar (see page 105).

Occasionally, test for hot spots by feeling with your hand. These may indicate a broken flue—a definite fire hazard that a mason should fix before you use the fireplace again.

How often a fireplace flue needs cleaning depends on how often you use it and the type of wood you burn. Pine and other sappy species produce creosote that cakes the flue and constricts the opening. The result: smoking and a possible chimney fire. Hire a chimney sweep to clean your chimney, or do the job yourself, as shown below. A faulty firebox design or downdrafts also can cause smoking (see page 104 for solutions to these problems).

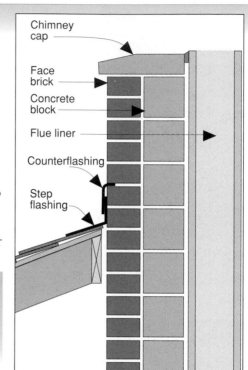

Chimney cap
Face brick
Concrete block
Flue liner
Counterflashing
Step flashing

YOU'LL NEED...

SKILLS: Basic masonry skills.
TIME: 1 to 8 hours.
TOOLS: Hammer, cold chisel, caulking gun, chimney sweep tools.

Rain erodes mortar joints. Chip away loose material, then repoint as explained on page 149.

Use silicone caulk around the flue for a flexible seal that rides out expansion and contraction.

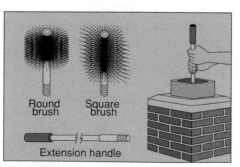

Round brush   Square brush   Extension handle

Buy chimney brushes and extension handles to fit your flue cross-section and length. Brush from the top down.

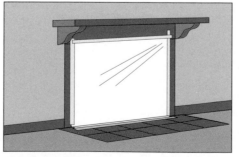

Before brushing, open the damper and seal the fireplace opening with a wet sheet, canvas, or polyethylene.

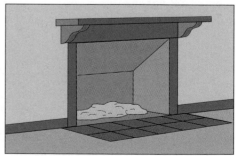

Wet down the soot before you clean out the firebox. Vacuum around the damper before closing it.

PREVENTING ATTIC CONDENSATION

An attic that cannot breathe properly has problems. During hot weather, temperatures may reach 150°F, adding a big load to the cooling system. During cold spells, the temperature difference between the attic and heated spaces below causes moisture condensation, which can lower the R-value of insulation, rot framing and sheathing, and shorten the life of your roof.

The solution to both problems is to provide adequate air flow through inlets at the eaves or soffits, then up and out via louvers near the ridge.

How much ventilation your attic needs depends on whether the insulation includes a vapor barrier (see pages 390–393). If it does, there should be 1 square foot of venting for every 300 square feet of attic floor space. If there is no vapor barrier, double this figure.

Illustrated below are the most common passive ventilation systems. To learn about buying and installing powered units, see pages 403–406.

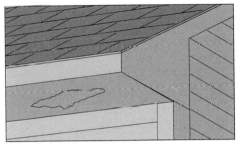

Paint peeling off soffits is a sign that the attic needs better ventilation. Also, check insulation for dampness.

Icicles sometimes form on roofing nails that penetrate the sheathing. To prevent dripping, clip off the nail ends.

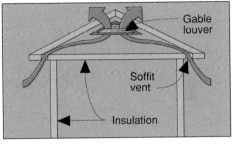

In an unfinished attic, you might get by with gable louvers at each end. Better yet, add soffit vents, too.

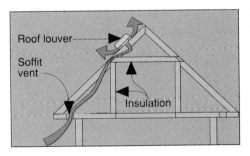

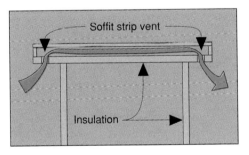

Finished attics need both soffit vents and roof louvers. Inlets and outlets should be about equal in area.

Flat roofs need ventilation, too. Strip-style soffit vents might be the answer here. Size them as explained above.

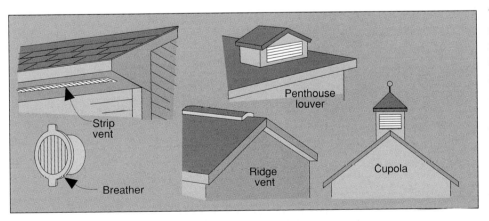

There are ventilation components for almost any roof. Breathers are easy to install, but you need many of them. Soffit strip vents provide greater air flow. Up top, you can choose gable or roof-mounted louvers (shown above). A ridge vent is an unobtrusive answer. Add design interest with a cupola. Penthouse louvers work well on big, flat roofs. Many of these projects are big jobs better left to a contractor, but you can install a roof louver using the skylight procedures on page 141.

Solving Roof Problems (continued)

REPAIRING AND MAINTAINING GUTTERS AND DOWNSPOUTS

When you consider that your roof's drainage system annually diverts thousands of gallons of water from your house's exterior and foundation walls, you can see why it merits a semiannual inspection.

Familiarize yourself with the system's key elements, illustrated below. There are three basic forms of gutter hangers: a strap nailed to the roof sheathing, a fascia bracket attached to the fascia, or a spike and ferrule driven through the gutter into rafter ends (see page 137).

All gutters must slope slightly toward their outlets. From there, an elbow connects with a leader, then another elbow, the downspout, and a third elbow that directs the spout outlet away from the wall.

Check gutters and downspouts every spring before heavy rains begin and late in fall after leaves have fallen. Remove all debris that is clogging the system, look for rust or corrosion, and be vigilant for low spots where water may be standing.

Because standing water causes most gutter problems, make sure the gutters slope toward their outlets. To check this, pour some water into the gutter and watch what happens.

Eliminate sags by lifting the gutter section slightly. Look for and repair loose hangers, or bend up the hanger with a pair of pliers. If this doesn't do the trick, install an additional hanger.

> ### YOU'LL NEED...
> **SKILLS:** Basic and ladder skills.
> **TIME:** 4 to 6 hours for a medium-size house.
> **TOOLS:** Hose and sprayer, wire brush, putty knife, ladder, hammer, hacksaw, pliers.

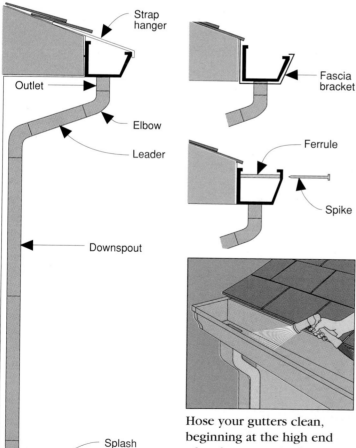

Strap hanger

Outlet

Elbow

Leader

Downspout

Splash block

Fascia bracket

Ferrule

Spike

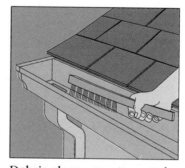

Debris clogs up gutters and downspouts and holds moisture that causes rust, rot, and corrosion.

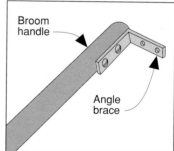

Broom handle

Angle brace

Fasten a metal angle to the end of a long pole or board, then use it to rake debris toward you.

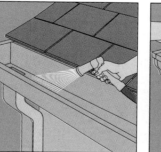

Hose your gutters clean, beginning at the high end of each run—or in the middle of runs having spouts at both ends.

Often you can blast out spout blockage with water pressure or a plumber's snake. Otherwise, you may have to dismantle the downspouts.

If the inside of a gutter is rusting, scrape and wire-brush it clean, then apply a thin coat of roofing cement.

Sand wooden gutters down to bare wood, apply linseed oil, let dry, then apply two coats of roofing cement.

Lift shingle. Nail the strap hanger to the sheathing, then seal the nailheads with roofing cement.

Pull spout strap from the wall and coat the underside with roofing cement. This seals the nails.

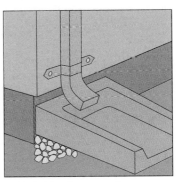

Splash blocks must be pitched away from the foundation walls. Raise and shim underneath with gravel.

You can install perforated roll-up hose. It extends like a party noisemaker when the water comes down.

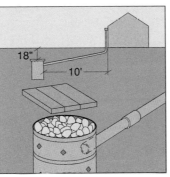

For serious runoff problems, you may have to use a dry well. One common do-it-yourself type is shown here.

Screen guards keep leaves out of gutters. Slip the inner edge under the first course of shingles.

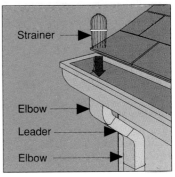

Wire cage strainers eliminate downspout clogging. You still have to clear debris from around the cages.

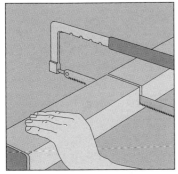

Cut downspouts with a fine-tooth hacksaw. Mark a line around the circumference so the edges will be square.

To join downspouts, crimp the end of one so it will slip into the other. The upper section always goes inside.

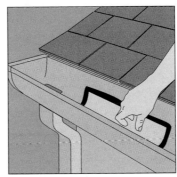

Patch a rusted-out gutter with metal flashing. Cement in place, then coat with more roofing cement.

Installing New Roof Products

No one likes to spend a lot of time on ladders or moving around on steep roof surfaces. Fortunately, most roofing components (except shingles) are relatively lightweight and easy to install.

If you will be working on the roof, consider investing in a pair of roof brackets. These simple devices support a level plank upon which you can rest materials. To install, just lift a shingle, drive a nail, then hook the bracket on it.

Always wear sneakers or other slip-resistant shoes when working on a roof. Don't burden yourself with a heavy belt full of tools that could throw you off balance or injure you in a fall. Keep them in a tool bucket that you can haul up and down with a rope (see page 122).

MATERIAL MATTERS · CHOOSING GUTTERS AND DOWNSPOUTS

Today's gutter and spout systems consist of a series of modular pieces that you simply assemble to suit your house's situation.

Before you order, make a list of the components shown below, then inspect your house and write down how many of each you'll need.

Most gutters come in 10-foot lengths and require a downspout every 35 feet. Longer runs should be pitched toward an outlet at either end. Gutters should always be pitched away from valleys and toward corners.

If you are replacing only parts of a system, be sure you don't mix metals; copper, steel, and aluminum are not compatible with each other.

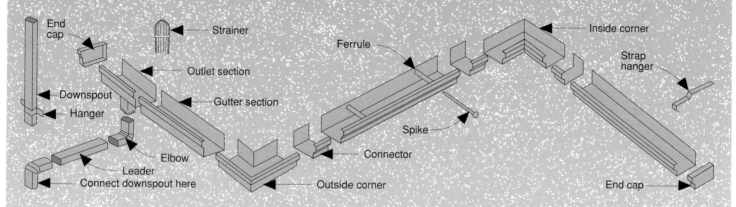

GUTTER MATERIALS SELECTION GUIDE

Material	Features	Maintenance	Life Span/Cost
Steel	Plain galvanized or enamel finish	Prone to rusting; should be painted	15 years; inexpensive
Aluminum	Enamel or plastic-clad finish; easy to install, but fragile	Resistant to corrosion, but may need occasional repainting	15 to 20 years; moderate
Vinyl	Sturdy and durable; can be tricky to install; available in white or brown	Immune to rot and rust; cannot be painted	50 years; expensive
Copper	Durable; not widely used; joints must be soldered	Does not rust or corrode, but leaky joints require soldering	50 years; most expensive
Wood	Vulnerable to rot; very heavy	Requires frequent waterproofing and painting	10 to 15 years; moderate

PUTTING UP NEW GUTTERS AND SPOUTS

Installing new gutter systems is not quite a do-it-yourself job because it calls for two ladders and an extra pair of hands. With a partner, the job is easy because the preformed components make it basically a cutting, assembling, and hanging job.

If you're repairing part of an existing system, dismantle it as little as possible and measure for the new parts. If you're installing a new gutter system, repaint peeling fascia boards first—or install one of the many prefinished fascia products offered by gutter manufacturers.

Cut aluminum and steel gutters with metal tin snips. For heavier-gauge metal or vinyl, use a hacksaw. Assemble the sections with slip-joint connectors and caulk all joints and nailheads with manufacturer-recommended caulk. Newer gutter types with neoprene-gasketed slip connectors don't need caulk.

With aluminum gutter systems, never use anything but aluminum nails, screws, and rivets. Use rust-resistant steel fasteners with steel gutters and downspouts. As a general rule, use fasteners made of the same metal as the metal gutter.

You have a choice of gutter hangers. Strap hangers only work with flexible roofing materials, such as asphalt shingles, that you can lift up to put the hanger under. If your roof has rigid wood shingles or slate, use fascia brackets or spike-and-ferrule hangers. Spikes are easiest to install, but they may sag under heavy loads of ice and snow if used in northern, high-precipitation areas.

YOU'LL NEED...

SKILLS: Basic carpentry and ladder skills.
TIME: 1 day for new gutters for a medium-size house.
TOOLS: Hammer, hacksaw, level, caulking gun, two ladders, pliers, tin snips or metal shears.

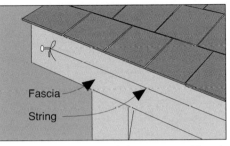

Gutters slope toward the spouts. Check the manufacturer's recommendations, then tack up a string for a guide.

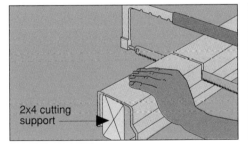

Insert a 2×4 when sawing gutter sections. Always file cut edges to smooth off sharp burrs.

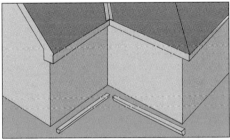

Assemble gutter runs on the ground first, caulking and screwing or riveting all joints, except those at the corners.

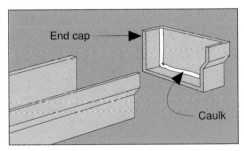

Most end caps simply snap onto gutter sections. Apply a bead of caulk or joint sealer to prevent leaking.

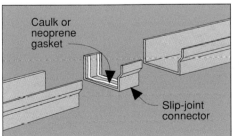

Caulk slip-joint connectors unless gasketed. These important components are the most susceptible to leaking.

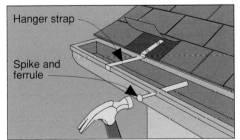

Space hangers 24 or 32 inches apart. Spikes go into rafter ends. Predrill holes before lifting the run into place.

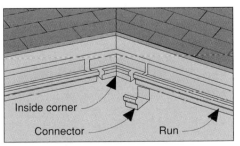

Connect two runs with corner sections. Caulk, then fasten with rivets or sheet-metal screws.

Installing New Roof Products (continued)

INSTALLING NEW SHINGLES

Unless your home already has slate or tile shingles, you can rule out these heavyweights because ordinary framing won't bear the weight load.

Wood shingles and shakes offer high insulation value, superior durability, and classic good looks. However, they require a relatively steep roof pitch and are prohibited by fire codes in some communities. For more about wood shakes and shingles, see page 139.

Asphalt shingles come in a broad array of colors, shapes, textures, and qualities. Like all shingles, they are sold by the square—the amount of material needed to cover 100 square feet. They often are rated by their weight per square—the heavier, the better (and the more expensive).

In comparing weights, do not rate asphalt shingles from one class against those from another. Class C shingles, which have an organic felt base, offer only moderate fire resistance. Class A shingles, which are backed by noncombustible glass fibers, are highly fire-resistant.

Premium Class A shingles should not rot, blister, or curl. A few of the most expensive resemble wood shingles and shakes.

In general, you can apply new shingles and shakes—either asphalt or wood—over any existing roofing, except shakes. This saves the trouble and expense of tearing off the old roof. If you already have two layers of asphalt shingles, you probably will have to remove them because a third layer would exceed the roof's weight limitations.

Reroofing with Asphalt Shingles

Use your old shingles as guides and you'll find that a reshingling project can go quickly. Before you begin, nail all loose or curled shingles, and replace any that are missing. Reset popped nails, too. Shingles measure 1×3 feet, with cutouts that divide the shingle into three tabs. Simply butt each new shingle against the bottom edge of an old one, staggering the tabs from course to course.

YOU'LL NEED...

SKILLS: Basic roofing skills.
TIME: 3 hours for each 100 square feet.
TOOLS: Regular or roofing hammer, utility knife, ladder, tools for flashing if needed (see page 130).

1. Check drip-edge flashing at the eaves and rakes. If it is failing, replace as you would any other flashing (see page 130).

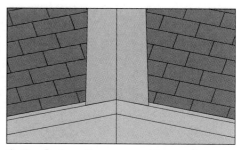

2. To flash valleys, use either roll roofing or sheet metal. Valley flashing should project about 1 inch beyond the eaves.

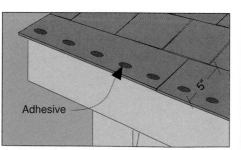

3. For the starter course, trim off shingle tabs to make strips only as wide as the old exposure—usually 5 inches. Fit them as shown.

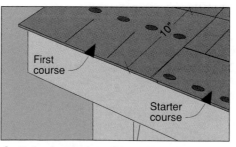

4. Completely lap the starter course with the first finish course. Always stagger end joints from one course to the next.

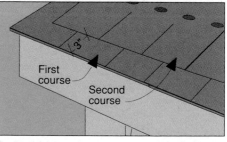

5. Build later courses stair-step fashion. The first course will have only a 3-inch exposure, but a gutter (not shown) will conceal this.

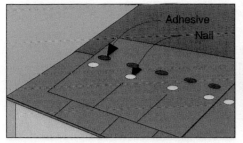

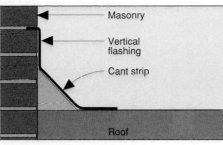

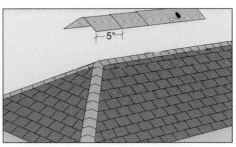

6. Each shingle requires four nails, about ½ inch above the cutouts. Do not sink the nailheads into the surface.

7. A cant strip at the base of a vertical surface improves runoff. For more about chimney flashing, see page 131.

8. Cover the ridge of the roof with special shingles, or cut ordinary ones into three separate tabs to fit.

Reroofing with Wood Shingles and Shakes

To lay up wood shingles and shakes, you use the same basic techniques illustrated previously—but you need a couple more tools and a little more preparation work. Additional tools include a multipurpose roofer's hammer for nailing, trimming, and gauging courses and a lightweight power saw for more precise cutting. Purchase the best shingles or shakes you can afford. Wood shingles can be installed over the top of asphalt shingles, depending on the weight of the layer(s) already on the roof.

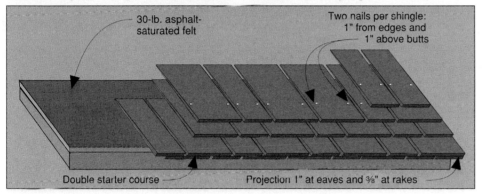

1. Start a wood shingle roof with a double starter course, projecting over the edges as shown. Stagger the joints of succeeding courses. Maximum exposure depends on shingle length (see manufacturer's recommendation).

> ### YOU'LL NEED...
> **SKILLS:** Basic carpentry and roofing skills.
> **TIME:** 4 to 6 hours per 100 square feet.
> **TOOLS:** Roofer's hammer, utility knife, lightweight power saw, ladder.

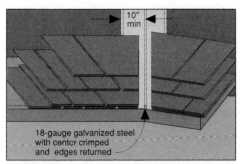

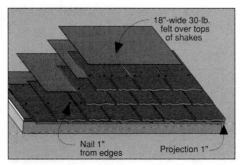

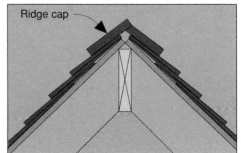

2. Flash valleys with 18-gauge galvanized sheet metal, crimped and rolled by a metal shop.

3. Install shakes the same way as shingles, but interleave 18-inch-wide strips of 30-pound roofing felt.

4. Cover the ridge with overlapped 1×4 or 1×6 boards. Caulk the overlap to prevent leakage.

Installing New Roof Products (continued)

INSTALLING A SKYLIGHT

A skylight brightens interior rooms in a way no artificial source can match. Even on cloudy days, a skylight provides a surprising amount of light—and the operating cost is nil.

Prefabricated kits—available in various domed, rectangular, and square shapes—include an acrylic window (or "light") and a flanged metal frame that you nail to your roof deck.

Getting through the roof requires only modest framing and flashing expertise. Keep in mind, however, that you also will need to construct a light shaft through your attic, unless your home has a flat roof or an integral roof-ceiling deck.

Work from the inside out, framing the ceiling opening and building the shaft before you cut into the roof. Skylights are designed to span two or three rafters on typical 24-inch spacings; often it is necessary to cut and tie off rafters and ceiling joists to accommodate the shaft. Caution: Be sure that you shore up the ceiling with T-braces (see page 169) before cutting open the ceiling. (For more information about ceiling framing, see page 59.)

The drawings below show three shafts designed for different situations. Regardless of the one you choose, construct a sleeve with ½-inch plywood, check it for fit, then paint the inside white to ensure maximum reflective value.

For a flat-roof installation, just frame the opening, paint the rafters and headers around it, then install the skylight. Note that you may also need to raise the unit with nailers, as shown on page 141.

YOU'LL NEED...

SKILLS: Moderate carpentry and roofing skills.
TIME: 8 hours per skylight.
TOOLS: Hammer, drill, screwdriver, caulking gun, saw.

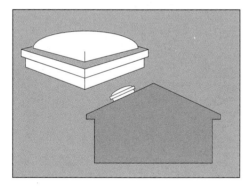

Domed skylights are suitable for installation on flat or pitched roofs. Some also include a cranking system so you can open them for ventilation.

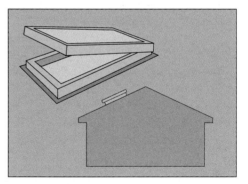

Dormer skylights make sense only for pitched roofs. Good skylights are double-glazed, with an air space to cut heat loss.

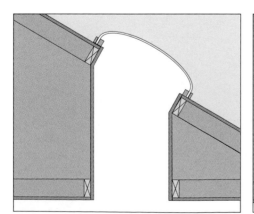

If you locate a skylight directly above the ceiling opening, you can get by with a simple straight shaft.

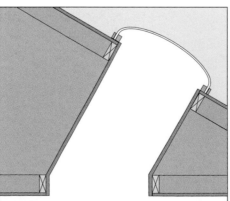

A tilted shaft lets you offset the roof and ceiling openings somewhat. These are trickier to construct, of course.

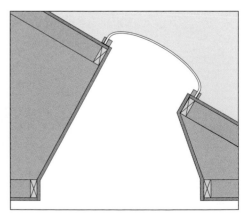

The ceiling opening can be bigger than the skylight. A splayed shaft disperses daylight over a broad area.

Going Through the Roof

Once you have built a skylight shaft, topping it off with a prefab skylight takes a day or less. First, you must cut and tie off the rafters with headers, as you did with the ceiling joists. Locate the opening by sliding the shaft into position and marking around its perimeter.

When you set the unit in place, fit its flange under roofing at the top and sides, but let overlap the shingles on the down-roof side.

YOU'LL NEED...

SKILLS: Moderate carpentry and roofing skills.
TIME: 8 hours per skylight.
TOOLS: Saw, hammer, drill, keyhole saw, utility knife, caulking gun, tin snips for flashing if needed.

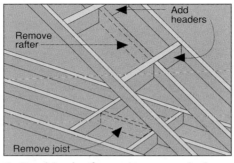

1. Double-check measurements before cutting into framing, and install headers before cutting the sheathing.

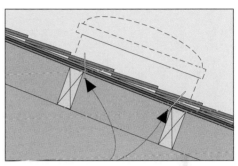

2. To mark the opening, drive long nails through the roof at each corner, then chalk an outline on the top side.

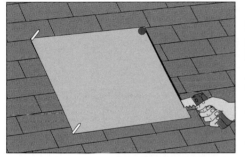

3. Remove shingles and building felt with a utility knife. When you saw the sheathing, don't let it fall below.

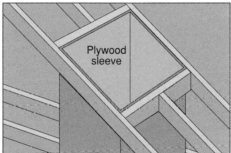

4. Slide the shaft up from below and nail it to the framing. If the floor is insulated, insulate the shaft, too.

5. Seal under the flange before you nail it, then cement the shingles to it with roofing cement for a watertight joint.

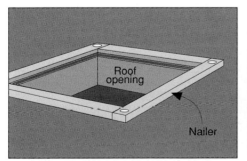

6. On flat roofs, install nailers around the opening. Otherwise, standing water may overflow the frame.

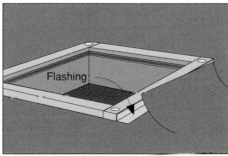

7. Seal under nailer with roofing cement, then slip flashing under the roofing and up the sides of the nailer.

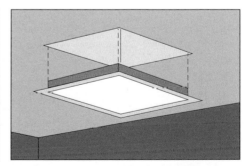

8. If you want to add a light diffuser, just screw its frame to the inside of the shaft. Wipe the shaft clean first.

EXTERIOR WALLS, WINDOWS, AND DOORS

Regardless of your home's exterior skin, its skeleton probably looks like the one shown here. The sill plate and box sill sit on top of the foundation wall. If your basement ceiling is open, periodically check the box sill, sill plate, and sill seal. Attend to any moisture immediately because rot here could cause structural damage.

The wall consists of a sole plate—2×4 or 2×6 studs, spaced 16 or 24 inches on center—that does the support work and a pair of 2×4s or 2×6s that makes a top plate upon which rest the rafters or framing for a second story.

Insulation between the studs conserves heat (see pages 390–400 for more about insulation). Wood or composition board sheathing adds further insulation and strength. Then a layer of air wrap, either asphalt-saturated building paper or plastic, seals the sheathing.

Outside, siding faces the elements and gives your home its visual character. Shown here is lap siding, so-called because the boards overlap each other. Don't assume, however, that what looks like a board or shingle is actually made of wood. A variety of manufactured materials (see pages 154–159) give the appearance of wood without its

high maintenance requirements.

Regardless of its composition, siding deserves a careful, semiannual inspection. You should scan its surface systematically, using binoculars for closeups of high places if necessary. Look for cracks, splits, peeling paint, and evidence of rot or insect damage. Any breaks in your home's skin—no matter how small—will eventually admit water into wall cavities. Neglect the repairs explained in this section (see pages

144–151) and moisture could wreck insulation, framing, or even interior wall surfaces.

If a new paint job seems imminent, see pages 553–564. To learn about basic wall building techniques, turn to pages 50–53.

During your inspection, if you suspect a wall might be infested with termites or other insects, read the information about identifying insects and what to do about them on pages 152–153.

ANATOMY OF A FRAME WALL

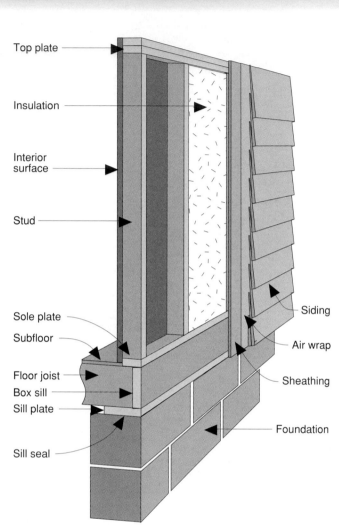

Top plate

Insulation

Interior surface

Stud

Sole plate

Subfloor

Floor joist

Box sill

Sill plate

Sill seal

Siding

Air wrap

Sheathing

Foundation

ANATOMY OF A BRICK OR STONE WALL

Most "brick" or "stone" houses do not have solid masonry walls. Instead, builders face conventional framing with a masonry veneer—combining the weather resistance of brick or stone with the lighter weight and superior insulating qualities of wood stud construction.

Check the section view at right. Studs, not bricks, bear the load. A single tier of brick connects to the studs with short metal strips called ties. Between the brick and sheathing is an air space, which drains away moisture that might penetrate the brick surface.

One big difference between masonry and frame walls occurs at the foundation. With masonry-veneer construction, the foundation must support the heavy masonry skin as well as the framing system. The foundation must be designed to support this load at the time it is built. Thus, it is not feasible to veneer an existing frame wall with conventional masonry materials.

Although masonry-veneer walls are relatively impervious to weather and time, inspect them periodically, paying particular attention to mortar joints that may need to be repointed (see page 149). Solid masonry walls—usually used today only for garages, garden walls, and commercial structures—may consist of several tiers of brick or stone, or concrete blocks that have been veneered. To learn more about these materials, see pages 203–213.

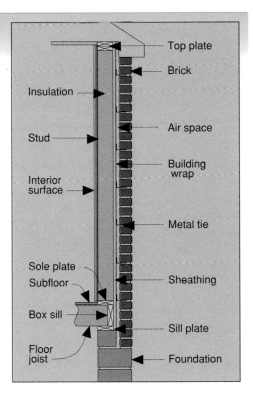

ANATOMY OF A STUCCO WALL

Stucco walls also usually begin with wood-stud framing, although stucco can be applied directly to masonry surfaces. As the drawing at right shows, spacer strips are nailed to the sheathing and a ground of metal lath is attached to the spacers. Then, stucco—a cement-based plaster—is troweled onto the ground.

As with interior plasterwork, it takes three layers of stucco to build up a smooth surface. The first, the scratch coat, oozes through the ground for a good grip; the brown coat smooths out major irregularities in the surface; and the finish coat completes the job. Newer, vinyl-based materials are sprayed on.

As with concrete (see page 184), you can trowel, scrape, stipple, and

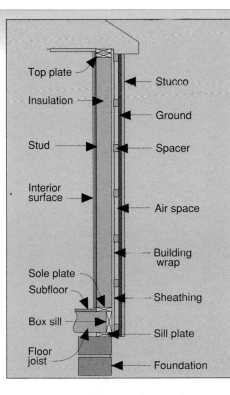

spatter stucco textures ranging from glassy smooth to rugged rustic. You also can add coloring pigments to the finish coat of both cement and vinyl stucco for an exterior that will never need painting.

Properly applied, stucco lasts for decades with little attention. Watch, though, for cracks that may develop around windows, doors, and chimneys. If not remedied, these may admit moisture that could eventually rot framing. As with masonry-veneer walls, keep your eye on long, running cracks that might indicate settlement.

For information about patching cracks and holes, see page 151. If you are planning to paint stucco, be sure to use a coating formulated for concrete (see pages 553–554).

Solving Wall Problems

Preventive maintenance is the key to prolonging wall life. With just a few tools, tubes of caulk, a garden hose, and a ladder, you probably can tone up your walls in a single day.

Start by giving wood siding and trim a good scrubbing. As dirt washes away, watch for mildew, popped nails, and minor cracks that need caulking. You can deal with most of these problems during a semiannual bath, as shown below.

Split siding or masonry that is in need of repair are best treated at another time (see pages 147–151).

CLEANING AND MAINTAINING EXTERIOR WALLS

Wash wood surfaces with a detergent solution, then rinse well. Pay particular attention to areas under eaves, porches, and other sheltered places. House paints are designed to chalk, or gradually wear away, with exposure to rain—a sort of self-cleaning action that does not occur in protected zones.

A dark, rash-like spot that won't wash off is mildew. This fungus thrives in high humidity and shade.

Masonry surfaces sometimes suffer from efflorescence, a white, powdery residue that resists scrubbing. Both mildew and efflorescence are easily treated, as explained below.

Include nails and screws in your tool bucket so you can make minor repairs as you go along. Choose screw-type or ring-shank nails for better holding power—and drill pilot holes so you don't split the wood. Use rust-resistant, galvanized aluminum or brass nails and screws; otherwise, they'll eventually stain the paint around them.

YOU'LL NEED...

SKILLS: Basic skills.
TIME: 1 day depending on the size of your house and extent of repairs needed.
TOOLS: Power washer, brushes, hammer, nail set, drill, putty knife.

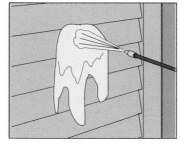

Borrow or rent a pressure washer to remove loose paint as well as entrenched dirt and grime.

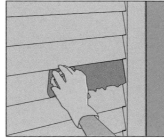

You can remove mildew with a trisodium phosphate solution or regular household laundry bleach.

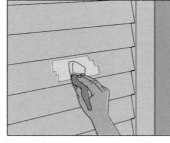

If mildew has damaged the paint, strip and bleach with oxalic acid. Refinish with mildewcide paint.

Using a nail set, drive in all popped nails beneath the surface. Fill the holes with wood putty or latex caulk.

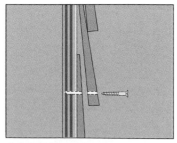

Warped boards resist nailing. Drill pilot holes, countersink rustproof screws, and caulk screw heads.

Scour efflorescence with a 1:10 solution of muriatic acid and water. Clean small areas one at a time and rinse.

Undercut cracks in stucco, as shown on page 37. Pack with patching cement, then smooth with a putty knife.

To see if cracked masonry is settling, bridge the crack with tape. A twist in the tape indicates movement.

SEALING WITH CAULK

Different building materials swell and shrink at different rates, resulting in cracks where siding meets masonry, where siding butts trim, and where flashing contacts roofing. Use caulk wherever unlike materials meet. The illustration below shows typical spots to check.

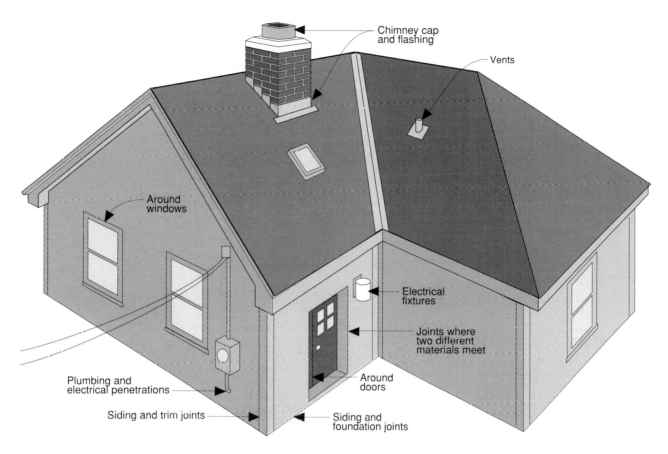

Chimney cap and flashing

Vents

Around windows

Electrical fixtures

Joints where two different materials meet

Plumbing and electrical penetrations

Around doors

Siding and trim joints

Siding and foundation joints

MATERIAL MATTERS

Caulking material falls into two categories—rubber-derived formulations, such as latex and butyl, and synthetic-based, high-performance materials. The type you select depends upon the job you want it to do.

Before buying, read the product data for preparation requirements, materials the caulk will adhere to, and paintability. The chart at right compares the common sealants.

CHOOSING SEALANTS

Type	Where to Use	Cost
Acrylic latex	Good general-purpose, fast-drying sealant; ideal for filling small cracks and joints; paintable	Inexpensive
Vinyl latex	Highly adhesive and waterproof; good for wet areas, such as tubs and showers	Moderate
Butyl	Excellent exterior caulk for gutter seams, flashings, storm windows, and large joints; paintable	Moderate
Silicone	Exceptional adhesion and life; great for around tubs and showers; some brands are paintable	Most expensive

Solving Wall Problems (continued)

USING CAULK

If you have never used caulk, start in an inconspicuous area. Some types stick more readily to fingers and tools than to the surfaces they're sealing. It takes a tube or two to learn how hard to squeeze and how fast to move the nozzle for a smooth, unbroken bead.

For most jobs, use an inexpensive half-barrel gun. Its squeeze handle pushes a plunger against the bottom of a disposable cartridge, forcing caulk through the nozzle.

To apply caulk, first scrape out old, cracked caulk and flaked paint, and be sure the surfaces are dry.

Hold the gun at a 45-degree angle and pull it toward you in a smooth, steady stroke, maintaining an even pressure on the trigger. Remove excess and smooth irregularities with a moist fingertip or putty knife. You should not caulk at temperatures below 50°F.

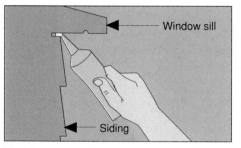

Toothpaste-style tubes are handy for minor touch-up jobs, but are costly if you have much caulking to do.

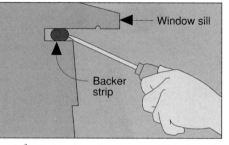

Pack ¾-inch or wider gaps with closed-cell foam backer strips, then complete the seal by caulking.

For a big job, save money by buying a full-barrel gun and loading it with compound that is sold in bulk.

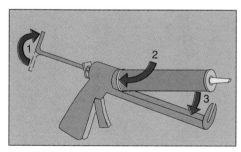

To load a half-barrel gun, invert its plunger handle, pull all the way back, and slip in a cartridge of caulk.

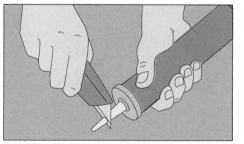

Snip off the nozzle's tip. The closer to the tip, the narrower the bead will be. Puncture inside seal with a nail.

Between perpendicular surfaces, bisect the angle with the gun's nozzle to make a smooth concave bead.

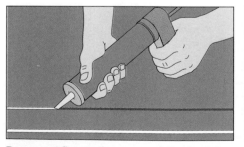

Between flat surfaces, straddle the joint with the nozzle and pack it so that the caulk bulges out.

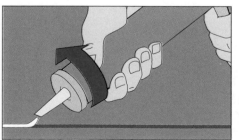

At the end of a stroke, lift the tip with a twist to catch caulk oozing from the nozzle, then pull back plunger quickly.

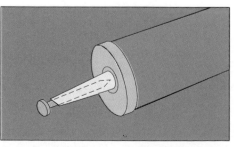

Save partial tubes by sealing them with a nail. Or, invert the cut-off tip of the nozzle and stuff it into the opening.

REPAIRING WOOD SIDING AND SHINGLES

Damaged siding lets moisture enter exterior walls and rot away their framing. Make repairs as soon as you spot damage. Pack small cracks, splits, and open seams at board ends with latex or butyl caulk. If more than a few boards or shingles are failing, however, consider re-siding the entire wall (see pages 154–159).

You may be able to repair badly split pieces by applying waterproof glue directly into the split. If not, you'll have to replace the damaged board or shingle—an operation that requires careful, but not skilled, carpentry. The problem is that each course of lapped siding is held in place by nails driven through the course above it. The drawings below show how to repair lapped wood siding. Use the same steps to replace wood shingles, but don't try to pry out the nails; cut them underneath the shingle with a hacksaw.

YOU'LL NEED...

SKILLS: Moderate carpentry skills.
TIME: 1 to 3 hours for a single course of siding.
TOOLS: Chisel, hammer, pry bar, hacksaw blade, square, putty knife, caulking gun.

1. To remove an entire length of siding, work a chisel under its lower edge, then switch to a pry bar.

2. If the nails begin to come out with the board, jam the nail with a pry bar and tap the board down.

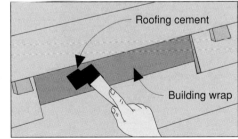

3. If the nails aren't accessible from the surface, slip a hacksaw blade underneath the siding and cut them.

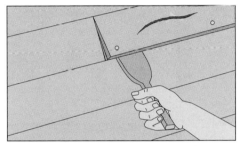

4. In a small area, tap wedges under the course above and use a square to mark the saw cuts. Cut along marks.

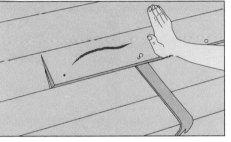

5. Split damaged area along the grain and remove a piece at a time. Remove all remnants under the board above.

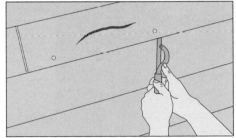

Roofing cement

Building wrap

6. If you puncture the building paper underneath, seal it with a liberal coat of roofing cement.

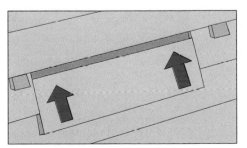

7. Cut the replacement for a tight fit, then slide it under the board above, tap into place, and remove the wedges.

8. Finally, nail the new board at the top and bottom, fill nail holes and the vertical seams with caulk, then prime and paint.

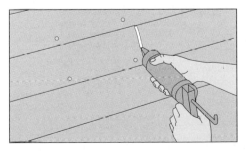

Solving Wall Problems (continued)

REPLACING A VINYL SIDING STRIP

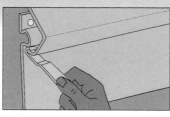 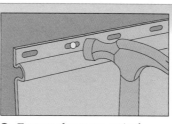 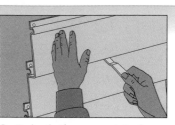

1. Remove strip by inserting zip tool under lip above, pulling down, and sliding. Pull nails with a pry bar.

2. Fasten the new strip by nailing through the centers of the nail slots. Do not drive the nails tightly.

3. Relock the new strip by pulling down and sliding the zip tool while pressing in on the bottom edge.

PATCHING ALUMINUM SIDING

 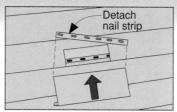 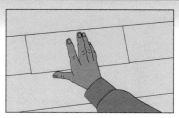

Detach nail strip

1. With a utility knife, cut top and sides of rectangle around damage, bend down tab, and cut bottom.

2. Cut a patch of matching siding 3 inches wider and remove its nailing strip. Clean surfaces to be glued.

3. Apply clear silicone sealant to back of patch, press and lock in bottom. Clean up excess sealant.

REPLACING ALUMINUM SIDING END CAPS

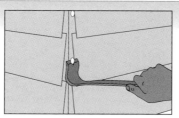 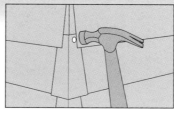 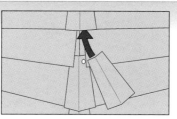

1. Remove all of the damaged corner caps. Remove remaining nails with a small pry bar.

2. Starting at the lowest, slide replacement caps under bottom lips of courses; nail with aluminum nails.

3. Cut nailing strip off top cap, apply silicone sealant to back side, slide cap under lips of side strips and press.

REPAIRING ALUMINUM SIDING DENTS

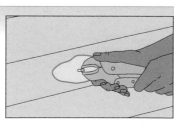 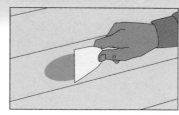 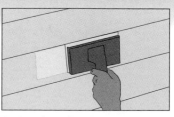

1. Drive a No. 6 self-tapping screw into deepest point of dent, then pull dent partway out with locking pliers.

2. Sand dent area until bare. Apply two-part auto-body filler with a wide putty knife and smooth flush.

3. Sand with 120-grit paper until smooth. Paint with color-matched paint suited to aluminum siding.

REPAIRING BRICKWORK

Though far more permanent than wood siding or shingles, brick walls also require occasional attention. Their most common malady is crumbling mortar. You can repair deteriorated joints by tucking mortar into them with the point of a trowel—a process masons call pointing or tuck pointing.

Some specialized tools will help you do the job. You'll need a pointing trowel, which is slightly smaller than an ordinary masonry trowel, and a joint strike, used to shape the concave joint. Also handy is a hawk, which you can buy or make by screwing a short length of dowel or broom handle to a square of plywood. Practice on a less visible area first if you're inexperienced with masonry work.

Pack the joints with mortar mixed with a liquid latex binder. You also can use conventional mortar mix (see page 206) or vinyl patching cement, which is easier to apply but doesn't look like mortar. After you have filled and smoothed the joints, strike or shape them to match the other joints. (For typical mortar treatments, see page 211.)

You also can point long vertical cracks, whether the cracks are only in the joints or in the bricks themselves. A better solution is to grout cracks, as shown on page 150. Don't overlook a broken brick, either (see page 150). The freezing and thawing of any water that gets in the crack could cause more extensive damage.

As with all masonry repairs, keep the mortar damp for several days—rapid drying weakens the bond. Mist the repair daily, or tape a sheet of plastic over it to keep it moist.

> ### YOU'LL NEED...
> **SKILLS:** Moderate masonry skills.
> **TIME:** 1 to 2 hours to repoint an 8×8-foot area.
> **TOOLS:** Cold chisel, hammer, brush, pointing trowel, hawk, joint strike.

Repointing Bricks

Clean out all loose mortar to a depth of about ¾ inch. Take care not to chip the brick itself.

Brush the joints with a scrub brush, then wet them down so the bricks won't draw water from the mortar.

Mix mortar to the consistency of peanut butter. Pick it up by slicing off a hunk and slipping a trowel under it.

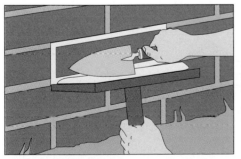

A hawk brings mortar right to the work. Pack mortar into the joint with the trowel's tip, then slice off excess.

After pointing eight to ten bricks, rub the joints with a soft, wet brush. This further compacts the mortar.

Strike joints with a joint strike (see page 184). Dampen occasionally for the next two or three days.

Solving Wall Problems (continued)

REPAIRING BRICKWORK (continued)
Grouting Long Cracks

Before filling a vertical crack like the one at right, apply the test on page 144 to see if the wall is settling. If it is, you should consult a contractor. If not, loosen clinging material with a small screwdriver, then remove debris with a vacuum cleaner.

Force grout into the crack with a pointing trowel. Use vinyl-based grout, which has the elasticity to move with expansion and contraction of surrounding material.

Replacing a Damaged Brick

If your home is old, the most difficult part of replacing a brick will be finding a matching brick. Chip out a piece and take it to a used brick dealer. Also note the face dimensions of the brick; sizes may vary substantially.

For the work, you will need mortar, a bricklayer's chisel, a heavy hammer or mallet, a trowel, and a tool for striking mortar joints (see page 211). When working with the hammer and chisel, protect your eyes with goggles or safety glasses and your chisel hand with a leather work glove.

The illustrations at right show how to replace a full brick. (If you must cut a brick, see page 210.) Coat porous bricks (unglazed bricks) with silicone masonry sealer to minimize water absorption and future repairs.

1. Chip out the damaged brick one piece at a time. Remove the old mortar, too. Thoroughly clean out dust and debris from the cavity.

2. Dampen the surrounding bricks to retard water absorption from the mortar, then lay fresh mortar on the bottom and sides of the cavity.

3. Wet the brick, mortar its top, slide it into place, and pack mortar into the joints. Scrape off excess mortar.

4. Match existing joints with the proper technique (see page 211). Use a mason's jointer or a piece of pipe.

> ### YOU'LL NEED...
> **SKILLS:** Moderate masonry skills.
> **TIME:** 30 to 60 minutes to replace one brick.
> **TOOLS:** Cold chisel, hammer, trowel, hawk, joint strike.

REPAIRING STUCCO WALLS

Of all wall materials, stucco is one of the most difficult to patch. Small cracks can be filled easily (see page 144). But if the damage is more extensive, you must chip away the old material down to the lath or masonry underneath, then build up a new surface in three layers.

Problem areas larger than 4 feet square usually require that the entire wall be restuccoed—a job for an experienced masonry contractor. Small, do-it-yourself patching jobs can be done during mild weather when there's no danger of freezing. Plan on the project taking at least three days. Wait at least six weeks before painting, then prime and paint with a concrete coating (see pages 553–554).

Colored stucco is difficult to match. Experiment with pigments, keeping in mind that colors will fade as much as 70 percent by the time the stucco dries. Never let the coloring pigment exceed 3 percent of the batch's total volume.

To blend the patch's final surface with surrounding areas, use one of the concrete finishing techniques described on page 184.

YOU'LL NEED...

SKILLS: Moderate to advanced masonry skills.
TIME: 3 working days for a large patch extended over 10 to 12 days to cover drying time.
TOOLS: Trowel, improvised rake, spray hose, metal straightedge.

1. Apply the first coat of stucco to a depth about ¼ inch below surrounding surfaces. Press with the trowel to embed it firmly in the lath.

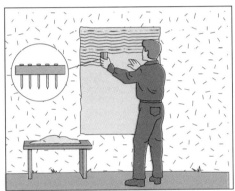

2. When the stucco begins to firm up, scratch it with an improvised rake made by driving nails through a piece of wood.

3. Mist the scratch coat with fine spray, keeping it damp for two days. In windy or sunny weather, repeat several times daily.

4. Apply the second (brown) coat to within about ⅛ inch of the surface and level it off with a metal straightedge, as shown.

5. "Float" the brown coat by working it with a trowel until water comes to the surface. (See page 183 for more about floating).

6. Mist the brown coat for two days, wait a week, moisten again, and smooth on the finish coat. Texture it within one-half hour.

Solving Wall Problems (continued)

GUARDING AGAINST TERMITES

Watch for these devastating insects in early spring and fall, when reproductive members of termite colonies sprout wings, take off on mating flights, discard the wings, and establish nesting places. If you find a pile of wings, suspect a colony nearby.

Termites fall into two groups—subterranean (those that eat wood but nest underground) and nonsubterranean (those that live in the wood itself).

Nonsubterranean wood-boring insects, including powder-post beetles and carpenter ants, as well as several termite species, remain above ground. Sometimes, you can spot their entrance holes in the wood's surface; a pile of sawdust pellets is another telltale sign.

If you suspect termites, call a licensed pest exterminator. Don't panic—although these pests can demolish a house, it would take years to do so.

Exterminators surround the house with what amounts to an underground moat of insecticide, usually by injecting chemicals into the soil with special equipment. Isolated from the earth, worker termites in the house soon die of thirst; the remainder of the colony starves or moves on.

Nonsubterranean termites confine their activities to limited areas, such as the inside of a porch column, a window, or a door frame. If the wood has not been weakened structurally, extermination consists of boring holes into the wood and injecting a liquid or powdered chemical. If the damage is more extensive, the wood member must be cut away and replaced with new treated lumber.

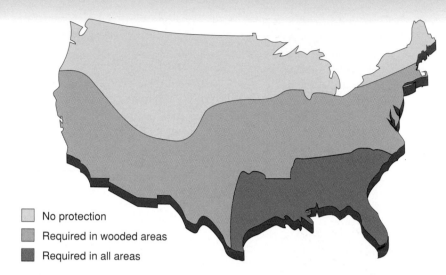

☐ No protection

☐ Required in wooded areas

☐ Required in all areas

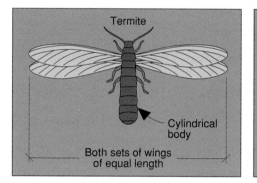

Termites resemble ants, but have cylindrical bodies. During the mating season, they have two pairs of equal-sized wings.

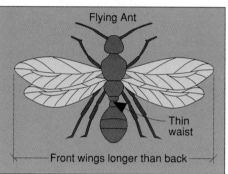

Flying ants have thinner waists than termites, and one pair of wings is shorter than the other.

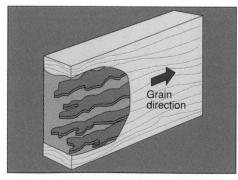

Subterranean termites form tunnels in the direction of the wood grain, sometimes leaving nothing but a shell.

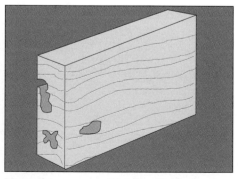

Nonsubterranean termites burrow across the grain. Occasionally their tunnels break through the surface.

APPLYING TERMITICIDE

Most termites live in the forest, where they have an abundant supply of food in the form of dead and fallen trees. They don't distinguish between wood in its natural state and wood that has been through a sawmill, however. If you don't want termites to picnic on your house, the first steps are to clear the site of any construction debris and block the easy routes from the soil into your home's wood structure.

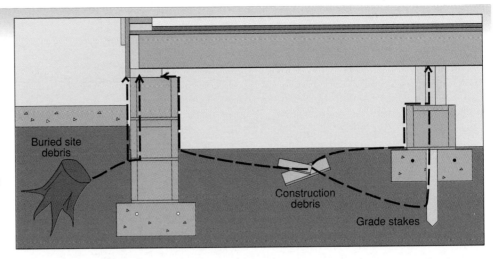

Most homes in termite-infested areas are built on crawlspace foundations. Termiticide should be applied around the bases of all rigid structures that are between the soil and the sill or floor framing. These structures include masonry walls, masonry piers, and plumbing pipes. As a second line of defense, foundation walls and piers should be capped with sheet-metal termite shields.

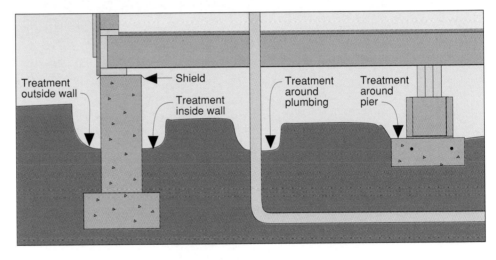

Full-basement foundations are treated as if they were boats floating in a sea of termites. The soil outside the wall is treated all the way to the footing, and termiticide is applied to the entire soil surface before the basement floor slab is poured. If the foundation wall consists of hollow masonry blocks, the wall is capped with solid concrete and a sheet-metal shield.

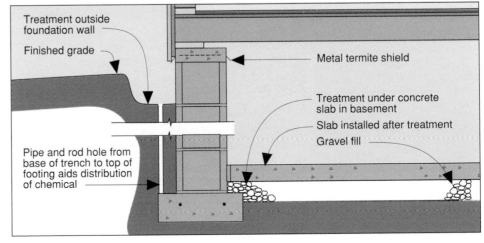

Installing New Siding Materials

No other improvement can do as much for your home's appearance and livability as a new exterior surface. Re-side to create an entirely different appearance, or duplicate the old look using a low-maintenance product that won't need painting for decades, if ever. The range of siding materials and styles available (below and on page 155) is almost staggering.

But before you choose a siding for your house, examine what's underneath. Tightly interlocked new siding greatly reduces air infiltration through exterior walls. It won't make up for lack of insulation and sheathing, however. If you're looking for energy savings, you might be wise to strip walls to their sheathing or studs and upgrade the R-value with insulation (see pages 390–391). Or, perhaps the answer is to beef-up existing insulation with a polystyrene backing that's available with some manufactured sidings (see page 159).

MATERIAL MATTERS   CHOOSING SIDING

Material	Appearance	Features/Price	Durability
Wood, plywood	Widest range of styles, textures and finishes; available preprimed, presealed, or vinyl-clad	Difficult to apply over existing siding; prices vary from low (yellow pine, fir) to high (redwood, cedar, plywoods)	Depends upon species and pretreatment
Hardboard	Lap and vertical panel styles with a variety of textures and prefinished colors; also available in preprimed form	No problems with grain, splitting, or knots; large panels mean fewer joints for easier installation and greater weather resistance; color selection limited; moderate price	Vinyl-clad types guaranteed up to 30 years; preprimed types must be repainted periodically
Fiberglass	Shingles, shakes, and a few lap designs; usually textured	Of some insulation value; resistant to fire and termites; prone to splitting; low price	Guaranteed up to 20 years, but appearance deteriorates
Aluminum	Wide range of lap, vertical, shingle, and shake styles; broad selection of prefinished colors	Most popular; choice of baked enamel or plastic finishes at prices ranging from moderate to high; lightweight, unaffected by fire and termites; Drawbacks include dents easily, noisy, conducts electricity	Guaranteed up to 35 years for plastic-clad types; easily cleaned; needn't be repainted
Vinyl	Limited choice of lap and vertical styles; more and more colors becoming available	Impervious to most perils; color is impregnated all the way through; higher rate of expansion and contraction makes application critical; most costly	Lifetime guarantees; cannot be repainted

CHOOSING AND BUYING SIDING

Wood—once the only practical choice for nonmasonry walls—has now become the standard against which other materials are compared. Its competitors include hardboard, fiberglass, aluminum, and solid vinyl. The chart on page 154 summarizes the properties of these materials.

The type of siding that you select depends largely on the appearance you want, local availability, and how much you're willing to invest against maintenance savings later on. All types simulate wood styles with varying degrees of success (see below). If you like the look of painted boards or shingles, any manufactured siding will come close. Imitations of natural wood finishes and textures are less convincing.

Most of the alternatives to wood eliminate its susceptibility to rot, splitting, warping, and termites. And most—including wood—now are available with factory finishes that do not need to be repainted. Vinyl formulations, the best of these coatings, protect surfaces from deterioration for up to 35 years. Solid vinyl siding is so tough that it's often guaranteed for the life of your house.

Manufactured sidings have made giant strides, but wood still remains the most popular. Redwood and cedar heartwoods naturally resist rot and insects and never need painting. You can stain them or let the weather bleach the boards over time to a silvery gray. Less expensive woods are available presealed for a low maintenance, natural appearance. If you decide against prepainted wood or hardboard siding, you can buy these materials preprimed with an undercoat that increases the life of the final finish.

Although more expensive than board sidings, plywood types offer several advantages. The 4×8-, 4×9-, or 4×10-foot panels go up faster and seal tighter than individual boards or shingles. In certain instances, you may not need sheathing underneath the plywood siding. (See page 158 for more about plywood siding.)

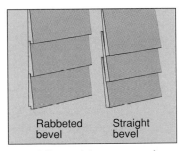

Lap siding, either squared off or beveled, is applied horizontally, with boards lapped about 1 inch.

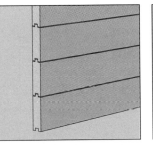

You can install tongue-and-groove siding horizontally, vertically, or even diagonally.

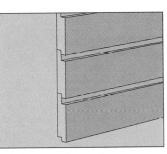

Shiplap or channel-groove siding has rabbeted edges to interlock boards. Install horizontally or vertically.

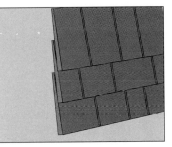

Shingles have a smooth appearance, adapt readily to misshapen walls, and are easy to apply.

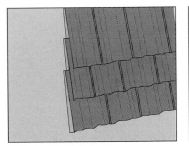

Shakes are like shingles, but have an irregular, hand-split look. They're more expensive than shingles.

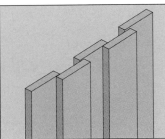

Board-on-board siding is applied vertically and lapped about 1 inch. Widths may be random or regular.

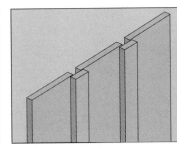

Board-and-batten siding is vertical. With reverse board and batten, the battens are applied first.

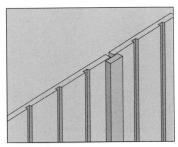

Grooves give plywood sheets the appearance of boards. Joints may be shiplapped or covered with battens.

Installing New Siding Materials (continued)

APPLYING WOOD SHINGLES AND SHAKES

Of all siding materials, shingles and shakes are the easiest to install. The job is repetitive, but requires only basic carpentry skills. Nail up a batten guide strip for each course, fit each piece ⅛ inch from its neighbor, and drive in two or three nails.

You can apply shingles and shakes directly over old wood siding. If your house has wood or plywood sheathing, you can remove the old siding, repair defects, and put up new building wrap first. You can use the same techniques shown here for wood shingles and shakes to install fiberglass or composition types also, but be sure to check manufacturer's recommendations.

Shingle grades run from 1 to 4, in a variety of sizes and textures. Choose No. 1 or No. 2 grade material for exterior walls. No. 3 and No. 4 grade are fine for outside use, but only where appearance isn't a factor, as in the first layer in double-course shingling.

To apply double-course shingles, nail up two layers, one on top of the other (see below). This lets you expose more of the shingle surface and creates a deeper shadow line between courses. Expose slightly less than one-half of the shingle for single coursing, about two-thirds for double-course applications.

For a neat, uniform look, carefully plot exposures so they'll line up with window tops and sills, then hold courses exactly level. If you want to add design interest, you can nail them such that the bottom butt edges are random lengths.

Shingles up to 8 inches wide need two rustproof shingle nails each; with wider shingles, use a third nail.

Soak bundles of shingles for several hours before you begin, or the wood may expand and pull away during the first heavy rain.

> ### YOU'LL NEED...
> **SKILLS:** Basic carpentry skills.
> **TIME:** 6 to 8 hours for a 10×25-foot wall.
> **TOOLS:** Saw, level, and hammer (renting a pneumatic nailer speeds up large jobs).

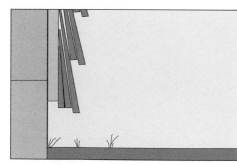

1. Use two shingles for the first course, three if you'll be double coursing. Overlap the foundation about 1 inch.

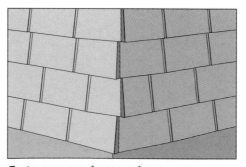

2. Drive nails ¾ inch from each edge and at least an inch above where the butt edges of the next course will fall.

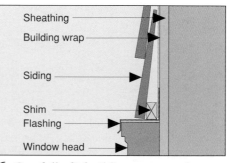

3. To keep butts perfectly level, nail up a guide strip as shown. Always stagger edge joints from course to course.

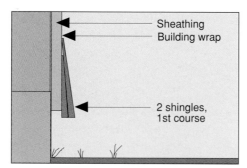

4. For double-coursing, use longer nails. Edges of the outer course should be ½ inch below the undercourse.

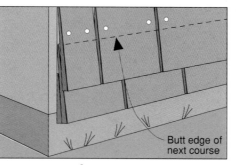

5. At corners, butt each course alternately, mitering edges or covering them with wood or metal molding.

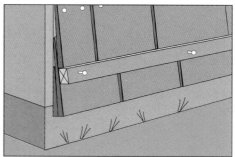

6. Carefully fit building wrap and shingles over flashing atop windows. Shim with partial shingles to shed rain.

APPLYING BOARD SIDING

Installing horizontal wood siding is much the same as installing wood shingles and shakes (page 156). The work calls for much more precise calculations, however, and may require extensive carpentry, as well.

You must decide first whether to retain the existing siding as a nailing base or to rip it off and start over. With old tongue-and-groove boards, you'll have a flat surface to which you can nail directly. The new siding will make your walls about ¼ inch thicker, so remember that you'll have to fur out door and window frames by that amount.

With old lap siding, you must fur out the walls first (see below). The ¾-inch air space between new and old sidings adds valuable insulation space, but it means door and window openings may be recessed by as much as 1½ inches.

Ensure that boards will remain perfectly level from course to course, and that courses will line up with the tops and bottoms of door and window frames. Carpenters typically calculate locations for lap joints in advance with the aid of a story pole (see page 209). Then they mark the laps on frames and on walls around the corner from the one they're working on. Plan to overlap boards by at least 1 inch. Increase this slightly, if necessary, for a proper fit around openings and at the eaves.

Vertical applications—especially with random-width boards—require fewer painstaking calculations.

Consider openings and corners before you get to them, though, and be sure to plumb each board.

Handle all siding lumber carefully, especially prefinished and preprimed types. These relatively soft woods often split when nailed near an edge. To keep this from happening, drill pilot holes first or use special preblunted siding nails.

YOU'LL NEED...

SKILLS: Intermediate to advanced carpentry skills.
TIME: Several days to side an entire house.
TOOLS: Hammer, drill, handsaw, miter saw, level, chalk line.

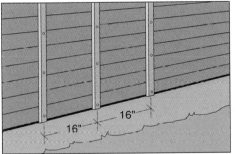

Apply horizontal siding over lap siding by nailing up 1×3s; drive nails through old siding into studs beneath.

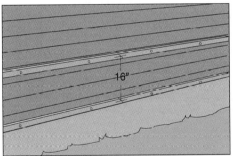

Nailing strips for vertical siding should run horizontally. Space them uniformly, 16 inches from center to center.

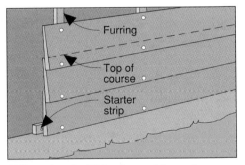

Siding that is 10 inches wide or less requires two nails driven into each stud. Wider siding requires three nails.

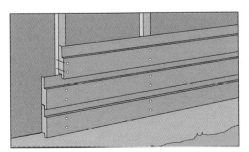

Channel-groove siding gets two nails across the width of each board. Nail about 1 inch from the board's edge.

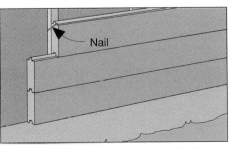

Tongue-and-groove siding is nailed through the tongue of each course. Wide boards may need a second nail.

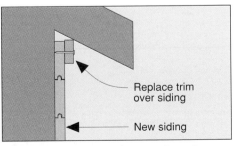

Siding should extend up under trim boards that conceal rafter ends. Reuse trim you pried loose or replace it.

Installing New Siding Materials (continued)

APPLYING PANEL SIDING

Large hardboard and plywood panels cover a wall rapidly—and with panels as slender as 7/16 inch thick, panels minimize trim problems around doors and windows. To install them yourself, you'll need a good grounding in basic carpentry techniques plus an assistant to help handle the sheets.

Some panels come with rabbeted edges that interlock to make a vertical shiplap joint; others simply butt together, their seams covered by a batten strip or special T-shaped molding (shown below).

Panels should be nailed to studs, spacing nails 6 inches apart on edges and 12 inches apart on intermediate studs. Use rust-resistant ring-shank nails or color-matching nails that are available from the manufacturers of prefinished siding materials. Never drive panels tightly together; compensate for expansion by leaving a 1/16-inch space and filling the space with caulk.

Cut paneling with the good face down if you're using a saber or circular saw or with the good face up with a hand or stationary power saw. An inaccurate cut will spoil an entire panel, so plot dimensions on graph paper and double-check them before you begin sawing. Remember to seal cuts in preprimed and prefinished panels before installation (check the manufacturer's specifications for the right sealer).

Metal accessories, similar to the ones shown on page 159, simplify fitting panels together at corners and around doors and windows. Or, if you'd rather, you can fabricate your own corner treatments, as shown below. (For more about working with plywood and hardboard, see pages 504–509 and 512–513.)

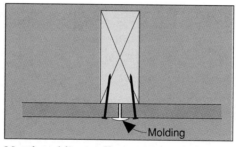

To nail shiplap joints, nail up one sheet, caulk, then install the next. Don't try to drive one nail through both lips.

Metal moldings offer an inconspicuous way to finish off butt joints. Some prefinished moldings simply snap into place between the panels.

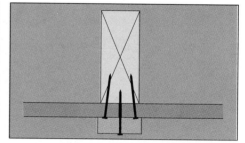

You also can cover butt joints with wood battens. For a board-and-batten effect (see page 155), space more vertical strips across the panel's width.

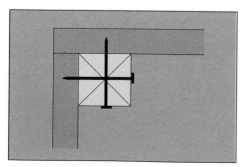

Finish inside corners with 2×2 trim, as shown. You can also select from a variety of cove moldings milled for this purpose.

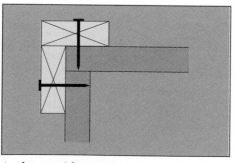

At the outside corners, lap a pair of 1×3s or 1×4s. To accommodate expansion, nail them to the siding, not to each other.

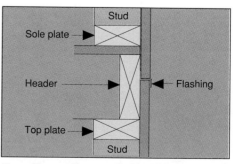

On taller walls, you'll encounter horizontal joints. Nail bottom panel in place, caulk, lay flashing in place, and nail top panel.

APPLYING MANUFACTURED SIDING

Aluminum, steel, hardboard, mineral fiber, and vinyl sidings are designed especially for re-siding applications and are relatively easy to install. Check the warranty, however, to see if you risk voiding it by doing the work yourself. If not, install the siding by closely following the manufacturer's instructions.

Aluminum, steel, and vinyl siding have top and bottom lips. You nail one course through prepunched holes in the top lip, then interlock the top edge with the bottom of the next. Install mineral fiber, plywood, and hardboard types as you would conventional lumber (see page 157), or attach them to metal channel moldings between courses.

All manufactured sidings use standardized, lightweight components that go up fast and fit snugly, with none of the warping and splitting problems prone to wood. Vinyl siding, however, can turn brittle at low temperatures and may lose its shape with exposure to very strong sunlight. Hardboard siding can absorb condensation from within walls, so don't use it unless there is a vapor barrier in the wall. Metal siding must be grounded because it conducts electricity.

Aluminum and vinyl siding expand and contract considerably with temperature changes. That's why they come with slots, instead of holes, for nailing. Locate nails near the center of these slots—and don't drive the nails so tightly that they'll impede the inevitable movement.

Beware of siding companies that approach you with hard-sell presentations and too-good-to-be-true financing arrangements. The vast majority of siding contractors are reputable, but there are always a few fast-buck operators in the field.

YOU'LL NEED...

SKILLS: Basic carpentry and sheet-metal skills.
TIME: Several days but manufactured siding can be applied more quickly than wooden lap siding.
TOOLS: Hammer, drill, saw, zip tool (often provided by manufacturer).

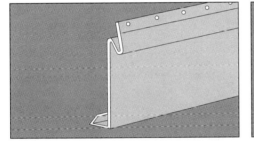

Aluminum and vinyl sidings come in strips with interlocking top and bottom flanges for tight joints between strips.

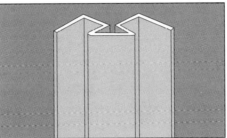

Inside corner posts usually are installed first, carefully caulked, then plumbed so each course will be level.

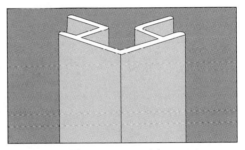

Cover outside corners with continuous strips (shown) or put individual caps over each course. Caps go up last.

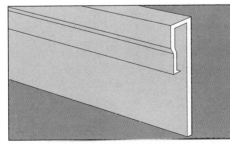

Because manufactured sidings are fairly thin, they present few problems around openings. This channel fits under windowsills.

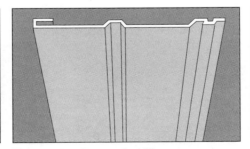

Using manufactured soffits, you can extend a new siding job up under the eaves, thereby avoiding chronic repainting and repair problems.

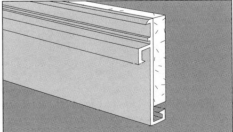

Insulation-backed siding does a good job of muffling noise—a problem with metal sidings. Thermal resistance is only fair, however.

Solving Window and Door Problems

There are few houses that don't occasionally suffer shattered glass, a torn screen, or other minor damage to windows and doors. Because few repairmen find it worth their while to make house calls for these simple ailments, finding someone to do the work can be a big problem. If you'll take the time to learn the techniques on the following pages, however, you needn't be at anyone's mercy.

Note that this chapter covers only the exterior parts of windows and doors or parts, such as glass, that are normally repaired from the outside. Interior jobs are explained on pages 67–76. To learn about weather stripping, see pages 385–389.

REPLACING BROKEN GLASS WINDOWPANES

Faced with a broken window, you have three choices: 1) remove the sash and take it to a hardware store or glass shop for reglazing; 2) buy a new pane that is cut to size, and install it yourself; or 3) cut the glass yourself from standard-sized sheets kept on hand for such emergencies.

Dismantling a window (see page 67) sometimes is far more work than simply replacing the glass. Cutting glass (page 161) isn't difficult, but you might break a pane or two before getting the knack. If you opt for the second course, you can make the repair yourself in under an hour.

Before buying glass, measure carefully, as shown below. Check the thickness, too (most panes are ⅛-inch). You'll need glazier's points, or spring clips if the frame is metal, and a can of glazing compound. Try to get the push-in-type glazier's points (shown on page 161)

because they are easier to insert.

Caution: Always wear heavy gloves when handling broken glass. Take care with the sharp edges and corners of new panes, too.

> ### YOU'LL NEED...
> **SKILLS:** Basic skills.
> **TIME:** About 30 minutes a pane.
> **TOOLS:** Putty knife, scraper, caulking gun, brush.

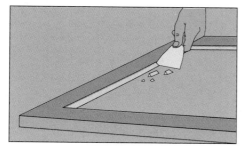

1. Chipping off old glazing compound can be the hardest part of the job. Use a putty knife or old chisel, or soften old glazing with a soldering iron.

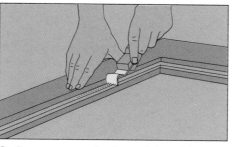

2. Scrape away the last of the old compound, then roughen the groove with a scraper so the new glazing compound will adhere properly.

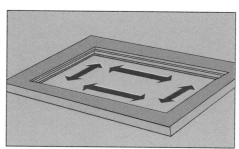

3. Sashes aren't always perfectly square, so measure at several points, then subtract ⅛ inch from each dimension to determine glass size.

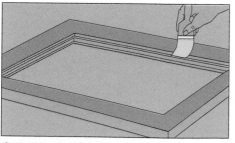

4. Prime the groove with linseed oil, turpentine, or oil-base paint. Untreated wood will draw oil from the glazing compound, shortening its life.

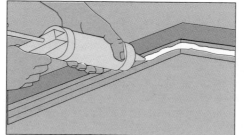

5. Before you insert the new pane, apply a ⅛-inch-thick bead of glazing compound. This helps seal and cushion the glass.

6. Line up one edge of the pane in the sash, lower it into place, and press gently with your palm or fingertips to seal it into the glazing compound.

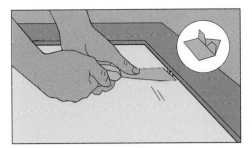

7. Press glazier's points into the sash with a putty knife. Don't push too hard or you may crack the glass.

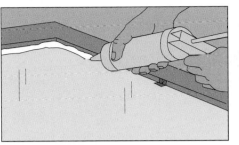

8. Apply a ¼-inch bead of glazing compound. Press it into place to make sure it sticks to both glass and wood.

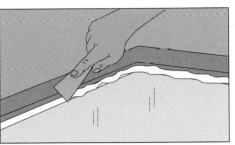

9. Bevel the compound with a putty knife. If compound sticks to the knife, wet it with turpentine.

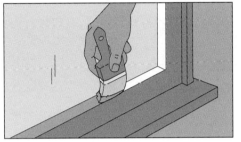

10. Let the compound dry for a week before painting. Paint should overlap the glass about ¹⁄₁₆ inch for a tight seal.

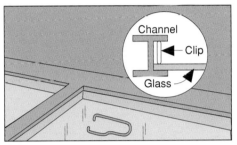

Spring clips substitute for glazier's points in steel sashes. Install as shown. Metal windows needn't be primed.

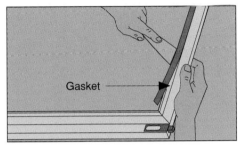

In an aluminum storm window, a rubber gasket, forced into place with a putty knife, holds the glass.

CUTTING GLASS

When you cut glass, you take advantage of its inherent brittleness. Scoring it with a cutting wheel focuses all its breaking tendencies along a single line. A smooth, even score lets you snap the glass with ease. The trick is to make the right score in a single stroke. If you exert too little pressure on the glass, the cutting wheel will skip; if you exert too much pressure, the edges will crack or chip.

When cutting glass, always work on a flat, clean surface. Use a carpenter's square—or guide the cutter with a strip of hardwood that has been dampened so it won't slide across the surface. Don't wait too long after scoring to snap glass—it tends to heal itself. Because of its properties, do not attempt to cut safety glass

YOU'LL NEED...

SKILLS: Basic skills.
TIME: 5 to 10 minutes per pane.
TOOLS: Glass cutter, brush, square, tape measure, wooden straightedge, linseed oil or other lubricant.

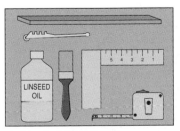

1. Tools include glass cutter, wooden straightedge, brush, linseed oil, square, and measuring tape.

2. Lubricate the line, then draw the cutter along the straightedge in one firm, smooth stroke.

3. Make the break by laying glass with the scored side up over a board and pressing down on both sides.

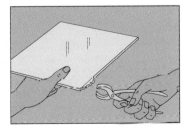

4. Nip away irregularities with pliers. Teeth in the glass cutter also are designed for this purpose.

Solving Window and Door Problems (continued)

REPLACING SILLS AND SADDLES

Windowsills take a terrific beating. Rain not only hits them directly but also cascades onto them from windows and siding. Angled as they are, windowsills catch plenty of sunlight as well. This alternate soaking and baking process eventually makes them veritable sponges that can't hold paint for very long periods.

The best preventive is a couple of coats of paint applied annually. If a sill is too far gone for that, there are two alternatives. First, rebuild it with a fiberglass-type product made especially for the purpose. Second, install a new sill. Door sills, called saddles or thresholds, also fail over time. Replace either with the procedures illustrated here.

Determine if the sill or saddle fits under the jambs on either side, then measure, and buy a new piece. The drawings below show how to install a new piece of wood in either situation—but you might opt to replace a saddle with a preformed, predrilled metal or plastic unit.

Remove the old saddle or sill. This probably will be the most difficult part of the job. Use a chisel or old screwdriver to probe for nails that may be holding the piece in place. If you can't get the nails out, in the end you simply may have to saw out a section, as shown below, or demolish it by splitting it along the grain with a hammer and chisel, then pulling out the splintered remains.

If you can get the old one out intact, use it as a template for marking the replacement. If not, measure carefully so you get a snug fit.

Prime all sides and edges of a new sill before installing it. For more about how windows and doors are put together, see pages 67–68 and 79. To learn about weather-stripping-type thresholds, see page 389.

> ### YOU'LL NEED...
> **SKILLS:** Basic carpentry skills.
> **TIME:** 1 to 2 hours per sill.
> **TOOLS:** Backsaw, chisel, hammer, nail set, drill, caulking gun.

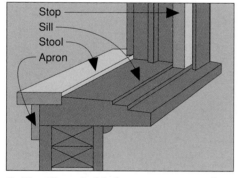

1. You'll probably have to remove the apron, stool, and stop molding to remove a sill. Pry out these pieces carefully to avoid damage.

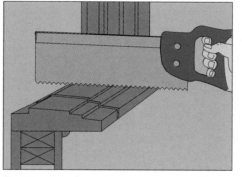

2. You may have to saw out a section from the center of the sill, then drive the end pieces inward. Use these as patterns for the new piece.

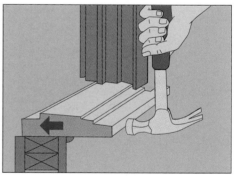

3. Gently tap the new sill or saddle into place. Don't force it. If it resists, remove and sand the ends, beveling them slightly.

4. Using rust-resistant nails, secure the sill from underneath. Countersink the nails, then caulk the nailheads and the ends of the sill.

5. Nail a saddle at both ends and in the middle. Countersink and hide nailheads with putty. Caulk both ends of the saddle.

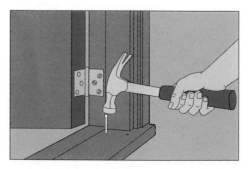

REPAIRING AND MAINTAINING SCREENS AND STORMS

Rustproof screen materials (see page 164) and combination screen/storm sashes (see page 165) have taken the semiannual drudgery out of securing a home against drafts and insects. But even low-maintenance types of screens and storms require occasional attention. Check caulking around the frames of combination units. Clean oxidized aluminum with car polish. Vacuum dirt from screening. Mend punctured screening with a dab of quick-drying household cement. Darn a tear in metal screens with fine wire or fishing line, but patch larger holes, as shown below. If you have plastic or fiberglass screens, you're better off replacing the entire screen.

Wood-frame screens and storms are more trouble, but careful monitoring and diligent maintenance will minimize hassles. Check each unit when you take it down, set aside those that need help, and repair them at your leisure.

Consider, too, how many windows you actually open up during the summer months. Leaving a storm window in place not only saves you some work, it also helps keep a room cool.

Adjust or replace screen/storm door closers as soon as they begin to malfunction—doors that slam or flap in the breeze don't last long.

Adjustments vary widely. Look for a knurled knob, screw, or ratchet at one end of the pneumatic tube. On some types, the tube itself rotates.

Paint wood frames whenever they need it. Shrinkage and warping reduce their weather-stripping value. (For information about weather stripping storm windows and doors, see pages 385–389.)

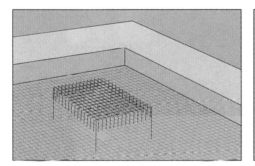

To patch metal screens, cut a patch, unravel a few strands, fit patch over hole, and bend strands back.

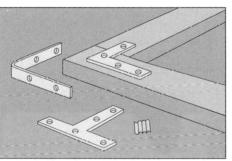

Reinforce corner joints with mending plates. Corrugated fasteners also work well for mitered joints.

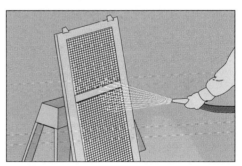

Clean screens with a blast from a hose; scrub metal screens with a stiff brush. Don't forget the frame's edges.

Paint rusty steel screens with a pad. To unclog holes, rub back side with a dry pad. Let dry; then paint back side.

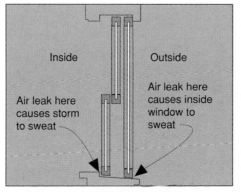

Air leaks around interior sashes or storms cause sweating. Condensation forms on the sash that is not leaking.

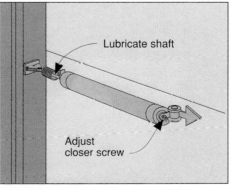

Lubricate door closers every fall by wiping the shaft with oil. Check the adjustment for proper operation, too.

Solving Window and Door Problems (continued)

REPLACING SCREENING

You install screening in much the same way an artist stretches a canvas—fasten it at one end of the frame, pull the material taut, then secure at the sides and other end. The drawings below show how to improvise a "stretcher" with some 1×2s and wood wedges for wood-frame windows. Aluminum frames have a spline-and-channel structure that stretches the screen.

When removing moldings from wood frames, begin with the middle rail and spring the molding loose with a chisel or putty knife. Always work from the center to the ends, applying pressure near brads. If a molding breaks, you can find a reasonable facsimile at a lumberyard. Ask for screen molding.

For the screen material, you can choose aluminum, plastic, fiberglass, copper, or bronze. Aluminum is inconspicuous, but is subject to staining; fiberglass and plastic won't stain, but their filaments are thicker, which affects visibility; copper and bronze must be coated with spar varnish periodically to prevent staining. Buy 18/14 mesh or finer.

> **YOU'LL NEED...**
>
> **SKILLS:** Basic skills.
> **TIME:** 30 minutes per screen.
> **TOOLS:** Chisel or putty knife, scissors or shears, utility knife, staple gun, saw, spline roller.

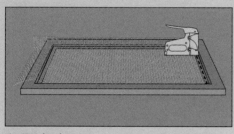

1. With shears, cut material slightly wider and at least 1 foot longer than the frame, then staple the top edge.

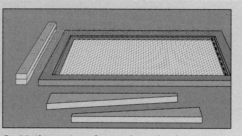

2. Nail a strip of wood to the bench or floor, roll screen over it, and nail another strip on top of the first.

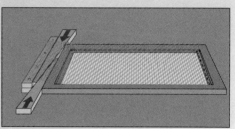

3. Insert wedges between the cleats and frame on either side. Gently tap the wedges until the screening is tight.

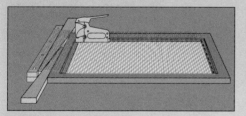

4. Staple screening to the bottom edge, then the sides. If the frame has a center rail, fasten screening to it last.

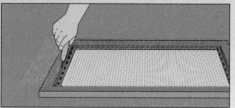

5. Trim off excess and refit the moldings with small brads. Countersink brads and fill holes with wood filler.

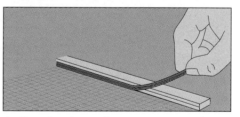

1. For aluminum frames, remove the old mesh by prying out the spline. You may need to buy new splining.

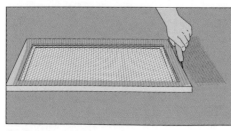

2. Square up the frame, lay new screening over it, and cut screen the same size as the outside of the frame.

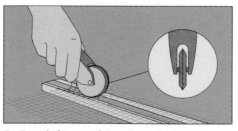

3. Bend the mesh's edges and force them into the channel with the convex wheel of the spline roller.

4. Force the tubular spline into the channel with the concave wheel of the spline roller, tightening the mesh.

Installing New Combination Windows and Storm Doors

Door and window units for new construction arrive with doors or sashes already hung in their frames. Carpenters build "rough" openings, tip the units in place, and add trim.

Combination screen/storm doors and windows also arrive assembled. Because openings for these units are finished, combinations usually are made to order. Installation may be included in the purchase price, but you may save 10 to 15 percent by installing them yourself (see below).

Prehung exterior doors are installed in much the same way as interior ones (see pages 85–86).

> ### YOU'LL NEED...
> **SKILLS:** Moderate carpentry skills.
> **TIME:** 2 to 4 hours for a window.
> **TOOLS:** Hammer, drill, screwdriver, caulking gun.

CHOOSING AND BUYING COMBINATION UNITS

Combination windows and doors pay for themselves with energy savings. Beware of shoddy products, however. Poorly made or poorly fitted units leak air, are difficult to operate, and eventually turn into eyesores.

What are the considerations? Check the corners of the frames.

Lapped joints are stronger and tighter than mitered ones. If you can see light through the joints, you can be sure that they'll admit air.

Combinations come in double- or triple-track designs. With double-track units, you must remove and replace the bottom sash (either storm or screen) seasonally. Triple-track units have tracks for the top and bottom storm sashes and the screen sash,

and thus are self-storing—you don't have to remove the storm or screen sash you are not using. Generally speaking, the deeper the tracks are, the higher a unit's insulation value will be.

After installing combinations, make sure each window and door is well-caulked, operates smoothly, and seals tightly. Clean and lubricate the tracks annually to lengthen their life span.

INSTALLING COMBINATION WINDOWS

Installing combinations is quick; the effect on comfort is noticeable; and the chore of switching storms and screens is past. The key to buying and installing these units is accurate measurements. Check and double check. Do not assume that any of your windows are the same size.

Make sure your units have two or three ventilation holes in the bottom frame members to let moisture out.

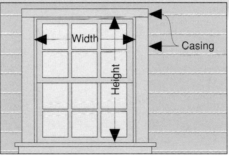

1. Measure the width between the inside edges of the side casings and height between top casing and sill.

2. Place the combination on the sill, center it between side casings, and trace outline with a pencil on casings.

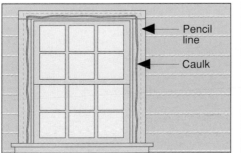

3. Using a caulk gun, run a bead of acrylic caulk around the casings about 1 inch inside the pencil line.

4. Align the window frame with the pencil line, press into caulk, and fasten to casing with aluminum screws.

5. Caulk around the frame where it meets the top and side casings. Smooth caulk with a wet finger.

Installing New Combination Windows and Storm Doors (continued)

INSTALLING A STORM DOOR

Assuming your exterior door is the standard 3-foot-wide × 6-foot, 8-inch-high door, you can use a prehung storm door of standard size.

A combination storm door features interchangeable glass panels for winter and screen panels for summer. Some have both upper and lower glass and screen panels. These maximize solar gain during the winter and ventilation during the summer. There are versions with solid lower panels, which are more practical if you have children and/or animals that constantly push against and damage the lower screen unit.

Don't be too frugal when it comes to doors that handle a lot of traffic. Only the highest quality door will withstand children running in and out and parents carrying grocery bags and firewood in both arms.

> ### YOU'LL NEED...
> **SKILLS:** Basic carpentry skills.
> **TIME:** 2 hours.
> **TOOLS:** Hacksaw, screwdriver, drill, caulking gun, hammer, level, tape measure.

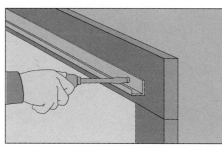

1. Temporarily screw the top drip cap to the top casing at the height specified by the door manufacturer.

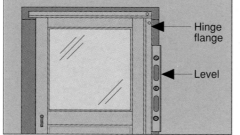

2. Measure from bottom of drip cap to sill along hinge side casing. Cut hinge flange ⅛ inch shorter than this length.

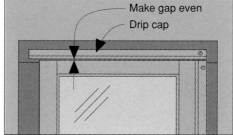

3. Using acrylic caulk, lay a bead of caulk along the back side of the hinge flange where it will meet the casing.

4. Line up the top of hinge flange with the edge of drip cap and fasten flange at the top with an aluminum screw.

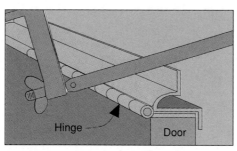

5. Plumb the hinge flange in the opening, then fasten it to the casing with the remainder of the screws.

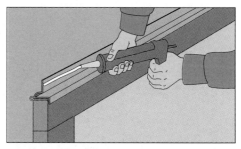

6. Remove the drip cap, caulk its back side, and reinstall it so that the gap between door and cap is even.

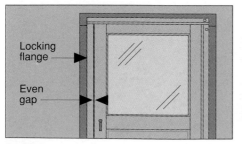

7. Measure, cut, caulk, and install the latching flange so that the gap between the door and the flange is even.

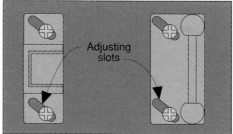

8. Test the door latching action. Adjust the latching pin, if necessary, so that the door closes easily but snugly.

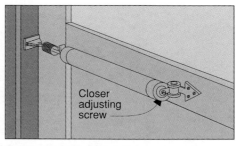

9. Install and adjust the pneumatic door closer. Install and adjust the door sweep if there is one.

Installing New Windows and Doors

Doors and windows require special framing around them to provide structural support to the floor or roof above and a sturdy framework to attach the door to.

The framing for a door consists of a header supported by king studs and jack studs on either side of the door. These studs transfer the weight of the home's structure to the sole plate below. Headers are built from two 2×8s, 2×10s, or 2×12s that sandwich a ¾-inch-thick piece of plywood. Windows have a similar framing around them, but they also have cripple studs below to support the window's sill.

Although the framing for a sliding door is shown here, the framing for a standard hinged door is similar. The opening for a hinged door may have only one cripple stud above the header because the opening is narrower. See page 32 for an illustration of framing around a hinged door.

Manufacturers of doors and windows usually specify the size of the rough opening needed, so consult the measurements provided with a new window before you start to build the framing. Custom windows can be ordered from several manufacturers but are frequently more expensive than standard size windows.

Because exterior doors and windows can be heavy, have a helper assist you when placing the unit in position. You'll also need someone to hold the window or door in place for the brief time when you shim the unit so that it is plumb and level.

ANATOMY OF FRAMING FOR A SLIDING DOOR

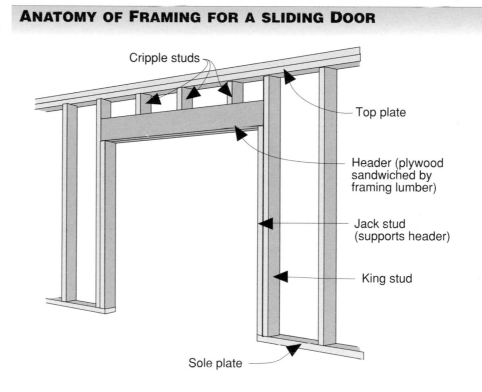

Cripple studs

Top plate

Header (plywood sandwiched by framing lumber)

Jack stud (supports header)

King stud

Sole plate

ANATOMY OF FRAMING FOR A WINDOW

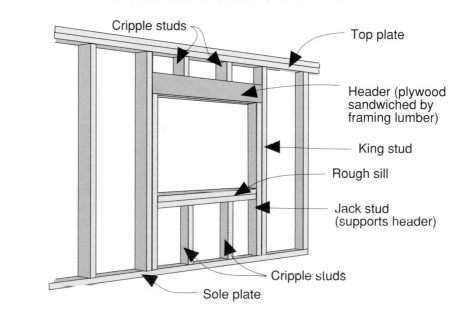

Cripple studs

Top plate

Header (plywood sandwiched by framing lumber)

King stud

Rough sill

Jack stud (supports header)

Cripple studs

Sole plate

Installing New Windows and Doors (continued)

INSTALLING WINDOWS

Installing windows up to 3½ feet wide can be a do-it-yourself project, but it does require advanced framing experience. You must know how walls go together (see page 32) and how to keep everything plumb, level, and square.

Carefully plan the window's location. Will you run into plumbing, heating, or electrical lines? It's relatively easy to relocate wiring, but difficult to move pipes or ductwork.

Make sure you know the rough-in dimensions of the new window. The exterior opening has to be only slightly larger. Work from the inside out. Mark the window location, then remove the wall surface from ceiling to floor to the inner edge of the first stud on either side of the rough-in measurement. Cut the exterior sheathing and siding just before you insert the window.

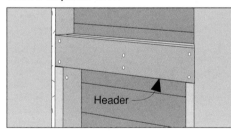

1. Mark the opening and cut from ceiling to floor along adjacent studs; leave sole plate intact. Use a chisel, then a keyhole saw.

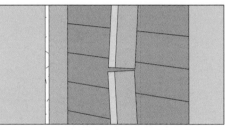

2. Remove studs interrupted by the window. Cut in the center and pry them carefully away from the sheathing.

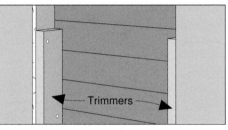

3. Nail 2×4 trimmers to the studs at either side of the opening. The trimmers support the window's header.

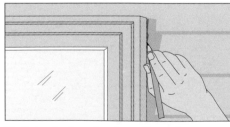

4. Build a header using two 2×6s with a scrap of ½-inch plywood sandwiched between them. Install the header on top of the trimmers.

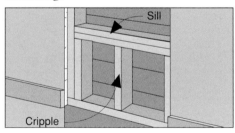

5. Construct a 2×4 sill, supported by cripple studs. Nail 2×4s between header and sill to frame side jambs at rough-in-dimension width.

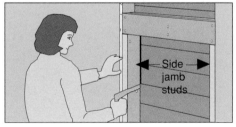

6. Cut out the exterior sheathing and siding from either the inside or outside. If you cut from outside, first drill pilot holes to mark corners.

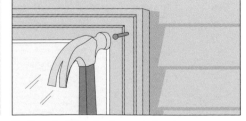

7. Set window in place from the outside, level and plumb, then trace around molding. Cut away siding to trace line.

8. Level the window again, insert shims, and nail the window to the framing through the exterior casing into the studs.

9. Inside, insert shims and nail jambs to studs. Insulate between frame and studs, refinish interior wall, attach inside casing, then caulk the exterior.

INSTALLING A SLIDING GLASS DOOR

The procedure on page 168 works for rough openings up to 3½ feet wide. For broader openings, such as large bay windows or a sliding glass door (shown here), you need larger headers: 2×8s for up to 5 feet of length, 2×10s for up to 6½ feet, and 2×12s for up to 8 feet.

Because exterior walls usually bear the weight of upper floors, you must devise a temporary support to carry the load while you modify the wall. Install braces, as shown below, and protect flooring with planks or plywood under the vertical supports.

Replacing a window with sliding glass doors that open to an outdoor living area entirely changes a home's character. So before you settle on a location, consider privacy, light, ventilation, and the traffic pattern.

Don't forget that glass loses heat rapidly at night and gains heat rapidly on sunny days. Minimize energy losses by choosing units with insulating glass and by orienting them away from prevailing winds.

Sliding glass door units are sold both with and without glass and are framed in aluminum, steel, or wood. Standard sizes are 5, 6, and 8 feet wide by 80 inches high. Unglazed types are not difficult for two people to handle. Be relatively sure you can count on good weather the day you cut through the exterior of the house. (Because it's easier to remove framing from a wide opening if you first pull off the sheathing and siding, your home's interior will be exposed throughout most of the project.) Also, be sure to have help

available to lift the header into position and install the door.

If your sliding glass door will replace an existing window, you can remove the old unit intact—sash and all. Wait until the studs are exposed on both sides, then pry them away from the window frame.

Making an opening in a brick-veneer wall calls for quite a bit more work—probably a job for a mason.

YOU'LL NEED...

SKILLS: Advanced carpentry skills.
TIME: 12 to 14 hours.
TOOLS: Hammer, chisel, carpenter's square, reciprocating saw, nail set, level, circular saw, caulking gun, tools to repair plaster or drywall.

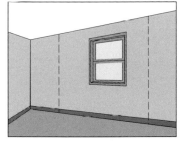

1. Mark cut lines and saw away the wall surface flush with studs on either side of the rough-in width.

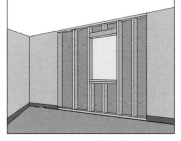

2. Remove or relocate any electrical wiring, plumbing, or heating ducts (see pages 232 and 278).

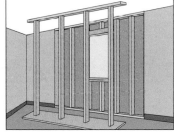

3. Set up bracing. You'll need one person to hold a 2×4 against the ceiling while you wedge in the verticals.

4. With a reciprocating saw, cut siding and sheathing at the top and sides; then cut through the sole plate.

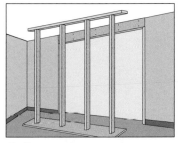

5. Cut trimmers and use them to wedge header into position. Nail trimmers to studs and toenail header.

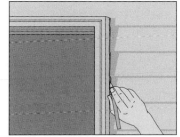

6. Place frame in opening, and mark and trim sheathing. Reinsert frame and secure loosely with screws.

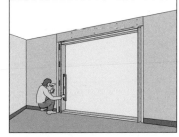

7. Level and plumb the door frame with shims. Tighten screws. Insulate between the frame and the opening.

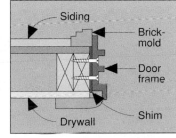

8. Molding bridges the gap between frame and siding; caulk joints. Inside, patch the wall and apply molding.

PORCHES, PATIOS, AND DECKS

Outdoor living spaces can be welcome enhancements to your home, whether they be for living, entertainment, play, or service. But sooner or later, weather takes its toll on porches, patios, and decks. The first few pages of this chapter show how to undo damage that may have occurred to porches, patios, or decks and to prevent its recurrence.

But the biggest problem with outdoor living space is that there's just not enough of it. So we've devoted the bulk of this chapter to ways you can remedy that situation. We will show you how to lay a simple brick-in-sand patio, pour a concrete slab, or get a sturdy deck project off the ground—outdoor improvements that can do wonders for the livability of outdoor spaces around your home—spring, summer, fall, or even winter.

ANATOMY OF A PORCH

Wooden porches vary in appearance, but underneath, most have the basic construction illustrated here. Wood or masonry posts rest on piers or footings. The posts, a ledger attached to the house, and one or more beams support floor joists. Decking is nailed directly to the joists. Columns extend the piers and posts to support the roof and railings. Up top, porches have virtually the same system of rafters, sheathing, and roofing as your house (see page 120). Finally, face boards on the roof and deck and a skirt below the deck conceal the various structural elements from view.

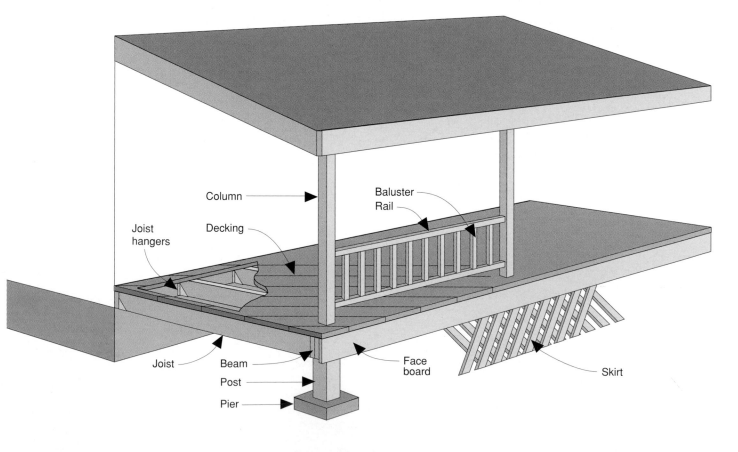

Column — Baluster — Rail — Joist hangers — Decking — Joist — Beam — Face board — Post — Pier — Skirt

Solving Porch Problems

One of the unhappy side effects of exposure to weather is rot. Whether your porch is suffering from rot caused by neglected maintenance, prolonged exposure to water, or fungi working away at seasoned wood, the cures are the same. You must repair the damage or, if the damage is severe, replace the rotten members. The sketches below show how to repair and replace porch columns, the most difficult elements to deal with.

Porches are susceptible to other maladies, too—pier or footing settlement; roof leaks; or damaged decking, porch steps, and railings. Inspect your porch annually. If there are problems, deal with them early. See pages 130 and 134–135 for help with repairing flashing and gutters.

REPAIRING ROTTED COLUMNS

As soon as you notice column damage (or damage to any porch element), determine its extent. Probe into the wood with a pocketknife. If the blade sinks in easily and the wood crumbles, replace the old column with a new one. If the damage is confined to the surface only, you can repair it fairly easily.

Before you make repairs, try to ascertain what caused the problem. If only the surface is rotted, chances are good that weather is the culprit. If water seems to be getting inside somehow, you'll need to find and seal the leak. And if you suspect termites, see pages 152–153.

Before you remove a column, be sure to brace the porch roof. Either improvise bracing with 4×4s or rent metal jack posts.

YOU'LL NEED...

SKILLS: Moderate carpentry skills.
TIME: 10 to 12 hours.
TOOLS: Hammer, chisel, saw, jack posts, concrete-working tools.

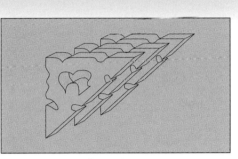

If the columns have fancy trim, you may be able to duplicate it by gluing together scrap boards, then cutting out patterns with a coping saw or router.

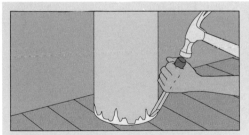

1. If only the outer edges of a column have rotted, chisel away the damage. Don't remove more wood than needed.

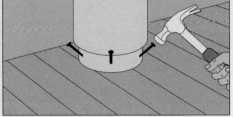

2. Coat the bare solid wood with preservative, then toenail large nails through the column into the floor.

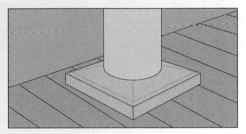

3. Conceal repair by building a form; pouring concrete, tapered as shown; and painting. Repeat on other columns.

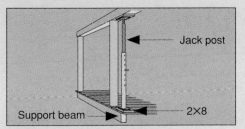

Jack post

Support beam — 2×8

1. If the column is beyond repair, brace the roof and remove the column; saw through it and pry out the pieces.

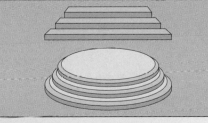

2. Make a new base to match others on the porch. Bevel the edges of the base so that it will shed water.

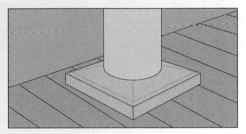

3. Toenail the new column to the new base. Nail the base to the floor. Caulk around both base and column.

Solving Patio Problems

Even brick, concrete, stone, and other hard-surface patio materials can't resist the effects of weather all of the time. Frost is the greatest enemy of patios. Thawing of the ground each spring creates a heaving effect that puts the surface to the test.

If your patio falls prey to the elements or to accidental damage, such as dropping a heavy object on it or staining, make repairs as soon as possible. The tips below and on the next page will help you make those repairs.

ANATOMY OF A PATIO

Regardless of a patio's surface—a poured concrete slab, flagstone, brick, or concrete pavers—that surface material usually rests on a sand base, as shown in the illustration at right. Large concrete slabs require expansion strips between them and other structures (for example, house foundations) and control joints to help keep possible cracking in check. Large concrete slabs also require reinforcing mesh or rods for strength and to prevent cracking. Brick and stone units "float" on the sand base or rest in a bed of mortar.

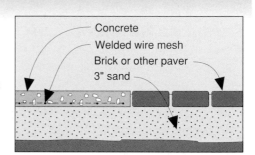

Concrete
Welded wire mesh
Brick or other paver
3" sand

HELPFUL HINTS   REMOVING PATIO SURFACE STAINS

Stain	Remedy
Food, grease, oil, lipstick	Mix dishwashing detergent in warm water. Work the mixture into the stain with a stiff brush or broom. Don't skimp. Rinse with clean water. If this doesn't work, add ammonia to the detergent and water mixture, following the same rinsing procedures, or scrub well with mineral spirits.
Paint and candle wax	Remove all the paint or wax you can with a regular or putty knife. Scrub the area with a metal bristled brush and cold water. If this fails, apply mineral spirits to the area. If the stain is on concrete and these treatments don't work, try aluminum oxide abrasive or an abrasive brick.
Blood, coffee, juice, feces	Use dishwashing detergent in cold water. Remove the stain as soon as possible. Work with a stiff scrub brush or broom, and flood the area with the detergent mixture. Rinse with clean, cold water.
Tar and heel marks	Try dishwashing detergent in warm water. If you're unsuccessful, scour the area with a stiff bristled brush and mineral spirits. Don't use a scouring pad. If some residue remains, flood the area with mineral spirits and blot it up with a soft absorbent cloth. This may take several applications.
Efflorescence	Rub the area with a wire brush. This should remove the white stain, which is caused by salts in the masonry mixture. If this doesn't work, many commercial stain removal mixtures are available that will remove the stain. They contain an acid, so be sure to wear gloves and safety glasses.
Dirt and grime	Hose down the surface with water and scrub it with a stiff broom. If this doesn't work, mix dishwashing detergent or trisodium phosphate with warm water and go over the area with a stiff brush or broom.
Soot	Apply detergent and water. If this doesn't work, apply a 1:1 mixture of muriatic acid and water. Be sure to wear gloves.

REPAIRING PATIO SURFACES

You repair a patio surface in much the same way a dentist fills a tooth: Clean away the old debris, prepare the cavity, and fill the void.

Don't try to fill cavities in concrete with more concrete; you won't get a good bond with the old surface.

Instead, use one of the commercial concrete patching materials listed in the chart below.

For stone and brick surfaces, you can simply lever out the damaged piece, replace it with a new one, and pack around it with mortar or sand. For more about brick repairs, turn to pages 148–149.

Practice the "dentistry" illustrated below, and your patio will look new again in no time—and with surprisingly little effort.

MATERIAL MATTERS · SELECTING CONCRETE PATCHING

Type	Uses	Description/Mixing
Latex, vinyl, epoxy	General-purpose repairs, such as hairline cracks, small breaks, patches, and tuckpointing; use latex or epoxy for patios	Sold in powdered form with or without liquid binder; mix with appropriate binder to a whipped-cream consistency
Hydraulic cement	Plugging leaks in masonry walls and floors; fast-drying formulas allow repair even while leaking	Available in powdered form; mix small amount with water or commercial binder, then work quickly
Dry premixed concrete	Replacing whole sections of concrete	Mix with water; the thicker the mix, the faster it sets up

YOU'LL NEED...

SKILLS: Basic skills.
TIME: 1 to 2 hours for hole about 12 inches across, not including drying time.
TOOLS: Hammer, cold chisel, wire brush, whisk broom, hose and sprayer, trowel, pry bar.

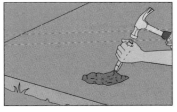

1. For holes in a concrete slab, chip away cracked material to solid concrete; clean with wire brush.

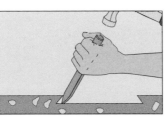

2. Undercut edges of the damaged area to provide a "key" to lock in the patch. Remove all loose materials.

3. Dampen the area to be patched. Some patches call for priming with a water/portland cement mixture.

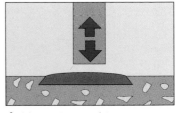

4. Tamp in patching compound. Pack it firmly and mound it a bit to compensate for shrinkage.

5. When the patch begins to set up, smooth it with a trowel. Cover patch and let it cure for one week.

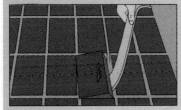

1. For stone or brick patios, remove damaged item. If mortar joints are damaged, use a latex or epoxy patch.

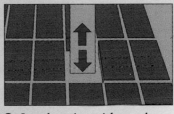

2. Level cavity with sand or mortar; tamp well. Replace brick or stone and tap level, then remortar.

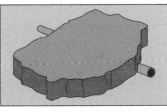

To move masonry slabs, roll on a length of pipe. When lifting heavy chunks, use your legs, not your back.

Solving Deck Problems

Decks, especially if neglected, but even if well cared for, develop many of the same problems that plague porches—rot and a host of structural maladies. Posts, beams, and joists particularly are prone to rot, as they're near ground level and covered by decking. Steps and railings work loose through normal use, and finishes, no matter how tough, give way to weather.

A twice-yearly inspection is your best protection against letting your deck's condition decline. If problems develop, tend to them quickly. The chart below describes what to do for several common ailments.

ANATOMY OF A DECK

A deck uses a simple post-and-beam construction. The decking rests on joists and beams, which rest on posts and piers or footings. The deck is tied to the house by a ledger. Joists sit on edge on the ledger and beam. House joists may be extended past the foundation wall to form a support for the decking. In some cases, the posts extend up through the decking to support the railing. On other decks, balusters are fastened to the joists or beams. A cap rail stabilizes and protects the other railing members.

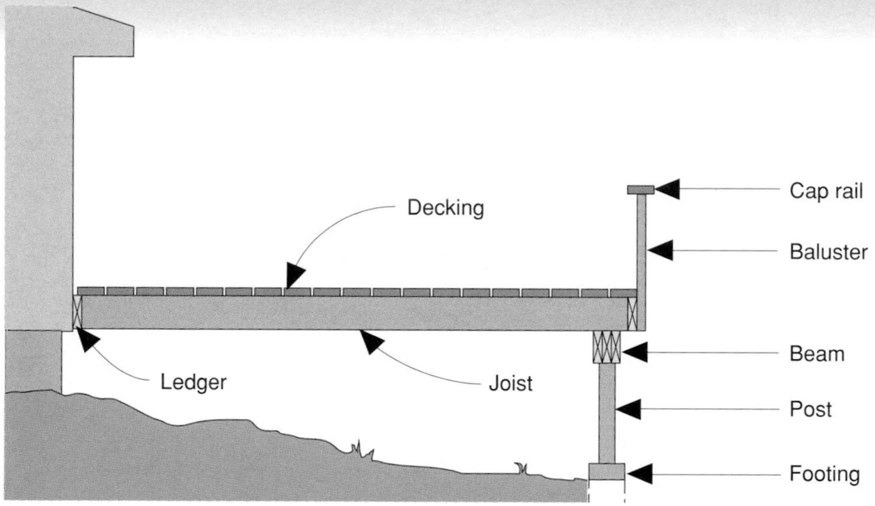

HELPFUL HINTS — SOLVING DECK PROBLEMS

Problem	Solution	Problem	Solution
Dirt, grime, grease, stains	Wash the area thoroughly with mild household detergent; rinse; see the stain removal chart on page 172	Sapstains, finish bleeds, finish failure	On unfinished wood, remove sap with mineral spirits; prime bleeds and finish failures with clear shellac; refinish
Mildew	Scrub the area with a mixture of water and household bleach, or use a commercial mildewcide	Damaged decking or components	Replacement parts are the best solution; see pages 185–190 for components used in deck construction

APPLYING STAINS AND PRESERVATIVES

The finish that protects your deck eventually will succumb to the ravages of time and weather. Not even redwood, cedar, or pressure-treated wood will hold up forever.

Stains work well on decks, so wherever possible use them. But if your deck has been painted before, you'll have to scrap off the old paint and apply a fresh coat.

If you opt to use stain, be sure to buy one formulated for exterior use, preferably a penetrating oil stain that is labeled "water repellent." These penetrate beneath the surface to provide long-lasting protection as well as good looks. If you want the wood's grain to show through, use a clear or semi-transparent stain. If you prefer a painted look, buy a solid-color stain. Do not apply such clear finishes as polyurethane or varnish because they do not hold up well against sunlight.

Adding Outdoor Living Areas

Your family's lifestyle can change dramatically with the addition of a patio or deck. You'll find that a well-planned outdoor living area can take pressure off interior spaces by providing alternative spots for cooking, eating, and relaxing.

Thoughtful planning is well worthwhile; a master plan will preclude later regrets. Below are some potential solutions for typical lots. Each has the three ingredients you should include in your plan: an outdoor living area, storage facilities, and a service area. Add a play area if you have children. And if you like to grow your own food or love flowers, don't forget to plan for your vegetable and flower gardens.

Start with the outdoor living area first. The slope of your lot will help you decide whether to plan a deck or patio. On flat lots, you have a complete range of choices, from brick-in-sand patios to an on-grade deck. If you must work on a slope, you may find that an elevated deck is the only practical alternative.

Study the area's relationship to the interior floor plan. You'll want convenient access, so take advantage of existing doors or consider installing a sliding glass door (see page 169). With these generalities in mind, plan the location and size of storage units to hold your yard and garden or recreational equipment.

The third ingredient is a service area. Make it large enough for garbage cans, a stack of firewood, potting benches, or whatever your family requires.

Check with your local zoning or building department for restrictions. Many zoning regulations require outbuildings and decks to be a specified distance from lot lines. Be sure you don't build on a part of your lot on which there's an easement or over an underground utility, such as a septic system. You may want to use graph paper to sketch out ideas to scale, or you may find it easiest to stake out the areas on a trial-and-error basis.

Finally, plan for privacy and screening. Consider the plantings you have and those you want to add, as well as fences you might want to build (see pages 191–213).

With goals established, you're ready to work out the details, such as the exact size of your deck or patio, what material to use, and the cost. With the know-how that follows, doing it yourself will yield worthwhile results—convenience, comfort for years to come, and more money in your pocket.

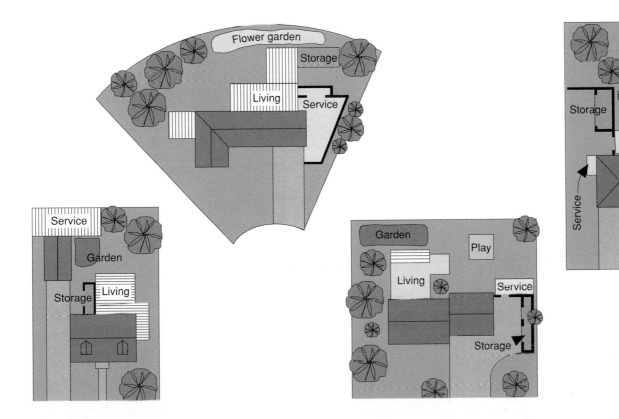

Adding Outdoor Living Areas (continued)

CONSTRUCTING A PATIO IN SAND

If you want a patio, but you don't like concrete, consider laying bricks, flagstones, slate, paving blocks, or precast patio blocks in sand. The procedures are relatively simple, and you won't need many special tools—a mason's hammer, brick chisel, shovel, nail hammer, garden hose, broom, and a level will see you through.

In addition to the surface material, you'll need sand to serve as a base. The amount required depends on the site, which must be level. For a 10×20-foot patio, you'll need 2 cubic yards of sand to provide a 3-inch base; in a well-drained area, you could get by with a 2-inch base—and only half as much sand.

The sketches below show the different patterns you can achieve by using brick for your patio. Note that bricks also can serve as borders for your patio.

Buying Paving Bricks

If you visit brick suppliers in your area, you will be amazed by the large selection of paving bricks available—standard-size bricks in many colors and textures, as well as jumbo and irregular-shaped ones.

Ask the supplier to estimate your needs based on the type of paving brick you choose. You will need about 460 bricks per 100 square feet of patio, allowing for breakage. Because bricks generally are sold in multiples of 500, you'll need one pallet of them. Brick costs vary considerably. Delivery to the job site is additional.

If you are a fan of used bricks, be sure that the ones you buy are hard; some will crumble when you tap them with a hammer. Also, if there is old mortar sticking to them, you've inherited a big brick cleaning job that must be done before you can begin laying your patio.

SURFACING

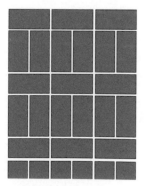

Basket weave

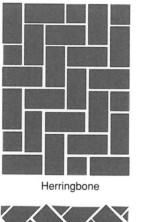

Herringbone

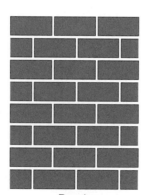

Running

BORDERING

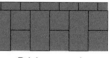

Bricks on end

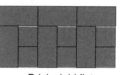

Bricks laid flat

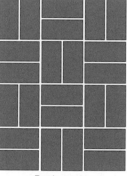

Capped herringbone

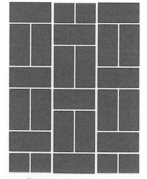

Diagonal herringbone

Double basket weave

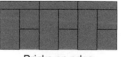

Bricks on edge

Sawtooth

Laying Bricks in Sand

Because the sand under bricks alleviates drainage problems, you needn't do a lot of site preparation for a brick-in-sand patio. However, the area must be level. If you have a large amount of dirt to move, hire a grading contractor to solve the problem. As you shovel or grade, keep in mind that the bricks are laid over a 3-inch sand base. You must consider brick thickness, too. Both affect the grade depth.

Using forms to define the patio perimeter makes sense even when setting bricks. Whether or not you use internal forms is a design consideration. See page 179 for help on setting up forms. If you plan to remove the forms, use economy-grade lumber. If they'll be part of the design, however, use redwood, cedar, or pressure-treated wood, fastened with galvanized nails.

> ### YOU'LL NEED...
> **SKILLS:** Basic brick handling skills.
> **TIME:** 8 to 12 hours for a 10×10-foot patio area.
> **TOOLS:** Shovel, hose and sprayer, heavy hammer or sledge, saw, string, level, brick chisel, broom.

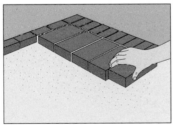

1. Stake out the area and level the surface. For brick-on-end borders, dig a trench along the perimeter.

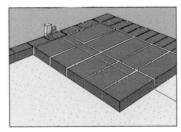

2. Spray the ground with weed killer. Then cover with dark 4-mil polyethelyne to prevent plant growth.

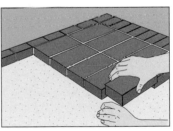

3. Install edging; set bricks on end, edge, or flat. If you are using forms, stake them every 2 feet (see page 179).

4. Spread 3 inches of coarse sand. Level it with a shovel. Soak the area thoroughly with water.

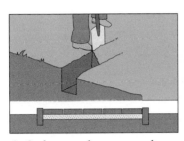

5. Screed the sand in 3-foot-square sections using a 2×4 notched to the depth of a brick and fitting over edging.

6. Set the bricks into place as carefully as possible. Try not to disturb the sand.

7. To help keep the bricks level, stretch a mason's line. Also, periodically check the units with a level.

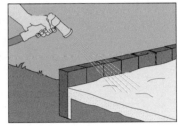

8. If you find a low brick, lift it out and sprinkle more sand underneath. If too high, remove some sand.

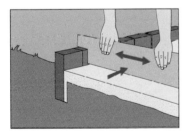

9. To cut a brick, place it on a firm surface, score the break line with a brick chisel, and tap with sledge.

10. Spread shovelfuls of damp sand on the surface and let it dry. Sweep the sand into the joints.

11. Wet the area thoroughly with a fine spray so the sand settles into the joints but does not wash away.

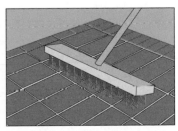

12. Repeat the sanding and watering several times until the cracks are full. Sweep the surface a final time.

Adding Outdoor Living Areas (continued)

WORKING WITH CONCRETE

Cement is a dry, powdery substance that serves as a binding agent to make mortar or concrete. Mix it with sand and water, and you get mortar, the stuff used to bind bricks, blocks, or stones together. Mix it with sand and gravel, and you get concrete.

All projects that involve concrete are strenuous jobs. First, you have to level off the area you'll be surfacing. Then, you have to build temporary or permanent forms to hold the concrete while it sets. Next, you have to place the concrete where you want it—heavy work that also

has to be done quickly before the mix sets. Finally, you have to level (screed) the surface, float it to work out irregularities, and finish it—again while the concrete is still wet. The following pages take you step by step through each of these stages.

HELPFUL HINTS

Before you begin, check with your city or county building department. You may be asked for such information as the size of the project, its location, approximate cost, and so on. There's often a small building permit fee, too.

When planning your project, ask yourself the following questions:
■ Does a concrete truck have access to the job site? If not, you'll need a couple of wheelbarrows and help on hand.

DOING YOUR HOMEWORK

■ Must electric or telephone lines be disconnected so a concrete truck can gain access to the site? If so, notify the utilities in advance.
■ Does the site require drainage? Usually, sloping or crowning the area can provide adequate water drainage, but problem drainage areas may require you to install drain tile beneath the concrete.
■ Does the project require special

grading? If so, have the utility companies locate and mark all buried cables or lines where you are digging.
■ Will the job require special concrete reinforcement, such as welded wire mesh or reinforcing rods? Driveways and walkways over which cars and trucks will be driven require reinforcement. Generally, it's a good practice to place reinforcing in all concrete projects.

TOOL TALK

A mason's hammer drives stakes; breaks stone, block, and brick; and chips away crumbling concrete. Lay out jobs with a 50-foot tape, mason's line, and line level. For smoothing and finishing concrete, you'll need a darby, a float or bull float, and a finish trowel. Have a hoe (a concrete hoe has holes in the blade to help mix the material) and shovel on hand to mix and distribute concrete.

To distribute your weight over the fresh concrete so you don't sink into it, make a knee board from lumber or plywood. Use a jointing tool to create dividing lines, such as the lines dividing a sidewalk into sections. An edger smooths and finishes the edges of concrete; use it while the forms are still in place. Quality concrete tools are not expensive, so buy the best.

TOOLS FOR CONCRETE WORK

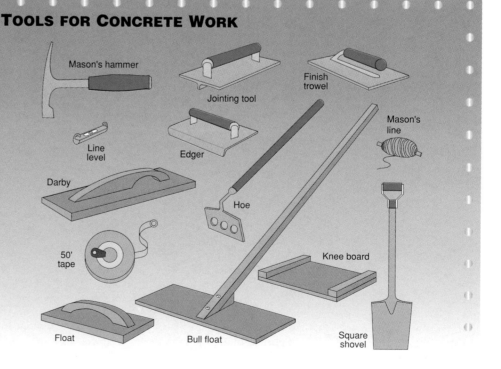

Mason's hammer
Jointing tool
Finish trowel
Line level
Edger
Mason's line
Darby
Hoe
50' tape
Knee board
Float
Bull float
Square shovel

BUILDING FORMS

Building concrete forms is not a finish carpentry project. Strength is more important than good looks, so spend your effort on secure bracing.

The material for concrete forms depends on the job. Economy-grade 2×4s (or 2×6s for thicker slabs) work well for straight runs. Use ¼-inch exterior plywood or tempered hardboard for curves.

Most often, you'll disassemble and remove the forms after the concrete sets. A light coat of used motor oil on wood forms prevents them from sticking to the concrete. It also will be easier and less time-consuming if you secure the forms with double-headed nails. Allow the concrete to set a day or two before removing the forms (as it sets, concrete will change color—from a dark gray to its characteristic light gray color).

If the forms will be a part of the permanent design, use cedar, redwood, or pressure-treated lumber.

YOU'LL NEED...
SKILLS: Basic carpentry skills.
TIME: 1 to 2 hours.
TOOLS: Hammer, saw, small sledgehammer.

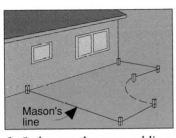

1. Stake out the area, adding 2 inches on sides for forms. Scrap 2×2s, pointed at one end, make good stakes.

2. Mark the ground by pouring sand over the mason's line. Remove the stakes and the line.

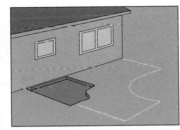

3. Excavate to allow for the depth of the sand bed and the slab. Dig about 1 foot wider than the outline.

4. Dig out rocks and roots and fill depressions. Wet and tamp the area to compact the base.

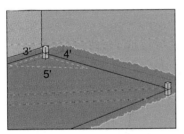

5. Reposition corner stakes, making sure corners are square, using the 3-4-5 method (see page 185).

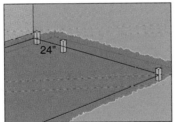

6. Drive more stakes every 24 to 30 inches. Stakes should be about 24 inches long and well set.

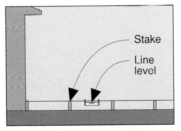

7. Stretch a line level from the first to the last stake in each row. Pitch line slightly to permit drainage off slab.

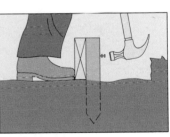

8. Secure forms to stakes with double-headed nails. The stakes must be flush with or below the forms.

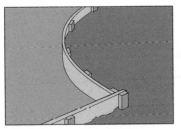

9. Outline curves with rope or garden hose. Stake hardboard every 18 inches.

10. Securely brace the forms at each corner and at other potential weak spots.

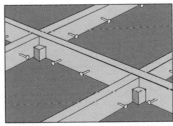

11. If you divide a patio into grids, stake inner forms as shown. Partially driven nails help to hold the concrete.

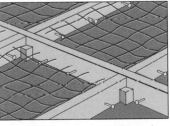

12. Pressure-treated boards make excellent permanent forms. Add reinforcing rods or mesh, if desired.

Adding Outdoor Living Areas (continued)

MATERIAL MATTERS

Knowing what material is available and the type of concrete suited to your job is the secret to buying concrete. Here is a brief rundown.

Ready-mix concrete. To order concrete already mixed, simply call one of the many concrete companies in your area. Tell them what the concrete is intended for and the area of the project. It's as simple as that. Before you call, be sure you have prepared the site completely. Don't expect the truck

BUYING CONCRETE

driver to sit and watch you rebuild incorrect forms, place reinforcement mesh, or hunt for your tools. Excess time spent at a job usually results in an extra charge. Make sure, also, that the truck has access to the site or that you have wheelbarrows to transport the mix. Keep in mind that most ready-mix companies won't deliver less than 1 cubic yard of concrete.

Premixed concrete. This product comes in bags. You simply add water

and stir. Use premixed bags for small jobs and repairs. One bag, typically 60 pounds, will make about ½ cubic foot of concrete.

Mix-it-yourself concrete. You can order all the materials—cement, sand, and gravel—and mix concrete yourself. For large jobs, rent a concrete mixer; for small jobs, mix the materials in a bucket or mortar box. The cost is fairly inexpensive, but if it's a large job, you may have a material storage problem.

Estimating Your Needs

Calculating how much concrete you need is easier than you think. If your project is rectangular, multiply the width by the length by the thickness in feet. If you're purchasing ready-mix, divide the result by 27, the number of cubic feet in a cubic yard, which is the unit in which concrete is sold.

To determine the square footage of a circle, multiply the square of the radius by 3.14. Then, multiply by thickness (in feet) and divide by 27. For all irregular shapes, it's best to draw the project to scale on graph paper, with

each square representing 1 square foot. This way, you can count the full, half, and quarter squares to determine the square footage fairly accurately.

Ready-mix companies probably will still want to know the square footage and thickness of your project. Accept the salesman's estimate—unless it is vastly out of agreement with your own.

If you're going to mix your own concrete, you'll have to order enough of each material—cement, sand, and gravel—according to the "mix" you are going to make (see below).

CONCRETE NEEDS
(Expressed in cubic yards)

Thickness (inches)	Surface Area (square feet)				
	20	50	100	200	500
2	0.1	0.3	0.6	1.2	3.1
4	0.2	0.6	1.2	2.5	6.2
6	0.4	0.9	1.9	3.7	9.3

Note: If the ground is sloped but the finish surface is level, you must use the average thickness of the concrete.

Choosing a Mix

The type of project you're undertaking determines the strength or "mix" of the concrete you need. Patios and sidewalks, for example, don't need the same strength a footing or driveway does. A thicker slab requires less cement proportionally than does a thinner one because of its greater mass.

For most home improvement projects, the regular mix of three parts gravel mix to two parts sand to one part cement will give you the desired

results. When mixed with water, this mixture contains enough cement powder to coat each particle of sand and gravel, and thereby create the bond that gives concrete its strength.

The amount of water added to the mixture is vitally important—use only enough to make the mixture workable (see page 181). If you are mixing your own concrete, move the mixing container as close to your project as possible. This will allow you ready

access to keep the mixture thick and strong, yet workable.

If you order from a ready-mix company, specify a minimum bearing capacity of 3,500 pounds per square inch at 28 days' cure.

During cold weather, add or ask for additives that will speed the concrete's curing times. These additives lessen the concrete's vulnerability to freezing, which can weaken it.

MIXING CONCRETE

Mixing concrete is much like mixing cake batter: You have to follow the recipe (or adapt it slightly) to obtain the very best results. Just as you can ruin a cake by adding too much liquid, you can weaken concrete if you add too much water in proportion to the other materials. On the other hand, too little water makes the concrete difficult to pour and to finish properly.

The amount of water needed depends on the sand. You'll need less water with wet sand than with dry sand. Test the wetness by balling some sand in your hand. If water runs out, the sand is too wet. If the ball compacts, like moist clay, the sand is perfect If the ball crumbles, the sand is too dry.

As you mix the concrete, add very small amounts of water at a time. At the outset, the concrete may crumble, but as you add more water, it will begin to flow together like thick mud. When it becomes one color—a medium gray—and has a shiny, plastic-like sheen, it's ready.

YOU'LL NEED...
SKILLS: Moderate concrete skills.
TIME: 20 to 30 minutes to mix a small batch by hand.
TOOLS: Shovel, concrete hoe, trowel.

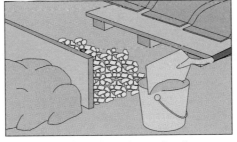

1. Mix batches of concrete in a wheelbarrow, on a piece of plywood, or on any flat, waterproof surface that you can hose off later.

2. Measure the ingredients by the bucketful, leveling off the material with your shovel. Proper amounts are very important here.

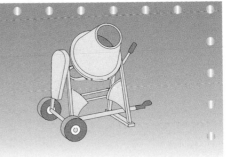

3. Use a concrete hoe or a shovel to thoroughly dry mix the correct proportions of cement, sand, and gravel. Roll one into the other.

4. Make a well in the center of the pile and pour in water gradually, mixing the components to a thick consistency.

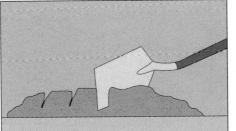

5. Test the batch by smacking it with the back of a shovel, then jabbing it lightly to make a series of grooves.

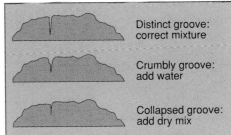

Distinct groove: correct mixture

Crumbly groove: add water

Collapsed groove: add dry mix

6. If the surface is smooth and the grooves maintain their separation, the mix is the right consistency.

TOOL TALK

If you need to mix more than a few cubic feet of concrete, you'll save many hours of labor by renting an electric- or gasoline-powered concrete mixer.

To use a mixer, add all of the gravel needed for the batch and some water,

USING A POWER MIXER

and switch on the mixer. Then add the sand, the cement, and, finally, more water. Mix for 3 minutes, gradually adding water until the mix achieves a uniform color. Stop the mixer often, removing some mix to test the batch as shown above.

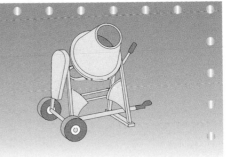

Adding Outdoor Living Areas (continued)

PREPARING FOR A CONCRETE POUR

To ensure a successful concrete pour, you must have everything prepared before the concrete is ready. Conversely, few things can cause more aggravation than a hasty setup. Start a day early by doing the preparation work shown here.

Make sure all the forms are in the correct position, and drive all stakes flush with the top edge of the forms.

Place expansion joints along the edges of foundations, other slabs, and other structural members. The joints allow for movement of the concrete with temperature changes

Have utility companies remove wire or cable obstructions. Also remember to make arrangements for reconnecting utilities.

Get together your concrete tools—shovels, hoes, floats, and trowels. Recruit helpers if the project calls for a large amount of concrete.

> ### YOU'LL NEED...
> **SKILLS:** Basic carpentry skills.
> **TIME:** 1 day.
> **TOOLS:** Tape, shovel, gloves, wire cutters, hose and sprayer, screed.

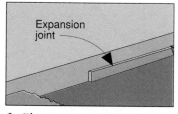

1. Place expansion joints between the slab and all abutting structures, such as a foundation, and every 8 to 10 feet in large slabs.

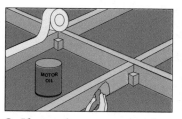

2. If you plan to remove the forms, coat them with oil. If the forms will remain as part of your design, protect the edges with masking tape.

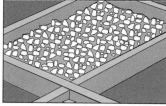

3. Make a bed for the concrete by spreading sand, cinders, or gravel. Generally, a couple inches of any of these materials will do.

4. Screed the base material to level the surface. Tamp the material lightly so it is well compacted and completely level.

5. Use welded-wire mesh for reinforcement. Have a helper stand on one end, then unroll the mesh and cut it. Wear gloves.

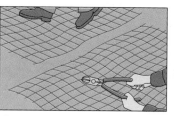

6. If working with grids, cut the mesh to fit, then flatten it out by walking on it. Heavy bolt cutters make easy work of the cutting.

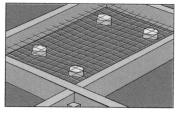

7. Lay the mesh into the area, and use rocks to prop it up so it's about midway up the forms. Avoid walking on the mesh.

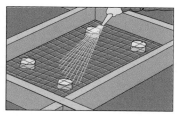

8. Wet down the area the day before pouring the concrete. Sprinkle it again just before pouring to slow the drying time.

HELPFUL HINTS · GETTING READY FOR READY-MIX

A concrete truck weighs tons and can ruin any walk or lawn over which it passes. You may want to use wheelbarrows to move the concrete. If the project is within 18 to 20 feet of the street, park the truck at curbside and use the truck's chute to move the material to the site. If the truck must roll over your lawn, make a road for it with 2-inch-thick planks of lumber.

Allow about 12 feet of overhead clearance as well. If there is a power or phone line in the way, call the respective utility to have it moved.

For wheelbarrow runs, lay down plywood or 1-inch-thick boards to ease the task of moving the heavy concrete. Pick a smooth route and use a helper.

POURING CONCRETE

For all its strength, concrete is a fussy building material. More than anything else, it needs time to cure. If you pour concrete over frozen ground, it will break up when the ground thaws. Pouring it over extremely dry ground also is bad, as the ground will absorb the water in the concrete mix and the concrete will set before you can finish it.

After concrete has been poured, you'll notice that a thin layer of water forms over the top of it. Don't remove the water! If you trowel the surface now, it will "craze" (or crack) and flake after the concrete has cured. Pour the concrete, screed it, float it, and then trowel it. Do all of this quickly; if your project is a large one, have helpers available.

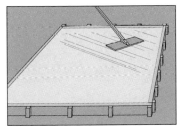

1. Pour concrete in the most remote area of the form. Build a bridge if you must use a wheelbarrow.

2. Spread the concrete with a concrete hoe so it's only slightly higher than the top edges of the forms.

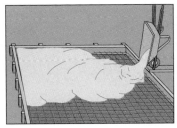

3. Dump succeeding loads against the first one, not on top of it. Pull up reinforcing mesh with rake.

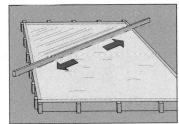

4. Screed with a straight 2×4 after the concrete has been poured. See-saw the 2×4 to fill in low spots.

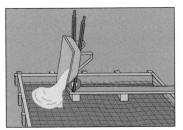

5. Floating levels the surface and pushes down aggregates. The float produces a rough, but level, finish.

6. Float small areas with a darby, swinging the tool in an arc. Stop when water bleeds onto the surface.

7. When the surface looks dry, test by scraping it with a finish trowel. If wetness appears, don't finish it yet.

8. Run a trowel between the form and concrete to separate them. Run the edging tool along the edge.

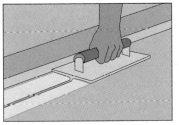

9. Make control joints by running a jointing tool across the slab, use a 2-inch board as a straightedge.

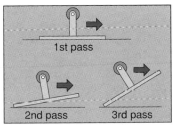

10. For a slick finish, trowel the surface three times. Move your arm in a wide arc using medium pressure.

1st pass
2nd pass   3rd pass

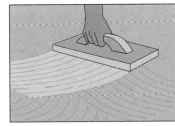

11. A wooden trowel, float, or brush produces a rough, skidproof surface. You'll need only one or two passes.

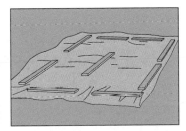

12. Cover with polyethelyne to hold moisture in. Or sprinkle with water daily for a week until concrete cures.

Adding Outdoor Living Areas (continued)

CUSTOM-FINISHING CONCRETE

There's a bit of the artist in us all, and there's no better time to use that talent than when you're finishing the surface of your concrete project.

Duplicate one of the designs shown below or, if you're really feeling creative, dream up a design of your own. Decide on the surface you want in advance, because you'll need all the time you can get to execute the design.

You also can color concrete to achieve a special look. Ready-mix companies will add coloring—usually red, brown, green, or black—for an additional charge. If you are mixing your own, purchase a coloring powder and mix it with the other ingredients as specified. Or you can spread on the coloring powder during the finishing process.

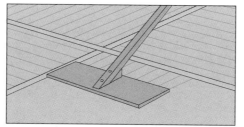

Swirl design. By working the trowel across the surface in an arc, you can produce this subtle, yet intriguing look. Using the edge of a finish trowel, lightly work the concrete, making sure that you don't dig the edges of the trowel into the surface. Don't try to establish any particular pattern. Just "freewheel" the trowel, forming a series of random, interconnecting arcs.

Checkerboard. This texture requires relatively little work. In fact, the less trowel work, the more interesting and skidproof the final effect will be. Especially attractive with a grid, checkerboarding will work on large expanses as well. Use a bull float, darby, or wooden hand float. Floats with a sponge-like surface will create a more pronounced texture effect.

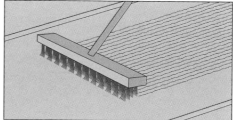

Brooming. For more texture and skidproofing, treat the surface with a broom after you float the concrete and it has hardened somewhat. For a light texture, use a soft-bristled broom; for coarser effects, use a broom with heavy straw or steel bristles. You can create similar special effects with a bamboo or steel lawn rake. Test the design before making a total commitment.

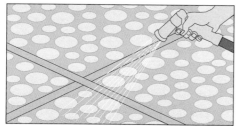

Exposed aggregate. Spread aggregate on the floated surface and press it into the concrete with a float, darby, or wide board until the pebbles are no longer visible. After the concrete begins to set, hose and scrub the surface with a stiff broom until you see the tops of the pebbles. Let the concrete set for about three to four days, then wash the surface with a 1:5 solution of muriatic acid and water.

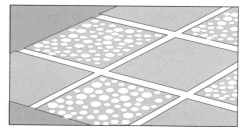

Geometric. Any series of lines that meet at random points falls into this category. The example above mimics the effect you'd get if you laid flagstones. A joint strike makes a perfect tool for creating this design. Use a light hand with it, however, because deep recesses will collect dirt. Work in the design after the surface has set long enough to support you on a knee board.

Combination effects. You can combine two or more designs to come up with other unique surfaces. The one depicted above combines exposed aggregate and a smooth troweled look, along with permanent forms in a grid pattern. It's best to sketch out your ideas ahead of time. Often, you can adapt or duplicate ideas found in magazines, outside public buildings, or on a neighbor's patio.

BUILDING A DECK

Decks, especially well-constructed ones, may look difficult to build. A few are truly complex and require advanced skills, but most are within reach of the average do-it-yourselfer. The purpose of the next few pages is to make this entirely possible project possible for you.

Using the correct materials and providing adequate support are the two most important aspects of deck building. If the deck can't withstand the impact of weather, or if it's so shaky that no one feels comfortable on it, your hard work and money will go to waste.

Use only woods specially intended for outdoor use, such as cedar, redwood, or pressure-treated lumber. Even then, take steps to protect that wood (see page 174). To ensure that the deck you raise is structurally sound, build it in compliance with the span tables at right and the building basics that follow.

YOU'LL NEED...

SKILLS: Moderate carpentry skills.
TIME: Several days.
TOOLS: Hammer, circular saw, chisel, level and line level, plumb line, drill, screwdriver, posthole digger, shovel, wheelbarrow.

BEAM AND JOIST SPAN TABLE

Beam Size	Maximum Distance Between Posts	
4×6	6 feet	
4×8	8 feet	
4×10	10 feet	
4×12	12 feet	

Joist Size	Maximum Distance Between Beams	
	Joists 16" apart	Joists 24" apart
2×6	8 feet	6 feet
2×8	10 feet	8 feet
2×10	13 feet	10 feet

Getting Started

Design your deck on paper first. Many books are available to give you planning ideas, based on your intended use of the deck. Using your rough plan dimensions, stake the deck out with 1×2 stakes. Determine the height of the deck by marking where you want the deck surface to meet the house. These procedures tell you if the deck site and size are suitable for your needs. If they aren't, shift the location, alter the size, or both, then redo your plan. Once you are happy with your design, obtain the necessary city or county building permits.

Mark the location of the ledger strip, which supports the joists along the house (not needed for freestanding decks). Build batter boards at the corners. Use a mason's line to level and square the deck. To check the corners for square, measure 3 feet along one string line and 4 feet down the adjacent line. The distance between the two end points should be 5 feet. The deck is square also when the lengths of the two diagonals are equal.

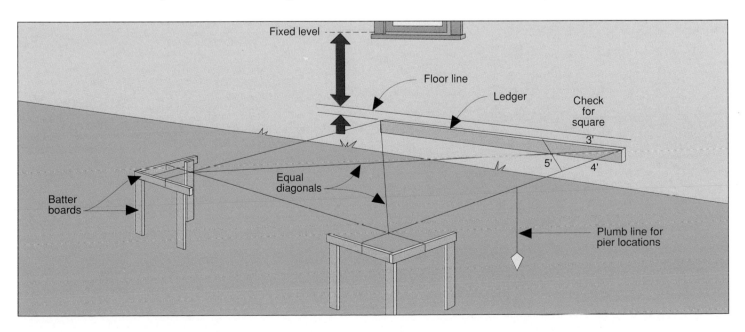

Fixed level

Floor line

Ledger

Check for square

3'

5'

4'

Equal diagonals

Batter boards

Plumb line for pier locations

Adding Outdoor Living Areas *(continued)*

BUILDING A DECK *(continued)*

Setting Posts

You should always use pressure-treated lumber for posts. Set posts directly in concrete or on top of a concrete footing. Otherwise, they will rot quickly.

If you set posts in concrete, first pour a footing that is several inches larger than the post and that is below the frost line (check with local contractors for proper depth). Unless your project is large, you should be able to use premixed bags of concrete rather than ready-mix. While the concrete is still wet, set and plumb the post. Attach outrigger stakes (see page 192) to steady the post until the concrete sets.

To set posts on concrete piers, first pour the footing and position and plumb one of the anchoring devices shown below in the still-workable concrete.

For most deck projects, 4×4 posts provide adequate structural support. Just be sure the posts are plumb (check each twice, taking readings from your level on sides at right angles to each other) and in perfect alignment with each other along your mason's line. For more about erecting posts, see pages 196-197.

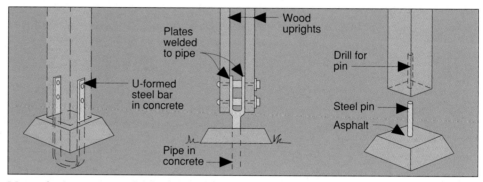

When you set posts in concrete, taper the concrete at ground level to help shed water, which otherwise collects around the post and leads to rot.

Many devices are available that will serve as stable post anchors. You can also get adjustable post bases that fit over machine or carriage bolts that have been set in the concrete footing or slab. These type of anchors allow you to make minor lateral adjustments of the posts.

HELPFUL HINTS

There are several options for attaching deck beams to posts. If you run the post up through the decking to serve as a support for a railing, fashion the beams from two lengths of 2× material sandwiched on either side of the post.

If your deck is on-grade, in which case you won't need a railing, or you don't want to run the post through the decking, cut the post to the correct height and fasten the beam on top of it, using a method shown at right.

For maximum strength, use bolts or large wood screws. Deck movements can work nails loose too easily.

ATTACHING DECK BEAMS

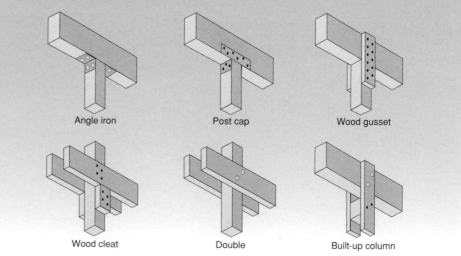

Angle iron Post cap Wood gusset

Wood cleat Double Built-up column

Attaching Ledgers and Joists

Unless your deck is freestanding and depends on posts for primary support, you must fasten a ledger strip—usually a 2×8 or 2×10—to your house using one of the fastening options shown below. Regardless of which option you choose, bear in mind that all vertical measurements must allow for the thickness of the decking material you'll be using.

Decide if you want the joists to rest on the ledger or flush with it, as would be the case if you're using joist hangers. If you use joist hangers, make sure that the bottom of the ledger is level with the top of the beam at the outer edge of the deck. Double-check the ledger's position by running a string with a line level from the top of the beam to the house. (You could have a very slight pitch toward the beam to allow for water runoff away from the house.) With your measurements confirmed, attach the ledger.

The joists come next. Joist size depends on the spans involved, but 2×6s, 2×8s, and 2×10s are most common. If you are using joist hangers, nail them along the ledger, usually at 16-inch intervals. Position the joists on the beams and in the hangers and secure them. If you're setting the joists on the beams and ledger, toenail them into position with galvanized nails.

YOU'LL NEED...

SKILLS: Basic carpentry skills.
TIME: 1 hour for a ledger and several hours for joists, depending on size and complexity of deck.
TOOLS: Hammer, drill, screwdriver, level and line level, socket wrench.

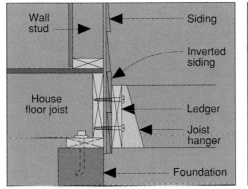

To attach a ledger strip to the band joist of the house, use lag screws. If the house has lap siding, invert a piece of siding for a shim.

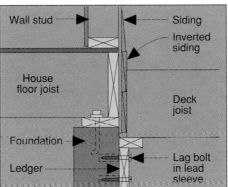

Fasten ledgers to a foundation with lag screws in lead anchors. You may have to double the ledger or put a strip on top of the ledger for the joists to sit on.

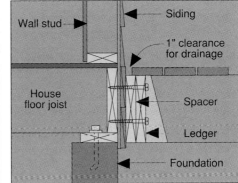

Install flashing to protect the ledger from sitting water. Or, use spacers to set the ledger 1½ inches from the house so water can run through.

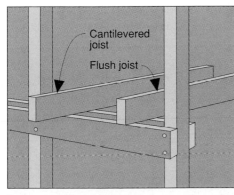

Joists can be cantilevered over the edge beam or flushed with it. You might prefer the cantilevered effect if you don't skirt the deck.

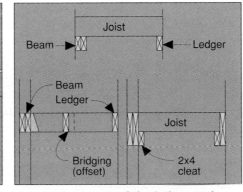

Rest joists on top of the ledger and beam, then toenail them. Or, use a flush connection by butt-joining or cleating and toenailing.

Adding Outdoor Living Areas (continued)

BUILDING A DECK (continued)
Constructing Stairs

Laying out a stairway is a challenge. Not only do you have to accurately compute angles, you must maintain equal riser and tread spacing from top to bottom. Building an open-riser, open-stringer stairway is an excellent introduction to this advanced carpentry task.

Stairs basically divide a difference in elevation into a series of equal steps. Measure this distance—the total rise—and the distance from your deck to where you want the stairs to end—the total run.

Ideally, each step should have a rise of 7 to 8 inches and a run of 10 to 11 inches. Divide your choice of these riser and tread numbers into the total rise and run to see if you get a whole number of treads and risers. You probably won't, so just adjust the riser height or tread run slightly until you get an even number. Don't forget to include the thickness of the tread material in your rise computations.

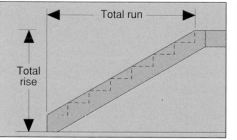

1. Measure from top of the deck to the ground (total rise) and from deck to where stairs will end (total run).

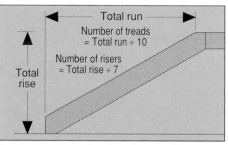

2. Divide these by the acceptable rise and run figures above to determine the number of treads and risers required.

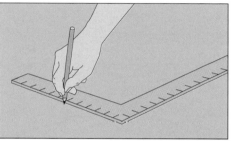

3. Mark the riser height on one leg of a framing square and the depth of the tread on the other leg of the square.

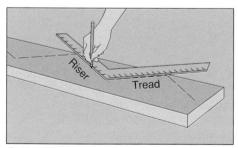

4. Lay the square against a 2×10 or 2×12 stringer, then scribe the marked points onto the lumber.

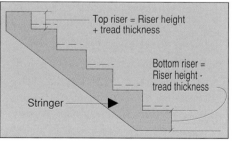

5. For evenly spaced risers, subtract tread thickness from the bottom riser and add it to the top.

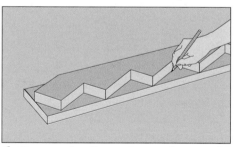

6. Cut out the first stringer, then use it as a template for the second. Be sure to allow for the saw kerf when you cut it.

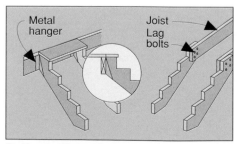

7. Fasten the stringers to the sides of a joist or header using metal hangers. Or, bolt the steps to the joists.

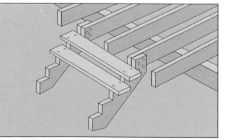

8. Nail on the treads, using galvanized finishing nails. Cut tread material flush with the stringer or let it overlap.

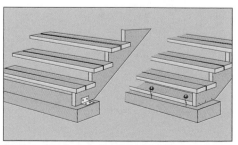

9. Set the bottom of the steps on concrete and fasten it with expansion anchors and lag screws or angle irons.

Building Stairs Without Notching Stringers

If you don't want to notch the stringers for a stairway, use cleats on the insides of the stringers to hold the treads. The same design calculations apply (see page 188) whether you cut out the riser and tread notches or use cleats as shown here.

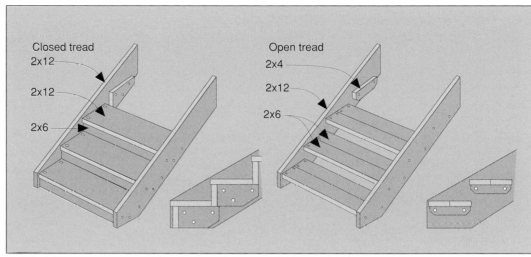

Laying Decking

Because the decking is the most visible element of your project, it's important that you lay it correctly.

Most people run the decking across the joists, as it not only yields an attractive look, but also is the easiest design to lay. With a little more work, you also can create a number of special-effect surfaces. You might, for example, want to fashion a parquet block design or run the decking diagonally. Just keep in mind that you'll need adequate joist support beneath each piece of decking.

Start laying the decking at the house and work outward. Make certain that the first piece is square to the house. This first piece serves as the all-important guide for the rest of the decking. Use ¼-inch spacers to separate subsequent pieces. After laying every three or four strips, double-check for square by running a line from the house to both ends of the same piece of decking. Butt the ends of the decking pieces together for a snug fit.

Check the end grain of each board before you nail it. Notice that the tree rings hump toward one side of the board—called the bark side. Nail all decking bark-side-up to minimize future cupping of the lumber.

If the lumber you're using is slightly warped, nail one end of it to a joist, then "pull" the loose end into position and nail it, working from joist to joist.

You can use 10d galvanized nails or 3 inch noncorrosive deck screws to secure the decking to the joists. If you notice that the decking splits as you're nailing it, blunt the nail points slightly with a hammer. Or, drill pilot holes for the nails or screws, especially at the ends of the lumber, where splitting usually occurs.

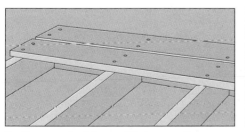

1. Secure decking with two nails or screws at each joist. Don't worry about cutting the decking to exact length yet.

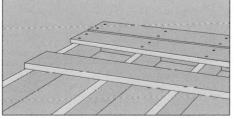

2. Maintain proper spacing with a ¼-inch spacer strip. Stagger end joints as you go across the deck.

3. After all boards are nailed, snap a chalk line along the edges and trim with a saw. Use a board as a guide.

Adding Outdoor Living Areas (continued)

BUILDING A DECK (continued)
Adding Deck Railings

You can come up with a multitude of designs for deck railings—as long as the design relates in scale to the deck and the structure adjoining it. The primary purposes of railings are to provide safe passage from the deck to the ground and to prevent people falling off the deck, so build it strong. If children will frequent the deck, use a close spacing sequence for the rails.

The sketches below show three typical railing options. Duplicate one of them or, if you'd rather, dream up a one-of-a-kind treatment.

Secure all railing posts to the decking superstructure with lag screws or carriage bolts. Nails don't provide the needed holding power. Tie the railing into the structure's posts, beams, or joists; don't rely on the decking strips themselves to properly hold a railing in place.

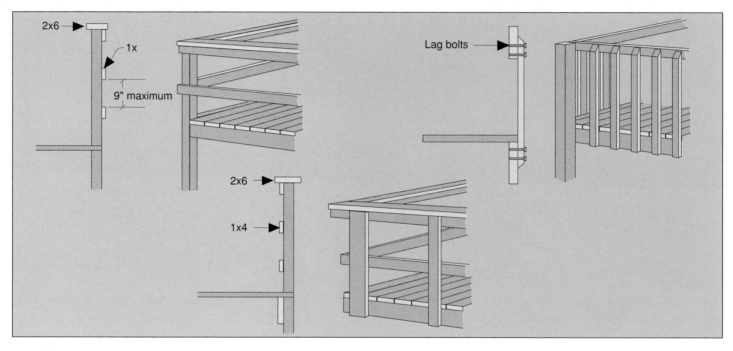

Adding a Bench to a Deck

A bench makes your deck more useful and often conserves deck space by moving the bench to the perimeter of the deck. If used on the deck's perimeter, a bench also can serve as a railing. The example at right, again, is just one design that is easy to construct.

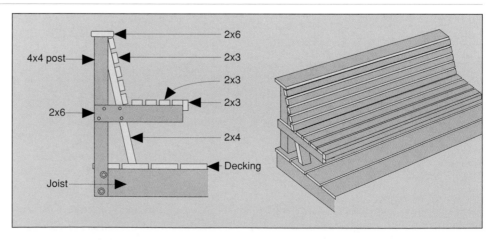

FENCES AND GARDEN WALLS

Examine the drawing below and you will see a skeleton common to almost all nonmasonry fences. Posts at the ends, corners, gates, and "along the line" support rails at the top, bottom, and sometimes in the middle of the fence.

The individual character of a fence is achieved when you add screening—pickets are shown here,

but there are dozens of other possibilities, as well. To learn more about the many shapes a fence may take and how to build fences, see pages 193–202.

Build a masonry fence and you've got what is known as a screen wall; position it to hold back a slope, and it's a retaining wall. More about both beginning on page 203.

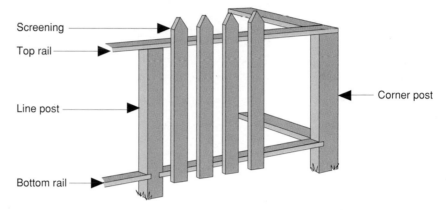

Screening — Top rail — Line post — Corner post — Bottom rail

Solving Fence Problems

REPAIRING DAMAGED RAILS

Rot is a fence's worst enemy and typically attacks bottom-rail joints first. If you catch decay early, you can saturate the damaged spot with a preservative, then mend it as shown below. If the rail has broken away, you'll have to replace it. Use

treated lumber for your repairs.

To minimize rot around fences, make sure posts are set in concrete and cut back surrounding vegetation. Plants often keep areas moist and thereby contribute to the effects of moisture on wood.

> **YOU'LL NEED...**
> **SKILLS:** Basic carpentry skills.
> **TIME:** 30 to 60 minutes to fix a rail; additional time for painting.
> **TOOLS:** Hammer, chisel, saw, nail set, caulking gun, screwdriver.

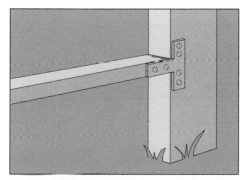

Chisel out rotted material. Secure rails to posts with steel T-braces, drilling pilot holes for screws.

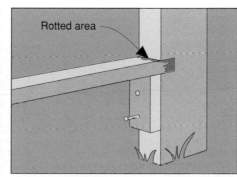

Alternatively, shore up rails with short 2×4s butted tightly against the rail and fastened to post with galvanized nails.

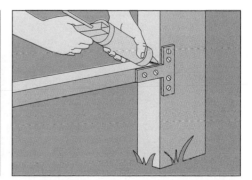

At the rail/post joint, apply butyl caulk, which will remain flexible to deter rot. Paint the brace to match the fence.

Solving Fence Problems (continued)

STABILIZING WOBBLY POSTS

Posts wobble because they weren't set properly or because moisture, freezing, and thawing have loosened their buried ends.

You can steady a wobbly post with stakes or splints, but if they have rotted away at ground level, you'll have to replace them. This is a big job, because the rails must be dismantled and reassembled.

To remove posts, rent a post puller or inch them out of the ground with a wrecking bar, using a piece of a 4×4 for leverage. Digging away the earth around the posts will make the job easier.

See page 197 on how to install new posts. Double-check your measurements; enlarging the holes may have put spacings slightly off.

> ### YOU'LL NEED...
> **SKILLS:** Basic carpentry skills.
> **TIME:** 30 to 90 minutes per post.
> **TOOLS:** Shovel, hammer, posthole digger, drill, wrench, concrete tools.

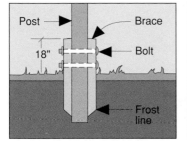

Shore up posts with 2×4 stakes. Bevel driving ends, apply a preservative, drive stakes, and bolt together.

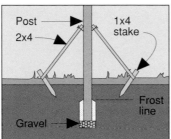

For a more permanent repair, enlarge postholes, pour concrete, and tamp. Brace posts while you work.

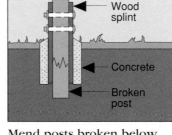

Mend posts broken below ground with splints. Enlarge hole, position and bolt splints, and pour concrete.

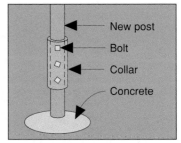

To repair rusted pipe posts, cut old pipe and replace with new pipe, using a collar and bolts to secure the joint.

REPAIRING SAGGING GATES

Check gate posts to make sure they're firmly anchored in the ground. If not, fix them using one of the methods illustrated above.

If the posts are plumb but the gate binds, examine the hinges. Chances are, they're loose, worn, bent, or not sturdy enough to support the weight of the gate. If so, replace the hinges.

Moisture makes a wooden gate swell. The tendency then is to force the gate open or closed, which loosens the hinges and causes the gate to sag.

> ### YOU'LL NEED...
> **SKILLS:** Basic carpentry skills.
> **TIME:** 1 hour to fix a wooden gate.
> **TOOLS:** Hammer, screwdriver, saw, drill, wrench.

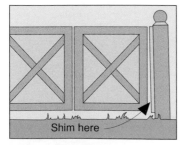

If the gate is hung on a post, remove hinges and shim them as shown. If the latch side binds, plane it.

If hinges are loose, remove them, fill holes with dowel plugs, and replace hinges using longer screws or bolts.

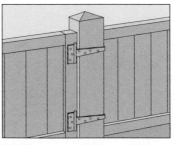

Replace worn hinges with larger ones. To make a strap hinge stronger, bend its tip around the post.

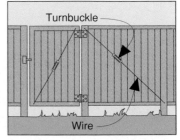

Brace gate frames with turnbuckles and wire. Attach wire to screw eyes in the gate or fence frame.

Building New Fences

Want to build a new fence? Don't underestimate the amount of time and effort involved in building it— it's hard work! Luckily, however, erecting a fence is not complex. If you are reasonably handy and if you heed the advice given on the next few pages, you won't have much difficulty.

PLANNING A FENCE

As with so many other home improvement projects, the building of your fence is only one part of the project. The up-front time involved in planning is equally important.

You should check your local building codes first. Many ordinances specify the maximum height a fence may be, the distances you can build from property lines and the street, and even the type of materials you can and cannot use.

Find out also if you'll need a building permit. (If the fence will protect a swimming pool, for example, you almost certainly will.) To apply for a permit, you'll have to submit a plan for approval. Pick up the forms and relevant regulations from your local building department.

If a new fence abuts neighbors' properties or affects their views, talk with them about your plans. Double-check property lines (hiring a surveyor if needed) and clarify that you will maintain the fence. This will forestall future disputes or lawsuits.

What do you want your fence to do? Must it mask trash cans or a work area? Provide privacy or security? Define a garden or patio? Screen the sun or buffer wind? A well-planned fence often does several of these jobs at once.

Visualize your design in context with present or future landscaping. Will you need a gate? Alternatively, consider a series of freestanding fence panels, staggered in such a way that they provide privacy yet let people walk through easily.

Choose materials and styling that complement your home's style. If a new fence will be visible from the street, it should harmonize with your neighborhood's character.

Proper scale is important, too. A fence that is too tall will visually overwhelm a low ranch house, while a short fence will look squatty beside a tall house.

BUFFERING WIND

It might seem that a solid fence would make an excellent windbreak. But as you can see from the sketches below, solid construction actually may aggravate a wind problem. What's more, a severe storm might flatten the entire fence.

If the wind in your area is consistently strong, slow it down with open work screening, such as slats, latticework, or bamboo. Louvers not only reduce the air's velocity considerably, they redirect it as well. You can use trees and shrubbery to help control wind, too.

Before you orient a windbreak, check with the local weather bureau or your county extension service for the direction of prevailing winds and advice on height and size of such a windbreak.

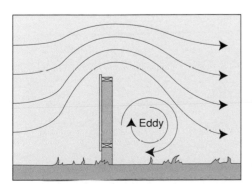

Wind striking a solid fence "hops" over it, creating a vacuum on the lee side that pulls the air down again.

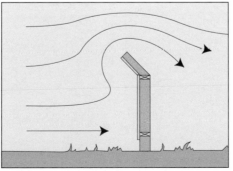

Adding a 45-degree cap at the top of the fence increases the wind-protected area on the other side.

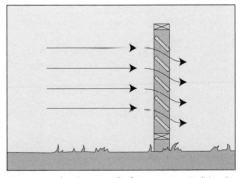

An open latticework fence won't block the wind totally, but will slow its velocity to a more comfortable level.

Building New Fences (continued)

COPING WITH A SLOPE

Don't let a sloping site discourage you from building a fence. In fact, building on uneven terrain often makes a fence more visually interesting. The drawings at right show two methods that you can use, depending largely on the severity of the slope.

On gentle slopes, you'll have to "rack" the rails as you install them. Sink the end posts first, then stretch a line between them and lay out the rails to locate positions for the line posts (see page 196). Dig a hole for the first line post and cement it into place (see page 197), making this post several inches taller than the fence will be.

Fasten the bottom rails to the end post and pull them up or push them down until they're parallel to the ground. Fasten them to the line post. Repeat this procedure down the line.

After you've installed all bottom and top rails, go back and trim off the post tops to the proper height, cutting them at an angle so that rain and snow will not collect on top.

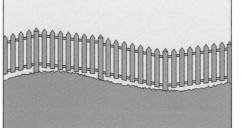

On a gentle slope, let the fence follow the land's contour. Open styles are better suited to this than solid ones.

On steeper grades or if you use solid screening, step the fence. Construct one section at a time.

CHOOSING A FENCE STYLE

You may have a general fence style in mind to achieve the look you want in your yard, but there are so many styles that it might be worthwhile to look around to see what other people have done. Some typical styles are shown below. Many other books and magazines offer good ideas that you can duplicate or modify to your desire.

You may find that home center stores can help you choose a style. Their personnel usually have a good idea of what styles of fences will work well in various situations. Also, many stores now sell some styles in prefab form, which saves a lot of cutting and fitting.

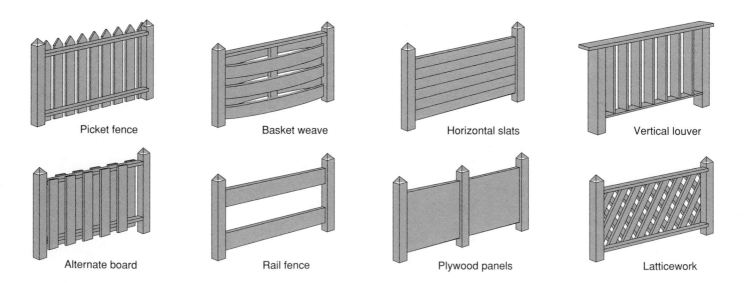

Picket fence

Basket weave

Horizontal slats

Vertical louver

Alternate board

Rail fence

Plywood panels

Latticework

CHOOSING MATERIALS AND A SCREENING STYLE

Before making a materials list, visit home centers to look at available options. Your first decision is whether to use pressure-treated or untreated lumber. For posts in the ground and rails lying close to the ground, the question is a no-brainer—always use pressure-treated. For screening, compare the slightly greater cost of pressure-treated lumber to the advantage of a fence that won't rot in your lifetime.

The next decision is how much intricate cutting you want to do yourself. You may be surprised at the number and variety of styles of precut fencing material—milled posts, rails, post caps, and many styles of pickets.

Picket styles are limited only by your imagination (some examples are shown at right). Pick a precut one or design one yourself. Pickets with straight cuts are simple to turn out with a tablesaw, chopsaw, or radial-arm saw. Before you decide to make your own pickets with intricate curves, however, count the number you will need, then time yourself making several. How long will it take to make all you need? At some point of no return, precut pickets may look pretty reasonable.

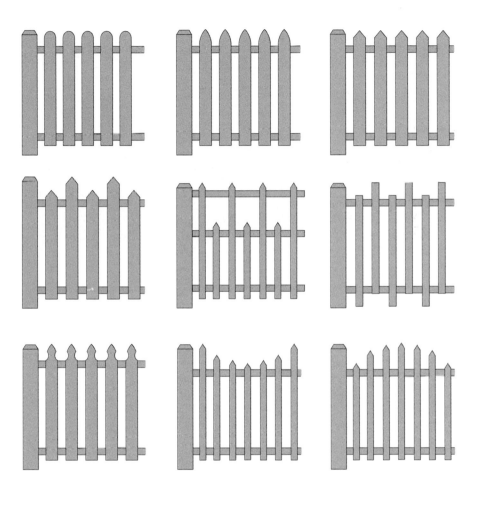

MAKING PICKETS WITH A BANDSAW

Unless you need only a dozen pickets, forget about using a sabersaw. The only tool for making identical, repetitive curved cuts on a hundred or more pickets is a bandsaw. Use a template to ensure that your pickets are uniform. Gang four or more pickets together, predrill the top and bottom nailing holes, and loosely nail them together while you make the cuts.

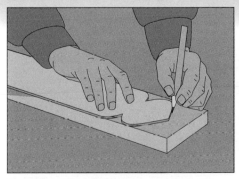

1. Make a template from tempered hardboard or other sheet material, and trace outline onto pickets.

2. Drill and nail four or more pickets together, top and bottom, then cut picket outline with bandsaw.

Building New Fences *(continued)*

LAYING OUT A FENCE

Take your time in laying out a fence project. The reason: A measurement that's just an inch off at the outset can become a foot down the line.

Start by marking end and corner posts, then stretching a mason's line between them. Step back and look at your layout from several angles. If it looks good, sink end posts, then mark positions for line posts.

If your fence is long, a 50-foot tape measure will make your layout job a lot easier. For stakes, use 1×2s or 2×2s that have been pointed at one end with a hatchet.

1. Locate terminal posts (corners and ends) and mark with stakes. Then locate and mark gate post positions.

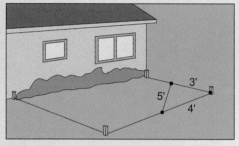

2. Square the corners, using the 3'-4'-5' method. Tie a mason's line between the posts to mark the fence line.

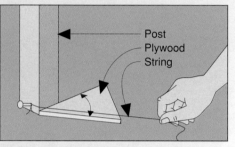

Post
Plywood
String

3. If a corner won't be 90 degrees, compute the angle on graph paper and cut a template from a plywood scrap.

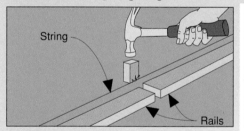

String

Rails

4. Locate line posts by laying precut rails along the line. Drive stakes where the rail ends butt.

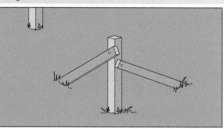

For a stepped fence, set and plumb lower post and use a tape measure to locate stakes for line posts upslope.

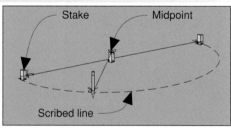

Stake   Midpoint

Scribed line

For a curve, stake ends. Stretch a line between them and find midpoint. Trace arc with a line and a stick.

TOOL TALK

Set fence posts from 24 to 30 inches into the ground. It's best to dig below the frost line if you can.

Sink end, corner, and gate posts slightly deeper than line posts. To give yourself leeway for getting everything plumb and straight, make the holes larger than the posts.

Always set terminal and gate posts first. Then dig a hole for the first line post, set it, and move on to the next. Space line posts 6 to 8 feet apart.

USING POSTHOLE DIGGERS

If you're digging just a few holes in rock-free earth, use a clamshell or auger posthole digger for the job.

If you have a lot of holes to dig, rent a power-driven auger. These generate lots of torque, so you'll need a helper.

SETTING FENCE POSTS

For strength and long life, always set end, corner, and gate posts in concrete. You can anchor line posts in soil only, unless the fence will be extremely tall, heavy, or subjected to strong winds. You'll add life to line posts, however, if they're set in concrete also. (See page 196 for tips on digging postholes.)

Because the posts are set one at a time, consider buying premixed bags of concrete. Premixed material has the correct amount of sand and gravel added to the cement; all you need to do is add water and mix.

Otherwise, you can buy the cement in bags, order sand and gravel, and mix the concrete yourself (see pages 180–181). Mixing it yourself is less expensive, but the convenience of premixed usually is worth the extra money. In either case, you will need some gravel for the bottom of the postholes.

YOU'LL NEED...

SKILLS: Basic carpentry and concrete handling skills.
TIME: 4 to 6 hours for a four-sided fence with one gate.
TOOLS: Posthole digger, shovel, level, hammer, circular saw, tamping rod or board, and, if you're mixing your own concrete, a wheelbarrow or mixing box and concrete hoe.

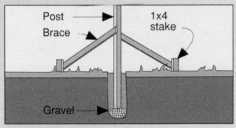

1. Shovel 3 inches of gravel into hole. Set post in place, plumb it on two sides, and brace with outriggers.

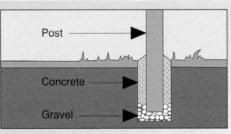

2. Add more gravel around post. Pour in concrete, tamping as you fill to remove air bubbles in the mix.

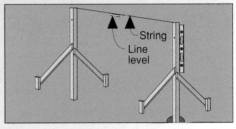

3. Set next terminal post. Plumb and brace it. Stretch line between posts to ensure equal heights. Add concrete.

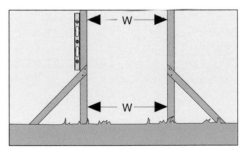

To square gate openings, measure between posts at top and bottom. Measurements must be equal.

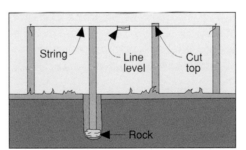

If you dig a posthole too deep, use a rock as a filler. If holes are too shallow, dig deeper or saw off post top later.

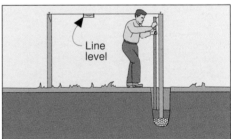

To set posts in soil, lay a gravel base, then have a helper shovel dirt into the hole while you tamp. Mound earth.

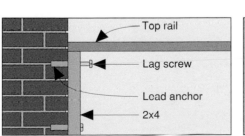

Attach a terminal post to a masonry wall using lead expansion anchors and lag screws. Drill with a masonry bit.

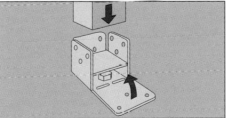

Fasten posts to a concrete slab with metal post anchors held in place with expansion anchors and lag screws.

For a watertight seal around posts in concrete, wait for a dry spell to apply butyl caulk around post base.

Building New Fences (continued)

MATERIAL MATTERS   APPLYING FINISHES BEFORE ASSEMBLY

Tom Sawyer discovered that it takes a lot of time to work a brush into all the nooks and crannies of a fence. Even a short fence soaks up a surprisingly large quantity of paint or stain.

Unless you are like Tom and have gullible friends, your best bet is to finish the fence pieces before you assemble them. So, after the posts are set, cut the rails and screening, lay them out on sawhorses or another support system, and apply the finish of your choice with a roller or paintbrush.

Use a good exterior paint or stain (see page 553). Both wood and metal must be primed first; this properly seals the surface so that the top coating will hold up longer under exposure to severe weather.

Spraying paint (see pages 568–569) makes this job even faster, but the overspray wastes a lot of finish and may kill nearby vegetation if you're not careful. You also must be careful to spray on calm days or you risk getting wind-blown paint on houses and cars that are in the area.

Once your prefinished fence is assembled, you'll have to go back and touch up spots that have been marred by hammer tracks, saw cuts, and other knocks and dings. Just to be on the safe side, apply a third coat to the tops of the posts and to the joints between the rails and the posts.

PUTTING UP RAILS

Fastening rails to posts calls for simple joinery techniques. Once the posts are plumb and aligned, simply cut each rail squarely, fasten it to one post, then level and attach it to the next post.

The illustrations below show seven different ways to secure rails. The one you choose depends on your tools and skills. It's tough, for example, to cut dadoes, notches, and mortises and tenons without power equipment. On the other hand, butt joints supported by blocks or metal angles call for only regular hand tools and nailing know-how. Toenailed joints are easy, too, once you have mastered the knack of making them (see page 51).

For fasteners, use ceramic-coated screws or hot-dipped galvanized nails. Other types stain the finish.

Space bottom rails at least 6 inches above the ground—far enough away so that vegetation doesn't touch them and transfer moisture to them. You can place them higher to make mowing easier. Fences taller than 10 feet may need a third rail spaced equally between top and bottom rails.

YOU'LL NEED...

SKILLS: Basic carpentry skills.
TIME: 15 minutes per post.
TOOLS: Drill, screwdriver, chisel, hammer, circular saw.

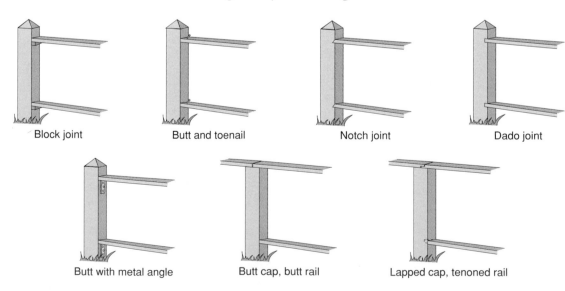

Block joint   Butt and toenail   Notch joint   Dado joint

Butt with metal angle   Butt cap, butt rail   Lapped cap, tenoned rail

PUTTING UP SCREENING

Now comes the fun part of building a fence—fleshing it out with screening material. As with all carpentry projects, you must keep the parts both square and level.

You can purchase precut fence screening such as pickets, wooden panels, and gates. Other types of screening must be custom-made—an easy but repetitious job. For a custom fence, adapt the basic screening techniques shown below.

YOU'LL NEED...

SKILLS: Basic carpentry skills.
TIME: 2 hours for a 30-foot fence.
TOOLS: Drill, screwdriver, hammer, saw.

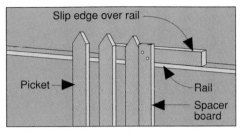

To space pickets, slats, and boards, ripsaw a strip to width and nail a cleat to one end. Hang cleat on top rail.

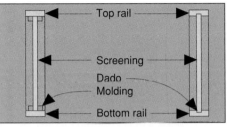

Nail screening to the sides of posts and rails. Or, sandwich it between molding strips or into dadoes in the rails.

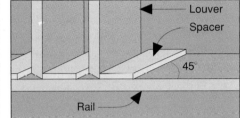

For a louvered fence, cut spacer blocks from 1×3 boards. Cut at 45-degree angles so each louver fits perfectly.

BUILDING A GATE

A gate that is strong and true will give you years of trouble-free service; a poorly constructed one will cause all kinds of grief. Hang the gate on the gate posts before attaching the screening to the fence in case it's necessary to correct an out-of-square opening.

YOU'LL NEED...

SKILLS: Basic carpentry skills.
TIME: 2 to 3 hours.
TOOLS: Saw, drill, screwdriver.

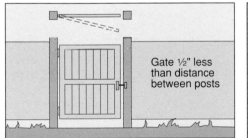

1. Square opening. Make the frame ½ inch narrower than the opening. For very heavy gates, allow ¾ inch.

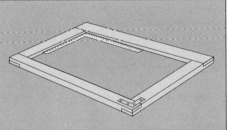

2. Use lap joints at corners of frame. Metal angle plates add strength at corners. Check square when assembling.

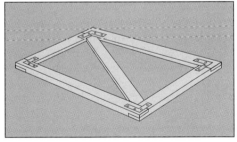

3. For strength, run a diagonal brace from the top of the hinge side to the bottom of the latch side. Add screening.

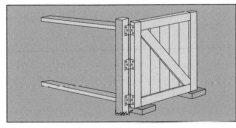

4. Screw or bolt hinges to the gate. Prop gate open in a level position, then fasten hinges to the post.

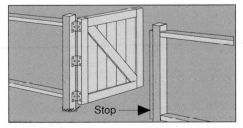

5. With the gate closed, mark its inside edge on the latch post then nail up a strip of wood to serve as a gate stop.

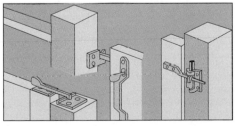

6. Mount latches on the top or the side of the gate. The thumb latch (center) requires boring a hole in the gate rail.

Building New Fences (continued)

USING VINYL FENCING

"Vinyl is final," was the pitch that converted contractors and homeowners alike to vinyl siding. The thought of never having to paint a house again has convinced many people to switch from traditional wood siding to vinyl materials.

Next came vinyl lawn furniture and rain gutters—and now fencing. Good-quality vinyl fencing is expensive, but, as its manufacturers point out, the extra cost is justified by the advantages. It won't rot or corrode; fade or discolor; chip, crack, or peel; and it cleans up with soap and water.

Vinyl fencing installs in much the same way as wood fencing. The fencing comes in kit form, knocked down, in 6- or 8-foot sections. Posts are laid out and set in the ground to a depth of 24 to 30 inches. Gate posts, which suffer the most abuse, are filled with concrete and ½-inch reinforcing rod. Terminal, corner, and line posts are filled with 60-pound bags of concrete mix, followed by a bucket of water.

Rails fit into premade sockets in the square posts. Pickets sit in sockets in the bottom rail and pass through, or are capped by, the top rail. Hardware and fasteners are made of stainless steel.

Both posts and pickets may be capped off with a variety of molded caps to achieve the style of fence you prefer. The style shown in the anatomy drawing at right is a classic picket fence. But you will find privacy, lattice, and farm styles, too. No matter what style you choose, you'll never again have to worry about hiring Tom Sawyer to whitewash this fence.

ANATOMY OF A VINYL FENCE

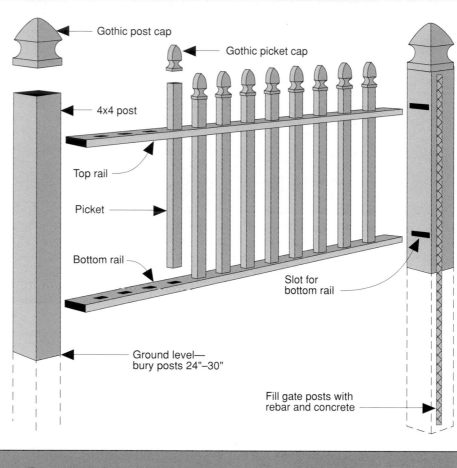

Gothic post cap

Gothic picket cap

4x4 post

Top rail

Picket

Bottom rail

Slot for bottom rail

Ground level—bury posts 24"–30"

Fill gate posts with rebar and concrete

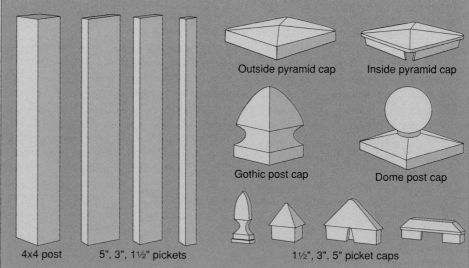

4x4 post

5", 3", 1½" pickets

1½", 3", 5" picket caps

Outside pyramid cap

Inside pyramid cap

Gothic post cap

Dome post cap

ANATOMY OF A CHAIN-LINK FENCE

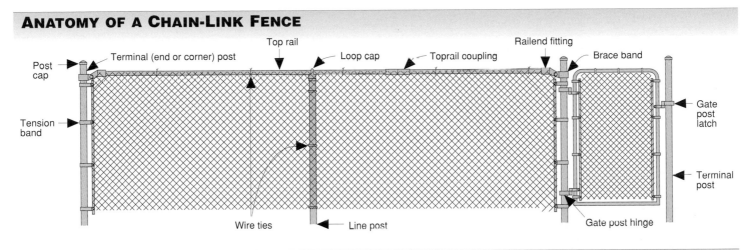

INSTALLING CHAIN-LINK FENCING

Despite its appearance, chain-link fence is relatively simple to install. It comes in several different heights, and dealers will deliver material with fence posts cut to the correct height. The only special tools needed are a posthole digger and fence stretcher.

Chain-link fence is no more expensive than a wood fence, lasts a lifetime if you buy quality material, requires little or no maintenance, offers excellent security, and adapts well to uneven terrain.

Wood and plastic slats threaded vertically through the links offer privacy and a wind screen. Or, for a more natural look, encourage vines to grow up the fence.

YOU'LL NEED...

SKILLS: Basic mechanical skills.
TIME: 2 to 3 hours to set posts, 2 days for concrete to dry, 4 to 6 hours to install fencing.
TOOLS: Posthole digger, shovel, level, fence stretcher, hammer, pliers, adjustable wrench.

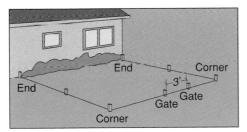

1. Mark locations of terminal posts—ends, corners, and gates. Allow 3 feet, inside-to-inside, between gate posts.

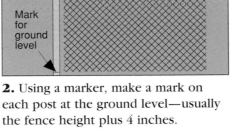

2. Using a marker, make a mark on each post at the ground level—usually the fence height plus 4 inches.

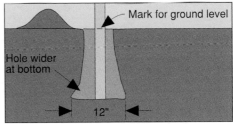

3. Using a clamshell digger, dig the holes for the terminal posts to the depth of your mark on each post.

4. Set posts in concrete. Just before the concrete sets, plumb the posts and adjust height so the mark you made (see Step 2) is at ground level.

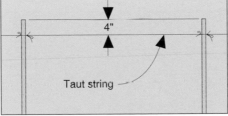

5. After concrete dries a day, stretch taut lines between terminal posts 4 inches below their tops as guides for line posts.

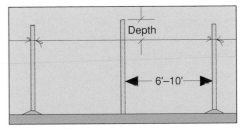

6. Space line posts evenly every 6 to 10 feet between terminal posts. Hold posts to string and mark. Dig holes to the depths marked.

Building New Fences (continued)

INSTALLING CHAIN-LINK FENCING (continued)

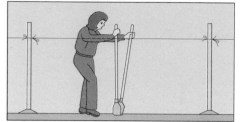

7. Dig the line postholes. Verify the depths by inserting the posts in the holes and holding them up to string.

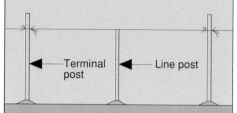

Terminal post — Line post

8. Set the line posts plumb in concrete with the tops even with, and centered under, string. Let concrete cure a day.

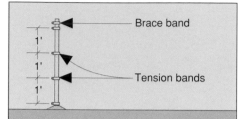

Brace band

1'
1'
1'

Tension bands

9. Slip on tension bands (one per foot) and brace bands (one per end and gate post; two per corner post).

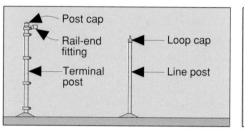

Post cap

Rail-end fitting

Loop cap

Terminal post

Line post

10. Cap terminal posts with post caps. Place a loop cap on each line post. Fasten rail-end fittings to brace bands.

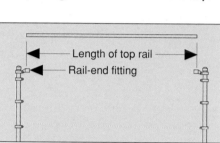

Length of top rail

Rail-end fitting

11. When measuring top rail length, include socket depth in measurement. Begin inserting rails at one end fitting.

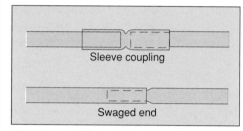

Sleeve coupling

Swaged end

12. Depending on product, the rail sections fit together with couplings or by inserting small end into large end.

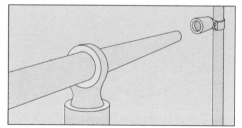

13. Insert top rail through loop caps. Cut last rail to length, remove other fitting, slip onto rail end, and refasten.

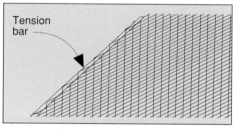

Tension bar

14. Unroll fencing on the ground outside posts. Slide a tension bar through the links at one end.

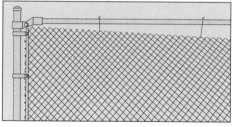

15. Lift fence and attach tension bar to terminal post tension bands. Lift and tie fence loosely to top rail with wire ties.

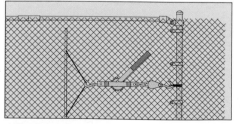

16. Thread a tension bar through fence 4 feet from other terminal post and stretch fence taut with fence stretcher.

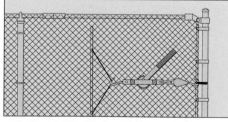

17. Hold third tension bar to tension bands and "cut" fence by removing a vertical strand. Feed bar through end.

18. Attach bar to tension bands and remove stretcher. Secure fence to top rail and line posts with wire ties.

Solving Wall Problems

Garden walls fall into two broad categories: screen walls, which are little more than fences made of masonry, and retaining walls, which are stronger to hold back a slope and prevent soil erosion.

Both usually stand on concrete footings and consist of successive courses of bricks, block, stone, or other material bound together with mortar—a mixture of cement, sand, and water. Dry walls are laid without mortar (see pages 204–205).

Brick walls, such as the one shown above right, ordinarily have two or more tiers, interlocked periodically with metal wall ties.

Retaining walls include the same basic elements as screen walls, plus additional features. Reinforcing rods strengthen the wall itself and tie it into the earth it retains. Weep holes allow excess water to escape, keeping pressure off the wall.

Many masonry garden walls are topped with a concrete or stone cap. Below and alongside, there may be a drainage system to carry off water.

Water is a masonry wall's mortal enemy. Freezing and thawing water can heave footings, crumble mortar joints, and topple caps. Trouble points on retaining walls include blocked drainage tiles and weep holes and soil erosion directly behind the wall where it meets the soil. Plantings and additional buried drainage tile will help stop erosion.

Check walls twice a year. Pay particular attention to the situation at ground level. Maintain and repair masonry walls as you would other exterior masonry (see page 149). Keep mortar joints in repair by tuckpointing them, and patch damaged wall caps. If the wall is wood, replace any rotting wood members with pressure-treated lumber.

ANATOMY OF A SCREEN WALL

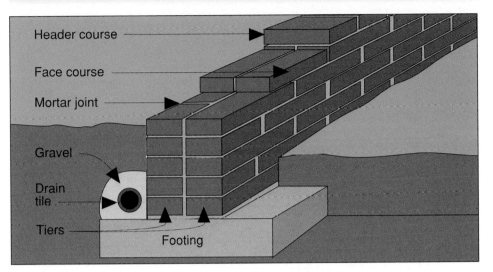

Header course
Face course
Mortar joint
Gravel
Drain tile
Tiers
Footing

ANATOMY OF A RETAINING WALL

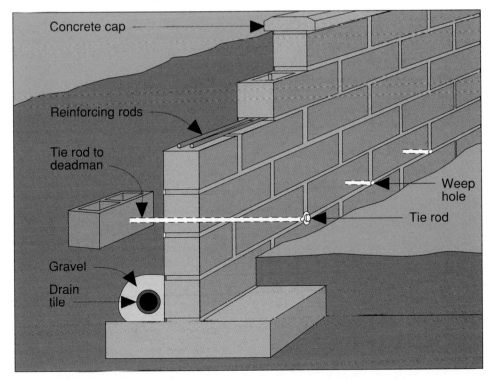

Concrete cap
Reinforcing rods
Tie rod to deadman
Gravel
Drain tile
Weep hole
Tie rod

Building New Walls

Building a garden wall is hard work and requires some masonry skills, but it's by no means beyond a do-it-yourselfer's skills.

Dry walls (those without mortar) go up in a hurry because you just pile up layer upon layer of stone—either freestanding or against an earth embankment. Many home centers now sell interlocking blocks that look like natural rock—an easy option for a rustic look. Wet walls require more skill to build because they use mortar for strength.

Plan the wall's placement for maximum effect—visual and practical. Make sure that building codes don't restrict where and with what materials you can build. And overestimate your material needs so you won't be caught short.

DRY WALLS

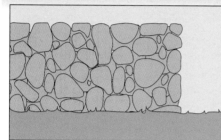

Rubble-stone walls are like jigsaw puzzles. Simply stack them up—against a bank or freestanding (see page 205).

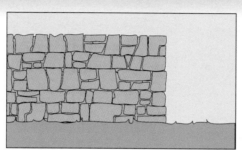

Ashlar stonc is cut on four sides so it's easy to stack. You still may have to do some final cutting for a neat fit.

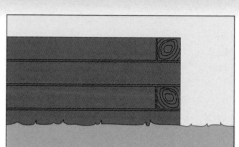

Used or new railroad ties make terrific walls. Stack and tie them together with large spikes or steel reinforcing rods.

WET WALLS

Brick walls gain strength from mortar and usually require footings (see pages 206–207 and 210–213).

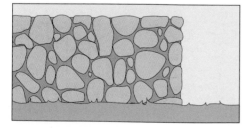

Like brick, a mortared concrete block wall needs footings, but it goes up faster (see pages 207–209).

Field stone must be cut and fitted. Such walls require more mortar than brick or concrete block walls.

Poured concrete walls require forms, which you can rent. These sturdy walls have footings and are reinforced.

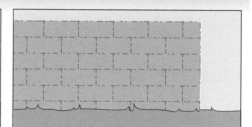

Build a wall quickly by dry-laying blocks, then bonding them together with fiberglass-reinforced mortar.

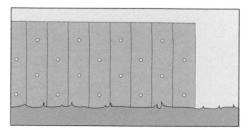

LAYING UP A DRY STONE WALL

Stacking stone is the oldest way to build a wall. Excellent for building retaining walls, stone also makes nifty looking, freestanding decorative walls. But a dry stone wall usually won't work as a screening wall because you can't dry-stack the stones high enough to achieve the screening effect.

Generally, you won't need to lay footings when erecting a dry stone wall. The wall will ride out frost heaves, and if damage does occur, you can repair it quickly.

If the wall will be freestanding and is for decorative purposes only, level the ground with a shovel and lay a gravel bed before stacking the stone. This especially applies to ashlar stone. A level base allows you to lay up the stones like bricks.

If you have the opportunity, pick and choose your stones when you purchase them. Select medium to large stones, instead of smaller ones, because they fill up space faster. For the smaller stones that you'll need to fill in holes around the larger ones,

break the stones with a mason's hammer. If you can't pick and choose and are stuck with a potpourri of sizes, use the larger stones as the base for the wall and lay the smaller ones on top.

YOU'LL NEED...

SKILLS: Basic masonry skills.
TIME: 2 days for a 20-foot-long wall that's 2 feet high.
TOOLS: Mason's hammer, brick chisel, shovel, wooden stakes, mason's line, wheelbarrow.

1. Lay out the wall using stakes and a mason's line. Dig a trench 6 to 12 inches deep and about 1 foot wider than the wall.

2. Fill the trench to within an inch of grade with pea gravel or small rocks and level the base. This base provides drainage and serves as a footing.

3. Begin the wall with stones that are large enough to span the gravel bed. Save smaller stones for the top courses.

4. For the second and succeeding courses, stagger the joints for greater strength. For retaining walls, tilt courses into the embankment.

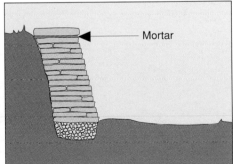

Mortar

5. For a tight cap, spread 2 inches of mortar along the next-to-last course. Press flat stones into the mortar, filling the gaps with small stones.

Building New Walls (continued)

WORKING WITH MORTAR

For convenience, most people prefer to buy premixed mortar, even though it costs a bit more than it does to purchase the ingredients.

If you mix your own, a good "mix" for garden walls is one part masonry cement to three parts sand. Always use new masonry cement, and be sure the sand is clean. You'll need four bags of masonry cement and 12 cubic feet of sand for a brick wall 4 inches thick and 100 square feet in surface area.

You can mix the mortar in a mortar box or the bed of a large wheelbarrow; you'll need a hoe to blend the cement, sand, and water.

Store unmixed mortar cement in a dry place (again, don't use old cement that you've stored for a while). Have the truck driver dump the sand near the job site to save you time and effort. Keep the sand covered with plastic film. When you squeeze a handful of sand, it should stay in a ball without crumbling or exuding water (see page 181).

To mix mortar, combine the cement and the sand and blend it together with a hoe until its color is consistent throughout. Then add the water a little at a time, stirring the mixture with the hoe until it is smooth like thick mud. Test its consistency with a trowel, as illustrated below. Mix small amounts of mortar at a time; it sets quickly and becomes useless after an hour or so (even faster in hot weather).

TOOL TALK

USING A TROWEL

A trowel is used to place and trim mortar on bricks and blocks. It's also handy for making wall repairs (see pages 149–150). Beginners should pick a lightweight trowel. If you buy a good one, it should last a lifetime.

Practice makes perfect when it comes to working with mortar. So before attempting a finished project, build a test wall. You can reclaim the bricks or blocks, so your only "education expense" is the mortar.

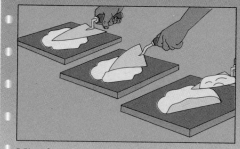

Mix the mortar so it slumps slightly. Slice off a section of "mud" and pick it up with a twist of your wrist.

Flick your wrist as you would flip a pancake, "throwing" the mortar in a smooth, lengthwise movement.

Run the trowel down the center of bricks to furrow the mortar. For concrete blocks, lay two lines initially.

Butter one end of the brick and set it down (don't slide it). Press dampened brick or dry block on the mortar.

Use the edge of your trowel to slice off mortar that oozes out. Use this excess to butter the next brick end.

Using a joint strike or piece of pipe, smooth mortar joints when they begin to stiffen (see page 211).

TOOL TALK

For brick and block walls, you'll need a mason's level, mason's hammer, cape chisel, line blocks, and mason's line. Make a hawk and a mortarboard from ¾-inch exterior plywood and 2×2s. Other handy tools include a brick chisel, sledgehammer, and a story pole to align bricks or blocks as the courses are laid. Make the story pole (see page 209 or 212) with a straight 1×3 the same height as the wall, marked off in vertical increments equal to the height of a block or brick.

OTHER MASONRY TOOLS

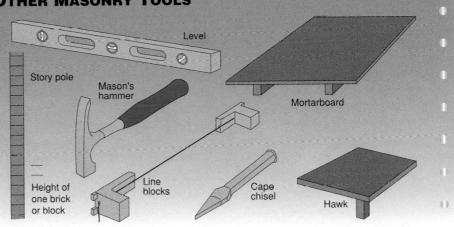

POURING FOOTINGS FOR WALLS

Wet walls require footings. As with all footings, those for walls should be below the frost line to prevent frost heaving. If you're unsure how deep the frost line is in your area, check with your local building department or extension service.

Because footings usually require lots of concrete, it's best to buy premixed material and have it trucked in. This will save you time and plenty of back-breaking work.

YOU'LL NEED...

SKILLS: Intermediate concrete skills.
TIME: 1 day.
TOOLS: Shovel, hammer, mason's line, level, rake, screed.

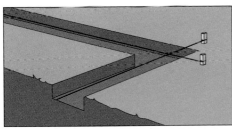

1. Stake out lines for the wall. Dig a trench twice the width of the footing. First wall courses will be below grade.

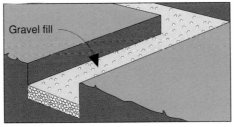

2. Place 6 inches of gravel in the trench for drainage and level it using a garden rake.

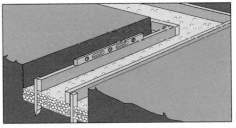

3. Stake the forms, making sure they are perfectly level and square. Drive stakes on the outside of the forms.

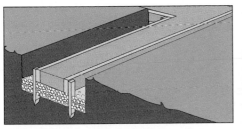

4. Coat forms with old motor oil for easy removal later. Pour concrete to top of forms.

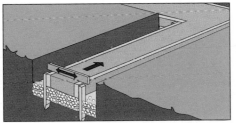

5. Screed concrete by seesawing a 2×4 along top edges of forms, removing excess concrete as you go.

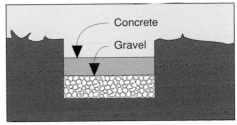

If the ground is hard, you can pour concrete without forms. Dig a straight-sided trench the width of the footing.

Building New Walls (continued)

MATERIAL MATTERS

WORKING WITH CONCRETE BLOCK

The illustration below shows various types and sizes of concrete blocks. Some blocks are sized to accommodate a ½-inch mortar joint.

Concrete blocks aren't as visually pleasing as bricks, stone, lumber, and other materials. You can solve this problem by using decorative blocks, which are manufactured in a variety of patterns and some special shapes.

Block walls need footings placed below the frost line. Lay out your concrete block wall in multiples of 8 inches. This will save work cutting the blocks to fit. Determine the number of blocks you need from this standard measurement.

As with brick walls, use a mortar mix consisting of one part cement to three parts sand. The mix should be drier than that for bricks because the heavy blocks will compact the mixture. So use less water. Unlike bricks, which must be dampened with water before they're laid, concrete blocks should be bone dry as they're mortared and set.

You'll need a trowel, mason's hammer, brick chisel, joint strike, level, carpenter's square, line blocks and mason's line, and a story pole.

Dimensions listed as W×L×H

Partition
$3\frac{5}{8}\times7\frac{5}{8}\times3\frac{5}{8}$"

½ Partition
$3\frac{5}{8}\times15\frac{5}{8}\times3\frac{5}{8}$"

Partition
$3\frac{5}{8}\times15\frac{5}{8}\times7\frac{5}{8}$"

Double ends
$3\frac{5}{8}\times7\frac{5}{8}\times7\frac{5}{8}$"

Plain ends
$7\frac{5}{8}\times7\frac{5}{8}\times7\frac{5}{8}$"

Double ends
$5\frac{5}{8}\times15\frac{5}{8}\times3\frac{5}{8}$"

Double ends
$5\frac{5}{8}\times11\frac{5}{8}\times3\frac{5}{8}$"

Double ends
$5\frac{5}{8}\times7\frac{5}{8}\times7\frac{5}{8}$"

Half jamb
$5\frac{5}{8}\times7\frac{5}{8}\times7\frac{5}{8}$"

Half block
$7\frac{5}{8}\times7\frac{5}{8}\times7\frac{5}{8}$"

Half-high double end
$7\frac{5}{8}\times15\frac{5}{8}\times3\frac{5}{8}$"

Half-high
$7\frac{5}{8}\times15\frac{5}{8}\times3\frac{5}{8}$"

Half-high stretcher
$7\frac{5}{8}\times15\frac{5}{8}\times3\frac{5}{8}$"

Half-high
$7\frac{5}{8}\times7\frac{5}{8}\times3\frac{5}{8}$"

Double ends
$7\frac{5}{8}\times11\frac{5}{8}\times7\frac{5}{8}$"

Double end
$7\frac{5}{8}\times15\frac{5}{8}\times7\frac{5}{8}$"

Regular
$7\frac{5}{8}\times15\frac{5}{8}\times7\frac{5}{8}$"

Stretcher
$7\frac{5}{8}\times15\frac{5}{8}\times7\frac{5}{8}$"

Steel sash jamb
$7\frac{5}{8}\times15\frac{5}{8}\times7\frac{5}{8}$"

Plain ends
$7\frac{5}{8}\times11\frac{5}{8}\times7\frac{5}{8}$"

Cutting Concrete Blocks

Mark a cut line around the block. With a chisel and hammer, tap along line. The block will crack at the line.

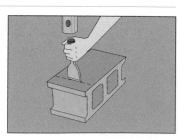

Reinforcing Block Walls

For walls that are higher than 4 feet, sink reinforcing rods into the footing as you pour it. Slip blocks over rods and fill cores with mortar.

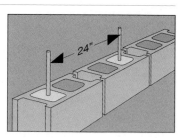

LAYING A BLOCK WALL

"Start even and square; finish even and square," is an old adage that's especially true when laying blocks or bricks. If you're off at the start, the error compounds with each added block. Also, the mortar joints must remain consistent in width so the blocks will align properly.

Set the ends, first course, and corners first. Check that the first blocks are level and square. To ensure that you lay the blocks level and plumb, stretch a mason's line between line blocks at either end of the wall. Move the line up after each course is complete. Don't rely on the line blocks alone, though. Use a story pole to guide you, and check every three blocks with a level as you go. If you spot an error, remove the blocks and start again.

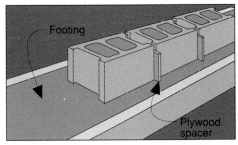

1. Before mixing mortar, dry lay first course on footing. Use wood strips for joint spacing. Mark spacings on footing.

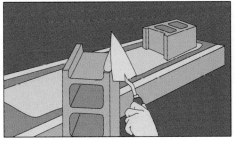

2. Set the end block in a bed of 2-inch-deep mortar. Butter and set second block with smaller holes down.

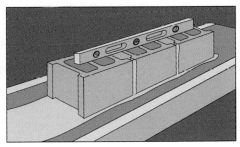

3. Check for level and plumb every three blocks. Tap blocks into mortar with trowel to make adjustments.

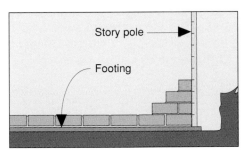

4. Build corners or ends after first course. Check with level and story pole. If off, pull blocks and start again.

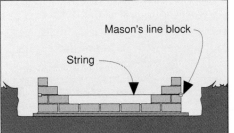

5. When corners are four courses high, stretch a line between them. Mason's line blocks hold line taut.

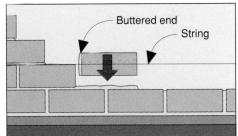

6. Lay blocks between corners level with line. Lift blocks into position; don't slide them. Alternate block joints.

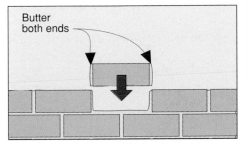

7. Butter both ends of last block in a course and ends of adjacent blocks. Carefully slip block into position.

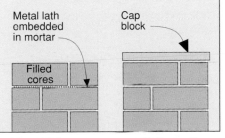

8. Use solid caps to top off the wall. Or, sandwich mesh in last mortar joint and fill block cores with mortar.

9. Use joint strike or pipe to smooth mortar (see page 211). Finish by wiping joints and faces with burlap.

Building New Walls (continued)

WORKING WITH BRICK

Laying up a brick wall is one of those projects that's more time-consuming than difficult. For every square foot of wall surface, you'll need to place about seven bricks. So, even a short wall translates into a lot of work.

Many of the same tools and techniques that are used for block walls work equally well for brick walls. Before you undertake your project, refer to pages 206–207 for information on tools, pouring footings, and working with mortar.

When shopping for bricks, you'll find a variety of sizes, colors, and styles. But you're first basic choice is between three options: SW (severe-weathering) brick, used mainly in cold climates; MW (moderate-weathering) brick, for areas with moderate temperatures year-round; and NW (no-weathering) brick, for use in mild climates and interior construction, such as fireplace facades. For exterior retaining walls, use SW brick because it withstands frost better below grade.

You also can choose between standard, jumbo, or irregular sizes. This is pretty much a matter of personal preference.

You'll need seven bricks for every square foot of wall surface. For strength, brick screen and retaining walls should be made of two tiers (one column of bricks set next to another) rather than one tier. This doubles the number of bricks you'll need. You'll also have to order double the cement and sand for the mortar. To be safe, overestimate your needs so that you won't run short in the middle of your project.

Plan ahead for delivery, bearing in mind that your yard or driveway may not withstand the heavy load. For small quantities of brick, you may be able to wheelbarrow the bricks from the curb to the building site. Store bricks up off the ground on a wooden palette, and cover them with polyethylene so they don't absorb water.

Fitting Bricks Together

Although bricks are rectangular, you can lay them in a surprising number of ways that not only add strength to the wall but also give it a distinct character of its own. The illustrations on page 211 show some of the more popular bonds.

To get the design you want, you'll have to cut some of the bricks to fit. Tools needed to cut brick include a marking pencil, hammer, and brick chisel. Mark all four sides of the brick where you want to cut it. Then score the brick along the line by tapping the brick chisel gently with a hammer. The brick should break cleanly along the score line.

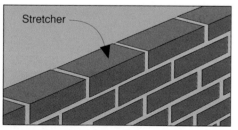

Stretchers, laid flat, with face out, are an integral part of every brick wall, regardless of the bond you choose.

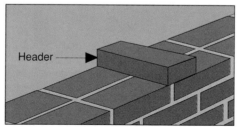

Headers run at right angles to stretchers. Laid every few courses, or on top of a wall, they add strength.

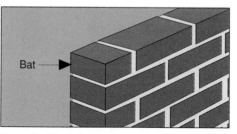

Bats (half-bricks) are used on ends of walls and as closure units for header courses. Split bricks to make bats.

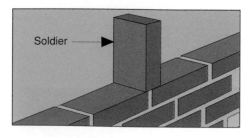

Soldiers are bricks set on end, facing outward. They add variation but little strength.

Rowlock headers are set across stretchers with their edges up. Rowlocks often are used to cap off a wall.

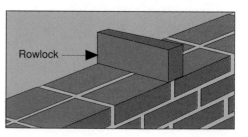

Choosing a Bond

The pattern in which you set your bricks is called a bond. As the bricks are laid, they are staggered so that vertical joints never align (except for stacked bond). Staggered joints give the wall strength.

You also can strengthen two-tiered walls with metal wall ties placed between tiers. The ties, positioned at various intervals along the wall, lay across the bricks.

Before you make a decision on the type of wall bond you want, it's a good idea to buy a hundred or so of the style of bricks you want and build a test wall without mortar. Try several different bonds, then make your commitment.

Running bond. All bricks are laid as stretchers. Use this bond for walls less than 4 feet high.

Common bond. Headers are used every six courses. Bats still are needed to get correct joint arrangement.

English bond. Header and stretcher courses alternate. Bricks split lengthwise stagger vertical joints.

Garden wall bond. Trios of stretchers are separated by headers. It's weaker than the English bond.

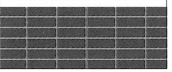

Stack bond. Joints are not staggered. A weak wall, so build a two-tiered wall and keep it shorter than 4 feet.

Flemish bond. Stretchers and headers are alternated in each course. This is an exceptionally strong bond.

Choosing a Mortar Joint

Pointing or striking a mortar joint helps make the joint watertight by sealing off tiny hairline cracks in the mortar. It also gives the wall a professionally finished appearance.

If your home has a brick veneer, you may want to finish your wall's joints to match. Buy an inexpensive joint strike, or you can use a piece of pipe, an old spoon, or a trowel for a pointing tool.

Struck joint. Make with the edge of a trowel before the mortar starts to harden. Test with a finger—mortar should be pliable to the touch. Stop to point after laying every two courses.

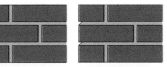

Struck joint   Weathered joint

Weathered joint. Make with the edge of a trowel. Keep the bottom of the mortar line flush against the bricks below, controlling the trowel so the point doesn't dig into the mortar.

Concave joint. Form with a pipe or joint strike. This technique allows water to drain from the joints. Point the vertical joints first, then the horizontal joints.

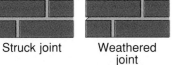

Concave joint   Flush joint

Flush joint. Simply cut excess mortar from the face of bricks. Make this joint at the same time you lay the bricks.

Vee joint. Make with a brick jointer or a piece of metal angle. The trick is to strike the joint quickly after the brick has been laid. Otherwise, the mortar will bunch up.

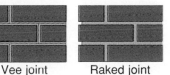

Vee joint   Raked joint

Raked joint. Make with a piece of wood the width of the mortar joint. Keep the end of the wood wet to keep the mortar from sticking to the strip.

Building New Walls (continued)

LAYING A BRICK WALL

String loose bricks along the length of the wall footing so they're in easy reach as you build the wall. The bricks should be wet when laid; sprinkle them with a hose before you start and keep them in a bucket of water as you work. If possible, have a helper mix the mortar as you lay the bricks. This will speed the job and keep the mortar fresh.

Begin building your wall from the ends or corners, then fill in the middle of the wall. The starter, or first, course of brick must be absolutely level and square on the footing. If not, remove the bricks from the footing, clean away the mortar on both the footing and the bricks, and start again. Continue with the next bricks and courses, double- and triple-checking each with a level, square, and story pole.

YOU'LL NEED...

SKILLS: Intermediate masonry skills.
TIME: 6 to 8 hours for a 4-foot-high, 20-foot-long section
TOOLS: Shovel, wheelbarrow, trowel, mason's line and line blocks, level, story pole, brick chisel, hammer, hose, bucket.

Building Up Corners and Ends

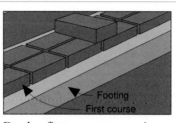

Dry-lay first course, spacing bricks ½ inch apart. Check spacing between tiers by laying a brick across them.

Soak bricks before laying. Dry bricks absorb water from the mortar and, as a result, weaken the wall.

Start at an end or corner. Pick up a few dry-laid bricks; throw and furrow mortar line. Lay bricks; check level.

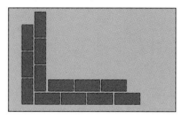

Corners are crucial, so check your layout carefully. Note that joints between bricks are staggered.

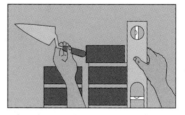

Check carefully for brick alignment, as well as level and plumb. Tap misplaced bricks gently into place.

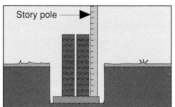

Build up corners, ends, and a section every 10 feet in long walls. Use a story pole to check for alignment.

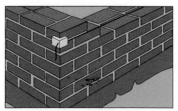

To ensure that courses remain aligned and level, use mason's line stretched between line blocks.

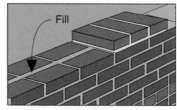

Lay headers every sixth course on common-bond walls. Trowel mortar between tiers for strength.

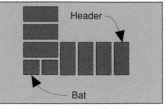

Turn headers around corners as shown. Cut a few bats from full bricks to form the proper corner bond.

Completing the Courses

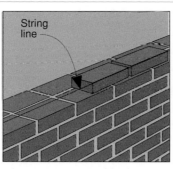

Align intervening bricks using a mason's line, raising it after each course. If a brick is out of line, remove it and start over.

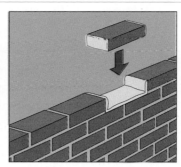

To lay a closure brick, butter both ends of it and the ends of bricks already in place. Gently set brick into place.

A level makes an excellent straightedge. Check work by holding it horizontally, vertically, and diagonally.

Strike joints after every three or four courses—verticals first, then horizontals. (See page 211 for different striking techniques.)

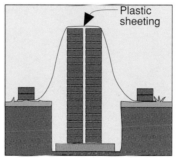

Before finishing for the day, scrub the bricks to remove loose mortar. Wet down the wall and cover it with polyethylene sheeting.

After three weeks, scrub the bricks with a mild solution of muriatic acid. This removes mortar that remains on them.

Capping Off a Brick Wall

When possible, top a wall with coping—bricks, stone, or precast concrete—to keep water off the bricks below. The coping should slope just enough to shed water and should project about ½ inch out from the face of the wall so water won't run down the wall.

Pitch the cap by building the mortar bed higher on one side of the wall. To add more strength to the entire unit, stagger coping joints with the vertical joints in the wall.

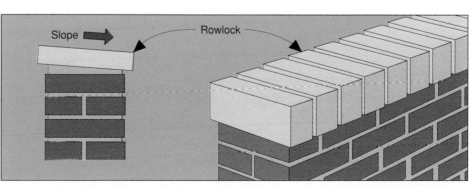

A course of rowlocks is the simplest way to top a wall. Choose bricks at least 1 inch longer than the width of the wall.

WALKS, STEPS, AND DRIVES

Paving includes everything from a stepping-stone walkway to a highway. Materials commonly include concrete, brick, stone, asphalt, even wood and gravel.

This chapter covers aspects of home paving not treated elsewhere. For more about working with concrete, see pages 173 and 178–184; to learn about setting bricks or stones in sand, see pages 176–177.

Paving of any type depends on proper drainage to protect it against damage from freezing and thawing.

Underneath, a porous base—usually sand or gravel—drains away water before it can harm the surface.

Ignore a paving problem and it will get worse. The repair techniques shown on the following pages call for only modest time and money.

Laying new paving materials is a bigger job, of course, but you can master the basics (see pages 218–221). Because even a large paving project usually can be broken down into a series of smaller ones, the work need not be overwhelming.

Solving Paving Problems

LEVELING WALKS

To even up a heaved or sunken walk, pry up the out-of-keel piece and add to or remove what's underneath. Flagstones, bricks, and small pieces of concrete lift out with little persuasion. Bigger slabs may demand a pick, wrecking bar, or pipe. Chop away roots you encounter with a hatchet or ax.

Frost, settlement, de-icing compounds, and tree roots all take their toll on the best-laid paving. Fortunately, all you need for most repairs is a few dollars' worth of patching materials and hand tools.

Before you attack a problem, however, find out what caused it. In chronic situations—usually the result of an inadequate base—you may be better off to rip up all of the old paving and start from scratch.

YOU'LL NEED...

SKILLS: Basic skills.
TIME: 30 to 90 minutes to repair a crack or one bad sidewalk section.
TOOLS: Sledgehammer or mason's hammer, cold chisel, pry bar or wrecking bar, caulking gun.

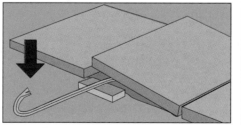

1. Work a wrecking bar under the settled section, lift it high enough to get under, then prop it up with a 2×4.

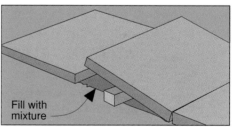

Fill with mixture

2. Fill underneath with equal mixture of sand, sifted dirt, and cement. Tamp or overfill to allow for settling.

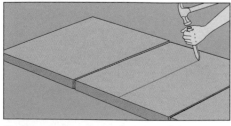

3. If a section is too large to lift, score near center and break with a chisel and hammer. Wear goggles and gloves.

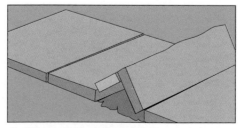

4. When a piece breaks free, pry and block it up. Add fill if low or remove soil or chop out roots if it's high.

5. Level the section and cement pieces together, or fill crack with asphalt. Sand asphalt to prevent foot tracking.

REPAIRING MASONRY STEPS

Damaged masonry steps pose serious safety hazards. If you neglect repairs, you could end up replacing the entire structure. Clearly, it pays to attend to problems right away.

Some steps have a brick superstructure underneath and concrete treads. Others are all brick; still others are solid concrete.

With brick-and-concrete construction, you must guard against moisture getting into the mortar joints of the bricks. Repoint crumbling material (page 149) and patch the treads as you would any concrete surface (see page 173).

If your steps are constructed of brick, check for mortar damage in the treads, where the treads meet the risers, and in joints between the steps and house or walk. Repoint these joints if necessary.

To replace a broken brick, chisel out the mortar around it, chop out the pieces, and replace it (see page 150). Repairs for solid concrete steps are shown below. Note that it's important to "undercut" old concrete so that the patch can get a secure hold. Use a cold chisel or brick chisel to do this, then thoroughly flush away debris with a hose. Keep the crack damp until you fill it.

For patching material, mix one part cement with three parts sand and just enough water to make it doughy. Or purchase special premixed patching compounds available in cartridges. Trowel this mixture into the damaged area, packing with the trowel's tip and smoothing with its edge.

To repair small chips, sections that are spalled, and other damaged areas that you can't undercut, use special epoxy patching cement mixed with sand according to the manufacturer's specifications.

YOU'LL NEED...

SKILLS: Basic concrete skills.
TIME: 30 to 60 minutes to repair a single step edge.
TOOLS: Hammer, cold chisel, trowel, wrecking bar, caulking gun.

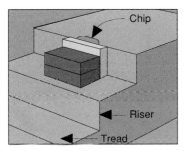

Often, you can glue pieces back in place with epoxy cement. Clean area, press piece in place, and hold with board and concrete block.

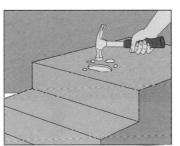

Epoxy cement revives spalled surfaces, too. Clean away loose concrete, then trowel on mix, feathering the edges.

Level a settled stoop as you would a slab (see page 214). You may need a helper for the job and maybe a second wrecking bar.

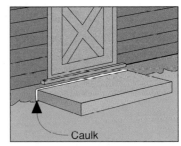

Fill joint between foundation and stoop with concrete joint filler, latex caulk, or a filler like oakum, foam, or an asphalt expansion strip.

1. If an entire edge is broken, chisel a V groove along it to help hold the patch in place. Clean the area thoroughly, then wet.

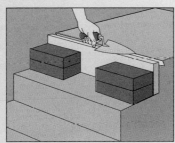

2. Press a board the height of the step against the riser to serve as a form. Apply concrete, packing groove full. Level with top of board.

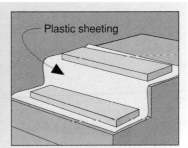

3. To strengthen the patch, keep it damp for about a week. Cover the repair with plastic sheeting and weight it down with scrap lumber.

Solving Paving Problems (continued)

PATCHING ASPHALT

Asphalt paving is made by mixing asphalt with gravel. Because asphalt paving is softer than concrete, it has enough plasticity to ride out minor heaves and settling. When a crack or pothole does appear, you can patch it with a mix sold by the bag or by combining asphalt sealer and sand.

Try to patch asphalt when the temperature is 60°F or higher. Asphalt is brittle when cold. If you must work in cool weather, store the compound indoors in a warm place. Break up any lumps by walking on the bag before opening it.

Asphalt paving needs sealing every two years or so—whenever the surface becomes checked with hairline cracks or dries out. To do the job, buy 5-gallon buckets of sealer and apply as shown in the last illustration below.

Beware of promoters who offer to seal your drive for a cut-rate price. Their sealers usually disappear as fast as they do.

> ### YOU'LL NEED...
> **SKILLS:** Basic skills.
> **TIME:** 1 hour for a larger pothole.
> **TOOLS:** Shovel, trowel, tamper, asphalt sealer broom.

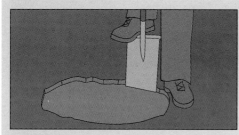

For cracks in asphalt up to ⅛ inch wide, partially fill crack with sand and pour in a liquid sealer.

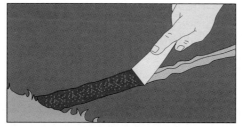

For larger cracks, mix sand with sealer, making a paste. Pack mixture into crack with a putty knife or trowel.

Seal asphalt regularly. Pour out sealer and work it into the surface with an asphalt sealer broom. Apply two coats.

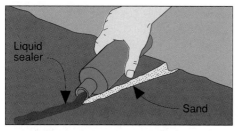

1. To fill holes, remove dirt and debris down to solid material. Cut edges vertical and tamp around top of hole.

2. For deep potholes, add stones to conserve on patching material. Fill with gravel to within 4 inches of top.

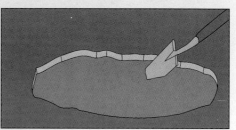

3. Add asphalt mix, slicing it with a trowel or spade to remove any air pockets and to compact the mix.

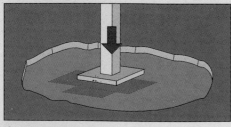

4. When the mix is within an inch of the top, pack it with a tamper made from a 2×2 and a scrap of plywood.

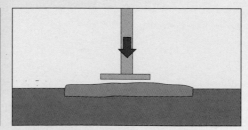

5. Add more patching material, mounding it slightly above the surface. Tamp the patch as firmly as possible.

6. Sprinkle the patch with sand to prevent tracking. Compact it by driving a car back and forth over the repair.

REVIVING A LOOSE-FILL DRIVE

Loose-fill materials, such as gravel, pebbles, crushed rock, cinders, or slag, make a drive that's relatively inexpensive and impervious to freezing and thawing cycles. The major problem with a loose-fill drive is that repeated use and erosion tend to move some of the fill material onto your lawn or flush it down the street's storm sewers, forcing you to replenish the material every few years.

If your drive slopes steeply, loose fill simply can't stay put. Consider paving with a hard surface material, such as concrete or asphalt. On fairly level terrain, retain the fill by installing curbing as shown below.

Before you begin, however, wait for a heavy rain and see what happens to the water. If it stands in puddles on the drive itself, you need to build up the low spots. To do this, spread out sand or a mixture of sand and crushed limestone, then add the loose-fill topping.

If water flows across the drive, taking loose fill with it, regrade the drive before adding the edging.

YOU'LL NEED...

SKILLS: Basic skills.
TIME: 2 to 3 hours.
TOOLS: Shovel, garden rake, hose, hammer, wheelbarrow.

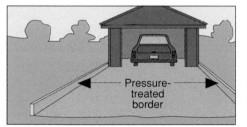

1. Add pressure-treated wood to sides of the driveway, anchoring with stakes. Or, install solid partition block.

2. Surface should be as level as possible. Level high spots and fill low ones with sand and limestone fill.

3. Saturate the ground with weed killer to keep vegetation from peeking through the loose fill.

4. A sand base aids drainage. Use 2 inches of sand for every 3 inches of fill. Level sand, then wet to compact.

5. Dump fill in a series of piles along your drive. Spread out the fill with a shovel and rake.

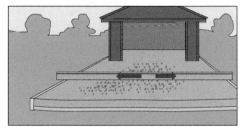

6. Level the fill with a 2×4 screed, dragging its ends along curbing and shoveling away excess as you screed.

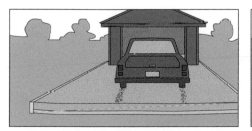

7. To compact the fill, drive a car back and forth across the surface. After several passes, add fill to low spots.

8. In spring and fall, level the fill, adding more where necessary; compact with car. In spring, apply weed killer.

Laying New Paving Materials

Garden paving is an excellent way to learn the basics of working with masonry. Unlike the bigger jobs of constructing a patio (see pages 176–184) or planning a drive (see page 221), you needn't move a lot of earth, prepare extensive footings and forms, or master special techniques.

Certain projects go faster than others, of course. For a rustic pathway that rises and falls with the terrain, you need to excavate only a few inches, pour a loose-fill base of sand or gravel, then lay one of the materials shown below. On land that's high and drains reasonably well, you may not even need a base.

For the more formal look of an arrow-straight walk, you'll probably need a concrete base, but it need not be more than 4 inches thick and does not require reinforcement.

If you're doing extensive paving, use materials that you can make yourself or buy at home centers. This way, you can do a few sections at a time, without a weekend-after-weekend work hangover.

YOU'LL NEED...
SKILLS: Basic to intermediate masonry skills, depending on the material and the landform.
TIME: 5 to 6 hours for a short walk.
TOOLS: Shovel, garden rake, wheelbarrow, masonry tools (see page 207).

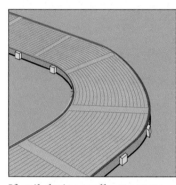

If soil drains well, concrete walks can be as thin as 3 inches. Make forms with 1×4s and shape curves with ¼-inch tempered hardboard. Broom-finish surface.

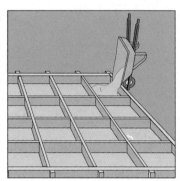

To cast your own stepping stones, build a temporary form on a level surface. Add a layer of sand and 2 inches of concrete. Screed the units with a 2×4.

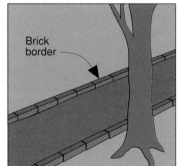

Asphalt is an economical paving material, but it needs a firm base of rock or tamped sand. You can color asphalt with special paints.

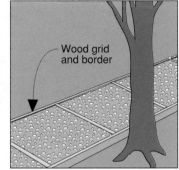

Retain loose-fill materials with wood, brick, or block edging. Build forms as you would for a loose-fill drive (see page 217). Use various gravels for interest.

Brick works well in formal or informal settings. Set bricks on sand as you would a patio (see page 176) or mortar them (see page 219).

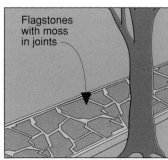

Set flagstones on sand or in mortar. Use a minimum of 2-inch-thick stones on a sand base; ½- to 1-inch stones on a concrete base.

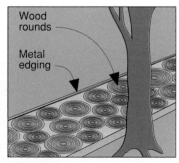

Wood blocks or rounds are made by slicing timbers or logs. Use redwood, cypress, cedar, or treated wood. These can be set in sand.

VENEERING A WALKWAY

For a durable, dressy walk—to a front entry, for instance—consider veneering a concrete slab with flagstones, slate, or quarry tiles.

Flagstones are simply big flat rocks. They come in irregular shapes or precut squares and rectangles. Because flagstones aren't uniformly thick, you must lay them on sand or in a 1-inch mortar bed.

Slate tiles are available in a variety of colors and standard thicknesses ranging from ¼ to 1 inch. Choose regular or irregular shapes. To trim slate, you'll need to rent a slate cutter. Slate should be set in a ½- to ¾-inch mortar bed.

Quarry tiles are made in many colors and are ⅜ or ½ inch thick. Choose square, hexagon, or curved shapes, and be sure to get a type meant for outdoor use. Trim and set quarry tiles as you would slate.

The drawings below illustrate the dry-set method of veneering with stones and tiles. You bond the paving units to the concrete with mortar, then fill the spaces in between with mortar or grout.

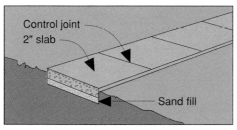

1. The concrete base—existing or new—must be at least 2 inches thick and poured over 1 to 2 inches of sand.

2. Dry-lay units with ½-inch joints to test pattern. Align joints with those in slab. Adjust later if necessary.

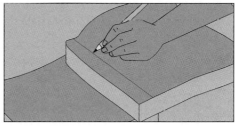

3. Mark units by overlaying adjacent stones, then tracing a line. For tile or slate, you'll need a special cutter.

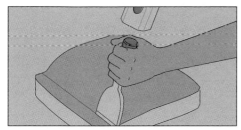

4. To cut flagstone, lay it on a solid surface and score along the line with a brick chisel; score other side, too.

5. Slip a board under the scored line and gently tap with a sledge or mason's hammer until the stone fractures.

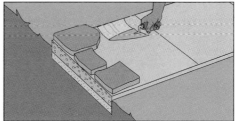

6. Remove several units. Wet concrete well and trowel on a layer of 1:3 mortar mix or special dry-set mortar.

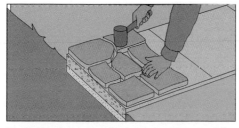

7. Embed stones and tap in place with a mallet. After laying several pieces, check for level; units must be true.

8. Let mortar set 24 hours, then pack joints with 1:3 mortar mix or premixed grout. Trowel joints smooth.

9. When mortar is nearly dry, wipe off excess with damp burlap. Cover with plastic and keep damp for a week.

Laying New Paving Materials (continued)

BUILDING IN-GROUND STEPS

In-ground steps not only get you from one level to another, they also limit soil erosion. Plan them as you would a retaining wall (see pages 204–213). Notch steps into slopes wherever possible.

Select materials to match the existing pathways that the steps connect. Some options are shown below. Be sure to firmly anchor the material and provide adequate drainage. It's best to pitch treads slightly downhill or to one side so water will run off.

After deciding on the materials to use, you'll need to answer three questions. How many steps will you need? How deep should each tread be? How high should each riser be?

Begin by measuring the total rise from the bottom to the top level.

Drive a tall stake at the bottom and stretch a line from the stake to the top. Level this line, then measure from the line to the stake bottom.

The height of each riser can vary from 3 to 9 inches. Low risers—usually with deep treads—provide a leisurely transition from one level to another; plan shallow treads and higher risers where you want to get from one level to another rapidly.

To determine the total run, measure the length of the line you stretched from the stake to the top of the slope. By varying the run and the height of the risers, you can compute the number of steps you'll need and the depth of each tread.

Treads should be a minimum of 10 inches deep. For a graceful, terraced effect, the step treads can

be up to 3 feet deep or more.

Excavate using a spade, keeping the sides of the cuts straight. When calculating how deep to dig, include a couple of inches for a sand or gravel base and don't forget to allow for the thickness of the treads in planning the height of each riser, especially at the top and bottom. If you use masonry, be certain to pour footings first.

If you prefer wooden stairs other than railroad ties, check out the open-riser staircase on page 188.

open-riser staircase on page 188.

YOU'LL NEED...

SKILLS: Basic to intermediate skills, depending on the material.
TIME: 10 to 14 hours.
TOOLS: Depends on materials used.

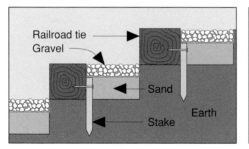

Railroad ties make good risers. Treads here are gravel, but you also can use brick, block, concrete, or more ties.

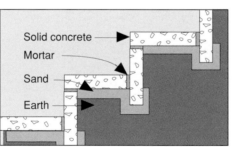

Solid concrete blocks offer a quick way to build steps. Set them in a sand base pitched slightly forward for drainage.

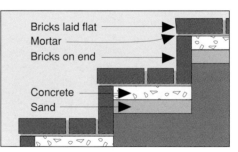

For brick steps, lay down a sand bed and set concrete slabs on top. Then set the bricks in mortar.

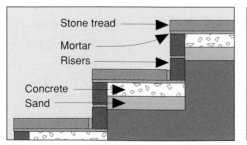

Flagstones can rest on brick, wood, or stone risers. Set on sand/concrete pads in mortar for the best stability.

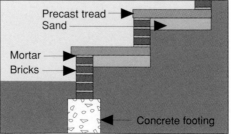

Precast slabs are heavy enough to hold themselves in position. But put them on a firm base for stability.

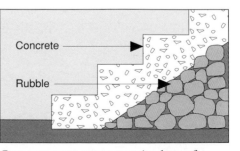

Cast concrete steps require lots of form-building and material. Dump clean stones or bricks into form first.

PLANNING A DRIVEWAY

Because of the magnitude of the project, most people don't attempt to pave a driveway themselves. Although the planning and forming work isn't too difficult, the mixing, screeding, floating, and troweling can be back-breaking.

If you decide to do the entire job yourself, be sure to order premixed concrete. The additional cost of having concrete delivered is small when you consider the rental expenses you'd incur if you mixed the concrete yourself. The same is true for asphalt surfaces.

You can save dollars, however, if you design, lay out, and prepare the forms. Then, you can have a contractor pour the concrete.

If the site for your driveway is firm and has good drainage, don't disturb the soil. Just skim off the vegetation from the ground, set the forms, lay down a bed of sand, then pour the concrete.

If the earth is not solid, add a 4- to 6-inch-thick base for the concrete. For details on how thick the base needs to be, check with a concrete supplier in your area.

Single car drives vary in width from 10 to 14 feet, or about 3 feet wider than a car. Allow 16 to 24 feet for two cars or a two-car garage.

If heavy trucks will frequent the drive, plan for 6 to 8 inches of concrete. If only pickup trucks and cars will use the driveway, a depth of 4 to 6 inches will suffice.

If you're working with a level slope, pitch the drive away from the garage at ¼ inch per running foot.

Use 2×4 or 2×6 lumber for the forms. Or, you may be able to rent metal forms for less than you'd pay for the lumber. The forms are held by stakes on the outside of the forming members. Sledgehammer the stakes into the ground, spacing them 24 to 30 inches apart. Drive the tops of the stakes below the top edges of the forms; the concrete can't be leveled easily if the tops of the stakes are in the way. (See pages 178–184 for more about concrete.)

You may need a polyethylene moisture barrier and reinforcing rods or mesh for strength. Ask your materials dealer about this because conditions vary with locality.

> ### YOU'LL NEED...
> **SKILLS:** Basic carpentry skills.
> **TIME:** 10 to 14 hours to excavate and build forms.
> **TOOLS:** Shovel, wheelbarrow, saw, hammer, sledgehammer, mason's line, level and line level.

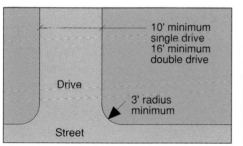

At the street, plan on a 3- to 5-foot radius curve. Other curves and turns in the drive need wider radii.

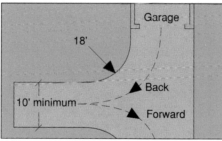

For a turnaround, plan an 18-foot radius and at least a 10-foot width. Make turnaround wider for parking.

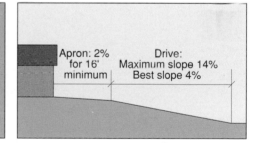

Grade must not exceed 1¾ inches per running foot. If greater, cars will bottom out on humps or at street level.

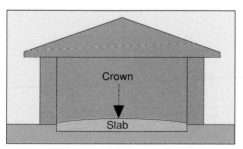

If the slope won't be severe, give the driveway a crown center so water will roll off to both sides of the drive.

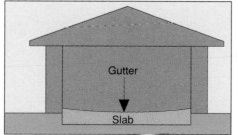

For long drives, plan a gutter center that will carry runoff water down the drive into street.

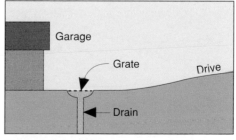

If garage is below street level, plan a gutter center with a drain outletting to a dry well or the storm sewer.

GARAGES

A garage can be one of the best used and most serviceable areas of your home. Yet all too often people relegate the area to junk storage, leaving just enough space to squeeze in the car.

One reason your garage may not be giving you the service you expect is a difficult-to-use garage door. After all, if it's hard to get into the garage, it's hard to use the space efficiently.

Adjusting a garage door, repairing an automatic-door-operator remote control, or making any number of other minor repairs or improvements will put your door and garage back on the active list. If you plan to install a new garage door, look for a product manufacturer that provides complete instructions with the garage door opener.

As you can see from the anatomy sketches below, garage doors are not overly complex. Most doors ride on a set of tracks. A cable and pulley system usually does the actual lifting, with help from some type of spring system that supplies the required tension. The doors either mount to the door jambs with vertical mounting brackets or ride in tracks that mount to the jambs.

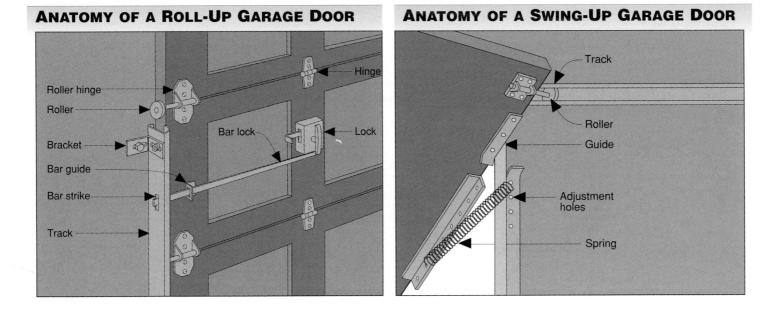

ANATOMY OF A ROLL-UP GARAGE DOOR

Roller hinge
Roller
Bracket
Bar guide
Bar strike
Track
Hinge
Bar lock
Lock

ANATOMY OF A SWING-UP GARAGE DOOR

Track
Roller
Guide
Adjustment holes
Spring

ANATOMY OF DOOR-LIFTING MECHANISMS

Torsion spring
Axle
Cable drum
Cable
Anchor
Track

Anchor
Cable
Pulley
Spring
Header
Jamb
Track
Cross tie

Solving Garage Problems

TROUBLESHOOTING GARAGE DOORS

Unlike an electrical or plumbing problem, which may take a professional to diagnose, garage door maladies are not difficult to locate. If the door opens or closes too easily, look to the spring system. If the door sticks, check out the tracks or the door trim.

The illustrations below show several common garage door problems that, when discovered, are easy to remedy.

Why do garage doors malfunction?

Though not the sole culprit, moisture plays a large part. It warps doors, rusts hardware, and causes framing members to rot away. So while you're looking for problems, check to make sure that water is not building up around or dripping onto the door. If it is, find the source of the water and make the needed repairs at once.

With swing-up garage doors, sagging is the biggest problem. The reason: The lifting mechanisms

usually aren't adequate to support the weight. If this is the problem, replace—don't repair—the mechanisms with extra-heavy-duty ones. Position them so the screws will be driven into new, solid wood.

Never try to repair or replace the spring on torsion spring doors. These springs are under tremendous tension and can cause severe injury if not handled properly. Call in a garage door contractor to repair or replace these.

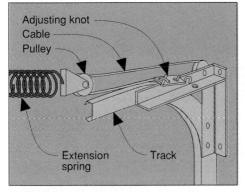

Cable slack causes pulley-type doors to malfunction. Tighten the cable without stretching the spring.

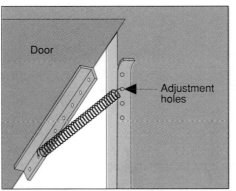

On doors with tension springs, tighten the spring by hooking it into the next hole in the door framing or track.

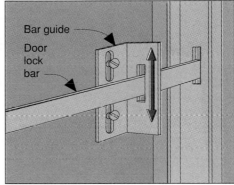

Bar locks won't lock if the assembly is out of alignment. Adjust either the lockset or the bar guide.

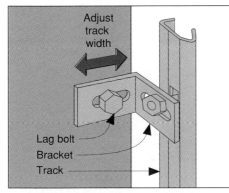

Tracks must be parallel or the door will bind. Measure between them in several places and make adjustments.

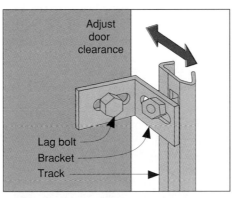

If the door rubs against the trim, move the molding back or adjust or shim out the track brackets.

Solving Garage Problems (continued)

MAINTAINING GARAGE DOORS

As long as they continue to operate, garage doors don't get a second thought around most homes. That's unfortunate because this lack of attention almost always results in a back-wrenching episode at some time or another when the door won't open or close.

Keeping your door hardware clean and lubricated will prevent most problems. The illustrations below show the techniques involved.

Another thing to keep an eye out for is failing paint or rust on a metal door—a sign that moisture is beginning to take its toll on the door. Blackish marks near the base of a wood door signal rot. Tend to these signs of danger as soon as possible to keep trouble to a minimum.

If your door is wood, remove the peeling or flaking paint down to the bare wood. Then prime the bare areas and apply two coats of exterior paint. If the door is metal, remove the rust or corrosion to the bare metal, prime the spots with metal primer, and apply two finish coats. You may have to repaint the entire door—wood or metal—so the new paint patches don't show.

Replace damaged hardware, such as hinges, locksets, and tracks. These nonfunctioning parts put additional strain on other components and result in future damage.

> ### YOU'LL NEED...
> **SKILLS:** Basic mechanical and painting skills.
> **TIME:** 30 to 40 minutes for regular maintenance.
> **TOOLS:** Screwdriver, wrench.

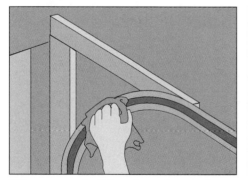

Wipe grease buildup from the tracks with a rag. Grease, combined with dirt, can cause the door to bind and jump.

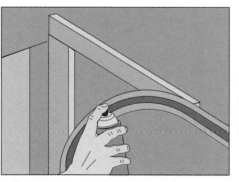

Lubricate the tracks with graphite or light machine oil. Distribute lubricant by opening and closing the door.

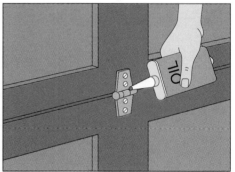

Oil hinge pins, too. If the pins are rusty, remove and clean the metal with steel wool or fine sandpaper.

Lubricate rollers and make sure they are in alignment with the track. Wheel supports usually are adjustable.

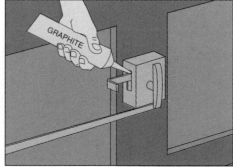

Use graphite, not oil, for locks. Puff the powder into the mechanism and into the key channel.

Keep door edges, panels, and bottoms sealed with paint. Repair damaged concrete at the base of the door.

WEATHERPROOFING GARAGES

Even attached garages leak a surprising amount of air, mostly through and around garage doors. Implement the remedies shown here to weatherproof your garage.

If your garage doubles as a workshop or a crafts or play area, you'll probably want to insulate the sidewalls and rafters or ceiling. For more about insulating these surfaces, see pages 390-400.

more about insulating these surfaces, see pages 390-400.

YOU'LL NEED...

SKILLS: Basic mechanical skills.
TIME: 30 to 60 minutes.
TOOLS: Screwdriver, hammer, wrench, caulking gun.

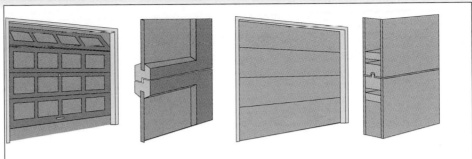

Raised-panel doors leak air where they are hinged. Keep hinges tight and joints free of dirt and paint globs.

Flush-panel doors have the same problems. For tight joints, adjust tracks, rollers, and all the hinges.

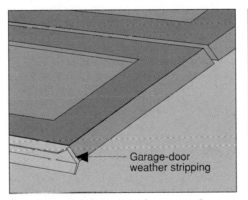

Seal bottom of door with garage-door weather stripping. It compensates for unevenness in the threshold.

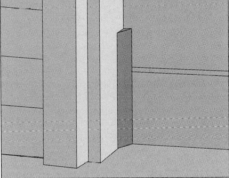

Outside, apply weather stripping to the top and side jambs to seal them when the door is in its closed position.

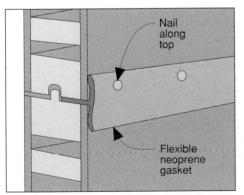

Apply a neoprene gasket to seal air and water out of joints. This weather stripping comes in several colors.

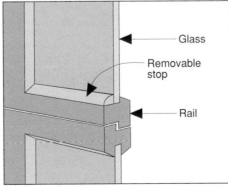

Replace broken windows as you would any window (see page 160). Glazing is held by a removable stop.

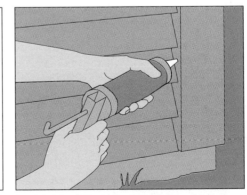

Seal joints between window and door trim and the siding with an exterior caulk (see page 145).

Solving Garage Problems (continued)

TROUBLESHOOTING ELECTRIC DOORS

Occasionally, automatic garage door operators go bad. But before you start sleuthing for a problem in the unit, make sure that it is not the garage door that is at fault. Also, make sure there is electric current going to the operating unit by plugging another appliance into the receptacle used by the opener.

If all is well, pull the emergency release cord or chain (see anatomy drawing on page 227). If you still can't move the door up or down, check to see if there are obstructions in the door tracks or if something is caught in the chain or screw drive. Also check to see if the door has been damaged, for example, by an accidental hit by a car bumper.

When you are satisfied that none of the above conditions exist, let the opener motor cool for about 10 minutes, then try to open the door with the wall-mounted push-button control. If this doesn't work, the control could be defective.

If the opener works when you push this control but not when you use the remote transmitter, replace the batteries in the transmitter with new ones and try it again.

If the door opens for no reason, a neighbor's transmitter may be operating on the same frequency code as yours. Most transmitters made today are designed to guard against thieves so this would be a rare case. If it's possible with your unit, try changing the code.

If the door opens partially, then stops, the trouble may be in the travel adjustment. A door that starts down but stops before it's closed completely requires adjustment.

Finally, if the transmitter activates the drive unit but the door doesn't move, chances are that the drive belt needs tightening.

YOU'LL NEED...

SKILLS: Basic skills.
TIME: 15 to 20 minutes.
TOOLS: Screwdriver, wrench.

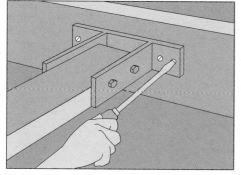

Through use, the header or door bracket can work loose, causing binding. Correct alignment and secure with long screws.

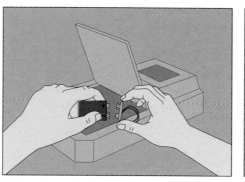

If the door won't open or close, the problem may be weak or dead batteries in the transmitter. It's smart to replace them annually.

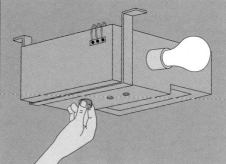

If the door reverses on its way up or down or won't reverse when obstructed, adjust the sensitivity of the safety control.

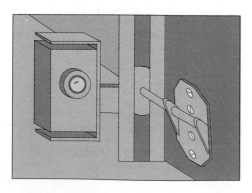

Many new doors have electric eyes that keep the door from closing if there is anything underneath it. Adjustments to electric eyes vary, so check manufacturer's instructions.

If the door doesn't open or close all the way, adjust the height adjustment screws. Sometimes, they're located inside the unit's housing.

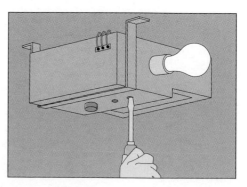

Making Garage Improvements

MATERIAL MATTERS   CHOOSING AND BUYING GARAGE DOOR OPENERS

An automatic garage door opener is one of those I-really-don't-need-one-of-those products that people thoroughly appreciate once they begin using it. Unlike many so-called convenience products, automatic door openers really do make sense in terms of effort saved—not to mention the added security they offer.

The safety and convenience features are intertwined. Once the door is down, the opener locks it automatically, and the only ways the door can be opened are with the transmitter, the auxiliary push-button control or coded keypad, or the manual emergency release cord inside the garage. A light, timed to shut off a minute or so after the door touches down, allows you time to exit the garage safely at night.

Most automatic openers have a safety device that either stops the door or immediately reverses it if the door meets an obstruction while moving. Assuming the unit has been adjusted properly, the slightest resistance to the moving door will stop it from traveling any farther. Many building codes now require the additional safety of an electric eye that reverses the door if it detects an obstruction.

If the push-button or keypad transmitters malfunction, you can pull an emergency release cord to disengage the unit from the door so you can operate the door manually. Most operators feature motor-overload devices that automatically deactivate the motor if it overheats.

The anatomy sketch below shows the relatively simple makeup of garage door openers. The drive unit is the heart of the opener. It houses the motor, control terminals, a belt and pulley system, and a series of relay switches and gears or sprockets—all of which combine to make the unit work.

A trolley, attached to an opener arm, which in turn is connected to a door bracket, rides along a track to raise or lower the door upon receiving instructions from a remote control. The way in which the trolley rides along the track depends on whether your opener has chain drive or screw drive. With chain-drive units, the chain, activated by the motor/belt/pulley, moves back and forth around a series of sprockets, taking the trolley with it. With screw-drive units, the trolley moves via a threaded rod that rotates in one direction to open the door and in the other direction to close it.

The controls consist of a transmitter and a receiver. The portable transmitter sends out a coded signal to the receiver mounted either within the drive unit or on the ceiling in the garage. The signal activates a relay switch, and the switch releases a low-voltage impulse, which activates the motor drive.

ANATOMY OF AN OPENER

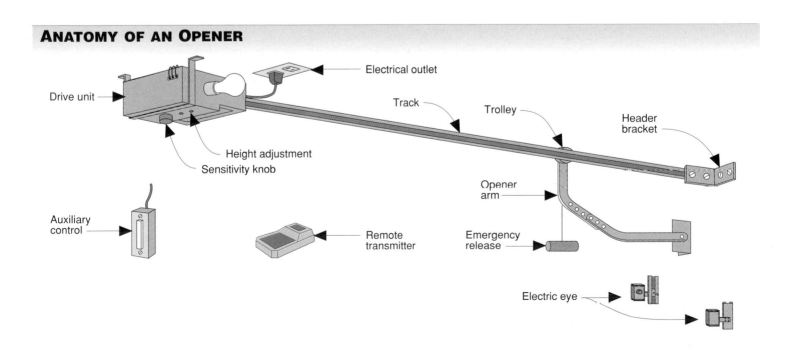

Making Garage Improvements (continued)

INSTALLING A GARAGE DOOR OPENER

When you get home with your opener, sit down and thoroughly study the assembly and installation instructions. They'll familiarize you with the unit and its parts and lead you step-by-step through all the procedures necessary to install the unit correctly. The sketches below depict some of the steps involved in a typical installation. Some manufacturers now provide a videotape demonstration of how to install the door.

Check with your local building department to see if an electric eye is required for safety. Give the garage door the once-over to make sure it's operating smoothly. Balky doors put a severe strain on the small motors that power openers, so go over the points listed on page 224. Make sure especially that the tracks are parallel to each other and that the rollers roll freely.

Disengage door-locking devices so they can't be used. The opener has a built-in lock that secures the garage adequately. Besides, additional locks may damage the opener.

After installing the unit, you most likely will need to make minor adjustments to ensure that the door opens and closes completely and that it stops or reverses itself if obstructed on its downward path. Again, refer to the installation instructions for these adjustments (also see page 226).

(also see page 226).

YOU'LL NEED...

SKILLS: Basic skills.
TIME: 1 to 2 hours.
TOOLS: Drill, screwdriver, wrench, stepladder.

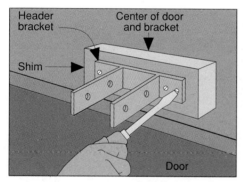

1. Locate the vertical center of the door, then fasten the header bracket about 2 inches above the highest point traversed by the door as it opens.

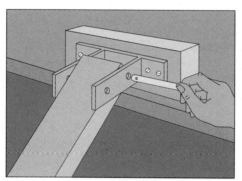

2. Slip the track into the bracket and secure it in position. You'll have to support the other end of the track until you attach it to the drive unit.

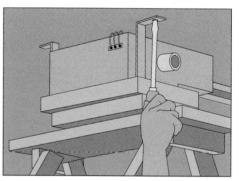

3. Align track perpendicular to the door; mark position for and then fasten the drive unit to the garage ceiling or to the rafters or collar beams.

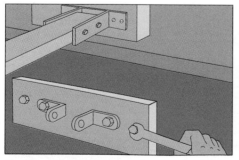

4. Mount the door bracket as shown, making sure the opener arm will pull straight up when connected to it. Otherwise, it may bind.

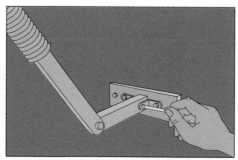

5. Close the door, then mount the opener arm parts to the track trolley and to the door bracket. The electrical connections are the last step.

CREATING STORAGE SPACE IN A GARAGE

This page is dedicated to those people who, once or twice a year, decide it's high time they clean up the garage "once and for all."

Most garages have far more storage potential than we give them credit for. Here, the name of the game is to get everything off the floor, making way for the more important things, such as the family car(s), which garages were designed for. Obviously, you can't hang your lawnmower or motorcycle up on the wall, but you can lift most everything else out of the way.

The sidewalls of your garage are natural spaces for storing a multitude of items. So is the back wall. Hang garden tools and other smaller items from nails fastened to the studs or top plate. You can also purchase hanging brackets intended for this purpose from hardware or home improvement centers. Or, devise a series of shelves mounted on the surface or between studs. (See page 92 for shelf hardware options.)

For larger items, consider making or buying cabinets, which can be as simple as a plywood box with a door on the front or as fancy as used kitchen cabinets.

Don't forget overhead storage, either. Adding cross ties and nailing up plywood opens an entire level of new space. This area is good for storing seasonal gear.

Study the storage ideas below, do a little designing on your own (see pages 88–101 for more ideas), and maybe this time you will get your garage shipshape once and for all.

YOU'LL NEED...

SKILLS: Basic carpentry skills.
TIME: 2 to 3 hours.
TOOLS: Saw, hammer, screwdriver.

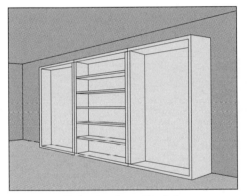

Section off the back wall of the garage with plywood boxes fastened to the wall with metal angles. Fit shelves between the uprights.

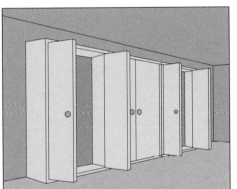

Build custom plywood cabinets that use the space from the floor to the ceiling. Or, buy similar metal cabinets.

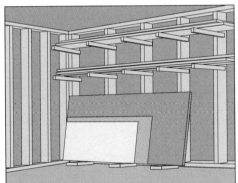

A storage setup with shelves up high keeps scrap lumber and sheet goods handy without taking up too much space or looking cluttered.

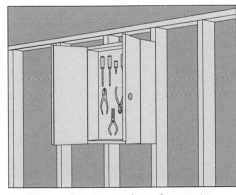

Locking cabinets are best for storing expensive tools, chemicals, paint, and other items that attract children.

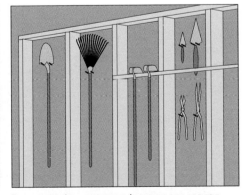

Inexpensive storage is easy to create with nails and scrap lumber. Determine your needs and divide up the space.

YOUR HOME'S SYSTEMS

ELECTRICITY

Getting to Know Your System

To most people, a household electrical system seems mysterious and even dangerous. Actually, its principles rest on elementary logic. If you master them and observe a few precautions that will soon become second nature, you can safely pull off a wide variety of electrical repair and improvement jobs.

Let's take a quick look at the overall system that keeps you comfortably supplied with electricity. Power from the utility comes in through a service entrance either in overhead or underground wires to a meter that keeps track of your household's electrical consumption. That electric meter may be inside your house or, more commonly now, outside. The power continues to a service panel, which distributes it to different circuits that serve various zones of your house or particular appliances. Fuses or circuit breakers in the service panel control individual circuits and protect against an electrical fire, which could develop if there is a short circuit or if a circuit draws more current than it's designed to handle.

ANATOMY OF A SIMPLE ELECTRICAL SYSTEM

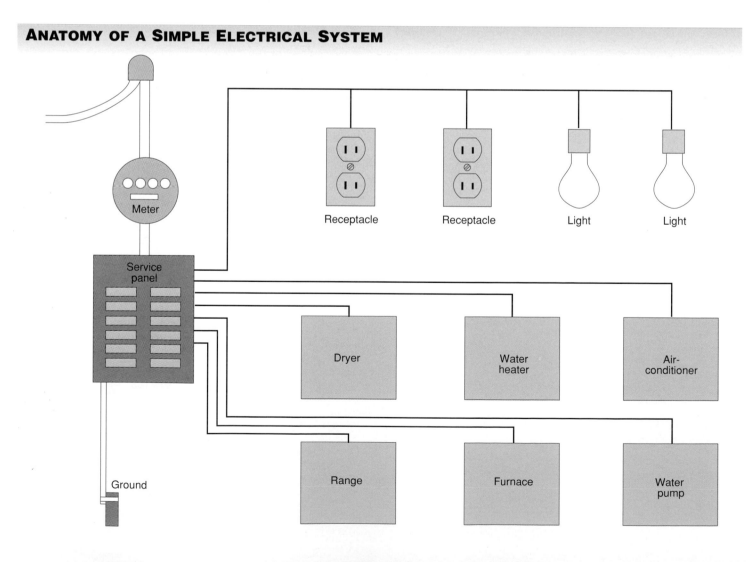

Meter

Receptacle

Receptacle

Light

Light

Service panel

Ground

Dryer

Water heater

Air-conditioner

Range

Furnace

Water pump

UNDERSTANDING ELECTRICAL TERMINOLOGY

Electrical current flows—under pressure—through the wiring in your house. That flow would come to an absolute halt if you were to disconnect every appliance, light, or other device that you have. But as soon as you turn on one device, the flow in that particular circuit begins.

The amount of current going through a wire at a given time is measured in amperes, or amps for short, and is equal to the number of electrons passing a certain point each second. The pressure that forces these electrons along their route is known as voltage, which is measured in volts.

If you were to increase the voltage, you would not accelerate the flow of current; current travels at a constant speed—the speed of light. But you would increase the power in your lines. That power is measured in watts and is the product of amps times volts. Your utility bills are based on the number of watts and hours of use. The billing unit is a kilowatt-hour (kwh), or 1,000 watt-hours used after 1 hour.

When current flows from the service panel to, for example, a plug outlet, the electrons travel through what is called a hot wire, which is black (or, in rare cases, a white wire with black paint or tape to indicate that it is functioning as a hot wire).

After current has flowed through a light or appliance, the electrons seek a direct route to ground (see page 237) and travel in white neutral wires to get there. These neutral wires, also known as system grounds, complete every circuit in the system by returning the current to the ground.

Modern electrical circuits have three wires; the third is a bare or green one that serves as an equipment ground. Its role is to ground metal parts throughout the installation, such as conduit, armored cable, motors, and major appliances. This grounding wire protects against the danger of short circuits.

HELPFUL HINTS   LEARNING ABOUT CODES AND INSPECTIONS

The National Electrical Code, published by the National Fire Protection Association, is the most complete, detailed set of guidelines you are likely to find anywhere. If you are planning a major wiring job, get a copy; the book is full of helpful tips. Despite the code's strong influence nationally, the last word on what you can and cannot do comes from your local building code. Its provisions are law and take precedence over anything you'll see in a national code.

A few localities don't even allow do-it-yourselfers to work on their own wiring; others make you get a temporary permit first. Some areas permit homeowners to undertake all but the final connection at the service panel. Check with your city or county code official. And then expect to have your work inspected.

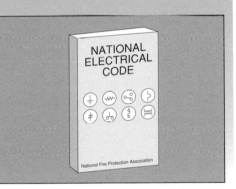

READING A METER

Most electric meters have four or five dials. The leftmost dial indicates tens of thousands of kilowatt-hours; the next one to the right, thousands; and so on.

Read from left to right. If a pointer is between two digits, read the lower number. If the pointer is on a number and the dial to the right of it has not yet passed zero, read the next lower number.

Your usage will be the number you read minus the number you read at the previous meter reading.

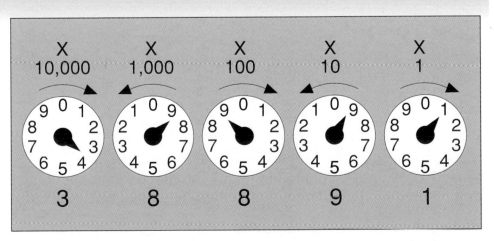

Getting to Know Your System (continued)

KNOWING YOUR SERVICE PANEL

Most electrical projects begin at the service panel—also called a breaker box or fuse box. It's the heart of your system and home base for protective devices that automatically disconnect power to the entire house or to individual branch circuits in case of overloads (a circuit drawing more power than is intended) or a short circuit (a break in a wire or a hot and ground wire accidently coming in contact with each other). The panel is also where you'll shut off the current manually when needed.

Caution: Always shut off the power to the circuit(s) you will be working on before you start an electrical project, then use a tester to make sure the power actually is off.

Working with a Circuit Box

In newer service panels, the safety devices protecting your home are called circuit breakers. The typical circuit breaker box (at right) will have one main cutoff breaker and a number of smaller breakers, each controlling a branch circuit. A breaker may be "tripped" off by a short or an overload. After you find and correct the problem that caused the breaker to be tripped to the off position, reset the breaker by flipping the toggle switch to the on position.

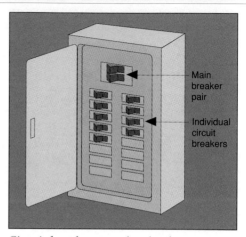

Main breaker pair

Individual circuit breakers

Circuit breaker panels, also known as service entrance panels, are rated by the size of the main breaker pair at the top: 100-, 150-, 200-amp, etc.

Working with a Fuse Box

If you have an older home in which the original wiring is intact, chances are your service panel is a fuse box rather than a breaker box. Instead of tripping a breaker when a problem occurs, fuses "blow."

Whenever the current builds up beyond the level intended for a particular circuit and its fuse, the thin strip of metal that carries the current through the fuse simply melts in a flash. When this happens, the circuit is open and current flow comes to a screeching halt.

In the fuse box, you'll usually find a main pullout block with two cartridge-type fuses (see page 235) mounted on its backside. To shut off the electric current to the entire house, grab the handle and pull out the block. (Some older boxes also have a shutoff lever.) Large 240-volt circuits for major appliances may be protected by pullout blocks also. Most 120-volt branch circuits are protected by 15- or 20-amp screw-in plug fuses.

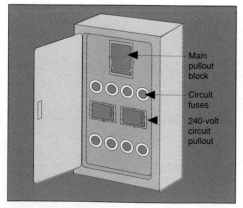

Main pullout block

Circuit fuses

240-volt circuit pullout

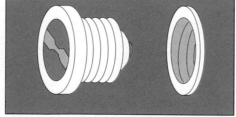

A plug fuse screws into the fuse box like a bulb. Handle only the rim when replacing this type of fuse.

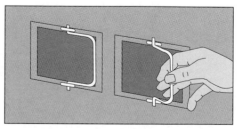

Large 240-volt circuits for water heaters and ranges are protected by pullout blocks with cartridge fuses.

MATERIAL MATTERS

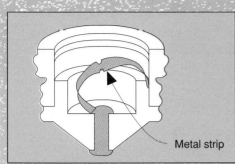

Metal strip

In the most common type, the plug fuse, a metal strip melts and breaks the circuit in case of a short or overload.

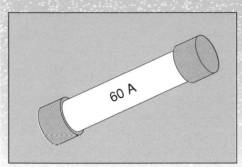

60 A

Circuits carrying greater than 30 amps require cartridge fuses. The ferrule-contact style goes up to 60 amps.

IDENTIFYING FUSE TYPES

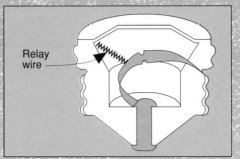

Relay wire

Use time-delay fuses for overloads of a few seconds. The fuse blows only for shorts or continuous overloads.

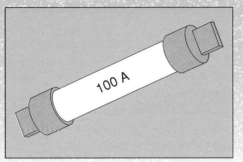

100 A

Knife-blade fuses are rated for 60 amps or higher. Both types of cartridge fuses can have time-delay features.

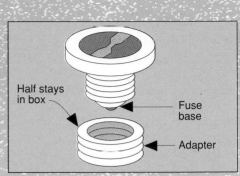

Half stays in box

Fuse base

Adapter

Type-S fuse bases are sized by amp rating. Adapters in the box accept only matching fuse bases.

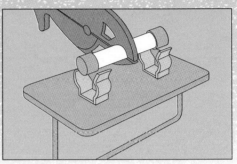

Use a plastic fuse puller to remove a cartridge fuse from an auxiliary fuse box or the back of a pullout block.

HELPFUL HINTS

Diagnosing a blown fuse is easy, mainly because the culprit usually leaves a telltale sign. If a short has occurred, an ordinary plug fuse will have a blackened window. In case of an overload, the metal strip will be broken (see drawings at right). Time-delay fuses react the same way to shorts as do plug fuses. But if an overload hits a time-delay fuse, solder in the bottom of the fuse loosens and releases a metal strip that is pulled upward by a coiled wire.

"READING" A BLOWN FUSE

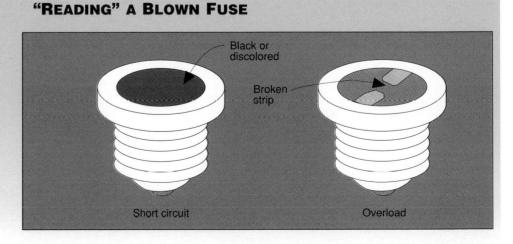

Black or discolored

Broken strip

Short circuit

Overload

Solving Electrical Problems

CALCULATING YOUR HOUSE POWER

Has your electrical system kept up with the demands placed on it by all the modern work savers—electric ranges, microwaves, air-conditioners computers—you've accumulated? Chances are, it hasn't. A 100-amp main service used to be sufficient for most homes. Today, you're likely to need 150 or 200 amps.

If a constant harassment of overloads keeps you busy resetting breakers or changing fuses and juggling appliances from one outlet to another, you already know you have a problem. Here's a scientific way to track it down.

Because circuits are rated at the service panel in terms of amps, you'll have to do some elementary arithmetic to get an amp rating for every electrical device in your house. Before you start calculating, however, you should take a complete survey of your house, identifying which outlets, lights, or appliances are on which circuits and listing every electrical appliance. When you're through, post a duplicate of that circuit plan next to, or inside the door of, your service panel. It will tell you at a glance which breaker to flip or fuse to pull when you want to work on a specific outlet or switch.

The formula, amperage equals watts divided by volts, allows you to figure the amperage requirements of each electrical device on each circuit. Most circuits are 120 volts, and you should be able to find either a wattage figure or amperage figure on every bulb, appliance, and other electrical item you have. If you are lucky enough to find an amperage figure, you don't need to make a calculation. If all you find is a wattage figure, divide it by 120 to determine the amperage.

The last step is to add up all of the amperage figures for each circuit and compare that total with the amperage capacity that appears on the appropriate breaker or fuse. By doing so, you'll know for sure if that circuit would face an overload if every device on that circuit called for current at the same time.

If your survey turns up some nerve-jangling results, add circuits, shuffle outlets from one circuit to another, or do a little of both.

General-purpose circuits need 15-amp breakers or fuses. Circuits that serve large appliances require greater capacities. In addition to the circuits shown below, kitchens should have at least two 20-amp small-appliance circuits. Also, workshops should have their own—or a seldom used—20 amp circuit.

Individual 240-volt circuits are in order for central air-conditioners, electric ranges, electric dryers, electric water heaters, electric furnaces, and heat pumps.

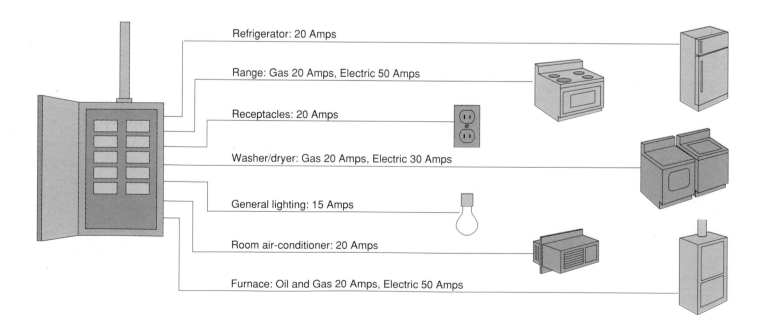

Refrigerator: 20 Amps

Range: Gas 20 Amps, Electric 50 Amps

Receptacles: 20 Amps

Washer/dryer: Gas 20 Amps, Electric 30 Amps

General lighting: 15 Amps

Room air-conditioner: 20 Amps

Furnace: Oil and Gas 20 Amps, Electric 50 Amps

GROUNDING YOUR ENTIRE SYSTEM

There are two kinds of electrical grounding. System grounding is the grounding of current-carrying wires. Equipment grounding is the grounding of noncurrent-carrying portions of your wiring installation, such as the housings of motors and appliances as well as smaller metal items, such as conduit, armored (BX) cable, and metal boxes for fixtures, switches, and receptacles.

Proper grounding starts in the service panel at the grounding bus bar, which is connected to earth by a cable known as the ground wire. This wire is fastened to the grounding bus and either to a metal rod driven into the earth outside your house or to your incoming water-supply pipe, which leads into the earth. The bus bar, in turn, has solderless connectors or screw terminals to which two other types of wires are connected—grounded wires and grounding wires.

Grounded wires are the white neutral wires that complete each of the circuits by returning current to its source and, in so doing, ground the system. Also connected to the bus bar is the incoming neutral wire from the utility company. Grounding wires—usually bare, green, or green with yellow stripes—are the wires that ground the equipment.

It is important to have equipment grounded. For example, if a short circuit should occur inside a motor, the motor might still run and the circuit breaker might not trip. The outside case of the motor could then be "live." Anyone touching the case would complete the circuit through their body to the ground. A properly installed grounding wire routes the errant current safely back through the bus bar and into the ground.

There are two ways to ensure equipment is grounded, depending on the type of wiring in your house. For circuits with metal conduit or armored cable, the conduit or cable must be mechanically connected to each box and to the service panel. Where nonmetallic (NM) cable is used, the cable must contain three wires—hot, neutral, and bare grounding. The grounding wire must extend from the metal switch or outlet box to the bus bar. Some older homes have neither type of cable. The only solution in that case is to rewire the entire house.

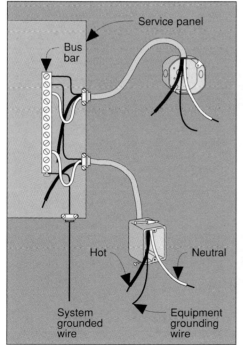

The bare equipment-grounding wires and white system-grounding neutrals connect to terminals on the bus bar.

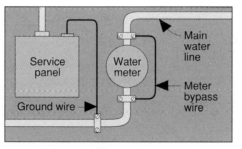

Add a bypass to the water-supply pipe to keep the grounding complete in case the meter has to be replaced.

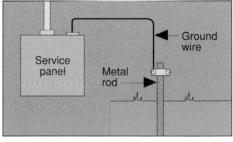

You can also attach the system ground wire to a metal rod that's been driven into the earth.

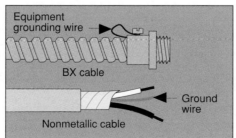

Two equipment grounds: BX cable makes metal-to-metal contact; its ground strip adds extra insurance.

A plug adapter is grounded only if the screw holding the pigtail is in contact with a properly grounded outlet box.

Solving Electrical Problems (continued)

TOOL TALK

TOOLS FOR ELECTRICAL REPAIRS

You probably already have on hand a number of the tools you'll need for electrical work—old standbys, such as a hammer, drill, keyhole saw, chisel, screwdrivers, hacksaw, measuring tape, and the like. But there are a few special tools you will want to buy, rent, or borrow before you take on an electrical project of any size. If you decide to buy them, choose only high-quality tools. They work much better and last much longer than their bargain-basement look-alikes.

The examples below represent the bulk of the tools you'll need to solve the electrical problems treated on the next four pages. (See page 249 for more items necessary for bigger jobs.)

The fish tape can be bought with or without a reel. Both electrical testers are musts (see page 239). Some electricians like to use the combination tool because it can both cut and strip wire and crimp special fasteners, whereas others prefer to stick with a simpler wire stripper. You'll use the side-cutting pliers to snip wires in tough-to-reach places. Similar lineman's pliers have heavy square jaws that are ideal for twisting wires together. Needle-nose pliers make quick work of curling loops on the ends of wires.

Round up a sharp straight-bladed pocketknife or utility knife to slit the sheathing lengthwise on nonmetallic cable. Use a nut driver to reach into places wrenches can't touch.

Wire connectors are not actually tools, as you use them up just as fast as you do wire. But be sure to have a collection of various sizes and colors of screw-on connectors available; they'll make quick work of wire-to-wire connections.

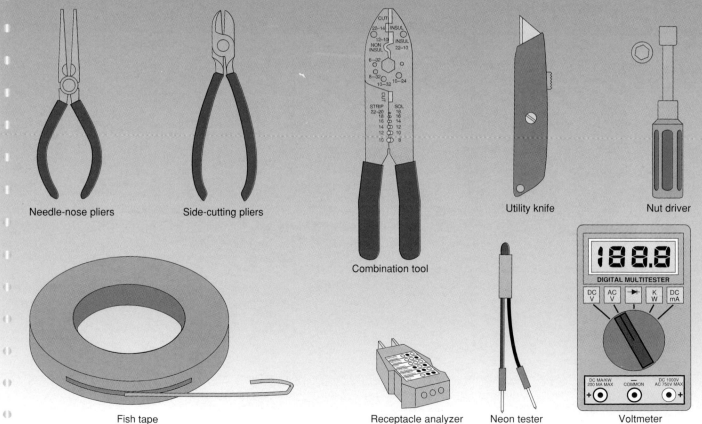

Needle-nose pliers   Side-cutting pliers   Combination tool   Utility knife   Nut driver

Fish tape   Receptacle analyzer   Neon tester   Voltmeter

TESTING CIRCUITS

It's good to have several types of electrical testers to help you find circuit problems. A receptacle analyzer (shown on page 238) is good for testing modern receptacles with large and small prong slots and a grounding hole. A neon tester detects the presence or lack of a current. Use a voltmeter to test a circuit for a variety of conditions—the voltage, whether it is hot, if a short circuit exists, even how many amps a fixture or device is drawing.

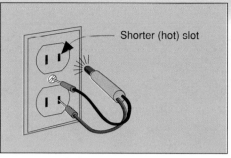

Shorter (hot) slot

To check if older receptacles are grounded, see if the neon tester lights up when touched to a receptacle box as shown.

Voltmeter selector on KΩ

A lamp socket is good if the voltmeter shows zero resistance with the probes held as shown. Replace the socket if it doesn't check out.

MAKING WIRE CONNECTIONS

Whether you're joining wires to switches, receptacles, or in mid-circuit, all connections must be made inside a box. Switches and receptacles can have one of two types of terminals (or both)—screws and grip holes.

With the screw type, you simply loosen the screw, strip and curl the end of the wire, and place the loop around the screw clockwise. Then securely tighten the screw.

Although grip holes can be wired quickly, electricians use the screw terminals instead. Screw terminals hold wires more securely and are less likely to come undone as you push the receptacle into the box.

Screw-on connectors make the job of joining wires simple. Keep a good supply on hand.

YOU'LL NEED...

SKILLS: Basic skills.
TIME: 10 minutes per receptacle.
TOOLS: Wire cutter and stripper or combination tool, pliers, screwdriver.

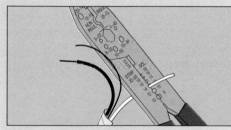

1. Remove about ¾ inch of insulation from each wire with a stripper. Wire size is indicated alongside each hole.

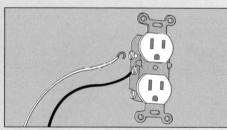

2. Use needle-nose pliers to bend the wire end into a loop, then curl it around the terminal screw.

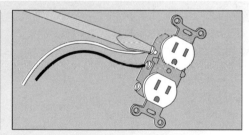

3. Be sure the screws are tight—but not so tight that they crack the plastic body of the receptacle.

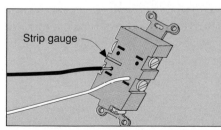

Strip gauge

Receptacles with grip holes have a strip gauge on them to show exactly how much wire insulation to remove.

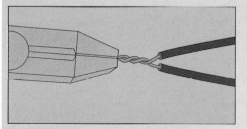

1. To ensure a solid connection with wire connectors, strip the wires and twist them together with pliers.

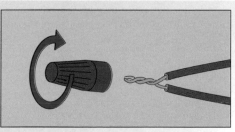

2. Push the wire into the connector and turn clockwise as far as it will go. Make sure no bare wire is exposed.

Solving Electrical Problems (continued)

HELPFUL HINTS

A table lamp is one of the simplest examples of electricity at work. It's also one of the easiest things to troubleshoot. Whenever a lamp doesn't light, the first thing to check is the bulb. If a new bulb doesn't solve the problem, the next place to look is the receptacle. The easiest way to find out if it's hot is to plug in another lamp. If it works, you've narrowed the problem to one of three remaining areas, shown in the table at right—the plug, the cord, or the socket.

TROUBLESHOOTING LAMPS

Symptom	Cause	Cure
Won't light	Loose connection	Tighten connection.
	Broken wire	Replace cord.
Blows fuse	Frayed cord	Tape or replace cord.
	Defective plug	Replace plug.
	Defective socket	Replace socket.
Light flickers	Loose connection	Tighten connection.
	Defective switch	Replace switch.

REPLACING A LAMP CORD

Worn lamp cords not only can cause serious shocks or short circuits, they're also fire hazards. So why take a chance? Make the repair as soon as you spot the trouble. If you think the socket is old and needs replacement, now's the time to do that also. Tape the new cord to the old one before you pull out the old cord. That way as you pull the old cord out, you'll pull the new cord into place.

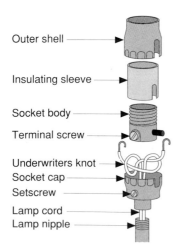

- Outer shell
- Insulating sleeve
- Socket body
- Terminal screw
- Underwriters knot
- Socket cap
- Setscrew
- Lamp cord
- Lamp nipple

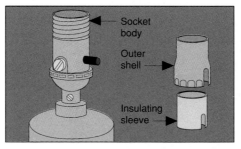

1. To expose the socket, press on the outer shell where it says "PRESS" and pull off the shell and insulating sleeve.

Socket body / Outer shell / Insulating sleeve

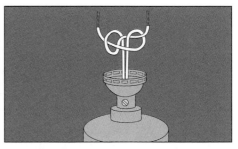

2. Loosen terminal screws, remove old cord (installing a new one as explained above), and tie an Underwriters knot.

3. Twist the braided strands tightly, curl as shown, and screw one wire to each terminal in a clockwise direction.

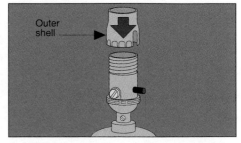

Outer shell

4. Pull the wire from below to draw the socket against its base, then replace the insulating and outer shells.

REPLACING PLUGS

If a plug has loose prongs, a cracked body, or a blackened spot, replace it immediately. Replace the plug also if you are replacing the cord—they're most likely of the same vintage.

There are two basic types of cord plugs—those for round cords and those for flat cords. Vacuum cleaners, irons, and other high-amperage appliances usually have round cords. Flat cords are found on low-amperage devices, such as radios, clocks, and lamps. Your replacement plug must be the same type as the original.

YOU'LL NEED...

SKILLS: Basic electrical skills.
TIME: 10 to 15 minutes.
TOOLS: Wire cutter and stripper or combination tool, screwdriver, pliers.

Hook up plugs designed for round cords (right, above) as shown below. The other two plugs shown at right are for flat cord, also known as zip cord. To connect these, insert the squared-off end of the flat cord into a slot on the plug and depress a lever (or push two parts together). Internal prongs pierce the wire insulation and connect the prongs to the wires in the cord.

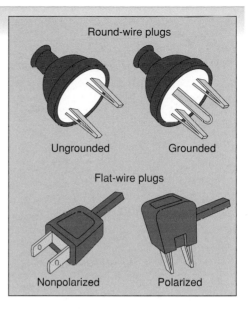

Round-wire plugs

Ungrounded   Grounded

Flat-wire plugs

Nonpolarized   Polarized

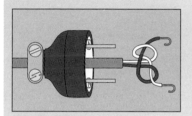

1. Remove sheath, insert cord, and tie Underwriters knot. Strip ¾ inch of insulation from both wires.

2. Twist strands of each wire, loop each clockwise around a screw, and tighten screw. Tuck in stray strands.

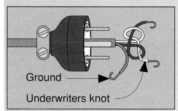

Ground

Underwriters knot

1. With grounded plugs, insert cord, tie three wires together, and pull the knot snugly into the plug.

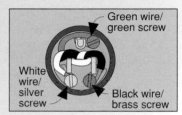

Green wire/green screw

White wire/silver screw

Black wire/brass screw

2. Strip insulation, twist strands, loop, and fasten under screws. Replace protective insulating cover.

TOOL TALK

You usually can get by around the house with a few 10-amp, two-wire extension cords. But it's a good idea to have at least one cord of a larger capacity—say, a 20-amp size—for hooking up appliances that draw more current than a radio or vacuum cleaner. In your workshop, you will want a large-capacity, three-wire cord, usually made of No. 14 wire, to handle power tools.

The longer the cord, the greater the voltage drop, so use the shortest cord possible. Check the table at right for buying guidelines.

SELECTING EXTENSION CORDS

Use	Length	Size
Lamps, clocks, etc., up to 7 amps	To 25 feet	No. 18
	To 50 feet	No. 16
	To 100 feet	No. 14
Small appliances, up to 10 amps	To 25 feet	No. 16
	To 50 feet	No. 14
	To 100 feet	No. 12
Large appliances, power tools	To 25 feet	No. 14
	To 50 feet	No. 12
	To 100 feet	No. 10

Note: The larger the wire size, the smaller the wire's diameter (see page 244).

Solving Electrical Problems (continued)

PROTECTING AGAINST VOLTAGE SURGES

Voltage surges are momentary jumps in the voltage coming into your home. While they typically last less than a second, they easily can wipe out delicate electronics, such as personal computers, televisions, and stereo systems. They may be caused not only by lightning strikes but by surges when power is restored after an outage; when your utility reroutes power from one station to another; or even by static electricity.

Surge protectors typically are a combination of two devices. Solid-state metal-oxide varistors shunt the excess voltage and current to ground in less than one-millionth of a second. Also, inductor coils resist sudden changes in voltage.

The best surge protection units offer protection for multiple AC outlets, as well as incoming cable television and telephone lines.

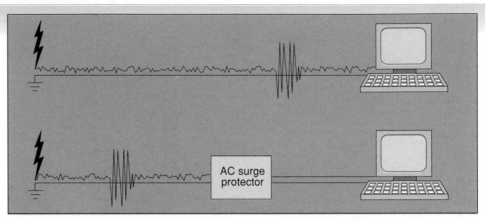

CHOOSING A SURGE PROTECTOR

In shopping for a surge protector, be careful of units that look like they offer surge protection but are merely multiple outlet boxes. Look for units with the following features and specifications:

■ **UL 1449 Rating:** the maximum voltage allowed through the unit; 400 volts is typical; lower is better.

■ **Response Time:** how long it takes for the protector to react to a surge; 1 nanosecond (one-billionth of a second) is typical; less is better.

■ **Surge Current:** the maximum current the unit can absorb without failing; 20,000 amps is typical; more is better.

■ **Joules:** the maximum energy the unit can absorb without failing; 200 joules is typical; more is better.

■ **Line Protection:** the number of conductors (hot, neutral, and ground) protected; should be three.

■ **EMI/RFI:** reduction of "noise" on incoming line; 30 decibels is typical; more is better

■ **Protected Outlets:** the number of protected receptacles; six is typical.

In addition, look for in and out jacks for cable TV and telephone lines, a circuit breaker for overloads, an on/off indicator light, and an audible alarm that signals when a surge occurs and the unit has failed.

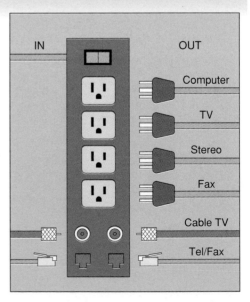

REPLACING RECEPTACLES

If a receptacle goes bad, all you have to do is wire the new outlet exactly as the old one was done— hot (black) wire to the brass terminal screw and neutral (white) wire to the silver screw. If there is a ground wire, it is connected to the green screw on the receptacle. If you replace an old two-prong outlet with a three-prong one, the ground prong will be active only if the receptacle box is grounded back to the service panel. See page 237 for more information about grounding.

> ## YOU'LL NEED...
> **SKILLS:** Basic electrical skills.
> **TIME:** 15 minutes.
> **TOOLS:** Screwdriver, tester.

1. Before you start, turn off the power at the main service panel. Remove the single screw holding the faceplate.

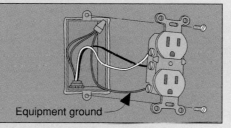

Equipment ground

2. Remove screws that fasten the receptacle to the box at top and bottom; pull out the receptacle.

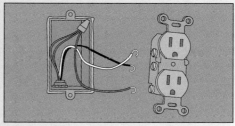

3. Before you disconnect the old wires, make a sketch to help you remember where each wire goes.

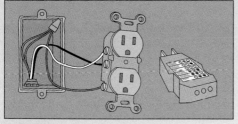

4. Hook up the new receptacle, using your sketch. Test your handiwork with a receptacle tester.

Side-by-side installations are just as easy. Just remember to sketch the wiring layout.

If you have small children, use child-proof safety covers. You have to remove the cover to expose the slots.

REPLACING SWITCHES

The most common household switch is a single-pole (one switch) variety. It has two brass-colored terminals and, in some cases, a grounding terminal. A switch is wired only into the hot line. Remember to always turn off the power at the service panel before working on a circuit.

> ## YOU'LL NEED...
> **SKILLS:** Basic skills.
> **TIME:** 15 minutes.
> **TOOLS:** Screwdriver, tester.

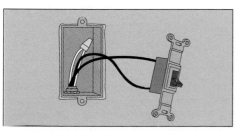

The neutral wires here are independent of the switch and continue all the way back to the service panel.

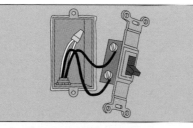

Switch terminals aren't always positioned the same way. Most often, however, they face the side.

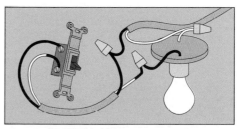

The ends of the white wire in this nonmetallic cable are taped black to indicate that it serves as a black wire.

Running New Wiring

Extending or adding a circuit calls more for careful thinking than actual skill or hard work. Most components fasten together surprisingly easily. Your hardest task will be to become familiar with the array of electrical materials on the market. After reviewing the next few pages, you may want to visit a well-stocked home center store and take a look at the products on display. If things still look complicated, a salesperson can lend you a hand. Or, if you can tour a new house that is still at the wiring stage of construction, the whole story, from panel to light switch and all points in between, will be laid out before you.

MATERIAL MATTERS — SELECTING WIRE SIZES AND TYPES

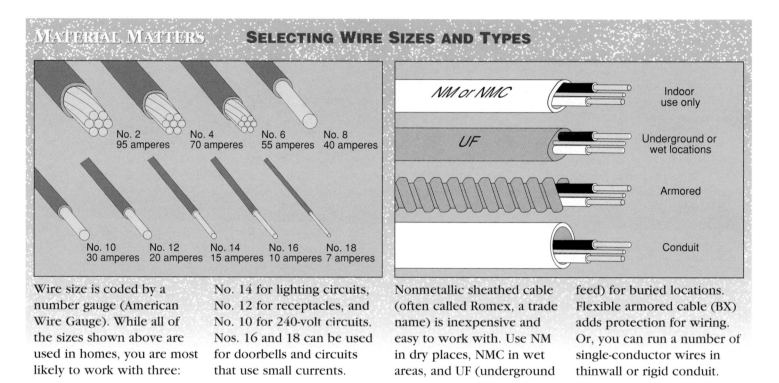

No. 2 95 amperes
No. 4 70 amperes
No. 6 55 amperes
No. 8 40 amperes
No. 10 30 amperes
No. 12 20 amperes
No. 14 15 amperes
No. 16 10 amperes
No. 18 7 amperes

NM or NMC — Indoor use only
UF — Underground or wet locations
Armored
Conduit

Wire size is coded by a number gauge (American Wire Gauge). While all of the sizes shown above are used in homes, you are most likely to work with three: No. 14 for lighting circuits, No. 12 for receptacles, and No. 10 for 240-volt circuits. Nos. 16 and 18 can be used for doorbells and circuits that use small currents.

Nonmetallic sheathed cable (often called Romex, a trade name) is inexpensive and easy to work with. Use NM in dry places, NMC in wet areas, and UF (underground feed) for buried locations. Flexible armored cable (BX) adds protection for wiring. Or, you can run a number of single-conductor wires in thinwall or rigid conduit.

HELPFUL HINTS — "READING" CABLE MARKINGS

Building codes specify the type of cable you may install. Most permit Type NM for indoor uses. Its sheath is a moisture-resistant, flame-retardant plastic that is easy to strip. You'll find two or three insulated conductors inside protected by a paper wrapping. If two, one will be black, the other white; if three, you'll see a red one, too. There also may be a bare grounding wire.

The markings at right on the top wire indicate the cable contains three No. 10 wires and a grounding wire.

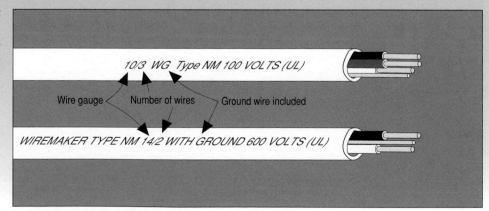

10/3 WG Type NM 100 VOLTS (UL)

Wire gauge — Number of wires — Ground wire included

WIREMAKER TYPE NM 14/2 WITH GROUND 600 VOLTS (UL)

WORKING WITH WIRE CABLES

Nonmetallic (NM) or armored cable comes with wires inside. NM cable is easier to work with, but some local codes may require armored cable.

Most often, both are concealed within walls where they run little risk of being damaged. Run them vertically between the studs or horizontally through holes drilled in the studs. (Be sure holes are at least 1½ inches back from the front face of the stud.)

When you buy armored cable, stock up on anti-short bushings, which prevent sharp cable edges from damaging the wires' insulation.

YOU'LL NEED...
SKILLS: Basic electrical skills.
TIME: 10 minutes to strip each end of the cable and clamp in place.
TOOLS: Utility knife, combination tool, screwdriver, hammer.

Using Nonmetallic Sheathed Cable

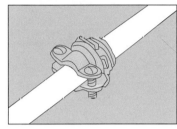

1. To attach NM cable to a box, slip a box connector 7 inches onto the cable and tighten the screws.

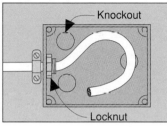

2. Remove a knockout from one side of the box and insert the connector. Then screw on the locknut.

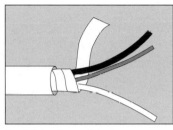

3. After the cable is anchored, slit and remove the sheath and cut away the protective paper lining.

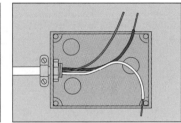

4. Use a combination tool (match hole size to wire) to remove ¾ inch of insulation from both wires.

Using Armored Cable

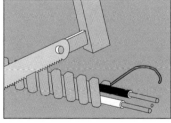

1. Partially cut armored cable at an angle with a hacksaw. Don't nick the insulation on the wires.

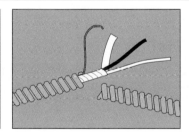

2. Twist end and pull it off. Unwind protective paper as far as you can and cut it off.

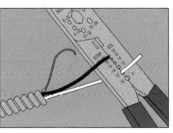

3. Strip both wires back about ¾ inch. A wire stripper is the best tool, but you also can use a knife.

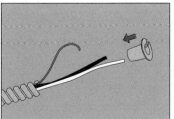

4. Because cut edges of steel armor are sharp, you must insert an anti-short bushing to protect the wires.

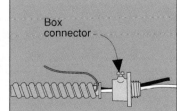

5. Fold back ground wire and push a box connector onto cable as far as it will go. File any sharp edges.

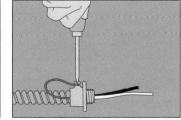

6. Wrap ground wire around the screw of the connector and tighten screw firmly.

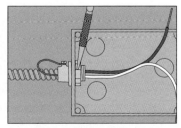

7. Remove a knockout, insert connector, and screw on locknut. Pound a nail set against lugs to tighten nut.

Running New Wiring (continued)

TIMELY TECHNIQUES

WORKING WITH CONDUIT

Unprotected electrical cable—unless inside a wall, floor, or ceiling—is susceptible to damage. Whenever you run wiring in an unfinished space or garage, protect it with conduit.

There are four types of conduit available. But for residential uses, you will probably encounter only the thinwall type. It's sold in 10-foot lengths that you can join end to end with couplings and to boxes with connectors (shown below).

The trickiest part of working with conduit is bending it to get around corners or to make the small offsets

necessary at each box. To do this, you slip the conduit into a bender (see page 249), as illustrated, then gently lever the bender toward you. Make a bend gradually, with a series of tugs along its radius. If you pull too sharply at any one point, you will crimp the tubing. The importance of making smooth bends becomes clear after you have installed a run of conduit, fitted boxes at either end, and started to pull wires through the conduit. Too many bends—and any crimping at all—will hang up the wires and risk breaking a wire or damaging its insulation.

You should limit bends in any run between boxes to a total of 360 degrees. If you have to traverse more than the equivalent of four one-quarter bends, install an additional box.

Most codes specify that you use Type TW wires in conduit. You'll need at least two conductors (one black, one white). To pull the wires, thread a fish tape (see page 238) through the tubing and attach the wires to it, then pull the tape back through the conduit. Never splice wires inside conduit—a poorly made connection could render the entire conduit run "live."

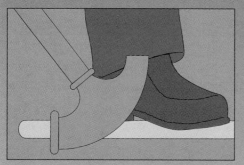

Bend conduit first, then cut it to length. Make a few practice bends before you start your job.

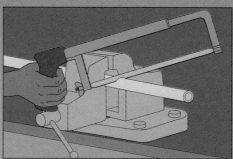

Hold the conduit in a vise while you cut it with a hacksaw. File off burrs so they won't damage the wiring.

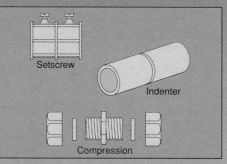

Shown are the three types of conduit couplings. The indenter type requires a special crimping tool.

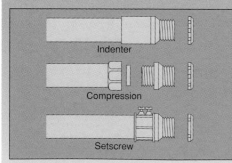

Box connectors, which match the three couplings above, secure the conduit safely in place.

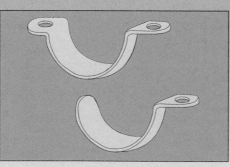

Use clamps to anchor ½-inch thinwall conduit to walls or ceilings near boxes and at least every 10 feet.

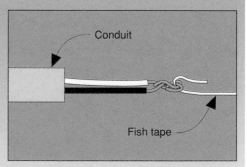

For short runs, you can push wires through conduit. For long runs, pull the wires with a spring-steel fish tape.

USING SURFACE RACEWAYS

Although less attractive than hiding the wiring in the wall, surface-mounted wiring raceways, either metal or plastic, are easy to install.

Raceway channels attach to the wall with couplings, clips, and straps; some are available with self-sticking mountings. After mounting the hardware, pull the wiring through the channels and make the connections. A variety of fittings help you build a raceway system suited to your needs.

YOU'LL NEED...

SKILLS: Basic electrical and carpentry skills.

TIME: 30 to 45 minutes for a 20-foot section with two receptacles.

TOOLS: Screwdriver, combination tool, drill.

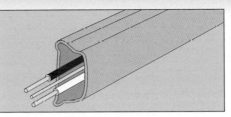

For safety codes, one-piece raceway must be exposed, except when it runs through a wall into the next room.

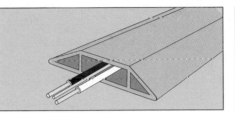

A one-piece "pancake" channel is available for installations that require running wiring on top of the floor.

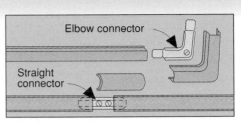

Elbows, T-connectors, reducing connectors, and even receptacles and switches tie into raceway systems.

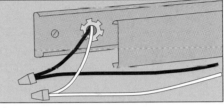

Two-piece raceway doesn't require a box. Power enters via cable connected to the wall-mounted backing plate.

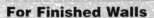 **SELECTING BOXES AND ACCESSORIES**

For Exposed Walls

Because all switches, receptacles, fixtures (except fluorescent lights), and wiring junctions must be protected by a box, you can appreciate why there are hundreds of different boxes on the market. Boxes come in metallic, nonmetallic, and waterproof types.

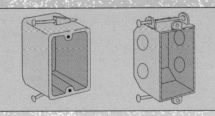

You can nail these boxes to the side of a stud with their own 16d nails. One is plastic; the other steel.

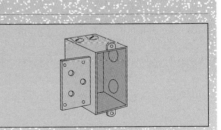

These boxes are nailed to the front of a stud. The brackets are recessed for the thickness of a normal drywall surface.

For Finished Walls

The products at right make installing a new box in an existing finished wall fairly simple. The most difficult part is fishing the new cable through the wall. Before you begin, refer to pages 32–33, 55, and 252 for information about cutting different wall materials.

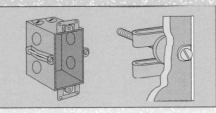

Push this box into an opening to the ears. Turn the two clamp screws to tighten the box against the wall.

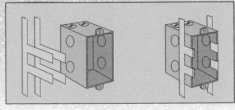

Slip metal box supports alongside the box, then fold the tabs into the box to hold it snug against the wall.

Running New Wiring *(continued)*

The Basic Box

You'll get a lot of mileage out of this box, especially if you use the style that comes with internal clamps. The two-hole ears at top and bottom are adjustable and removable to suit differing wall thicknesses. Electrical codes allow you to "gang" together two or more of these boxes.

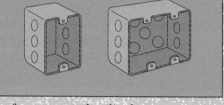

The top internal clamp accommodates armored cable; the bottom clamp can be used for nonmetallic sheathed cable.

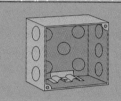

To gang boxes, remove a side from each and join them with the screws that formerly held the sides in place.

Utility and Junction Boxes

All boxes must be at least 1½ inches deep to comply with electrical codes. Most junction boxes are octagonal or square and are available only in the 4-inch size. If you must mount a box on the surface of a wall, use the round-cornered variety, which is called a utility or handy box; these, however, cannot be ganged.

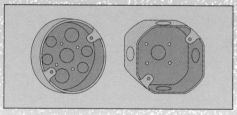

Surface-mounted utility boxes come in 2- and 4-inch-wide sizes. Use the square type of this box for junction boxes.

If the box won't be exposed, use a sharp-cornered type. There are more sizes available than for utility boxes.

Ceiling Boxes

Ceiling boxes, from which you can hang fixtures, are usually round, octagonal, or square. Because of the weight of fixtures, you must anchor the box very securely. If you can't gain access to the ceiling joists, you'll have to mount the box in the plaster or drywall span between joists (see page 253).

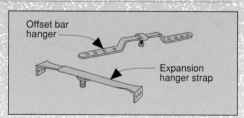

Offset bar hanger

Expansion hanger strap

Ceiling boxes have internal clamps and/or connector knockouts. Boxes nail to or are hung between joists.

Straps on the top hanger are recessed into plaster and nailed to joist bottoms. Install the other type from above.

Accessories

Many accessories are available to solve wiring problems. For example, if you've installed thick planking over your old walls, your existing switch boxes will be recessed too deeply. But a depth ring extends the box so that it's flush with the new surface. Check electrical suppliers for more accessories.

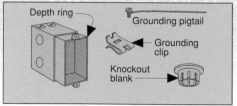

Depth ring

Grounding pigtail

Grounding clip

Knockout blank

Some accessories include a depth ring, grounding screw with pigtail, grounding clip, and knockout blank.

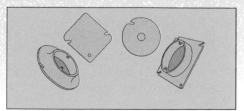

Every box must be covered. Covers come in all sizes and shapes, ranging from metal disks to complex designs.

MATERIAL MATTERS   SELECTING THE CORRECT BOX SIZE

An overcrowded electrical box increases the chances of a short circuit. The chart below shows the sizes and number of wires that you can safely fit inside boxes of various sizes, depending on wire size.

As you make your determination, keep in mind these exceptions: (1) Wires from a fixture on the box connected to wires in the box are not counted. (2) A wire that enters and leaves the box without a splice counts as just one wire. (3) If the box contains a cable clamp, hickey, or fixture stud, reduce the number of permitted wires by one. (The reduction is only one, no matter how many items are in the box.) (4) External, attached connectors aren't considered as devices in the box; count each internal connector or clamp as one. (5) Reduce count by one wire for each receptacle, switch, or other device in the box. (6) If a wire starts and ends in a box, such as a ground wire from the green terminal to the box, don't count it. (7) When one or more bare grounding wires from a nonmetallic sheathed cable run into a box, reduce by one the number of wires allowed.

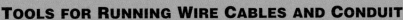

Box Type	Size (inches)	Maximum Wires				Box Type	Size (inches)	Maximum Wires			
		#14	#12	#10	#8			#14	#12	#10	#8
Basic boxes	3×2×1½	3	3	3	2	Ceiling and	4×1½ round	3	3	3	2
(switches and	3×2×2	5	4	4	3	junction boxes	4×2⅛ octagonal	5	4	4	3
receptacles)	3×2×2¼	5	4	4	3		4×1½ square	5	4	4	3
	3×2×2½	6	5	5	4		4×2⅛ square	6	5	5	4
	3×2×2¾	7	6	5	4		4×1½ square	7	6	5	4
	3×2×3½	9	8	7	6		4¹¹⁄₁₆×2⅛ square	7	6	5	4
Utility boxes	4×2⅛×1½	5	4	4	3						
	4×2⅛×1⅞	6	5	5	4						
	4×2⅛×2⅛	7	6	5	4						

TOOL TALK   TOOLS FOR RUNNING WIRE CABLES AND CONDUIT

The Tool Talk on page 238 showed tools you need to make general repairs. For those long runs between basement and attic, you'll need a few additional tools.

Start with a ⅜-inch electric drill with a spade bit that can eat its way through 2×4s and their inevitable knots. You also may need an extension bit to bore through double top plates and a carbide-tipped masonry bit to drill into block walls.

Round out your arsenal with a conduit bender of the correct diameter for the conduit you'll be using, a pipe cutter (some professionals still prefer a hacksaw), the fish tape you bought for general repairs, and a keyhole saw to cut openings for new boxes.

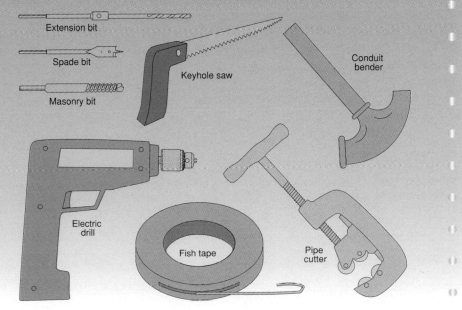

Extension bit
Spade bit
Masonry bit
Keyhole saw
Conduit bender
Electric drill
Fish tape
Pipe cutter

Running New Wiring (continued)

EXTENDING EXISTING CIRCUITS

If you want to add just a couple of outlets or a new light fixture, you shouldn't have to run new wire all the way from the service panel. The easiest places to access wiring and power are junction boxes and duplex receptacles.

If you have a basement, look for junction boxes there. If the circuit has excess capacity (see page 236) and your needs won't tax it, start your new line at the box. Or, you might find a box or two in the attic.

In a finished house, look for a nearby receptacle. Tie into one that has two unused terminals (provided the circuit has power to spare).

YOU'LL NEED...

SKILLS: Basic electrical skills.
TIME: 1 to 2 hours.
TOOLS: Screwdriver, needle-nose pliers, wire stripper.

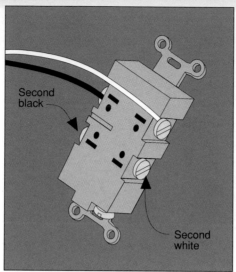

Second black

Second white

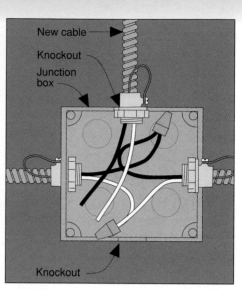

New cable

Knockout

Junction box

Knockout

Most duplex receptacles have four terminals—two hot (generally brass) and two neutral (generally silver). Extend a circuit by tying into the two unused terminals. If all terminals are in use, you'll have to look for another receptacle with available terminals.

Extending a circuit from a junction box in the attic or basement isn't difficult. Remove one of the knockouts, attach your new cable, and tie the wires into the existing connections. You'll have to use larger wire connectors to accommodate the additional wires.

Finding a Place to Tap In

Tapping into existing circuits to add a receptacle or fixture is not that difficult. Look for junction boxes between exposed joists in the basement or the attic. Check all walls in the room where you want to add a receptacle to see if there is a receptacle box in an adjoining room. It's then easy to tap power from that box.

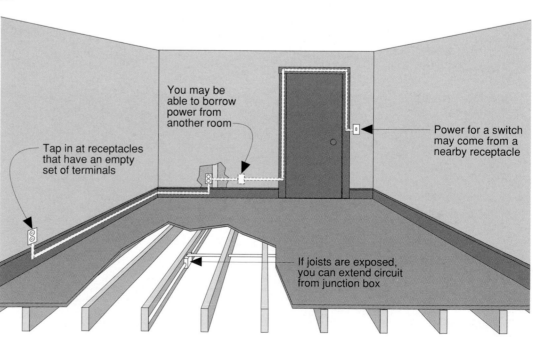

You may be able to borrow power from another room

Power for a switch may come from a nearby receptacle

Tap in at receptacles that have an empty set of terminals

If joists are exposed, you can extend circuit from junction box

FISHING WIRES

Getting wire from one spot to the next is usually the biggest challenge in adding or extending circuits in an existing house. It takes time, patience, and a basic knowledge of construction techniques. But it can be the most rewarding part of the job, because once you've pulled your wires through that "impossible" maze of walls, ceilings, and floors, you will feel like you've really accomplished something.

Expect to find a 2×4 plate in the bottom of each wall, double plates at the top, and possibly 2×4 fire blocking crosswise between studs halfway up the walls. If you have a chimney on an interior wall, running wire alongside it may be the best path from the attic to the basement.

You'll have some wall patching jobs facing you when the wiring is completed, so check pages 35–40 for a quick refresher course.

check pages 35–40

Getting Wires From Unfinished Spaces

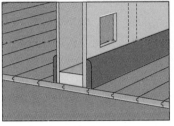

1. Check to make sure you won't cut into a stud (see page 33), then cut opening.

2. Remove the baseboard, drill a hole in the floor, and place a 16d nail in the hole.

3. Find your locator nail, then drill up through the sole plate from below.

4. Push up fish tape from below, having a helper guide it through the outlet hole.

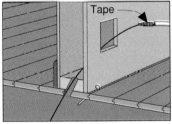

5. Hook the cable to the fish tape. Wrap with electrical tape to ensure a smooth pull.

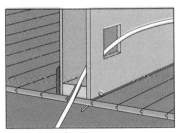

6. Pull cable into the basement. Wire the outlet and mount it in the wall.

Getting Through Finished Walls

1. To get cable to a new ceiling fixture, cut a hole in the wall near the ceiling.

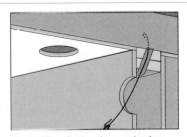

2. Drill a hole through the top plates, fasten tape to cable, and push into cavity.

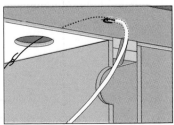

3. Fish second tape into ceiling, hook onto the first one, and pull the cable.

Running New Wiring (continued)

MOUNTING WALL BOXES

When you have access to exposed studs, you can mount a box in five minutes or less. But if you have to hunt for the studs (see page 33), cut openings, and run cable, plan on spending at least 30 minutes or more per box.

Switches should be installed 48 to 50 inches above the floor; receptacles, 12 to 16 inches above the floor. The national code requires that receptacles be placed so that no point along any wall is more than 6 feet from an outlet. Mount boxes so they are flush with the finished wall surface.

In finished spaces, your order of attack should be to locate and cut the opening, dry-fit the box, fish the cable, attach it to the box, then install the box permanently. From that point, it's a matter of patching the walls and hooking up your new switches, receptacles, and fixtures.

> ### YOU'LL NEED...
> **SKILLS:** Basic carpentry skills.
> **TIME:** 5 minutes in unfinished space; 30 minutes in finished space.
> **TOOLS:** Hammer, screwdriver, drywall saw, chisel, drill.

Installing Boxes In Unfinished Spaces

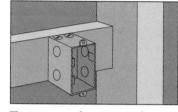

To mount a box away from a stud, nail a 2×4 crosspiece between studs and screw the box to the crosspiece.

Simply hold this box where you want it and pound the pre-attached 16d nails into the side of the stud.

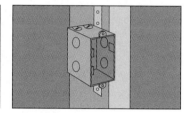

Place this type of box in position on the wall, then nail it through the bracket and into the stud.

Installing Boxes In Paneling And Drywall

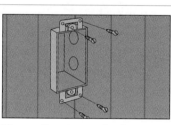

If paneling is sturdy, just cut a hole in it, insert the box, and screw through the two ears into the paneling.

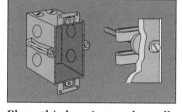

Place this box into a drywall hole, then tighten the screws, which draw up holding clamps on each side.

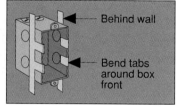

Position these supports on each side of box behind the drywall and bend the flaps to anchor the box to the wall.

Installing Boxes In Lath and Plaster

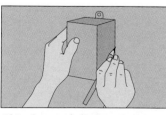

Chisel a peek hole so you can center the box ears on a lath. Then draw around the box to mark the cut.

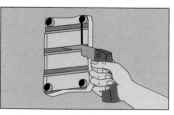

Cut away plaster with a chisel, drill starter holes, then carefully cut the lath with a sharp keyhole saw.

Enough lath should remain at the top and bottom to screw the box (through its ears) to the lath strips.

MOUNTING CEILING BOXES FROM ABOVE

Mount ceiling boxes from above if you have easy access to the joists from above or if you can patch the floor above once you've opened it up. Carpeted floors above lend themselves to this method because the carpet hides the floor patch.

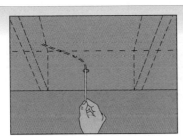

1. Drill ¼-inch hole, slip an L-shaped wire into it, and spin wire to confirm that there is space for box.

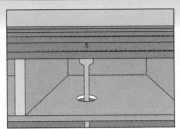

2. Widen hole to 1 inch and bore a locator hole in the floor above using an extension bit.

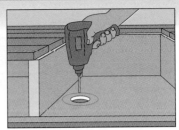

3. Cut out flooring, trace box outline, and drill holes around perimeter of the cutline.

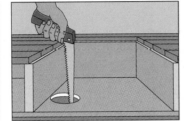

4. Cut opening with keyhole saw. Score plaster from below with utility knife.

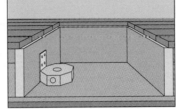

5. If the hole abuts a joist, mount a box equipped with a bracket.

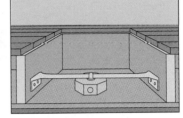

6. Otherwise, use a box on an adjustable bar hanger. Screw hanger ends to joists.

MOUNTING CEILING BOXES FROM BELOW

If you do not have access from above, you'll have to do all the work from below. The most difficult parts of such a project are working with tools over your head and refinishing the ceiling once you've installed the box.

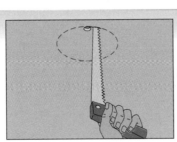

1. Mark box hole, check to make sure there is room for box (see above), and cut out with a keyhole saw.

2. For lightweight fixtures, insert and rest bar hanger on ceiling. Don't use this method for heavy fixtures.

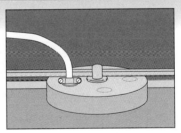

3. Remove ceiling box center knockout, slip the box onto the hanger's stud, and screw on nut inside box.

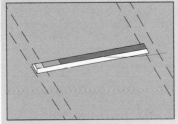

1. For heavy fixtures, cut groove in ceiling to joists on either side of fixture hole.

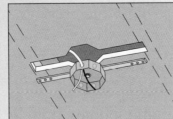

2. Cut hole in center, screw offset bracket-and-box to joist bottoms; patch plaster.

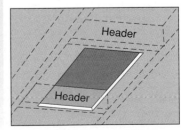

For a full-access installation for a recessed fixture, you should add support headers.

Running New Wiring (continued)

WIRING RECEPTACLES AND SWITCHES

Once you have run wires through walls and ceilings, hooking up receptacles doesn't take long. You simply connect the black, hot wire to one of the brass terminals on each device, and the white, neutral wire to the silver-colored terminal. If the circuit will continue on from there, connect a continuing set of hot and neutral wires to the second set of terminals.

Switches, on the other hand, require a bit more thinking. You first must determine where the switch is located relative to the power source and the fixture it will control. Will power flow through the switch to the fixture, or vice versa? A switch interrupts only the hot leg of the circuit. If the current will come to the fixture first, you must make a "switch loop" by connecting the white wire to the power source and switch and the black wire to the switch and fixture. Because the white wire serves as a hot lead, it must be marked with black tape at each end.

If the current goes to the switch first and then to the fixture, you needn't connect the neutral wires to the switch. Attach the black wires to each of the switch's terminals and "jump" the neutrals, as shown in the next-to-last drawing below.

For more about wiring switches and receptacles, see page 243; turn to pages 267–277 for more about installing fixtures.

> ### YOU'LL NEED...
> **SKILLS:** Basic electrical skills.
> **TIME:** 15 minutes.
> **TOOLS:** Combination tool or wire stripper, screwdriver, needle-nose pliers.

Wiring Receptacles

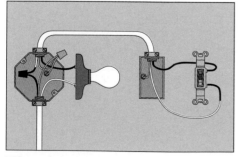

Slot-type receptacles let you push the stripped end of a wire into a hole in the receptacle. But the slots don't hold wire as well as screw terminals.

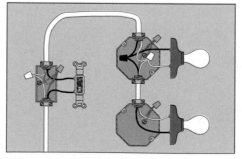

To add a receptacle to an existing circuit, run wires from the empty terminals on the existing receptacle to the new one.

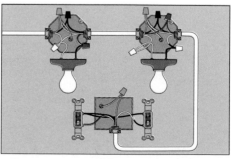

Fold wires carefully into the box, then screw the receptacle to the box; align cover plate before tightening screws.

Wiring Two-Way Switches

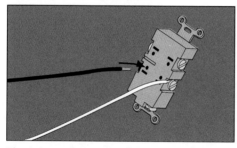

When the switch is beyond the fixture, wire it like this. The white wire from the switch must be coded black.

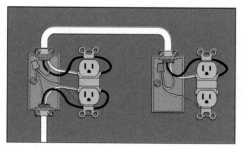

When the switch is in the middle of the run, wire it this way to control one or more fixtures.

When two switches in the same box control separate fixtures, use a three-wire cable. Power comes from the left.

WIRING THREE- AND FOUR-WAY SWITCHES

Three-way switches aren't what their name implies. They control fixtures from two locations, not three. For example, you might install a switch at the top of a stairway and another at the bottom, so that both operate the same fixture in the stairway. Three-ways are adaptable to many other lighting situations also.

Although three-way switches are different from their simpler two-way cousins, they're easy to understand if you learn three bits of information: (1) A three-way switch has three terminals—a dark-colored one for the "common" wire and two light-colored ones for the "traveler" wires. (2) Always attach the incoming hot (black) wire to the common terminal of one switch, and always run a hot wire (black or a white wire marked black) from the common terminal of the second switch directly to the black wire of the fixture. (3) Always connect the two traveler terminals of one switch to the traveler terminals of the other.

Four-way switches control a light from more than two locations. Install one three-way switch nearest the power source, one nearest the light, and a four-way switch in between.

The wiring diagrams below show the most common installations. The grounding wires have been left out of the illustrations to make the sketches easier to follow.

> ### YOU'LL NEED...
> **SKILLS:** Intermediate electrical skills.
> **TIME:** 20 to 30 minutes.
> **TOOLS:** Combination tool or wire stripper, screwdriver, needle-nose pliers.

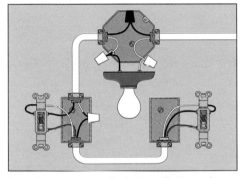

In a three-way switch installation, the hot wire from the source goes through the fixture box and connects to the common terminal of the switch at left.

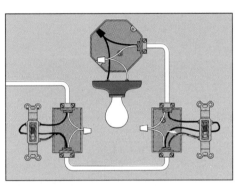

Here, when the power source comes to the switches before the fixture, the white neutral wire isn't pressed into service as a hot wire.

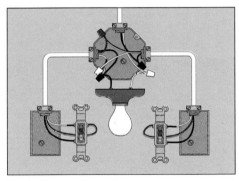

In this case, the white wire serves as a traveler between switches and must be painted or taped black to indicate that it's serving as a hot wire.

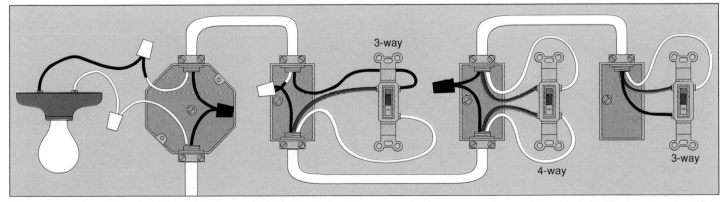

A four-way switch is wired between two three-way switches in this circuit so the light can be controlled from three locations. A two-wire cable (plus ground) is all that's needed between the fixture and the first switch. But three-wire cable is required between switches. The neutrals act as travelers from one switch to the next and as the hot wire returning from the switches to the fixture. You can easily spot a four-way switch; it has an extra terminal.

Running New Wiring (continued)

ADDING NEW CIRCUITS

The first step in adding a circuit to a new living space is to get from the service panel to the location of the new circuit. From then on, you should be installing wire after the rough framing is done, but before the walls are finished.

Start at the service panel, but don't connect the wires to the box's terminals yet. Instead, fish all of your wiring through the walls, floors, and ceilings as necessary (see page 251). You probably will be running nonmetallic sheathed cable to the new space because you can't use rigid conduit without tearing out a

lot of framing and finish materials. Some local codes require the use of armored cable; be sure to find out what is acceptable in your area.

If you only need a couple of new circuits, you can run a single three-conductor cable from the panel. For a multicircuit add-on, consider running heavier cable from the main service panel to a new subpanel in the new space, then splitting off new circuits from the subpanel.

When you get the cable to the new space, use a spade bit to drill wiring holes through the centers of the studs and joists. This minimizes

the chances of a nail being driven into the wire later. If you must drill a hole closer than 1½ inches from the front edge of the stud, cover the front of the stud at that spot with a piece of metal plate at least ¹⁄₁₆ inch thick to prevent a nail from penetrating the stud and any wires.

After the wiring is in, mount the boxes where needed (see pages 252–253). This should go quickly because you simply nail the boxes to the sides of the exposed framing. Then install the switches, receptacles, and fixtures (see pages 254–255 and 267–277).

Connecting to the Service Panel

Some experts recommend hiring a licensed electrician to do work inside the service panel; some codes may even require it.

If you do your own connections at the panel, the first thing you want to do is to remove or open the front cover and flip off the main breaker or pull the main fuses. (Caution: This shuts off all the branch circuits in your home, but the large, main wires coming into the box at the top will still be live!) Strip the wires you'll be bringing into the box, making sure they are long enough to curl around inside the box and reach the proper

terminals. Remove a knockout from the side of the box and anchor the cable or conduit to the box with a cable clamp or conduit connector.

For a fuse box, connect the black wire to the terminal screw on the fuse holder and the white wire to the bus bar to which all of the other white wires are connected. Attach the ground wire to the ground strip, which in some cases may be the same bus used for the white wires. Screw in a fuse, replace the inner cover of the box, and reinstall the main fuses to test the circuit.

For a circuit-breaker box, attach

the white neutral wire and bare grounding wire to the neutral bar. Fasten the black wire to a new circuit breaker, and press it into an empty slot. Flip the main breaker on and test the circuit. Remove the proper knockout(s) to accommodate the new breaker(s) before you put the panel cover on again.

> ### YOU'LL NEED...
> **SKILLS:** Intermediate electrical skills.
> **TIME:** 20 minutes.
> **TOOLS:** Combination tool or wire stripper, screwdriver.

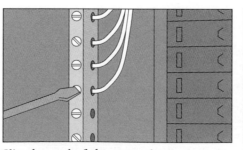

When working inside a service panel, you are safest standing on a dry board with one hand in your pocket.

Slip the end of the neutral wire into an empty slot on the bus bar, then drive in the screw tightly against the wire.

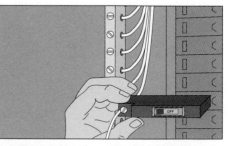

Installing a breaker usually is a one-handed job; simply push the breaker contacts into the appropriate slots.

WORKING WITH HEAVY-DUTY CIRCUITS

Heavy-duty circuits for major appliances (120/240 volts or 240 volts only) must be wired according to strict guidelines; so find out what local codes require. You'll usually be working with special heavy duty receptacles and plugs—even for built-in appliances that you might expect to be wired directly to a junction box. That is because the national code requires that you be able to disconnect a built-in unit in case of electrical emergencies. In some cases, this means a separate switch wired from the service panel, but usually the disconnect device is simply a heavy-duty receptacle into which a matching cord-connected plug is inserted.

Heavy-duty receptacles and plugs are identified as 2-pole, 2-wire; 2-pole, 3-wire; 3-pole, 3-wire; 3-pole, 4-wire; and so forth. The number of poles indicates the number of wires that normally carry current. If there is one more wire than poles, the receptacle or plug has an extra terminal for a separate grounding wire. Never connect a current-carrying wire to this terminal.

Wiring 240-Volt Plugs And Receptacles

Hook together two 120-volt circuits and you have a 240-volt circuit. Such a circuit consists of just two hot wires, plus an equipment ground. This means that if you use black and white cable, you should mark the ends of the white wire with black tape to indicate that the white wire also is hot.

Receptacles and plugs for 240-volt appliances are designed such that a plug of a certain voltage and amperage will fit only a receptacle with identical characteristics.

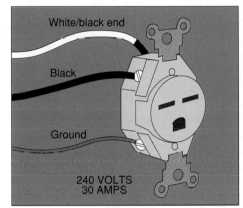

In this 240-volt, two-wire-plus-ground receptacle, the top two terminals are for the current-carrying wires.

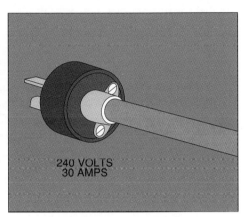

This 240-volt plug is a mate for the receptacle at left and is wired identically. A sleeve covers the wiring.

Wiring 120/240-Volt Plugs And Receptacles

Electric ranges require 120/240-volt power supplies because the burners need 240 volts at high heat but 120 volts for lower heat. Timers and lights also run off 120 volts. Special three-prong plugs and receptacles are made for this installation.

Heavy-duty components come in many configurations, each for a specific voltage and amperage. The chart on page 258 shows some common types. Some plugs are designed so they can't be inserted or removed without twisting.

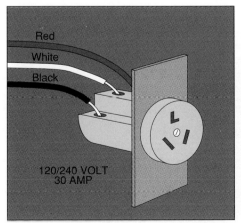

This 120/240-volt receptacle has three current-carrying wires—white neutral, and red and black live.

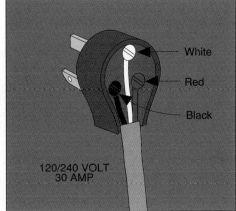

Simply match up plug terminals with receptacle terminals, then wire by color accordingly.

Running New Wiring (continued)

INSTALLING MAJOR APPLIANCES

If you're running wiring for a new appliance, read the sections of the National Electrical Code that pertain to appliance circuits. The main decisions you'll face are the size of wire and circuit breaker (or fuse) and what types of plugs and receptacles to use for the job.

The chart below provides a summary, but be sure to check an appliance's rating before you size the circuit. If the rating is in watts, remember that you simply divide watts by voltage to get amperage.

Note, also, that 240-volt plugs and receptacles are not as standardized as those for 120-volt devices. Not only do their configurations vary according to their amperage ratings, but sometimes even a receptacle and plug rated at the same amperage will not mate. The chart shows only some of the dozens of possibilities.

Will you even need a special heavy-duty plug and receptacle? The national code distinguishes between three types of appliances—portable, stationary, and fixed—and spells out different requirements for each. A portable appliance, such as a microwave oven, is one that is quite mobile. The stationary variety, for example, a slide-in range or a dryer, can be moved fairly readily but usually remains in its original place of installation. Fixed appliances, such as water heaters, cooktops, and wall ovens, are installed in permanent locations.

MATERIAL MATTERS   SIZING HEAVY-DUTY CIRCUITS

Appliance	Electrical Requirements	Wire Size	Receptacle
Electric dryer	120/240 volts, 20 to 30 amps	#10	 30-Amp 120/240-Volt
Electric water heater	240 volts, 20 to 30 amps	#12 for 20 amps or less #10 for 30 amps	 20-Amp 240-Volt or  30-Amp 240-Volt
Electric range	Typically 50 amps at 120/240 volts; check local code for plug and receptacle requirements.	Two #6 hot wires and a #8 neutral; for small units, two #8 hot and a #10 neutral	 30-Amp 120/240-Volt or  50-Amp 120/240-Volt
Separate oven and cooktop	Connect both to a single 50 amp, 120/240-volt circuit or provide separate 30-amp circuits for each.	For a single circuit, see electric range above; otherwise, 30-amp circuits take #10.	 50-Amp 120/240-Volt or  30-Amp 120/240-Volt
Microwave, refrigerator, dishwasher, clothes washer, gas dryer	Typically, 15 or 20 amps at 120 volts; each should have a separate circuit, however.	#12	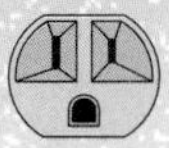 15-Amp 120-Volt
Window air-conditioner	From 15 amps at 120 volts up to 30 amps at 240 volts; more about air-conditioners on pages 378–379.	#12 for 20 amps or less #10 for 30 amps	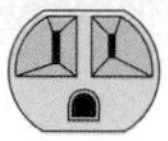 15-Amp 120-Volt or  30-Amp 240-Volt

GROUNDING APPLIANCES

Appliances must be grounded to prevent a shock if a circuit's fuse or breaker fails to react when needed. If receptacles are properly grounded (see page 237), the third wire of the appliance's power cord will ground the unit. Otherwise, or if your local code requires it, ground appliances by running a wire from the ground terminal of the appliance to a pipe of your plumbing system.

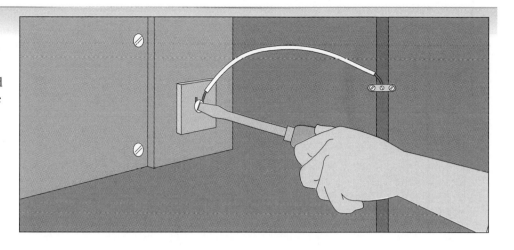

TROUBLESHOOTING APPLIANCES

When an electric appliance or tool stops working properly, you may need professional repair help. Before you call for service, however, see if you can isolate the cause of the fault using the process of elimination.

Start with the most obvious possibilities. Is the machine plugged in? Are the controls properly set? Check the service panel for a tripped breaker or blown fuse on the circuit. If you find one, reset the breaker or replace the fuse.

If the circuit trips off again, you can be fairly sure there is either a short in the unit or its cord or the circuit is overloaded. Often, just unplugging an appliance and peering into its innards will reveal a bare wire that has grounded out.

If you don't find a breaker or fuse out, you know that the circuit is live. Double-check this by testing the receptacle with a neon tester.

The drawings below illustrate where to look for other problems. To learn about troubleshooting heating and cooling equipment, see pages 338–357.

If jiggling the plug gets an appliance going again, either the plug or—more rarely—the receptacle is faulty.

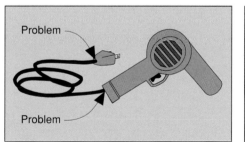

When a cord goes bad, it usually happens at an end. See pages 240–241 to replace cords and plugs.

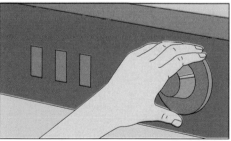

If wiggling a switch gets results, the switch should be replaced—a job you may be able to do yourself.

Motors that spark, smoke, or smell usually need new motor brushes. Don't use the device until it has been repaired.

With larger appliances, you may be able to track down the source of a malfunction by listening carefully.

Running New Wiring (continued)

WORKING WITH LOW-VOLTAGE WIRING

Doorbells, chimes, intercoms, thermostats, and some lighting systems run on voltages that are "stepped down" by a transformer from 120-volts to between 6 and 30 volts. These circuits can be installed without boxes, circuit breakers, fuses, or grounding.

Working with low-voltage circuits is ideal for do-it-yourselfers because

the small voltage is not dangerous to work with.

Replace old low-voltage wiring with bell wire—a No. 18 gauge wire with a thin coat of plastic insulation. You splice it the same way as you splice standard wire. Be sure to buy different colors of wire so you will know which is which when you make the final connections. Before

you buy the wire, find out if you are working on a two-wire or a three-wire system.

To install a new low-voltage device, first run a circuit from the service panel to a conveniently located junction box. Install the transformer at that point and go from there.

Wiring Doorbells and Chimes

The most popular use for low-voltage wiring is the common doorbell—or, in some installations, chimes. The low-voltage part of the system starts at the transformer, which is usually in the 6- to 8-volt range for doorbells or 15 to 20 volts for chimes. On a few models you have the option of choosing the terminal—and voltage—you need.

Transformers vary, so if you are replacing a bad one, be sure to get a unit that is compatible with your existing system.

In older installations, you may find the transformer mounted near the junction box or even on the box cover. In newer homes, transformers usually are fastened to the side of the service panel.

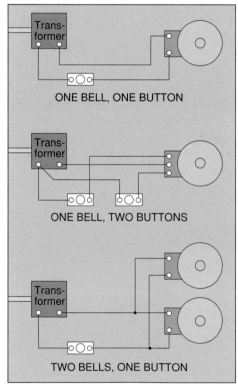

ONE BELL, ONE BUTTON

ONE BELL, TWO BUTTONS

TWO BELLS, ONE BUTTON

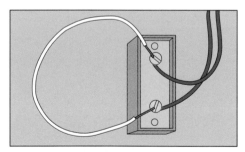

To check a doorbell button, use a jumper wire as discussed below. If the bell rings, the button is shot.

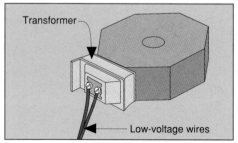

A threaded fitting on this transformer extends through a knockout in the box and is held by a nut.

Troubleshooting a Doorbell

Finding a problem in a doorbell is a process of elimination. If the bell works sporadically, check out the button first. Unscrew it from the wall and hold a jumper wire across the two contact points. If the bell now rings, clean the contact points with emery cloth.

If the button works, check the bell and transformer for loose connections. If they are tight, hold a screwdriver across the transformer's bell-wire terminals. If you don't get a weak spark, replace the transformer. If you see even the faintest spark, the transformer is fine, and the

problem is the bell or the wiring.

To check the bell, disconnect it and hook it directly to the bell-wire connections at the transformer. If it doesn't ring, the bell is shot; if it does ring, you had better start replacing the wire—a tedious, last-resort measure.

WORKING WITH TELEPHONE WIRING

Your local telephone company is responsible only for the wiring up to the network interface, which is usually close to where the wire first enters your house. The telephones and all of the interior wiring belong to you and are your responsibility, unless you have a maintenance contract with the phone company to cover problems with interior wiring. The illustration at right shows a typical phone wiring system.

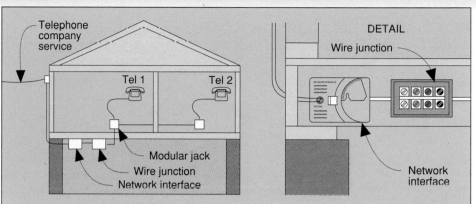

Understanding Wire Types

Flat line cord is used only to attach a phone or modem to an outlet jack.

Telephone wire (round with white jacket) runs from the wire junction to the outlet jacks. The most common version has four conductors (red, green, yellow, and black). If you encounter other types of wire, the table at right shows you which colors correspond to the common-version wiring.

TELEPHONE WIRE COLOR CODES			
Insulation Body/Stripe Colors			
4-Wire	**4-Wire**	**4-Wire**	**6-Wire**
Red	Blue (B)	B/W	B/W
Green (G)	White (W)/B	W/B	W/B
Yellow	Orange (O)	O/W	O/W
Black	W/O	W/O	W/O
			G/W
			W/G

Troubleshooting

No Dial Tone

■ Dial a number. If the number does not ring, plug a different phone into the jack. If the number now rings, phone one is broken and must be replaced.

■ If the number does not ring on the second phone, plug phone one directly into the network interface. If this works, the trouble is in the wire between the interface and the jack. Remove both interface and jack covers and substitute yellow for red and black for green wires.

■ If the dialed number does not ring on phone two, even when connected to the interface, the problem is in the phone company's wiring. Call for service.

Continuous Dial Tone

■ If you hear a continuous dial tone while dialing a number, the red and green conductors are reversed between the network interface and the phone.

■ If all phones have the same problem, reverse the red and green conductors leading out of the network interface.

■ If the problem is in one phone only, reverse the red and green conductors from the modular jack to the phone.

Noise on the Line

■ Install a plug-in radio interference filter between the jack and the phone. If that doesn't work, call the phone company.

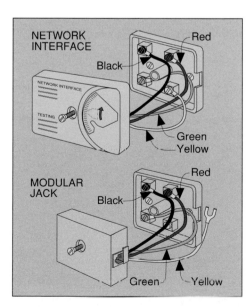

Running New Wiring *(continued)*

WORKING WITH TELEPHONE WIRING *(continued)*

Adding a Telephone To an Existing Line

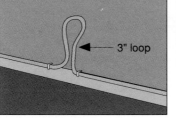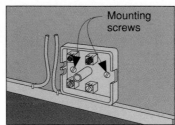

1. Remove staples and pull up a 3-inch loop of wire. Cut at top of loop.

2. Use two screws to mount the base of a modular jack next to the loop.

3. Remove knockouts, strip wire ends, and insert wires under color-coded screws.

Running a Line from An Existing Jack

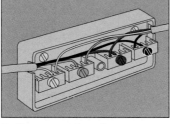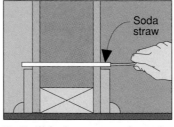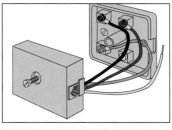

1. Loosen colored screws, insert color-matched wires, and tighten screws.

2. Drill holes, run and staple wire to baseboard, feed wire through walls as shown.

3. Mount a modular jack, strip wires, and insert wires under color-matched screws.

Converting an Old Telephone to Modular Jacks

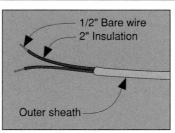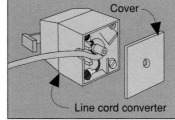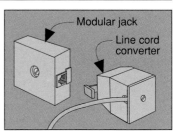

1. Cut cord near wall outlet; strip back sheath 2 inches and wire insulations ½ inch.

2. Remove cover of a line cord converter. Fasten wires under color-matched screws.

3. Replace cover and plug converter into a working modular jack.

Converting an Outlet To Modular Jacks

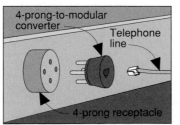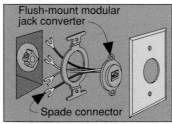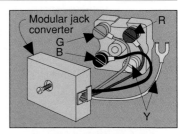

If existing outlet has four holes, plug in a four-prong-to-modular converter.

If a hard-wired flush-mount, replace with a flush-mount modular jack converter.

If a hard-wired baseboard block, replace with a modular jack converter.

Using Outdoor Wiring

Whether you're just installing an outdoor receptacle or are taking on a more extensive project, such as running a branch circuit to a new shed or backyard light, the principles you learned for interior work still apply outdoors. Only the material changes—and then only slightly.

Outdoor wiring does involve a few added precautions, however. For example, whenever you undertake an outdoor wiring project, use either metal conduit with Type TW wires pulled through it or UF (underground feed) cable, a tough, highly moisture-resistant sheathed cable. Some local codes specify one in particular, so check with a local electrician or your building code authorities. You also should check to see if there are restrictions on who does exterior electrical work and how it is to be done.

If you use UF cable, you still are required to protect it with conduit when it is above ground. UF cable must be buried at least 12 inches below the surface. Rigid conduit need be only 6 inches underground; thin-wall conduit needs 12 inches of earth protection.

To guard against serious electrical shocks, codes require you to protect outside circuits that include receptacles with a ground-fault circuit interrupter—GFCI. (See page 266 for more about these units.)

Outdoor components (see below) are similar to those used inside but have watertight features, such as gasket seals, spring-loaded covers, and rubber-sealed connections.

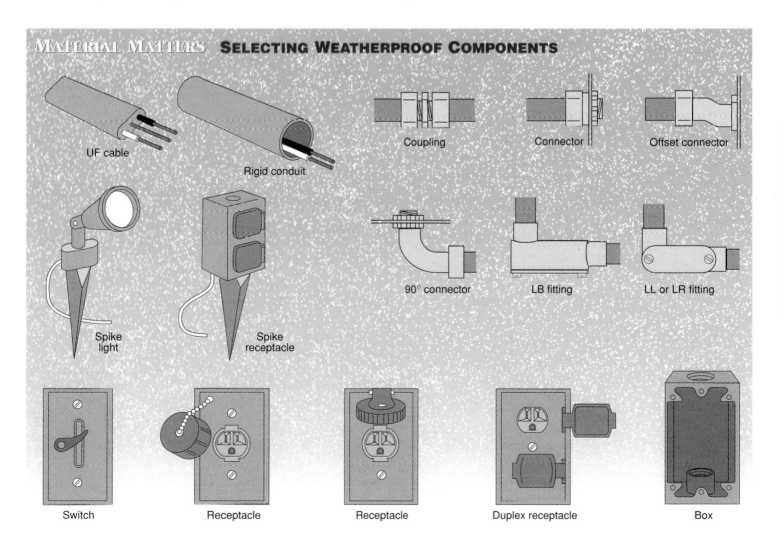

MATERIAL MATTERS   SELECTING WEATHERPROOF COMPONENTS

UF cable

Rigid conduit

Coupling

Connector

Offset connector

Spike light

Spike receptacle

90° connector

LB fitting

LL or LR fitting

Switch

Receptacle

Receptacle

Duplex receptacle

Box

Outdoor Wiring *(continued)*

GETTING WIRES THROUGH A WALL

Cutting a hole in an exterior wall requires prior planning. Where you make the incision depends on your success in finding a circuit that has underused capacity, as well as how far you have to go to tie into a feeder line. Also, you must check out what might be inside the exterior wall (see page 142).

In some locations, you can run sheathed cable through a wall to an exterior box; in other places, you must use conduit or armored cable. Find out what your code permits.

In most cases, it is best to install a junction box back-to-back with the exterior box, then connect the two with conduit or armored cable (see top middle illustration, page 265).

Another option is to tap into an existing outdoor fixture. Special fittings and adapters make it easy to tie into the old fixture box. Before deciding on this approach, make sure that the present circuit has the capacity you need for the extra receptacle or fixture (see page 236).

INSTALLING EXTERIOR RECEPTACLES

Installing an outdoor receptacle is a simple job. It amounts to little more than locating it where you want it and cutting the hole in the exterior

wall, then mounting a weatherproof box on the surface or recessing it into the wall (the best way to go, though it requires more work).

Remember that a ground-fault circuit interrupter (GFCI) must be installed in any outdoor circuit.

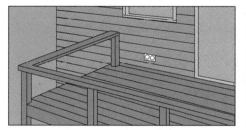

An obvious location for an exterior receptacle is the exterior house wall facing a deck or patio.

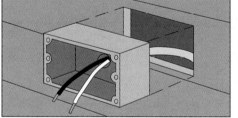

Carefully size the opening so the waterproof box will fit into it snugly, minimizing heat-robbing gaps..

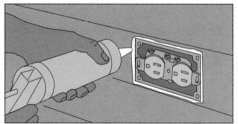

Install the receptacle (see page 266 for a GFCI type) and caulk before screwing on the faceplate.

INSTALLING EXTERIOR LIGHTS

These days, security isn't far from anyone's mind. It's comforting to know that a flick of a switch can turn a dark, shadowy backyard into

one flooded with light. If you can't perform such magic, you would be smart to install a security light. (See pages 265, 277, 409, and 416 for

ideas on types of security lights and where to put them.) One of the easiest locations to work with is under an overhang.

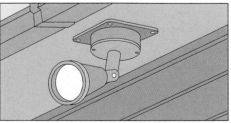

Make an opening for a switch box in the room below, then fish a cable to it through an opening in the soffit.

Fasten the cable to an outdoor fixture box with a box connector, screw the box to the soffit, and wire the fixture.

After connecting the cable wires to the fixture wires with wire connectors, mount the outdoor fixture to the box.

RUNNING WIRES UNDERGROUND

If you plan to run underground wiring, also plan to spend some time in the trenches. For a lengthy run, consider renting a trencher for a few hours. Though expensive, this tool makes quick work of this otherwise laborious task. (See page 263 for depth requirements for cable and conduit.) **Caution: Always contact your gas, water, electric, and phone companies to have them locate buried utility lines before digging any trench.**

Start your project by planning your routes, including where you want to go through the wall. Run power to a new interior junction box nearby and drill through the wall. It's best to use a short piece of rigid conduit to make the through-the-wall connection between the box and an exterior connector called an LB fitting. This fitting enables you to make the sharp 90-degree turn downward and also has a removable plate that makes it easier to pull wires through the conduit.

You must use conduit from the fitting to the bottom of the trench and again between the trench and the receptacle or lamppost at the other end.

YOU'LL NEED...

SKILLS: Basic excavating and electrical skills.
TIME: 4 to 6 hours.
TOOLS: Shovel (or trencher for long runs), wire stripper, conduit bender, needle-nose pliers, hacksaw, drill, screwdriver.

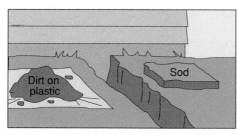

Remove and save the sod before you dig the trench; pile the loose dirt on a tarp or piece of plastic sheeting.

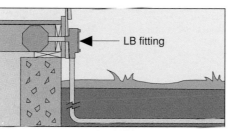

Tie the exterior LB fitting to an interior junction box with rigid conduit. Run conduit from LB fitting into trench.

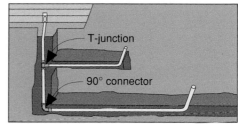

If you use rigid conduit, you can buy special tee and elbow fittings to make the junctions and turns required.

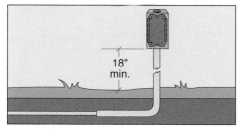

An outdoor receptacle must be at least 18 inches above ground. Protect its wiring above grade with conduit.

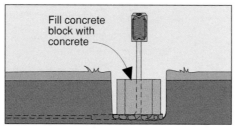

Stabilize receptacles with concrete; use either a big coffee can or a concrete block as your form.

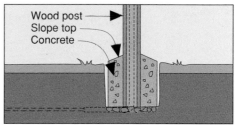

For lampposts, run conduit/cable up center of the post; set post in concrete with a sloped top (see page 197).

INSTALLING AUTOMATIC LIGHTING CONTROLS

To be sure your security light is on every night, wire it directly to an automatic control—a photocell or a timer. Both usually come with easy-to-follow instructions. Photocells must be installed outdoors; timers, inside. Lights also come with motion detectors that turn on the light when movement occurs nearby.

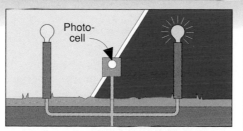

Photocells turn lights on at dusk, off at dawn. Include a switch so you can manually override the photocell.

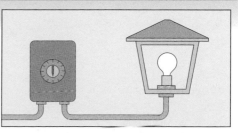

Timers let you choose when the lights go on and off. Some models take the place of standard light switches.

Outdoor Wiring (continued)

INSTALLING GROUND-FAULT CIRCUIT INTERRUPTERS

As few as 200 milliamperes (about enough to light a 25-watt bulb) can kill you if you happen to touch a hot wire or appliance while touching plumbing components or standing on wet earth. That is why electrical codes require that all new bathroom circuits and outdoor receptacles be protected by a ground-fault circuit interrupter (GFCI).

A GFCI is an amazing device that trips the circuit whenever even a tiny leakage occurs. The shutoff action is so fast (¹⁄₄₀ second or less), that there is not enough time for you to be injured. Shown at right are two commonly available types of GFCI devices.

> **YOU'LL NEED...**
>
> **SKILLS:** Basic electrical skills.
> **TIME:** 15 minutes.
> **TOOLS:** Combination tool or wire stripper, needle-nose pliers, screwdriver.

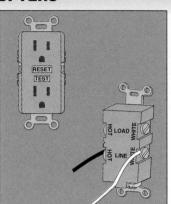

A GFCI receptacle replaces a standard receptacle. It may protect just itself or other receptacles down the line.

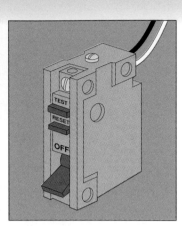

This GFCI breaker replaces a standard circuit breaker. It protects all receptacles on its circuit.

HELPFUL HINTS

Ever wondered how much it costs to burn a light or run an appliance? To find out, simply multiply the wattage of the device by the hours it runs. Divide the result by 1,000 and multiply that result by the price you pay per kilowatt hour for electricity. If you can't find a wattage figure on an appliance's rating plate, simply multiply the unit's amperage by its voltage.

The table at right lists some ways to reduce the amounts of energy appliances use. To learn about the even greater savings possible with heating, cooling, and water heating equipment, see page 381. For more about lighting, read the next chapter.

USING ELECTRICITY WISELY

HOW THRIFTY ARE YOUR APPLIANCE HABITS?

Appliance	Relative Operating Cost	How You Can Save
Freezer, Refrigerator	The biggest energy eaters in the kitchen; models with automatic defrost use much more energy than manual-defrost models.	New models are much more energy-efficient, so upgrade if you can afford to. Open doors as little as possible.
Range	Usually the number two energy consumer, depending on your family's cooking and baking needs.	Cook small meals in pressure cookers or small appliances. Meat thermometer minimizes opening oven.
Dishwasher	Third or fourth energy consumer; most of the energy goes into heating water and drying cycle.	Eliminating the drying cycle cuts operating costs by one-third.
Washer, Dryer	Third or fourth energy consumer; the less water a washer uses, the less the operating cost; dryers with auto-dry settings save energy.	Run cold water loads if possible and use the lowest water level necessary. Longer spin periods remove more water and cut down drying times.
Water heater	Electric water heaters are more expensive to operate that gas-fired ones; baths use more hot water than showers.	Set thermostat to 125°F or lower. Take short showers instead of baths. Wrap heater with insulation jacket. Insulate hot water pipes (see page 396).

LIGHTING

Vision specialists maintain that 90 percent of what we know comes to us via our eyes, making lighting one of the most important of your home's systems. In too many households, however, lighting is one of the most neglected aspects.

Few of us live totally in the dark, of course. Because our eyes compensate for light levels that are a bit too dim or too bright, it is easy to ignore a lighting problem that causes eyestrain, fatigue, or even accidents.

If your lighting system is inefficient, you may also be wasting energy. For example, without enough illumination in a particular area of a room, you may turn on every lamp in the vicinity, thus overcompensating with high-wattage bulbs.

How much lighting is enough? And what can you do to achieve the proper level? This chapter answers the first question, then explains how to approach the second.

Good lighting starts with the right bulb. For most of the lamps and fixtures in your home, the majority of people prefer the warm color quality and high adaptability of incandescent bulbs. In these bulbs, electricity flows through a metal filament, causing it to glow white hot. The lower the filament's electrical resistance, the more watts it consumes and the more light it produces.

Wattage is not the amount of light that a bulb puts out. Light output is measured in lumens, and not all bulbs are equally efficient on a lumens-per-watt basis. You will find a lumen output rating on the bulb's paper sleeve, though not on the bulb itself.

Incandescent bulbs are the least energy-efficient. Much of the energy they consume is wasted producing heat, which eventually burns up the filament. Long-life bulbs give off less heat, and correspondingly less light, for the same amount of electricity.

Although each has its own drawbacks, fluorescent and high-intensity discharge (HID) lighting use far less electricity per lumen output than incandescent bulbs. Both can last 10 to 30 times longer than incandescent bulbs. More about these money- and energy-savers on pages 274–277.

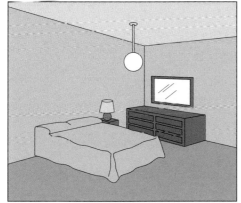

General lighting visually expands a room's size and provides basic brightness. It usually consists of a ceiling or wall fixture, supplemented with convenient portable lighting. For living and sleeping areas, lighting experts recommend that you allow 1 watt per square foot with flush or pendant fixtures (see page 269) or 1½ watts per square foot for recessed lights. Kitchens, baths, and laundries need as much as 4 watts per square foot for incandescent bulbs, or 1½ watts for fluorescent tubes.

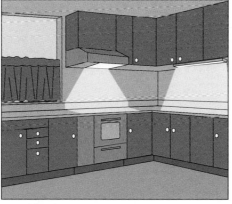

Task lighting lets you get a good look at what you are doing by focusing light directly on the working area.

Most tasks require 150 watts of incandescent or 40 watts of fluorescent light. For prolonged reading, you need 200 to 300 watts of incandescent or 60 to 80 watts of fluorescent light.

For countertops and workbenches, provide 120 watts of incandescent or 20 watts of fluorescent lighting for each 3 running feet of work surface. Fixtures should be mounted 14 to 22 inches above the surface.

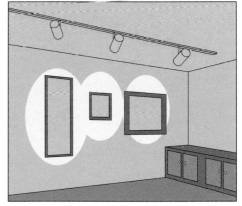

Accent lighting provides architectural flavor, and sometimes does the job of general lighting as well. Use it to wash a wall, play up interesting textures, spotlight a fireplace, or dramatize a dining table. Let your imagination be your guide as to how much light is enough. Do try, however, to give rooms a variety of accent lights, separately switched, so you can vary moods and suit different requirements. A wide spectrum of fixtures and bulbs—incandescent, fluorescent, and HID—adds even more possibilities.

HELPFUL HINTS   RECOMMENDED LIGHTING LEVELS FOR THE HOME

Room	Application	Recommendations
Bathroom	Mirrors	75-watt incandescents or 20-watt warm fluorescents at each side of mirror; add a 100-watt incandescent or 40-watt fluorescent ceiling fixture.
	Large mirrors	36- to 48-inch diffused fluorescent along top of mirror; for a less efficient, but more interesting effect, install 15-watt G bulbs along both sides and top of the mirror.
	Shower light	60-watt incandescent bulb in a waterproof ceiling fixture
Bedroom	General	10 lumens per square foot of incandescent ceiling fixtures (a 60-watt incandescent bulb produces about 900 lumens); 60-watt fixtures in closets
	Reading in bed	100-watt bedside lamp with bottom of the shade at eye level; optionally, a 50-watt headboard lamp for each person, 30 inches above mattress level
Dining room	Chandelier	200 to 300 watts of incandescent lighting, 30 inches above the table surface; for ceilings higher than 8 feet, raise chandelier 3 inches per additional foot of height.
Entry	Foyer	About 2 watts of incandescent fixtures per square foot of floor area
	Outside	60-watt incandescent fixtures at each side of door, 5 feet, 6 inches above landing
Hall	Ceiling or wall	One 60-watt incandescent ceiling or wall fixture per 10 feet of hall length
Kitchen	Ceiling	50 lumens per square foot of fluorescent ceiling fixtures
	Sink	Two 75-watt reflective bulbs, 18 inches apart and 24 inches out from wall
	Under cabinet	8 watts per foot of fluorescents under front edge of cabinets
	Island	Two 75-watt reflective incandescent bulbs, 24 inches apart over center
Living room/	General	Wall lamps and wall-washing track lighting for 10 lumens per square foot average
Family room	Reading	100-watt floor or table lamp with bottom of the shade at eye level
Stairway	Stairs	Ceiling or wall fixtures at top and bottom; both controlled with 3-way switches
Study	Desk	100-watt incandescent lamp with bottom of shade 15 inches above desk top
Shop	Bench	Hang double 48-inch fluorescent bulbs, 48 inches above and over front edge of bench.

Selecting Fixtures

The most difficult thing about selecting light fixtures is narrowing down the huge selection available. There is a fixture for every need and every budget. The possibilities are almost limitless once you realize that many lamp shops and hardware stores stock lamp components that you can put together yourself.

The chart below discusses types of fixtures and some of their uses. After digesting this information, you may want to visit a lighting store, where the personnel will be able to guide you toward the most appropriate products for your needs.

MATERIAL MATTERS — CHOOSING LIGHTING FIXTURES

Fixture Type	Use
Surface-mounted 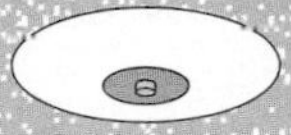	Mount on the ceiling's surface, distributing even, shadowless lighting; must be shielded with translucent material to minimize glare and should have sockets for several smaller bulbs rather than one or two big ones.
Dropped or suspended 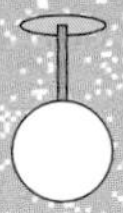	Have many of the same characteristics as surface-mounted fixtures; because these are closer to eye level, glare may be a problem—try dimmer switches; hang fixtures 12 to 20 inches below an 8-foot ceiling or 30 to 36 inches above table height.
Recessed 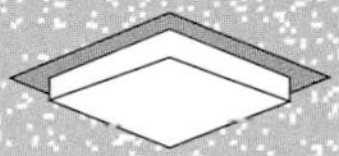	Include downlights that are fixed or can be aimed, incandescent or fluorescent bulbs shielded by plastic diffusers, and luminous ceilings; if a diffuser is used, it will require more wattage—up to twice as much—for the same amount of light.
Wall bracket 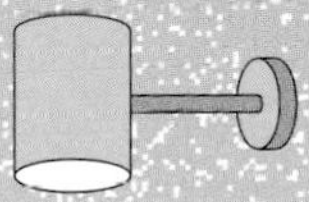	Conserve space in tight quarters, serving as either task or accent lighting; for reading lights, mount them 15 to 20 inches to the left or right of the page and 48 inches above the floor.
Track 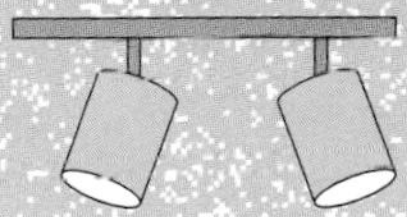	Have the flexibility of being able to add, subtract, or rearrange a broad range of modular fixtures at will, aiming them in any direction to create limitless lighting effects; see page 272 for how to install track lights.
Cornice 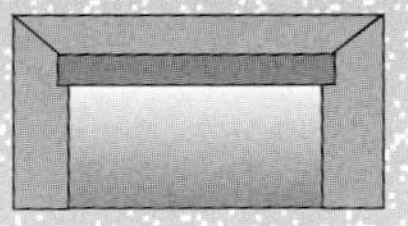	Bathe a wall with soft downward light to dramatize draperies or other wall treatments; build a cornice with 1×2 and 1×6 lumber; mount the tube 6 inches from wall.
Valance 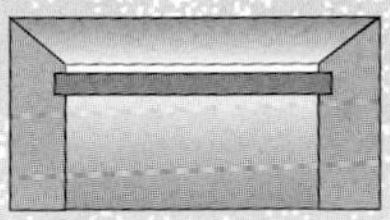	Provide both uplight and downlight; to build, you'll need 1×2 and 1×6 lumber and angle brackets; top the unit with translucent plastic and you have a lighted display shelf. 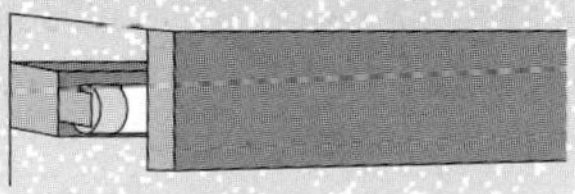
Cove 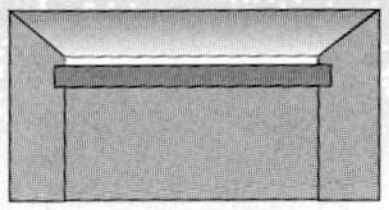	Dramatizes a ceiling; make your own with wood and angle brackets; mount bulb about 1 foot below ceiling level; paint the inside white to maximize reflection. 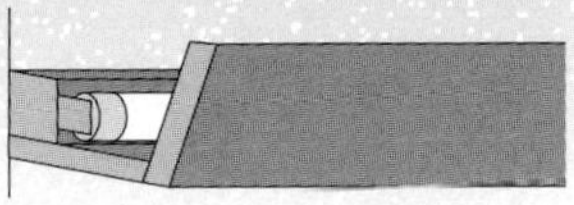
Under-cabinet 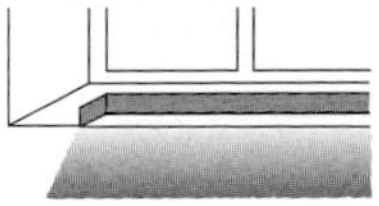	Shed light on countertops; shield with skirting; use the longest tubes that will fit and fill at least two-thirds of the counter's total length.

Incandescent Lighting

Incandescent ceiling or wall fixtures operate much like the table lamp shown on page 240. A pair of leads serves as the cord, connecting the fixture's socket to house wiring. For saftey reasons, these connections are made in a ceiling box.

Many of these fixtures do not permit as much air circulation and so get hotter than table lamps. Thus, bulb holders usually are made of nonmelting material, such as porcelain. This is also why you should never exceed the wattage specified on the fixture—heat could melt the wires' insulation, causing a short circuit and/or a fire.

Support systems for ceiling fixtures vary (see below), but all of them secure the fixture to its electrical box—usually a 4-inch octagon—and in some cases to the ceiling or joists as well. Never support a fixture only with its leads.

ANATOMY OF A CEILING FIXTURE

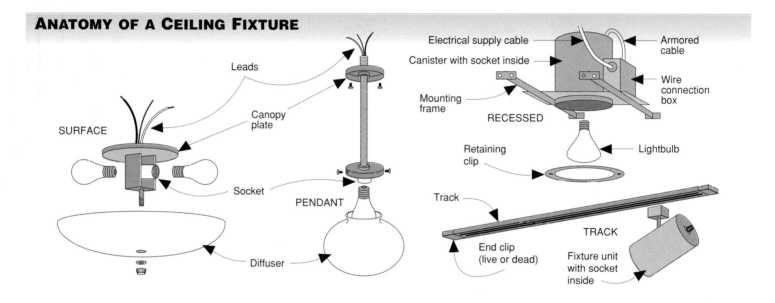

SURFACE

Leads

Canopy plate

Socket

PENDANT

Diffuser

Electrical supply cable

Canister with socket inside

Mounting frame

RECESSED

Armored cable

Wire connection box

Retaining clip

Lightbulb

Track

End clip (live or dead)

TRACK

Fixture unit with socket inside

HELPFUL HINTS

With electrical tape, a screwdriver, pliers, and a neon test light, you can solve most fixture problems. To avoid

TROUBLESHOOTING FIXTURES

shock, shut off power to the light, then double-check with your tester before touching the fixture. You may have to turn on the power later to perform some of the tests called for below.

Symptom	Causes	Cures
No light	A burned-out bulb; a broken or loose wire in the ceiling box; a bad switch	Replace bulb. Drop the fixture as shown on page 271, then check and tighten all connections. Check the switch with a neon tester (see page 239); to replace switch, see page 243.
Fixture blows fuses	Frayed wires in the ceiling box may be shorting out; defective bulb socket	Drop the fixture and examine the wires carefully; tape any bad spots. Test the socket with a voltmeter (see page 239). Some sockets can be replaced easily; with others, you will have to buy a new fixture.
Light flickers	Melted insulation or a bad socket; failing dimmer	Tape or replace wires that look dubious. Test the socket; if you still have a problem, you may have to replace the dimmer.

REPLACING A CEILING FIXTURE

Replacing an old fixture usually takes only a few minutes, if you have the right hardware. **First, shut off the power to the appropriate circuit at the service panel.**

Examine how the old fixture is attached. Some secure with bolts to a strap (first drawing below); others mount with a hickey to a stud in the center of the box (third drawing); still others use a combination of these systems.

Once you have determined what you are working with, follow the sequence illustrated below. Take care not to undo other connections that you may find in the box. Handle fixtures gently—most are made of lightweight metal that can be bent easily.

See pages 250–253 for information about running power to a location that did not have any before.

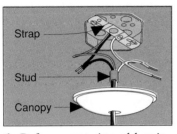

1. Before removing old unit, note assembly. Strap mounting works best with lightweight fixtures.

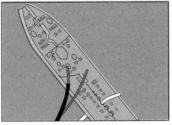

2. Strip ¾ inch of insulation from new leads. If wires are the stranded type, twist bare ends slightly.

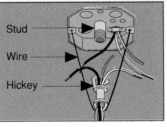

3. You can temporarily support a heavy fixture with a coat hanger or strong cord.

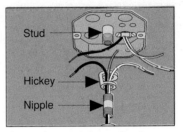

4. Wires exit through the hickey's side. Screw a nipple into hickey; thread hickey onto stud.

5. After the fixture is mechanically secure, make the electrical connections, then carefully coil up wires inside the box.

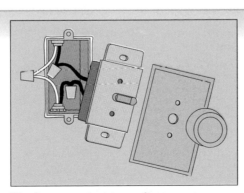

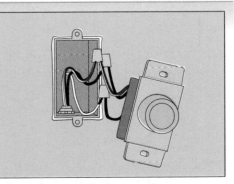

6. Check your installation by turning on the power. If the fixture lights up, shut off power again and raise and secure the canopy.

INSTALLING A DIMMER SWITCH

Dimmers let you select lighting levels according to your needs and moods. Install one as you would a switch (see page 254). Don't overload the dimmer beyond its wattage limits. For three-way installations, make sure to use a dimmer designed for that purpose.

Incandescent dimmers must be used only in incandescent lighting circuits, not to control fluorescent lighting or motors. Special dimmers are available for fluorescents.

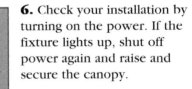

Hook up a rotary-type dimmer as shown. Tuck in the switch, wires, and connectors carefully—space can be tight in the box.

Like ordinary switches, ordinary two-way dimmers cannot be used in three-way lighting circuits. Use one designed for three-way circuits, as shown.

Incandescent Lighting (continued)

INSTALLING TRACK LIGHTING

Track lights might be called "unfixed fixtures." Instead of a single light source overhead, a track system lets you encircle a room with soft, balanced illumination, play up a ceiling, or spotlight architectural details—then change it all around whenever you feel like it.

Lightweight and modular, track light components assemble easily. But even a modest layout may require a dozen or more different pieces. Plan carefully so you'll know exactly how many of each you need.

Tracks come in 2-, 4-, and 8-foot sections that can be plugged end-to-end to any length you desire. T, X, and L couplings let you change direction. With two- or three-circuit

components, you can wire in separate switches to control different lights at any point along the runs.

In plotting out an installation, you first must provide a power source. Most tracks can be fed from one end, at a coupling, or (in some cases) at any point in between. If the room already has a switch-controlled fixture, you probably can tap into its box, but you may have to fish cable and install a new box (see pages 250–253) at the correct spot for your track system.

If you don't already have power where you need it, see pages 244–255 for how to run wire or check with an electrician for the cost of installing a ceiling box and wall

switch. Or consider running a switch-controlled power cord from a receptacle to the ceiling.

You also must decide how to attach the tracks to the ceiling. You can buy kits to attach the track to the T-bars of a suspended ceiling or for dropping it a foot or so below a conventional ceiling.

> ### YOU'LL NEED...
> **SKILLS:** Basic carpentry and electrical skills.
> **TIME:** 2 to 4 hours for an 8-foot-long system, if electric source is ready.
> **TOOLS:** Wire stripper, drill, miter box and backsaw, screwdriver, chalk line, ladder.

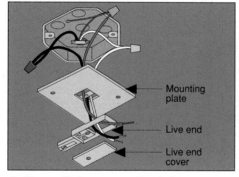

Mounting plate
Live end
Live end cover

1. Shut off the power first, then mount a connector—either the live-end type shown here or a center-feed—to the ceiling box.

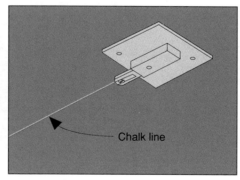

Chalk line

2. Snap chalk line from the connector's center along the route you want the tracks to follow. Measure carefully.

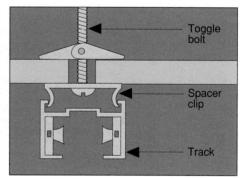

Toggle bolt
Spacer clip
Track

3. Spacer clips drop the tracks a bit so they can ride out uneven surfaces. Mount the clips first, then snap the tracks into them.

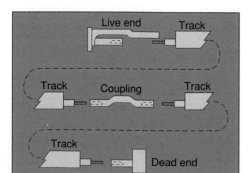

Live end
Track
Track
Coupling
Track
Track
Dead end

4. Push the couplings and tracks together as you go. Snap-on covers give the installation a finished appearance.

5. If, at the end of a run, you must cut a track, use a backsaw and miter box. Once a unit has been cut, however, you cannot add to it.

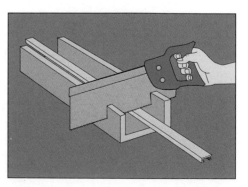

INSTALLING A RECESSED LIGHT FIXTURE

Before installing a recessed light fixture, be aware that 97 percent of the electricity it uses ends up as heat. Never install a higher wattage bulb than recommended by the fixture manufacturer. Also, you should never install such a fixture in a ceiling below an attic; the heat will simply escape into the attic, adding to heat buildup problems during summer months.

When you replace a recessed fixture, match the old fixture so that you can reuse the old mounting frame and trim.

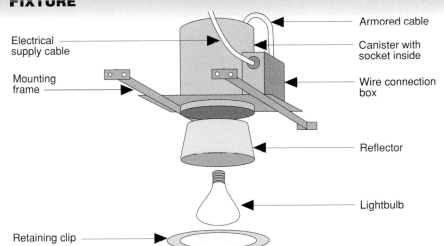

Armored cable

Electrical supply cable

Canister with socket inside

Mounting frame

Wire connection box

Reflector

Lightbulb

Retaining clip

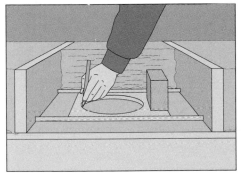

1. Remove insulation. Adjust the frame and place the fixture between the joists. Trace the outline of the canister on the ceiling.

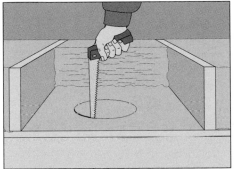

2. Cut out the canister opening from above with a keyhole saw. If the ceiling is plaster, first score it deeply from below to avoid cracking.

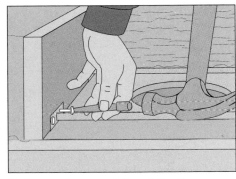

3. Insert the round lip of the frame into the ceiling hole from above. Adjust the frame against the joists and nail the frame into place.

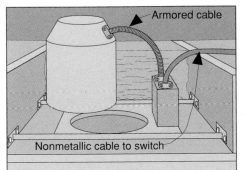

Armored cable

Nonmetallic cable to switch

4. If it hasn't already been done, insert armored cable from the canister into the electrical box. Run nonmetallic cable from wall switch into box.

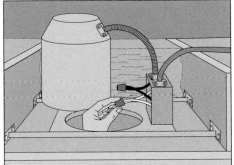

5. Strip wires and connect with wire connectors—black to black, white to white. Install box cover plate. Replace insulation with required clearance.

6. Place canister in the frame and attach it to the unit. Install the bulb reflector and ceiling trim. Screw in the recommended bulb and test.

Fluorescent Lighting

Switching on the power to a modern-day rapid-start fluorescent light kicks off a chain reaction. First, a ballast sends current to cathodes at either end of the tube. These excite a gas, creating barely visible ultraviolet rays. The rays then strike a phosphorous coating on the tube's inner surface, causing it to glow. Some older fluorescents also have an additional starter that preheats the gases in the tube for a faster startup.

Because fluorescent lights don't "burn" the way incandescent lights do, they operate much more efficiently. A 40-watt fluorescent tube, for instance, produces 2,000 lumens of light, compared to 450 lumens from a 40-watt incandescent bulb (see chart at right).

Because fluorescent lights operate at cooler temperatures, they last much longer, too. In fact, a tube's life span is determined by the number of times you start it—not the length of time it runs.

Thrifty as it is, however,

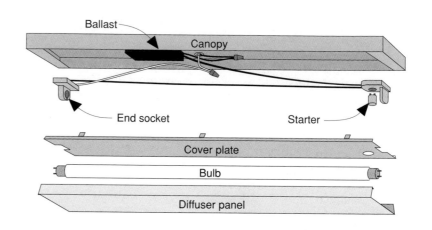

fluorescent lighting has a few drawbacks. It is much less flexible than incandescent lighting because you can't interchange tubes of different wattages in the same fixture. Fluorescent lighting also has a diffuse, flat quality that is ideal for task lighting but monotonous in other situations.

You needn't settle for the bluish cast that emanates from "cool white" tubes, however. "Warm white" and "warm white deluxe" versions more closely resemble incandescent light.

LAMP EFFICIENCIES		
Lamp Type	**Watts**	**Lumens/Watt**
Incandescent	40	12
	60	15
	100	18
Halogen	20	15
	45	22
Fluorescent	9	67
	30	79
	40	79
Mercury	100	37

REPLACING INCANDESCENTS

Incandescent light is close in spectral (color) output to natural sunlight and, thus, is easy on the eyes. It is not easy on the pocketbook, however, being the least efficient of today's common light sources.

Manufacturers have ingeniously adapted fluorescent bulbs to take the place of incandescents. All you need is an adapter, which has a built-in ballast, and an incandescent screw-type lamp base. Some bulbs come with both; some require a separate adapter. All, however, share high efficiency and long life. Make sure the replacement bulb fits the fixture before you purchase it.

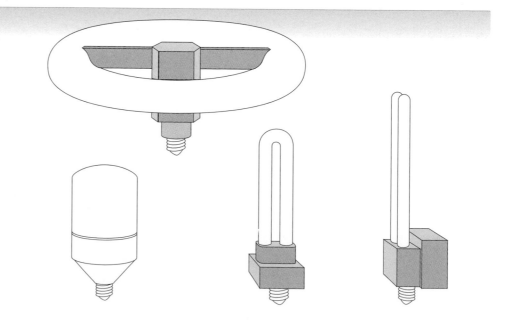

HELPFUL HINTS — TROUBLESHOOTING FLUORESCENT LIGHTS

Problem	Causes	Solutions
No light	It's rare for a fluorescent tube to abruptly burn out the way an incandescent bulb does.	Check connections (see page 276); then replace the starter, tube, and ballast—in that order.
Partial light	Ends light up but the center doesn't. Ends are blackening. Uniform dimming	Replace the starter. Tube is failing; replace. Tube is dirty or is failing; clean or replace.
Flickering light	Tubes blink when brand-new, at temperatures below 50°F, and just before they go out.	Make sure tube and/or starter is seated properly.
Humming; acrid smell	Almost always indicates a ballast problem	Tighten ballast connections; replace if necessary.

REPLACING A TUBE

The gases in fluorescent tubes are hazardous, and tubes should not be disposed of with your normal waste. Check with your waste collection agency for proper disposal techniques in your area.

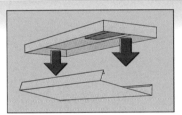

1. Turn off power. Remove diffuser panel by pulling one edge up and out.

2. Remove bulb by rotating one-quarter turn in socket and pulling one end down.

3. Align new bulb pins with socket, push up, and turn 90 degrees. Replace diffuser.

REPLACING A STARTER

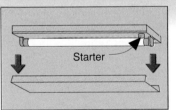

Starter

1. Turn off power. Remove diffuser panel and locate starter, if there is one.

2. To remove starter, push in, twist counterclockwise, and pull out of socket.

3. Push new starter into socket and twist clockwise as far as it will go.

REPLACING A BALLAST

As with fluorescent tubes, ballasts contain hazardous wastes. Again, check with your waste collection agency for proper disposal techniques in your area.

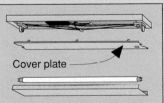

Cover plate

1. Turn off power. Remove diffuser panel, bulb, and electrical cover plate.

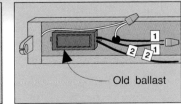

Old ballast

2. Label wire pairs; remove wire connecting nuts; remove ballast.

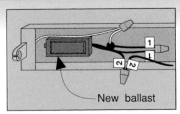

New ballast

3. Install new ballast. Connect wires. Replace cover plate, bulb, diffuser.

Fluorescent Lighting (continued)

INSTALLING FLUORESCENT LIGHTING

Installation procedures for a fluorescent fixture are essentially the same as for a ceiling incandescent fixture (see page 271)—secure it to the ceiling electrical box. You may, however, need to provide additional support, depending on the fixture's length and whether its electrical feed is at one end or in the center.

Making the electrical connections is equally simple—just hook the fixture's black wire to the black house wire, and the white to the white. Note, however, that most fluorescents also have a third, green

grounding wire. If the ceiling box has a separate ground wire, connect it to this; if not, attach the ground to the box itself with a screw or special grounding clip.

If you are installing a series of fluorescent fixtures, such as you would for a luminous ceiling system (see page 66), plan to provide intensity controls so you can vary lighting levels to suit your needs. The best way to do this is to connect some fixtures to one switch and others to another switch. Or, you can hook them all to a single,

fluorescent-only dimming control (ordinary dimmers don't work with fluorescent lighting). The trouble with these, though, is that you must install a special ballast in each fixture—a costly and time-consuming proposition.

YOU'LL NEED...

SKILLS: Basic electrical skills.
TIME: 30 to 45 minutes for one light fixture.
TOOLS: Wire stripper, screwdriver, needle-nose pliers, drill, ladder.

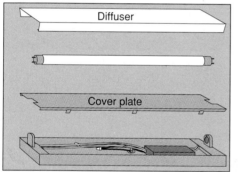

Remove the diffuser, tube, and cover plate. A series of knockouts in the fixture's metal frame lets you bring in power from almost any direction.

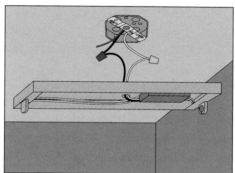

For a center-feed installation, remove the center knockout and mount the unit to a hanger strap in the box as you would an incandescent fixture.

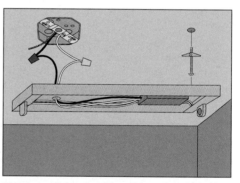

If you will be feeding the power from one end or the other, support the other end with a screw into a joist or a toggle bolt into the ceiling.

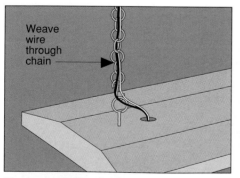

To drop a light closer to a work surface, you can suspend the fixture with lightweight chains. Thread the electrical wires through the links.

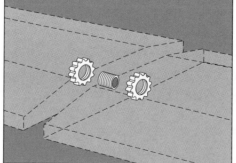

Additional knockouts and threaded nipple couplings let you tie two or more fixtures together end-to-end or side-to-side.

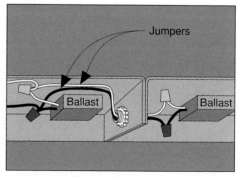

With multiple installations, you can make electrical connections within the fixtures, as shown here, without adding more electrical boxes.

HID Lighting

High-intensity discharge (HID) lighting combines elements of both fluorescent and incandescent lighting. These efficient lamps use a ballast to energize the same chain of events that takes place inside a fluorescent tube (see page 274). In contrast to tubes, HID bulbs can be aimed almost as effectively as incandescent lights. The result: brilliant, economical illumination that floods your yard, drive, or entry walk with light just as it does public roadways and parking lots.

HID lights vary in efficiency (see below), but all put out far more lumens than incandescent bulbs and last up to 30 times longer.

HID lights take up to 15 minutes to warm up, however, so don't use them for frequent on/off situations. Carefully select the wattage you need—you can't change bulb size unless you change the ballast, too.

MATERIAL MATTERS	COMPARING HID LIGHTS	
Type	**Properties**	**Uses**
Mercury	From 50 to 1,500 watts; twice as efficient as incandescent bulbs; some close to matching incandescents' color quality	Fixtures range from classic home-style post lanterns to industrial styles. Use a 50- or 75-watt lamp to illuminate a yard or drive, 175-watt eaves lights for security.
Metal halide	From 175 to 1,000 watts; four times as efficient as incandescent lights; cast a strong green/white light	Best for floodlighting a yard. Control them with either a switch or an automatic light-sensitive control.
Sodium vapor	Available in 250, 400, and 1,000 watts; six times as efficient as incandescents; cast a yellow hue	Most economical source for a lot of light; combining these with metal halide lamps helps cool the color.

Low-Voltage Lighting

Low-voltage systems "step down," or reduce, 120 volts to 6 to 30 volts, which means you can safely string together a series of fixtures like so many Christmas tree lights.

Indoors, low-voltage lighting allows you to add new fixtures almost anywhere, hooking them up with surface wiring that resembles ordinary telephone cable. You can run it easily along baseboards, window casings, and other trim.

Outdoors, low-voltage lighting is even more versatile. Simply plug a transformer into a standard 120-volt receptacle and run lightweight cable to spiked fixtures, such as the ones shown here. Because there is little shock hazard, you can bury the cable a few inches below ground or lay it right on the surface. Contrast this with the far more arduous job of installing underground 120-volt wiring (see page 265).

Don't count on low-voltage equipment for all your outdoor lighting. Low-voltage bulbs are limited to 50 watts and don't produce as many lumens as comparable 120-volt lights. For more about working with low-voltage wiring, see page 260.

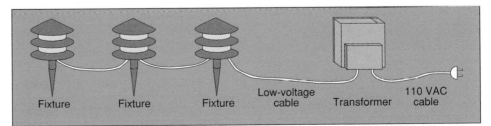

Low-voltage transformers typically provide enough power to supply about 300 watts of lighting up to distances of 100 feet. Yard or drive lighting systems like the one shown come with easy-to-use installation instructions.

PLUMBING

The oldest and simplest of a home's systems, plumbing seems mysterious only until you realize it relies on just two basic principles: gravity and pressure. Turn on a faucet full blast, and you can feel the pressure that pushes water through pipes to your fixtures. In most water systems, this pressure comes from the "head" created by the difference in height of the nearest water storage tower and the elevation where the water comes out of the system in your house. Pull a drain plug and gravity carries the water away.

Because of the simplicity, the hidden parts of a plumbing system—the pipes and the fittings that tie them together—rarely produce trouble. When something goes wrong, it usually happens at a fixture or inside a pipe, either of which you can service yourself.

This chapter introduces you to your plumbing system's inner workings, explains how to cope with plumbing emergencies and repairs, then illustrates what you need to know about upgrading your home's waterways.

Getting to Know Your System

Your water, from either a municipal system or a private well, enters your house through a sizable pipe. If you are on city water, this pipe connects to a meter that records the amount of water entering. Next to the meter is a shutoff valve that lets you stop all flow of water, if necessary. A branch of the supply pipe then travels to a water heater. In the case of private well systems, it may go to a pressure tank first and then to a water heater.

From the top of the water heater emanates a hot water supply line. This line and a cold water supply line run parallel throughout your home to serve the various fixtures, such as water faucets, lavatories, bathtubs, and toilets, and appliances, such as washing machines and dishwashers. The supply lines are under pressure—usually 50 to 60 pounds per square inch.

The drain-waste-vent (DWV) system carries away wastewater and sewage waste to a city sewer or a septic system. It also vents harmful gases to the outside. Not under pressure, these pipes depend on gravity to perform their function.

ANATOMY OF A PLUMBING SYSTEM

Stack vent

Roof vent

Loop vent

Trap

Water supply

Drain and vent system

Cold supply

Hot supply

Water meter

Floor drain

To sewer or septic tank

SHUTOFF VALVES

Supply systems have shutoff valves—sometimes called stops. Think of them as on/off switches that provide an easy-to-find, quick-to-close turnoff network in the event the piping system springs a leak or if you want to make repairs to any of the system components.

Look for shutoffs near where supply lines enter an appliance or fixture. If you don't find them there, use the main shutoff valve on the side of the meter from which the water enters from outside. Closing this valve turns off all your water.

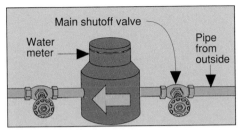

At a meter, you will find two shutoffs. Use the one on the supply side so pressure doesn't damage the meter.

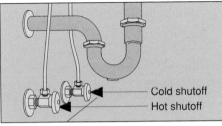

Supply lines at sinks and toilets may have shutoff valves. Water heaters will have one, too.

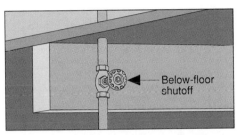

With some fixtures, such as tubs, the shutoff may be beneath the floor or hidden behind an access panel.

TRAPS

Traps prevent sewer gas from backing up into your home. These simple devices work by creating an automatic water seal (see right), which forces gas to rise up the soil stack vent. Running water flushes the trap, but gravity ensures that some water remains in the trap.

"S" trap

Running trap

"P" trap

PLUMBING CODES

For everyone's protection, a national plumbing code spells out specific guidelines for all plumbing operations. Most cities, towns, and communities have adopted this code or amended it to meet local requirements and conditions.

Before you install new plumbing, check out the plumbing code in your area to make sure your project conforms to it. A permit probably will be required for new plumbing work. You also may have to have a plumbing inspector check your finished installation.

READING A METER

Regardless of type, reading a water meter involves subtraction.

With dial types, note the pointer positions (see page 233), wait a few days, and note their positions again. Subtract the first reading from the second for the gallons or cubic feet of water used.

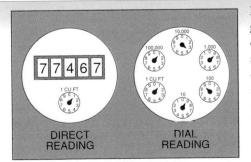

DIRECT READING

DIAL READING

If you suspect you have a water leak, give the water meter a leak test. Turn off all your faucets and water-using appliances. Watch the 1-cubic-foot dial on your water meter for 20 minutes or so. If the dial moves at all, the water supply system is leaking, probably behind a wall or underground.

Solving Plumbing Problems

When confronted with a plumbing problem—even one of those nuisance repairs, such as fixing a dripping faucet or unclogging a drain—too many people simply throw up their hands and call a plumber. Then, often as not, they wait hours or days for a repair that takes only a few minutes, but costs a lot of money.

If that has happened at your house, the next 20 pages are for you. They delve into difficulties you may encounter, explain the relatively simple components you'll have to deal with, and present the know-how you need to handle a situation confidently and effectively.

After you have mastered these basic repair techniques, you may want to try out some of the home improvements covered later in this chapter.

Note that one aspect of home plumbing is not covered here—the subsystem of pipes, valves, and appliances that use natural or LP gas. These problems and solutions are covered on pages 328–335.

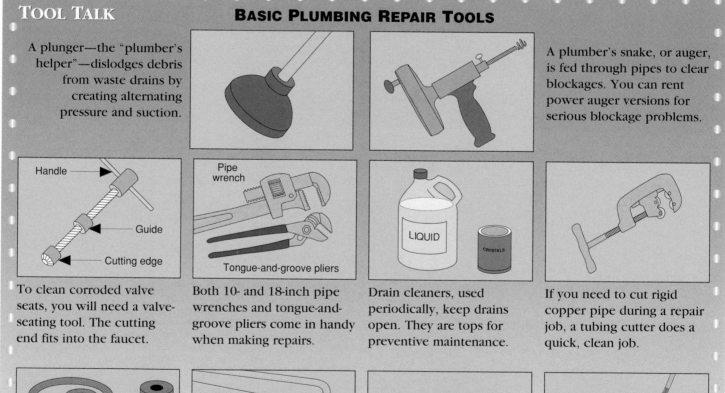

TOOL TALK

BASIC PLUMBING REPAIR TOOLS

A plunger—the "plumber's helper"—dislodges debris from waste drains by creating alternating pressure and suction.

A plumber's snake, or auger, is fed through pipes to clear blockages. You can rent power auger versions for serious blockage problems.

To clean corroded valve seats, you will need a valve-seating tool. The cutting end fits into the faucet.

Both 10- and 18-inch pipe wrenches and tongue-and-groove pliers come in handy when making repairs.

Drain cleaners, used periodically, keep drains open. They are tops for preventive maintenance.

If you need to cut rigid copper pipe during a repair job, a tubing cutter does a quick, clean job.

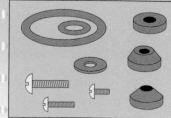

For faucets, buy a box of assorted washers, which usually includes the necessary screws.

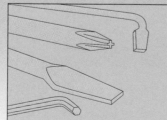

For fixtures, you'll need standard, Phillips, and offset screwdrivers. Allen wrenches also are handy.

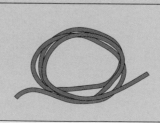

Packing for faucet nuts looks like heavy twine coated with wax. Keep the packing tightly sealed.

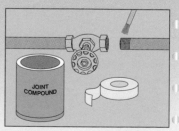

Use joint compound (pipe dope) or pipe tape to seal threads when you assemble, or reassemble, piping.

FIRST AID FOR LEAKS

Sometimes it seems as if pipes schedule leaks to correspond with the closing hours of hardware stores. If this happens, you may be able to make a temporary emergency patch.

The patch can be made of any material that will stop the flow of water: a piece of rubber and a C-clamp, plastic tape, even a length of garden hose split and clamped around the pipe. Better, though, is an emergency patch kit—bought at the store when it was open.

When you notice a leak, turn off the water at the main valve or a shutoff valve (see page 279). Then, diagnose the damage. If the leak is behind a wall, in a ceiling, or under a floor where you can't get at the pipe, shutting it off is about all you can do. If the leak is visible and patchable, apply one of the patches illustrated below.

If water drips, rather than squirts, from a pipe or joint, it may be water condensation, not a hole. If this is the problem, see page 396.

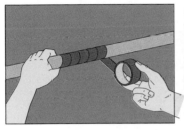

For tiny leaks, dry the pipe and wind electrical tape at least 6 inches on either side of the hole.

Epoxy putty works well for leaks at connections. Spread epoxy with a putty knife; it hardens quickly.

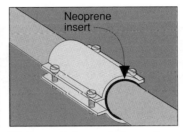

This special metal clamp has a rubberlike inner lining. Tighten the clamp with a screwdriver to stop the leak.

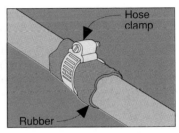

A hose clamp and sheet rubber make an excellent emergency leak stopper until you can replace the pipe.

THAWING FROZEN PIPES

Before applying any thawing technique, open the faucet the frozen pipe supplies. The steam created by the heat must be able to escape. Otherwise, your pipe may burst from steam pressure.

If the frozen pipe is well behind a wall or in a ceiling or floor, all you can do is turn up the house heat and wait—or tear out the wall.

Do not use a propane torch or other open flame to thaw pipes. Too many house fires have been caused by such techniques.

If freezing pipes are a constant threat in your area, jacket your pipes with pipe insulation or install thermostatically-controlled heat tape.

If pipes freeze under a sink that is along an outside wall, just open the sink cabinet doors and let room heat keep the pipes warm.

YOU'LL NEED...

SKILLS: Basic skills.
TIME: 10 to 30 minutes, depending on the accessibility of the pipe.
TOOLS: Blow dryer, heat lamp, pot.

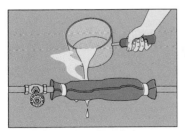

You can thaw a pipe by taping layers of cloth to the pipe and pouring hot water on it. This, however, can be a messy solution.

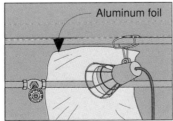

A heat lamp is excellent for exposed or concealed pipes. Protect materials around the pipe because a heat lamp can scorch.

For exposed pipes, use a blow drier. Open the faucet first. Work from the faucet toward the frozen area.

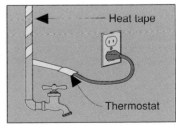

Electric heat tape runs on house current. Wrap it around the pipe and plug it into an outlet. A thermostat controls the temperature.

Solving Plumbing Problems (continued)

OPENING CLOGGED DRAINS

A house has three types of waste drains: fixture drains, such as those at sinks and toilets; main drains, which lead from the fixture drains to the main pipe that carries waste from your house; and sewer drains, which run underground to the sewer or septic tank.

A blockage may originate in any of the three, so your first chore is to locate the blockage. Usually, it will be in a trap or in or next to a pipe connection that makes a turn.

Open a faucet at each sink, tub, or other fixture—but don't flush a toilet; it could overflow. If only one fixture is stopped up, the problem is nearby. If two or more fixtures won't clear, something has lodged in a main drain. If no drains work, the blockage is near the point where the main drain connects to the sewer drain or in the sewer drain itself.

The fact that wastewater always flows downward lets you logically ferret out an obstruction. The techniques shown here explain what to do once you know the general vicinity of the blockage.

> ### YOU'LL NEED...
> **SKILLS:** Basic plumbing skills.
> **TIME:** 10 to 30 minutes.
> **TOOLS:** Hand auger or closet auger, plunger, tongue-and-groove pliers.

Unplugging Sinks

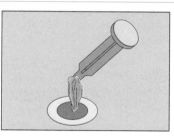

To remove a lavatory stopper, turn and lift. Debris may accumulate around the lifting mechanism.

Plungers with molded suction cups are best for toilets or rounded lavatories.

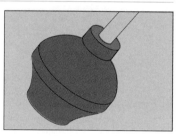

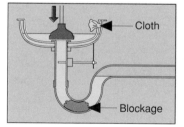

Plug overflow outlet with a wet cloth. Make sure the plunger seals tightly over the drain, then push down.

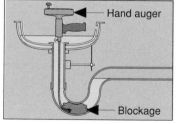

Thread a plumber's snake down the trap, or open the cleanout on the bottom of the trap to work from there.

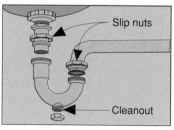

Remove the trap (see page 292) and flush it. This also lets you get a snake into the main drain.

Unclogging Toilets

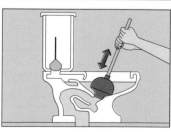

Apply a plunger to the outlet hole. Try a suction stroke upward first, then a pressure stroke downward.

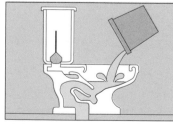

If the bowl is empty, fill it to the rim. Spread petroleum jelly on the rim of the plunger to aid suction.

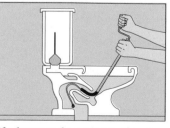

If plunger doesn't work, use a closet auger. As you crank. it wends its way down through passages.

Unclogging Tubs

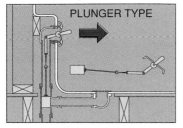

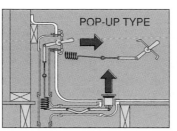

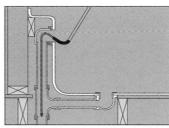

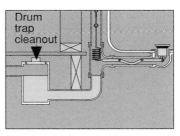

For plunger-type drains, remove and clean the stopper and strainer. Try a plunger; block the overflow drain with a wet cloth.

For pop-up type drains, remove the pop-up assembly. Try the plunger here first also.

If the plunger doesn't work, run a snake down through the overflow pipe, not the tub drain.

Some tubs have a drum trap in or under the floor near the tub. Clean it out by removing the cleanout plug.

Unclogging Main Drains

There may be more than one cleanout in your drain system. If so, find the cleanout plug nearest the sewer line and loosen it. If water forms around the threads, the trouble is between this plug and the sewer. If no water forms, the clog is further back from this cleanout. Move to the next cleanout back and check there for water. Once you find where the clog is, insert your snake and be ready for a messy job.

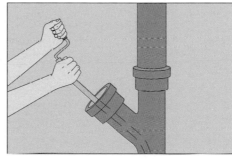

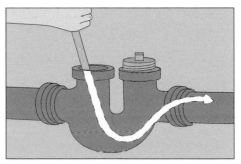

Unscrew the cleanout plug. Have a large bucket handy to catch residue and protect your floors. Sewage residue is messy stuff to work with.

Thread an auger or snake into the cleanout opening toward the sewer line. Once you break through, flush with a garden hose.

On a U-trap, work from the cleanout plug nearest the sewer line. If the obstruction isn't in the trap, continue up the main drain, then toward sewer.

Unclogging Sewer Drains

The sewer drain rarely gets clogged. If it does, remove the cleanout plug and try threading a garden hose into the line and turning on the water full blast. Push the hose through the blockage, letting the water clear away the debris. If that doesn't work, insert a power auger snake into the pipe and twist it through the blockage. If your problem persists, you'll probably need a professional to look at the problem.

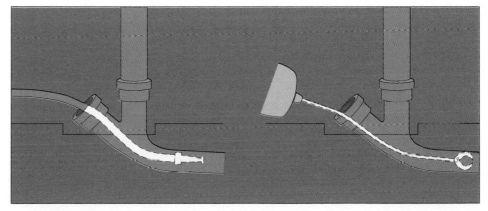

Solving Plumbing Problems (continued)

MAINTAINING SEPTIC SYSTEMS

Many rural homeowners don't realize the purpose of a septic system until it is too late—that is, until the system is destroyed. The purpose of the concrete tank, hidden out of sight under the lawn, is to provide a factory where anaerobic bacteria (bacteria that live without oxygen) digest and separate organic (human and otherwise) waste into liquid effluent, solid sludge, and floating scum.

By digesting the waste, the bacteria reduce its volume and render the liquid effluent relatively harmless. The solid sludge settles to the bottom of the tank. The liquid overflows into a distribution box from which it flows to rows of perforated pipes in a drainage field of gravel and sand. Some of the liquid evaporates, while the rest sinks into the ground.

If the sludge accumulates to the bottom of the outflow pipe, the waste doesn't linger for the bacterial action, but shoots right through, solids and all, to the distribution system. The solids clog the gravel bed, and the untreated wastes float to the surface. At that point, the gravel bed has to be replaced—a very expensive proposition. As with teeth, it is far less costly to perform regular preventive maintenance than to replace them. Call a cleanout service before it is too late.

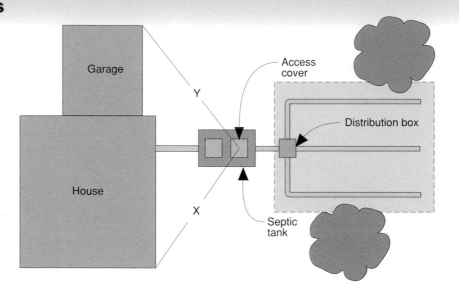

MANAGING YOUR SEPTIC SYSTEM

Do:

■ Keep a plot plan showing the location of the septic tank access cover and layout of the distribution field. (As shown above, plot the X and Y distance from corners of your house on your house deed and keep this in a safe place.)

■ Have the septic tank cleaned—or at least inspected—every two years.

■ Flush ½ pound of brewer's yeast dissolved in warm water down a toilet twice a year to help promote bacterial digestion.

■ Space out the interval between baths, showers, and clothes washer loads if you have an influx of guests.

■ Locate gutter downspouts to divert rainwater away from the distribution field.

Don't:

■ Use a garbage disposal to dispose of food waste through the septic system. Instead, create a compost pile. The compost will be invaluable in your garden.

■ Use commercial drain cleaners any more than you have to because they kill the anaerobic bacteria.

■ Flush coffee grounds, paper goods other than white toilet tissue, or grease down any drain.

■ Pour chemicals, such as paint thinner, paint stripper, bleach, pesticide, or photographic developer, down a drain.

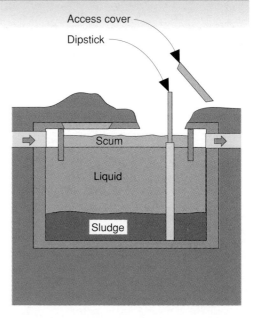

MAKING FAUCET REPAIRS

Unless your ears have tuned out such noises, it probably hasn't been long since you heard the plop-plop-plop of a leaky faucet. You can bet you'll hear it again. Wishing away leaky faucets doesn't work, so you had better learn how to repair them.

Faucets vary widely in style, but all fall into one of two broad categories: compression and noncompression faucets. Chances are you have both in your home.

Compression types, also known as stem faucets, always have separate hot and cold controls. Turning a handle to the off position rotates a threaded stem. A washer at the bottom of the stem compresses into a seat to block the flow of water, as shown in the first anatomy drawing below. To learn how to repair stem faucets, see page 286.

Most noncompression faucets have one lever that controls the flow of both hot and cold water. Inside a single-lever, noncompression faucet will be one of the three operating mechanisms shown below.

A disk faucet mixes water inside a cartridge. At the bottom of the mixing chamber, a pair of disks raises and lowers to regulate the flow of water and rotates to control the temperature mix. For repair information, see page 287.

A rotating-ball faucet consists of a ball with openings that line up with the hot and cold inlets and the spout. Rocking its lever adjusts both the temperature and the flow. Repairs are shown on pages 287–288.

A sleeve-cartridge faucet operates something like a disk type. Lifting the handle controls the flow, moving it from side to side regulates the temperature. Inside, however, the workings include a cartridge and sleeve arrangement instead of disks. For repair procedures, see page 288.

All four types of faucet have aerators, diverters, and strainers that may clog and choke the flow of water. If you have a problem with any of these items, turn to page 290.

ANATOMIES OF FAUCETS

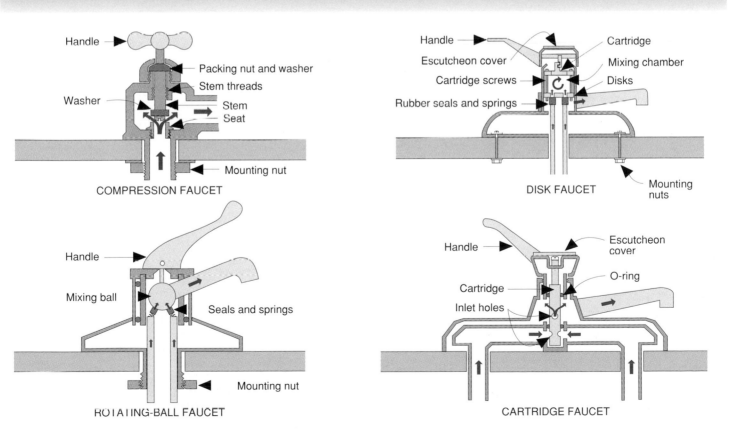

COMPRESSION FAUCET

DISK FAUCET

ROTATING-BALL FAUCET

CARTRIDGE FAUCET

Solving Plumbing Problems *(continued)*

MAKING FAUCET REPAIRS *(continued)*
Repairing a Stem Faucet

Stem faucets are the most leak-prone of all faucet types. They develop the sniffles for one or more of the following reasons: a worn washer, a pitted or corroded valve seat, or deteriorated packing.

As the first anatomy drawing shows (see page 285), the washer must withstand the pressure of repeated openings and closings. As the washer wears, you have to apply more and more force to turn off the water—until, finally, no amount of turning stops the flow.

Fortunately, replacing a washer is a simple procedure, as illustrated below, that requires only basic tools and a faucet repair kit that includes an assortment of washers to fit various stems. The package generally also includes O-rings and new screws for attaching the washers to the stems.

If you have to replace the faucet washers often—every month or two—you are probably dealing with a pitted or corroded valve seat. Abrasion here wears out washers rapidly. Again, the solution is simple, but you will need a special tool— the valve-seating tool shown below and on page 280.

Washer and seat problems cause drips. On the other hand, if a faucet leaks around the handle, the packing probably has worn out. With newer faucets, which don't use packing, the problem may be a worn O-ring.

While you have a faucet apart, note if the threads around its stem show signs of heavy wear. If so, it's a good idea to replace the entire unit, preferably with a washerless noncompression type. Installation is fairly easy; see pages 317–318.

Whenever you work on a faucet, first be sure to turn off the water at the main valve or at the shutoffs below the sink or lavatory (see page 279. If you forget this step, you'll have a real mess on your hands.

YOU'LL NEED...
SKILLS: Basic plumbing skills.
TIME: 1 hour.
TOOLS: Screwdriver, wrench, seat grinder.

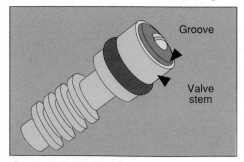

1. After prying out the escutcheon on the handle, back out the screw and remove the handle. Lift it straight up.

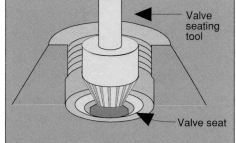

2. Remove the packing nut with an adjustable wrench or tongue-and-groove pliers. Screw out the stem.

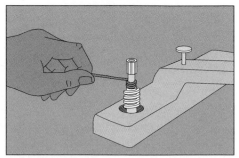

3. The washer, held in place by a screw, is at the bottom of the stem. Replace the O-ring(s) now, too.

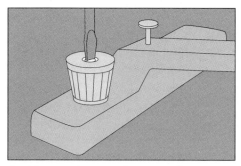

4. A worn washer has grooves in it. When you replace it, clean the entire valve stem with fine steel wool.

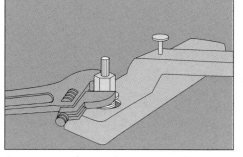

5. To smooth a seat, insert the valve seating tool, apply light pressure, and twist clockwise. Vacuum out filings.

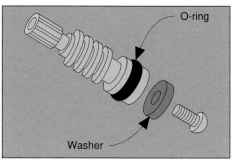

6. Before reassembling an older faucet, wind new packing around the stem, then install the packing nut and handle.

Repairing a Disk Faucet

The disks in most disk faucets are ceramic and won't wear out. But their inlet holes (see below) may become constricted by lime deposits from the water. When this happens, you have to dismantle the faucet and clean out the deposit. If the faucet leaks around its base, you must replace the inlet seals in the cartridge's underside. If only one of the seals appears worn out, replace them all now because the others will soon wear out also.

Another type of disk faucet (not shown) resembles the compression versions shown on pages 285–286 in that it has separate hot and cold controls. Take one apart, though, and you will find a cone-shaped rubber diaphragm at the end of the stem where you would expect to see a washer. If this is worn, pry it out and replace it. These are sometimes called "washerless" faucets.

You can buy repair kits for both ceramic and diaphragm-disk faucets, but take along the old assembly when you shop because sizes vary. As with all faucet repairs, shut off the water and drain the tap before you begin repairs.

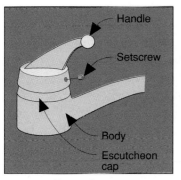

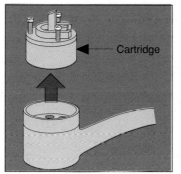

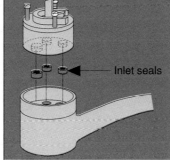

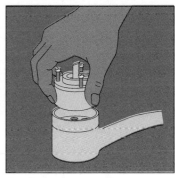

1. Pry off any decorative cap present, then remove the screw and handle. With some types, you have to pry between body and handle.

2. Remove the screws holding the cartridge in place and lift out. The entire cartridge unit can be replaced if necessary.

3. Check to be sure dirt hasn't lodged between the disks and that the inlet seals are in good condition.

4. Reinsert the new or repaired assembly, aligning it so the screws mesh with the holes below.

Repairing a Rotating-Ball Faucet

Ball faucets usually serve for years with no trouble. When one begins to drip, you can be certain that its springs and seats need replacing. Leakage around the handle, on the other hand, means it needs new O-rings. Neither repair is difficult.

The procedure for getting at faucet parts depends on whether the faucet has a fixed or a swiveling spout. With fixed-spout models, simply remove the handle and the cap underneath (see drawings on page 288). With swivel-spout types, you have to lift off the spout as well.

While you have the unit apart, check the ball itself for wear or corrosion and replace it, too, if necessary. Repair kits include springs, seats, O-rings, and other seals—but you'll need the make and model number or the old parts to get the right components.

Reassemble the parts in order and replace them in the housing. With a swivel-spout model, push the spout straight down until you hear it click against a slip ring at the base of the housing. Because the O-rings create a great amount of tension, you'll have to push hard.

Solving Plumbing Problems *(continued)*

MAKING FAUCET REPAIRS *(continued)*
Repairing a Rotating-Ball Faucet *(continued)*

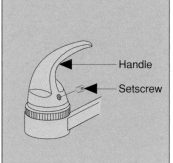

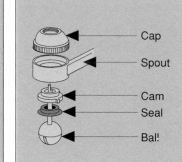

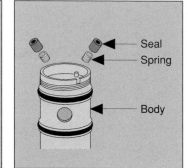

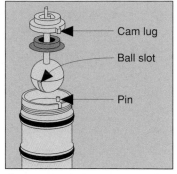

1. After turning off the water, loosen, but don't remove, the handle's setscrew with an Allen wrench. Remove the handle.

2. The cap and spout come off next. Pull out the cam, the ball, and the stem. Remove and replace the O-rings if they are worn.

3. Remove seals and springs with needle-nose pliers. Replace these according to directions that come with the repair kit.

4. When you replace the ball, be sure to align the slot in its side with the pin inside the housing. The cam has a lug key, too.

REPAIRING A SLEEVE-CARTRIDGE FAUCET

When a sleeve-cartridge faucet goes bad, replace either its O-rings (if there are any) or the entire cartridge.

The key to dismantling this type of faucet lies with a small retainer clip in the handle assembly. With some faucets, you can see this clip at the point where the handle meets the base. With others, you must first remove the handle and, in the case of a swivel-spout faucet, the spout.

Under the handle, you will probably find a ring or tube that simply slides off to expose the retaining clip. Pull out the clip with needle-nose pliers and the cartridge will pull out with little difficulty.

If the hot and cold water are reversed when you replace the cartridge, remove it, rotate the unit 180 degrees, and replace.

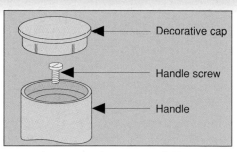

1. With a screwdriver, carefully pry off the decorative cap and back out the screw in the handle. Remove the handle and spout.

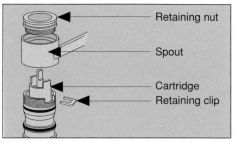

2. The retaining clip may not be hidden at all. Some faucets also have a second retaining clip located near the handle. Once the clip is removed, the cartridge will pull out.

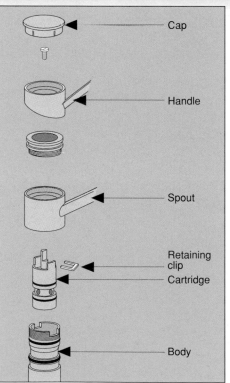

A typical cartridge faucet looks like this when disassembled. A retaining ring must be pulled back to expose the retaining clip for removal.

YOU'LL NEED...

SKILLS: Basic plumbing skills.
TIME: 30 minutes
TOOLS: Screwdriver, needle-nose pliers, tongue-and-groove pliers.

REPAIRING TUB FAUCETS AND SHOWERHEADS

Like sink and lavatory faucets, wall-mounted faucets fall into two categories: compression and noncompression types. Compression faucets, the two-handled types, feature O-rings and washers that you can replace (see at right). The noncompression version usually has a single handle pull-on, push-off configuration, with a cartridge assembly beneath. When it leaks, the whole cartridge assembly usually requires replacement (see below).

Problems with shower heads usually stem from lime deposits and/or corrosion. Often, you can disassemble the head and clean its moving parts. If you can't take the unit apart, replace it with a new one.

YOU'LL NEED...

SKILLS: Basic plumbing skills.
TIME: 30 to 60 minutes to disassemble, clean, and reassemble.
TOOLS: Screwdriver, tongue-and-groove pliers, socket wrench with extra-deep sockets if your faucet stems are recessed in the wall.

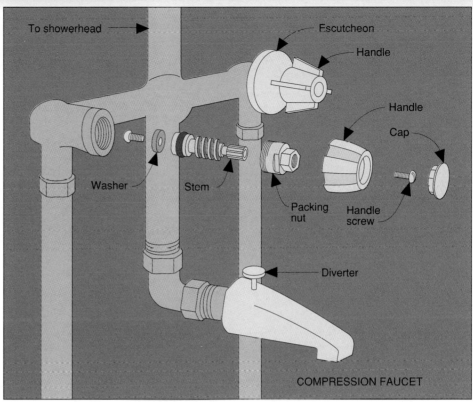

COMPRESSION FAUCET

To repair wall-mounted compression faucets, pry out the cap and remove the handle. Under this, you will find a packing nut. Loosen the nut, replace the handle on the stem, and turn the

handle to remove the stem. If the stem O-rings or seat washer are worn, replace them. Coat O-rings with heat-resistant lubricant. Replace worn packing, too, if the stems have it.

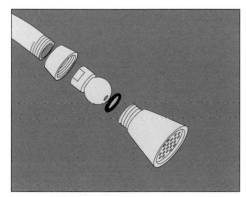

Unscrew showerheads as shown. This will expose the screens, strainers, and O-ring for cleaning or replacement.

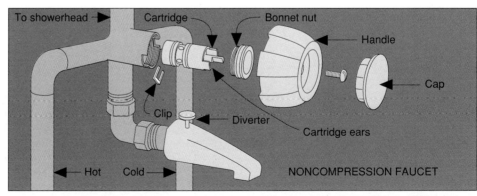

NONCOMPRESSION FAUCET

To repair leaky noncompression faucets, you'll probably need to replace the cartridge. Remove the handle and retaining clip, then the cartridge. To

insert the new cartridge, push it into the housing unit until the ears are flush with the housing. Align parts, then insert retaining clip.

Solving Plumbing Problems (continued)

REPAIRING DIVERTERS, SPRAYS, AND AERATORS

When diverters, sprays, or aerators act up, the problem often is a worn out washer or a clogged strainer.

Diverters channel water from a faucet to a showerhead or spray attachment. Make minor repairs, such as replacing worn O-rings, packing, or washers, by backing out the diverter assembly. If the diverter assembly is leaking, you'll have to replace it. Take the old unit to a plumbing shop so you can match it.

With single-faucet tubs, the diverter is in the spout. If it breaks or wears out, you'll have to replace the entire spout.

Sprays have a hose and spray nozzle head. Trouble can develop in connections, washers, or the nozzle. Before you rip into the assembly, try tightening the connecting nuts to stop leaks, and make sure the hose is not kinked.

Aerators, the tiny devices on the ends of faucets, are screwed to the spout. Clean out rust or lime deposits blocking the strainers or screen. If the malfunctioning aerator is old, replace it with a new one.

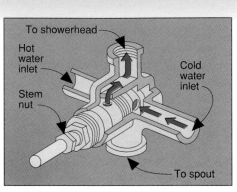

YOU'LL NEED...

SKILLS: Basic skills.
TIME: 20 minutes.
TOOLS: Tongue-and-groove pliers, screwdriver.

For tubs with separate diverter valves, remove the handle, unscrew the stem nut, and remove the diverter valve assembly. Compression-type valves can be repaired, but cartridge-type ones will have to be replaced.

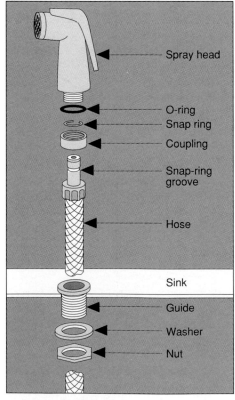

A spray attachment has washers and couplings that can leak. To stop most leaks, tighten these connections.

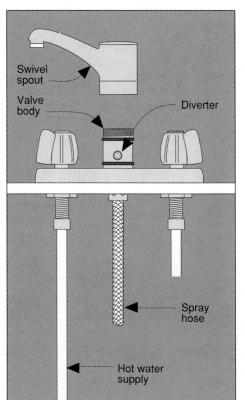

Sink faucet diverters are positioned on top of the faucet housing. The spray hose connection is under the sink.

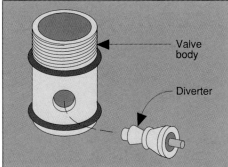

Lime deposits clog a faucet's diverter. With the type shown, remove and clean or replace the assembly.

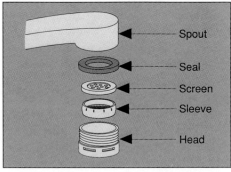

Assemble aerators in this order. Clean the screen by flushing it with water or brushing the mesh.

REPAIRING DRAINS AND TRAPS

Compared to faucets, drains are relatively simple. Because gravity does most of the work, drainage systems don't have to be designed to handle pressures such as those in water supply systems. Except for rudimentary linkages that operate pop-up and trip-lever assembles, there are no moving parts beneath a lavatory, sink, or tub. Trouble here almost always falls into one of two categories—a clog or a leak

If a drain is clogged, see pages 282–283 for helpful hints. If the flow just seems slower than it should be,

try running hot water for about 10 minutes; often this will be enough to dissolve accumulated grease or soap. If hot water doesn't do the job, try drain cleaner, following the manufacturer's instructions to the letter. Don't use drain cleaner in a completely stopped-up fixture—if it doesn't work and you have to dismantle the trap, you'll be working with dangerously caustic water.

To find a leak, set up a strong light under the fixture and wipe all drainage components dry. Run warm water (cold water can cause

misleading condensation) and check each connection, starting at the top where the drain exits the fixture. Check for moisture by wiping each fitting with your fingertips.

If you find a leaking connection, tightening its slip nut may solve the problem. When you do this, however, take care not to apply too much pressure; drain fittings can be easily cracked or crushed. If tightening doesn't eliminate the leak, prepare to dismantle the assembly (see page 292).

Adjusting Pop-Up and Trip-Lever Mechanisms

Have you ever filled a lavatory or tub, stepped away, and returned to discover that the water level had dropped? If so, the fixture's pop-up or trip-lever mechanism is letting you down.

Start by lifting or turning out the stopper and flushing away any hair, soap, or other debris that might be preventing it from seating properly. After you replace the stopper, check to see if the lifting assembly pulls it down so it fits snugly.

If you're dealing with a lavatory pop-up that doesn't seat, get under the basin and take a look at the pivot rod. It should slope slightly upward from the pivot to the clevis. To adjust the pivot rod, loosen the clevis's setscrew, push down the stopper, and retighten the setscrew. If the lift rod now is difficult to operate, adjust the linkage between the pivot and clevis so they meet at nearly a right angle.

A sink pop-up often leaks at its pivot ball. Sometimes tightening the retaining nut here may stop the drip. If not, remove the nut and replace the washer or gasket inside the nut.

Tub pop-ups—and a variation called a trip-lever—work in much the same way, except that the mechanisms are housed within the

tub's overflow tube. To adjust them, remove the stopper, unscrew the overflow plate, and pull out the entire assembly.

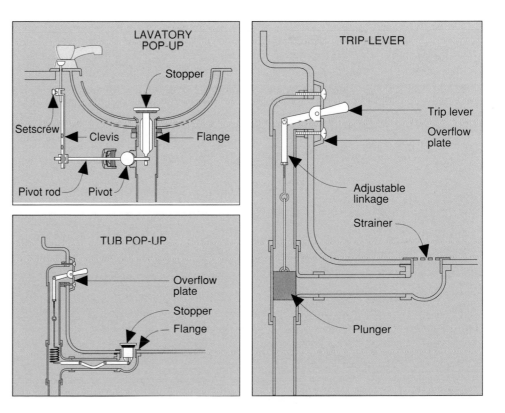

LAVATORY POP-UP — Stopper, Setscrew, Clevis, Flange, Pivot rod, Pivot

TUB POP-UP — Overflow plate, Stopper, Flange

TRIP-LEVER — Trip lever, Overflow plate, Adjustable linkage, Strainer, Plunger

Solving Plumbing Problems (continued)

REPAIRING DRAINS AND TRAPS (continued)
Dismantling a Trap

Clogged drains, the wear and tear of time, and the ring or other piece of jewelry that inevitably falls down a drain ensure that you'll have to take apart a trap at some time or another. The secret to how trap components fit together lies with slip-joint connections. Only the trap pipe is threaded, not the tailpiece or drainpipe that slips into either end. This system lets you twist everything to align the assembly. Then, you tighten the slip nuts to secure it.

Although most slip fittings use rubber washers, some older slip fittings may be packed with lamp wick, which looks like ordinary cotton string but makes a more watertight seal.

Whenever you have a trap apart, inspect it for corrosion. It usually shows up first at the bend along the sides and bottom. Before buying a new trap, measure the diameter of the tailpiece—usually 1¼ inches.

> ### YOU'LL NEED...
> **SKILLS:** Basic plumbing skills.
> **TIME:** 30 to 45 minutes.
> **TOOLS:** Tongue-and-groove pliers or a pipe wrench.

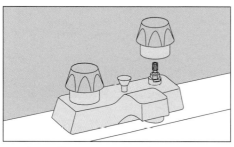

1. Shut off water at the shutoff valves. Or, remove the knobs so you don't chance turning on faucets accidently.

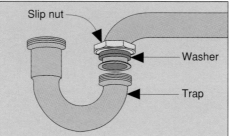

2. Slip a bucket underneath trap to catch water. Open the cleanout if the trap you're working with has one.

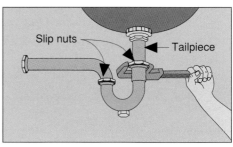

3. When you loosen slip nuts at the tailpiece, this type of trap will simply drop loose or come off with a tug.

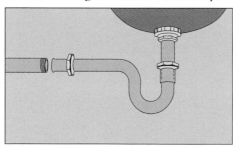

4. With a fixed trap, slide down the tailpiece, then turn the trap loose from the drainpipe.

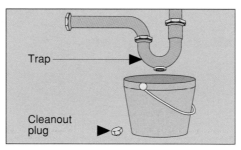

5. Leaks often result from worn washers. Tighten the slip nut or replace its washer.

7. Then use a wrench to tighten it another one-quarter turn. Pad wrench jaws so they don't mar the plating.

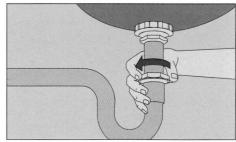

6. When you reassemble drain fittings, be careful not to overtighten them. Start by turning the slip nuts hand-tight.

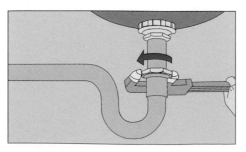

8. To test a trap for leaks, fill the basin with water, open the drain, and check all connections closely for signs of moisture.

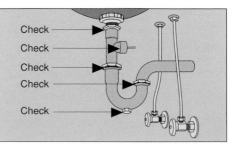

REPAIRING TOILETS

Most toilet maladies happen inside the tank, where all the mechanical parts are located. Only rarely will other problems develop.

Lift the top off a toilet tank and you'll find an assortment of balls, tubes, and levers similar to those in the anatomy drawing at right. Flipping the handle sets in motion a chain of events that releases water to the bowl, then automatically refills the tank and the bowl.

Flipping the handle activates a trip lever that lifts a flush ball at the bottom of the tank. Water then rushes through a seat into the toilet bowl. After the tank empties, the flush ball drops back into its seat.

Flushing also triggers the refill cycle. A float ball moves down along with the water level and opens an inlet valve. This brings fresh water into the tank through a refill tube and sends water to the bowl through a second refill tube that empties into an overflow tube. As the water rises in the tank, so does the float. When it reaches a point ¾ inch below the top of the overflow, the float shuts off the inlet valve, stopping flow to both the tank and bowl.

The following pages take you step-by-step through just about everything that can go wrong inside a toilet tank.

ANATOMY OF A TOILET TANK

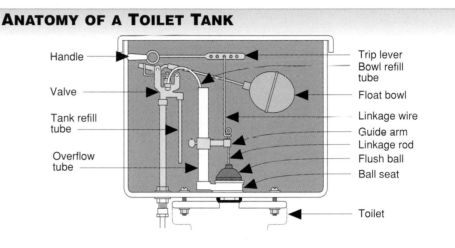

Handle — Valve — Tank refill tube — Overflow tube

Trip lever — Bowl refill tube — Float bowl — Linkage wire — Guide arm — Linkage rod — Flush ball — Ball seat — Toilet

HELPFUL HINTS   TROUBLESHOOTING TOILETS

Problem	Solution
Water runs, but tank won't fill properly	Check the handle, trip lever, guide arm, flush ball, and connections to make sure all are working. The handle may be too loose; the trip lever or guide arm, bent or broken; or the connection between the trip lever and guide arm, out of adjustment so it doesn't raise the flush ball enough.
Water runs constantly after the tank is filled	The handle and trip assembly may be malfunctioning (see above). Check the flush ball for proper seating, the seat for corrosion, and the float ball for water inside it.
The water level is set too high or too low	You may have to adjust the float ball downward. Check to make sure it's not damaged—it could be full of water. The inlet valve washers may be leaking and need replacement. Check to see that the flush ball is seating properly. Check the ball seat for corrosion.
Toilet won't flush properly	Gently bend the flush tank float downward to lower the water level. Bend it upward to raise the water level. Or, use the adjustment screw on top of the inlet valve to set the float arm. The water should be ¾ inch below the top of the overflow tube.
Water splashes in the tank while it refills	Water may be too low in the tank. If so, bend the float ball up to permit sufficient water to flow into the toilet bowl.
Tank leaks at the bottom	Adjust the refill tube that runs into the overflow tube. You may need to replace the washers in the inlet valve. Tighten all the nuts at the bottom of the tank. If this doesn't work, replace the washers.

Solving Plumbing Problems (continued)

REPAIRING TOILETS (continued)
Repairing Flush Mechanisms

An occasional gurgle, a constant flow of water—both are signs that your toilet has troubles. But don't panic! Almost all of the time, you can trace the problem to the flushing mechanism, which controls the water in the flush tank. Usually, correcting the problem involves only a simple adjustment or, in some cases, a few new parts.

If the working parts are metal (usually brass) and not too old,

you're best off replacing the individual malfunctioning parts. If the parts are plastic or have been in service for several years, replace the entire assembly. Tank assemblies come in kit form with easy-to-follow installation instructions.

> **YOU'LL NEED...**
> **SKILLS:** Basic plumbing skills.
> **TIME:** 45 minutes to replace the entire assembly.
> **TOOLS:** Screwdriver, pliers.

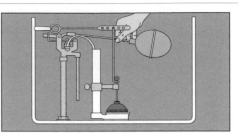

1. Does water keep flowing after the tank has filled? Lift the float rod gently. If the water now shuts off, the float ball position has to be adjusted slightly so the valve will close.

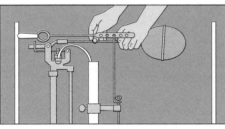

2. To adjust the position, bend the rod so the float ball is about ½ inch lower. Flush the tank to check the float.

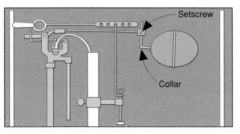

3. A collar allows more accuracy when adjusting the float. Look for a setscrew on the inlet valve arm.

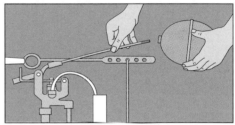

4. Half of the float ball should submerge. If it sinks lower, check it for leaks. Replace the float, if necessary.

1. If the above steps don't help, you'll have to repair the valve assembly. Turn off water below tank or at water meter.

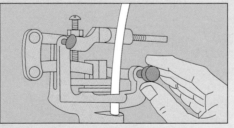

2. Worn valve washers may be the problem. Flush water out of tank. Open valve by removing two pivot screws.

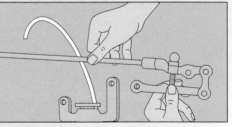

3. Slide the float, rod, and linkage out of the valve. On some assemblies you remove a cap covering the inlet valve.

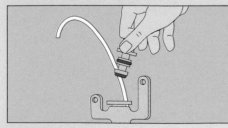

4. Pull the plunger upward. If it's stuck, use a screwdriver to pry it out gently. Don't damage the metal.

5. A washer at the plunger base shuts off the water. In most cases, simply push the new washer into position.

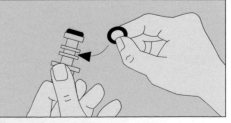

6. Another washer may be in a groove in the valve; replace it also. Brush any corrosion from the plunger.

Repairing a Flush Ball

Several conditions can cause water to leak around the tank flush ball into the bowl: a misaligned guide arm and wire, a bent linkage wire, a worn flush ball, or a pitted or corroded flush-ball seat. Usually, you can pinpoint the problem by flushing the toilet and watching these parts operate. (See anatomy drawing on page 293.)

To check the ball seat, lift the ball with the flush handle and run your fingers over the seat. If it's rough, it probably is corroded or pitted—a job for an abrasive or steel wool.

If the problem is a worn flush ball, upgrade the assembly with a new flapper-type ball unit or a "water saver" valve-and-ball device. Both are easy-to-install replacements that you'll find at most home center stores (see below).

> **YOU'LL NEED...**
> **SKILLS:** Basic plumbing skills.
> **TIME:** 20 to 30 minutes.
> **TOOLS:** Steel wool or scrubber pad.

1. Raise the linkage rod and test the flush ball for wear. To replace, unscrew rod by hand or with pliers.

2. With the flush ball removed, clean the ball seat. Use fine steel wool to buff the metal seat until it's shiny.

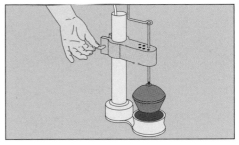

3. Adjust the linkage rod so it allows the ball to seat. To adjust the guide arm, loosen the setscrew as shown.

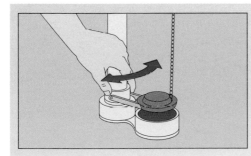

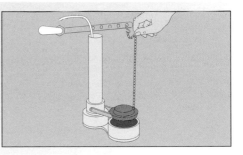

1. Align a flapper-type ball over the seat by twisting it on the overflow tube. A chain serves as the linkage.

2. Adjust chain to length and fasten to trip arm. If lift chain is broken or badly corroded, replace it.

Upgrading a Flushing Mechanism

Like anything mechanical, a flush-tank assembly eventually wears out. Its life span depends on how often it's used and the hardness of the water in your area. Some municipal or well water corrodes plumbing parts quickly and clogs up parts with lime deposits.

Almost all flush-tank mechanisms are replaceable by the piece, so you don't have to buy the entire unit. Flush balls, floats, lifts, and guides are standard, so they fit most any flush-tank make or model. If you're having trouble with the assembly, however, it might be smarter to replace the entire unit, a slightly more advanced project, but still a do-it-yourself one.

Many new flush-tank mechanisms depart from traditional designs. One, a flapper-ball unit, produces quiet flushes and has an extremely long life span.

Another type, called a water-saver, does not use a float-ball. Instead, water pressure regulates the water-inlet valve. The valve, in turn, meters out the exact amount of water needed in the tank for a full flush. This feature, in time, saves a considerable amount of water and eliminates the need to adjust a float arm and float ball.

If you choose to stick with a standard tank assembly, invest in a quality product. It may cost you a bit more at the outset, but your troubles with the unit should be minimal.

Solving Plumbing Problems *(continued)*

REPAIRING TOILETS *(continued)*
Adjusting Tank Linkage

A toilet's handle mechanism is the key to starting the flushing cycle. It's also the most prone to malfunction. The tank linkage is made up of a handle, trip lever, linkage wire or chain, and connecting devices. If any one of these items gives out, it affects the entire assembly.

Corrosion, the assembly's biggest enemy, usually occurs around the handle where it goes through the flush tank and connects to the trip lever. If you spot trouble here, remove the handle by loosening the nut that holds it with an adjustable wrench. Be extremely careful when you remove the handle. Too much pressure can crack the flush tank. If this happens, you'll have to buy a whole new tank. If you can't loosen the nut, cut through the bolt with a hacksaw. Again, take care that you don't crack or chip the tank.

Clean the parts with fine steel wool. Lightly coat the parts with a waterproof grease and reassemble.

Trip-lever troubles start when the lever gets bent or misaligned with the lift chain or linkage wire. The lever is set at a slight angle to the handle so it can operate freely without rubbing against the tank, inlet valve, or overflow tube.

Flip the handle several times to make sure the trip lever is operating freely. If it isn't, try gently bending the arm toward the center of the tank for necessary clearance. As you bend the arm, hold it with one hand near the flushing handle.

The chain between the end of the trip lever and the flush ball often fails to work when corroded. Replacing the chain is simple. A new one made of brass will last longer.

> ### YOU'LL NEED...
> **SKILLS:** Basic plumbing skills.
> **TIME:** 20 to 30 minutes.
> **TOOLS:** Adjustable wrench, hacksaw.

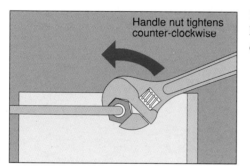

Handle nut tightens counter-clockwise

1. Take care when tightening or loosening the handle nut. Clean and coat the parts with waterproof grease.

2. Straighten the linkage wire connected to the trip lever. Lift the flush ball off the seat to prevent suction.

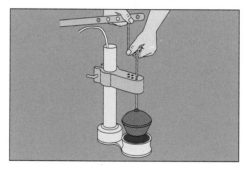

Stopping Tank and Bowl Leaks

Occasionally a toilet develops an external leak at one of three points: the supply pipe, the point at which the tank joins the bowl, or around the base.

For a leaking supply pipe, tighten the nut that holds the fitting to the tank. If that doesn't work, shut off the water, empty the tank, remove the fittings, and install new washers or a new pipe, if necessary.

A leak where the tank joins the bowl may simply mean the tank's hold-down bolts have come loose. Drain the tank and tighten the bolts as shown at right. If that doesn't work, remove the bolts and install new washers.

With older toilets, the tank may be connected to the bowl via an elbow. Tighten the elbow's slip nuts or repack them.

If the toilet leaks around its base at the floor, check the hold-down bolts. Chances are, they've come loose and allowed the bowl to rock. Tightening the bolts might solve the problem. If not, you may have to remove the toilet and install a new wax seal (page 320).

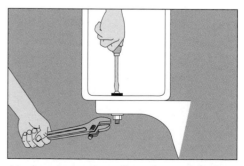

Apply penetrating oil to the tank bolts, loosen them, then carefully retighten. Too much pressure will crack the tank.

MAINTAINING A WATER HEATER

Today's water heaters generally provide years of trouble-free service. Just a little effort on your part, however, can extend your water heater's life and cut down on its energy consumption.

Some manufacturers recommend that new gas or electric units be drained partially every two months during their first year of operation, then every six months after that. This removes sediment or other debris that has settled out of the water at the bottom of the tank.

To drain a water heater partially, turn off the water shutoff valve at the top of the water heater or at the main water meter. Place a bucket under the tank's drain valve, or fasten a hose to the valve and run it to a floor drain. Open the drain valve and let out water until it runs clear, then close the drain valve and reopen the supply valve.

Check the heater's pressure-relief valve to be sure it's capable of letting off steam if pressure builds up in the tank. Just lift the valve handle; if it's functioning properly, hot water will be released through the overflow.

If your water heater is gas-fired, inspect the flue assembly every six months to make sure there are no obstructions. The burner ports may have to be cleaned, too, as explained in the chart below. If you're plagued with a pilot light that just won't stay lit, see pages 329–330 and 343.

ANATOMY OF A WATER HEATER

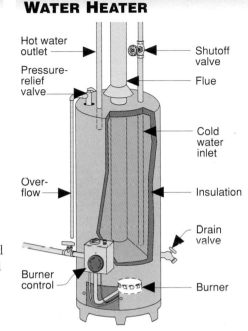

- Hot water outlet
- Pressure-relief valve
- Over-flow
- Burner control
- Shutoff valve
- Flue
- Cold water inlet
- Insulation
- Drain valve
- Burner

HELPFUL HINTS   TROUBLESHOOTING WATER HEATERS

Problem	Solution
Water won't heat (electric)	Check the fuse box or circuit breaker for a blown fuse or a tripped switch. Reactivate; if the heater blows fuses or circuits often, call in a professional.
Water won't heat (gas)	Pilot light isn't burning; relight it (see page 329). Unclog burner ports as explained below. Make sure the gas connection shutoff valve is fully open. Check temperature control knob for proper setting.
Water too hot	Turn back thermostat setting; if the thermostat is not functioning, call in a professional.
Water tank leaks	Turn off the water and gas or electrical supplies and drain the tank. It probably will have to be replaced (see pages 321–322).
Water supply pipes leak	Tighten pipe fittings; if this doesn't work, turn off the water and replace fittings. If water condenses on the cold water supply pipe, wrap the pipe with standard pipe insulation (see page 396).
Clogged gas burner ports	Remove the debris with a needle or the end of a paper clip; do not use a wooden toothpick or peg, as either can break off in the portholes.
Gas flame burns yellow	The burner may not be getting enough air. Also check the pilot light (see page 330); the flame should be about ½ inch long. The burner should be serviced professionally every 24 months or so.
Heater smells of gas	Immediately turn off the main gas supply valve and open windows. Coat the pipe connections with soapy water and turn on the gas again. If bubbles appear, the connection is leaking.

Solving Plumbing Problems (continued)

WINTERIZING A PLUMBING SYSTEM

Many homeowners have found out the hard way what happens to pipes in vacant houses that have little or no heat. Completely shutting down a plumbing system is neither difficult nor costly.

Turn off the water at the meter. Or, better yet, arrange to have your municipal water department turn off the water service at the valve outside your home. Then, starting at the top of the water supply system, open every faucet—bathtub, shower, lavatory, and so on. Be sure not to miss any you don't normally use, such as an outside sill cock or an underground sprinkler system. (These should be drained every fall anyway, whether your home will be heated or not.)

Turn off the power (gas or electricity) to the water heater and drain it. By the time you reach the system's lowest point, the supply pipes should be completely empty. Make sure, however, that there's an open outlet at the lowest point. This might be the water heater, a basement laundry tub or washing machine, or a valve installed specifically for draining the system.

Go through the entire house a second time to freeze-proof the drainage system. Start by removing the cleanout plugs on all sink and lavatory traps. If a trap doesn't have a cleanout plug, dismantle and empty the trap itself (see page 292). After you've emptied each trap, replace it or its cleanout plug, then pour in automotive antifreeze mixed with water in the proportions specified for cars in your climate.

You won't be able to drain some traps, such as the ones in toilets and perhaps those under tubs. For toilets, flush them, pour a gallon of the antifreeze solution into each tank, then flush again. With bathtubs and other traps you can't get at, use a quart of full-strength antifreeze.

Water collects in dishwashers and washing machines, too. You'll have to siphon out these completely—but don't pour antifreeze into these appliances or any fresh-water pipes. Finally, fill your home's main trap with antifreeze.

To refill a drained system, turn off all faucets, then open the main water supply valve gradually. Expect some sputtering at first as the water pushes air out of the lines. Don't worry about the traps; antifreeze that was poured into them will be washed away by wastewater.

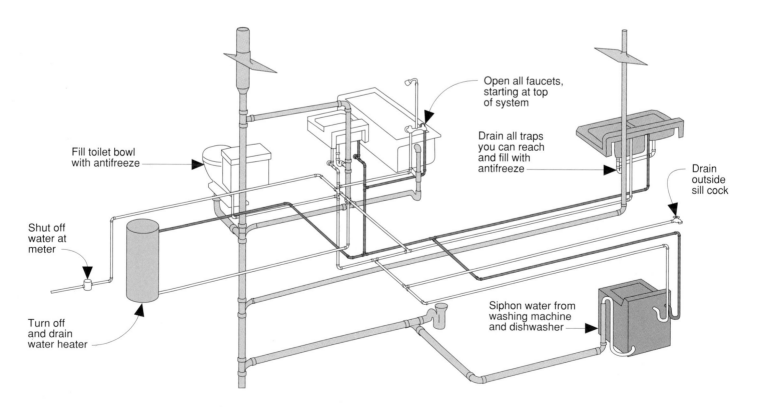

Open all faucets, starting at top of system

Fill toilet bowl with antifreeze

Drain all traps you can reach and fill with antifreeze

Drain outside sill cock

Shut off water at meter

Turn off and drain water heater

Siphon water from washing machine and dishwasher

QUIETING NOISY PIPES

Pressure can get to any of us from time to time, and believe it or not, the same thing is true of your water system. Under the considerable load of 60 pounds of pressure per square inch, your home's water pipes often can make a nerve-racking array of noises. But don't assume that you can't do anything to silence them; you can. The more common maladies and how to cure them are discussed here.

Water hammer is the loud bang you hear when you open a faucet, run the water, and quickly close the faucet. Hammering is terribly common. Automatic washing machines also may produce this sound when a solenoid valve snaps shut. Most house fixtures have an air chamber, which eventually fills with water and causes the hammering.

The solution is to drain, then refill, the system. The air chambers will fill with air again and shouldn't act up for several years.

If your system isn't outfitted with chambers, install one at the faucet fixture. This chamber provides a "cushion" of air on which the bang can bounce (see below).

Machine-gun rattle signals a faucet problem. Try replacing the washers in the faucet (see pages 285–289).

A whistle indicates that a water valve somewhere in the system is closed partially. The water, under pressure, narrows at the valve and causes the whistle. Open the valve as far as you can. If a toilet whistles, adjust the inlet valve (see page 294).

If you hear water running through the system, check for leaks at toilets, sill cocks, the furnace humidifier, and your water softener.

Soft ticking or cracking usually can be traced to a hot water pipe that was cool, then suddenly reheated with water. Insulate the pipe to muffle the noise.

Bangs may result from water pressure in the pipes that causes them to bang against metal hangers or wall studs. Have someone quickly open and close the faucet to cause a bang while you watch to see if the pipes move.

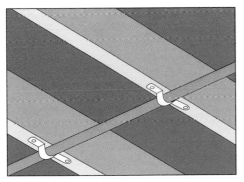

To stop bangs and squeaks, nail pipe hangers as shown. Do not use galvanized hangers on copper pipes.

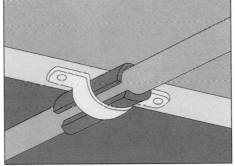

Soundproof pipes that rattle against hangers using short lengths of rubber hose, split lengthwise.

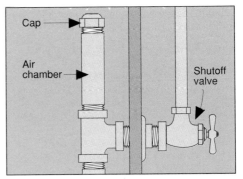

An air chamber is a length of pipe above the supply pipe, usually located near a faucet or fixture shutoff.

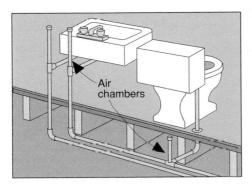

If you're remodeling or building a new house, here's an air-chamber diagram for a lavatory and toilet.

Some air chambers are designed to be added to your washer hookups and are available at plumbing stores. To install them, unscrew the supply hoses and insert the chamber between the valve and hose.

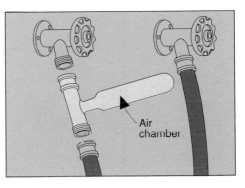

Solving Plumbing Problems (continued)

COPING WITH PRESSURE PROBLEMS

Water pressure is one of those things of which you can have too much or too little. If you have too much pressure in your lines, you need a pressure-reducing valve, which you can install easily.

If you're suffering from too little pressure, your immediate task is to locate the source of the problem, assuming it's not a problem with your municipal supply system.

Start by removing aerators and showerheads from fixtures. If the strainers are blocked with sediment and lime deposits, clean them. Make sure all shutoff valves are opened fully; partly closed valves slow water flow considerably.

If your water source is a well with an automatic pump, the pressure regulator at the pump may be set too low. Also check for a loose pump belt. During winter months, a frozen pipe or pressure switch can cause low pressure.

If none of the obvious checks produce any results, break a connection in the water system. If you find lime deposits inside the pipe, you may need new plumbing.

Do not try to flush a limed system with chemicals. Professional plumbers, however, can flush sediment from the pipes.

If liming is a problem in your area, the cheapest and easiest way to correct it is to install a water softener on cold as well as hot lines (see page 326).

But before calling in a plumber, call the municipal water department and ask them to check the water main leading into your home. It could be faulty.

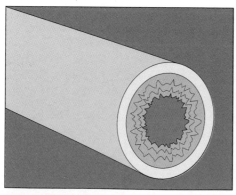

Open all supply valves, then turn off water at the main and check valve parts for damage, corrosion, or liming.

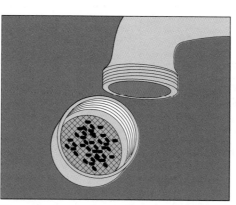

Unscrew aerators on faucet spouts to clean out debris. If the wire strainer is badly corroded, replace it.

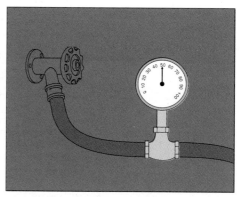

A pressure gauge is an easy way to check the water pressure. It should be 50 to 60 pounds per square inch.

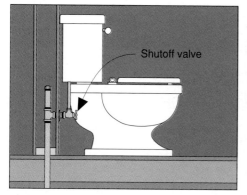

Limed pipes slow water to a trickle. If flushing the system doesn't help, the house will need to be replumbed.

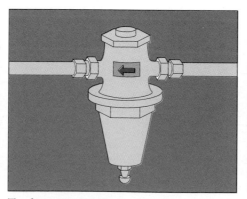

To decrease pressure, install a pressure-reducing valve. The further open the valve, the less the pressure.

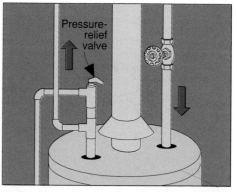

If the water heater doesn't have a relief valve, install one. Without one, water pressure could reach dangerous levels.

Making Plumbing Improvements

Like carpenters, plumbers divide their work into two general categories—roughing-in and finishing. In the roughing-in stage, sections of pipe are cut to length and pieced together with a variety of standardized fittings. The job is finished off by hooking a fixture to the new lines.

The balance of this chapter takes you step-by-step through both phases of a plumbing project—from those critical first measurements to the moment you turn on the water and check your work for leaks.

The key to visualizing how a plumbing run will go together lies with the fittings illustrated on page 302. Plumbing components are made from a wide variety of materials (see page 303), but all are joined together with similar elbows, couplings, tees, and other connecting devices.

Note, however, that the chart on page 303 indicates different materials for water supply and drain-waste-vent (DWV) piping. These fittings are not interchangeable, even when they're made of the same materials. That's because drainage fittings have smooth insides to allow water flow. On the other hand, because supply fittings are under pressure, their slight restrictions don't critically impede the flow.

MEASURING PIPES AND FITTINGS

Before you buy parts for any pipe-fitting project, you first must establish the diameters and sometimes—especially if you're purchasing prethreaded stock—the exact lengths of the pipe you'll be dealing with. Computing both dimensions is not tricky once you learn a few rules.

Pipes always are sized by their inside diameters. Thus, the best way to determine accurately what you need is to saw open a section of the pipe run you'll be tying into and measure the pipe—not its fittings—as illustrated below.

Don't be surprised to discover that the inside diameter turns out to be slightly larger or smaller than a standard pipe size. So-called 1-inch steel pipe, for instance, may be slightly greater or slightly less than 1 inch inside, depending on the thickness of its walls. Rounding off your measurement to the nearest 1/8 inch will give you the nominal dimension you need.

The thing to keep in mind when you're figuring lengths is that you have to account for the distance each pipe engages in its fittings, as well as the distance between fittings. To do this, first measure from face to face, then add on the socket depths, as shown below. Socket depths vary somewhat from one pipe material to another, but remain the same for all fittings of a given material.

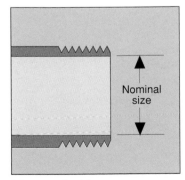

Measure inside—not outside—pipe diameters. Actual and nominal dimensions can vary by 1/16 inch or so.

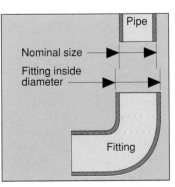

Fittings are sized according to the pipes' inside dimensions, so measuring a fitting doesn't tell you much.

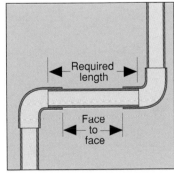

A pipe that's too short may leak at one or both ends. For accuracy, compute the length from face to face.

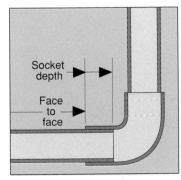

Check socket depths. Pipes have fittings on both ends, so multiply by two, then add the face-to-face length.

Making Plumbing Improvements (continued)

MATERIAL MATTERS · KNOWING PLUMBING FITTINGS

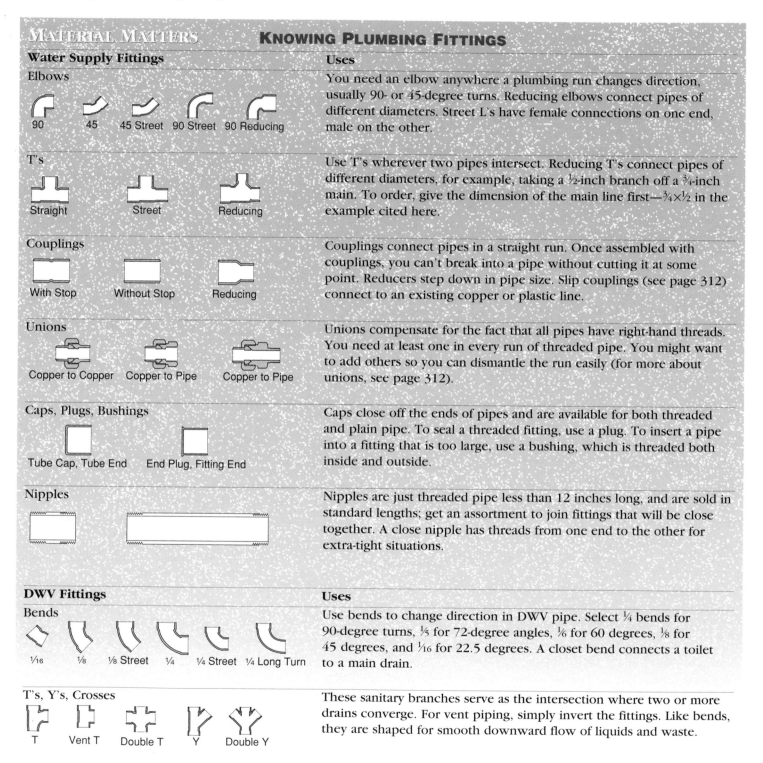

Water Supply Fittings | Uses

Elbows

90   45   45 Street   90 Street   90 Reducing

You need an elbow anywhere a plumbing run changes direction, usually 90- or 45-degree turns. Reducing elbows connect pipes of different diameters. Street L's have female connections on one end, male on the other.

T's

Straight   Street   Reducing

Use T's wherever two pipes intersect. Reducing T's connect pipes of different diameters, for example, taking a ½-inch branch off a ¾-inch main. To order, give the dimension of the main line first—¾×½ in the example cited here.

Couplings

With Stop   Without Stop   Reducing

Couplings connect pipes in a straight run. Once assembled with couplings, you can't break into a pipe without cutting it at some point. Reducers step down in pipe size. Slip couplings (see page 312) connect to an existing copper or plastic line.

Unions

Copper to Copper   Copper to Pipe   Copper to Pipe

Unions compensate for the fact that all pipes have right-hand threads. You need at least one in every run of threaded pipe. You might want to add others so you can dismantle the run easily (for more about unions, see page 312).

Caps, Plugs, Bushings

Tube Cap, Tube End   End Plug, Fitting End

Caps close off the ends of pipes and are available for both threaded and plain pipe. To seal a threaded fitting, use a plug. To insert a pipe into a fitting that is too large, use a bushing, which is threaded both inside and outside.

Nipples

Nipples are just threaded pipe less than 12 inches long, and are sold in standard lengths; get an assortment to join fittings that will be close together. A close nipple has threads from one end to the other for extra-tight situations.

DWV Fittings | Uses

Bends

¹⁄₁₆   ⅛   ⅛ Street   ¼   ¼ Street   ¼ Long Turn

Use bends to change direction in DWV pipe. Select ¼ bends for 90-degree turns, ⅕ for 72-degree angles, ⅙ for 60 degrees, ⅛ for 45 degrees, and ¹⁄₁₆ for 22.5 degrees. A closet bend connects a toilet to a main drain.

T's, Y's, Crosses

T   Vent T   Double T   Y   Double Y

These sanitary branches serve as the intersection where two or more drains converge. For vent piping, simply invert the fittings. Like bends, they are shaped for smooth downward flow of liquids and waste.

SELECTING PIPES AND FITTINGS

The type of pipe you'll need may depend on the plumbing code in your area. You also must consider the function the pipe will serve. Some types of pipe can be used only in drain-waste-vent (DWV) systems; others can't carry hot or drinking water. Also, you'll need to know what type of pipes currently are in your house. You needn't stick with the same type—but you'll need special fittings if you're going to join pipes of different materials.

We've divided the possibilities into four categories: copper, threaded, plastic, and cast iron.

Copper pipe is the most widely used, and virtually all codes permit it. It is more expensive than other types, but it's lightweight, versatile, and resistant to corrosion.

Threaded pipe is rarely used today. Cutting, threading, and turning threaded pipe is difficult. Also, steel limes up and rusts out in a decade.

Plastic pipe is the easiest to work with, but you can't use it in every situation and under some codes.

Cast iron pipe is the heaviest and most difficult to work with, although no-hub clamps make smaller jobs feasible for do-it-yourselfers.

MATERIAL MATTERS COMPARING PIPE MATERIALS

Material		Uses	Joining Techniques/Features
Copper	Rigid	Hot and cold water lines; DWV	Joints usually sweat-soldered (see page 304); its light weight makes it easy to handle
	Flexible	Hot and cold water lines	Solder or compression joints (see page 305); comes in coils; easily bent; too soft for exposed locations; fittings expensive
Threaded	Galvanized steel	Hot and cold water lines; DWV; don't use for gas	Comes in 21-foot lengths that you cut, thread, and join with fittings; time-consuming
	Black steel	Gas and steam or hot-water heating lines	Same as galvanized pipe, but not used for household water due to rust
Plastic	Rigid ABS	DWV only	Cut with saw; solvent-weld (see page 307); light and easy to work with; not allowed by all codes
	Rigid PVC	Cold water and DWV only	Same as ABS
	Rigid CPVC	Hot and cold water lines	Same as ABS
	Flexible polybutylene	Hot and cold water lines	Join with fittings shown on page 308; expensive and not widely used
	Flexible polyethylene	Cold water lines only; used mainly for sprinkler systems	Same as polybutylene
Cast-Iron	Bell and spigot	DWV only	Joints packed with oakum, then sealed with molten lead
	No-hub	DWV only	Join sections with gaskets and clamps (see page 310); not too difficult for do-it-yourselfers

Making Plumbing Improvements (continued)

WORKING WITH RIGID COPPER PIPE

Rigid copper pipe comes in 10- and 20-foot lengths and in one of three different wall thicknesses. The thinnest of these, Type M, is approved for interior use by most local codes. A few codes call for medium-wall Type L. Type K has a thick wall and is required for underground runs. Fittings include most of those shown on page 302.

Professional plumbers preassemble runs of copper pipe, fluxing and dry-fitting each joint, without soldering them. When everything fits together properly, they go back and solder all the joints.

After you solder a joint, examine it for gaps around its perimeter. Leaks that don't show up until after you turn on the water mean you have to completely disassemble the joint to resolder it.

When you're using a blowtorch, protect nearby flammable surfaces with sheet metal.

YOU'LL NEED...

SKILLS: Intermediate plumbing skills.
TIME: 10 to 20 minutes per joint.
TOOLS: Tubing cutter or hacksaw, round file, steel wool, flux brush, blowtorch.

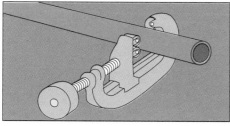

1. A tubing cutter does a fast, neat job of cutting copper pipe to length. If you use a hacksaw, keep the cut square.

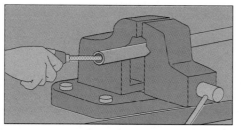

2. If you cut pipe with a hacksaw or a pipe cutter's reamer, use a file to remove all metal burrs from the cut.

3. Shine the ends of the pipe with a fine-grit abrasive or steel wool to remove grease and dirt.

4. Apply rosin-flux (not acid-flux) soldering paste to the outside of the pipe's end and inside the pipe fitting.

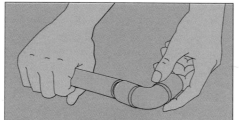

5. Slip the fitting onto the pipe. If the fitting has a hub or shoulder, make sure the pipe is seated against it.

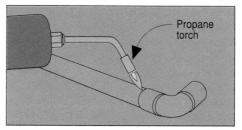

Propane torch

6. Heat the pipe and fitting where they join. The tip of the inner flame on a blowtorch produces the most heat.

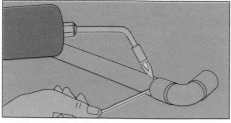

7. Test the pipe for temperature. If the solder melts, the temperature is right. Solder will flow into the connection.

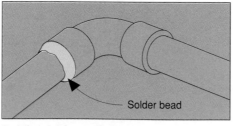

Solder bead

8. The solder will flow around the joint. When the bead is complete, quit applying solder and remove heat.

9. For a professional appearance, wipe the joint with a cloth. Be careful not to get burned, though.

WORKING WITH FLEXIBLE COPPER TUBING

Flexible copper tubing is very workable. Use care when bending it, however, because it kinks easily. Once kinked, it's almost impossible to bend back into its original round shape and should not be used because it impedes water flow.

There are two weights of flexible copper tubing: Type K, generally used for underground installations, and Type L, for interior runs. Both come in 15-, 30-, and 60-foot rolls at plumbing and home center stores.

You can assemble runs with solder and standard connections (see page 304), with flare fittings, or with (see page 304) compression fittings. Flare and compression fittings cost more than solder fittings, but assemble more easily and don't require heat for soldering, an advantage when working in close quarters between wall studs and floor joists.

Consider soldering connections that you'll never need to break; save the more costly fittings for hooking up fixtures that might need to be removed someday.

To form flare fittings, you'll need a flaring tool (see below). Be sure to put flare nuts on the tubing before flaring the ends. Then, once you've flared the tubing ends, you just screw special fittings together.

With compression fittings, simply slip a compression ring over the tubing. The ring compresses and seals when the fittings are screwed together. The drawings below show how to join flexible tubing with both types of fittings.

YOU'LL NEED...

SKILLS: Intermediate plumbing skills.
TIME: 10 to 20 minutes per fitting.
TOOLS: Spring bender, wrenches, flaring tool.

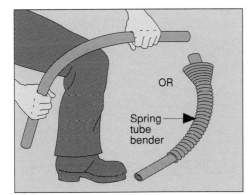

Bend flexible copper tubing over your knee or with a spring tube bender. Make gentle bends, not acute angles.

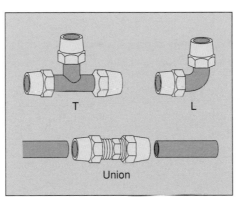

Fittings include T's, L's, unions, and a variety of adapters for hooking to other types of pipe.

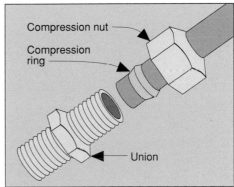

A compression joint has a ring that compresses under pressure of the fitting, producing a leak-free joint.

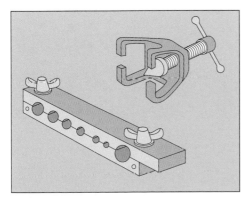

A flaring tool is a two-piece unit. Different-sized beveled holes in the block fit different sizes of tubing.

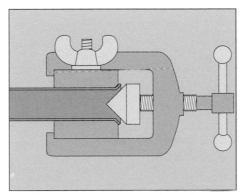

Put flare nuts on pipe, then clamp pipe in the block. Center the flaring part of the tool over the tubing, then tighten.

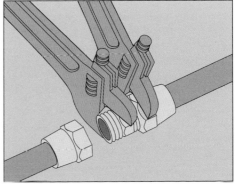

After making the flares, use wrenches to connect the joint. If the joint leaks under pressure, reflare the joint.

Making Plumbing Improvements (continued)

WORKING WITH THREADED PIPE

Although copper and plastic pipe now offer better alternatives, plumbers have been threading together steel, iron, brass, and bronze pipes for a century or so. Unless your home is fairly new, at least some of its plumbing may consist of this old-fashioned system.

If you need only a few sections of threaded pipe, measure carefully, then order them precut and prethreaded. For larger jobs, it may pay to thread your own pipe. You'll need a vise; pipe cutter; a threading die and die stock, which you can rent; and a reamer.

The key to threading pipe is to start the die squarely on the pipe. You must get it right the first time or the threads won't thread.

The length of the thread varies with pipe diameter. For ⅛-inch pipe, you should have ¼ inch of threads. For ¼- and ⅜-inch pipe, use ⅜ inch of threads; for ½- and ¾-inch pipes, ½ inch of threads; and 1-inch pipe requires ⁹⁄₁₆ inch of threads.

To measure the length of pipe needed, measure between the face of each fitting, plus the distance into the fittings. For example, if you're working with ¾-inch pipe and the distance between the face of each fitting is 4 feet, you'll need a piece of pipe 4 feet, 1 inch long.

If you're replacing a piece of pipe and threading the pipe yourself, remember to include a union fitting in the measurement. The same threading distance applies to unions as for the other fittings.

> ### YOU'LL NEED...
> **SKILLS:** Intermediate plumbing skills.
> **TIME:** 15 minutes to thread both ends of a pipe.
> **TOOLS:** Pipe cutter, reamer, vise, threading die and die stock, pipe wrenches.

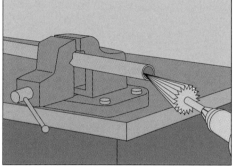

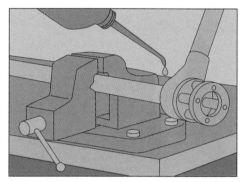

1. To cut pipe, clamp it tightly in a vise and cut with a pipe cutter. The sharp metal wheel does the cutting.

2. Remove burrs from the inside of the pipe with a reamer powered by a brace or drill. Remove just the burrs.

3. Lock the die in the stock. Place the die squarely on the pipe and begin turning. Apply oil to aid cutting.

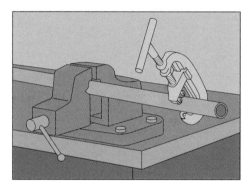

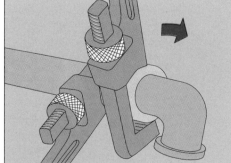

4. Apply pipe dope or Teflon pipe tape (clockwise) to the pipe threads (not to the fitting threads).

5. Hold pipe with one pipe wrench, as you turn the fitting onto the pipe with another. Tighten as far as possible.

WORKING WITH RIGID PLASTIC PIPE

Rigid plastic pipe offers great opportunities for professionals and do-it-yourselfers alike. It's the lightest of all pipe materials, cuts with an ordinary saw, and glues together with fittings and special solvent cement.

Be warned, however, that because plastic pipe is relatively new to plumbing, a few localities still prohibit or restrict its use. So before you spend a dime on plastic pipe or fittings, check the plumbing codes in your area to find out if plastic is allowed and in which situations.

There are three types of plastic pipe—CPVC (chlorinated polyvinyl chloride), PVC (polyvinyl chloride), and ABS (acrylonitrile butadiene styrene). Only CPVC pipe can be used for hot water supply lines. Don't mix these materials; they require different joining solvents and expand at different rates.

Keep expansion in mind, too, when you're assembling runs of plastic pipe, especially CPVC. Plastic pipe does expand when hot water runs through it. Provide plenty of clearance between fittings and framing, and bore oversized holes where the pipes pass through wood. Otherwise, the system will creak, squeak, groan, and maybe even leak every time you turn on a water tap or run hot water into a drain.

Solvent-welding plastic fittings calls for no special tools or skills.

Alignment is critical, however, because once you've made a connection, the joint is permanent. Make a mistake and you have to cut out the fitting and install a new one.

Solvent-welded joints don't reach working strength for 16 to 48 hours. Thus, your family may have to do without running water for a full day or more after you've completed an installation.

YOU'LL NEED...
SKILLS: Basic plumbing skills.
TIME: 10 minutes per joint.
TOOLS: Backsaw, miter box, utility knife.

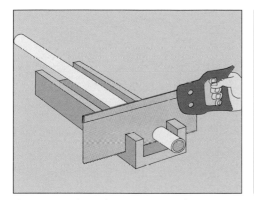

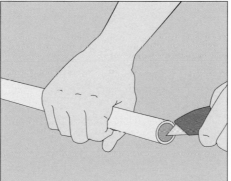

1. Using a bench jig or miter box, cut rigid plastic pipe with a backsaw. Be sure the cut is absolutely square.

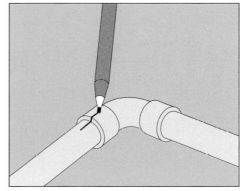

2. Carefully remove the burrs made by the hacksaw with a sharp knife. Tip the pipe so debris will fall out.

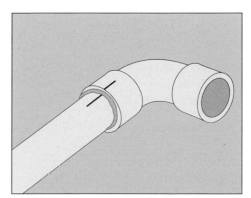

3. To ensure proper alignment, dry-fit pipe and fittings, making alignment marks, before applying solvent.

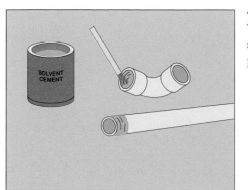

4. Lightly sand the outside of the pipe. Wipe it with a clean cloth and apply solvent cement to the outside of the pipe and the inside of the fitting.

5. Assemble the connection with a quarter turn to distribute the solvent cement. A bead of solvent should form around the fitting.

Making Plumbing Improvements (continued)

WORKING WITH FLEXIBLE PLASTIC PIPE

Flexible plastic pipe is available in polybutylene (PB) or polyethylene (PE) types. PB tubing can be used for hot and cold water supplies with pressures up to 100 psi (pounds per square inch) and temperatures up to 180°F. PE tubing, used for cold water systems only (such as sprinkler systems), can withstand pressures up to 125 psi and 100°F temperatures.

Unlike rigid plastic, flexible plastic pipe fits together with clamps or compression fittings instead of cement. You can buy many kinds of fittings—T's, L's, and straight connections—in a variety of diameters to fit various pipe sizes. Conversion fittings let you join the pipe to metal plumbing pipes.

Although flexible plastic pipe is "flexible," don't overdo it; it can kink. Bend it into gentle curves. The product is rigid enough to support itself on long runs, but it's best to use support hangers every 32 inches.

There are no special tricks in working with flexible plastic pipe. You can cut it with a hacksaw or even a utility knife. PE pipe softens when it becomes warm. Connections on aboveground installations may expand during hot summer months, causing leaks. Check and tighten these joints regularly.

Plastic pipe used outdoors should be drained during cold weather to prevent frozen water from cracking and breaking it. Because the plastic is weather-resistant, you needn't disconnect and store the system during cold weather.

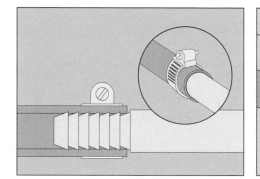

For PE tubing, use stainless steel worm-type clamps to fasten fittings. Position the clamp so it tightens on the entire shoulder of the fitting.

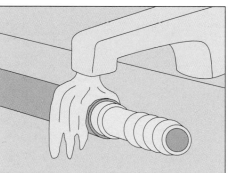

To break loose a clamped connection on PE tubing, soak it under hot water to expand the PE tubing. Do not use a propane torch.

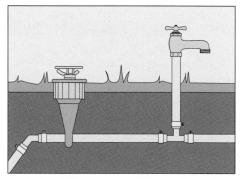

Because tight bends will kink flexible tubing, use T and L fittings to turn corners and make connections, such as on underground sprinkler systems.

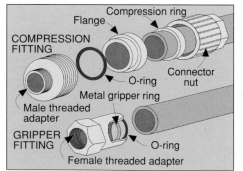

PB plastic tubing fits together with either compression or gripper fittings. T's, L's, and other fittings are available.

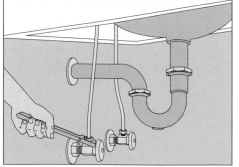

Because PB tubing can be used for hot or cold water supplies, it makes a good choice for stop-to-fixture hookups.

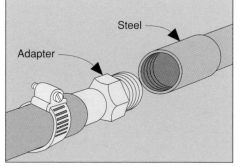

Many adapters are available to join either PE or PB plastic pipe to other plumbing materials.

WORKING WITH CAST-IRON PIPE

Until recently, installing cast-iron DWV systems was all but out of the question for do-it-yourself plumbers.

A new system, however, uses no-hub cast-iron pipes. With these, you simply couple sections with a special neoprene gasket and an automotive-type clamp (see page 310). You need no special tools, and if a fitting comes out a little cockeyed, it takes only a minute to loosen the clamp, twist everything the way you want it, and retighten it.

Best of all, no-hub components are compatible with hub-and-spigot piping, so if you ever have to cut into an existing cast-iron soil pipe, you can simply cut out a section and slip in a no hub T (see page 310).

No-hub joints eliminate most, but not all, of the hassles involved in working with cast-iron. Wrestling 5- and 10-foot lengths of this heavy material into place is hard work. Cutting cast-iron pipe can be a problem, too, unless you rent specialized equipment or measure and buy precut lengths.

Faced with a sizable DWV installation that calls for a new soil stack, it's best to have a professional install the stack. You can run drain and vent lines from the fixtures to the stack. (For more about DWV systems, see pages 311–312.)

Be sure, too, that you properly brace the pipes with supports at each fitting and every 4 feet on straight runs. Drawings on page 310 show commonly available hangers.

YOU'LL NEED...

SKILLS: Basic plumbing skills.
TIME: 10 to 15 minutes to cut a pipe.
TOOLS: Hacksaw, cold chisel, small sledgehammer, chain cutter.

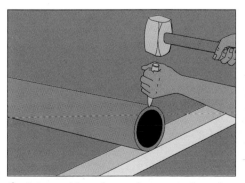

1. To cut cast-iron pipe, measure the length you need. Scribe the cutoff line on the pipe with a wax pencil.

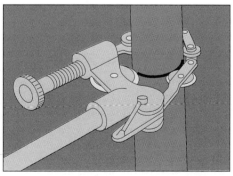

2. Elevate the pipe on a scrap piece of lumber and make inch-long cuts around the pipe's circumference.

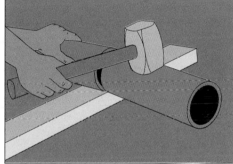

3. Along the saw kerf, rap the pipe smartly with a small sledge; it should fracture cleanly at the cut.

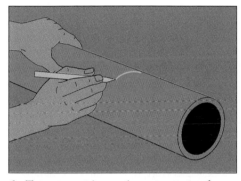

4. A jagged break can be evened up by tapping with a cold chisel and hammer. Edges don't have to be glassy smooth.

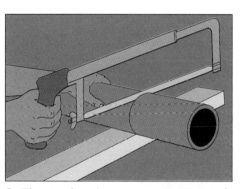

5. Use a chain cutter for large-diameter pipes. The chain secures the pipe as the cutting wheel scores the surface.

Making Plumbing Improvements (continued)

WORKING WITH CAST-IRON PIPE (continued)

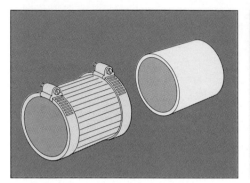

A no-hub connector consists of a neoprene sleeve and metal clamp that tightens with worm-drive screws.

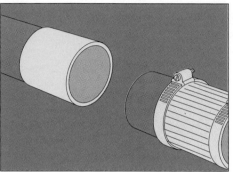

To assemble joints, remove burrs from the pipe ends, then slip the clamp and neoprene sleeve onto the pipe.

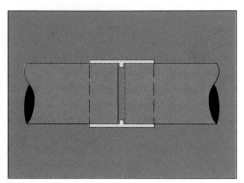

Push the pipes together so that the ends butt, separated only by the inner ridge of the sleeve.

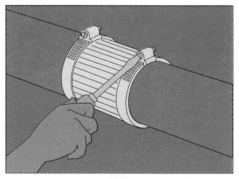

Center the clamp over the sleeve and tighten with a screwdriver or special T-wrench. Don't overtighten.

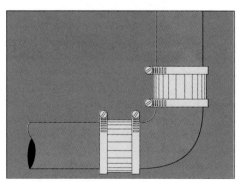

Bends and all other fittings go together the same way. You'll need a sleeve and clamp for each end of the fitting.

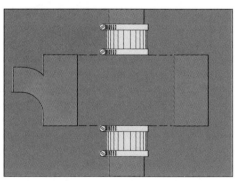

Here's how to fit a no-hub T into an existing run. Slip clamps over the ends, then position the fitting.

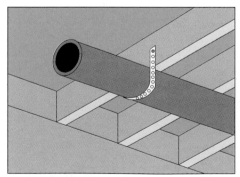

Support horizontal runs with pipe straps or hangers. This type attaches to the faces of floor joists.

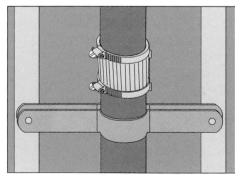

Two-piece hangers serve as a clamp to hold vertical runs. Install one below each joint and at floor level.

CONNECTING TO DWV LINES

Thinking about adding a new fixture in your house? If so, you've probably wondered where the water's going to come from—and where it's going to go.

Of the two parts to this problem, the first is relatively easy to solve. Small-diameter supply lines zigzag easily through tight spots. Because they're under pressure, you can extend them almost any distance.

DWV lines are another matter. These pipes are much larger and more difficult to conceal. And even more critical, you have to ensure that a new fixture is properly vented. Otherwise, vacuum in the drainage system could suck water from the fixture's trap and let sewer gas back up into the house.

Does this mean you have to install a vent, as well as a drain, for each and every fixture? Fortunately, most plumbing codes let you dispense with individual venting under certain circumstances (see below).

The most common of these exceptions—wet venting—requires locating the fixture within a specified distance from your home's soil stack (see bottom, left illustration)—and the fixture must drain only liquid wastes. This means you can wet-vent a lavatory, tub, or shower, but not a toilet or kitchen sink. Get advice from a professional plumber before you plan DWV hookups for such solid-waste carriers.

It makes sense to situate a new fixture as close as possible to existing lines. The alternative is to install an entirely new stack—something you might consider if you're contemplating a major installation, such as a new bathroom.

When you're measuring distances, don't neglect to allow for a slope of ¼ inch per foot (or whatever local code calls for) from the fixture to the main drain. It may be necessary to elevate a tub or shower to provide proper drainage.

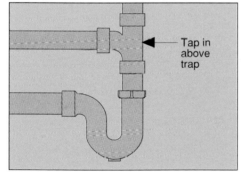

You can drain two lavatories or sinks into the same trap, provided that their drain outlets are no more than 30 inches apart.

Unit venting allows fixtures to be placed back to back, discharging into the same vent-waste line. Each fixture has its own trap.

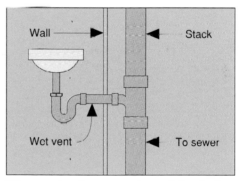

Wet venting lets a portion of the drain line also serve as a vent. Not all fixtures can be wet-vented (see above). And not all codes allow wet venting.

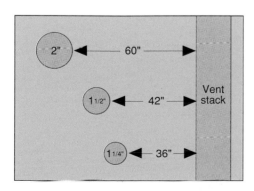

Maximum wet-vent distances depend on the size of the fixture's drain. The specifications shown are typical, but check your local code.

Existing fixtures may tie into a stack via a circuit vent. If so, you can install a new fixture between the main stack and the circuit stack.

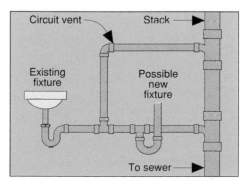

Making Plumbing Improvements (continued)

TAPPING INTO SUPPLY LINES
Using Saddle T's

Looking for a way to run a new pipe without breaking a connection in the old run? Simply clamp on one of the saddle fittings shown at right, drill a hole, and hook up your new run.

Turn off the water, open a faucet to drain the pipe, strap on the saddle, and mark the hole with a center punch. Remove the saddle and drill a hole in the existing pipe. File away rough edges.

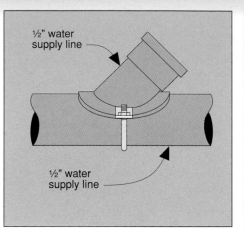
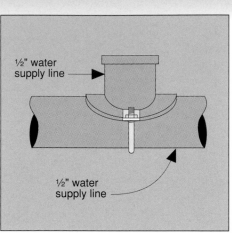

Using Slip Rings

Copper, threaded, or plastic rigid pipe doesn't have enough flex to pop a T into an existing run, so you have to install either a union (see below) or a slip ring. For a slip ring, cut the line and remove a section large enough to fit the T and a spacer that will help tie the T into the existing line (see right). Fit the T, spacer, and slip ring into the run, slide the ring into position, and solder or solvent-weld the joints.

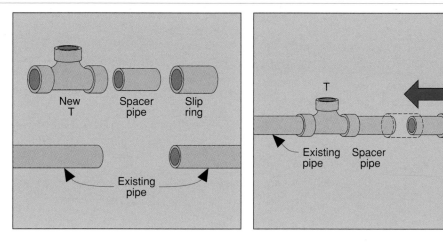

Using Unions

Unions compensate for the fact that all pipe threads in the same direction. If there's a union in the existing run, loosen its union ring, pull apart the fitting, and remove pipe on one side or the other. Now, install a new T and nipple, then reassemble, as illustrated.

If there's no union in the existing run, simply cut into the line wherever you need to add one.

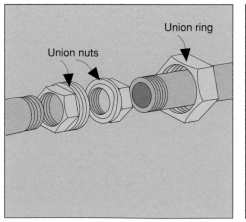
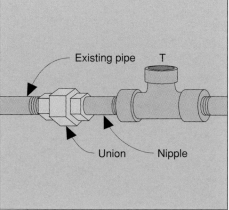

ROUGHING-IN PLUMBING LINES

Plotting Dimensions

Once you know where and how you're going to tie into your home's existing plumbing system, it's time to pinpoint exactly where new lines will go. The best way to do this is to purchase your new fixture(s), then mark the rough dimensions on the floor and wall, as shown.

Don't let the word "rough" mislead you. Accuracy is essential. The measurements shown here are typical ones, but check your fixtures for specifics.

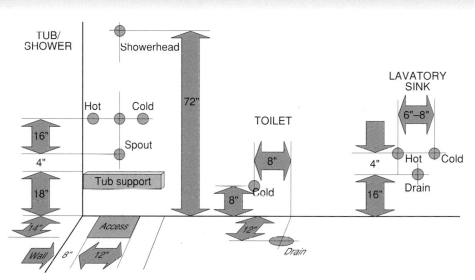

Supporting Exposed Pipe

Pipe runs must be supported to take the weight off threaded, soldered, or cemented connections. This is done with pipe hangers, wood scraps, or wire hangers. If you are using metal pipe, be sure to use only hangers that are made of the same metal as the pipe or plastic hangers.

Space hangers every 3 feet. Plastic and copper pipe, however, need more support than galvanized steel. Although plastic and copper won't kink, they belly-down when filled with water. The weight can break connections and cause a serious leak. Plastic also needs more room for expansion, as explained on page 307. Where a pipe makes a 90-degree turn, support it with wood brace or use a strap hanger to support it.

If the pipe snakes along a masonry wall, hangers often can be installed with concrete nails. Drive the nails flush with the hangers, then stop hammering—extra "finishing" taps will loosen the nails.

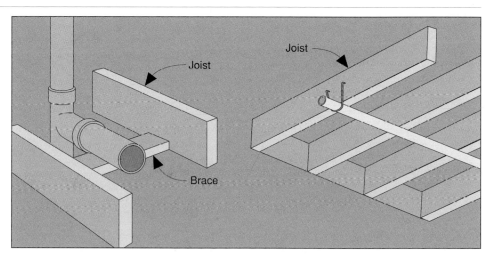

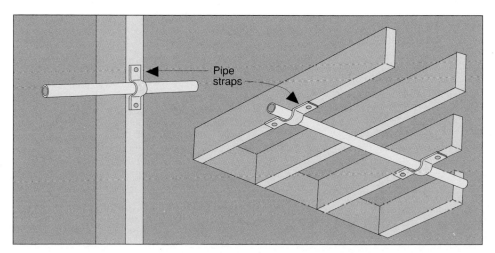

Making Plumbing Improvements (continued)

ROUGHING-IN (continued)
Notching Studs and Joists

Supporting pipes that pass through walls, under floors, or over ceilings is easy—just cut notches in the framing members or bore holes through them. Some plumbers prefer to notch; others like to bore. Boring weakens a member less than notching, but may create problems when assembling long runs.

If a notch will be located in the upper half of a stud—usually 4 feet or more above the floor—you can safely cut away up to two-thirds of the stud's depth. In the lower half of a stud, don't notch more than one-third of its depth, unless you reinforce it as shown below. You can bore anywhere along a stud's length, provided you leave the clearance indicated.

Never notch a joist more than one-fourth of its depth—and keep the notch toward the ends. Always reinforce joists.

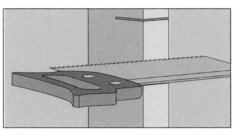

Make notches in studs with a handsaw. Measure and lay out the cuts; don't guess at the width, depth, or height.

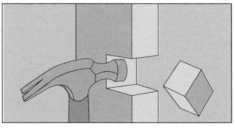

With a chisel, score a line between the ends of the saw kerfs, then knock out the notches with a hammer.

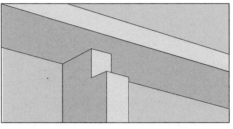

If the notch is next to a header or sill, cut notch with a hacksaw, as you may encounter nails. Renail the member.

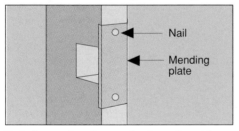

Nail

Mending plate

Reinforce deeply notched studs with metal mending plates. You'll have to mortise it if the studs will be covered.

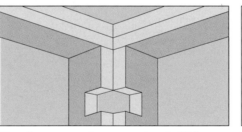

Notch a corner by removing half from each framing member. A 90-degree pipe L will fit snugly in the notch.

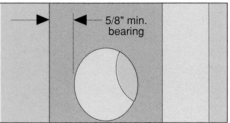

5/8" min. bearing

Leave ⅝ inch of wood around bored holes. Pipes should fit fairly snugly; but plastic pipe needs room for expansion.

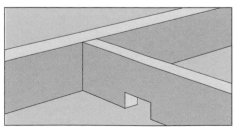

Notch joists near ends, not near the center. Cut the notch to fit the pipe. Big, sloppy cuts weaken the framing.

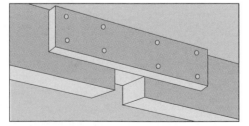

Always reinforce joists with wood strips nailed to both sides of the joist. You can notch the patch, too.

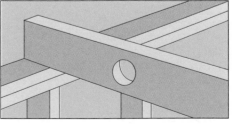

Holes bored in joists should be located near another support member to avoid undue stress on the joist.

INSTALLING SINKS AND LAVATORIES

Once you've roughed in supply and DWV pipes for a new sink, all that remains is to fasten a faucet assembly to the fixture (see page 317), mount the fixture, and fit it with a trap (see page 292).

Sinks and lavatories (bathroom sinks) are made of stainless or enameled steel, porcelainized cast-iron, fiberglass, vitreous china, or synthetic marble products. Deck-mounted types fit into a countertop or cabinet; wall-hung versions rest on brackets and sometimes legs.

Most deck-mounted sinks come with a pattern or basic dimensions to make a cutout template. Take care in laying out the cut, paying special attention to how the drain and supply lines will tie into the fixture. Cut the opening with a sabersaw. In a butcher-block countertop, you may need to make pocket cuts with a circular saw (see page 440), then finish with a sabersaw.

Deck-mounted units may be either rimmed or self-rimming (see drawings below). With some, you need to cut a recess around the opening. The manufacturer usually supplies full installation instructions.

Mount the faucet assembly before you set a sink or lavatory into place. With the bowl upside down or on its side, you'll find it much easier to get at the faucet's locking nuts, rather than working from underneath the sink in often very tight conditions.

Hanging systems for wall-mounted lavatories vary. With most, you fasten a bracket to the wall with toggle bolts or recess a hanging strip into the wall (see below). Make sure the brackets are level, then align slots or lugs in the lavatory's back and lower it into place.

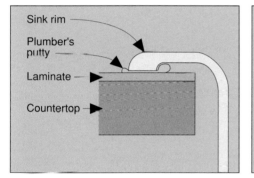

Self-rimming fixtures have a ridge around the bowl that creates a tight seal. The countertop or cabinet may need to be recessed to accept the rim.

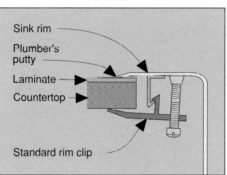

On lightweight self-rimming sinks, such as a stainless steel kitchen sink, screw-down rim clips, like the one shown, hold down the sink tightly.

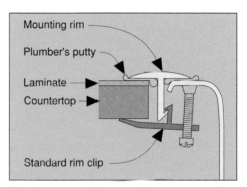

Flush-mounted rimmed fixtures usually have metal strips that sandwich the edge of the fixture. Secure these with rim clips or screws.

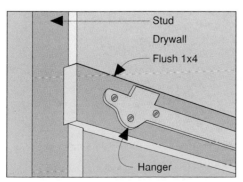

For wall-mounting brackets, recess a 1×4 into studs, making sure the face of the 1×4 is flush with the finished wall.

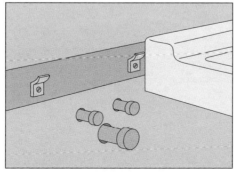

Screw hanging brackets to the 1×4. The bracket style depends on the fixture design. Brackets must be level.

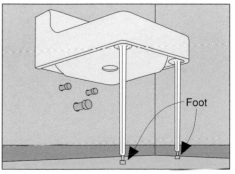

If the sink has legs, attach them under the fixture apron. Unscrew feet until they fully support the fixture's weight.

Making Plumbing Improvements (continued)

INSTALLING TUBS AND SHOWERS

If you're constructing an all-new bath, plan your framing around the installation of tubs and showers. Start by selecting the unit you prefer. Standard tubs measure 4½, 5, and 5½ feet long, but you'll also find plenty of nonstandard sizes.

Enameled-steel tubs are relatively lightweight and inexpensive. They're prone to chipping, however, and are noisy unless you insulate under and around the unit.

Porcelainized cast-iron tubs are more durable, costly, and heavy. Beef up floor joists under these.

Though more expensive than steel or cast-iron versions, fiberglass tubs often include molded wall panels so you needn't worry about tiling or waterproofing around them.

For a shower, you can buy a standard receptor base and build your own enclosure with panels or ceramic tile. Or, you can purchase the entire unit base, walls, and a sliding or folding door—in knockdown kit form.

If you're replacing an old tub with a new one, prepare for a much bigger task. First, you must get the old tub out—major surgery that usually involves chopping into tiling or possibly removing a wall. Next, you have to wrestle the new unit in and adapt framing and plumbing to its dimensions.

The drawings below illustrate typical tub/shower installations and how each of these fixtures fits into new framing. Drain connections call for dropping a trap below the floor. If this isn't feasible, you'll have to elevate the tub. Position faucets, spout, and shower head, as shown.

> ### YOU'LL NEED...
> **SKILLS:** Intermediate plumbing, carpentry, and finishing skills.
> **TIME:** 2 to 3 days.
> **TOOLS:** Pipe cutter, blowtorch, wrenches, hacksaw, handsaw, hammer, screwdriver, drill.

Tying into Framing and Plumbing

The drawing at right shows a typical tub/shower installation. Drain connections call for dropping a trap below the floor. If this isn't feasible, you'll have to elevate the tub.

The enameled-steel tub shown has a flange around its edges that rests on 1×4 cleats; the flange also is nailed to the studs. Recess another 1×4 into the studs to support the showerhead and valve assembly.

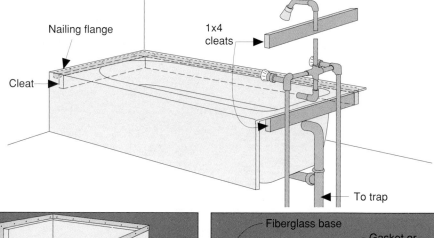

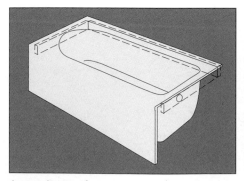

A cast-iron tub rests on 1×4 cleats. Its heavy weight keeps it stable, so you needn't nail it in place.

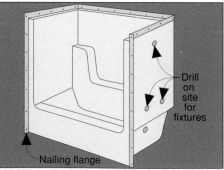

Molded fiberglass tub/shower units have flanges for nailing to studs. Some units dismantle to get into spaces.

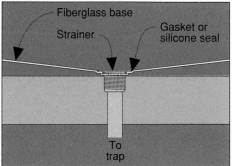

You can position a shower base over a basement floor drain. Seal the drain according to manufacturer's directions.

INSTALLING NEW FAUCETS

Selecting a new faucet is like choosing a pair of shoes—you pick from plenty of styles, then you make sure it fits properly.

If you're replacing an existing faucet, measure the distance between the water supply pipes, as shown below. Or, disconnect the old unit and take it to the store. The new faucet must fit the holes in your fixture exactly.

If, on the other hand, you'll be installing an entirely new fixture, choose the fixture first, then buy a faucet that's compatible. Don't worry about supply connections; flexible plastic tubing connectors let you compensate for differences between the faucet spacing and shutoffs.

Disconnecting an old faucet can be tricky if the old connections are corroded or tough to get at. Shut off the water and slip a bucket under the shutoff valves to catch water that may remain in the pipes. Carefully fit a wrench to the connector nuts (you may need a basin wrench as shown below), and make sure the wrench has a good grip before you apply pressure.

If the connections won't budge, apply penetrating oil, wait for 20 minutes or so, and try again. As a last resort, heat the nuts with the flame from a propane torch, then turn them loose.

The water supply lines to faucets typically connect with compression fittings that thread onto their inlets and are threaded or soldered to the supply lines. If you have to solder, dismantle the faucet's working parts first (see pages 285–288) so they won't be damaged by the heat.

Installing Deck-Mounted Faucets

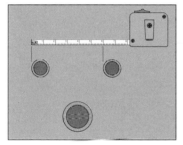

1. For the distance between centers of pipes, measure from the outside edge of one to the other's inside edge.

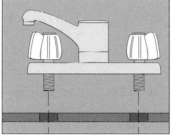

2. Insert the faucet connections in the deck holes. Refer to installation instructions for particulars.

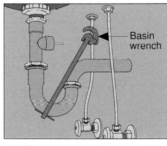

3. To connect pipes in tight quarters, you may need a basin wrench. It can adjust to several positions.

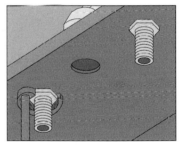

4. Tighten locknuts below the deck before connecting water supply pipes.

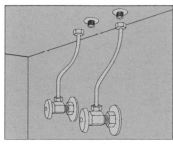

5. Some copper tube connections have flared or compression fittings. Take care not to kink the tubing.

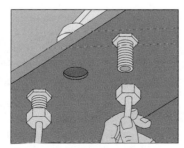

6. If using copper tubing, bend to fit the connections, but don't kink it. Use pipe dope or tape on threads.

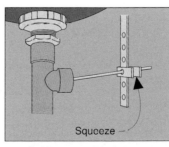

7. The faucet may have a sink pop-up. If so, install the connection on the slide rod below the unit.

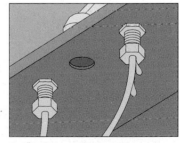

8. Turn on the valves and test pipes and faucet for leaks. If you spot any, tighten the connections.

Making Plumbing Improvements (continued)

INSTALLING NEW FAUCETS (continued)

Installing Wall-Mounted Faucets

Although you gain access to wall-mounted faucets differently than deck-mounted faucets, the same installation techniques apply. Measure the distance between the water supply lines, or take the old faucet to the store to match the fittings on a new faucet.

Because the fittings of wall-mounted faucets usually are chrome-plated, pad the jaws of tools with adhesive tape or bandages.

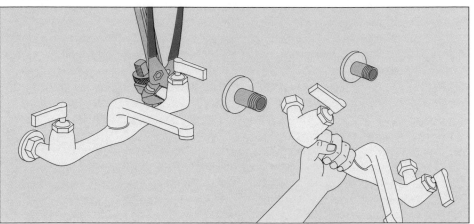

Installing Tub/Shower Faucets

To replace or add faucets to shower and tub assemblies, you must get in back of the finished wall to reach the connections, either through an access panel or by poking a hole in the wall. Whether you cut into the wall from the front or the back, make sure the panel you cut allows plenty of working room.

Close the shutoff valves to the tub and disconnect the faucet. If you're removing soldered connections, protect the wall surfaces from your heat source.

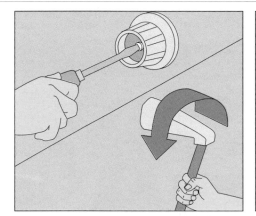

Start by removing the faucet handles, escutcheons, and spout, as shown. Don't mar plated parts.

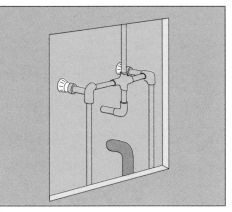

If you must cut an access panel in the wall with a keyhole saw, see pages 34–39 for repair techniques.

Installing a Hand Shower

Hand-held showers mount at either the showerhead or the spout. Combination hand and stationary showers, however, connect to the shower pipe. A showerhead usually is connected to the supply pipe with a threaded fitting. Loosen the fitting to remove the showerhead. If you don't have a shower, replace the tub spout with a diverter type that has a hand shower connection.

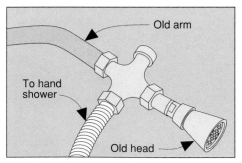

A standard or cross-T fitting may be used for a hand shower. Make sure the T fits all three connections.

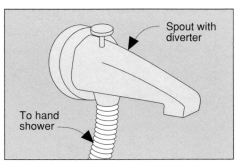

Diverter spouts also channel water to the hand shower. Make sure the new spout threads match those of the pipe.

SELECTING A TOILET

All of a toilet's mechanical action takes place in its flush tank. We show its components and explain how to make repairs there on pages 293–296.

When shopping for a new toilet, it also helps to know the anatomy of the whole unit, illustrated at right. Both tank and bowl are molded of vitreous china. This produces a glaze that's impervious to almost anything but chipping, scratches, and cracks.

Flushing actions differ. All depend on water pressure to create a siphoning action—but some do this more efficiently and quietly than others. The table below compares the three basic modern types. A fourth type, the wash-down toilet, is all but obsolete and prohibited by some codes. If you need to replace one of these, so much for the better.

Regardless of design, floor-standing toilets mount in the same way. A closet flange sits atop a closet bend and accommodates hold-down bolts. These bolts, plus the unit's considerable weight, maintain pressure on a wax or rubber bowl seal that prevents leaks.

ANATOMY OF A TOILET

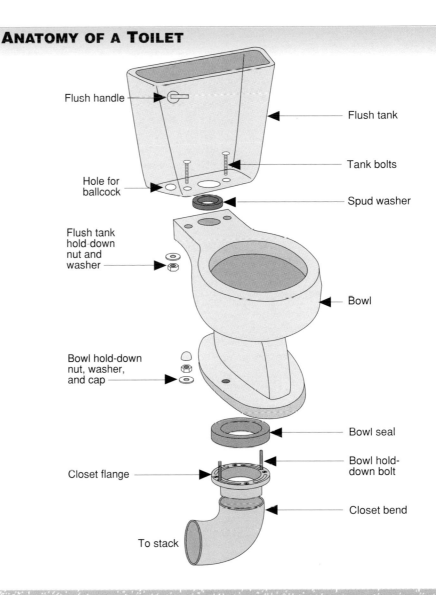

When buying a new toilet, check the distance from the wall (not from the baseboard) to center of closet flange, usually 12 inches. A 10-inch version fits tight situations.

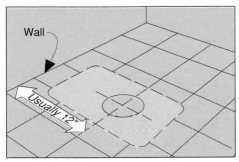

MATERIAL MATTERS FLUSHING ACTION IN TOILETS		
Flow Method	**Description**	**Advantages**
Reverse Trap	Flush through the back of the base for an efficient siphoning action	Relatively quiet flushing action
Siphon Jet	A modification of the reverse trap	Greater water surface area and larger passages within the base reduce likelihood of clogging.
Siphon Vortex	Designed to produce swirling action	Even greater water surface area and whirlpool action ensure efficient flushing.

Making Plumbing Improvements (continued)

INSTALLING A TOILET

Setting and hooking up a toilet is a surprisingly simple operation. With an existing fixture, shut off and disconnect the supply line, flush the tank, then swab out remaining water with an old towel or sponge.

Older tanks attach to the wall via screws through the rear and have an elbow connection to the bowl. Disconnect these and remove the tank. If the tank sits on the bowl, the toilet can be removed in one piece, but separating the tank and bowl makes them easier to handle.

Pry off the caps covering the bowl's hold-down bolts. Remove the nuts—or cut the bolts with a hacksaw if they're rusted on. Lift the bowl off the flange. Keep the flange in place. If it is damaged, you may have a large job that calls for a pro.

Before you install the new bowl, temporarily set it on the flange and check for level. Shim, if necessary, with rustproof metal washers.

Lift off the bowl again, turn it upside down, and fit a wax seal around the bowl's outlet. Run a bead of putty around the outer rim of the bowl's base, so dirt and water won't get underneath. Set the bowl in place, check for level again, and install nuts on the hold-down bolts. Tighten until snug; don't overtighten or you may crack the china.

Fit a spud washer and the tank over the bowl's inlet opening, secure with bolts, and hook up the water supply. If there's no shutoff valve on the supply line, now's the time to install one.

> ### YOU'LL NEED...
> **SKILLS:** Basic plumbing skills.
> **TIME:** 2 to 3 hours.
> **TOOLS:** Wrenches, screwdriver, putty knife, hacksaw.

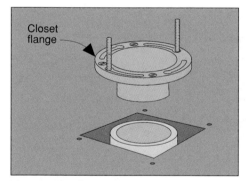

To install a flange on new installations, apply cement to the drain pipe and flange and screw flange to the floor.

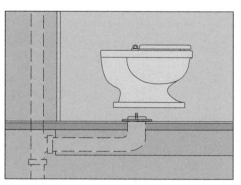

Set the bowl in place with a slight twisting motion but don't rock or lift it again—you could break the seal.

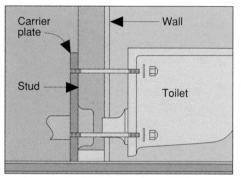

Wall-mounted toilets attach to a plate behind the wall. These have a similar flange-and-gasket arrangement.

INSTALLING FIXTURE SHUTOFFS

Shutoff valves save trips to your home's main water valve every time you work on a fixture. Before you set out to buy the parts, measure the supply pipe or pipes you'll be attaching to and note whether they're threaded steel, copper, or plastic. Each requires different fittings or adapters. For installation, refer to the appropriate pipe-fitting techniques on pages 301–308.

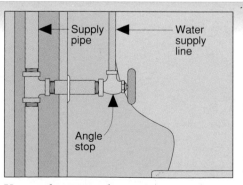

Use angle stops where pipe exits from the wall. Connect to tank with flexible tubing and compression fittings.

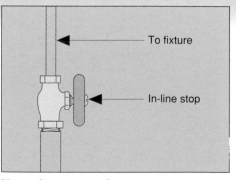

Use in-line stops when pipes come out of the floor. Stops usually are smaller in diameter than house plumbing.

INSTALLING A WATER HEATER

Sooner or later, all water heaters succumb to rust and corrosion and need replacement. There's nothing difficult about hooking up a water heater. You usually can find a replacement with about the same dimensions as the old one. This spares you the trouble of retailoring plumbing lines.

Also, unless there are special considerations, you'll want to stick with the same kind of heater you have now, either gas or electric. But you may want to upgrade the size of the unit if you find your hot water demands are increasing

Before you rush out to get a new heater, make sure it's really the tank that's leaking—not the overflow or a poor connection. (See page 297 for troubleshooting water heaters.)

If you do need a new unit, have a helper on hand when it arrives. Traversing stairs with a tank that weighs 125 to 200 pounds can be tricky. An appliance dolly makes the job a lot easier, too.

Set up your new heater next to the old one, study the installation instructions, and determine if you need new plumbing or flue fittings. Some plumbers don't bother to install union connections or shutoff valves. If that was the case when your heater was installed, you'll have to cut the hot and cold water lines to remove the water heater. To save trouble in case anything goes wrong in the future, invest in a couple of unions and a shutoff valve, too.

For information about saving water heating energy, see page 381. And to learn about the principles of solar water heaters, turn to page 375.

For information about saving water heating energy, see page 381. And to learn about the principles of solar water heaters, turn to page 375.

YOU'LL NEED...

SKILLS: Intermediate plumbing skills and basic electrical skills if the heater is electric.
TIME: 5 to 6 hours.
TOOLS: Hacksaw, pipe wrench or adjustable wrench, screwdriver, level, brush.

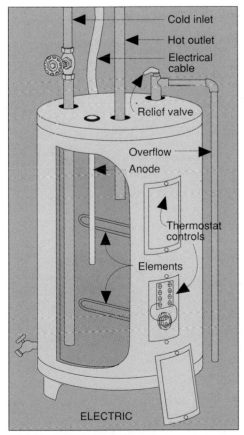

An electric water heater has four hookups: hot and cold water supplies, electricity, and a pressure-relief valve.

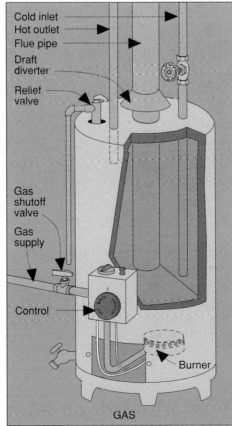

A gas heater, in addition to hot and cold water hookups and a relief valve, also has a gas line and a flue stack.

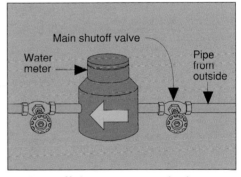

1. Turn off the water near the heater or at the water main. You must do this before starting any other work.

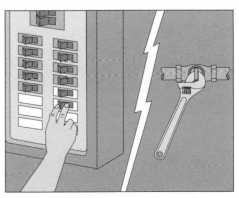

2. Shut off electricity at the service panel or gas by closing the shutoff valve leading to the water heater.

Making Plumbing Improvements (continued)

INSTALLING A WATER HEATER (continued)

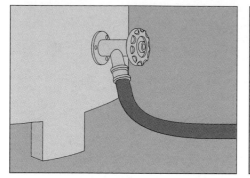

3. After turning off the water, drain the tank. With a bucket this could take several hours, so connect a hose from the drain valve to a floor drain.

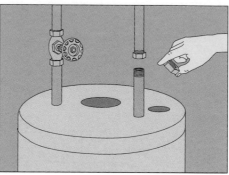

4. Disconnect hot and cold water lines (see pages 304–308 if you have to cut pipes) and gas or electricity lines. Slide the old unit out of the way.

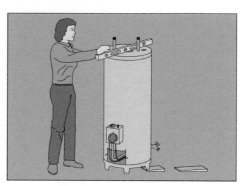

5. Don't make any of the connections on the new heater until it's level. You can level it with cedar or other rot-resistant shims.

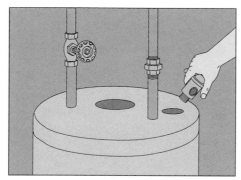

6. Reconnect the hot and cold water lines (with unions or flexible tubing), the pressure-relief valve, and the gas or electrical lines.

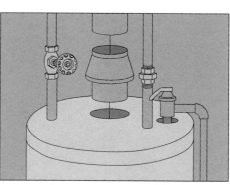

7. On gas models, install the draft diverter, position over the flue baffle, and connect the flue pipe. Use parts included with new heater kit.

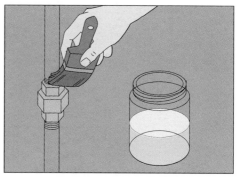

8. After opening main gas shutoff, check for leaks by swabbing union joint with a solution of soapy water. Watch for air bubbles indicating a leak.

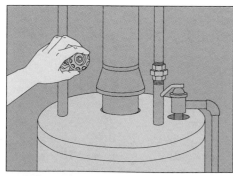

9. Open cold water shutoff to fill the tank. Open a hot water faucet in the kitchen. After water flows into sink, light the gas pilot or turn on electricity.

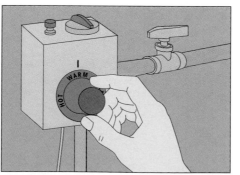

10. Set the thermostat at about 125°F. Lowering the setting by a few degrees will save some energy. (See page 381 for other energy-saving ideas.)

11. Extend a water heater's life by draining off 2 to 3 gallons of water from it every two months during the first year; every six months thereafter.

CONNECTING AN AUTOMATIC WASHER

Washer hookups are semipermanent. You simply connect hoses from the washer to valves on hot and cold water supply lines and insert the drain hose into either a standpipe, as shown at right, or a laundry tub.

Connect the supply hoses before moving the washer into place. Watch that the hoses don't kink when you make these hookups and when you push the washer into place. Be sure, too, to install filter screens in the hose fittings to protect the inner workings of your washer from debris in the plumbing system.

After pushing washer into place, be sure to level the machine by adjusting leveling legs at the corners. Make sure all four feet are in firm contact with the floor and that you tighten up their locknuts securely against the washer frame. The washing action of the machine generates a lot of vibrations that can cause the machine to "walk" around if it is not level.

If the washer drains into a standpipe installation, ward against overflow by making sure the top of the standpipe is higher than the machine's water level. Also, the pipe must be of a larger diameter than the hose. This provides an air gap so the machine can't back-siphon dirty water from the drainage system.

YOU'LL NEED...

SKILLS: Basic plumbing skills.
TIME: 30 to 60 minutes.
TOOLS: Tongue-and-groove pliers or adjustable wrench, level, open-end wrench.

ANATOMY OF A WASHER HOOKUP

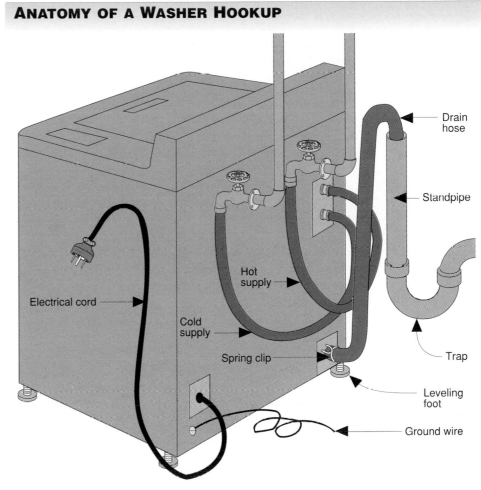

Drain hose

Standpipe

Hot supply

Electrical cord

Cold supply

Spring clip

Trap

Leveling foot

Ground wire

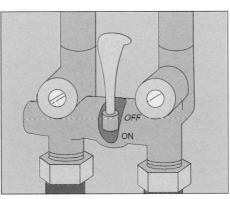

A lever valve lets you shut off hot and cold water with a single control. Close the valve when not in use to keep water pressure from damaging the internal parts of the washer.

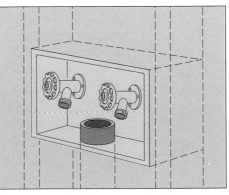

For a tidy installation in a finished room, recess the hose valves and the standpipe into the wall. Make sure the valves are easy to reach and the supply lines don't bend so much as to kink.

Making Plumbing Improvements (continued)

CONNECTING A DISHWASHER

Uncrate the machine and study its installation instructions. Most units are designed to replace a 24-inch-wide kitchen base cabinet, so your first job will be to remove a cabinet, tailor a space to fit (see pages 94–97), or remove an old dishwasher that you're replacing.

Determine where you can tie into the water and drain lines. If your new dishwasher will be located near the sink, that's the logical place to go. But you also can drop through the floor and connect to plumbing in the basement.

For the water supply, use flexible copper tubing. A saddle T (see page 312) will make quick work of this connection. Be sure to provide a shutoff. (For more about flexible copper pipe and shutoffs, see pages 305 and 320, respectively.)

Dishwashers drain through a hose that you clamp either to a new T under the sink or—if you have a garbage disposal—to a fitting on the side of the disposal. Some codes require an air gap to ensure that the dishwasher can't accidentally back-siphon water from your home's drainage system. The drawings below depict all three options.

For electricity, you'll need a separate 15- or 20-amp branch circuit. Locate a junction box near the unit so you can easily disconnect it for repairs. In some communities, you also must ground the machine's frame. (To learn about running new circuits and grounding appliances, see pages 244–259.)

> ### YOU'LL NEED...
> **SKILLS:** Intermediate plumbing and carpentry skills.
> **TIME:** 1 to 2 hours to replace a dishwasher; 4 hours to install a new dishwasher.
> **TOOLS:** Handsaw, drill, wrenches, pipe cutter, screwdriver.

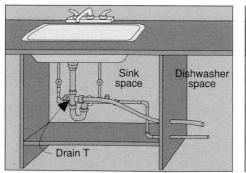

Before running supply and drain lines, check directions to see where they can be located. Areas shown are typical.

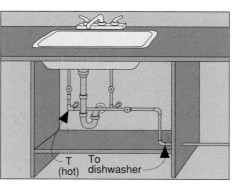

The easiest way to bring hot water to a dishwasher is to tap a sink supply. Make final connections at the front.

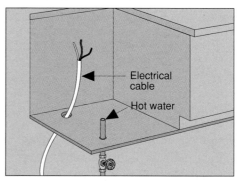

Electricity probably will have to come from below. You can connect to water there, also; install shutoff below floor.

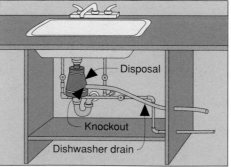

To hook drain into a sink drain, you'll need a special drain T fitting. (For more on drains, see pages 291–292 and 311.)

To hook drain to a disposal, remove knockout or plug, then connect the drain. Dealers have installation kits.

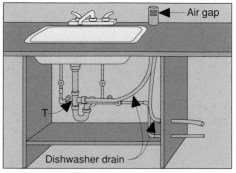

If the plumbing code requires an air gap, you'll need to make a hole in the sink or countertop to install it.

TREATING WATER

Hardness—far and away the most common water-treatment problem—results from an excess of calcium and magnesium in your water. These minerals combine with soaps and detergents to inhibit cleaning action. Heated hard water also builds up constricting scale inside pipes, faucets, water heaters, and other appliances—reducing their efficiency and shortening their life spans.

To find out if you have a hard water problem, draw off a pint of tap water into a bottle you can cap, add 10 drops of detergent, and shake well. If the solution foams readily, your water is relatively soft. If you get a curdlike film instead of foam, consider investing in a water softener. Or, call your water department and ask how much calcium carbonate is in your community's water supply. Water with less than 1 grain of calcium carbonate per gallon is considered soft; from 3.5 to 7.0 is hard; and greater than 7.0 is very hard.

Water softeners remove calcium and magnesium through a process called ion exchange. Water passes through a bed of plastic resin beads that absorbs the minerals and replaces them with sodium, which is derived from common salt. Periodic backwashing removes the built-up calcium and magnesium and also replenishes the "salts."

Removing iron and/or manganese and hydrogen sulfide calls for one or a combination of devices. An oxidizing filter removes excessive iron deposits. An automatic chlorine feeder, in tandem with an activated carbon filter, gets rid of manganese or hydrogen sulfide and disinfects water from a questionable source.

Neutralizing filters include a cellulose element that strains out sediment, silt, and cloudiness. A reverse osmosis filter has a plastic membrane that catches dissolved sodium salts, pesticides, detergents, and organic matter. (For more about all of these, see page 327.)

HELPFUL HINTS   TROUBLESHOOTING WATER TREATMENT PROBLEMS

Problem	Symptoms	Cures
High iron	Stains on fixtures and laundry; bad taste; water appears somewhat rusty after it stands for several minutes; rust dust on surfaces	Install a water softener; if amounts of iron are excessive, use a special iron (oxidizing) filter in the water softener unit.
High manganese and iron	Cloudy or hazy tap water; may leave blackish stains on fixtures or hard surfaces, such as kitchen countertops or bathtubs	A water softener with iron filters and a chlorine feeder may solve the problem; chlorine is removed from the water by charcoal filters.
High corrosive hydrogen sulfide	Water has rotten-egg odor	Use a water softener with the chlorine treatment; also helpful is a neutralizing filter and water purifier with an activated carbon element and a cellulose element.
High sodium, pollution	Salty, black-colored water	Install a reverse-osmosis and deionization unit.
"Hard" water	No suds when detergent is added to water	Install water softener (see page 326).
Bacteria	Sickness among family members, typically stomach upsets or diarrhea	Chlorination; a private well may be "shocked" with pool chlorine tablets; let well set for 12 hours, then run water until chlorine smell disappears.

Making Plumbing Improvements (continued)

GETTING WELL WATER TESTED

Whether you have just drilled a new well or purchased a home with an existing well, it is a good idea to have the water tested. The chart at right lists some water tests that are good to make or that are required by certain home lending agencies.

Start in the telephone book's classified section under "Well Contractors." They know what testing services—including any from the state—are available and the prices. If that doesn't produce a recommendation, look under "Water Analysis." Some water-treatment equipment dealers offer free tests.

TAKING YOUR OWN WATER SAMPLES

A water analysis is only as good as the water sample you provide. Before collecting the sample(s), remove aerators and other tap attachments that may harbor contaminants. Let the tap run at least 5 minutes for a well in daily use or at least 1 hour for a new well that has never been tested or used.

For a bacteria test, avoid contamination of the sterile bottle and cap. Wash your hands and have the water running before you break the bottle seal. Leave a small air space at the top and seal the bottle tightly. Mail the sample immediately.

TYPICAL WATER ANALYSES

Safety Check	Bank Mortgage	FHA/ HUD
Nitrate	Nitrate	Nitrate
Nitrite	Nitrite	Nitrite
Bacteria	Bacteria	Bacteria
	Iron	Iron
	Manganese	Manganese
	Copper	Copper
	Chloride	Chloride
	Hardness	Hardness
		Color/odor
		Turbidity
		Sodium
		Lead

CONNECTING A WATER SOFTENER

When selecting a water softener, you have three options: Buy one outright, rent a unit and maintain it yourself, or have the equipment installed on a service basis.

Buying or renting costs less in the long run. But owner-maintained water softeners require drain and electrical connections that enable you to periodically flush and recharge the units. Service units don't require these; instead, the dealer simply brings a fresh tank and regenerates the old one.

Treat only water that's used for cleaning, dishwashing, and bathing. You can divert hard water to toilets and outside sillcocks with the T fitting illustrated. From that T, water flows through the softener, then on to cold-water faucets and the water heater. A bypass valve lets you service the unit without shutting down the entire water supply.

ANATOMY OF A WATER SOFTENER HOOKUP

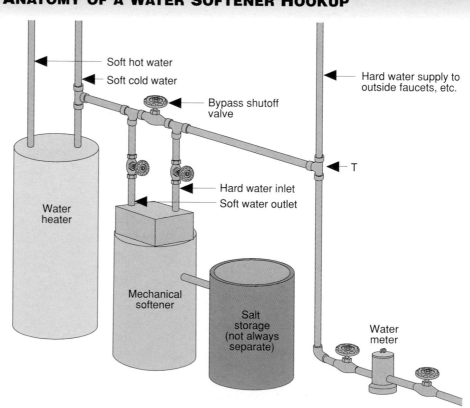

Soft hot water
Soft cold water
Hard water supply to outside faucets, etc.
Bypass shutoff valve
T
Hard water inlet
Soft water outlet
Water heater
Mechanical softener
Salt storage (not always separate)
Water meter

CONNECTING A WATER PURIFIER

Water softeners only improve water's cleaning power; they don't clean the water. Several types of water purifiers are available to remove contaminants from your water.

Two-stage water purifiers combine neutralizing and carbon filters to provide crystal clear, good-tasting water. Another type includes a reverse-osmosis module that catches dissolved contaminants. A chlorine feeder system chemically treats all household water.

For a two-stage purifier, you simply break into a supply line and hook in the unit. Reverse-osmosis filters need an additional drainage connection that you can make with flexible ¼-inch tubing. Most come with installation instructions that a do-it-yourself plumber can follow.

Installing Countertop Units

Countertop water purifiers treat cooking and drinking water only. They generally are the simplest to install, requiring no cutting or assembling of pipes. Typically, you just replace the existing faucet aerator with a special diverter. Most units mount on the wall or under a cabinet to save counter space.

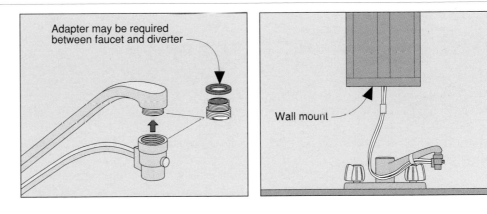

Adapter may be required between faucet and diverter

Wall mount

Installing Undersink Units

An undersink filter also serves just one tap. Most units that you insert in the middle of a supply run must be installed horizontally. In a vertical run, such as under the kitchen sink, you'll need to use the plumbing arrangement shown (near right) for the unit to work properly. Make sure to include a shutoff valve on the supply side so you can change the cartridge easily.

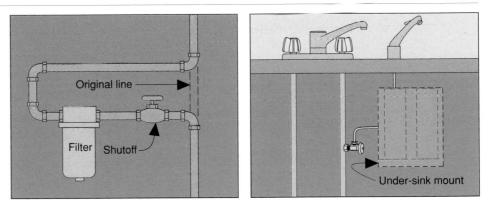

Original line

Filter   Shutoff

Under-sink mount

Installing a Feeder-Filter System

A feeder-filter system injects a controlled concentration of bacteria-killing chlorine into water that comes from a private water source. A pressure storage tank holds the treated water long enough to kill the bacteria. Water needing no further treatment comes straight from the tank. Potable water goes through a filter that removes the chlorine.

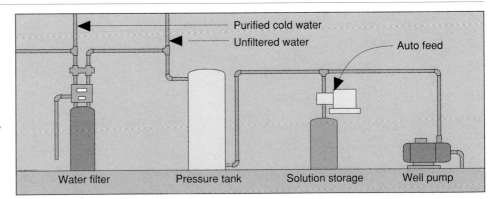

Purified cold water

Unfiltered water

Auto feed

Water filter   Pressure tank   Solution storage   Well pump

GAS

Think of a gas system as a special, simplified sort of plumbing network. Like its water-carrying cousin, a gas system consists largely of pipes that thread their way under floors and through walls to supply fixtures or appliances. Unlike other plumbing, however, gas systems have no drainage lines—and, of course, their medium is a gas, not a liquid.

Most people are wary of gas—and with good reason. A leak can cause fire, explosion, or suffocation. Gas, itself, is odorless. That's why suppliers add a scent to their product so you can smell a heavy concentration of gas. If you ever do, first open doors and windows, extinguish all flames, then shut down the system. Don't try to make repairs yourself—call the gas utility or a plumber or heating contractor.

Getting to Know Your System

The anatomy drawing below shows the pathways gas follows through a home. Liquefied petroleum (LP gas) or natural gas enters via a supply main. If the gas comes from a utility, a meter here keeps track of usage. Gas then travels to the various units it serves through black steel pipes.

Shutoff valves located at the meter and at each unit allow you to shut down the entire system or any individual component. Some shutoffs have handles that can be turned by hand; others have a key that can be turned only with a wrench (see insets below). Both types are open when their handles are parallel with the pipe; they're off when handles are perpendicular to the pipe.

Vent pipes on gas furnaces and water heaters complete the system by carrying off harmful carbon monoxide gas produced during combustion. On water heaters, a draft diverter prevents outside air from coming down the vent stack and blowing out the pilot light.

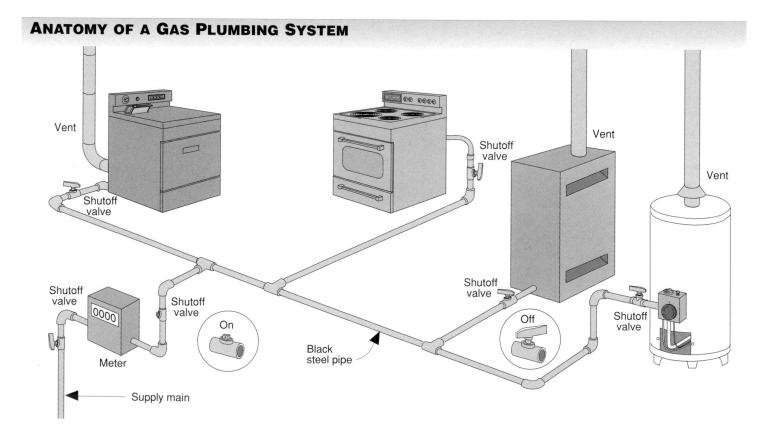

ANATOMY OF A GAS PLUMBING SYSTEM

Vent

Shutoff valve

Shutoff valve

Vent

Vent

Shutoff valve

Shutoff valve

Shutoff valve

Shutoff valve

0000

On

Off

Meter

Black steel pipe

Supply main

Solving Gas Problems

Because they're so simple, gas systems usually are trouble-free. When a problem occurs, you'll most likely find the cause at a pilot light—a small, continuous flame that ignites the main burners in most older gas appliances. Most newer model gas appliances have electric ignition systems (see page 332).

A few other problems often arise. Tiny leaks—usually at a pipe joint that's been jarred—pose an obvious safety hazard. Poorly adjusted pilots may be wasting energy. And most burners need an occasional tune-up. Troubleshooting and repair tips for these problems are shown on this and the following two pages.

TESTING FOR LEAKS

All gas leaks call for immediate action. If you ever detect the unmistakable aroma of escaping gas, open doors and windows, extinguish all cigarettes and open flames, close the main gas shutoff valve, and call your gas utility company.

If you merely think you smell gas near an appliance, you can use the soap bubble method to check out your suspicion without the delay and expense of a service call.

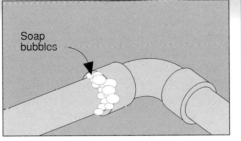

Brush a mixture of dish detergent and water onto a gas fitting that you suspect may be leaking. Bubbles indicate a leak.

If there's no odor of gas, check vents with a smoldering match. If the smoke is drawn to a joint, there's a leak. Don't use a match flame to check gas pipes.

LIGHTING PILOTS

Most of us are called on to light a pilot light at some time or other. The exercise can be a frustrating one if you don't follow the manufacturer's instructions to the letter.

Range burner pilots rarely pose a problem; just touch a match to them, as shown below. But other appliances—such as ovens, furnaces, and water heaters—require a slightly more complicated procedure, usually spelled out on a plate affixed to the unit's control unit.

The difficulty is because these pilots include an important safety device—a thermocouple, a bulb-like sensor that's warmed by the pilot flame. The thermocouple tells the main burner control if the pilot is burning. If it's not, the thermocouple cools and shuts off gas to the appliance's burners and pilot.

To relight the pilot, you need to either warm the thermocouple for a moment with a match (this works with most ovens) or temporarily bypass the thermocouple by holding down a reset button.

Procedures vary, so check the instruction plate on the pilot assembly. If the plate is missing or illegible, see below, or, for a gas furnace, see page 343.

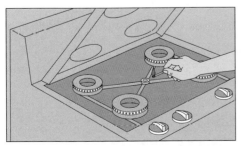

To light a range burner pilot, turn off the controls, then hold a match to the pilot. You may have to lift the top.

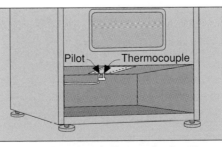

For an oven pilot, remove the broiler. Let the match warm the thermocouple, and the pilot will light.

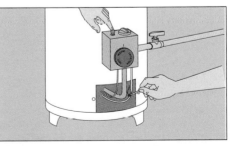

With other pilots, turn the burner knob to "pilot," hold a match to the pilot, then hold down the reset for a minute.

Solving Gas Problems (continued)

ADJUSTING PILOT LIGHTS

You may be paying for more gas than necessary. Natural gas pilot light flames should be blue with just a tinge of yellow at the tip. An LP pilot should have a blue-green inner flame, again, with no more than a fleck of yellow at the tip.

Before you make adjustments to pilots, be sure that the gas supply line is turned completely to its open position. Also, make sure that the unit is getting an adequate air supply for combustion. Boxes and other paraphernalia stacked too close to an appliance could be suffocating the flame.

Pilot light adjustments usually are made with a small screw that you turn in one direction or the other until the flame is just right. Manufacturers often conceal these (so they won't be tampered with), and the hiding places vary from make to make.

If you have the unit's operating and maintenance guide, it will probably tell where to look. If not, and if the screw isn't out in the open, remove control knobs, nameplates, or access doors to find the adjustment screw. If all else fails, call in professionals and watch what they do. Then you can do the job yourself the next time. The drawings below illustrate the basics of getting an efficient flame.

With a furnace or water heater, be sure to turn the control knob to its pilot setting before you make any adjustments. This prevents the main burners from firing while you adjust the pilot flame.

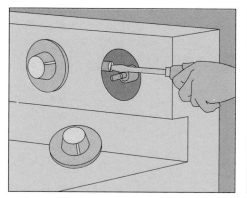

Pulling off a control knob provides access to the pilot adjustment screws for this range.

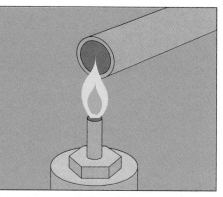

On a range, turn the adjustment screw until the flame tip is centered in the flash tube that leads to the burner(s).

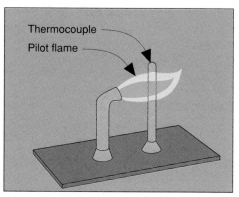

If the pilot has a thermocouple, adjust the flame to touch it about ½ inch from the end of the device.

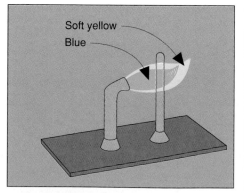

Lack of air causes a mostly yellow flame. Clean the tip of the pilot tube. The flame should look like this.

Dirt in a pilot tube will cause a split flame (left). A draft will cause the flame to flicker (right).

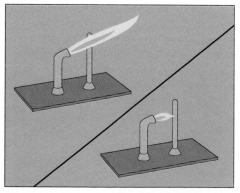

High gas pressure causes a lifting, flowing flame; low pressure, a small blue flame. Call your utility company.

ADJUSTING GAS BURNERS

If you have problems with gas range burners lighting, first check for a buildup of grease and corrosion before making any adjustment of the flame controls. Clear burners as shown below and keep them clean with regular household detergents.

The top burners of a gas range should be adjusted so they produce an inner-cone flame about ½ inch high. To adjust the flame height, slide the air shutter until a medium flame rises from the orifices.

Some newer gas burners feature an automatic-control thermostat that's stimulated by heat reflected from pots or pans on the burner. When the reflected heat reaches a certain level, the thermostat "turns down" the gas supply.

To adjust controlled burners, open the control knob completely and light the burner. Unscrew the knob and remove the trim. To lower the flame, turn the pilot screw clockwise. To raise it, turn the screw counterclockwise. The sensing head should be ³⁄₁₆ inch below the surface of the utensil grate.

Several conditions can cause oven burners to malfunction—a control knob that's not adjusted properly, an improperly set thermostat, or a faulty thermocouple. If the pilot light is working properly and the burner ports aren't clogged, call in a professional to make the necessary adjustments or repairs.

Burners in furnaces become clogged with combustion debris or rust. Have your furnace serviced before every other heating season. The money spent on a checkup may save you plenty on fuel, and it lessens the chance of having a malfunction on a cold, snowy night.

YOU'LL NEED...

SKILLS: Basic skills.
TIME: 15 minutes to completely clean one burner.
TOOLS: Screwdriver, pin or needle.

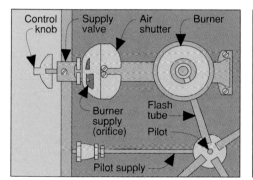

Typical range burners have a gas control, a burner unit with a perforated ring, and a flash tube from the pilot.

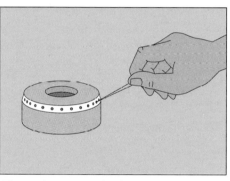

Clogged ports in the burner ring can cause an uneven flame. Clean these with a needle or pin.

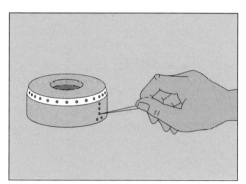

If a burner won't light easily, suspect dirt in the openings near the base. Clean these with a needle or pin also.

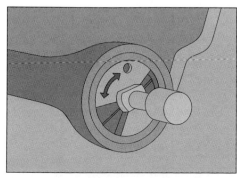

To adjust a burner, loosen the screw and turn or slide the air shutter. When you get it right, tighten the screw.

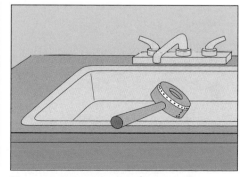

You can remove most burners for cleaning. Wash with warm water and detergent. Replace when dry.

Making Gas Improvements

If you're replacing an existing gas appliance, the work of running a gas pipe to the location was done long ago. However, if you're changing the location of an appliance or dealing with an entirely new installation, hiring someone who knows the tricks of the trade is money well spent. In this case, some fairly sophisticated hookups may be necessary. Also, installation work necessary for a new gas furnace usually is much too complicated for most do-it-yourselfers.

If you do decide to run a gas line yourself, make sure that the pipes and connections you use for the hookup meet your local code requirements. Call your gas utility for information; don't rely on an appliance dealer. Also, make sure to use pipe dope or tape on all joints, and use the soap-bubble method (see page 329) to check for leaks.

HELPFUL HINTS   CHOOSING AND BUYING GAS APPLIANCES

When purchasing a new range or other gas-fired appliance, you'll find a broad selection from which to choose. The features you choose depend on your needs and budget. In general, you'll usually find the best values with models that are one or two notches below the top of the line.

Why? To keep prices competitive, manufacturers often cut quality corners with so-called economy models. Medium- to upper-level-priced appliances, on the other hand, usually have the same basic machinery as the very best models—but with fewer frills.

Another good reason for aiming high is because that's where you'll find energy-saving devices that can pay for themselves several times over during an appliance's lifetime. These include electric ignition systems, heat sensors that automatically turn down burners, and humidity sensors that shut off clothes dryers when clothes are dry. Something as seemingly insignificant as a pilot light can account for one-third to one-half of the total fuel needed to operate some appliances. Manufacturers label their gas and electric appliances with the estimated annual energy consumption.

Many gas appliances can be adapted to burn either natural gas or LP gas.

Conversion usually involves just unscrewing and turning over a plug in the appliance's burner assembly. Ask the dealer to find out if this is possible with the unit you're considering.

When making your decision to buy, weigh the added convenience of each additional feature against the amount of money it will cost. You may find that you can get along quite nicely without this or that.

If you're considering replacing an electric appliance with a gas one, you'll have to consider the cost of running new gas lines, if you don't want to do the project yourself, versus the energy savings or other benefits you're anticipating from the gas appliance.

Also take your family's size and lifestyle into consideration when determining your needs. If you're in the market for a water heater, for example, you need a unit large enough to supply you with all the hot water you need whenever you need it. An oversized heater, on the other hand, can waste a lot of energy warming water you don't need. An average four-person family can get by with a 40-gallon water heater.

With water heaters, also take note of a unit's "recovery rate," which is the amount of water that it can heat in a one-half- or one-hour period. If your family doesn't use a lot of hot water, this probably won't make much difference. But if demand is heavy during certain periods of the day, a medium-sized, quick-recovery unit might use less gas overall than a larger, low-recovery model. Before making a commitment, ask the dealer the following questions. The answers will enable you to determine if you're buying the best for the least.

■ How long are parts warranted on the appliance? What is the replacement warranty, if any, on the entire unit?

■ Is there a charge for delivering the appliance to your home?

■ Is there a charge for connecting the appliance? Does this include the cost of parts?

■ What is the delivery timetable?

■ Will the dealer disconnect and haul away the appliance you're replacing? Is there any charge for this?

■ Does the dealer have a service department, or must you call in another repair service if you have trouble?

■ Does the dealer offer financing terms? If so, what are the terms?

■ Will the dealer give you a trade-in allowance for your old appliance?

INSTALLING A GAS RANGE

Provided you already have a gas line where you need it, hooking up a range calls for more homework than actual labor. Start by carefully reading the installation instructions that came with the appliance.

If instructions are not available, look for the unit's rating plate, usually affixed to the inside of its broiler or oven. Here you'll find the manufacturer's recommended clearances to combustible surfaces. Most modern-day ranges need zero clearance at the rear and to cabinets on either side, but must be situated 12 inches or more from a corner.

Check with your utility to see if the local code allows a flexible pipe connection, which is the easiest to make. If so, buy a connector only slightly longer than the distance from the black gas pipe to the connection on the range. If flexible pipe is not allowed, you'll have to make a rigid connection. Use black steel pipe (see pages 301–303, 306, and 312). Whichever type of connection you use, it's wise to install a branch line shutoff as well.

You also need to determine what electrical connection the range requires. Slide-in types, such as the one shown below, simply plug into a nearby receptacle. Most drop-in and countertop units, however, must be permanently connected to a wall box (see pages 244–259).

With these points settled, shut off the gas and make the connections. Make sure when you push the range into its final position that you don't damage the fittings you just made.

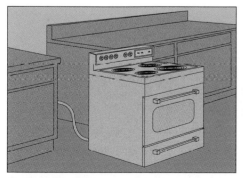

1. Coat pipe threads with pipe dope or tape, then install the shutoff. Use two pipe wrenches for a tight connection.

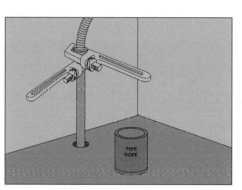

2. Apply more dope and attach the flexible connector. Exerting too much pressure may crack the fittings.

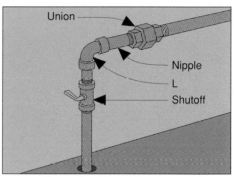

3. For a rigid connection, use nipples, an L, and a union. You may need a reducing fitting at the range gas inlet.

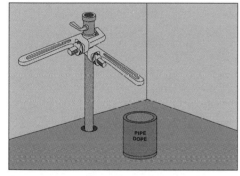

4. Slide in the range close enough to connect it. With most models, you remove broiler to get at connections.

5. Open the shutoff and a burner until you smell gas. Turn off the burner and check for leaks (see page 329).

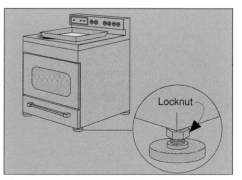

6. Place range in final position and level it with leg adjusters. A pan of water on top can replace a level.

Making Gas Improvements (continued)

INSTALLING A GAS DRYER

Hooking up a gas dryer involves about the same work as connecting a gas range. The only additional step is venting the unit to the outside.

The vent pipe can be of rigid metal, which requires an elbow at every change in direction, or flexible vinyl, which doesn't. For long runs, especially those that pass through interior walls, floors, or ceilings, use rigid metal ducts. Use flexible duct for out-in-the-open distances of 10 feet or less. Either type should be at least 4 inches in diameter.

Keep duct runs as short as possible. But don't exhaust a dryer into a chimney, under a floor, or into a crawlspace. Lint may build up in these spaces, creating a fire hazard. Don't put screws or a damper inside vent pipe, either. They catch and hold lint. Secure joints with duct tape instead.

Install a hooded damper on the outside wall to keep cold air from blowing back into the vent pipe. Add insulation around the pipe where it passes through an exterior wall or an unheated space. Cool pipes are prone to condensation, which also collects lint.

A dryer must be level and located on a firm footing or its spinning action may damage the machine. If the dryer is not on a concrete floor and the floor is at all shaky, beef it up with bridging between the joists (see page 11).

The drawings below illustrate only the steps in a dryer installation that differ from those for a range, so check page 333 as well.

> ### YOU'LL NEED...
> **SKILLS:** Basic plumbing skills and carpentry skills.
> **TIME:** 1 to 2 hours.
> **TOOLS:** Pliers, hammer, adjustable wrench, end wrench, drill, keyhole saw, utility knife, tin snips.

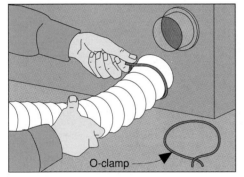

Flexible duct is easiest to install. It's available in kit form, complete with clamps and an outside hooded damper.

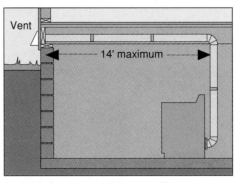

A rigid duct run with two elbows can extend up to 14 feet. Deduct 4 feet for each additional elbow.

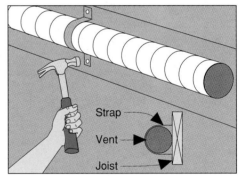

Both rigid and flexible ducts require hangers every 6 feet. Stretch flexible duct slightly; don't let it coil up.

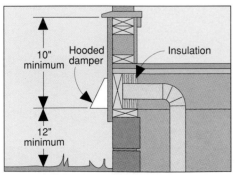

A vent should exit the house at least 12 inches above ground level and 10 inches below any window.

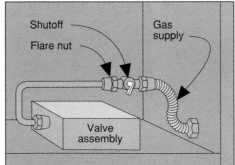

If the dryer won't fire, purge air from the line by loosening the flare nut for a few seconds.

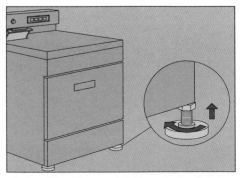

Make sure dryer is level and sits firmly on floor before loading it with clothes. Don't install a dryer on carpeting.

INSTALLING A GAS GRILL

A gas-fired grill takes all the bother out of outdoor cooking without sacrificing any of its fun and flavor. You can even install one indoors, provided you top it off with a powered ventilating hood to draw off smoke and odors (see page 407).

The key to the way a gas grill works lies with its permanent briquettes. Fired by natural or propane gas burners, these volcanic rocks catch meat juices, then smoke and flare up just as charcoal does. It's this action—not the smell of charcoal itself—that gives grilled food its unique taste.

Gas grills can be mounted permanently on a post or in a countertop on your patio; attached to a roll-around cart and plugged into the gas supply with a flexible, quick-connect hose; or supplied by a propane gas bottle that rides on the cart.

If you decide on a permanent mounting, make the hookup with small-diameter, flexible copper tubing, as shown below. Check with your gas supplier and ask how deep the line should be buried. You may want to hire a professional to connect it to your house system. (For more about working with copper tubing, see page 305).

Set the grill post in the ground with concrete, as you would a fence post (see page 197). On a concrete patio, use concrete expansion anchors and lag bolts to attach the post directly to the concrete. On a brick patio, remove a few bricks, dig a hole, and set the post.

> ### YOU'LL NEED...
> **SKILLS:** Basic excavating and plumbing skills.
> **TIME:** 2 to 4 hours.
> **TOOLS:** Shovel, spring bender, wrenches, level.

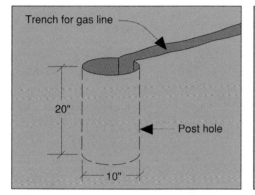

1. Dig a hole 10 inches in diameter and 20 inches deep for the post. Run the pipe trench after you dig the hole.

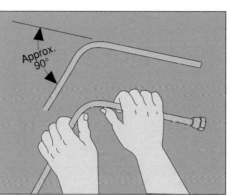

2. Gradually bend the tubing to a 90-degree angle. Bend as shown or use a spring bender to avoid kinks.

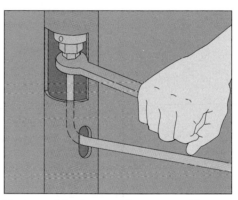

3. Assemble the regulator according to the manufacturer's instructions. Insert the tubing and connect it.

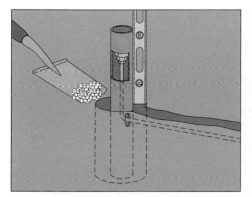

4. Set the post in the hole and the pipe in the trench. Keep the post plumb while you shovel concrete around it.

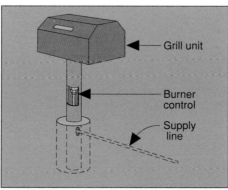

5. Connect the tubing to the gas. Turn off the controls, turn on the gas, and test for leaks. Then assemble the unit.

HEATING AND COOLING

How's the climate in your home? Whether you feel too hot, too cold, or just right depends largely on the temperature and humidity of the air around you. It's your home's comfort system—whether it be a forced-air, piped, or radiant one—that regulates the air temperature by adding or removing heat. Many systems also control the humidity level by adding or removing moisture.

This chapter explains how heating and cooling systems work, how you can maintain and improve their efficiency, what your choices are in new equipment, and—most importantly—what you can do to slow the flow of dollars to your gas, oil, or electric company.

Though heating and cooling components vary enormously, all take advantage of heat's inherent tendency to move from a warmer object or space to a cooler one. This means you can couple a heat source, such as a burner, electric resistance element, or heat pump, with a heating plant, usually a furnace or boiler, to send heated air, water, or steam via a distribution network to a home's various rooms. After the medium gives off its heat, it then recirculates to the heating plant. A control unit, almost always a thermostat, maintains a preset temperature by switching the heating plant on and off.

In a sense, this chapter presents more than you really need to know about heating and cooling. Because no one system includes all the components we show, you'll need to read selectively.

And yet, this chapter tells less than the full story. Equally important is the way you conserve heating and cooling energy with insulation and ventilation—that chapter comes next.

Getting to Know Your System

"Ducted" systems circulate air from a furnace to registers in each room via a network of ducts. Modern, forced-air versions have a blower that pushes treated air through supply ducts and pulls it back through return ducts.

An older home may have a less-efficient gravity system, which works the same way, but without a blower. Warm air rises from the furnace to the rooms, and cool air falls through the returns.

Blower-driven forced-air heating systems have one big advantage over steam and radiant systems: They can be adapted easily to centrally cool as well as heat homes.

Troubleshooting and maintenance tips for air furnace systems can be found on pages 338–347. For tips on air-conditioning problems, see pages 355–356.

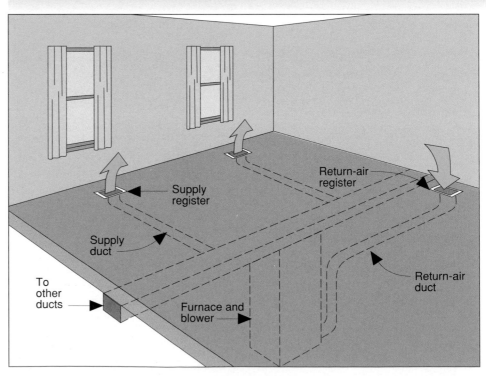

ANATOMY OF AN AIR SYSTEM

Supply register

Supply duct

To other ducts

Furnace and blower

Return-air register

Return-air duct

ANATOMY OF A WATER OR STEAM SYSTEM

In a "piped" system, water or steam distributes the heat. The heating plant, called a boiler, sends hot water or steam through supply lines to radiation units in each room. The radiators transfer heat to the air, then direct the cooler water back to the boiler via return lines.

Because steam rises, it doesn't need the circulator pump shown here. Not all hot-water systems have pumps, either. Gravity systems rely on water's tendency to expand when heated and contract when cooled. In forced, or hydronic, systems, a pump merely helps to move the water.

If your home has hot-water or steam heat, turn to pages 348–353 for more detailed information.

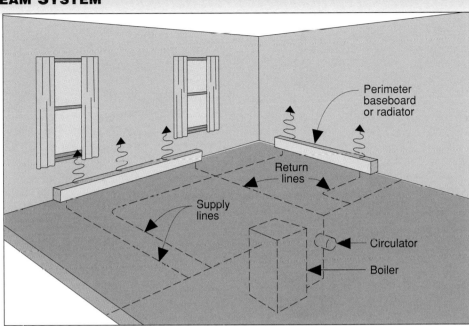

Perimeter baseboard or radiator

Return lines

Supply lines

Circulator

Boiler

ANATOMY OF A RADIANT SYSTEM

Radiant heating warms the floor, ceiling, or baseboard units in a room, providing silent and even heat. Some systems use electrical cables, as shown at right; others circulate hot water through small-diameter tubing embedded in concrete. Don't confuse radiant heating with the electric-resistance furnace on page 341.

Because they have no moving parts, electrical radiant systems rarely have problems. When they do, it's usually at the electrical circuit panel (see pages 234–235). If your home has this type of system, avoid boring or breaking into radiant surfaces or you may, indeed, have problems.

Not much can go wrong with a radiant water-distribution system, either. It depends, however, upon a boiler (see pages 352–353).

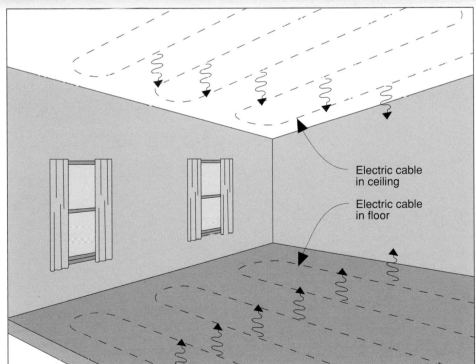

Electric cable in ceiling

Electric cable in floor

Maintaining and Troubleshooting Air Systems

If you consider that a forced-air heating/cooling system completely recirculates the air in your home as many as three times every hour, you can see that it has a big job to do. Fortunately, most of the components of a forced-air system are easy to take care of—once you know what they are and where they're located.

Begin by noting which registers supply treated hot air and which ones return cold air to the furnace (see anatomy drawing on page 336).

Most rooms have at least one hot-air supply register. Supply registers usually have movable dampers that let you modulate the airflow or shut it off entirely.

Cold-air return registers typically are larger and less numerous—many homes have only one per floor, located in a hallway or other central spot. Returns never have dampers, because shutting one off would suffocate the system to a degree.

While you are surveying the air registers, make sure none is blocked by furniture, draperies, or carpeting. Supply registers must have unobstructed space above; return registers must be open to air currents from all directions.

Take a trip to the basement next. If it has an exposed ceiling, you can easily trace the entire duct network. The drawing below shows how ducts connect to the furnace and what goes on in there.

KEEPING AIR MOVING

All forced-air furnaces work like the one illustrated here. Sizes and shapes may be different, but the principles are the same.

Return air passes through an air filter into a blower compartment. The blower then pushes air into a second compartment, where it's warmed by a heat source. This might be electrical heating elements (see page 341), a gas- or oil-fired heat exchanger (see pages 342 and 344), or a heat pump (see page 346). If you have central air-conditioning, a cooling coil in the supply duct above the heat source extracts heat from the moving air during hot months (see pages 355–356).

The heated or cooled air then moves into a plenum from which the supply ducts radiate to carry air to the various rooms.

Air enters this particular furnace configuration at the bottom and exits at the top. Known as an upflow type, it's best suited to basement installations. For types that fit other situations, see page 374.

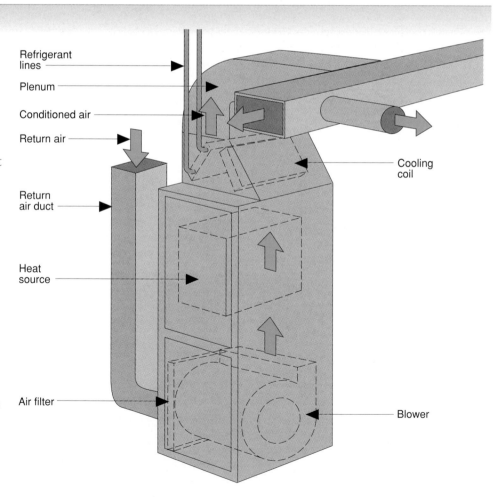

Refrigerant lines

Plenum

Conditioned air

Return air

Return air duct

Heat source

Air filter

Cooling coil

Blower

Replacing Filters

One disadvantage of forced-air heating and cooling systems is that blowing air stirs up dust and dirt. The key to clean forced air is that, as the air flows up through the furnace, the filter catches these particles.

If you neglect a filter, it can turn into a dam that throttles the airflow and makes the unit work harder, thus wasting energy. A severely clogged filter can even cause a furnace to overheat and shut down.

Filters are easy to replace, so check them monthly during the heating and cooling seasons. Just pull out the old one, and hold it up to a light; if you can see light through the filter, it's still usable.

Most filters consist of oil-treated fiberglass framed in cardboard. Install these so air strikes the oiled side first; you'll usually find an arrow on the filter indicating the direction of the airflow. Cleanable dry-foam

filters can be vacuumed or washed.

Standard filters trap only larger particles. To remove fine dust and pollen, consider an electrostatic air cleaner (see page 362).

YOU'LL NEED...

SKILLS: Basic skills.
TIME: 5 minutes or less.
TOOLS: No special tools; screwdriver to open some blower doors.

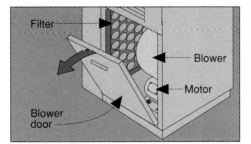

Most blower doors lift or swing open. On counterflow models, the door will be up top.

Simply slide the filter out of its channel. Look for dirt on or around the blower, too. Vacuum, if necessary.

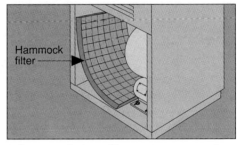

A hammock-type filter wraps around the base of the blower. They're also easy to replace.

Oiling and Adjusting Blowers

Make blower maintenance part of your seasonal tune-up schedule—and check out the unit whenever air seems to be moving faster or slower than usual.

Some blowers have direct-drive motors; others operate with an adjustable V-belt-and-pulley setup (shown at right). You needn't worry about adjusting the direct-drive type, but it may need oil, so check the manufacturer's instructions.

On either type, look for lubrication ports on the motor and

YOU'LL NEED...

SKILLS: Basic skills.
TIME: 20 to 30 minutes.
TOOLS: End wrench or socket wrench, screwdriver, oil can.

on the blower pulley on belt-drive units, as shown below. With an oil can, squirt a few drops of SAE-10 nondetergent oil into these ports at the beginning of each heating and cooling season.

Belt-drive blowers require the correct belt tension (see below,

right). Check the belt for fraying, cracks, and signs of wear—consider keeping a spare one on hand. An adjustable motor pulley lets you change the speed of a belt-drive model by loosening a setscrew and adjusting the distance between pulley faces.

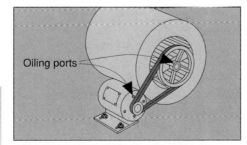

If a motor has oil ports, they'll be at each end of the shaft. Also, check for lube points on the blower fan.

Adjust the belt so it's loose without slipping; it should depress about one inch. Keep mounting bolts tight.

Maintaining and Troubleshooting Air Systems (continued)

KEEPING AIR MOVING (continued)
Balancing an Air System

If some rooms in your home are consistently too hot or cold, don't blame the furnace. Instead, take on a simple "balancing" project.

To balance a forced-air system, you reduce the airflow to a room that is too warm. Warm air then reaches colder areas, typically those farthest from the furnace.

You already may have tried balancing by partially or totally closing registers in the hotter rooms. This cools the room off, but it doesn't redirect the air. Instead, look for dampers in the ductwork. Dampers are controlled by a handle or a locknut arrangement (see below). You may find one at the point where each duct takes off from the furnace plenum. Not all duct systems have dampers, so consider installing them (see page 359).

Identify which ducts serve each room, and label their dampers. Close them one at a time to determine which room isn't getting air.

Wait for a cold day to begin the balancing procedure shown below.

If only one or two rooms have airflow problems, you might be tempted to adjust only the dampers. Because balancing is a robbing-Peter-to-pay-Paul proposition, however, you'll get better results by tuning the entire system.

YOU'LL NEED...
SKILLS: Basic skills.
TIME: 3 to 4 hours.
TOOLS: Thermometers, masking tape, ladder.

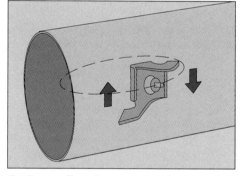

1. Open all registers; open dampers by loosening locknuts and turning the damper handles parallel to the duct.

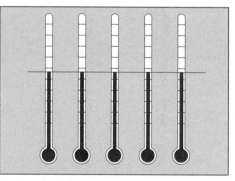

2. Synchronize several thermometers by laying them together for 30 minutes and noting differences.

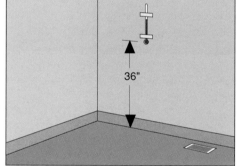

3. Place a thermometer in each room, 3 feet above the floor but not above a supply register.

4. Begin to partially damper rooms, beginning with the one where your home's thermostat is located.

5. Note any increase in air delivery to other rooms. Recheck temperatures and continue adjusting dampers.

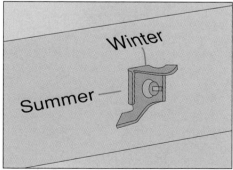

If you have central cooling, you may have to rebalance in the summer. Mark seasonal settings on the ducts.

UNDERSTANDING AN ELECTRIC-RESISTANCE FURNACE

To envision an electric-resistance furnace, think of a giant toaster with a fan blowing through it. As air pushed by the blower moves through the heating elements, it picks up warmth, then continues into the plenum and ducts to registers in each room.

Because no combustion occurs in an electric furnace, it doesn't require the flue or heat exchanger that gas and oil furnaces must have. Therefore, maintenance is almost nil. Operating costs, however, usually run substantially higher.

Check the anatomy drawing at right. An air-circulation switch—often on the house thermostat, but sometimes on the furnace—lets you run the blower continuously, if you wish. Underneath, accessible through a removable cover, there may be fuses or breakers for each of the heating elements. A transformer steps up amperage to the high levels needed for heating. Relays turn the elements on or off according to instructions from the thermostat.

The chart below lists the few things that can go wrong with electric-resistance furnaces and what you can do about them. Always shut off the furnace's main circuit breaker before removing the control or access panels. You'll find the breaker located next to the furnace or in your home's main service panel. Don't attempt to work on the heat elements—that's a job for a professional.

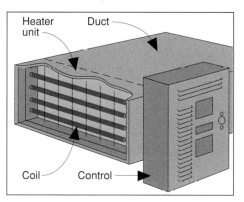

If your home has a heat pump, it may have resistance-type duct heaters, like the one shown here. These mini-furnaces automatically pitch in when the temperature drops below what a heat pump can handle by itself.

ANATOMY OF AN ELECTRIC-RESISTANCE FURNACE

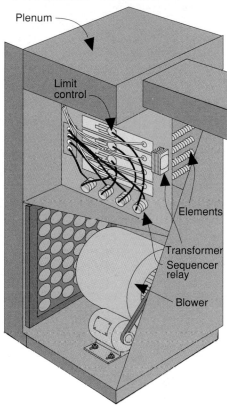

Plenum

Limit control

Elements

Transformer

Sequencer relay

Blower

HELPFUL HINTS TROUBLESHOOTING BEFORE CALLING FOR SERVICE

Problem	Causes	Solutions
No heat	Furnace switch or main breaker open; thermostat set too low	Check switch, fuse or breakers, and the thermostat. If the blower runs but there's no heat, check the fuse or breaker block.
Cycles on and off too often	Clogged filter or failing blower, causing unit to overheat	Replace the filter. Oil and adjust the blower (see page 339).
Not enough heat	Improper thermostat setting; defective heating element; clogged filter or duct	Check thermostat first, then the fuse or breaker; replace a blown fuse or flip on the breaker. If the fuse blows or breaker trips when you turn on the power, call a professional. Replace the filter.

Figure labels: Heater unit, Duct, Coil, Control

Maintaining and Troubleshooting Air Systems (continued)

UNDERSTANDING A GAS FURNACE

Burners in a gas furnace differ little from those on a gas range—they're just bigger. But the controls needed to automatically turn the burners on and off and to provide a foolproof safety system are more complex.

The burners and heat exchanger in the interior of the furnace can be examined through an inspection port (see anatomy drawing). A set of tubes—manifolds—feeds the burners a mixture of gas and air, which is ignited by the pilot. As the heat exchanger warms up, the blower pushes air through it and up to the plenum. Flue gases exit past the exchanger up the flue and chimney.

For safety, a combination valve is connected to the pilot. If the pilot goes out, the valve shuts off the gas. A second safety—the limit switch in the plenum—turns off the gas if the plenum gets too hot; it also stops the blower when the temperature in the plenum drops to a certain level after the burners have shut down.

Beyond checking for flue leaks, relighting the pilot, replacing filters, or servicing the blower, there's little you need do with a gas furnace.

ANATOMY OF A GAS FURNACE

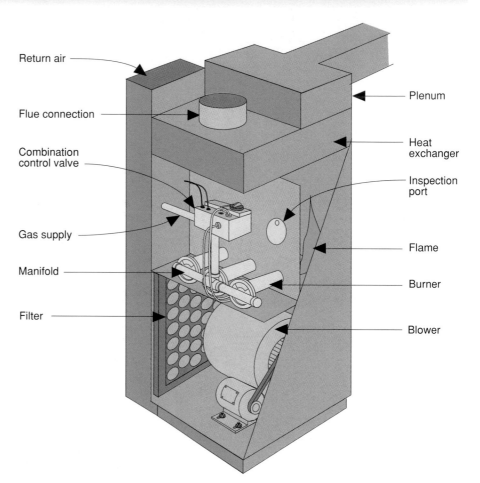

Return air — Plenum — Flue connection — Heat exchanger — Combination control valve — Inspection port — Gas supply — Flame — Manifold — Burner — Filter — Blower

Checking Out the Chimney and Flue

Flues can develop leaks, releasing highly lethal carbon monoxide into your home's air. Also, various things can clog a chimney.

These dangers warrant an annual checkup. Inspect all of the points illustrated at far right, paying special attention to the pipe between the furnace flue and the chimney. For more about chimneys and flues, see pages 105, 132, and 329.

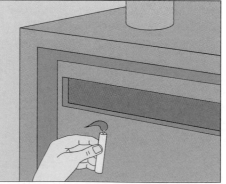

Hold a candle to the opening in the top access panel with the furnace running. A flue leak will blow out the flame.

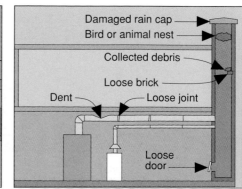

Damaged rain cap — Bird or animal nest — Collected debris — Loose brick — Dent — Loose joint — Loose door

Any of these problems may cause a carbon monoxide leak. If you suspect a damaged flue pipe, replace the pipe.

Lighting a Gas Furnace Pilot

Some gas furnaces ignite with an electrical spark system similar to the one used on oil burners (see page 344). Most, however, depend on a gas pilot light for firing—and when the furnace fails to operate, it's usually because the pilot has gone out or needs adjusting.

Procedures for relighting a pilot differ somewhat, so follow the steps listed on the instruction plate attached to the furnace. With most, you'll find a gas cock with three settings—off, pilot, and on. Turn the cock to "off," wait a few minutes for residual gas to clear, then switch to the "pilot" setting. Hold a lighted match to the pilot, depress a reset button, and hold it down for the time specified by the instructions.

If the pilot stays lit, turn the cock to "on" and the burners will fire. If the pilot goes out again after you release the reset, repeat the entire procedure, holding the reset down a little longer.

If you can't get the pilot lighted after two or three tries, call your utility company or a repair service. The failure most likely indicates a problem with the thermocouple, a sensing device that keeps open the main valve to the burners. When the pilot goes out or the thermocouple malfunctions, it signals the main gas valve to close.

A weak or wavering pilot flame also may cause a thermocouple to shut everything down. The flame should be blue, with the tip barely flecked by yellow. The flame should hit the sensing tube about ½ inch from its end.

If the pilot flame doesn't fit this description, make sure it isn't being buffeted by a draft. Then, try cleaning out the opening of the pilot tube with a needle or nail.

If that doesn't do the job, you'll need to adjust the pilot flame, as explained on page 330.

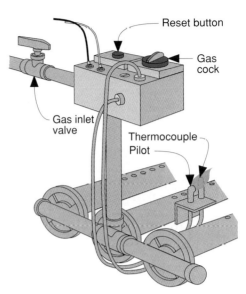

YOU'LL NEED...
SKILLS: Basic gas plumbing skills.
TIME: 10 to 15 minutes.
TOOLS: Matches.

HELPFUL HINTS — TROUBLESHOOTING BEFORE CALLING FOR SERVICE

Problem	Causes	Solutions
No heat	Thermostat too low; switch, fuse, or circuit breaker open; gas shut off; pilot out	Check thermostat, switch, and fuse or breaker. Relight pilot.
Cycles too often	Usually a clogged filter or a blower problem	Replace filter. Oil and adjust blower (see page 339).
Not enough heat	Again, a clogged filter; burners may need cleaning	Replace filter. Have burners cleaned by a professional.
Blower runs constantly	Fan switch set for continuous circulation; limit control out of adjustment	Reset fan switch on furnace or adjust limit control (page 363).
Furnace squeals or rumbles	Squealing: blower belt slipping or bearings need lubrication Rumbling with burners off: misadjusted pilot Rumbling with burners on: dirty burners	Oil blower and adjust belt (page 339). Adjust pilot (page 330). Have burners cleaned by a professional.

Maintaining and Troubleshooting Air Systems (continued)

UNDERSTANDING AN OIL FURNACE

Compared to gas and electric furnaces, an oil-fired, forced-air heating plant has more components. It has the same filter-and-blower unit common to the other furnace types, but the heat producer in an oil furnace—its burner—includes a second motor/blower setup. This one mixes oil with air, ignites the mixture with an electric spark, then blasts a torchlike flame into a fireproof compartment just below the heat exchanger.

Examine the anatomy drawing at right. The combustion air blower pulls in air through an adjustable shutter, mixes it with oil in an air tube, sets it afire with a pair of electrodes, then forces it through a nozzle into the combustion chamber. A transformer steps up voltage to the electrodes. In some models, a primary safety control keeps an electric eye on the flame; if it fails to light, the safety shuts down the burner. Other types do the same job with a heat sensor in the flue pipe.

The motor on the combustion air blower also drives an oil pump. This pulls oil through lines from the fuel oil tank. An automotive-type filter strains the fuel.

Despite this complexity, modern oil burners are reliable. They do, however, require annual tune-ups, which, if neglected, will add to your fuel oil bills. Here are the jobs that generally need doing before each heating season.

■ Clean or change the oil filter in the fuel line at least once a year. Some types of oil filters have a replaceable cartridge; other basket types must be washed out in kerosene. With both, make sure to install a new gasket when you reassemble the filter.

■ Clean the pump strainer annually, if your unit has one. Again, soak it in kerosene and replace the gasket.
■ Clean the fan blades monthly with a long-handled brush.
■ Lubricate the burner motor every month or two, unless it's permanently lubricated (in which case you won't find lubrication ports or the instruction plate will so indicate). Most require only a few drops of light, nondetergent oil.

Look for instructions on the housing.
■ Check all flue connections annually (see page 342).
■ Call for a professional tune-up at the start of the heating season. Insist that the service technician take instrument readings for combustion efficiency, smoke density, and draft. The technician also should check out the firing system, clean the ignition electrodes, and clean or replace the combustion nozzle.

ANATOMY OF AN OIL FURNACE

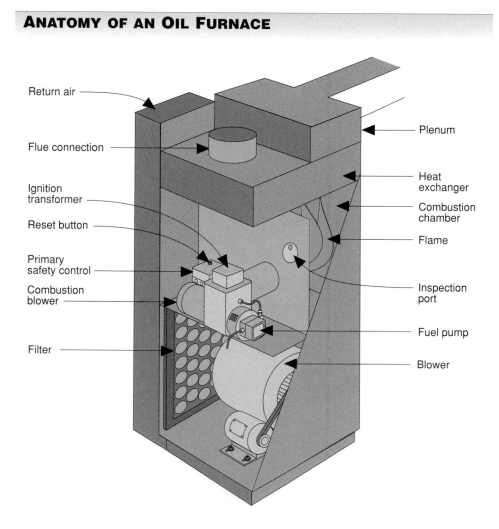

Return air

Flue connection

Ignition transformer

Reset button

Primary safety control

Combustion blower

Filter

Plenum

Heat exchanger

Combustion chamber

Flame

Inspection port

Fuel pump

Blower

Checking Safety Controls

Every oil burner includes a safety device that monitors its operation and turns off the unit if something goes wrong. Often, however, the reason for a shutdown lies with the "safety" itself.

Reset the safety and try again, as shown below. If the burner kicks off again, shut off all power—the burner motor and ignition may be protected by separate fuses or breakers.

If your burner has an electric-eye primary safety, look for an access cover that lets you get to its photocell. Wipe the photocell with a clean rag or tissue to remove soot, reassemble, turn on the burner, and see if the furnace fires.

The second type of safety—a stack switch—mounts on the flue. Remove the screw holding the unit to the stack, slide it out, and wipe off the sensor.

Don't continuously try to restart a balky oil burner. Unburned oil could accumulate in the combustion chamber and "flash back." If the furnace won't fire after three attempts, call for service.

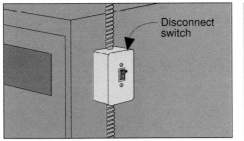

There may be a burner disconnect switch on the side of the furnace and another outside the furnace room.

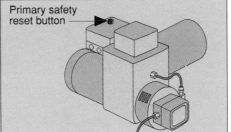

If the primary safety or stack switch shuts off, wait five minutes, then press the reset lever or button.

Combustion air blowers usually are protected by an overload device. Restart by pressing the reset button.

HELPFUL HINTS   TROUBLESHOOTING BEFORE CALLING FOR SERVICE

Problem	Causes	Solutions
Burner doesn't run	Thermostat setting too low; main switch, a circuit breaker, or fuse open; motor may be overheated	Set the thermostat 5°F higher than usual. Check switches, breakers, and fuses. Oil motor. Press reset.
Burner runs but won't fire	Oil or spark not getting to the unit; safeties sooty	Make sure oil valves are open and there's oil in the tank—dip a rod into it, don't trust the gauge. Clean safeties.
Burner cycles too often	Clogged blower filter or other blower problems; improperly set limit control	Replace filter. Oil and adjust blower (see page 339). Check and adjust limit control (see page 363).
Burner smokes or squeals	Combustion air blower motor needs oiling	Shut off the unit, let it cool, and fill the oil cups; check them again after the motor has run for an hour or so.
Chimney smokes	A cold flue causes this when the burner first fires; but if smoking persists, it's a sign of incomplete combustion, which means the unit is wasting fuel.	Call for service and request the instrument tests listed on page 344. Don't attempt to adjust a burner yourself.

Maintaining and Troubleshooting Air Systems (continued)

UNDERSTANDING A HEAT PUMP

Of all heating components, a heat pump is the most difficult to comprehend. Think of it as a reversible air-conditioner. Like an air-conditioner, it can lower indoor temperatures by removing heat from the air and dispelling it outside, but it's also capable of extracting heat from relatively cool outside air and pumping it indoors.

To do its job, a heat pump—like all refrigeration devices—takes advantage of liquid's tendencies to absorb heat as it expands and turns into a gas and to give off heat as it's compressed into a liquid (see anatomy diagrams at right).

The anatomy of a split-system heat pump (shown in the heating mode) shows that it has two sections. In the outdoor unit, a fan moves air through a coil that absorbs heat. A compressor then superheats the vapor and sends it through refrigerant lines to a second coil in the furnace. Here, a blower pushes return air through the coil, warming the air and forcing it into the ducts. Meanwhile, refrigerant travels back to the outdoor unit to begin another full cycle through the pump.

An automatic reversing valve reverses these flows. It has to be automatic because when the outside air temperature approaches the freezing mark, heat pumps tend to freeze up. When this happens, a sensor activates the reversing valve and the unit defrosts itself.

In some heat pumps, the compressor, fan, coils, reversing valve, and blower are enclosed in a single outdoor cabinet, as shown at right. Only the system's main supply and return ducts penetrate exterior walls; there is no separate furnace.

ANATOMY OF A HEAT PUMP

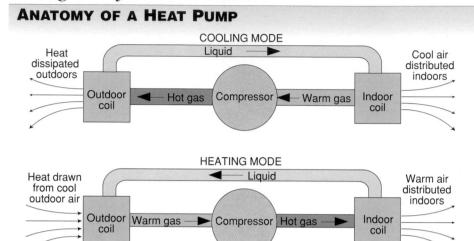

ANATOMY OF A SPLIT-SYSTEM HEAT PUMP

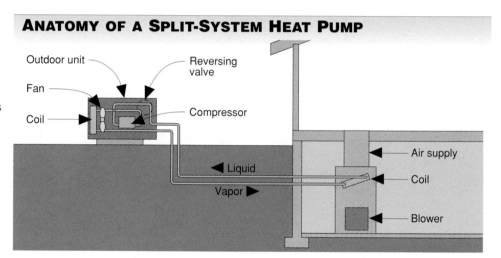

ANATOMY OF A SINGLE-UNIT HEAT PUMP

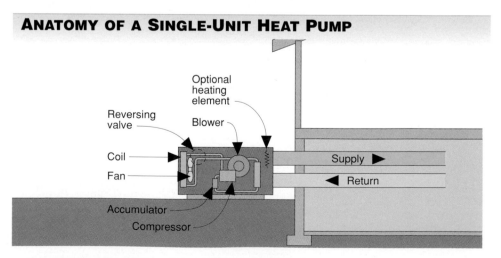

Operating a Heat Pump

Heat pumps work well down to temperatures of about 15°F. Below that, most require a backup heating source, usually electric-resistance elements installed in the furnace, ducts, or the pump cabinet itself. These units also take over for the pump while it's defrosting. If you live in a cold climate and have a heat pump, you no doubt have such a backup system.

When a heat pump's defrost cycle runs continuously—or not at all—the backup system takes over, a problem you might not be aware of until your electric bill arrives. That's why it pays to familiarize yourself with what happens during a normal defrost cycle.

You'll notice that when the temperature hovers around freezing, frost will form on the outdoor coil. When this occurs, the reversing valve should activate a cooling cycle to melt the ice. You may hear gurgling or see steam rising from the outdoor unit.

Heavy ice accumulation means the unit isn't defrosting. No ice or defrost cycles that last longer than 15 minutes indicate that the pump is stuck in its cooling mode.

For either condition, check the outdoor coil. Leaves, snow, or other matter may be cutting off airflow through the coil. Clear the obstruction and the system should return to normal operation.

If it doesn't and the coil remains coated with ice, the reversing switch may be stuck. Try freeing it by switching your house thermostat to the cooling mode. If the ice remains on the coil after an hour, flip the system selector switch to the "emergency heat" setting and call a heating contractor for service.

Note that if all electrical power has been off for more than an hour at temperatures lower than 50°F, because of either a power outage or a tripped circuit breaker, you should not attempt to restart a heat pump for at least six hours after the power has been restored. Instead, turn the system selector switch to "emergency heat," wait six hours, then return to the normal heat setting; turning the system switch to "off" doesn't shut off the heater. This time delay gives a heating element in the compressor's oil crankcase time to warm up the system's lubricant and prevent valve damage.

The chart below identifies the most common maladies of heat pumps and what to do about them. Like other heating units, it's good to have a heat pump serviced annually.

HELPFUL HINTS TROUBLESHOOTING BEFORE CALLING FOR SERVICE		
Problem	**Causes**	**Solutions**
Pump does not run	No power to the unit or the thermostat not calling for heat	Check thermostat setting, electrical disconnect switch, and fuses or breakers. Most pumps have a "reset" switch in the outdoor cabinet. (IMPORTANT: See above before restoring power.)
Short cycles	An obstruction blocking the outdoor coil; malfunctioning blower unit; clogged filter	Clear the outdoor coil (see above). Check the filter and blower unit (see page 339).
Long or frequent defrost cycles	Blocked outdoor coil could cause defrosting that lasts longer than 15 minutes or that occurs more than twice an hour.	See text above for symptoms and what to do.
Uneven heating	Heat pumps deliver a cooler flow of air than you may be used to. Also, indoor temperatures normally will drop 2° to 3°F when the outside temperature reaches the system's balance point differential, which is the point at which the backup heating kicks in.	Minimize airflow discomfort by carefully balancing the duct system (see page 340). To offset the balance point differential, you may have to raise the thermostat setting in colder weather.

Maintaining and Troubleshooting Piped Systems

The difference between hot water and steam might seem merely one of degrees, but that's not always the case. In many hot-water heating systems, the water temperature reaches 240°F, far above the 212°F needed for steam.

What actually distinguishes the two is that water systems are sealed, and contain only carefully controlled amounts of air in the radiation units, piping, and boiler. Steam systems, on the other hand, must "breathe."

This explains why you usually can hear steam going through the system, often to the accompaniment of banging pipes and hissing radiators. The steam has to push air ahead of it up the "risers" and out vents on each radiator.

Conversely, hot water has little air to impede its progress and circulates smoothly through the system, generally with nothing more than a few muffled thumps to let you know it's operating.

KEEPING STEAM OR WATER MOVING

Some steam-heat piping systems employ a one-pipe distribution network like the top one at right. A single pipe serves as both supply and return for each radiator.

Steam rises from the boiler to the radiators, gives off its heat, and condenses to water. The condensate drops back down the same pipe to a return main. This feeds the boiler with water to be boiled for the next steam cycle.

Most hot-water, and some steam, systems use the two-pipe network shown at the bottom right. Water or steam flows through radiation units and returns through separate pipes. The expansion tank serves as a cushion, allowing the water pressure to increase, which helps it circulate more readily.

In a "series loop" system (not shown), steam or water flows from one radiation unit to the next; there are no mains. Turning off one radiator stops the flow of steam or water, thereby shutting off all the other units.

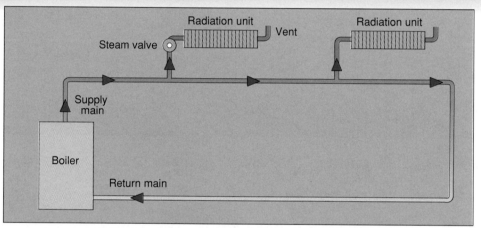

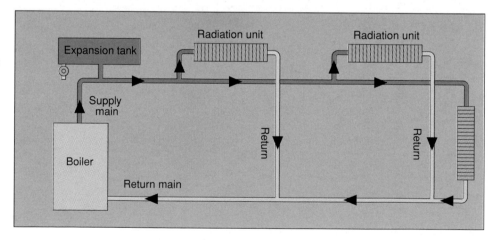

Maintaining Radiation Units

Steam and water radiation units—old-fashioned upright radiators or newer upright or baseboard convectors—are simply pipes that dissipate heat. Maintenance consists of making sure water or steam can flow through the pipes. If a unit doesn't heat, check its air vent. Liquids and gases can't get into a pipe that's full of air. Hot-water radiators—especially the ones farthest from the boiler—should be bled every fall. Steam radiators bleed themselves each heating cycle—if their vents are working.

Realize, too, that radiation units depend on pitch for drainage. If one doesn't slope toward its return outlet (or inlet, in a one-pipe system), trapped water will keep it from heating up.

What can you do about a radiation unit that's too hot? If you have a hot-water system, you might get some relief by adjusting its inlet valve. Better yet, balance the entire system, as you would with forced air (see page 340). With some piping, flow valves near the mains serve the same function as duct dampers. If your system doesn't have these, use the inlet valves on each radiator. When you get the balance you want, remove their handles so the settings can't be altered by someone else.

Steam radiators are difficult to regulate. Turning a valve to an in-between position won't modulate the heat; it causes the unit to bang. What you need is an adjustable air vent, available from some plumbing suppliers. Decreasing the size of the vent's aperture slows the rate at which steam enters the radiator.

YOU'LL NEED...

SKILLS: Basic plumbing skills.
TIME: 3 to 4 hours to adjust the radiators in an entire house.
TOOLS: Screwdriver, wire or pin.

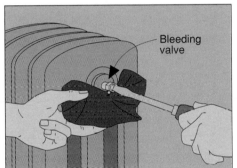

If an inlet valve leaks, try tightening its packing nut; if that doesn't work, repack it as for a faucet (see page 286).

Bleed a hot-water radiator by opening vent with a screwdriver or special key. When water squirts out, close it again.

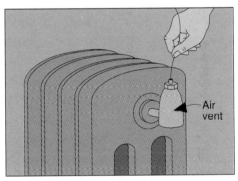

If a steam radiator won't heat, clean the air vent orifice with a fine wire. If plugged permanently, replace the vent.

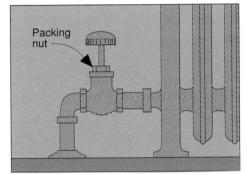

If a radiator warms only slightly, but evenly, water may be trapped inside. Make sure it's pitched toward return.

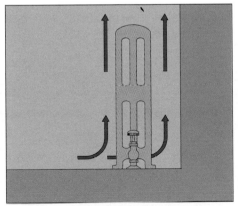

Radiators depend on air circulating freely. Don't obstruct with draperies, furniture, or solid enclosures.

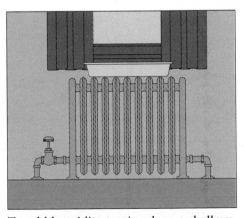

To add humidity to air, place a shallow pan of water atop a radiator. Some enclosures include pans.

Maintaining and Troubleshooting Piped Systems (continued)

UNDERSTANDING A STEAM BOILER

A steam boiler works like a giant tea kettle. A gas or oil burner heats water to the boiling point, sending steam to radiators in the house.

Modern-day boilers are more complex. The water doesn't simply lie inside a big kettle—that would take hours to heat up. Rather, water circulates around the heat source through a series of passages or tubes. Boilers also require controls to monitor and regulate their operation. These include a pressure gauge and regulator that shuts down the heat source when steam reaches a preset level, a pressure-relief valve that releases steam if the regulator fails, and a low-water cutoff that shuts down the system if the water level gets too low.

Some boilers also have an automatic feed, usually combined with the low-water cutoff, that supplies fresh "makeup" water when it's needed; with others, you have to manually open and close an ordinary valve.

Preventive maintenance includes checking controls monthly and occasionally flushing the boiler. Both are illustrated below.

To prolong boiler life and maximize efficiency, schedule an annual checkup in the spring just before you shut down the heating system. Rust thrives during periods when the unit is idle.

Ask the service technician about chemically treating the boiler water to reduce its oxygen content. Steam systems include air, and aerated water promotes rusting.

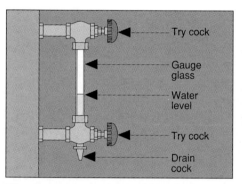

Check gauge glass monthly when boiler cycle is off for proper water level. To check level and make sure a gauge is working, open the try cocks.

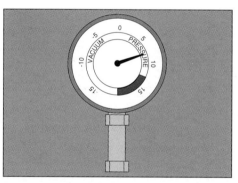

Steam pressure should not exceed the level shown by the fixed pointer on the pressure gauge. If it does, call for professional service.

Lift the lever of the relief valve to check operation. With the boiler working, it will release steam, then reseat properly. If not, have it replaced.

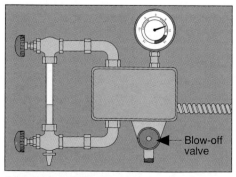

Open blow-off valve on the low-water cutoff monthly to flush sediment. Let water run until it's clear. Be careful because the water will be hot.

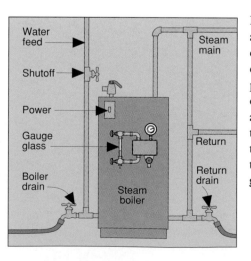

If the water in the gauge glass is rusty, and flushing through the blow-off valve doesn't clear it, it's time to flush the entire boiler. To do this, shut off the power and automatic feed, if you have one. Attach hoses to the boiler drain and return drain, open them, and let the water run out. Shut the drains, refill the boiler, and drain it again. Repeat the process until the water in the gauge is clear.

TROUBLESHOOTING A STEAM BOILER

When a boiler goes cold, check to be sure its main switch hasn't been inadvertently turned off, then look for a blown fuse or tripped circuit breaker. Also, try raising the thermostat setting.

If the boiler's burner unit is getting power, check the gauge glass to see if the boiler has enough water. When the water level drops below a certain point, the low-water cutoff turns off the burner or electric heating elements; otherwise, heat would "cook" the tank.

You can easily add water to a boiler—but first examine the return lines for leakage. Most steam systems gradually lose water through evaporation, but a big return leak will trip the low-water cutoff after just a couple of heating cycles. (Because supply lines carry only steam under relatively low pressure, they rarely develop leaks.)

If you have a leak in a supply or return, call a plumber, not a heating contractor. One of the techniques on page 281 might allow you to run the system until help arrives.

When you do add water to a boiler, be certain that you don't overfill it. Steam systems depend on an airspace above the waterline—called a chest—where the steam builds up a head. If you flood the chest, water could back up the return lines or trip the relief valve—both messy situations.

If your boiler has an automatic water-feeding device, you won't, of course, notice any problems with the water level; the automatic feed will make up any shortage with each heating cycle. This means that a leak could go unnoticed for quite some time, and constantly introducing fresh, cold water to the system will add to fuel and water bills. This is why you should shut off the feed every so often—most systems have valves or bypass piping for that purpose—and keep an eye on the water level for a few days.

Also, don't neglect to flush the automatic feed at the intervals recommended by the manufacturer. A feed that gets stuck open could flood the boiler.

HELPFUL HINTS TROUBLESHOOTING BEFORE CALLING FOR SERVICE

Problem	Causes	Solutions
No heat	No power to the unit; no water; burner problems	Check thermostat, switches, fuses or breakers, and water level. Boiler burners differ little from those on furnaces (see pages 342–345).
Poor heat	Rust and scale in a boiler, constricting passages and reducing efficiency; build-up on heating surfaces of soot from combustion	Flush the boiler (see page 350). Cleaning the heating surfaces is a job for a professional.
Chronically low water level	Leaking return lines or, more serious, a leak within the boiler itself	For return-line leaks, see main text above. Boiler leaks require major repairs or may mean you need to buy a new unit.
Clouded gauge glass	Usually, boiler needs flushing, but sometimes the glass itself needs cleaning	Flush boiler (see page 350). To clean gauge glass, turn off boiler, close try cocks, loosen nuts above and below glass, lift up the glass, pull it out, and clean it with a brush.
Noisy pipes	Probably water trapped in return lines or in the return main	Check the pitch of all returns—they must slope back toward the boiler. Adjust the slant, if necessary, with new pipe hangers.

Maintaining and Troubleshooting Piped Systems (continued)

UNDERSTANDING A HOT-WATER BOILER

Hot-water and steam systems use the same boilers, fired by similar burners, and both have pressure-relief valves designed to "blow" if pressure in the system gets too high. But hot-water heating systems are controlled by a different set of devices, and they have additional components that need tending.

The controls include a combination gauge, often called an altitude gauge, that lets you keep an eye on both water temperature and pressure and lets you know when the boiler needs water or is malfunctioning. With some systems, a pressure-reducing valve takes care of the water problem automatically. Both are shown below.

Hot-water systems also depend on an expansion tank that must be properly charged with air to prevent the water from boiling. With newer installations, you'll find this hung from the basement ceiling near the boiler, as in the drawing below, right. In older homes, it may be located in the attic.

Newer-type expansion tanks include a purge valve that simultaneously releases water and lets in air. Older versions have only a gauge glass, like the one on a steam boiler. For more about expansion tanks, see the page 353.

If your system is a forced-water (hydronic) system, look for one or more motor-driven pumps—called circulators—on return lines near the boiler. Some circulator motors are lubricated permanently and do not need maintenance. Others require a few drops of light oil annually. Read the instruction plate attached to the motor, however, because overboiling also causes problems.

Systems that have more than one circulator may be zoned to independently control temperatures in different areas of your house. Zoned systems have low-voltage, motor-driven zone valves on the supply lines. Each obeys orders from its own thermostat. These require no regular maintenance, but they can fail occasionally (see the Helpful Hints chart on page 353).

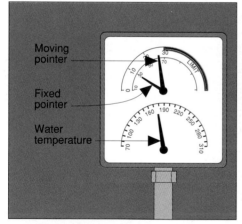

A combination gauge on the boiler has three indicators. The moving pointer shows actual pressure; the fixed pointer, the minimum pressure. If the moving pointer drops below the minimum, the system needs water. The lower temperature gauge shows water temperature. Maximum boiler water temperature is set by moving a pointer along the sliding scale of an aquastat (shown in far right drawing). Don't tamper with an aquastat setting.

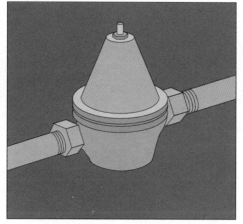

A pressure-reducing valve automatically maintains the correct water pressure. To be sure it's doing its job, check the combination gauge and call for repairs if necessary. If there's no pressure-reducing valve, you can manually feed the boiler by opening the feed water valve and closing it again when pressure reaches 12 pounds per square inch (psi). High water consumption means there's a leak in the supply or return piping or in the boiler itself.

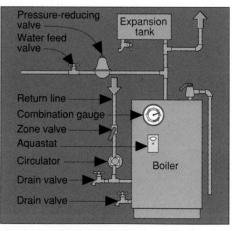

Hot-water boilers rarely need flushing, but check by draining off a bucket of water. If it's rusty, shut off power and open the drain cock and the air vents on the highest radiation units. If the boiler has a manual feed, open it, too. When the water runs clear, close the drain and vents and wait until pressure reaches 20 psi. Bleed each radiator until the pressure reaches 20 psi, drain off water; if the pressure falls below 12 psi, add more water.

TROUBLESHOOTING A HOT-WATER BOILER

Despite their complexity, hot-water boilers provide trouble-free service for years. When a problem does develop, it is usually with the expansion tank or a circulator, not the boiler itself.

Water spurting from a pressure-relief valve means there's not enough air in the tank. The tank has filled with water, which expands as it heats up and trips the safety. Check this by touching the tank. Normally the bottom half will feel hotter than the top; if the top seems hot also, it means the tank has filled with water and must be bled.

With most tanks, let the system cool, attach a hose to the tank's purge valve, and run off two or three buckets of water. The valve lets in air at the same time. An older tank might have an ordinary valve rather than the purge type. With these, first close a second valve in the line between the tank and boiler, then completely drain the tank.

After bleeding the tank, return all valves to normal settings and start the boiler. Let it run for about an hour, then check the system's pressure on the combination gauge.

When a circulator fails, its motor may continue to run, because the motor and pump are connected by a spring-loaded coupling designed to break if the pump jams. Usually, the broken coupling makes a loud clamor. A leaking circulator means the pump seal must be replaced. Call a service technician for all repairs to a circulator.

HELPFUL HINTS TROUBLESHOOTING BEFORE CALLING FOR SERVICE

Problem	Causes	Solutions
No heat	No power to the boiler; low water level; burner problems	Raise the thermostat. Check switches, fuses, circuit breakers, and water level. Troubleshoot the burner's safety controls.
Poor heat	A sudden change usually means too much or too little water; a gradual change results from deposits in the boiler or on the heat exchanger	Check the combination gauge, then the expansion tank. If problem developed slowly, try flushing the boiler, then call a professional for a tune-up.
Leaks	The circulator; pressure-relief valve; piping; or, more rarely, boiler tank	Is water coming from the pressure-relief valve, underside of a circulator, or supply or return pipes? Water may travel quite a distance from a leak, but always in a downward direction. Consider repairing pipes yourself (see pages 281 and 301–306) or call a plumber for service.
Only some radiators heat up	Suspect trapped air, especially in units far from the boiler. If an entire zone is cold, the problem lies with a zone valve or its circulator.	Bleed air from the cool units (page 349). Check the circulator (above). If a zone valve is stuck, you'll feel heat in the pipe up to the valve but not beyond.
Clanging pipes	A sudden racket usually means a circulator has gone bad. Chronic banging noises may be result of improperly pitched return lines.	Check the circulator. For banging, use level to check slope of all return lines (see Helpful Hints chart on page 351).

Troubleshooting a Thermostat

Pop the cover from a thermostat and you'll discover that your heating system's "brain" has remarkably few components. That's because it amounts to nothing more than a temperature-sensitive on/off switching device.

The sensing is done by a coil or strip of two metals that expand and contract at different rates. As room temperature drops below the setting you've selected, this bimetal coil or strip closes a set of electrical contacts, sending a low-voltage signal to a transformer that turns on the furnace or boiler. When air warms above the thermostat setting, the bimetal opens the contacts again,

shutting off the heat. Switching to the cooling mode, of course, simply reverses these cycles.

Thermostats are as reliable as any other switch. When a heating or cooling problem comes up, first make sure the temperature setting is at the right level—sometimes turning the dial up or down a few degrees will get things going again. Troubleshoot the system's other components, as shown on the preceding pages. If they're all in working order, shut off the main power switch, return to the thermostat, and try the procedures shown below. (For information about installing new energy-saving

thermostats, see page 370).

Programmable thermostats vary widely between manufacturers, so make sure you keep the instructions for adjusting them after they are installed. The primary advantage of programmable thermostats is that they can save you money in heating and cooling costs.

YOU'LL NEED...

SKILLS: Basic skills.
TIME: 10 to 20 minutes to clean a thermostat; 30 minutes to check the thermostat's accuracy.
TOOLS: Screwdriver, paper or dollar bill, fine brush, level, thermometer.

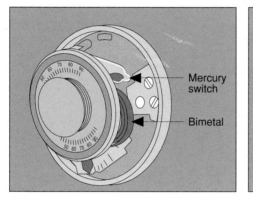

In some thermostats, contacts consist of a sealed mercury switch that never needs cleaning.

In older units, clean dirt from exposed contacts by drawing a new dollar bill or other piece of paper between them.

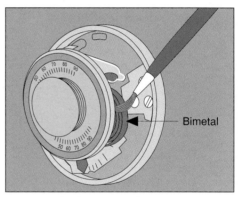

Dust on the bimetal will impair a thermostat's efficiency. Clean with a small brush or blow with dry air.

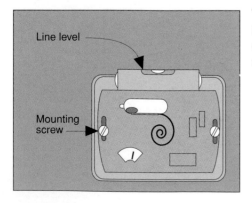

Thermostats with mercury switches must be level. To reposition, remove cover and adjust screws in the mounting plate.

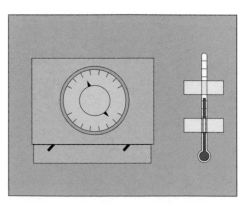

To check the accuracy of a thermostat, tape a thermometer to the wall. If recalibration is needed, call a service technician.

Maintaining and Troubleshooting Cooling Systems

You've probably noticed that degree for degree, cooling consumes far more energy than heating. Why?

The answer lies in the nature of the cooling process. The cooling unit must absorb heat from the air—a big task in itself. It also has to reduce humidity to a more comfortable level. It does this by overchilling the air, then pushing controlled amounts of warm, humid air through the cooling coil, causing moisture to form on the coil. This moisture is carried away through a condensate drain.

What's more, cool air weighs more than warm air, so, unlike heat, it doesn't tend to rise of its own accord. The result: First you pay dearly to lower the temperature and humidity of the air, then you need additional energy to move it around.

Any inefficiency in a room air-conditioner or a central system just compounds the already heavy electrical load it needs. To minimize this energy draw, you must keep your home's cooling equipment in top operating order. The following two pages show how.

Begin by familiarizing yourself with the two principal components of a cooling system. One of these is a condensing unit, in which refrigerant is condensed into a liquid. You'll always find this component located outdoors, where it can release heat (and most of the system's noise) to the outdoor air.

The condensing unit then sends the now-cool refrigerant to an evaporator coil inside the house. Here, a blower moves air through the coil to cool and dehumidify it. If yours is a central system, the evaporator coil is located in the furnace plenum, as illustrated below and on page 338, and the blower is the furnace's blower.

Room air-conditioning units house all their parts in a single, two-compartment cabinet (see page 357). Heat pumps—essentially two-way air-conditioners—have additional components (see page 346).

ANATOMY OF A CENTRAL COOLING SYSTEM

To trace the circuits of heat and cold through a whole-house air-conditioning system, study the drawing at right. Outdoors, a compressor and condenser coil "make cold" by pressurizing refrigerant gas, which loses heat as it turns into a liquid. The coil, a network of tubing and fins, transfers the heat to the outdoor air pulled through it by a fan. Cool refrigerant flows through tubing to the evaporator coil, where the refrigerant absorbs heat from air pushed through it by the furnace blower. Cool, dry air then moves into the plenum. Meanwhile, water that condensed from the air in the plenum runs down a condensate drain. The refrigerant, a hot gas once again, returns through another line to the condensing unit.

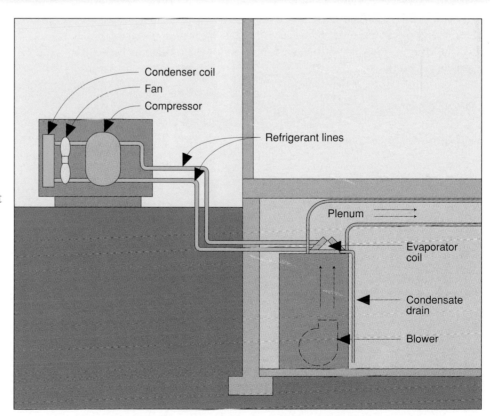

Condenser coil
Fan
Compressor
Refrigerant lines
Plenum
Evaporator coil
Condensate drain
Blower

Maintaining and Troubleshooting Cooling Systems (continued)

MAINTAINING A CENTRAL AIR-CONDITIONER

When something goes wrong with a central air-conditioner, call a service contractor. Better yet, don't wait until a unit breaks down before making that call. Schedule a tune-up for the start of every cooling season. For example, some of the refrigerant may have leaked out—a condition that gradually diminishes your system's efficiency.

Once a month keep an eye on the points illustrated below, making sure air flows freely through the condenser, evaporator coils, and your furnace's blower unit. Examine one of the coils and you'll see that it resembles an automobile's radiator—loops of tubing laced through a honeycomb of aluminum fins. Leaves, debris, or even a heavy accumulation of household dust on these fins chokes off the airflow upon which cooling systems depend.

When you clean the fins, treat them gingerly; they bend easily, and sharp tools may puncture the relatively soft copper tubing.

Don't neglect your furnace's blower unit, either. Moving cool, heavy air strains belts and bearings. To learn about keeping blowers blowing, see pages 338–339.

Keep the condensing unit clear for airflow. Hose out leaves and keep shrubs pruned back.

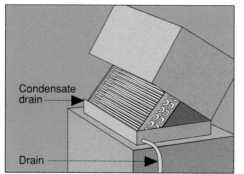

During humid weather, check the condensate drain to be sure that it's carrying off excess moisture.

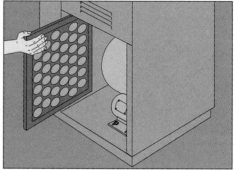

A clogged filter can shut down a unit. Change filters several times per season; never run a system without a filter.

HELPFUL HINTS TROUBLESHOOTING BEFORE CALLING FOR SERVICE

Problem	Causes	Solutions
System not running	Incorrect thermostat setting; no power to the unit	Be sure room temperature is above the thermostat setting. Check circuit breakers, main power switch.
System runs but doesn't cool	May need refrigerant; airflow problems	Check for a clogged filter or malfunctioning blower. Look for blockages at the condensing unit. Refrigerant must be recharged by a professional.
System cycles too often	May also indicate airflow problems; defective thermostat	Check condensing unit's airflow first, then the filter and blower. Check thermostat (see page 354).
Uneven cooling	If some rooms are too cool and others too warm, duct system needs balancing.	To learn about balancing an air system, see pages 340 and 359. If house doesn't cool sufficiently, the unit may be undersized.

MAINTAINING AND TROUBLESHOOTING A ROOM AIR-CONDITIONER

A window-installed room air-conditioner has all the same components you'd find in a central system, but they're scaled down to fit into a two-section enclosure.

The unit's smaller inside cell includes a blower, evaporator coil, and thermostat sensor that reads the temperature of air coming into the evaporator coil. The thermostat is located behind the control panel. A removable front panel covers everything and often holds the filter as well.

An isolation panel separates the components that are inside and those that are outside the window. The panel may have a shutter you adjust from the control panel to bring in outside air.

In the outside portion of the unit, a fan moves air through a condenser coil, where the refrigerant is liquefied and sent to the evaporator coil.

Most room air-conditioners are permanently lubricated. Routine upkeep consists of keeping their filters and coils clean.

When a unit refuses to run, make sure its filter is clean and that the power cord is plugged in. Check the main service panel for a blown fuse or tripped circuit breaker. Don't restart a room air-conditioner for 5 minutes after it kicks off, so that built-up heat can dissipate first.

If the unit cycles on or off too often or otherwise runs erratically, suspect thermostat problems. Often this means that the thermostat sensor has been knocked out of position. The sensor should be near the coil, but not touching it. Adjust it by carefully bending the wire.

If you hear a gurgling noise, or if water drips from the front panel, shut off the power and check with a level to make sure the cabinet's outer section slopes toward its condensate drain.

ANATOMY OF A ROOM AIR-CONDITIONER

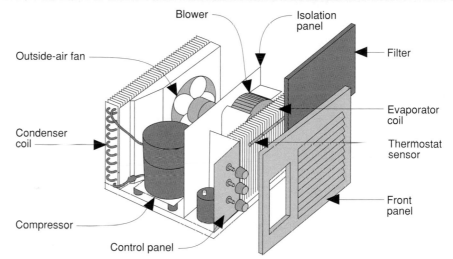

Blower — Isolation panel — Outside-air fan — Filter — Condenser coil — Evaporator coil — Thermostat sensor — Compressor — Control panel — Front panel

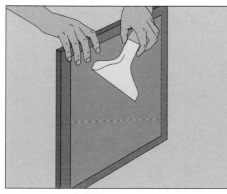

Some types of filters are vacuumed; others should be washed or replaced. Clean or change the filter every two to three weeks.

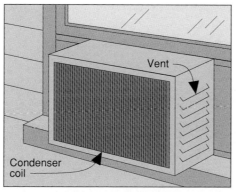

Vent — Condenser coil

Every month, check the condenser coil and intake vents for obstructions, such as leaves or dirt. Hose out this part of the unit every spring.

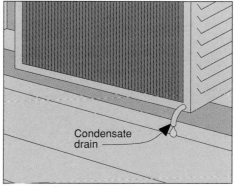

Condensate drain

Also, check the condensate drain outlet. If it's plugged up or the unit is not properly pitched away from the house, condensation can't run out.

Making Heating and Cooling Improvements

After studying the heating and cooling basics on the preceding pages, you may have already realized an anatomical fact. Though the "heart" of your home's comfort system is complex, its "arteries" and "veins" are just runs of ducts or pipes. Its thermostatic "brain" is really nothing but a temperature-activated on/off switch.

You'll want to leave heart surgery to a heating specialist, of course. But with only a few talents and tools, you can safely operate on your home's circulatory system, replace its brain with a more sophisticated one, and even implant another heart in the form of an auxiliary space heater. On the next 24 pages, you'll find many ideas on how to improve your heating and cooling system.

ADDING A WARM AIR OUTLET

Have you got a room that's too cool in the winter and too hot in the summer because it doesn't get enough air? Have you just finished off an unheated part of your house? How do you make these spaces comfortable? If your heating/cooling system isn't already running continuously in very cold or warm weather, extending the plenum or tapping into it, as shown below, is the answer. If, on the other hand, your system is already working at its capacity, consider solving the problem by installing one of the independent space heaters shown on pages 366–369.

Before going to a sheet-metal supplier for materials, draw a rough sketch of what you're trying to do. Measure the length of the new run and also the diameter of the pipe that's used for existing runs.

> ### YOU'LL NEED...
> **SKILLS:** Intermediate sheet-metal and carpentry skills.
> **TIME:** 2 to 3 hours to run a new warm air outlet.
> **TOOLS:** Tin snips, screwdriver, pliers, hammer, drill, keyhole saw.

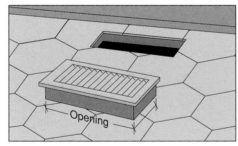

Try to locate registers along an outside wall, keeping supply run as straight and short as possible. Drill holes in corners, then cut out flooring with keyhole saw.

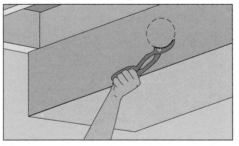

If you can't extend an existing supply line duct run, you can tap directly into the plenum. Cut opening in either its bottom or side.

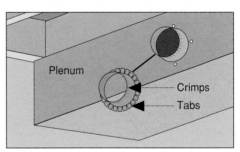

"Take-off" fittings come with flanges that are inserted into the plenum, then folded flat. Secure them with sheet-metal screws, drilling pilot holes first.

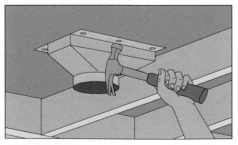

Most registers connect to their ducts with a "boot" fitting. Nail or screw it securely to the subfloor.

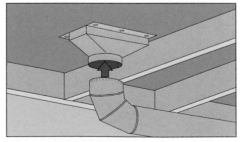

Fit an elbow to the boot and assemble the rest of the run. Secure connections with screws and duct tape.

ADDING AN IN-LINE DAMPER

Dampers—essentially doors located inside supply ducts—control the flow of heated or cooled air to room registers. Dampers let you cut down the flow to a spot that's getting too much air and redirect it to one that's not getting enough. This balancing process lets you adjust temperatures to make up for differences in exposures, length of duct runs, heat-producing appliances, or other anomalies (see page 340).

If your ducts don't already have dampers, installing them is simple. Just buy the right components and locate them in the right places.

Dampers for round ducts come preassembled in a section of duct that fits into existing runs, as shown below. When buying them, you'll need to know the diameter of your ducts—usually 5, 6, or 7 inches.

Rectangular supply ducts vary in size and cross-section, so you may need to have these made to order by a sheet-metal fabricator (find one in the Yellow Pages) or a heating contractor. They also can show you how to install them.

With an extended plenum system, such as shown on pages 336 and 338, install a damper in each supply line just past the point where it exits the plenum. To get at these, you may have to work your hands and tools into cramped quarters.

With a perimeter duct system, the ducts fan out from a central, boxlike plenum. Again, install dampers slightly beyond where the supply branches from the plenum.

Most duct runs dismantle more easily than you might think. They are secured with just one or two screws at each joint. Unscrew either end of a section, and maybe the boot as well, and you usually can create enough play to wrestle the section loose.

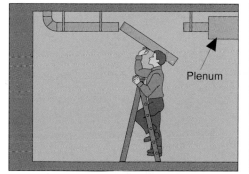

1. Pulling a section away from the end toward the furnace disengages its plain end. Then, slide the crimped end free.

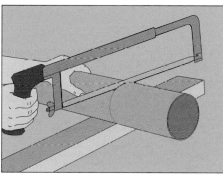

2. Cut a piece from the noncrimped end of the duct section that is 4 inches shorter than the new damper section.

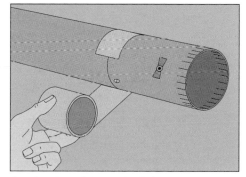

3. Slip the plain end of the damper section over the other duct's crimped end. Secure with screws and duct tape.

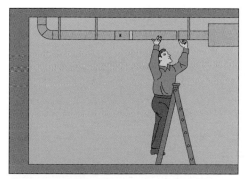

4. Reassemble the run with the new damper section. Crimped ends of the sections point away from the furnace.

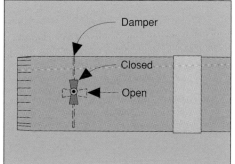

5. In the open position, the damper lever will be parallel to the duct; fully closed, it will be perpendicular.

Making Heating and Cooling Improvements (continued)

INSTALLING A HIGH-WALL RETURN

Warm air and cool air behave differently. That's why it's difficult to use the same duct systems for both heating and cooling your house.

In the heating mode, it makes sense to locate both supply and return registers at or near floor level. Heated air rises from the supplies, while heavier, cool air settles back to the return registers.

In the cooling mode, a furnace's blower pushes cooled air with enough force to boost it toward the ceiling. Unless warm air near the ceiling can get back to the cooling unit, however, the air in the room tends to stratify in layers—the warmest toward the ceiling, the coolest at the floor.

You don't need to rip open an entire wall to install a return register near the ceiling to solve this cooling problem. Interior walls are the best places for returns. They're usually not insulated, so there's no reason you can't use one of these hollow spaces as a return duct.

The drawings here show how to tap into a wall cavity—and possibly use space between the floor joists, as well. To pick the right spot, be sure to avoid other heating or plumbing runs. Don't worry about wiring, however; it won't impede airflow to an appreciable extent.

Study the anatomy of an interior wall (see page 32) and of a floor (see page 10) before you start. If the wall includes fire blocking, you'll need to make a third opening in the wall to remove it. How you cut into your walls and patch them depends on whether they're surfaced with drywall, plaster, or paneling (see pages 35–39).

Once installed, a high-wall return will make a big improvement in a room's comfort level. Your cooling system will run more efficiently, too. You may need to rebalance the system, however (see page 340).

> ### YOU'LL NEED...
> **SKILLS:** Intermediate carpentry skills.
> **TIME:** 4 to 6 hours.
> **TOOLS:** Drill, keyhole saw, backsaw, tin snips, hammer, screwdriver.

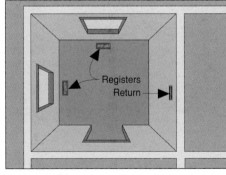

1. So air circulates through the room, locate the return on an interior wall opposite supply registers.

2. Returns should be about 6 inches from the ceiling. Locate studs, drill pilot holes, then cut out grille opening.

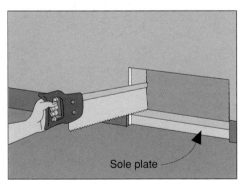

3. Make another opening directly below at the floor level. Saw out the sole plate and cut a hole in subflooring.

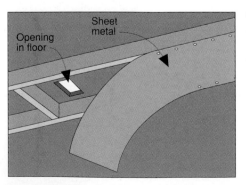

4. If joist cavities run in the right direction, use one as a duct by nailing sheet metal to it to enclose it. Connect this duct to the existing return system.

5. Or, you can drop a boot below the joists and run new duct back to your home's main return. You must seal the joist cavity around the boot.

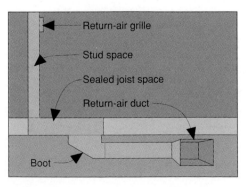

ADDING A POWER HUMIDIFIER

Many forced-air heating systems do more than heat the air they move: They add moisture to make up for the dryness that comes with winter weather. If your furnace isn't equipped with a humidifier, or if it has only a passive, evaporative plate humidifier (a small, drawerlike unit), you need something that can cope with the big volumes of arid air that pass through a heating system.

Power humidifiers can do so. Some motorized models spray a fine mist directly into the air stream; others rotate a porous water wheel through the heated air. Still others pull the air through a moist pad.

Better units are controlled by a humidistat. When the air's relative humidity reaches a preset point, the humidistat turns off the humidifier until the moisture level drops again. (Most people are comfortable in the 30- to 50-percent humidity range.) The unit also cycles on and off with the furnace blower.

Installing a power humidifier involves cutting a hole in a plenum or duct, hooking into a cold water line, routing water overflow to a nearby drain, and making electrical connections—all basic skills outlined in previous chapters.

If your home has copper or plastic plumbing, you can easily tap into an existing water line with a saddle-T. Most humidifier kits come with a self-tapping shutoff valve that connects into copper pipe. With steel pipes, use a conventional T-and-union connection. (See page 312 for these plumbing connections.) Your electrical connection can come from any nearby junction box (see pages 244–256.)

Most power humidifiers mount on the furnace plenum, as illustrated here. A few, however, attach to the main return or to a bypass between the two. Consult the manufacturer's instructions before installing these.

YOU'LL NEED...

SKILLS: Basic sheet-metal, plumbing, and electrical skills.
TIME: 2 to 3 hours.
TOOLS: Tin snips, drill, screwdriver, adjustable wrench, wire stripper, pliers.

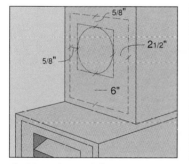

1. Most humidifiers come with a template you tape in place to locate the unit.

2. Drill pilot holes, then cut opening with tin snips. Drill holes for mounting screws.

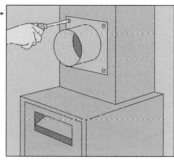

3. Slip mounting collar in place, caulk, and secure with sheet metal screws.

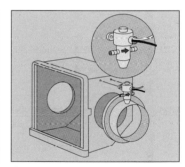

4. Make sure arrow on solenoid valve points in same direction as water flow.

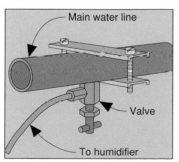

5. Install a shutoff valve, which usually comes with kit so you can easily remove the unit if it needs servicing.

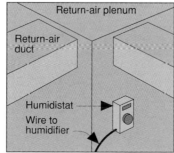

6. Locate humidistat on the main return duct. Follow manufacturer's directions for the electrical hookups.

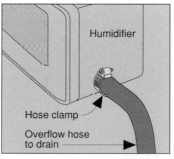

7. For overflow drain, attach a length of flexible rubber tubing to the humidifier outlet with a hose clamp.

Making Heating and Cooling Improvements (continued)

CHOOSING AND BUYING AN ELECTRONIC AIR CLEANER

The filter on an air-conditioner or a furnace—nothing more than a simple screen—does an excellent job of snaring large bits of dust. But pollen, smoke, bacteria, mold spores, and other small particles pass right through.

An electronic air cleaner uses a magnetizing process called ionization to remove more than 90 percent of the pollutants in your home's air. It does this by giving the very tiny particles a strong positive charge, then attracting them to a series of negatively charged plates. The collected particles then cling to the plates until they're washed away.

Electronic air cleaners range from portable models no larger than a radio to whole-house units that permit a heating/cooling/humidifying system to truly condition the air. All electronic air cleaners depend on a continuous flow of air through the unit—for maximum efficiency a unit usually requires enough airflow to change the air three times per hour. Maintenance consists of periodically washing the collecting plates. For some units, you also must replace a charcoal filter every three months.

Central air cleaners usually mount on the furnace's return side. Some models have a sensor light that indicates when the collector needs cleaning and a test button to let you know if the unit is working properly.

To install a furnace-mounted air cleaner, you need to tap into ductwork, make power connections, and sometimes—with wash-in-place models like the one shown below—provide a water line and a drain. Bigger, more complex systems are best sized and installed by a professional contractor. Others come in kit form, with instructions oriented to do-it-yourselfers.

Consider installing an electronic air cleaner if you live in a particularly dusty area. Also, if a family member has dust allergies, often you'll find that reducing the amount of fine particles in the air can alleviate allergy symptoms.

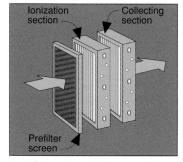

Prefilters catch big particles before the smaller ones are ionized and collected.

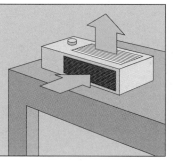

Tabletop units handle rooms up to 250 square feet in size. Plug these in anywhere.

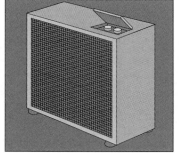

Console models handle spaces up to 500 square feet. Most have two-speed fans.

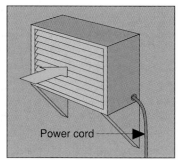

For small systems with one return, you can get a unit that doubles as a register.

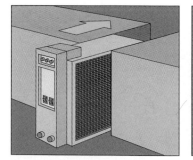

Others mount in the return duct next to the blower and adapt to furnace layouts.

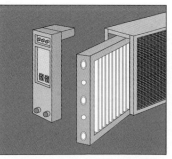

To clean most units, slide out the collector plate and rinse it in water.

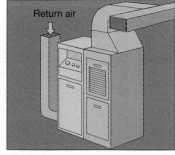

Wash-in-place cleaners install next to the furnace. You don't manually clean these.

SETTING A FURNACE FOR CONTINUOUS AIR CIRCULATION

Adjusting a furnace blower for continuous air circulation helps extract every bit of efficiency from heating, cooling, and humidifying equipment. Set on continuous circulation, your system will heat and cool more evenly. If the system has an electronic air cleaner, it will operate continuously, too.

Not everyone will find this option acceptable, however, especially on cold evenings between heating cycles. Air in motion draws off body heat and, consequently, tends to feel cooler than it actually is.

Adjusting a system for continuous circulation may or may not reduce total energy consumption. You may save on heating and cooling costs, but the electrical cost to run the blower constantly will increase. Whether or not that increase exceeds your fuel savings depends on what you're paying for the different forms of energy, how tightly your house is weather-stripped, and other factors.

Try using continuous air circulation for a month or so, keeping a careful tally of your energy bills. If family members are not comfortable with the blower on, you'll know sooner than that.

If continuous operation is not comfortable, try slowing down the blower, as explained below. For direct-drive blowers, a service technician may be able to make a simple electrical speed adjustment on the blower.

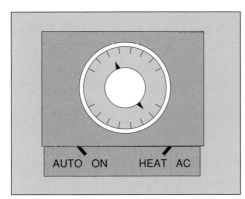

If your thermostat has a blower control, turn it from "auto" to "on" for continuous operation.

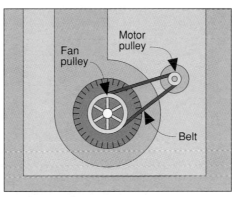

Increase airflow on a belt-driven blower by replacing the motor pulley with one that is one size smaller.

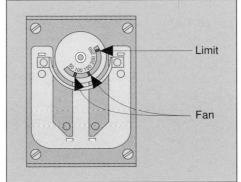

If the thermostat has no fan switch, adjust the fan's limit control, located on the furnace, as shown below.

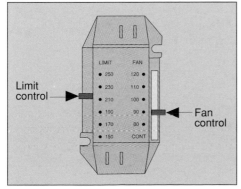

Remove cover on the limit control. If it looks like this, move the fan control to its lowest setting. Don't touch the limit setting; it controls burner temperature.

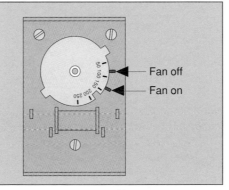

If limit control is like this one, move levers to lowest settings. You can adjust intermittent operation by resetting levers to 115°F on, 90°F off.

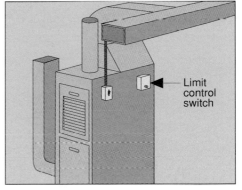

For a limit control like this, move fan levers to lowest settings. Be careful not to move the limit control, which should be adjusted by a professional.

Making Heating and Cooling Improvements (continued)

CHOOSING AND BUYING RADIATION UNITS

Radiation is a hot surface's tendency to "throw" heat into the air around it. Radiation accounts for only part of the way a so-called radiator works. Hold your hand above one and you can feel heated air rising from the top. This process, called convection, helps distribute the heat.

Whether a charming antique unit or a modern baseboard-style, the shape of the unit may be more important than physical size. Longer, lower types don't put out any more heat than upright units, but they spread it over a broader area.

A large unit may or may not radiate more heat than a smaller one. The square-inch area of the heating surface exposed to air passing through, as well as around it, is the critical factor. So, radiation units are sized according to the square inches of radiation a unit offers. With help from your heating contractor, you can calculate the number of square inches you'll need to warm a given area of your home.

In selecting a new or replacement unit, you also must consider the type of metal from which it is made. Cast iron gains and dissipates heat slowly, stretching the cooling-off period between heating cycles. Units made of steel, copper, aluminum, or combinations of these heat up rapidly and cool quickly. This means that a single fin-type convector (such as shown in the lower left drawing) in an otherwise iron system could result in a room that is alternately too hot and too cool.

The drawings below show various radiator/convector units. Baseboard types come in 1- to 8-foot-long sections that can be joined together.

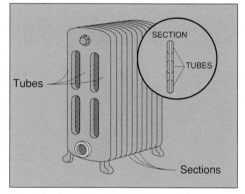

To calculate the "size" of a radiator, you must measure the surface area of all the tubes and sections.

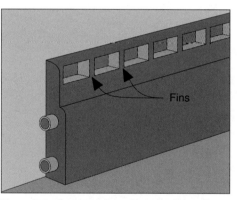

Type-RC cast-iron baseboards have fins inside and out to increase convection output. Use this type for shorter runs.

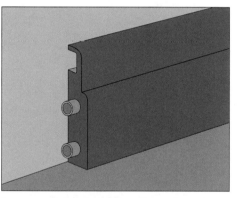

Lower-output, type-R units make sense for longer runs because they give off heat more evenly than shorter ones.

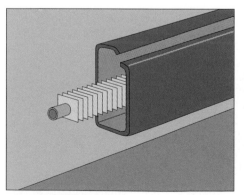

Fin-tube units rely on convection and heat and cool rapidly. Use them for hot-water—not steam—systems.

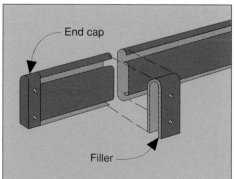

Dummy baseboard accessories are available to fill the spaces between convector units and to hide piping.

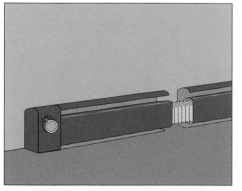

Electric baseboards warm mainly by radiation. Each one can be controlled by its own thermostat.

REPLACING OLD RADIATORS WITH CONVECTION UNITS

Thinking of replacing an unsightly old radiator with a sleek new baseboard system? If so, you have some moderate plumbing and carpentry chores—and one muscle job—ahead of you.

The heavy work involves wrestling that iron behemoth out the door. Don't try to carry a radiator; even small ones are amazingly heavy. Instead, with a helper, topple it onto a rug and drag it out, or rent an appliance dolly.

You'll have to assess your existing plumbing layout carefully. Ideally, baseboard units should run along outside walls and under windows—regardless of where the old radiator was located. This means you might have to repipe supply and return lines to the right spots—a not-too-difficult chore if you're familiar with the plumbing basics covered on pages 301–314. If major piping changes are needed, you may have a job best suited to a professional plumber.

You can use copper or threaded black steel pipe, in sizes specified by the manufacturer. Wherever steel and copper pipes meet, however, be sure to install a special adapter to prevent electrolytic corrosion. Don't forget to provide unions at either end, in case you ever need to disconnect the baseboard units.

You'll want to include a valve on the supply side and, most certainly, an air vent at the return side. For a steam system, get a "gate" valve; for a hot-water system, a "globe" valve. In some situations. you also may need a valve at the return outlet.

Mounting procedures vary, so follow the manufacturer's directions, bearing in mind that you always must provide enough pitch for condensate or cool water to drain to the return lines.

After you've finished installing your new units, fire up the boiler, wait an hour or so, then bleed air from the new run. To learn about this and other radiator basics, see pages 348–349.

YOU'LL NEED...

SKILLS: Basic carpentry skills and basic to intermediate plumbing skills.
TIME: 3 hours to replace one radiator, if system piping does not need revamping.
TOOLS: Hacksaw, screwdriver, pipe wrenches, tubing cutter, drill.

1. Count the tubes and sections in the old radiator. Knowing this, a dealer can size the new unit correctly.

Use a dolly—radiators are heavy

2. Turn off boiler, let system cool, and drain boiler and piping. Disconnect old radiator; remove with appliance dolly.

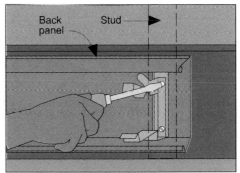

Back panel   Stud

3. Mark stud locations and screw the metal baseboard housing to the baseboard or wall at the stud marks.

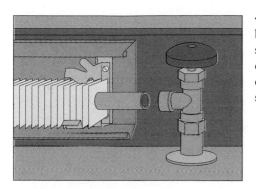

4. Cut and fit finned pipe sections between end fittings. If the locations or size of the new units and end fittings don't match, you'll need to use extensions and/or fittings. Fins are supported by brackets in the housing.

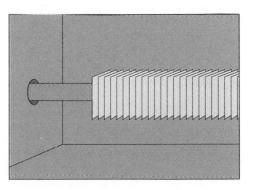

5. You can run pipes through walls, but leave a ⅛-inch clearance to allow for expansion.

Making Heating and Cooling Improvements (continued)

CHOOSING AND BUYING SPACE HEATERS

Many furnaces and boilers are bigger than they need to be, which means you easily can add more registers or radiation units, as shown on the preceding pages. If, however, you want to warm a sizable space, and especially if you need only part-time heat, an independent space heater might be a better alternative.

In shopping for a self-contained heating unit, you'll find a multitude of models from which to choose. The drawings below illustrate the major possibilities, and there are dozens of variations.

To narrow the field, ask yourself exactly what job the heater needs to do. Will it be used only occasionally or briefly for backup or auxiliary heating? If so, an electric wall, ceiling, or baseboard unit might be the answer. These are inexpensive, easy to install, and economical on floor space. Running one for extended periods, however, adds significantly to your electricity bill.

At the other end of the energy scale is the old-fashioned stove. Advances in wood-burning technology have turned the wood-burning stove into a truly efficient modern heater. Unless you cut your own wood, however, check on wood prices before you invest in wood-burning equipment. Also, remember that even the most efficient units must be tended once or twice a day. Veterans of wood heat point out that cutting wood, stacking and carrying it into the house, and removing ashes demand large expenditures of human energy.

What about fireplaces? We didn't include them in this lineup because most do not do a good space-heating job. While some do, many actually rob heated air from your home. For a complete discussion of fireplaces, see pages 102–111, and note the heat-efficient versions illustrated on page 106.

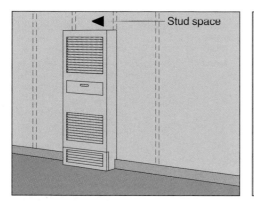

Wall furnaces take up little space, but must be vented outside and need fuel and power hookups (see page 367).

Electric heaters install anywhere and come in many different models (see page 368).

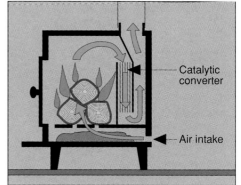

Airtight stoves use special drafting systems to extract maximum heat from each load of logs.

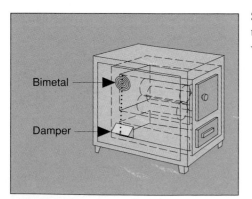

Some wood-burning heaters have thermostatic controls. They can warm a small house (see page 369).

Multifuel furnaces burn wood, coal, gas, or oil, producing heat even when you're gone for long periods.

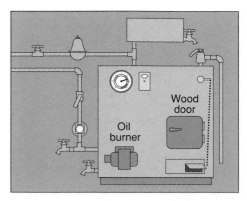

INSTALLING A GAS WALL FURNACE

A wall furnace packs all the elements of a forced-air heating system into a compact cabinet that mounts in or on an exterior wall.

With direct-venting models, a pair of metal pipes—one inside the other—penetrates the wall. One pipe supplies fresh air for combustion; the other exhausts fumes. With direct venting, you don't need to run a chimney to the roof. Also, because the fire is fed with outside air rather than house air, the system conserves indoor heat.

Check local community and building codes before buying a direct-vent furnace. Some restrict the type you can use and also may require professional installation.

Except for the gas line, there's nothing tricky about the installation. You'll need to make a wall opening, and if you choose a horizontal model, you may have to install a header (see page 168).

Position the furnace near the center of the wall, where doors, drapes, or furniture won't block the airflow. The outside vent should be at least 24 inches below eaves or other overhead projections and 12 inches above the ground.

Be careful not to crack the connections where the vent pipes attach to the furnace and where the door opens for access to the burner and pilot. Leaks here will blow out the pilot.

The drawings below show the procedure for installing a typical upright unit. For information on running pipes for gas hookups, see pages 301–303, 306, and 328. Tap electrical power from a nearby wall outlet or basement ceiling box (see pages 244–252).

YOU'LL NEED...

SKILLS: Intermediate carpentry, plumbing, and electrical skills.
TIME: 6 to 8 hours, including the electrical and gas lines.
TOOLS: Hammer, drill, sabersaw or reciprocating saw, screwdriver, pliers, wire stripper, tubing cutter, pipe wrench.

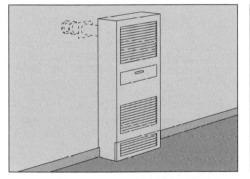

You can hang some units directly on the wall with brackets supplied by manufacturer; this reduces carpentry.

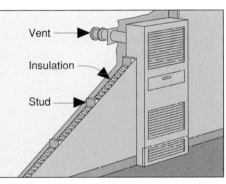

Many units are recessed into the wall. Locate studs, cut away drywall or lath and plaster, and remove insulation.

Determine where the flue will go, drill hole through exterior wall, and enlarge the opening with a sabersaw.

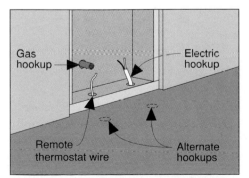

Drill holes for gas and electrical supply lines. These can come through either the wall or floor.

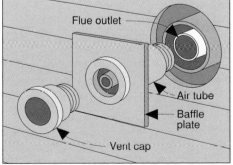

After you've installed the furnace, assemble the vent, making connections airtight by caulking the baffle plate.

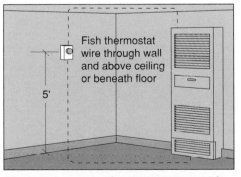

Place any remote thermostat to avoid hot and cold spots, corners, and alcoves. Run wire as shown.

Making Heating and Cooling Improvements (continued)

INSTALLING AN ELECTRIC HEATER

Electric heaters put out quiet, almost instantaneous heat—just what you need to take the nip from chilly bathroom air, warm a basement shop, or boost the temperature in a chronically cool room. Because electric heaters needn't be vented, you can tuck one almost anywhere.

Although these heaters aren't inexpensive to operate, using one strategically could help cut the cost of running your central heating system. Consider, for instance, installing a baseboard unit in a room that's used only occasionally. You could then shut off the room's registers or radiators and heat the space only when needed.

Electric heaters require lots of power. With small 500- to 1,000-watt models, you may be able to tap into a receptacle on a lightly used circuit, as shown below. (See page 236 to calculate your house power.) If a unit draws more than 1,000 watts, however, it should have its own 20-amp circuit. High-output heaters require 240-volt current—a job for a professional electrician.

An electrician also might be able to install a remote switch next to a door or in another convenient location. Timer switches save energy by shutting off a unit after it has operated for a preset time period.

For safety reasons, don't place either the heater or the switch within reach of a bathtub or other wet place. And make sure its grille can't be penetrated by a child's fingers.

Most units come with installation instructions. The drawings below show how to recess a fan-powered model into a wall. Ceiling, lamp-type heaters also may include an exhaust fan (see page 407).

YOU'LL NEED...
SKILLS: Basic carpentry and electrical skills.
TIME: 3 to 4 hours.
TOOLS: Drill, keyhole or sabersaw, wire stripper, screwdriver.

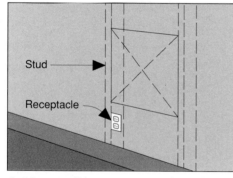

1. Most wall heaters are made to fit between studs. Locate studs, drill starter hole, then carefully cut out the opening with a keyhole or sabersaw.

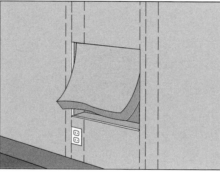

2. In outside walls, you'll probably find insulation in the cavity. Cut it off above and below the opening.

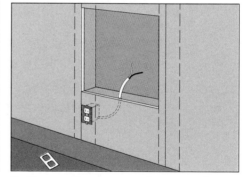

3. For small units, tap electricity from a nearby outlet box. For larger units, you'll have to run a new, separate circuit from the main service panel.

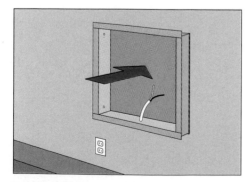

4. Most units come with mounting flanges for attaching to plaster or drywall. Run the electrical cable through the flange before installing it.

5. Complete electrical connections. Slip the heater into its flange box and screw on the grille to make it more tamper-resistant.

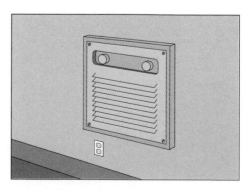

INSTALLING A WOOD-BURNING HEATER

Newer wood-burning heaters can keep a load of logs glowing for 12 hours or more. To top that, they burn so completely, you need to shut down the heater only once a week to clean out the ashes.

To maintain this long-burning fire, wood heaters carefully control the combustion process. Designs vary, but most feature airtight construction and an automatically regulated draft that provides the fire with no more air than it really need. The result: Wood-burning heaters draw very little air and lose a minimum of heat up the chimney.

You do pay a price for this efficiency, however. Slow-burning fires produce creosote, which can build up in a chimney and ignite. Because of this, you need to follow strict installation and maintenance procedures. Use only a masonry chimney or a metal chimney with a Class-A rating from Underwriters Laboratories. Follow the heater and chimney manufacturers' requirements to the letter, and check local building codes, too.

As you assemble a metal chimney, note that, unlike warm-air ducts, flue sections fit together with their crimped ends toward the heater. This allows condensation in the vent to flow back to the fire. For an airtight assembly, seal each joint with furnace cement and secure it with three metal screws.

To break in a new wood heater, light small fires for the first few times you use it. Otherwise, heat could crack a casting. Proper maintenance is important, too. Remove ashes at recommended intervals to prevent warping and burnouts, and clean the flue annually (see page 132).

When a wood-burning heater smokes or won't draw properly, make sure it's getting enough combustion air. If that's not the problem, your chimney might not be tall enough. More about these symptoms on pages 104–105.

YOU'LL NEED...

SKILLS: Intermediate masonry, carpentry, and sheet-metal skills.
TIME: 1 to 2 days.
TOOLS: Hammer, trowel, grout float, cold chisel, tin snips, screwdriver, drill, sabersaw.

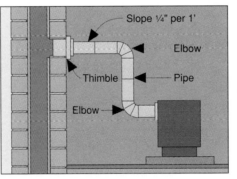

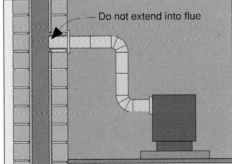

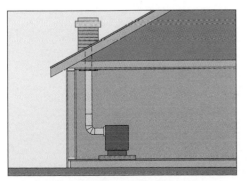

Check installation instructions for minimum distances to a combustible wall. Most also call for a masonry or other noncombustible base.

If location permits, it's easiest to connect to a masonry chimney, as shown. Keep flue pipe runs short, with no more than two elbows.

Make sure the flue pipe doesn't extend into the flue, causing an obstruction. Make the connection at least 18 inches below the ceiling.

If you don't have a masonry flue, you'll have to run a class-A metal flue through the ceiling and roof (see pages 107–109).

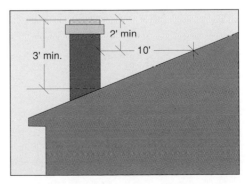

For a proper draw, the chimney should extend above the roof peak. If that would make it unwieldy, allow these minimum clearances.

Making Heating and Cooling Improvements (continued)

INSTALLING A PROGRAMMABLE THERMOSTAT

Programming a heating and cooling system usually results in a sizable reduction in energy bills. Generally, the greater the spread in degrees between the "home" and "away" (or day and night) settings—called the setback—the more energy savings you'll realize.

Timed thermostats include a 24-hour clock. You select the beginning and ending times for the setback period, then forget about it. Another type uses a photocell to switch from one setting to another at dusk and dawn.

Regardless of the type that best suits your needs, select a model that's compatible with your furnace's control circuit and electric current. In most cases, furnace switches operate on 15 to 30 volts, as do all timed thermostats. Don't try to connect one to a 120-volt system.

A thermostat needs good air circulation to operate properly. Locate it about 5 feet above the floor and away from drafts, direct sunlight, and dead air spots behind doors or in corners. Also, make sure there are no heating ducts, pipes, or flues in the mounting wall. Most often, your existing thermostat location will satisfy these criteria. If you need to move it to improve it's efficiency, you'll have to run new low-current wire to the new location (see page 260).

Adjusting the setback may call for experimentation. Begin by trying a setting 10°F lower or higher than your normal heating and cooling levels. If the house cools down or warms up too much, decrease the setback to 8°F. Also, adjust the timings on the setback cycle to accommodate your schedule.

If your home has a heat pump, consult your heating contractor before buying a timed thermostat. Using a programmable thermostat with a heat pump may actually add to your utility bills.

YOU'LL NEED...
SKILLS: Basic skills.
TIME: 20 to 30 minutes.
TOOLS: Level, screwdriver, wire stripper.

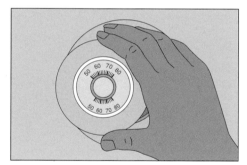

1. Shut off furnace and electricity. Disconnect old wires—don't let them fall into the wall—and label them as to which terminals they were connected.

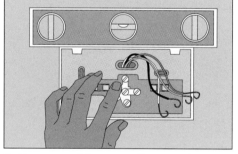

2. Remove old unit. Pull wires through new back plate. Mark level line on wall, install mounting screws, and check level again; then, tighten screws.

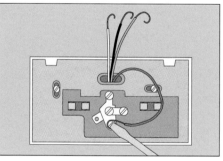

3. Connect wires to the appropriate terminals using your labels as guides; wires usually are color-coded.

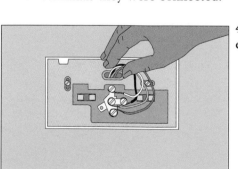

4. After wires are connected, push excess wire into the wall.

5. Attach cover to back plate. Turn on electricity and furnace and program the unit. Fine-tune settings over a period of a few weeks, as described above.

ZONING A FORCED-AIR SYSTEM

In a typical heating, ventilation, and air-conditioning (HVAC) system, a single thermostat located in a central location calls for warm or cool air, then the blower comes on to circulate the conditioned air throughout the home.

With a zoned system, as shown in the anatomy drawing below, individual thermostats call for warm or cool air for different zones. These zones—a single room, a floor, or a whole wing of the house—allow for different temperatures in these different areas of the home. You also have control over the fresh air that is fed into the blower unit.

Zoning provides several benefits:

■ The temperature can be tailored to the activity occurring in the zone.
■ By not overheating or overcooling a space, you save energy.
■ Because each zone calls for heating or cooling at different times, you generally can get by with a smaller system.

Generally, installation of a zoned system is not a do-it-yourself project. You should call in a qualified heating and cooling contractor. Why? Ducts are sized for an air pressure at the blower—due to resistance to airflow in the ducts—equivalent to that of 0.1 inch of water. At this pressure, air circulation is great enough to carry the required amount of heating or cooling energy, while the velocity is low enough to minimize the sound of rushing air.

When ducts are zoned, some may be shut off, leading to increased pressure, higher velocity in the open ducts, and a possible freeze-up of air-conditioning coils. The system may require a static-pressure regulating damper to automatically regulate air pressure and airflow at the blower. Measuring duct pressure and sizing ducts requires professional training and equipment.

Zone-control dampers (shown below) come in a variety of configurations and sizes. This allows a contractor to retrofit nearly any existing duct configuration.

ANATOMY OF A ZONED SYSTEM

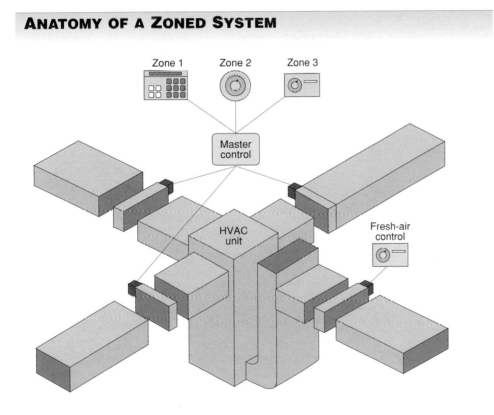

Zone 1 Zone 2 Zone 3

Master control

HVAC unit

Fresh-air control

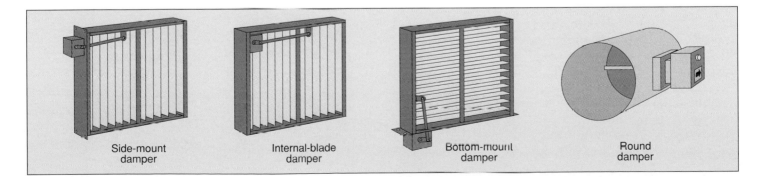

Side-mount damper

Internal-blade damper

Bottom-mount damper

Round damper

Choosing Heating and Cooling Equipment

The worst time to select a new furnace or air-conditioner is the day the old one takes its last breath. Split-second decisions then may result in years of higher-than-necessary fuel bills. With such

developments as high-efficiency furnaces, improved insulation, and others outlined in the next few pages, the choices can be confusing.

As you solicit contractors' bids, make sure that each one spells out

how much heating or cooling you're being asked to buy, as well as the ultimate price tag. The information presented here introduces you to some terms and should help you better understand those bids.

UNDERSTANDING HEATING AND COOLING TERMINOLOGY

■ A backup system is a second heating unit that kicks in when the main unit cannot handle the load.
■ A British thermal unit (Btu) is the heat needed to raise the temperature of 1 pound of water 1°F. Heating and cooling equipment is sized by the Btu delivered in 1 hour (Btuh).
■ Collectors are devices that capture heat in a solar installation.
■ Coefficient of performance (COP) is the ratio of total capacity of a heating unit to its total energy output. This gives you a measure

of the system's heating efficiency.
■ Design heat load is the rate of heat loss in Btuh when the outside temperature is at the design minimum temperature for the site.
■ The energy-efficiency ratio (EER) is the unit's Btu cooling capacity divided by its energy input in watts.
■ Heat gain is the Btuh of heat coming into your home from sources other than its heating and cooling system. Most heat gains come from the sun, but lighting, appliances, and even body warmth contribute.

■ Heat loss is the Btuh of heat escaping from your home.
■ Payback is the length of time it takes for energy savings from new equipment to equal your investment.
■ Tons is another way of expressing the output from an air-conditioner or heat pump. One ton of heating or cooling output equals 12,000 Btu.
■ A watt is a measure of the work energy of electricity; it's the product of amperes times volts. Electrical inputs—and your electric bill—are measured in kilowatt-hours (kwh).

SHOPPING FOR ENERGY

What are the relative costs of heating with oil, natural gas, liquid propane (LP) gas, or electricity? You probably don't have all of these options, but you may be able to choose between electricity and a fossil fuel. To find out which one would be the most economical, you need to get the unit cost of each form of energy from each utility, then do some math.

Energy units differ: Electricity is priced by the kilowatt hour (kwh); natural gas by 100 cubic feet (ccf); and oil and LP gas by gallons. Rating these might seem like comparing apples and oranges. But each unit yields a predictable number of Btu. It's Btu—millions of them—that you need to heat your home.

The table shows the Btu yields for different energy units and the

coefficients of performance (COP) for types of equipment. To figure the cost of each Btu generated by your new heating plant, divide the cost of each energy unit by its Btu yield. Energy forms are not equally efficient, so divide the cost per Btu you just obtained by the COP for the

equipment you're considering. Because a single Btu doesn't amount to much, multiply by 1 million. Your final computation should look like this:

Cost per million Btu = Cost of the energy unit ÷ its Btu yield ÷ COP × 1 million.

CALCULATING ENERGY YIELDS

Energy Form	Unit of Measurement	Btu Yield	Coefficient of Performance
Electricity	1 kwh	3,412 Btu	
Electric-resistance			1.0
Heat pump			1.5
Natural gas	1 ccf	103,000 Btu	0.70
Fuel oil	1 gallon #2 oil	139,000 Btu	0.70
LP gas	1 gallon	91,600 Btu	0.70

SIZING UP YOUR HEATING NEEDS

In the past, a heating contractor would walk around your house, guess its size, then order a furnace or boiler with considerably more capacity than you'd ever need.

Such seat-of-the-pants engineering guarantees that you'll be warm, but wastes energy. Now, knowledgeable contractors calculate the exact amount of your house's design heat load. They measure total heat losses, then compute the load for your geographic region using design temperatures. The result, in Btuh, provides a guide for sizing the heating plant. If, for example, your home has a total heat load of 93,000 Btuh, you'll need a furnace or boiler with at least that much output, perhaps up to 100,000 Btuh.

If you're replacing a furnace or boiler, make sure it wasn't oversized to begin with. Properly sized units run almost all the time in very cold weather; oversized ones will cycle off often.

Also, insulation, storm windows, and weather stripping substantially reduce your home's heat losses. So, you might consider upgrading these systems, as explained in the next chapter, to help save on energy bills.

Calculating Heat Loss

Every part of a house loses heat to the outdoors, but at different rates, calculated as an R-value (see page 390). To assess your home's heating needs, a contractor computes the volume of air and its exchange rate, then the heat loss value for each exterior surface—each surface's area divided by its R-value. Arrows on the drawing show relative rates of heat loss for roof, chimney, walls, windows, doors, and foundation. Longer vectors mean greater losses, but will vary according to materials used. For more about heat losses, see pages 75–78 and 390–400.

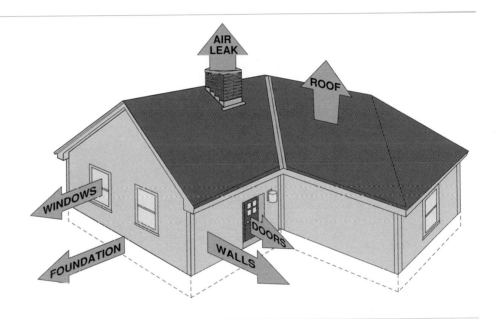

Using Design Temperatures

Once total heat loss has been tabulated, the contractor consults tables showing the design minimum (or coldest normal) temperature in your region. (See the map at right and note that these are not the coldest temperatures on record.) Subtracting this design minimum temperature from the inside temperature that you want to maintain provides the design temperature difference. This difference is multiplied by the total heat loss calculation to yield the design heat load—the load your furnace must handle.

Choosing Heating and Cooling Equipment (continued)

SELECTING A HEATING PLANT

Once your home's heating load has been calculated (see page 373), a knowledgeable contractor can go one step further. Using the energy-yield data (see 372) and heating degree days from the U.S. Weather Service, a contractor can come surprisingly close to estimating what you'd actually pay per year to operate a particular system.

Make sure to get this estimate. It helps you predict the payback period for equipment that might be more costly to begin with, but more economical in the long run. If, for example, heating unit A is priced

$500 more than unit B, but would save $100 a year in energy bills, its payback period would be five years.

Estimating payback periods calls for some guesswork, of course. Experts can't say exactly what will happen to relative energy costs in the years to come. It's also hard to make allowances for auxiliary equipment that adds to your comfort by cooling, humidifying, or cleaning the air, as well as heating it. Imprecise as they may be, payback calculations offer the best way to make sure you're getting your money's worth when

you purchase a new heating unit.

The drawings below show the different ways to install a forced-air furnace and its ductwork in a house that doesn't already have them. At the bottom of the page, you'll find information about two devices that improve the efficiency of a gas or oil furnace or boiler.

The payback period is even more important when you investigate more sophisticated (and expensive) equipment, such as solar units and heat pumps. Payback periods for these units can be lengthy (more about them on the following pages).

Selecting a Furnace Style

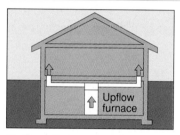

Upflow furnaces make sense for basement installations. Most ductwork is usually down there, too.

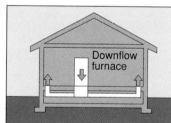

A downflow furnace can be concealed in a closet. Ducts then are run through a crawlspace or in the floor.

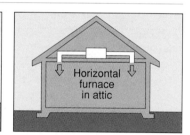

Horizontal furnaces and their ductwork can be installed in either an open crawlspace or an attic.

Energy-Saving Devices

Gas and oil furnaces lose about 20 percent of their heat up the flue. A motorized flue damper stops flue heat loss by closing the vent after a unit has cycled off.

Gas pilots that burn constantly waste even more fuel. Electric ignitions usually are coupled with the damper control. When heat is called for, the control opens a valve and lights the pilot, which ignites the burners, then shuts down.

To learn about getting fresh air to your furnace, see pages 401–402.

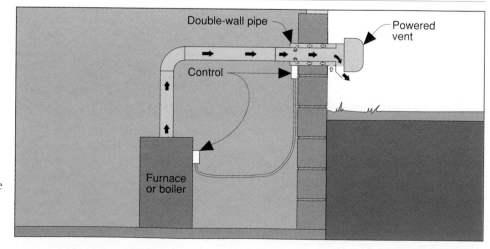

COLLECTING ENERGY FROM THE SUN

One of today's most promising energy sources is sunlight—an abundant; nonpolluting; and, best of all, free resource. Check the map at right for the average percentage of sunny daylight hours in your region. This figure gives you a rough idea of the theoretical savings solar energy could provide. The actual savings depends on what kind of solar heating systems you install.

Solar water heating (described below) and heat gains with passive solar strategies (described on page 376) are two possible energy savers. Active solar heating systems are big savers, but are beyond the scope of our discussions here.

If your area receives less sunshine than others, don't be discouraged. Because you've been buying larger quantities of energy to begin with, your actual dollar savings could still be substantial.

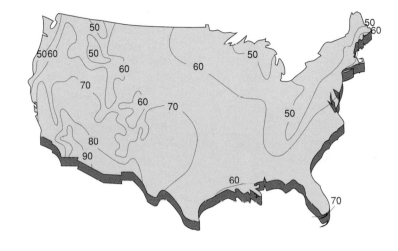

HEATING WATER WITH THE SUN

Water heating typically accounts for about 20 percent of a family's energy bill. Sunlight can greatly lighten this load and even take it over entirely during certain periods of the year.

The size of a solar hot-water system depends on your family's demands for hot water and the region in which you live. You'll need from one to five collectors like the one shown in the drawing. These send heat, via an antifreeze transfer fluid, to a storage tank located next to your water heater.

The fluid circulates through the storage tank's heavily insulated jacket, giving off heat to the water inside. A pump sends fluid back to the collector, continuing the cycle as long as the sun provides heat.

Solar-heated water can reach temperatures of 200°F or more. A tempering valve in the link between the storage tank and the water heater automatically adds cold water

to maintain the temperature needed for household use, usually 125°F.

If you are a moderately skillful do-it-yourself plumber and can make simple electrical connections, you

might be able to install modular components such as these yourself. Manufacturers usually provide kits with full instructions.

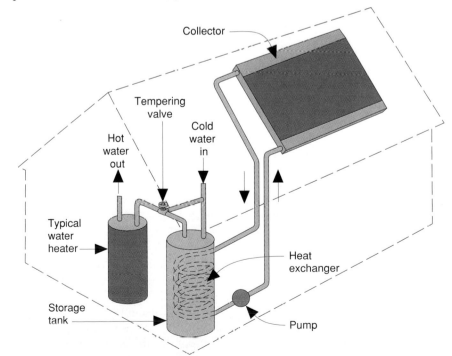

Choosing Heating and Cooling Equipment (continued)

HEATING YOUR HOUSE WITH THE SUN

Think about what happens to a car parked in a sunny spot. The interior temperature is much greater than the exterior temperature because the car's windows let in, then trap, more heat than they radiate back to the outside air. A solar heating system, using active solar collectors or passive heat gains, does the same thing with your house.

Heating your house with solar energy merits investigation, especially if you're building a new home. You'll need a site that gets lots of direct sunlight and a southern exposure. Solar components require lots of space: room on the roof for several sizable collectors and space for a several-thousand-gallon storage tank or an even bigger rock mass-storage pit.

Prepare yourself for a major initial investment. Solar systems easily cost two to three times as much as a conventional installation—in part because you also need a backup heat source that can take over during periods of prolonged cloudiness. This might be a gas, oil, or electric furnace; a series of radiant electric units; or a heat pump tailored for solar compatibility. Your payback calculations must account for the energy costs of operating the backup system, as well as the free heat you'll be getting from the sun.

TAKING ADVANTAGE OF PASSIVE SOLAR HEAT GAINS

If the payback period for an active solar system is unacceptably long or if you do not have the money to spend on a solar installation right now, you can try to plan solar capability into your new or existing home. For a new home, site it so that windows take advantage of passive solar heat gains and select a heating system now that you easily can plug solar components into later.

For existing homes, you've probably experienced the same effect of the parked car with sunny windows on room temperature in the winter. The effect is known as passive solar heating, heating by the sun without collectors, pumps, or storage systems. Whether building or remodeling, you can use this phenomenon to obtain more free heat from your windows.

During the heating season in the North Central United States, south-facing windows gain a lot more heat than north-facing ones. In fact, 1 square foot of south-facing glass takes in 175,000 Btu of solar energy, the equivalent of 175 cubic feet of natural gas, 1.2 gallons of heating oil, or 50 kwh of electricity.

But when the sun is not shining, which can be the majority of the time in the winter, the same window constantly loses heat as well. The amount of heat lost depends on the window's R-value (see page 77). Net heat gain—solar gain minus heat loss—is more important to evaluate. For example, for a double-glazed window with low-E glass or movable window insulation, south-facing windows still produce large net heat gains, nearly 150,000 Btu per square foot of window area, while north-facing windows show net heat loses.

The point is to concentrate your passive solar efforts on south-facing windows. You'll still want to insulate and weather-strip all windows to minimize heat losses (pages 77–78 and 382–400). But if you're remodeling or want to make your old house energy-efficient, look at replacing single-pane windows with double- or triple-pane units that are energy-efficient or even adding south-facing windows.

Be aware, however, that too much south-facing window area can be a poor investment. Once inside your home, the sun's rays are converted to heat. Some of the heat raises the air temperature; the remainder is stored in your home's building materials and furnishings, to be released to the air after the sun goes down. If the solar gain is too great, however, the air will overheat and you will find yourself opening windows to cool down. Or, if your thermostat is incorrectly located in that hot area, another part of the house may become cold because the thermostat will not turn on the furnace system.

How much south-facing window area can you have before your house suffers from overheating? A local heating contractor can calculate the number based on the heating-degree days for your region. The maximum window area—calculated as the percentage of window area to the total heated floor area of your home—ranges from 6 percent up to 15 percent. For example, if you live in St. Louis and your home is highly insulated, your house should have no more than 6 percent of the floor area in south-facing window area. If your house is 2,000 square feet, you could have up to 120 square feet of south-facing window area without causing overheating.

SELECTING REFRIGERATION EQUIPMENT

The energy efficiency rating (EER) of a cooling appliance is the ratio of a cooling unit's output in Btu and its input in watts (see page 372). Because a watt yields only a predictable number of Btu, why do EER ratings vary so widely? You might conclude that certain units put out two or three times as much energy as they consume. Can this be true?

Yes and no. A refrigeration unit can, indeed, sometimes deliver more than 100 percent of the energy it draws. That's because it's using those watts to move heat, not to produce it. An air-conditioner simply extracts heat from indoor air and moves it outside. Similarly, a heat pump squeezes heat from outside air and transfers it indoors.

Unlike combustion- or electric resistance-type heat producers, a heat mover's efficiency varies inversely to the difference between indoor and outdoor temperatures. As the temperature difference increases, EER drops. The coefficient of performance (COP), a measure of the heating efficiency of heat pumps (see page 372), has this same inverse relationship.

EER and COP ratings let you compare the relative efficiencies of different makes and models. The higher the COP or EER, the more heating or cooling per dollar you can expect. Manufacturers commonly give their units top EER and COP ratings. These ratings usually are certified by the Air-Conditioning and Refrigeration Institute (see below).

However, EER and COP figures don't help much in predicting your actual operating costs. To do this, you—or your contractor—also need to know the air-conditioning capacity required for your home and climate and the indoor temperature level you want to maintain. (For more about these, see page 378.)

Cooling specifications often include two sets of EER and COP ratings, one for each of the speeds at which the equipment was designed to run. Two-speed units loaf along at low speed during mild weather, then shift into high gear for extreme temperatures. Because the low speed uses about half as much power as the high speed, you don't pay for unneeded capacity.

You may find two-speed cooling units rated according to their seasonal energy-efficiency ratio (SEER), which basically is the EER prorated over an average cooling season. Here again, the higher a model's SEER, the better.

WATCHING OUT FOR LABELS

Cooling Capacity

Humidification Level

Sound Level

Heat Pump Capacity

Choosing Heating and Cooling Equipment (continued)

SIZING UP YOUR COOLING NEEDS

A grossly undersized air-conditioner just can't keep up on those really hot days. Oversized units can be even worse, however, because they cool in short, energy-wasting bursts, then shut down. Meanwhile, the indoor humidity level climbs and the air begins to feel clammy. Properly conditioned summer air, remember, is drier, as well as cooler.

Whether it's a room or central air-conditioner, a cooling unit should be just large enough to cope with prolonged hot spells. At those times,

you can expect it to run almost constantly, controlling humidity as well as temperature.

This means that the unit's output, in Btuh, must roughly equal the sum total of the heat gains of your house or room. If you're shopping for a central system, get bids from several installers and let them compute the gains, as explained below. For a room unit, you can do the figuring yourself without too much trouble (see page 379).

Some manufacturers size their

equipment's output in tons rather than Btu. To convert tons to Btu, multiply the tonnage by 12,000.

Chances are, you won't be able to get an exact Btu-for-Btu match between a model's capacity and your home's heat gains. Generally, it's safer to go to the next smaller size. With a slightly undersized unit, indoor temperatures might rise somewhat on really hot days, but continuous dehumidification will maintain a tolerable level of comfort.

Calculating Heat Gains

To calculate peak cooling demand, expect contractors to go through an even more lengthy and detailed process as that for heat losses (see page 373). Besides assigning Btuh gains to the exterior factors at right, they also need to know about hot or cold spots inside, how many appliances you have, and even how many people are in the family. For more about heat gains, see pages 75 and 382–407.

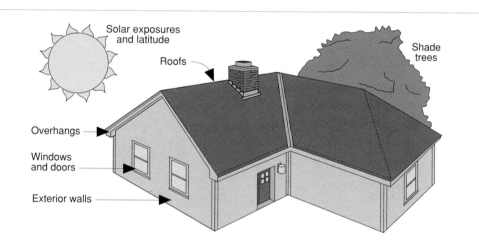

Solar exposures and latitude

Shade trees

Roofs

Overhangs

Windows and doors

Exterior walls

CHOOSING AND BUYING CENTRAL AIR-CONDITIONING

Once a contractor knows what your home's heat gains are, an installer will check the furnace blower and ductwork to determine if they can handle the heavier cooled air. While the plenum is being checked, ask if it can be modified easily to accept an electronic air cleaner, a power humidifier, or both. Even if you can't afford these items now, allowing for them will save on installation costs later. (More about humidifiers and air cleaners on pages 361–362).

You also may want to consider

installing a zoned system. Such a system could save on energy costs by keeping daytime temperatures higher in empty bedrooms.

Two-speed condensing units offer another way to minimize operating costs, matching a system's capacity to its needs. Lights on the thermostat let you know whether a two-speed unit is running at high or low speed, giving you a chance to raise the temperature setting and reduce demand when you choose.

Natural-gas-powered systems are

also available. Installation costs will be greater than for an electric air-conditioner, but you may recover the difference, and more, in lower operating costs, less maintenance, and longer life. This depends on your energy costs.

Finally, don't be surprised to find a wide range of prices for equipment with similar Btu capacities. Quality differences account for most of this variance. Some components are guaranteed for five years, others for ten.

CHOOSING AND BUYING A ROOM AIR-CONDITIONER

Central cooling is more efficient than a series of room air-conditioners. If you settle for less cooling, however, you might come out ahead by using room units.

The initial investment will be less, especially if you don't have forced-air heating to which you can add central air-conditioning. If you turn room units off or to a higher temperature setting when not using the spaces they cool, you can hold down operating costs, too.

Before shopping for a room unit, consider what you want it to do and where you'll be mounting it. A unit opposite a doorway may cool several rooms, but you may need to set up a fan to help air circulate.

Most room units are designed to fit into a double-hung window. If your windows are too narrow, shop for a narrow-chassis air-conditioner designed for casement windows. Or, consider a through-the-wall installation. Wall-mounted units don't obstruct views and run more quietly than window units. (See page 168 for how to make an opening in an exterior wall.)

Calculate the capacity you need, as explained below, then try to find an air-conditioner with a Btuh rating within 10 percent of that figure.

Compare energy efficiency ratings (EER) carefully (see page 377). The higher the EER, the less electricity a unit will draw. High-efficiency

models often also feature more sophisticated controls, such as timers and switches that let you choose whether or not the fan will run when the compressor is off.

Most room units come with installation instructions. Mounting one in a window will take a couple of hours. You'll need help to set the heavy, awkwardly balanced chassis in place.

Check for air leaks around the housing or sashes and seal gaps with an air-conditioner gasket or weather stripping. If you leave the unit in place year-round, you might want to custom-fit a storm window around it and replace the side panels with material of higher R-value.

Calculating Room Cooling Needs

Retailers size room units by the number of "rooms" you want to cool—figuring 6,000 Btuh for the first "room," and adding 3,500 to 5,000 Btuh for additional "rooms." Other factors come into play, however. How big is a typical room? And what about exposure, insulation, the number of windows and doors, heat gains from

appliances, and the number of people who will use the space?

You can use the chart at right to calculate your Btuh needs, going to the next larger size for hot spots and spaces with ceilings over 8 feet high. If you want an exact computation, ask a contractor for a cooling-load estimate form, along with the Btu factors they normally use.

COOLING NEEDS	
Cooling Area, square feet	Capacity, Btuh
265	6,000
300–350	7,500
350–450	9,000
450–520	10,000
520–600	11,000
600–750	12,500
750–900	15,000
900–1,050	16,500

Getting Power to a Unit

If your room unit is a small 120-volt model, you probably can plug it into an existing circuit. Make sure, however, that the connection is properly grounded (see page 237) and that the circuit has a fuse or circuit breaker that can handle start-up power surges.

Larger model 120-volt room air-conditioners and all 240-volt models need their own individual circuits. If you have a choice between 120- and 240-volt units, select the 240-volt

equipment. Higher-voltage air-conditioners use smaller conductors.

Plug and receptacle styles for 240-volt appliances vary according to amperage. The drawings at right show the ones you'll most likely encounter. Don't change receptacles unless the circuit wiring can handle the new load.

To learn about adding new circuits and installing major appliances, see pages 257–259.

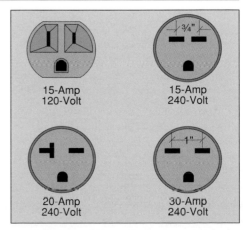

15-Amp 120-Volt

15-Amp 240-Volt

20-Amp 240-Volt

30-Amp 240-Volt

Choosing Heating and Cooling Equipment *(continued)*

USING EVAPORATIVE COOLERS IN DRY REGIONS

"Hot" and "humid" are terms that come to mind when you think of oppressive summer weather. That is because both temperature and relative humidity affect one's sense of comfort. The usual solution is a refrigerant-charged air-conditioner that wrings both heat and humidity from the air, at a high cost in electricity.

Some regions suffer from too-low humidity, however. In these areas, humidity can be traded for cooling through the simple and natural phenomenon of evaporative cooling, and at much lower cost.

Nature's equivalent to a man-made evaporative cooler is a thunderstorm on a hot day. We all have felt the dramatic drop in temperature that occurs after the rain stops. The cooling is due not to the rain itself, but to water evaporation after the storm is over.

An evaporative cooler consists of a water reservoir, a water-soaked fibrous pad, and a blower that pulls air through the wet pad. The blower draws in hot, dry air from outside and discharges the cooled air into the house. Leaving a window open in the room to be cooled allows the cooled air to flow through the room on its way outside.

Depending on how large of an evaporative cooler unit you need, it can be mounted on the roof, on the ground outside the house, in a wall, or in a window.

When the water evaporates from the cooling pad, any mineral content in the water is left behind on the pad. These mineral deposits build up rapidly in regions that have hard water. Check the pads once each month. Some pads can be demineralized by soaking them in a commercial lime remover; others must be replaced.

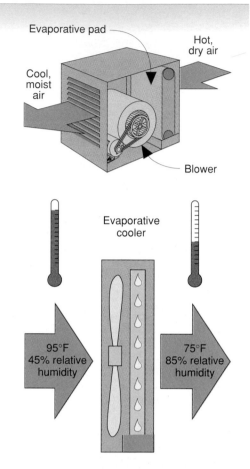

Sizing an Evaporative Unit for Your Home

Evaporative coolers are sized by the cubic feet of air they move per minute (cfm). To find the size of unit you require, follow these steps.

■ Compute the volume of your home's conditioned space in cubic feet; for example, 8×24×40 feet = 7,680 cubic feet.

■ In the chart at right, find the city nearest you and the recommended minutes per air change; for example, Phoenix, AZ—2 minutes.

■ Divide volume by minutes to find cooler cfm, for example: 7,680 cubic feet/2 minutes = 3,840 cfm unit. If your home is uninsulated, multiply by 2; if highly insulated, divide by 2.

RECOMMENDED MINUTES PER AIR CHANGE

City	Temp. Drop (°F)	Minutes per Air Change	City	Temp. Drop (°F)	Minutes per Air Change
AL, Birmingham	18	NR	NE, No. Platte	22	3
AZ, Phoenix	30	2	NV, Las Vegas	34	3
AR, Little Rock	18	NR	NM, Albuquerque	28	3
CA, Los Angeles	18	2	ND, Bismarck	22	3
CO, Denver	27	4	OK, Tulsa	22	1.3
GA, Atlanta	16	NR	SD, Rapid City	23	3
ID, Boise	25	4	TX, Dallas	22	2
KS, Topeka	20	3	UT, Salt Lake City	28	4
MT, Great Falls	25	NR	WY, Casper	27	4

NR = not recommended due to high ambient air humidity.

Conserving Energy

Energy conservation starts with efficient equipment that's also conscientiously maintained. The next chapter, "Weatherization and Ventilation," has information on ways to minimize the load on your heating and cooling equipment.

In the end, the way you operate your climate-control systems is as vital to fuel bills as your driving habits are to your car's fuel economy. Rushing to the thermostat every time you feel too hot or too cold wastes energy, just as a lead foot does on your car's accelerator.

The chart below lists how to control heating and cooling components with the same light, steady touch you use behind the wheel. For other energy-saving tactics, see pages 75–77 and 266.

HELPFUL HINTS FINE-TUNING YOUR HEATING AND COOLING HABITS

	Item	Tactic	How you save
Heating	Thermostat	Set back 8 to 10 degrees at night; set to 55°F when you're away from home for more than a day or two.	Savings of 8 to 15 percent are not unusual.
	Fireplace	Ordinary fireplaces will not reduce your heating bill; many draw off more heated air for combustion than they add. Most dampers leak heat even when closed; consider a glass fire screen (more about fireplaces on pages 102–111).	Tightly sealed glass screens definitely cut heating bills; close before retiring, and the fire will burn itself out.
	Ventilation	A range hood or bathroom fan can exhaust all the heated air in your home in about an hour. Control bath units with timers; use range hoods sparingly in cold weather (more about fans on pages 403–407).	Indiscriminate use of fans could be adding to your heating costs.
	Water heater	Lower setting 5° or 10°F, but not below 120°F. Add insulation blanket, which you can buy in kit form, around tank, especially if unit is in an unheated space (more about water heaters on pages 321–322).	Depends on where you live; lowering the setting saves more with electric units than with gas.
Cooling	Thermostat	Keep setting no lower than 78°F. On really hot days, turn it up even further. Regardless of the temperature outside, you'll feel comfortable if indoor levels are 15°F lower.	Dropping settings from 78° to 77°F costs 8 percent more; dropping to 72°F, costs 60 percent more.
	Appliances	Operate heat-producing appliances, such as washers, dryers, and dishwashers, at night or in early morning so heat and humidity don't add to the cooling load.	Energy savings will be greater if your utility has off-peak rates; comfort levels will be greater, too.
	Ventilation	An attic fan, coupled with proper attic insulation, can make a big difference in cooling load. Add power ventilators to dispel excess humidity in kitchen or bath if you don't have them (see pages 401–407 for both).	An attic or whole-house fan uses only about one-tenth the energy consumed by a central air-conditioner.

WEATHERIZATION AND VENTILATION

The preceding chapter dealt with heating and cooling equipment, the biggest energy consumers in most homes. Here, you meet their silent partners—the weather stripping, insulation, and ventilation systems that help you make the most of that precious energy.

These three elements work to control the heat your home loses in the winter and gains in the summer. Weather-stripping seals outside walls, windows, and doors, keeping outside air out and inside air in. Insulation retards heat transfer through solid surfaces. Ventilation exhausts excess heat, as well as stale air and humidity.

Chances are, your home could stand some upgrading on all of these counts (see the drawing below for points you should check). Why not start with your weather stripping? It's the easiest and least expensive component to deal with. You need a tight seal at all doors, windows, and anything else that opens. Caulk, a form of weather stripping, fills gaps between immovable elements where air could penetrate. For caulking basics, see pages 145–146. Window putty, also called glazing compound, seals joints between glass and wood (see pages 160–161).

Once your home is weather-stripped snugly, you can begin to assess the effectiveness of its insulation. You need the most insulation up top, either above your topmost ceilings or between the rafters. Next in line are the exterior walls. If your home sits atop a crawlspace or unheated basement, there should be insulation around ducts and pipes, as well as under the first-level floor or around the space's perimeter.

After you've tightened up your home's weather stripping and insulation, take a fresh look at its ventilation. Roof, soffit, and gable vents let an attic breathe (see page 133). Fans do the same for other areas (see pages 403–407).

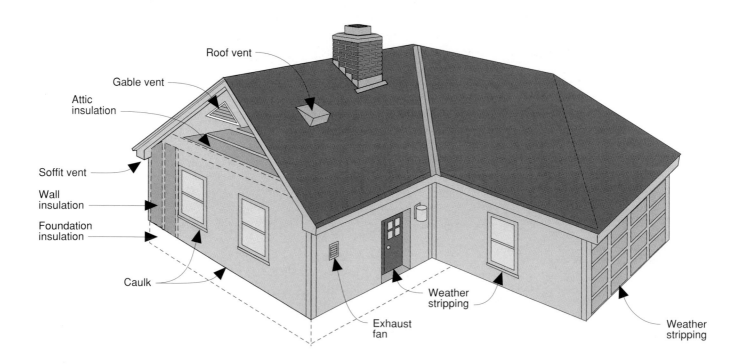

Roof vent

Gable vent

Attic insulation

Soffit vent

Wall insulation

Foundation insulation

Caulk

Exhaust fan

Weather stripping

Weather stripping

Plugging Hidden Air Leaks

You would never think of leaving a window open in the winter—unless someone else was paying the heating bill. Yet, the total of all of the miniscule cracks and holes in the floors, walls, and ceilings of the average older home is equivalent to an area of 2 square feet.

House doctors—technicians who specialize in finding and sealing such cracks—call these hidden heat leaks; hidden, because we never seem to see them.

The illustration at right points out the leaks you can uncover if you give your house a good once-over. The chart below shows the square-inch area of these leaks, both before and after treatment. After you've pinpointed the problem areas, use the techniques on page 384 to plug these leaks.

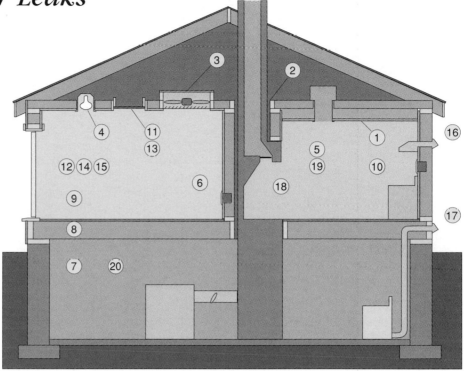

HELPFUL HINTS   SIZING UP TYPICAL RESIDENTIAL AIR LEAKS

Leak	Square inches
Ceiling	
1 Dropped/100 square feet	
no vapor barrier	78
with vapor barrier	8
2 Chimney, framing gap	12
gap weather-stripped	1
3 Whole-house fan, closed	8
covered with tight box	0.6
4 Lighting fixture, recessed	4
surface-mount	0.3
5 Pipe or duct, uncaulked	1
caulked at ceiling	0.2
Interior Wall	
6 Electrical outlet or switch	0.2
with cover gasket	.03
Exterior Wall	
7 Sill on masonry, uncaulked	65
caulked	13
8 Band or box sill, uncaulked	65
caulked	13

Leak	Square inches
Exterior Wall (continued)	
9 Floor/wall joint, uncaulked	27
baseboard caulked	7
10 Electric outlet or switch	0.2
with cover gasket	.05
Doors	
11 Attic fold-down	17
weather-stripped	8
12 Entrance	8
weather-stripped	6
with magnetic seal	4
13 Attic hatch	6
weather-stripped	3
Door and Window Frames	
14 Brick wall, uncaulked frame	2
caulked	0.4
15 Wood wall, uncaulked frame	0.6
caulked	0.1

Leak	Square inches
Vents	
16 Range, damper open	9
damper closed	2
17 Dryer, damper open	4
damper closed	1
Fireplace	
18 Damper open	54
average damper closed	9
clean, tight damper	5
with stove insert	2
Heating System	
19 Ducts in unheated space	56
caulked and taped	28
20 Furnace with flame-	
retention head burner	12
with stack damper also	9

Plugging Hidden Air Leaks (continued)

CAULKING AND SEALING AIR LEAKS

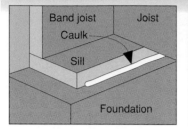

Seal the wood sill/masonry foundation joint with long-lasting polysulfide caulk.

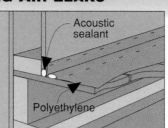

Staple polyethylene sheeting over nonhardening sealant to seal floor/wall joint.

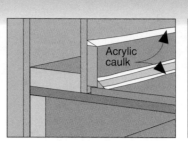

If there is a baseboard, seal with acrylic caulk; smooth caulk with a wet finger.

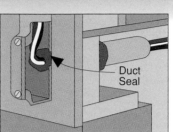

Seal service-entrance cable penetrations with nonhardening Duct Seal.

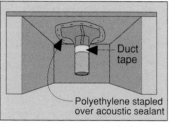

Large gaps around pipes can be sealed with polyethylene film over acoustic sealant.

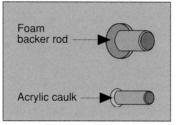

Another solution for large pipe gaps is foam backer rod or weather stripping.

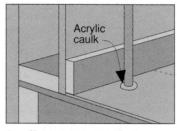

Smaller gaps around pipes can be filled with easy-to-use acrylic caulk.

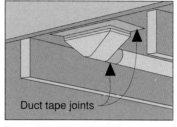

Duct joints and fittings should be sealed with duct tape.

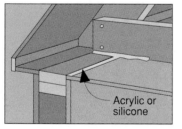

Seal joint between drywall and attic top plate with silicone or acrylic sealant.

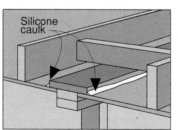

Seal the joint between drywall and wall top plate with silicone sealant.

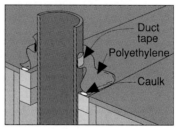

In attic, seal around vent pipe with polyethylene, duct tape, and caulk, as shown.

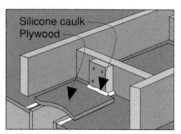

If an interior wall opens to the attic, caulk plywood pieces over the openings.

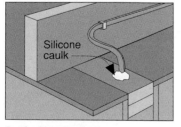

Seal electrical penetrations with silicone caulk.

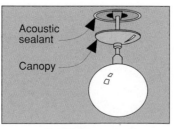

Use nonhardening caulk to seal fixture canopies.

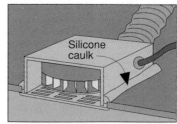

Seal a bathroom vent with silicone caulk.

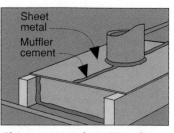

Chimneys get hot. Use sheet metal and muffler cement.

Solving Weather-Stripping Problems

Usually you can feel the heat leaks caused by inadequate weather stripping. Wait for a cool day and systematically pass your hand around the perimeter of a door, window, or any openable part of your home. Do you feel a breeze?

If so, you've located an air gap that needs to be sealed. Continue searching and you may find others.

Note that some other types of heat loss, such as radiation through single-pane windows, seem to produce a draft, but actually don't.

If you have doubts about whether you've found a leak or it's the effects of radiation, tape a sheet of polyethylene over the entire opening. If the plastic moves, there's an air leak around the opening and you need weather stripping.

CHOOSING AND BUYING WEATHER STRIPPING

As you make your survey for air leaks, carry along a tape measure and write down the dimensions of each door or window that needs weather stripping. If you feel a leak along just one jamb, you might be able to get by with adding or replacing material only at that edge—but take a close look at the others just to be sure. Total up your measurements and add about 10 percent for waste.

Make mental notes about how each window and door fits into its frame. You need to pay attention to this because weather stripping— whether it's made of metal, vinyl, felt, rubber, or a combination of these—depends on a tight fit to seal out drafts. Some materials work only with swinging doors or sashes; others fit sliding units, as well.

The chart below briefs you on the products you're likely to encounter. To learn what each looks like and how to install it, see the drawings on the following pages.

MATERIAL MATTERS COMPARING WEATHER-STRIPPING MATERIALS

Material	Installation	Cost	Durability
Spring metal	Fairly easy; cut it with snips, then tack in place to make an invisible installation.	Moderate	Excellent
Rolled vinyl and felt	Easy; cut with scissors or snips, then tack in place. These are visible when installed.	Moderate	Good
Self-adhesive foam	Very easy; snip it with scissors, peel off the backing, and press it in place.	Low	Fair
Interlocking metal strips	Several different configurations, all fairly difficult to install because you must align them exactly; work only on doors and casement windows.	High	Excellent
Door shoes, sweeps, and thresholds	Some mount on the bottom of the door; others replace an existing threshold. Installation can be tricky for some types, but relatively easy for others.	Moderate to high	Fair to excellent

Solving Weather-Stripping Problems *(continued)*

WEATHER-STRIPPING WINDOWS

Tightly zipping up a window against air infiltration calls for only a few tools and no special skills—but the job may take a while, depending on the number of sashes you have to seal. Plan your work for moderately cool weather because you'll have to open each window to get at its edges, and you'll also want to be able to feel for air leaks that might remain after you've finished.

Before you begin, inspect each window to make sure weather stripping is all it needs. Look for loose or missing glazing compound, which holds the glass panes in place on wood windows (see pages 160–161) or cracks in the exterior of vinyl or aluminum units.

Check for dried, broken, or missing caulk around the window's outer frame (see pages 145–146). Complete your exterior inspection by examining the sill. Weather-stripping along the window's bottom edge can compensate for some deterioration, but badly rotted sills and bottom rails let in moisture as well as air. (For sill replacement, see page 162.)

Inside, test latches to be sure they pull their sashes snug. Also, make sure each window is in smooth operating order (see pages 67–72).

In a big house, break down a thorough repair and weather-stripping project into phases, perhaps working on one exposure at a time. You'll begin to realize energy savings right away.

Installing Spring Metal Seals

Although not as easy to install as some weather stripping, bronze, aluminum, or stainless steel spring metal makes the best seal for windows. Designed to fit inside window channels or frames, its out-of-harm's-way location helps it survive years of openings and closings and renders the strips all but invisible.

Spring metal comes in kit form—with enough strips and nails to treat a typical window. Or, you can buy it by the running foot in coil form. Get the type with predrilled holes.

The drawings below show how to fit spring metal around double-hung and casement sashes, but you can easily adapt these techniques to suit other window types (see pages 67–68). Be sure the metal compresses when the window shuts.

YOU'LL NEED...
SKILLS: Basic carpentry skills.
TIME: 30 to 60 minutes per double-hung window.
TOOLS: Screwdriver, utility knife, tin snips, hammer.

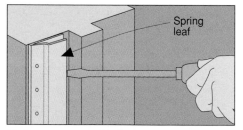

Nail strips in sash channel with spring side toward exterior. After strip is attached, pry leaf up to get best seal.

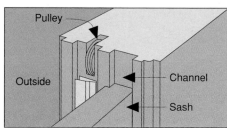

For double-hung windows, fit strips in the lower half of the inner channel and the upper half of the outer channel.

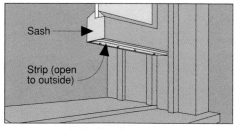

Fasten a strip to the bottom of the inner window's lower rail. Do the same to the top rail of the upper sash.

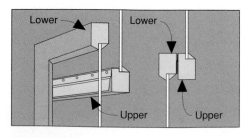

Where sashes meet, nail a strip to the bottom rail of the upper sash. Flatten the strip to make it fit.

On casement windows, nail strips to the frame. Install strips spring-side-in so sashes open freely.

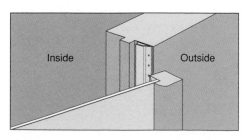

Installing Rolled Vinyl and Felt

Rolled vinyl, felt, and other gasket-type weather stripping attach to either the window frame or sash. When the window closes, they compress to seal air leaks. There are a wide variety of styles, including versions attached to rigid or flexible metal strips, as well as soft goods. Bulbous types provide more surface for better seals.

All are easy to install. Some, such as felt, must be mounted on the inside of windows and can be an eyesore. Felt also deteriorates fairly rapidly. Stretch the gasket material slightly as you attach it, making sure there are no gaps at corners.

Exterior installation provides a tighter seal and is less conspicuous. But you may need get out the ladder; avoid leaning way out of an upper-story window to drive in those last few nails.

YOU'LL NEED...
SKILLS: Basic skills.
TIME: 30 minutes per window.
TOOLS: Scissors or utility knife, hammer.

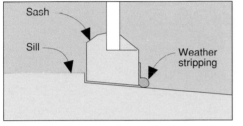

Nail on gasket weather stripping so its edge compresses when the window is latched. Bulbous types work best.

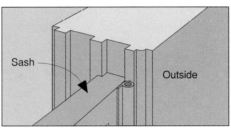

Along the sides of double-hung windows, attach strips to the outside face of the sashes.

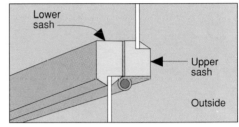

Seal between sashes by nailing a strip to the bottom of the upper sash, completely covering the gap.

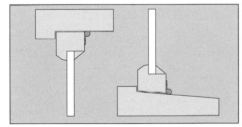

Seal the top and bottom sashes by attaching a strip to the outside of the upper sash's top rail and the outside of the lower sash's bottom rail.

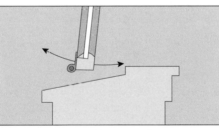

On casement windows, nail strips to the sash or the casing, whichever provides a tighter squeeze.

Installing Foam Strips

You may have discovered that self-adhesive foam tape doesn't resist friction very well. Even when you can keep it stuck, it doesn't last long. Still, there are compression-only situations where self-adhesive foam weather stripping works well. When foam flattens out, however, it's time to replace it. The only tool you'll need is scissors to cut the foam to length.

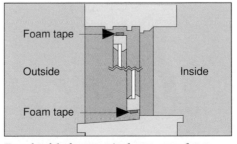

For double-hung windows, use foam only on the top and bottom of the rails. Foam can't take friction.

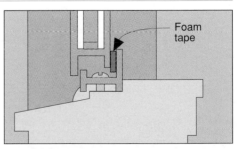

On metal casement or awning windows, stick foam tape on the frame. Apply to all four sides of the opening.

Solving Weather-Stripping Problems (continued)

WEATHER-STRIPPING DOORS

Doors leak twice as much air as windows. Coupled with the fact that doors also are used more often than windows, you can see why their seals merit careful inspection.

Check for crimped, flattened, or missing weather stripping at the top and sides. You might be able to adjust spring metal by prying lightly on the spring section. Other types probably will have to be replaced.

Feel along the threshold. Air infiltration means you need one of the bottom-of-the-door devices illustrated on page 389. And how's the door itself? Warping, an out-of-square frame, or deteriorated caulk around the edges give air a chance to make an "end-run" around even the tightest weather stripping. (See pages 79–82 for hints on repairing doors.) Examine storm doors, too. Some metal versions have a bulbous gasket along their lower edges; others employ a sweep. Both must be replaced periodically.

Check out any interior doors that open to an attic, garage, basement, or other unheated space. Builders often don't bother to seal these big heat-losers at all. Worse yet, some contractors cut costs by installing hollow-core doors that have little if any insulation value. If that's the case at your house, your best bet would be to invest in the far greater thermal efficiency of a solid- or foam-core door.

> **YOU'LL NEED...**
> **SKILLS:** Basic skills.
> **TIME:** 30 minutes per door.
> **TOOLS:** Scissors, utility knife or tin snips, hammer.

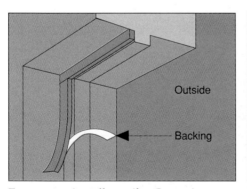

Foam tape installs easily. Cut strips to length, peel off backing, and press in place on the inside of the stops.

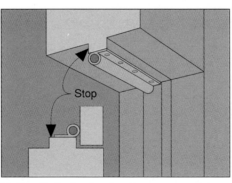

Nail rolled vinyl stripping to stop faces. Align so the bulbous edge projects, as shown in the inset.

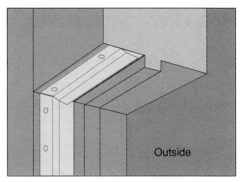

Nail spring-metal strips to the jamb inside the stop, fitting it carefully around the latch and lock mechanisms.

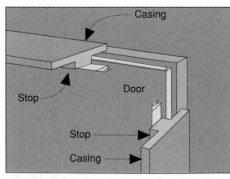

Interlocking metal channels form a good seal, but are tricky to align. Nail one part to door, other part to stop.

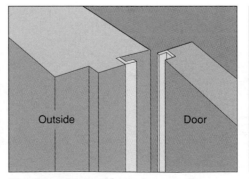

Metal J-strips seal best, but are the most difficult to install because you must rout a channel in the door.

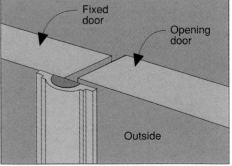

Use insulated molding to seal the gap between double doors. Nail to the face of the door that's usually closed.

Sealing Underneath Doors

A door's bottom edge poses two weather-stripping problems. First, the threshold has to withstand lots of traffic. Second, any seal attached to the door must clear carpeting or other uneven floor spots within the arc that the door traverses.

The devices shown here solve these difficulties with varying degrees of effectiveness. If your door has a badly worn threshold, consider replacing it with a metal one, such as the one shown below, or with a wood version (see page 162).

YOU'LL NEED...

SKILLS: Basic carpentry skills.
TIME: 45 minutes to replace a threshold, 20 minutes to install a door sweep.
TOOLS: Drill, screwdriver, hammer, handsaw.

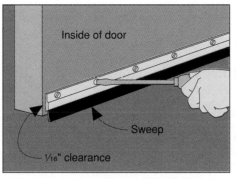

A door sweep works well if the floor is even. Simply attach it so the sweep seals against the threshold.

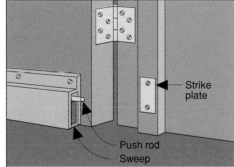

An automatic sweep uses a spring to raise itself as you open the door, then drops again when you close it.

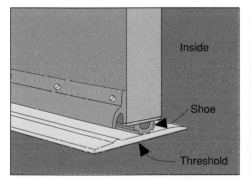

A shoe makes a durable seal. To install one, you must remove the door and possibly plane it, too.

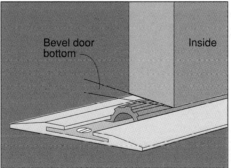

A bulb threshold works like a shoe. Bevel the door bottom, as shown. Replace the rubber bulb periodically.

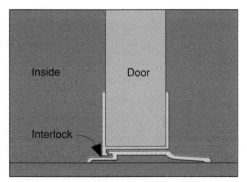

Interlocking thresholds make the tightest seal. Installing one calls for tricky carpentry and fitting, though.

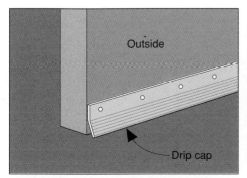

If water seaps under your door and into the house, nail a drip cap to its outside face.

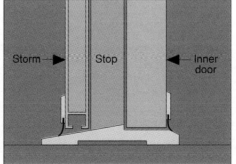

Don't forget storm doors. You can buy replacement rubber or plastic sweeps for these that install on the outside.

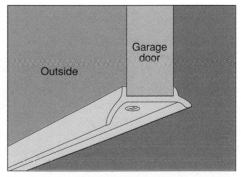

You can weather-strip the bottom edge of a roll- or swing-up garage door with a rubber door gasket like this.

Adding Insulation

If your home is an older one and has no insulation at all, you probably already know about the tremendous amount of heat that passes through its exterior surfaces. Proper insulation could cut this energy drain (and your energy bills) by 50 percent or more. Many newer houses, built before the energy crises of the 1970s, are just as underinsulated, with light doses of material in some critical places and often none at all in others.

Would it pay to upgrade your present insulation? How can you know for sure before you invest in upgrading? In most cases, the answer to the first question is yes. You can work out the answer to the second question on paper once you familiarize yourself with what R-values mean and do a little detective work around your house

R-values measure how well a material resists the flow of heat. The higher the R-value, the greater the

resistance, and the warmer your home will be in winter. Virtually every material—wood, masonry, fiberboard sheathing, even glass—offers some resistance to heat transfer. These factors differ only slightly from one house to another, though, so for your purposes you only need to determine what type of insulation you have and how much your house has. Insulation is rated by inches of thickness; to compute a material's total R-value, multiply the thickness of your present insulation by its R-value per inch.

To determine what kind and the amount of insulation you already have, start in the attic. Measure its thickness, taking care not to compact it, because the air spaces in insulation are a major part of its R-value. Check the chart on page 391 for R-value per inch. Do the same on the underside of floors over an unheated basement or crawlspace.

Examining exterior walls is a

bigger problem. Sometimes, removing the cover plate from a receptacle or switch lets you get a peek at what's in the wall. Usually, however, you'll have to make a small hole in the wall, then patch it

Don't poke into a wall with sharp implements. You could puncture a vapor barrier. Made of kraft paper, foil, or polyethylene, these membranes block moisture from seeping into the insulation (wet insulation has almost no R-value). If you have vapor barriers, they'll be facing the heated areas—just under floors, walls, and ceiling coverings.

Once you know the R-values for your home's various elements, you're ready to see how each one stacks up against the ratings (see below) for your area of the country. These ratings are maximums; it may not be cost-effective to bring your home up to these standards. You'll have to weigh the costs against the increased energy savings.

Determining Your Insulation Needs

The map at right divides the United States into six climate zones, and the table below lists different R-values for each zone—the first two for attics (with electric resistance-type heating or other type heating plants); the second for walls; and the third for floors. These standards, although widely used in new home construction, don't take into account several factors, the most important of which is the cost of energy in your area. Achieving R-values in excess of about 20 might be economically unattractive in terms of increased effectiveness. You may never be able to recover the amount spent.

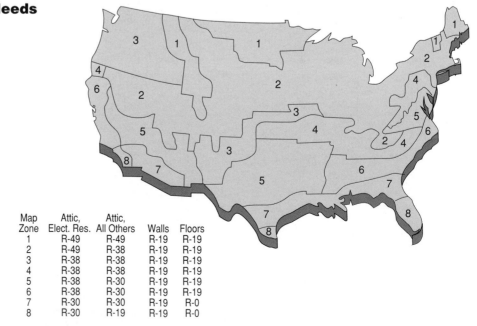

Map Zone	Attic, Elect. Res.	Attic, All Others	Walls	Floors
1	R-49	R-49	R-19	R-19
2	R-49	R-38	R-19	R-19
3	R-38	R-38	R-19	R-19
4	R-38	R-38	R-19	R-19
5	R-38	R-30	R-19	R-19
6	R-38	R-30	R-19	R-19
7	R-30	R-30	R-19	R-0
8	R-30	R-19	R-19	R-0

MATERIAL MATTERS CHOOSING AND BUYING INSULATION

When selecting insulation, judge it by its R-value, not its thickness. You'll find both the R-value and thickness marked on the wrapper. Having both lets you compare prices—but remember, buy Rs, not inches.

You'll need to pick an insulation type that fits the application. Types of home insulation are listed below.

Batts generally consist of fluffy fiberglass or rock wool in sections 15 to 23 inches wide, to fit joist and stud spacings, and 4 to 8 feet long. They're moisture- and fire-resistant and come with or without a vapor barrier. Although batts are easy to handle and install, you'll end up with more waste pieces than with blankets.

Blankets—also made of fiberglass or rock wool and sized to fit between framing—come in continuous rolls so there is less waste.

Loose-fill material can be poured or blown into cavities. The most common are fire-retardant cellulose fiber, vermiculite, perlite, fiberglass, and rock wool. This type is the easiest to install in walls and floor cavities that are already finished.

Foam also can be used to insulate finished walls, floors, and ceilings from the outside. Foam has a higher R-value than blown-in insulation, but it's much more expensive.

Rigid insulation consists of boards of molded or extruded polystyrene, polyurethane or polyisocyanurate. Polyurethane has a high R-value, but, along with polystyrene, it's combustible and must be covered with a ½ inch of drywall for fire safety.

Insulation Type	R-value per Inch	Uses	Installation Techniques
Batts			
Fiberglass	3.0	Unfinished attic floors, rafters, walls, crawlspaces, ceilings	Lay them in place or fit between studs or joists so friction holds them in place.
Rock wool	3.0		
Blankets			
Fiberglass	3.1	Unfinished floors, rafters, crawlspaces, walls, ceilings	Friction fit; those with vapor barriers usually have flanges that staple to framing.
Rock wool	3.0		
Loose-fill—Poured			
Fiberglass	3.1–3.3	Unfinished attic floors, especially those with irregular joist spacing or lots of obstructions; walls and other cavities	Easy if you can get at the cavity; just pour to the right depth, making sure you fill every cranny.
Rock wool	3.0–3.3		
Cellulose	3.7–4.0		
Vermiculite	2.0–2.6		
Perlite	2.0–2.7		
Loose-fill—Blown			
Cellulose	3.1–4.0	Finished ceilings, walls, floors, and other closed cavities	Rent machinery for this fairly tricky operation; better yet, hire a contractor.
Fiberglass	2.8–3.8		
Rock wool	2.8–3.8		
Foam—Urethane	5.3	Closed cavities	Injected into cavities; make sure the contractor is certified.
Rigid			
Polystyrene	4.0–5.4	Roofs, ceilings, walls, foundations, basement walls, and other places you need thin material with high R-values	Cement with adhesive, or friction-fit; the first two are combustible and must be faced with drywall.
Polyurethane	6.7–8.0		
Polyisocyanurate	8.0		

Adding Insulation (continued)

INSULATING AN ATTIC FLOOR

A poorly insulated attic squanders energy in both the winter and summer—sending heat right through the roof in cold weather and serving as an enormous solar collector on hot, sunny days.

How you approach an attic insulating project depends on how you're planning to use the area. If the space will be used only for storage, insulate the floor, as shown here. If it's finished or you intend to finish it later, insulate the ceiling and walls, as shown on page 393.

Either way, look first for leaks that might damage insulation (see pages 123–133), check to be sure you have adequate ventilation (see page 133), and decide if you want to cut summer heat buildup with an attic or whole-house fan (see pages 403–406).

If your attic has a floor, you have two installation choices: pull up sections and work the insulation under or hire a contractor to blow in loose-fill through holes bored in the floor. With unfinished floors, be sure to bring up some planks or pieces of plywood so you can get around on the joists without stepping through the ceiling below. Ceiling materials alone won't bear your weight.

Use batts, blankets, or loose-fill. If there already is a vapor barrier, use unfaced materials or slash the facing so moisture doesn't get trapped between the two barriers. Also, it's important you don't cover recessed light fixtures or exhaust fans; doing so could cause a fire. Instead, install baffles that keep the insulation about 3 inches away on all sides.

Caution: Some materials, such as fiberglass and mineral wool, are harmful to lungs and skin, so be sure to wear a painter's mask, gloves, and long sleeves if you'll be working with hazardous materials.

YOU'LL NEED...

SKILLS: Basic skills for batts and blankets; intermediate skills for blowing in loose-fill insulation.
TIME: 4 to 6 hours for an attic.
TOOLS: Utility knife, staple gun, rented blower for loose-fill.

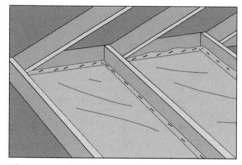

If you need a separate vapor barrier, staple 2-mil polyethylene between the joists. Seal seams with tape.

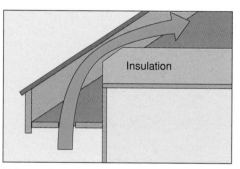

When placing batts or blankets, take care not to jam them against the roof; leave space at the eaves for airflow.

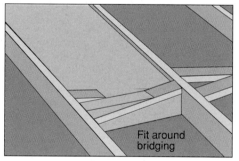

When you encounter bridging or other obstacles, cut for a snug fit. Otherwise, heat will slip through the gap.

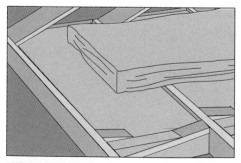

When trying to achieve a high R-value with two layers of insulation, place the second layer perpendicular to the first.

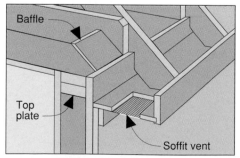

For loose-fill, nail baffles at the eaves. Insulation should cover the wall top plate but not obstruct airflow.

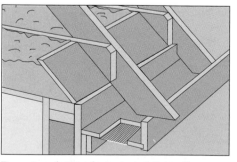

Pour insulation between joists, then level it with a board. Be sure you don't leave low spots or voids.

INSULATING A FINISHED ATTIC

Heating an attic that's underinsulated is a losing proposition. So, if you've got big plans for finishing off that space, better budget for plenty of the "fluffy stuff."

In an unfinished attic that doesn't have collar beams, you might be tempted to forget about them and run insulation right up to the ridge beam. Don't! That space above the collars, coupled with gable louvers at the ends (see page 133), gets rid of winter condensation as well as summer heat. Make the collars from 2×4s or 2×6s, depending on how heavy your future ceiling will be.

If your attic already is finished, you'll have to cut holes in the knee walls and the ceiling to gain access to insulate these areas. Fortunately, most walls and ceilings are not difficult to patch (see pages 35–39 and page 60).

YOU'LL NEED...

SKILLS: Basic skills.
TIME: 6 to 8 hours for an unfinished attic; additional time if you have to cut into and repair finished walls.
TOOLS: Utility knife, staple gun. Additional tools may be needed to construct collars or to refinish walls.

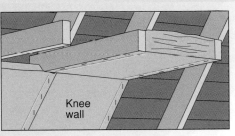

1. Add collar beams if your attic has none. Plan the height, cut beams to fit, then nail to the existing rafters.

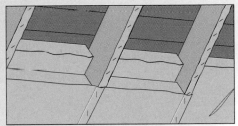

2. Staple blankets to collar beams, with vapor barrier side facing in. Continue down knee wall to floor.

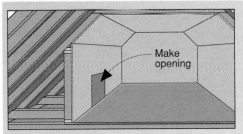

1. If you're adding to existing insulation, cut away its stapled flange and push it to the back of the cavity. Slash the old vapor barrier.

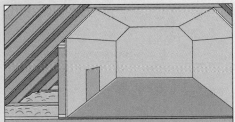

2. Place the new insulation over the old. Staple flanges to the rafters, with vapor barrier facing in, lap insulation joints (as shown) as you go.

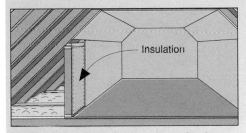

1. In a finished attic, make openings to get at spaces above collar beams and behind knee and end walls.

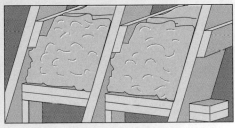

2. Lay loose-fill or blanket material between joists in the knee-wall space. Use a broom handle to push into "unreachable" spots.

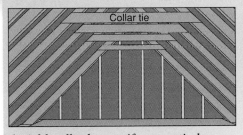

3. Don't insulate between roof rafters in the knee-wall space. Place material between the wall studs, with vapor barrier facing in.

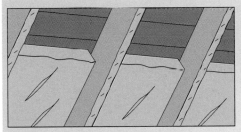

4. Pour loose-fill material between the rafters in the sloping part of the ceiling. Finish off with batts in attic above the collar beams.

Adding Insulation (continued)

INSULATING CRAWLSPACES

After attics, unheated crawlspaces are the next-most-vital places to insulate. You have two options: drape batts or blankets around the space's perimeter walls, or suspend material between floor joists, as shown on page 395.

Draping the walls creates a sealed air chamber, adding further insulation value. With some houses, however, you have no choice but to insulate the floor between the joists.

Wrapping up a crawlspace is a dirty but easy chore—providing you have enough space to crawl around. You'll need unfaced batts or blankets, 6-mil polyethylene sheeting to cover the ground, 1×2s and nails, and rocks or bricks. Wear goggles and other protective gear.

Close off unnecessary openings, but don't seal vents permanently; a crawlspace needs these for "breathing" in hot, muggy weather. For more about the importance of ventilation, see page 402.

Examine the underside of the floor. Joists run parallel to two walls, perpendicular to the other two. The first two drawings show the slightly different treatment for the walls that run perpendicular to the joists.

Warning: If you live in an extremely cold region, such as Alaska, the Northern Plains, or northern Maine, don't use the technique explained on this page; it could cause frost heaving that might damage your foundation. Check with local contractors or your building code department for techniques used in your area.

YOU'LL NEED...

SKILLS: Basic skills.
TIME: 4 to 8 hours, depending on accessibility of the crawlspace.
TOOLS: Utility knife, hammer, saw.

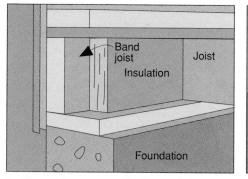

1. For walls perpendicular to joists, place insulation against the band joist. Cut pieces oversize so they fit snugly.

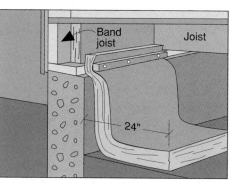

2. Unroll enough insulation to overlap band joist material and cover the earth at the wall's base. Secure with 1×2s.

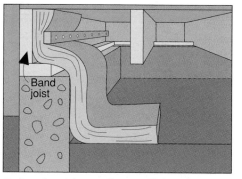

3. Insulate the walls parallel to the joists. Just let material cascade down the wall, as shown.

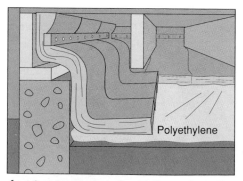

4. After insulating the walls, roll up the blankets and tuck a polyethylene vapor barrier on the floor. Tape it in place.

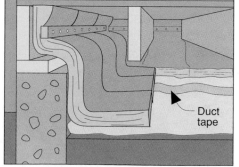

5. Tape joints between strips, or lap them at least 6 inches. Make sure you don't puncture the plastic.

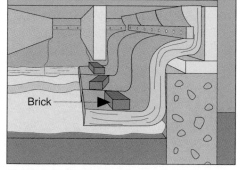

6. Weight polyethylene and insulation with rocks or bricks. Don't use wood— it could rot or attract termites.

INSULATING A FLOOR

Floors over basements, porches, garages, or other unheated zones need insulation, too. How you handle these heat-eaters depends on the situation underneath.

If the joists are covered, as with a finished garage ceiling, your best bet is to have loose-fill blown in by a contractor (see page 400). With open joists, install batts, blankets, or rigid planks, as shown below.

Use blankets or batts if the spaces between the joists aren't chopped up with lots of pipes, wiring, ducts, or bridging. Rigid planks allow you to drop below obstacles, but check building codes before you do so. You'll probably have to face rigid

urethane or polystyrene insulation planks with a noncombustible material; some building codes don't permit these types at all.

Unless you're simply adding another layer to existing insulation, get faced materials and install it with the vapor barrier side facing up (that is, toward the heated area). Foil facing works well here because it reflects heat back into living areas. Pay special attention to achieving good coverage at joists and headers around the floor's outside edges.

Cold slab floors present a special problem because you can't get material under them, where it would do the most good. It may help to

wrap the outside of your foundation, as illustrated below (bottom, right), but talk to a professional first. You might end up with a higher R-value by insulating the floor itself. To do this, glue down wood sleepers (see page 21), place rigid insulation planks between the sleepers, then lay new sub- and finish flooring.

YOU'LL NEED...

SKILLS: Basic skills.
TIME: 6 to 8 hours, depending on the number of obstacles, such as pipes, that you have to go around.
TOOLS: Utility knife, hammer, saw.

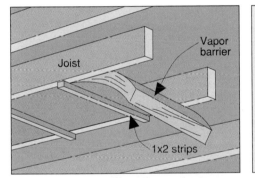

Support batts or blankets by nailing 1×2 strips to the undersides of joists. Space strips about 18 inches apart, laying insulation on top.

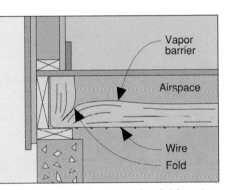

Start each insulation strip by folding it so that the insulation covers the band joist. You can use chicken wire stapled to the joists to support the batts.

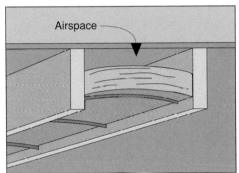

Or, you can support the insulation with friction-fit rods that slip between the joists. Leave some airspace between the insulation and floor.

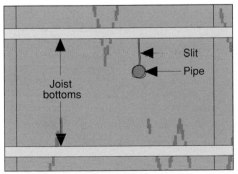

With a pipe or other obstacle, cut a slit in the insulation to the opening, then fit carefully. Seal slit with tape.

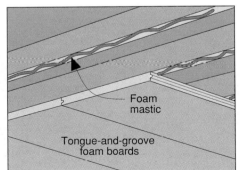

With rigid planks, apply adhesive to the bottoms of the joists and press the lightweight foam strips in place.

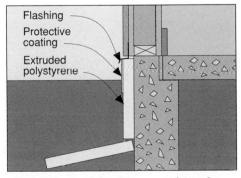

To insulate a slab, dig a trench to the frost line, then glue on 2-inch-thick foam planks from the siding down.

Adding Insulation (continued)

INSULATING DUCTWORK AND PIPES

When contractors compute heating and cooling loads, they tack on 10 or 20 percent for losses from the ductwork or pipes. If you insulate those that run through an attic, garage, or other unheated area, you can prevent most of this loss.

Heat also escapes from bare hot-water pipes, meaning water sitting in pipes cools down between uses; then you have to run extra water to get hot water out of a faucet. Wrapping these pipes will reap big dividends. Wrapping cold water lines won't save you energy dollars, but doing so will eliminate dripping and sweating from condensation, thus avoiding water spots or damage.

What about ducts that run through an unfinished or partially finished basement? Here you have a choice. If you're using the space as a living, play, or shop area even though it isn't finished, chances are you're depending on radiated heat from the ducts to keep things somewhat warm down there. In this situation, you would be better off to insulate the walls, as shown on page 397, and forget about the ducts.

If your basement gets only occasional use, consider installing a couple of new basement registers (see page 358) and insulating both the ducts and the floor above.

Duct insulation comes in 1- and 2-inch thicknesses. Get the thicker material, especially if your ducts are rectangular; 2-inch wrap cuts losses by about one-third more than 1-inch material. You'll also need several rolls of duct tape to seal all duct joints before you insulate.

If your ducts don't have dampers to balance airflow, add some before you insulate. Insulation ups the temperature of air at registers, and you'll want to do some fine-tuning afterward (see pages 340 and 359).

> ### YOU'LL NEED...
> **SKILLS:** Basic skills.
> **TIME:** 2 to 4 hours, depending on access to the ducts or pipes.
> **TOOLS:** Utility knife or hacksaw.

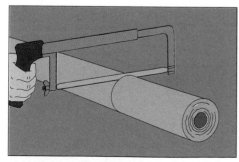

For ducts between joists, cut blankets and staple them to floor, as shown. Seal joints with duct tape.

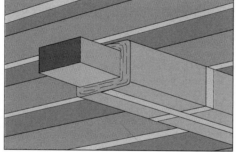

For other ducts, wrap insulation around all sides, sealing with tape. The vapor barrier should be on the outside.

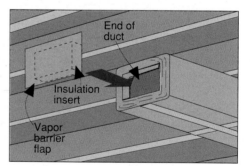

Extend insulation beyond the end of a duct, then cut an insert with facing flap. Fold and tape flap, package style.

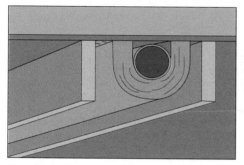

Cut pipe insulation with hacksaw or utility knife. At pipe ends or corners, cut short lengths to fill all spaces.

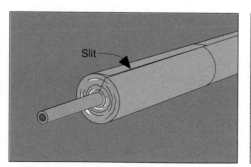

Pipe insulation comes in various lengths. A lengthwise slit lets you fit the sleeve on the pipe.

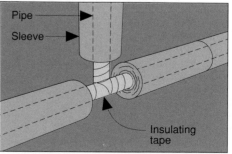

At junctions, wrap uncovered areas with spongy insulation tape. Just peel off backing and wrap.

INSULATING BASEMENT WALLS

Finishing off a basement? Rigid foam insulation planks or soft blankets or batts offer two ways to go. Which you choose depends on where you live and how much space you're willing to give up to the installation.

If your winters are mild, you can get by with a R-value of 7; in colder areas, aim for R-11. To achieve either of these R-values with batts or blankets, you'll need to frame out 2×3 or 2×4 stud walls over the masonry walls, then staple the insulation between the studs of your new built-out walls. You then can cover the wall surface with drywall or paneling.

Rigid foam insulation planks let you keep a new wall's thickness to a minimum because their R-values per inch are higher. Simply line the walls with furring strips (see page 47), then glue or friction-fit planks between the furring. But because of foam's combustibility, building codes require you to cover it with a minimum of ½-inch drywall—even if you're planning to install wood or hardboard paneling as your final finished surface.

Solve moisture problems before you begin. Seepage or leaks render insulating materials useless. Don't worry about mild condensation; insulation and a vapor barrier usually will eliminate this. (To learn about wet basement problems and their solutions, see pages 113–117.)

Insulation is less critical below ground level. To save money, you might insulate only that part of the wall the extends above ground level—although insulating the walls' full height will provide additional value. Either way, pay special attention to spaces above the sill.

As with crawlspace walls, these insulating techniques could cause frost-heave problems in extremely cold regions. Check your local building codes for approved insulation procedures.

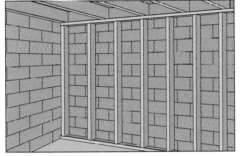

1. If you choose fiberglass batt or blanket insulation, frame up new stud walls (see pages 50–51).

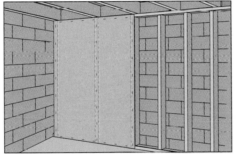

2. Staple insulation between the studs. Don't skimp on the staples. Drive one every 10 or 12 inches.

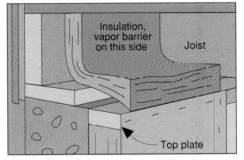

3. Above the sill, fit in small pieces of insulation. Secure with tape, staples, or wood strips (see page 394).

1. For rigid foam insulation, make a grid of 1×2s or 1×3s (see page 47 for more about these walls).

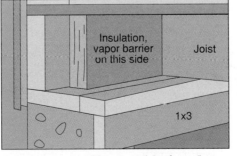

2. Use pieces of batts or blankets for spaces over the top of the sill. Vapor barriers always face inside.

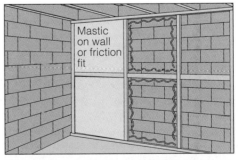

3. Cement planks to the walls between furring strips. Measure as you go to ensure tight fit. Cover with drywall.

Adding Insulation (continued)

INSULATING OUTSIDE FOUNDATION WALLS

Because a basement or crawlspace is so much warmer than outside air in winter, it is easy to believe that the earth is insulating a foundation. In fact, the average basement accounts for 20 percent of a home's heat loss.

The best location for foundation insulation is outside of a masonry wall, where it protects the masonry from damaging frost. In addition, the mass of the masonry acts to moderate the temperature swings of the outdoor air. The insulation also keeps the wall warmer in summer, reducing condensation and basement humidity.

YOU'LL NEED...

SKILLS: Basic excavating and carpentry skills.
TIME: 2 days for an entire house.
TOOLS: Shovel, wire brush, hammer, utility knife, paintbrush, roller.

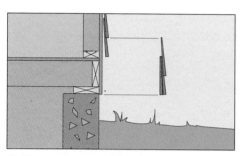

1. Remove several bottom courses of siding (see pages 147 and 157). Save the siding for reinstallation.

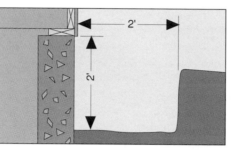

2. Excavate around the foundation to 2 feet below the sill and 2 feet wide. Place soil on sheets of polyethylene.

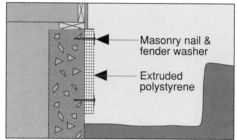

Masonry nail & fender washer

Extruded polystyrene

3. Fasten 1-inch sheets of extruded polystyrene to foundation with fender washers and masonry nails

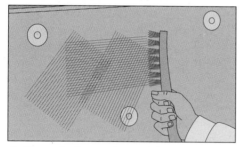

4. Scratch the surface of the foam with a wire brush to give the protective coating a "tooth" to adhere to.

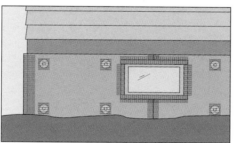

5. Apply self-adhesive fiberglass drywall tape to all joints and corners for reinforcement.

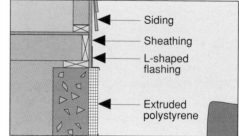

Siding

Sheathing

L-shaped flashing

Extruded polystyrene

6. Install galvanized or aluminum window flashing against the building sheathing and over top edge of foam.

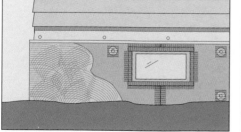

7. Brush on fiberglass-reinforced latex coating from flashing to several inches below the final ground level.

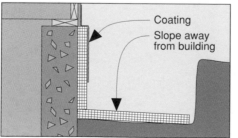

Coating
Slope away from building

8. Lay horizontal 2×8-foot sheets of foam so that they slope away from the foundation at 1 inch per foot minimum.

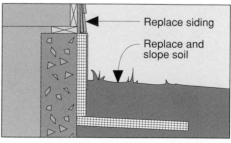

Replace siding

Replace and slope soil

9. Replace and grade the soil away from the building and plant grass. Replace the bottom courses of siding.

INSULATING EXTERIOR WALLS

The best time to insulate exterior walls is during construction. However, most people don't have this option. Because insulating such large areas is labor-intensive, the builder of your house may have skimped on insulation.

Even if the builder didn't, the 3½-inch cavities between 2×4 framing can hold only so much insulation—often not enough to achieve the R-value recommended. That's why the outer walls of newer homes often are framed with 2×6s spaced 24 inches apart or with 2×4s spaced on 16-inch centers, with rigid insulation panels on the outside and batts between the studs.

Don't assume that because your home is older and the walls are finished that you can't do anything

about these energy wasters. The techniques shown here and on the next page are used commonly to make walls more energy efficient. Be warned, however, that none is easy or inexpensive and that most require the services of a contractor with the specialized equipment and know-how to do the job correctly.

If your walls already have some insulation in them, you may find that it doesn't make economic sense to upgrade their R-value. If you decide to upgrade your insulation, shop carefully for a reputable installer and get several written bids that specify R-values as well as the amounts of material needed. A properly insulated 2×4 wall should have an R-value of 8 with fiberglass or rock wool insulation, R-10 for cellulosic

fiber, or R-11.5 for liquid foam. These values may not bring your home up to the standards listed on page 390, but they'll help a lot.

Unless you choose liquid foam, you'll also need a vapor barrier to protect the new insulation against condensation (see bottom of page 400 for how to install one without ripping apart the walls).

YOU'LL NEED...

SKILLS: Advanced insulation skills (often a job for a professional contractor).
TIME: Several days for an entire house.
TOOLS: Drill, wall refinishing tools, and specialized tools for blowing insulation into wall cavities.

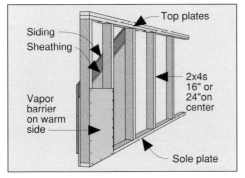

New, unfinished walls are a snap to insulate. Just friction-fit batts or staple up blankets.

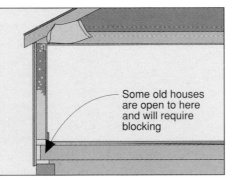

Determine if wall cavities run from attic to basement by dropping down a weighted string. If so, you can pour in loose-fill from the attic.

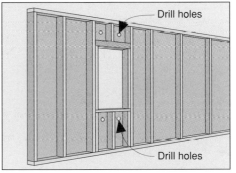

Most wall cavities have blocking, so a contractor removes exterior siding and bores a series of holes to gain access (see next page for details).

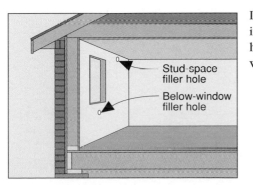

If your walls have a masonry veneer, it's best to work from inside, cutting holes in the interior wall surface, which then will have to be patched.

Liquid foam insulation fills in around pipes, wiring, and electrical boxes better than blown-in material—and provides its own vapor barrier.

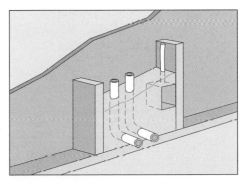

Adding Insulation (continued)

Installing Foam or Loose-Fill Insulation

Blowing or foaming insulation into walls calls for special expertise and machinery. These materials must be applied in the correct density, coverage, and thickness, or their insulating value will suffer—a job that requires savvy about house construction and an understanding of specialized equipment. Thus, this is most always a job that calls for a professional contractor.

The drawings below show the steps a professional would—and should—follow. To blow in loose-fill, contractors poke into stud cavities with a big hose, like the one on a vacuum cleaner. When they use foam, they pump it into the walls through a thinner hose with an applicator. In either case, specify to the contractor that you want proof the job has been done correctly. Special heat-sensing devices can pinpoint heat leaks.

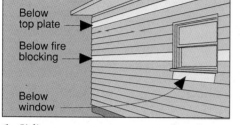

1. Siding courses are removed at the top, under windows, and maybe at the 4-foot level, where there's fire blocking.

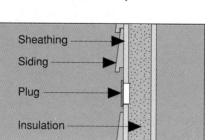

2. After peeling back the building paper, the installer uses a hole saw to bore holes into each cavity.

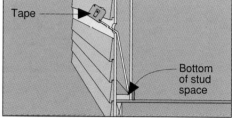

3. Professionals probe with a steel tape to see if there are obstructions that might create uninsulated pockets.

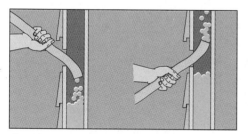

4. Material is blown into the cavity to the level of the inlet, then the nozzle is flipped up to fill the space above.

5. After each cavity is filled, a snap-in plug seals the hole. Then the building paper goes back in place.

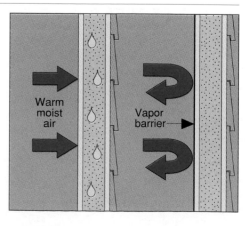

To save money, consider removing and replacing siding materials yourself. To learn how, see page 147.

Providing a Vapor Barrier

Without a vapor barrier, all insulation, except foam, will turn into a soggy mess in no time. Why? Temperature differences between a wall's warm and cool sides cause household moisture to condense inside the stud cavities, filling up pockets that trap air and negating the insulation's effectiveness.

Besides keeping insulation dry, a vapor barrier helps keep moisture inside the house, a feature you'll appreciate in the winter, when indoor air is dry.

But, how can you get a continuous waterproof membrane into a finished wall? You can't. However, you can seal the wall's interior surface for the same effect. Caulk cracks you find at the floor, ceiling, and around doors or windows. Then apply at least two coats of waterproof oil- or alkyd-base paint, or use a paint especially formulated for this purpose.

Solving Ventilation Problems

Like people, houses need to breathe—inhaling fresh or cooler outside air and exhaling moisture, unwanted heat, and odors. Even though weather stripping and insulation is meant to snug-up heated spaces, air must be allowed to pass through such areas as unheated attics and crawlspaces. Other areas and equipment require venting, too. The remainder of this chapter discusses your options.

Ventilation systems fall into two categories—static and powered. Examples of static ventilators are doors and windows. Opening one of these gets rid of smells and humidity in a hurry; it also can let them in and at the same time waste a lot of expensive heating or cooling energy.

Less perceptible—but just as vital to your home's well-being—are the static vents that circulate fresh air through an attic, crawlspace, even the combustion chamber of a furnace or boiler. Throttling these can lead to moisture-related problems, such as peeling paint, mildew, and rot.

Your home may already have a few powered ventilators—a hood over the kitchen range or a bathroom exhaust fan. If not, the following pages show how to install these household pollution-removers.

Power ventilation also reduces cooling costs by a surprising amount. A roof-mounted fan, working in tandem with static vents, removes heat buildup in attics and takes a big load off your cooling equipment. A larger fan in the attic floor may pull enough air through the house to cool it without using air-conditioning equipment.

GETTING FRESH AIR TO A FURNACE OR BOILER

Gas and oil heating plants consume more than just fuel. Their burners also require a steady supply of oxygen—and the flames don't care if it's warm or cool.

Chances are, your furnace or boiler draws its combustion air from the house. Don't confuse combustion air with the air that circulates through ducts and registers. Compartments within a furnace keep the two separate (see pages 342 and 344). Combustion air goes right up the flue—so why use house air that you just paid to heat for combustion purposes? Ducting outside air to the burner eliminates waste and may also improve the unit's efficiency.

Installing a fresh-air combustion feed is a fairly easy, straightforward job. But it's a job that should be done by a heating and ventilation contractor who can size the duct correctly for the amount of air your boiler or furnace needs.

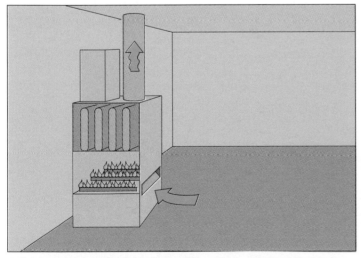

A furnace's combustion-air intake pulls heated air from the house, then sends it up the flue. In a tightly sealed home, this situation creates a vacuum that increases infiltration of cold, outside air.

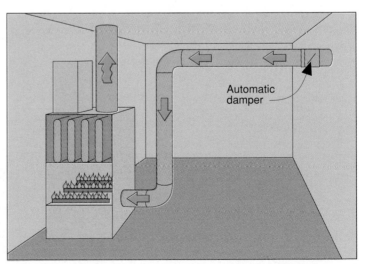

Automatic damper

A small-diameter duct feeds the flames with outside air, conserving warm, indoor air. A damper opens when the burner is on. Fuel savings often offset the installation cost in a single season.

Solving Ventilation Problems (continued)

VENTING A CRAWLSPACE

A crawlspace that can't breathe—even a well-insulated one—turns into a giant moisture chamber in hot, humid weather. Temperature differences between its inner and outer surfaces cause water to condense on joists, subflooring, and insulation, resulting in chilly floors, dank odors, and eventually rot that destroys your home's underpinnings.

That's why, if your house is built on a crawlspace, the builder most likely installed a couple of vents in the foundation walls. These should provide 1 square foot of vent space for every 300 square feet of the crawlspace's total area. Check these vents occasionally to make sure they aren't blocked. Also, shine a light inside to check for condensation.

You need airflow through a crawlspace only in the summer. Close up vents every fall to cut heat losses, possibly making covers, as shown below.

In a few homes, the crawlspace is permanently sealed so it can serve as a plenum for warm-air heating. In others, the furnace itself is located there and depends on air from the crawlspace for combustion. If either is the case at your house, refer to the last two illustrations below.

All of these recommendations presume that your crawlspace walls have been insulated and there is a vapor barrier on the ground (see page 394). Insulating ducts and pipes helps reduce condensation, too (see page 396).

If your crawlspace seems to be well-ventilated but you still see signs of moisture, water may be coming from a leak or seepage through the walls (see pages 112–117). You also should inspect the crawlspace for two other potential problems—termites (see pages 152–153) and rot (rot in any foundation members should be checked out by a professional contractor).

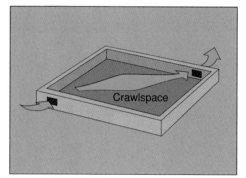

Every crawlspace (picture this with a house on top) needs at least two vents, located near opposite corners.

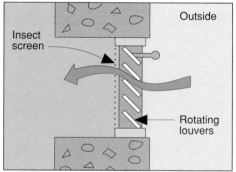

Good vents have louvers you can open and close. Open them for maximum airflow in warm weather.

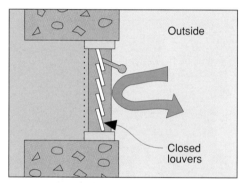

In cold weather, close the louvers or leave them open just a crack if winters in your area are damp.

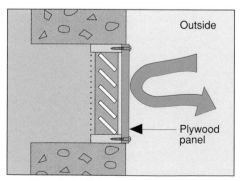

If your vents are open and inoperable, replace them or seal the openings with exterior plywood each winter.

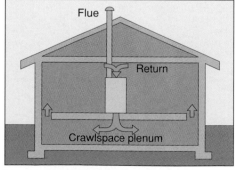

To dry out a crawlspace that's part of your heating system, run the blower a few times during the summer.

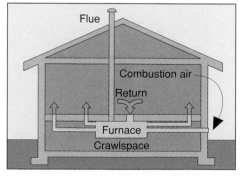

If your furnace is in the crawlspace, it will need a fresh-air combustion intake before you can close the vents.

CHOOSING AND BUYING FANS

Power ventilators, or fans, are quick-change devices that remove all the air within a space in just a minute or two—along with any heat, humidity, or odors the air might be carrying. That's why fans are sized according to the volume of air they move per minute. These cubic-foot-per-minute (cfm) ratings let you select a unit to match the space it must handle.

The chart below lists minimum cfm ratings for fans in different areas of your home. A 5×9-foot bath, for example, requires at least a 48-cfm fan. Because units are rated in 10-cfm increments, you'd shop for a 50-cfm model in this case.

Fans differ not only in the size, but also in the amount of noise they make. You'll find this measurement, in sones, on the unit's rating plate. The lower the rating, the quieter the fan. A 3-sone model would be one-half as noisy as a 6-sone model.

Before you buy an exhaust fan, you must give some thought to where the air it evacuates is going to go. Wherever possible, vent to the outdoors, even if that means running ductwork (see page 407).

You can vent a small bathroom or laundry fan into an attic or crawlspace—provided the space itself has enough ventilation to carry off excess humidity. Don't vent a kitchen unit into an attic or crawlspace; greasy air is flammable. If you can't duct the air outside, you'll need to purchase a ductless hood fan. These capture grease in washable filters and remove cooking smells with replaceable charcoal filters. However, ductless units don't get rid of heat or moisture.

You'll also need to decide what type of controls you want. For attic fans, you can choose thermostat-activated switches that automatically turn on the unit when temperatures in the attic reach a certain level. For a whole-house fan, a timer switch might make more sense.

In a bathroom, you might be tempted to connect a fan to an overhead light and operate them from the same switch, but an independent switch or a timer is better. Kitchen range hoods usually come with two-speed switches or variable-speed controls.

MATERIAL MATTERS   SELECTING THE RIGHT FAN FOR THE JOB

Location	Installation	Required CFM Rating
Kitchen range hood	Mount directly over the cooking surface, 21 to 30 inches from the burners; duct to the outside (see page 407) or choose a ductless type to remove grease and odors only.	40 times the lineal feet of the duct if placed along a wall; 50 times lineal feet for peninsula or island location
Kitchen wall or ceiling	Neither will exhaust air around the range as efficiently as a hood unit will; duct to the outside.	If ceiling is 8 feet high, double the kitchen's square footage.
Bath	Mount in ceiling or wall, ideally near the tub or shower and away from door; duct outside, if at all possible, or to well-ventilated attic.	Multiply the bathroom's square footage by 1.07.
Laundry	Locate as near as possible to the washer or dryer; duct outside or to a well-ventilated attic or crawlspace.	Multiply the room's square footage by 0.8.
Attic	Install in a gable-end wall or, better yet, the roof itself. If roofing is dark in color (and absorbs more heat), you'll need a bigger unit.	Multiply attic's square footage by 0.7; add 15 percent for dark colored roof.
Whole-house	Mount in the ceiling over a stairwell, central hall, or other spot where it can pull air from the entire house. Louvered shutters should close when not running or in case of fire. Units can be noisy, so check sone ratings before you buy.	Use cubic footage of whole house if you live in warm climates, half that size if you live in cold climates.

Solving Ventilation Problems (continued)

INSTALLING A CEILING FAN

Wind chill is the effect felt by the removal of heat from the skin by wind. While wind chill is associated with winter, it can work in summer to increase comfort. For example, 87°F air moving at 5 mph feels the same as 77°F still air.

Moving air with a fan at 5 mph is far less expensive than cooling air 10°F with an air-conditioner. Those slow-turning ceiling fans that we all associate with movies about the South increase summer comfort and quickly pay for themselves.

The simplest way to install a new ceiling fan is to substitute it for an existing ceiling fixture. Many ceiling fans also have light fixtures built into the units, so you won't be losing your lighting. See pages 244–254 for specifics about running new wiring.

Make sure the existing fixture box will support the weight of a fan. If not, install a metal brace between the joists, as shown below. Most fan canopies are large enough to cover the hole you'll need to make in the ceiling.

Consult the table at right to select the correct fan size for your room.

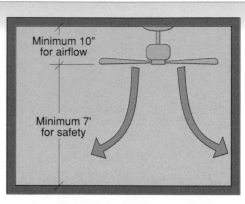

Minimum 10" for airflow

Minimum 7' for safety

YOU'LL NEED...

SKILLS: Basic carpentry and wiring skills.

TIME: 2 to 3 hours not including time to run new wiring.

TOOLS: Drill, hammer, keyhole saw, wire stripper, screwdriver, pliers, wrench.

RECOMMENDED FAN SIZE

Largest Room Dimension, feet	Diameter of Fan, inches
0–12	36
12–16	48
16–18	52
over 18	two fans

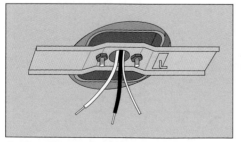

1. Turn off electricity at the service panel. Remove old fixture and its box. Use locknuts to attach the supplied stove bolts to the adapter plate.

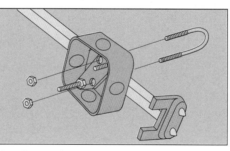

2. Place U-bolt over the brace bar and through bottom of a 1½-inch drop fixture box and adapter plate. Remove a knockout to receive the cable.

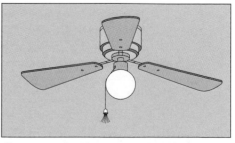

3. Position box in ceiling cutout (enlarged as necessary) with face of box flush with ceiling. Twist bar to extend braces. Tighten until secure.

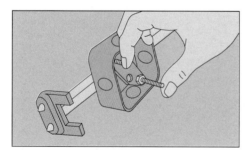

4. Thread old circuit wires through hole in mounting plate and attach plate to bolts. Secure plate with locknuts.

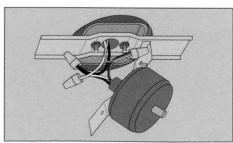

5. Temporarily support the fan motor and attach wires—black to black, white to white, bare to green.

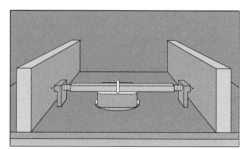

6. Secure the fan motor. Install the canopy to cover the ceiling hole. Assemble fan blades as instructed.

INSTALLING A ROOF-MOUNTED FAN

Vents and louvers help relieve the intense heat that builds up in an attic, and insulation retards heat transfer to the rooms below. But that's just not good enough during prolonged hot spells. A well-insulated attic holds heat for several hours after the sun sets, adding considerably to your home's overall cooling requirements.

That's why you should consider a roof-mounted power ventilator. Mounted on the roof near its peak and coupled with air intakes at or near the eaves, these units pull a steady breeze through the hot attic and can reduce cooling costs by as much as 30 percent.

However, if you do not have central air-conditioning and you don't plan to add it, a whole-house fan (see page 406) probably will provide you with more comfort.

Power roof ventilators are relatively inexpensive and come prewired in lightweight housings that tuck under roofing materials. Most units include thermostatic switches to turn the fan on and off as the temperature dictates. You also can add a humidity-activated control. Besides mounting the unit into the roof, a simple electrical hookup is all that's necessary.

Before you buy, compute the cfm capacity you need using the chart on page 403. You also may have to provide additional static venting at the soffits or in the lower part of the roof. Check the manufacturer's venting recommendations (also see page 133).

Because heat rises, you'll want to locate the ventilator as near to the roof's apex as possible, preferably in the center of a rear slope. For more about making an opening in your roof and flashing around it, see pages 130 and 141.

YOU'LL NEED...

SKILLS: Intermediate carpentry and roofing skills.
TIME: 4 to 6 hours.
TOOLS: Drill, hammer, sabersaw or reciprocating saw, caulking gun, wire stripper, screwdriver, pliers.

1. Measure recommended distance from the ridge. Find center between rafters; drill up through this point.

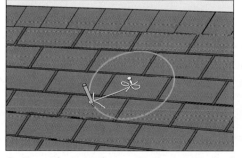

2. Outside, use that point as center and scribe a circle. Make this cut with a sabersaw or reciprocating saw.

3. Test-fit the housing, mark around its flashing, then peel back shingles around top and sides.

4. Turn the fan over and coat its edges with roofing cement to ensure a tight seal.

5. Slip into place; flashing fits under the rolled-back shingles on the top and sides, and on top of the lower shingles

6. Nail flashing to roof decking; apply roofing cement around flashing and to nails. Stick down top and side shingles.

Solving Ventilation Problems (continued)

INSTALLING A WHOLE-HOUSE FAN

Looking to lessen your dependence on airconditioning or to do without it entirely? A whole-house fan might be the answer. Such units pull large volumes of air through your home, exhausting it out through the attic.

A whole-house fan won't dehumidify and is run only when the temperature is lower outside than inside. Come sundown, one of these big units will draw off daytime heat buildup in a matter of minutes. Also, air in motion feels up to 10°F cooler than stagnant air.

A whole-house fan costs several times as much as the roof fan on page 405. The cfm capacity is much larger (see chart on page 403), and the units usually include a rubber suspension system to dampen vibration noises and an automatic shutdown system in case of a fire.

Installation requires more carpentry work, especially if you build the suction box (steps 4 and 5 below). Suction boxes allow you to ventilate only the attic during the day or while cooling equipment is in operation. These installations also are quieter. Before you build a suction box, however, read the instructions, paying particular attention to the recommended sizes for intake and exhaust openings. Constricting these may increase the air velocity and create wind noise.

You have plenty of flexibility in operating a whole-house fan, depending on which doors and windows you open. When the outdoor temperature begins to drop, you can raise the lower sashes of all windows to clear the air inside. Later you might shut some windows in areas that don't need ventilating. But don't close up all openings; these powerful units can suck soot out of your chimney.

YOU'LL NEED...

SKILLS: Intermediate carpentry and basic electrical skills.
TIME: 5 to 7 hours.
TOOLS: Hammer, measuring tape, saw, screwdriver, drill, wire stripper, pliers.

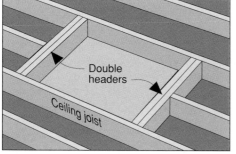

1. Cut an opening to size in the ceiling, allowing for double headers where you must remove a joist section.

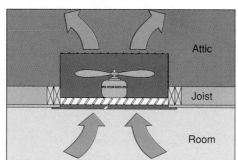

2. Horizontal mounting is easy. In this position, it ventilates the house but can't be used to cool just the attic.

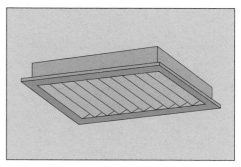

3. Cover the ceiling opening with an automatic shutter unit. Louvers open when the fan is running.

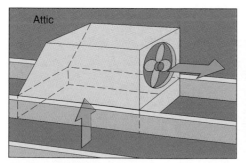

4. To cool either the attic or the house, build a suction box and mount the fan vertically, aimed at gable vents.

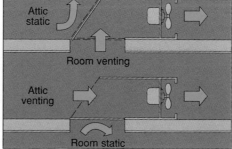

5. A trap door or automatic shutters let you exhaust the house (top) or vent the attic only (bottom).

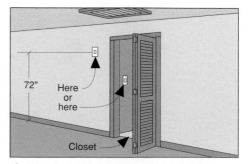

6. Locate switch where it won't be mistaken for a light switch. Or, install a timer to control the fan automatically.

INSTALLING A RANGE HOOD OR BATHROOM FAN

Tired of cracking open a window every time someone broils a steak or takes a shower? Kitchen and bath ventilating systems clear the air faster and use a lot less energy than what is lost through open windows.

Before you shop for a fan, refer to the chart on page 403 to determine the required cfm capacity, making special note of the installation data listed there.

As you survey the range of units available, compare sone ratings. Noise levels shouldn't exceed 8 sones for range hoods or 6.5 sones for bathroom fans. Most units are much quieter than this.

Units usually come with easy-to-follow installation instructions. Whether or not you decide to take on the job yourself probably will be governed by the carpentry work necessary to route a duct from your kitchen or bath to the outdoors. As noted on page 403, you can vent a bathroom or utility room fan into a well-ventilated attic, but don't vent a range fan into an attic.

The drawings below illustrate your major venting options. Choose the shortest run possible, with the least number of elbows; there should be no more than two elbows for ducts up to 5 inches in diameter, three for 6-inch or larger ducts. A duct run should be no longer than 25 feet, if at all possible.

Remember, too, that range hoods handle airborne grease. Because that greasy air is flammable, you should keep these ducts away from direct heat sources and clean out the hood's filter at the intervals specified by the manufacturer. Bathroom ventilators require virtually no periodic maintenance.

You'll also need a power source, of course. Because these units draw only small amperages, you may be able to tap into an existing circuit, as shown on pages 250–252.

YOU'LL NEED...

SKILLS: Basic carpentry and wiring skills.
TIME: 6 to 8 hours.
TOOLS: Hammer, measuring tape, saw, screwdriver, drill, wire stripper, pliers, tin snips.

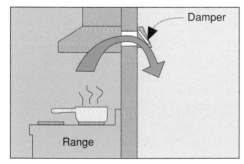

The easiest way to vent kitchen and bath units is directly through an outside wall.

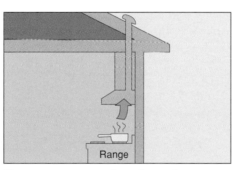

Or, you can run a duct through a cabinet above, then through the ceiling and out the roof.

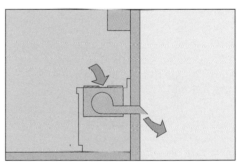

Self-venting ranges eliminate the need for a hood, but must still be ducted. Through-the-wall ducting is easiest.

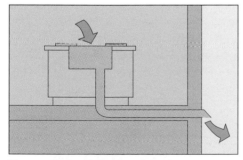

For a self-venting island range, run ducting between floor joists. Keep the duct run to a minimum.

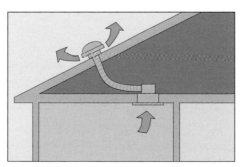

Use flexible ducting to vent a bathroom through a roof or wall, but don't use for range hood due to grease buildup.

SECURITY

To be "at home" is to have a sense of well-being that comes with feeling secure. If you haven't thought of security as one of the important systems in your home, now is the time to reorient your outlook.

To protect against break-ins and fire, you can use hardware devices, but your habits and procedures are as vital to security as water is to plumbing. You can, for example, void the protection provided by even the finest lock by "hiding" its key under the welcome mat.

This chapter deals mainly with security hardware. Before you get down to locks and bolts, however, test your safety awareness by reviewing the precautions outlined below, then "case" your house, as explained on page 409.

PROTECTING AGAINST BREAK-INS

Small-time thieves commit the great majority of household break-ins. They'll nab a purse through an open window, slit a screen door and make off with a TV set, even back a truck up to the garage and empty a house.

A surprising number simply walk through a door somebody didn't bother to lock. Insist on a 24-hour locked-door policy at your house—for a thief, routine daylight comings and goings often make a better crime cover than darkness.

When you're not home, make it look as if you are. Program timers to turn lights on and off at different times in different rooms (see page 416). Leave a radio playing loudly enough to be heard from just outside. Ask a neighbor to park a car in the driveway while you're on vacation. All of these strategies raise doubts in a prowler's mind.

Don't put your faith in such gimmicks as bogus detective agency decals and barking dog tapes; these fool only the people who buy them. Exceptions are programs run by many local police departments that allow you to electronically etch identification numbers on valuables. The police then provide a sticker for your door or window warning would-be burglars with a message like "All items of value on these premises have been marked."

If you come home to find a burglary in progress, don't panic, but don't try to apprehend the culprits, either. Get out and call the police, then wait until they arrive before you re-enter the house.

Properly securing your home's points of entry, as shown on the following pages, will keep out all but the most determined intruders. If you want to go further, consider the pros and cons of adding an alarm system (see pages 420–421). For even more protection, consult a reputable security service.

FIRE PROTECTION

Although houses may differ in many respects, almost all are built from uniform materials, assembled in basically the same ways.

Why don't builders exercise more creativity? The answer lies in your community's building code and its principal concern—the prevention of fire. Codes rate the relative combustibility of most construction materials, specify where and how they shall be used, and require that each of a home's components be capable of withstanding fire for a certain length of time.

Familiarize yourself with local building codes before you undertake structural changes. Insist that any contractors you hire do all work "to code." Building "out of code" may limit or even cancel an insurance settlement in the event of a fire.

The same goes for equipment that might cause a fire. This includes electrical, gas, and heating and cooling systems, as well as fireplaces and chimneys. For more about these hazards, check out the relevant chapters in this book.

Meeting modern building codes greatly reduces the risk of fire. Fire safety doesn't stop with the structural measures, however. Many fatalities occur because someone carelessly allowed a furnishing or appliance to ignite and fill a home with lethal smoke. Fumes and smoke overcome most victims well before the flames reach them (see page 417 for more about smoke detectors).

Make sure that every member of your household knows the ABCs of fire prevention promoted by your local fire department and the National Safety Council. If you haven't held a family fire drill lately, organize one now.

SIZING UP YOUR HOME'S DEFENSES

You should analyze the security at your house as if you were a prowler contemplating a break-in. Experts often do this with the zone approach illustrated here.

Perimeter defenses include all points easily seen from the street or from a casual stroll around the property. A well-groomed lawn deters prowlers. Trim back bushes near the house so intruders don't have a place to hide while they force open a window.

Keep your garage door closed, whether you're home or not. For convenience, consider a remote-control operator (see pages 227–228).

Make a second check at night, with all your exterior lights ablaze. They should illuminate the drive, as well as front, side, and rear yards. Use two bulbs at entries so you'll still have light if one burns out (more about exterior lighting on pages 277 and 416).

Points of entry are the most vital zones. Survey your doors first, because nearly 90 percent of all illegal entries happen there. Inside garage doors are favorite targets because an intruder can work on them without being observed.

Examine basement and ground-floor windows—plus all others that could be reached by scaling a tree or porch. To learn about securing points of entry, see pages 410–415.

Interior defenses include an intercom, with which you can communicate with someone at the front door. If your house is large, an intercom also can be used to monitor distant rooms. Alarm systems alert you to intruders and fire. Timing devices turn lights and radios on and off when you're away. See pages 416–421 for more about all these second lines of defense.

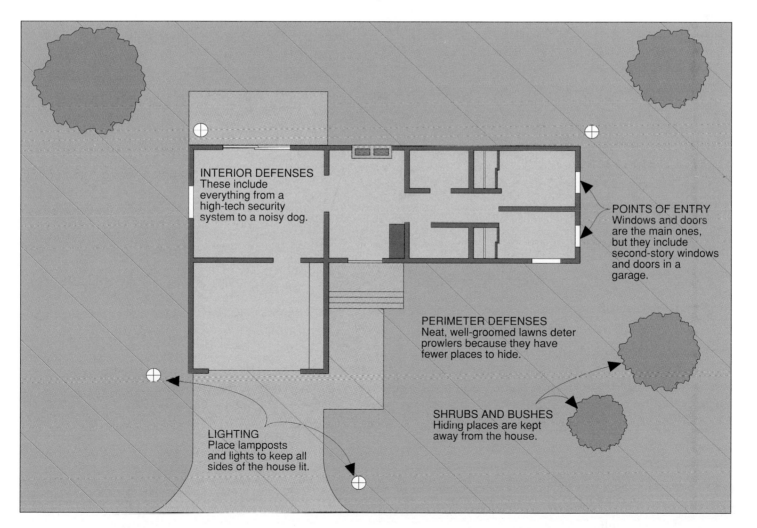

INTERIOR DEFENSES
These include everything from a high-tech security system to a noisy dog.

POINTS OF ENTRY
Windows and doors are the main ones, but they include second-story windows and doors in a garage.

PERIMETER DEFENSES
Neat, well-groomed lawns deter prowlers because they have fewer places to hide.

SHRUBS AND BUSHES
Hiding places are kept away from the house.

LIGHTING
Place lampposts and lights to keep all sides of the house lit.

Securing Points of Entry

There is no such thing as a totally burglar-proof door, window, or even bank vault. The question is, how long would it take a skilled professional to get in? The answer is usually a matter of minutes—sometimes seconds.

Fortunately, professional thieves like to be well-rewarded for their efforts and usually hit businesses and affluent neighborhoods. So-called "amateurs" also can break into almost any home. But if they find yours offers the kind of resistance that takes time to penetrate or attracts attention, most will move on to easier targets.

You can discourage thieves by beefing up points of entry, as shown here and on the following pages.

SECURING DOORS

Door security begins not with a good lock, but with the door itself and the frame into which it fits. Weak door assemblies can be broken with a single kick, popped open with a pry bar, or even pried out—frame and all—from the wall.

Strong exterior doors have solid cores—not hollow ones (see page 79). If they're sheathed in metal, so much the better. Unless your home is old or deteriorated, its front and rear entries probably boast stout doors. But what about those exterior doors leading to a basement or attached garage? Too often builders shave costs by installing flimsy units here. (To learn about hanging new doors, see pages 83–86.)

Open each door and examine its hinges. These should be heavy-duty types, well-fastened to the door and frame. Out-swinging hinges pose a special problem because their exposed pins are easily removed. Secure these as illustrated in last drawing, below right.

Pay attention to each door's frame and its exterior moldings. Gaps here pose not only an insulation problem, but an open invitation to pry-bar artists. Replacing an exterior door and frame assembly is not an extremely tough job—they usually come as a single unit—but one you might want to have done by a professional carpenter.

> **YOU'LL NEED...**
> **SKILLS:** Basic carpentry skills.
> **TIME:** 30 minutes per door.
> **TOOLS:** Drill, screwdriver, hammer.

Replace glass panes in a door with acrylic ones. Or, cover the inner face of the glass with a single sheet of acrylic.

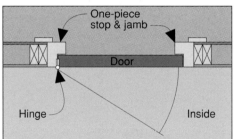

Exterior stops should be a part of the frame; if they're add-ons, nail and caulk tightly. Make sure the door fits snugly.

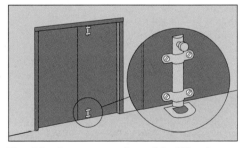

Double doors are vulnerable if both swing freely. Fix one by securing with bar or barrel bolts at top and bottom.

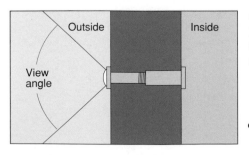

A wide-angle peephole viewer allows you to see who's at the door. Install one by simply drilling a hole and screwing together the units.

If a door has outside hinge pins, remove a screw from each leaf and drive a double-headed nail into the jamb to prevent hinge from being removed.

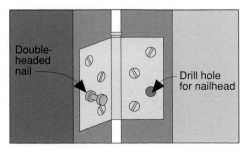

CHOOSING AND BUYING DOOR LOCKS

Burglars rarely pick locks. Why take the time when they can more easily slip the latch, strip out the lock innards with a screwdriver, or pry apart the door and frame? Cheap locks make foolhardy economy. Check your door locksets against the following rundown.

Key-in-knob locks offer the least protection. Many have a simple, beveled spring latch that can be slipped open by inserting a credit card between the door and frame, especially those on which the outside stops are not part of the frame, as explained on page 410. Better key-in-knob sets include a separate tongue that can't be opened this way. But, jabbing an ice pick or small screwdriver into the keyhole—or breaking off the knob—renders them useless.

Interior chain locks make sense only as supplementary hardware. They let you open a door far enough to see who's there and then check credentials. (See page 412 before installing one, however.)

Full-mortise locksets combine a separate deadbolt with an ordinary spring latch. They're so called because you must cut a deep mortise in the door's edge. Breaking off the knob or handle does the intruder no good.

Combination pad or keyless locks let you forget about lost keys. If you think someone has learned the combination, you can change it in just a few minutes.

Deadbolt latches let you add security without replacing the old knob set. To be effective, a deadbolt should have at least a 1-inch throw into the door jamb.

Vertical deadbolt cylinder locks make it impossible for an intruder to gain entry by forcing a pry bar between the door and frame, then separating them far enough to disengage the lock—a tactic that works with many horizontal deadbolts. You can surface mount some deadbolt latch types also—a much easier job than cutting in a full-mortise lockset.

Spring-latch rim locks are surface mounted cousins to ordinary, mortised spring-latch types—and just about as effective.

Sliding bar locks mount in the center of a door. Turning the key or inside knob drives long deadbolts into each jamb. These are highly jimmy-resistant, and even with the hinge pins out, you can't get the door open. They are not very attractive, however, and make a clanking noise when operated.

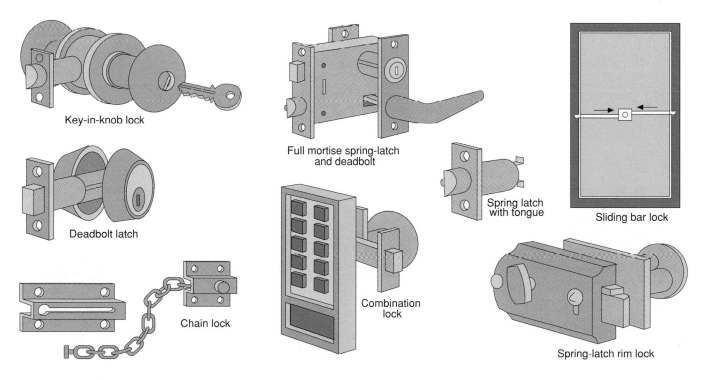

Key-in-knob lock

Deadbolt latch

Chain lock

Full mortise spring-latch and deadbolt

Combination lock

Spring latch with tongue

Sliding bar lock

Spring-latch rim lock

Securing Points of Entry (continued)

INSTALLING SURFACE-MOUNTED LOCKS

If you don't mind the utilitarian look of a surface-mounted lock, you can beef up a door's security in about half the time it takes to install a mortised dead bolt (see page 413). The simplest, but least effective, such solution is a chain lock (below, left). Unless attached into jamb studs with long screws, these can be dislodged by a strong intruder. If you select the vertical deadbolt type (illustrated below right), you'll get a stronger lock.

All surface-mounted hardware depends upon screws for holding power; if the screws that came with your lock don't penetrate at least halfway into the door, discard them and buy longer ones. For added strength, coat the screws with glue before driving them into pilot holes.

Double-cylinder locks require special one-way screws that you can turn in, but not out. Otherwise, an intruder could simply remove the assembly. The fittings with a double-cylinder lock generally include an extra set of conventional, slotted screws. Mount the lock and strike

with these, make any adjustments, then withdraw the slotted screws and replace them with the tamperproof versions.

Mount any surface lock about 8 to 10 inches higher than the existing knob set so you can see and operate it more easily. When you drill, work from one side of the door until just the point of the bit penetrates the opposite side of the door. Then switch sides to complete the hole. This prevents the drill from splintering the door's surface.

In assembling the lock, note that

its bolt mechanism and cylinder are actually separate components. If you want to rekey the lock, all you need to do is dismantle the unit and take the cylinder to a locksmith. To get a double-cylinder lock off the door, drill out its one-way holding screws

YOU'LL NEED...

SKILLS: Basic carpentry skills.
TIME: 30 minutes.
TOOLS: Screwdriver, pliers, drill, hole saw or spade bit for the diameter hole specified for lock.

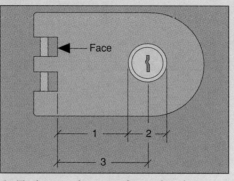

1. To locate distance from the door's edge to center of cylinder hole (3), add distance from door edge (1) to half of cylinder diameter (2).

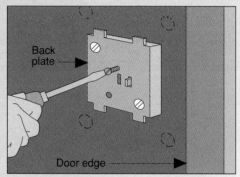

2. Attach the cylinder's back plate to the inside of the door. Then, turn the mounting screws through the plate into the cylinder.

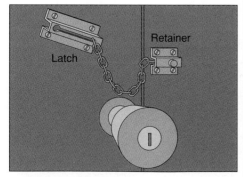

For quick, simple extra protection, you can install a chain lock, as shown. Mount the retainer with screws long enough to penetrate the jamb studs.

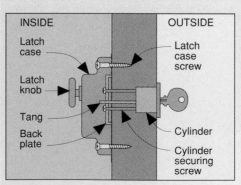

3. Slip the latch assembly over the tang, drill pilot holes, and screw to the door. The tang gives you a little adjustment leeway.

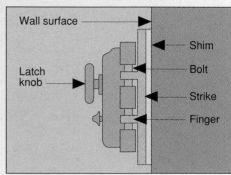

4. Mount the strike to the jamb. In order for the fingers to mesh with the bolt, you may need to shim underneath the strike plate.

INSTALLING A MORTISED DEADBOLT

Adding a deadbolt lock is an inexpensive way to back up a flimsy key-in-knob lockset—or provide supplementary security for any door. A mortised deadbolt looks like an integral part of the door itself, but is not as secure as a surface-mounted vertical deadbolt (see page 412),

Most mortised deadbolts now are made so that you don't need to hollow out a section of the door, as you had to with full-mortise locks (see page 87). Instead, you bore holes through the door's face and edge, then cut a shallow mortise for the bolt's strike plate and a deeper one for the jamb strike, as shown in the drawings below.

Measure the thickness of your door before you buy a deadbolt. Some locksets can be adjusted to compensate for varying thicknesses; others require special spacers or a shorter cylinder.

You also can select units with special "pick-resistant" cylinders. The biggest advantage to these high-security devices is that it's very difficult for a stranger who might have temporary possession of your key to get a duplicate. Usually, you have to write to the manufacturer for extras or provide proof of ownership to a licensed locksmith.

> ### YOU'LL NEED...
> **SKILLS:** Basic carpentry skills.
> **TIME:** 45 to 60 minutes.
> **TOOLS:** Awl, screwdriver, drill and hole saw or spade bit for diameter of hole specified for lock, hammer, chisel.

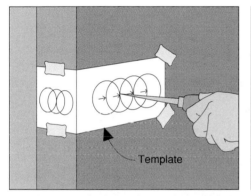

Template

1. Like most lock hardware, deadbolt sets include a template that helps you accurately locate where to bore holes.

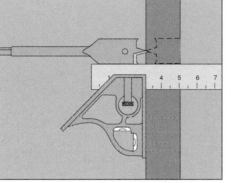

2. Make sure you drill holes absolutely square. To minimize damage, drill from one side, then the other, as shown.

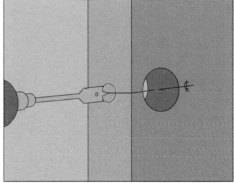

3. Bore a second hole—the one for the bolt—from the door's edge. Steady the door and keep everything true.

4. Insert the deadbolt, mark an outline for the strike plate, and cut a mortise for it using a hammer and chisel (see pages 83, 87, and 443).

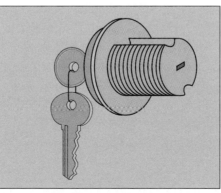

5. Assemble the components. Most mortised cylinders are threaded and have grooves for the setscrews that secure it.

6. Install the strike on the jamb as you would for any door (page 87). Often, you only need to bore a hole for the deadbolt itself.

Securing Points of Entry *(continued)*

SECURING WINDOWS

Intruders usually enter homes through doors, say police. However, you can't expect burglars to stand on tradition—especially if you have windows that they easily could force open and climb through without being noticed.

Don't worry about large expanses of fixed glass. The clatter from smashing a picture window probably would call attention to a break-in. Most burglars are cautious about being caught, so they don't bother with homes that are more secure, and move on to easier targets.

If the doors are locked, burglars will concentrate on smaller, operable windows. If the window can't be forced open, a burglar may stick

tape to a pane, break it, and quietly pull away the pieces to gain access to the latch.

The solution is to lock your windows in both their closed and open positions. Then, no one can reach inside and enlarge the opening. The drawings below and on page 415 show a variety of ways to secure windows and sliding doors. Be sure, however, that whatever method you use doesn't block a potential fire exit.

Most homes have many windows. Securing every one can be costly and time-consuming, so start with all sliding glass doors and windows accessible from ground level. Analyze which upper-level windows

could be reached from a balcony, garage roof, or tree. Enterprising second-story burglars may bring along a ladder to get at the ones you think are inaccessible.

Make sure all windows work properly. Sashes that wobble when you crank them, that rattle in high winds, or that have to be propped open offer only token resistance to break-ins. For window repairs, see pages 69–72 and 160–161.

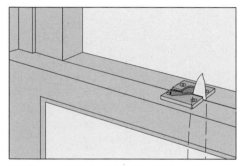

Ordinary sash locks offer little security because you can open most of them easily with a knife blade.

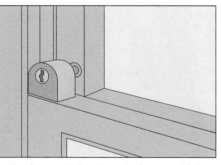

Key locks can't be jimmied, even if the glass is broken. Most let you lock the window in a partly open position.

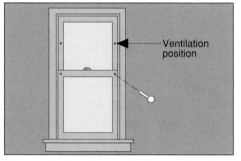

Secure double-hung windows closed or open with holes through the bottom sash and partly into top. Insert nails.

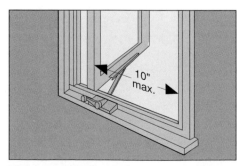

Many casement windows won't open enough to admit an adult. To check, open the window and measure.

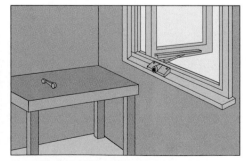

If a window is big enough to admit a person, after opening it remove the operator crank and set it out of reach.

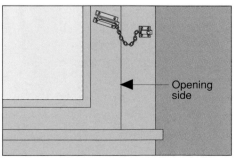

Install a door-type chain lock to keep windows from opening. Fasten it down with the biggest screws possible.

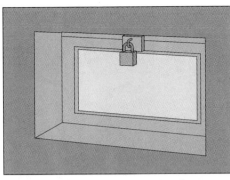

Install hasps on basement windows so you can secure them with master-keyed padlocks. Keep the key somewhere that's handy, but not on the sill.

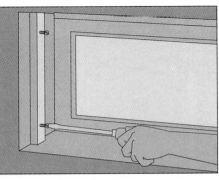

If your windows don't have hasps, drive long screws into a stop on either side. Leave a few inches to open the window for ventilation.

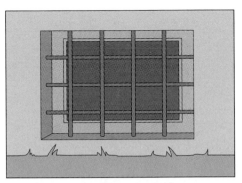

Custom-made grills mortared into foundation give basement windows a behind-bars look—but they provide peace of mind in high-crime areas.

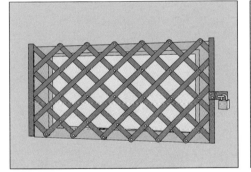

Scissors-type gates and hinged iron shutters can be padlocked from the inside, yet opened for escape in case of an emergency.

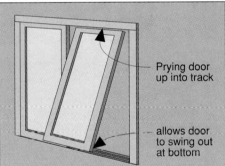

Prying door up into track

allows door to swing out at bottom

Thieves like sliding glass doors because some can be jimmied easily from their tracks, even when the door locksets are in a locked position.

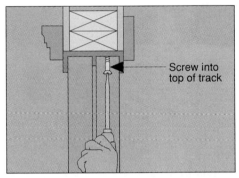

Screw into top of track

One solution for sliding glass doors is to drive sheet-metal screws into the top center of each upper track. Adjust them so the door just clears as it opens.

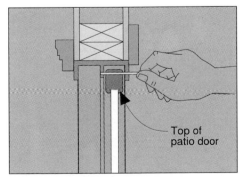

Top of patio door

Or, secure sliding glass patio doors by drilling holes through both the track and the sashes' frames. Slip nails into the holes to prevent opening.

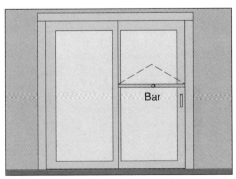

Bar

Accessory bars mount to the door frame to jam the sliding door. They preclude forcing the lock but don't protect against jimmying the door up.

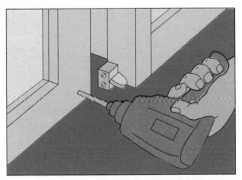

Toe-operated locks are convenient and the least obtrusive. You mount the lock on the casing and drill a hole in the sash into which a locking rod enters.

Establishing Second Lines of Defense

Smart homeowners don't stop at securing points of entry. They also take care to ensure that the lighting around the perimeter of the house is sufficient to dissuade would-be intruders. And, inside the house, they use one or more devices available today—electronic timers, smoke or fire detectors, fire extinguishers, intercoms, safes, and alarm systems. The rest of this chapter provides an overview and installation tips for these second lines of defense. Incorporating these items into your security plan will contribute significantly to the safety of all family members.

USING LIGHTS FOR SECURITY

If you ring your home with exterior lighting and use timers to orchestrate an at-home illusion, most night prowlers will shy away. Yard lighting can be expensive to operate, so consider hooking your system up to a photoelectric cell or timer, rather than just a regular switch. In this way, you can light only key areas on most evenings. (For more about exterior lighting, see page 277; and for switches, see pages 254–255.)

Inside, you can duplicate your family's nocturnal lighting habits with timing devices. For example, you might program lights to let a living room lamp burn until bedtime, then turn on your usual night light.

You can override most timers when you wish—and more-expensive versions control several lights on different programs.

The drawings below illustrate just a few of many ways you can use lights for added security. Check with a lighting dealer for other up-to-the-minute devices and techniques.

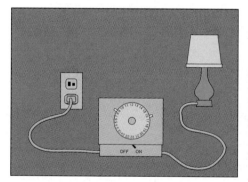

Moderately priced clock timers plug into an electric outlet, then a lamp is plugged into the timer.

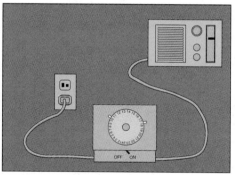

To make it sound as if you are home during the day, program a timer to turn on a radio in the morning, off at night.

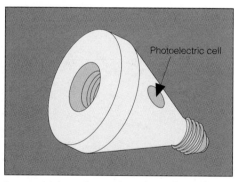

Inexpensive photoelectric cells sense darkness and turn lights on and off so you don't need to worry about them.

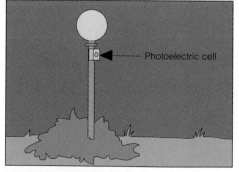

Photoelectric cells ensure that strategic outdoor fixtures will come on, whether you're home or not.

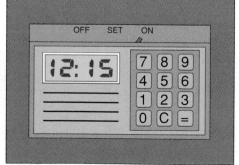

You can replace a regular wall switch with a programmable timer that turns lights off and on at preset hours.

A pair of eaves fixtures at one corner can illuminate two sides of your home with 40- or 60-watt floodlight bulbs.

HELPFUL HINTS   CHOOSING AND BUYING SMOKE DETECTORS

Even a relatively small, smoldering fire can fill a house with smoke in a matter of minutes—and smoke claims more lives annually than flames. Many local building codes and home insurance companies now require one or more smoke detectors in new houses.

There are two basic types of smoke detectors—photoelectric and ionization units. Photoelectric units include a beam of light and a photoelectric cell. When smoke enters the unit, it scatters the light, causing part of it to contact the photoelectric cell and trigger the alarm. Photoelectric smoke detectors react more readily to slow, smoldering

fires than to fast, flaming blazes.

An ionization unit ionizes the air inside the detector and gives it an electrical charge. Smoke particles cut down current flow, which sounds the warning. Ionization detectors respond more quickly than photoelectric units to fast, flaming fires.

Combination units are also available that provide the benefits of both types. These are more expensive, however.

Each type has its advantages and drawbacks. While battery-operated photoelectric models are available, many depend on house current, which means you lose protection during a

power outage or electrical fire and you must locate them near an electric outlet. Ionization units run on house current, batteries, or both. Besides reacting more slowly to smoldering fires, they're also more susceptible to false alarms.

Consider installing at least one of each—an ionization detector in your bedroom hallway plus a photoelectric unit in the living area. A deluxe system might also include a series of heat sensors wired in tandem with smoke detectors so that all the alarms will sound if any one senses heat or smoke. These require extensive wiring.

INSTALLING SMOKE DETECTORS

Smoke detectors take only a few minutes to mount. Knowing where to locate them, however, helps you decide how many you need.

Attach each unit to a ceiling or high on a wall about 8 to 10 inches below ceiling level. Ideally, you should have at least one detector on each floor in hallways leading to bedrooms and at the top of stairwells. Analyze your home's air currents and avoid dead corners where there is poor air circulation. Also, keep detectors away from smoky kitchen, furnace, garage, or fireplace areas.

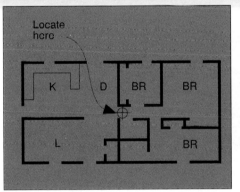

In a single-floor home with bedrooms clustered together, you can install one unit in a hallway between the bedroom and living areas.

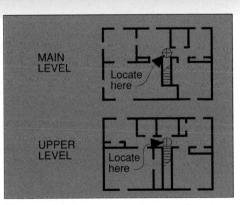

If your sleeping areas are spread out or are on different levels, you should use at least two detectors. Mount one at the top of the stairway.

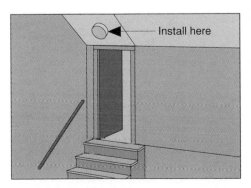

Protect your basement, too. Because smoke and heat always rise, install this detector at the top of the basement stairway, if possible.

Once smoke reaches the ceiling, it spreads out horizontally. This makes the center of a room the optimum location for a smoke detector.

Establishing Second Lines of Defense (continued)

MATERIAL MATTERS CHOOSING AND USING FIRE EXTINGUISHERS

A fire in your home can involve combustible solids, flammable liquids, or live electricity. To protect your family, arm yourself with a fire extinguisher rated to handle all three types of fires (see below).

When shopping, look closely at the label for a number that indicates the coverage it will provide. The larger the number, the greater the coverage.

When you get the extinguisher home, read the use directions in front of the whole family, check to be sure the unit is charged, then put it in an easily accessible place. You might want to have another extinguisher in your workshop or garage area, too. Check the unit's charge twice each year.

Type of Fire	Extinguisher to Use
Class A—Combustible solids, such as paper, wood, fabric, and most plastics	Pressurized extinguishers that expel water with a gas; an easily recharged pump type; foam also puts out Class A fires
Class B—Flammable liquids, such as grease, oil, gasoline, and kerosene	Foam, dry chemical, and carbon dioxide (CO_2) extinguishers all work against liquid fires; don't use water because it will spread the flames.
Class C—Live electricity; with power off, these become Class A or Class B fires.	CO_2 or dry chemical; never use foam or water on electrical fires, because you could suffer a serious shock and/or spread the fire.

CHOOSING AND BUYING AN INTERCOM SYSTEM

Of all home security devices, an intercom offers the most protection. You can learn who's at any door from a safe distance, control a buzzer-latch on your garden gate, monitor a sleeping baby, or even pipe music through the house.

Intercoms vary in complexity, but all operate on low voltages, stepped down via a transformer from your home's electrical system. This makes them relatively easy and safe for a do-it-yourself installation. You should pay close attention to installation instructions that come with the system, however. (More about low-voltage wiring on pages 260–261.)

Unless you are working with new construction, your biggest challenge will be unobtrusively routing or fishing wires from one room to another (see below and page 251). With flush-mounted wall components, you also will have to cut into walls, but usually you won't have to alter their framing.

The master station contains circuitry that lets you call any or all of the substations. It also may include a radio.

Substations have a combined speaker and microphone with switches that transfer from listen to talk modes.

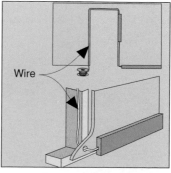

Outdoor substations often include a button to sound the doorbell or chimes. Others just beep or buzz.

Low-voltage wiring is similar to that used for telephones (see page 260). Often, you can run it along moldings.

CHOOSING AND BUYING A SAFE

Before you go shopping for a home safe, consider what you want it to do. Good safes carry Underwriters Laboratories (UL) ratings. Fire-resistant safes include fireclay insulation that will protect paper documents up to 1 hour at 1,700°F (Class C), up to 2 hours at 1,850°F (Class B), and up to 4 hours at 2,000°F (Class A).

These units also must pass tough explosion and impact tests. A fire-resistant safe costs less than any other type. Keep irreplaceable papers in this one.

Money chests, secured to your home's structure, generally are smaller in size and higher in price. These are UL rated, also, based on their ability to withstand attacks with tools (TL), torches (TR), and explosives (TX). TR and TX ratings apply primarily to large commercial units. Many, but not all, home safes are rated as TL. On those that are, the TL rating is followed by a number that indicates how many minutes the safe can resist an attack by an expert who knows the safe. A TL-15 safe, for example, will withstand 15 minutes of continuous drilling, under ideal conditions.

Money chests, although not always lightweight, can be pried out of a frame wall or floor, carried off, and cracked at the thief's leisure. Hiding the safe might remove it from an amateur's attention, but professional thieves know to look behind pictures, under throw rugs, and just about any place you might think of. That's why money chests are best installed in a masonry wall or floor, or soundly bolted to framing.

Combination safes consist of a burglar-resistant money chest inside a fire-resistant safe. These units have thick steel walls, an even thicker door, and a combination lock with a relocking device. This ensures that if a lock is attacked with tools, it will lock permanently until it is drilled out. A combination safe can be bolted into the floor to prevent the whole safe from being taken. Best of all is a safe that is set in concrete in a foundation wall.

OUTFITTING A CLOSET FOR SAFEKEEPING

No closet offers the security of a burglar- or fire-resistant safe. However, you can beef one up to protect a valued collection against grab-it-and-run thieves who commit most household break-ins.

Treat your "safe" closet's door as if it were a point of entry to your home. Use a metal-clad solid-core door—or at least a solid-core one. Make sure it's carefully fitted to its frame. An extra hinge in the center adds resistance to prying on that side. Because most closet doors swing outward, you'll want to secure all hinges with double-headed nails (see page 410). If it swings inward, secure the door stop with the largest screws possible.

On the latch side, install a strong deadbolt lock (page 413). Protect the door from being pried open by installing a heavy metal strip along the latch edge, as shown.

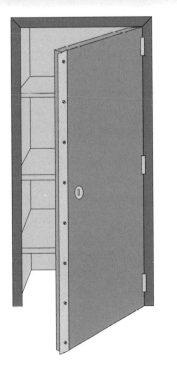

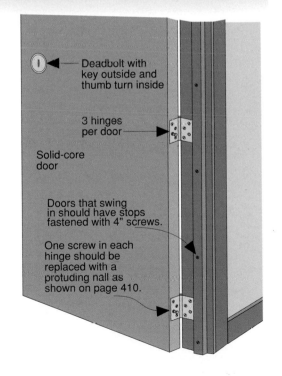

Deadbolt with key outside and thumb turn inside

3 hinges per door

Solid-core door

Doors that swing in should have stops fastened with 4" screws.

One screw in each hinge should be replaced with a protuding nail as shown on page 410.

Establishing Second Lines of Defense *(continued)*

CHOOSING AND BUYING AN ALARM SYSTEM

An alarm system will send almost any burglar packing. The same pandemonium also can create unpleasant headaches—for your neighbors as well as for you—if the system malfunctions or if you forget to disarm it when you enter.

You'll have to weigh the deterrent value of security alarm equipment against its nuisance potential. Check community ordinances, too; some regulate alarm system operation.

If you investigate electronic alarm systems, you'll find dozens of different ways to go. All employ a network of sensors that feeds information to a master control unit. The network may use lightweight, low-voltage wire strung from sensor to sensor or radio beams transmitted from the sensors to a receiver in the control unit.

When a sensor reports trouble, the control sets off the reporter—an alarm bell, siren, flashing light, automatic telephone dialer, or all of these devices. Most alarm systems include a time-delay setting so you can get out of the house and back in again without sounding the alarm. More expensive ones also offer smoke and heat detectors and even intercom systems.

Different types of sensors "feel," "hear," or "see" an intruder. Magnetic sensors feel when a door or window opens; pressure-sensitive mats and metal-foil alarm tape also are feelers. Ultrasonic detectors use inaudible sound waves to detect if anyone is moving about an area. Infrared detectors use light beams to sense the presence of an intruder.

Motion detectors often can be oversensitive, so get a model with a sensitivity adjustment. Also, keep in mind that motion detectors can be set off by a wandering child or pet.

Installing a wired system can be a lot of work. You have to run wire from the master control panel to one sensor, then the next, and so on, usually looping back to the master control at the end. Wired units cost less than radio systems, however, and with most, cutting any wire sets off the alarm.

With radio networks, you simply install a series of battery-powered transmitters and plug in the controller/receiver unit. One transmitter usually will handle several nearby doors or windows. The batteries in each transmitter must be checked periodically.

Security system control units may be powered by stepped-down house current, batteries, or both. Batteries won't let you down in a power failure, but you need a means of testing them, and the entire system, without activating the alarm.

ANATOMY OF A HOME ALARM SYSTEM

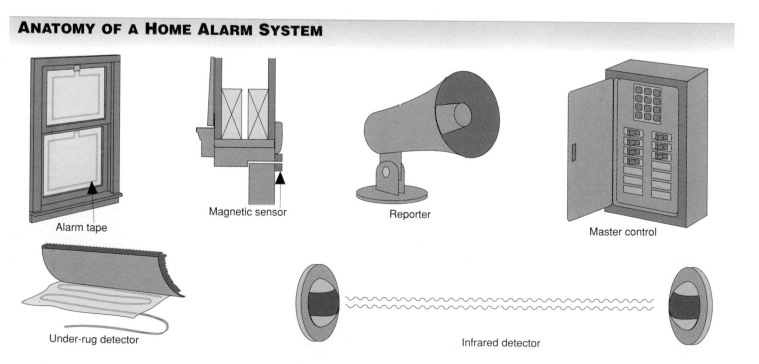

Alarm tape

Magnetic sensor

Reporter

Master control

Under-rug detector

Infrared detector

INSTALLING AN ALARM SYSTEM

Hooking up an alarm network can be a one-day job or an ongoing exercise in frustration. It depends on the care you take during installation.

Most problems are with magnetic sensors. The two halves—magnet and switch—must be in perfect parallel alignment, usually with no less than ⅛ inch or no more than ¼ inch between them. To maintain this tolerance, your doors and windows must fit snugly, with virtually no play. Otherwise, gusts of wind or a passing truck can set off the alarm. So, make sure doors (see pages 80–82) and windows (see pages 69–72) are in good working order.

Alarm circuitry varies somewhat. Most wired systems employ a "normally closed" circuit that keeps current moving as long as the unit is armed. Tripping or tampering with any sensor opens the circuit and sounds the alarm.

A "normally open" system—typically used with wireless setups—works the opposite way. Opening a door or window closes the circuit. If you understand which type you have, it will be easier to track down problems that occur during the installation or later on.

Mount the control unit in a convenient but inconspicuous location, such as inside a closet. Hook up the bell or siren and test it. Then install and test one sensor at a time before you move on to the next one. This way you know exactly where any difficulty lies.

Alarm kits include only a few sensors, but you usually can add any number of additional devices. Count your doors and windows and you'll see that full protection may require a lot of hardware. To save time and expense, consider permanently sealing shut windows that you never open, such as upper sashes in double-hung units.

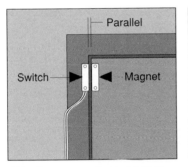

Attach a sensor's magnet to the door or window sash, its switch to the frame. These must be exactly parallel.

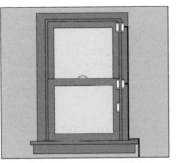

Another magnet on a double-hung sash lets you turn off the alarm, open the window, then rearm the system.

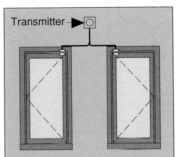

Here, top-mounted casement window sensors feed into a transmitter that broadcasts to a wireless master control.

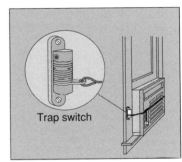

Trap switches let you string a wire across several in-swinging windows—or an air-conditioner.

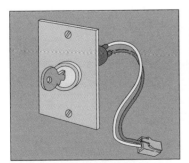

A key switch arms and disarms the system. Locate it outside the garage door or at the back door.

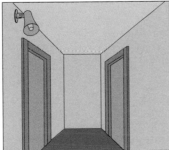

Mount interior reporter in a stairway, hallway, or other location that will broadcast its warning widely.

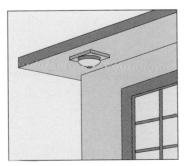

Place an outdoor reporter bell in an inaccessible spot so an intruder cannot silence it easily.

Basics You Should Know

TOOLS AND TECHNIQUES

"I'm just not handy," people often lament—as if others were born hitting nails squarely and sawing arrow-straight lines. Each of us starts out with no manual dexterity whatsoever, then gradually develops hundreds of skills that use hand-eye coordination—everything from grasping a rattle to driving a car.

This chapter is devoted to putting aside the myth of your unhandiness. If you master the basic techniques on the following pages, you can be an accomplished do-it-yourselfer.

Good craftsmanship begins with quality, well-cared-for tools. If, like most homeowners, you already have a few tools lying around, now is the time to take a critical look at them. Toss out those that are bent or broken and those that won't hold a cutting edge—and stay away from the bargain bins when you shop for replacement tools.

What makes a quality tool? Most manufacturers offer two or even three different lines. At the bottom are the low-cost "bargains"; don't waste your money on them.

Prices jump sharply at the next level, which is sometimes called the "homeowner" line. In this class are tools capable of performing most of the upkeep and improvement tasks around your house. For just slightly more money, however, you often can get professional-quality tools. Sturdily built to exacting standards, these will endure through years of hard use. In fact, some companies offer lifetime guarantees.

Take your time deciding on any tool, and find out what material it's made of. Several different alloys are used in metal implements. Carbon steel, a blend of iron and carbon, makes sense for hand tools that don't generate heat. Low alloy steel, which includes some tungsten or molybdenum, is slightly more heat-resistant. For high-speed cutting tools, look for high-alloy steel, which has a much higher tungsten or molybdenum content, or tungsten carbide. Power saw blades tipped with tungsten carbide will last years for the average do-it-yourselfer.

Metal tools differ, too, in the way they're made. Casting, the least expensive manufacturing technique, leaves flaws in the metal that make it prone to chipping and breaking. If you'll be hitting the tool, as you would with a chisel, don't buy the cast type. A broken tool can cause injury. Machined tools are suitable for all but the most severe duty. Forged or drop-forged tools are almost indestructible, an important quality for such items as hammers and cold chisels. Don't overlook a tool made partly of plastic, either. Fiberglass handles on hammers and axes, for example, are as strong as steel shanks, yet they have more resilience than wood handles.

Assemble your tool collection a few pieces at a time. Start with the basics, then add specialty items and power equipment as the need arises. In this way, you're more likely to invest in quality. As you gain proficiency, you'll also develop a clearer sense of what tools you would like to purchase next.

With about a dozen basic hand tools and an electric drill, you can make most minor home repairs. These include a measuring tape, straight- and Phillips-blade screwdrivers, regular and needle-nose pliers, an 8-inch adjustable wrench, a 16-ounce claw hammer, a push drill, a combination square, a crosscut saw, a hacksaw, a nail set, and a couple of chisels. We've included an electric drill among the basics because its versatility makes it an almost universal tool.

Except for the drill—and possibly an orbital sander for big finishing jobs—confine your initial purchases to hand tools. Power tools will do the same work faster, easier, and sometimes more accurately, but in the hands of an inexperienced person, they can wreck expensive materials in a hurry and cause personal injuries.

Power equipment falls into two categories—portable and stationary. The portables, such as a sabersaw or circular saw, go directly to the job. With stationary equipment—a tablesaw or radial-arm saw, drill presses, and the like—you must bring the job to it.

Use portable power equipment for around-the-house projects, up to and including major construction. Usually it doesn't make sense to invest in stationary power tools unless you're planning to pursue woodworking as a hobby or have mastered basic techniques and are considering a major home remodeling project.

Making and Using Blueprints

A key to any project—large or small—is a clear picture of what you are trying to create. Few people have the ability to picture an entire project in their imagination. This is where blueprints come in. If you draw out your project cleanly, clearly and accurately, you will find your project will follow suit. All it takes is a few simple tools and practice. Try it.

CHOOSING DRAFTING TOOLS

To make good drawings, you will need a smooth, flat surface that has one straight edge. You can buy a drafting board or use a scrap of pine-veneered plywood. The T-square produces horizontal lines; a triangle against the T-square, vertical lines. An architect's scale gives you dimensions at various scales. A compass and a protractor create arcs and measure angles. Also, get a good mechanical pencil and eraser.

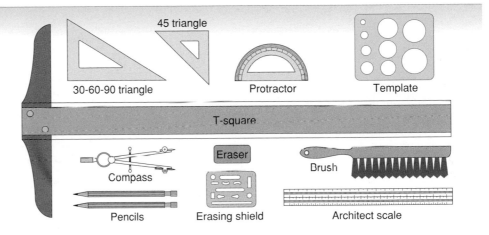

DRAWING TO SCALE

Draw your plans at a scale as large as your paper will allow. Typically this means ⅛ inch = 1 foot for a site plan; ¼ inch = 1 foot for a house; ½ inch = 1 foot for a room or deck. Use 1 inch = 1 foot for details.

An architect's scale is a triangular ruler that has six scales, ranging from ³⁄₃₂ inch = 1 foot to 3 inches = 1 foot. To lay out a dimension, start at the feet mark and end at the inch mark (end with finer spacing).

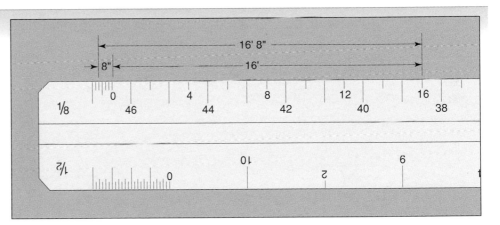

USING SYMBOLS

While you are free to create your own conventions or symbols, you will find that the architectural and building worlds have agreed on a few that are used universally. You will find it easier to read others' plans and to discuss your plans with professionals and suppliers if you speak the same language. At right are some of the common symbols that you will find most useful.

Earth		Surface light		Cold water	
Gravel		Duplex receptacle		Hot water	
Concrete		Weatherproof receptacle	WP	Vent pipe	
Brick		Range outlet	R	Waste pipe	
Finish wood		Telephone jack		Gas pipe	G — G
Framing lumber		Switch	S	90° elbow	
Fibrous insulation		3-way switch	S3	T	
Rigid insulation		Switch & receptacle	S	Clean-out	

Making and Using Blueprints (continued)

DRAWING AN ELEVATION VIEW

An elevation drawing is a view from the side. Because that is the perspective from which we normally view things, it is very much like a picture, except for the labels you may wish to add.

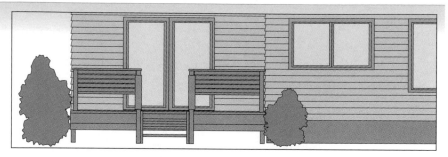

DRAWING A PLAN VIEW

A plan view drawing is a view from above (a bird's-eye view). It shows all of the important horizontal dimensions, such as total length and width, wall-to-wall room measurements, wall thicknesses, window and door locations, fixture and counter dimensions and placements, and sometimes even furniture placement. For an outside deck it may show walks and plants.

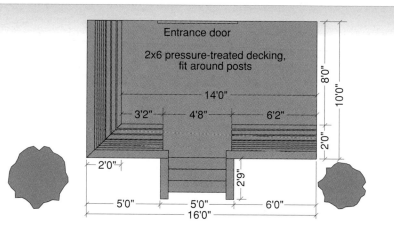

DRAWING FOUNDATION AND FLOOR FRAMING

Foundation and floor framing may be shown separately or combined. For a house, the foundation usually is shown with the first-floor framing. For a deck, the framing and foundation are so integral that they almost always are shown together. The view is a plan view, showing all of the structural members and how they connect. The length of each member often is called out.

2x8 ledger

2x8 joists @ 16" oc

2x4 seat supports

4x4 posts on piers

Double 2x10 beams

2x8 stringer

DRAWING DETAILS

Detail drawings are used when the other plans are insufficient to show the required level of detail. Thus, they are usually at a magnified scale, such as 1 inch = 1 foot or even 3 inches = 1 foot. They often are placed in an empty corner of one of the other drawings.

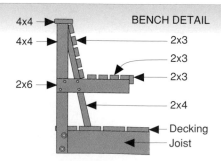

BENCH DETAIL

4x4

4x4

2x3

2x3

2x3

2x6

2x4

Decking

Joist

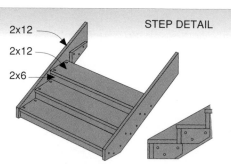

STEP DETAIL

2x12

2x12

2x6

Designing for Universal Access

Until recently, people with physical disabilities have been treated as a special class requiring specialized housing to accommodate their limitations. With research sponsored by the Veterans' Administration, and especially with the passage of the Americans with Disabilities Act, emphasis has shifted from specialized facilities and housing to a design approach that integrates accessibility into public facilities, the workplace, and housing.

As longevity increases, there is growing interest in homes "for the rest of your life." A small initial investment in accessibility and adaptability can make a home more manageable for senior citizens with diminished physical abilities, delaying the need to move into an assisted-living facility.

Before building or purchasing your next home, consider the handicap accessibility features shown here and on page 428. While designed to accommodate persons in wheelchairs, these plans also improve accessibility for those walking with canes and walkers.

DESIGNING ACCESSIBLE WALKS AND RAMPS

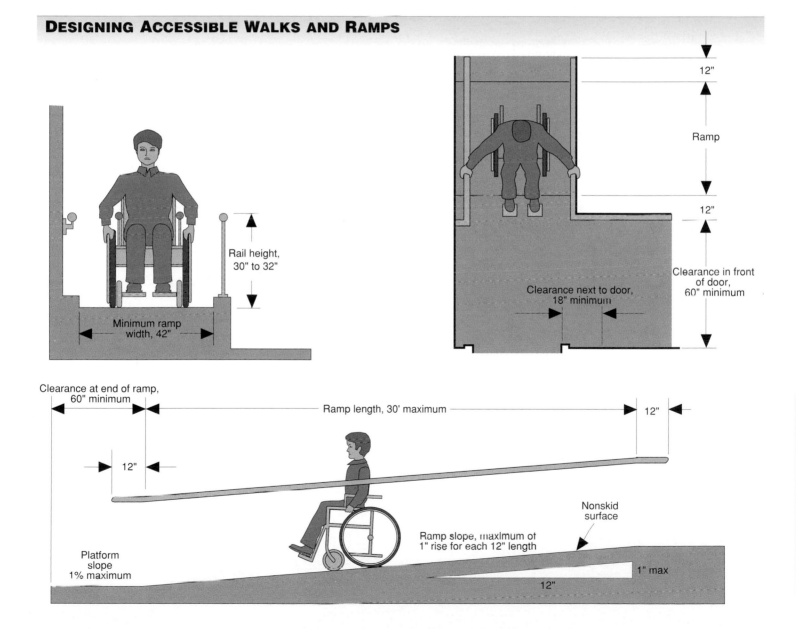

Designing for Universal Access (continued)

DESIGNING ACCESSIBLE BATHROOMS

Grab bar height above floor, 33"

Toilet seat height above floor, 20"

Hand-held shower on slide bar

Faucet and shower controls

Provide seat on end of tub, 18" minimum width

Tub height, 20" maximum

Tilted mirror
Outlet
Front of sink to wall, 27" maximum

Mirror height, 36" maximum

Sink height, 34" maximum

Undersink clearance, 27" minimum

Insulate pipes for protection

Controls

Hand-held shower on slide bar

Control height, 60" maximum

Seat

Nonslip surface

Grab bar height, 33"

Seat height, 20"
Width, 18" minimum

DESIGNING ACCESSIBLE KITCHENS

Clear width under counter, 36" minimum

21" maximum

Countertop height, 34" maximum

Undercounter clearance, 27" minimum

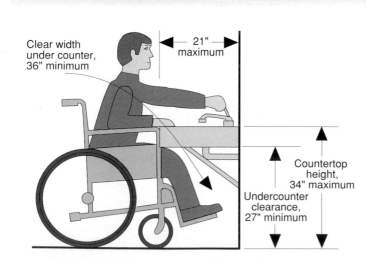

Maximum reach, 21"

Stagger burners

Front controls

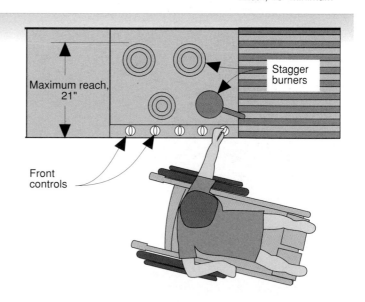

Measuring

Many home repair projects require a measurement of some sort, so you may as well develop the habit of clipping a steel tape to your belt or tucking a folding rule into your back pocket.

Simple linear measurements often aren't enough. Many times, you also must make sure that an object is square, level, and plumb.

It's surprisingly easy to misread or miscalculate a dimension—and mistaken measurements cost time and materials. Making careful and accurate measurements takes concentration and time. Sometimes you have to climb the ladder again or wriggle three times into a tight space. And sometimes, especially at first, you'll make a mistake. That's why you should follow the old adage that professional carpenters have passed down over the years: "Measure twice, cut once."

TOOL TALK — CHOOSING MEASURING TOOLS

With a 16-foot steel tape, you can make horizontal and vertical measurements, measure inside and outside curves, determine depths, and make round measurements. If you're laying out a large project—a patio, retaining wall, or deck—a 50-foot or longer cloth, fiberglass, or steel tape saves time.

A folding rule has multiple uses, too. This rule, whether wood or metal, makes short work of measuring across wide and open areas. Depth and inside measurements are the forte of the extension-type folding rule. A metal blade slides out of the rule to complete a measurement. This feature especially comes in handy in tight quarters where you can unfold only part of the rule.

A framing square, often called a carpenter's square, is designed for squaring and marking large objects, such as plywood and hardboard.

And you can use it to mark angles for rafter cuts and stringers for stairsteps.

A combination square often substitutes for a small try square, which is used for squaring and marking lumber for crosscuts. Most combination squares have a level in the handle. The square also may be used as a marking and depth gauge and as a miter square.

For building walls and checking grade slopes, a line level is used with a heavy cord (often called a mason's line). For determining or marking plumb, as when building a wall, use a plumb bob suspended by a cord. The chalk line shown here doubles as a plumb bob.

A short torpedo level helps you level foundation sills, tools on stands, and shelving. A 24- or 30-inch-long carpenter's level provides greater accuracy. Level bubbles indicate both level and plumb.

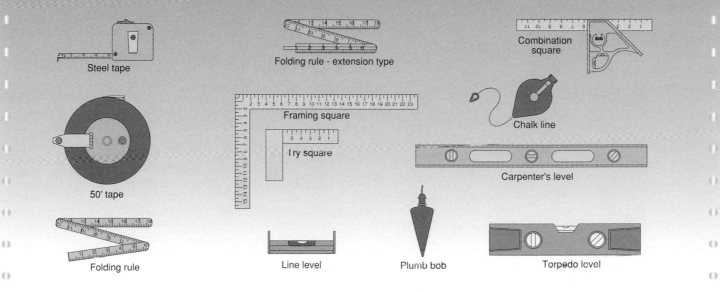

Steel tape

50' tape

Folding rule

Folding rule - extension type

Framing square

Try square

Line level

Plumb bob

Combination square

Chalk line

Carpenter's level

Torpedo level

Measuring (continued)

MAKING ACCURATE MEASUREMENTS

Learning that there is no such measurement as "about" will save you time, money, and frustration.

An equally important fact is that all materials aren't square, especially the ends of boards, dimension lumber, and timbers. However, almost all building material—wood, concrete, metal, plastic, and so on—has a factory edge. A "factory edge" is carpenters' vernacular for the milled edge of the material. This edge usually is true, or straight, so use it as a reference point for squaring the rest of the material.

To make accurate measurements, you'll need several tools, most importantly a rule or tape measure. Your best bet is a 16- or 25-foot steel tape. Buy one that is 1 inch wide so you can extend it over a long distance without it twisting.

You'll also need a sharp-pointed pencil to make accurate marks on your material. Carpenter's pencils, which have flat rather than round leads, work well for marking wood. For even more accuracy, use an awl, which looks like a short ice pick, or a scriber, which resembles a long toothpick. (Combination squares often come with a scriber.)

Another marking device, the chalk line, aids in laying down long straight lines. A chalk line is a roll of string inside a case filled with chalk. As you pull the line from the case, make sure the line has plenty of chalk on it; don't skimp. Tie the line to a nail on one end of your cutting mark and stretch it as taut as possible to obtain an accurate line. To make the mark, pinch the line between your thumb and index finger, pull the line out from the surface to be marked, and let the line snap back onto the surface. Snap the line just once.

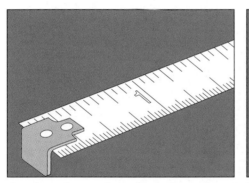

Good steel tapes have ¹⁄₁₆-inch markings on one edge, ¹⁄₃₂-inch marks for the first 6 inches on the bottom, and indicator marks every 16 inches for stud spacing.

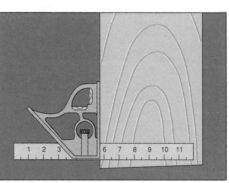

Before you make a measurement, check to be sure the end or edge of the board you're measuring from is square. If it isn't, square it up first.

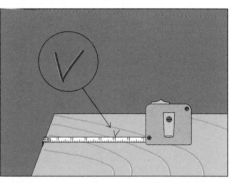

Make your cutoff-point mark with the tip of a V mark. A dot is too hard to see; a short line might veer one way or the other.

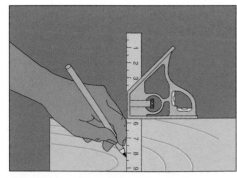

For narrow material with a factory edge, use a combination square to draw a fine line along the cutoff point.

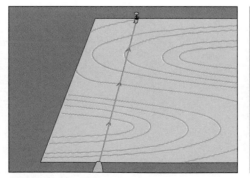

For wide stock, make V marks, then use a chalk line or straightedge to draw a line. Measure from the same end.

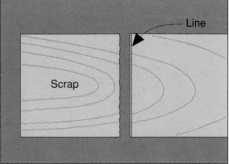

Saw on the scrap side of the line. Otherwise, material will end up a saw kerf shorter than the measurement.

USING SQUARES AND LEVELS

Before we discuss how to achieve "square," "level," and "plumb," you need to understand the meaning of these terms. Square refers to an exact 90-degree relationship between two surfaces. When a material is level, it's perfectly horizontal; when it's plumb, it's at true vertical.

Never assume that existing construction is square, level, or plumb. Chances are, it's not. To prove this to yourself, lay a level horizontally along any floor in your home, hold a level vertically against a wall section in a corner, or place a square on a door or window frame. Don't be alarmed at the results.

Variation is normal because houses usually settle slightly on their foundations, throwing square, level, and plumb out of whack.

When you make repairs or additions, you must compensate for the areas that are out of alignment. Three tools are needed to establish square, level, and plumb: a framing square, a level, and a plumb bob.

A steel framing (or carpenter's) square has two legs, each at right angles to the other. The "blade" side is longer and wider than the "tongue" leg. Usually marked in ⅛-inch increments, some squares also have scales so you can align

them for rafter and other angle cuts.

A level can be used to determine level and plumb. Hold it horizontally to determine level, vertically for plumb. When an item is level or plumb, the air bubbles in the liquid-filled glass vials are centered exactly between the lines on the vials.

How can you check if a level is accurate? Lay it on a horizontal surface and shim it, if necessary, to get a level reading. Then, turn the level end-for-end. If you don't get the same reading, the level needs to be adjusted or replaced. Some models allow you to calibrate the level by rotating the glass vials.

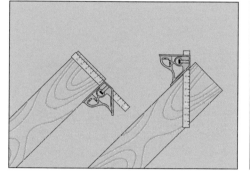

Use a combination square to mark 90- and 45-degree angles and measure depths. The blade slides through the handle; many have level vials, too.

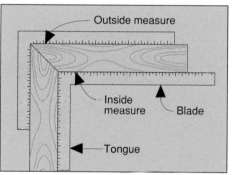

For large squaring jobs, use a framing square. When you mark measurements with it, be sure to read the proper inside or outside scale.

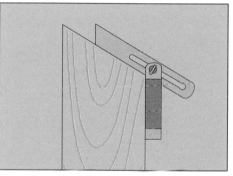

Duplicate angles with a T-bevel. Place handle on square edge of item, let the blade conform to the angle, then lock thumb screw.

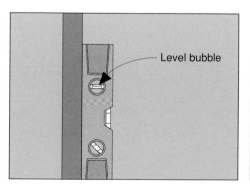

Set a level on the work and adjust the work until the bubble is centered. Some levels have a 45-degree vial.

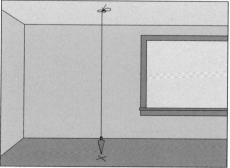

A plumb bob helps establish plumb. Suspend it from a cord with its point a fraction of an inch from the floor.

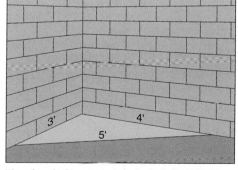

To check for square, mark 3 feet in one direction, 4 feet the other. The distance between the two points must be 5 feet.

Measuring (continued)

MAKING CURVES AND CONTOURS

The world of carpentry and home repair isn't all straight lines. To mark curves, circles, and angles, you need special tools, or tools that you can readily improvise.

For scribing contours, marking circles, and dividing lines, use a compass. Although you can't adjust a compass for large circles, it's more than adequate for marking materials that will be sawed or bored to accept pipes, electrical conduit, lighting fixtures, and so forth.

Dividers are used to step off, or repeat, a series of measurements along a scribed line. But you also can use them to scribe arcs, circles, and half-circles. Dividers are better

than a compass for transferring measurements from a tape measure to your material, or vice versa, with pinpoint accuracy.

To determine the outside diameter of such material as dowel rods, pipe, and conduit, use outside calipers. Used in combination with a tape measure, they also may be used to transfer measurements to material.

Inside calipers are used to measure the inside dimensions of pipe, conduit, or holes in most material. Touch the legs of the inside calipers to the edges of the material, lock the adjusting screw, then measure from one leg to the other.

While a compass is a basic

workshop necessity, dividers and calipers are classified as niceties. The reason: A compass can do the work of all three. When you invest in a compass, dividers, and calipers, buy tools with adjusting screws rather than those that just spread open.

When you get to intricate curves, another nice tool to have around is a contour gauge. This tool has a series of metal rods that you adjust to the item's contour, as shown below.

To draw curves and circles, you sometimes can improvise with a string or board and a nail; the bottoms of buckets, cans, or lids; coins—almost anything that is round or fairly round.

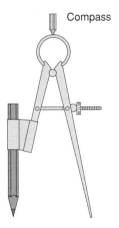
Compass

Dividers

Outside calipers

Inside calipers

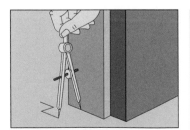
Scribe irregular surfaces by placing the compass point against the original; let the pencil mark the duplicate.

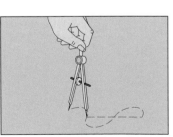
To use dividers (when you repeat measurements), keep one leg firmly planted while moving the other in an arc.

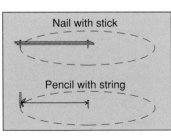
Nail with stick

Pencil with string

Make a compass by driving nails through the ends of a yardstick. Or, use a pencil tied to a cord.

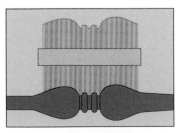
A contour gauge duplicates the profile of irregular surfaces. Lock in position and use to duplicate shape.

Cutting

There are few projects that don't involve cutting materials to fit. So, it just makes good sense to buy quality cutting tools and keep them in top condition. Sharp equipment makes cutting not only easier but safer, too (see pages 435, 444, and 447 for sharpening instructions).

Knives, the instrument from which all other cutting tools evolved, serve do-it-yourselfers in numerous ways. Your basic tool kit should include at least a utility knife.

Saws, actually a series of knives, are complex. Each of their many teeth must be kept sharp and in proper "set" so the saw slices, rather than tears, through the material.

Other cutting tools covered in this section are chisels, which are knives with sharpened ends; routers, basically electric chisels; threading taps and dies to cut threads in pipes; wire cutters and tin snips, best described as two knives on a pivot; and grinders and whetstones to keep your cutting tools sharp.

TOOL TALK

A saw actually makes two cuts, one on each side of the blade. Chipping away material on both sides gives the saw room to move.

The term "points" refers to a saw's number of teeth per inch. The more points a blade has, the smoother (and slower) a saw will cut. Wood-cutting blades typically have eight to 10 points per inch; metal-cutting blades, many more.

When selecting a saw, first check the blade. Quality versions use special alloys and have precision-ground teeth. Grip the handle. Does it feel awkward? You'll tire faster with an uncomfortable tool. Tired hands make errors. Finally, be prepared to spend some money on a good-quality saw.

CHOOSING HANDSAWS

Bargain-basement saws can chew up their savings by way of ruined materials in no time at all.

For most projects, your basic tool kit can include an eight-point crosscut handsaw, a keyhole saw, and a hacksaw. As you develop more skills, you may want to add some of the other handsaws shown below.

A crosscut saw works best across the grain of wood, the most common cutting operation. (For more about crosscuts, see page 434.)

A ripsaw is designed to cut along the length of the wood grain. Use it for sizing boards to the widths you need (see page 435).

A coping saw makes curves and tight-quarter cuts. Its narrow blade swivels in its frame so you can use it from any direction (see page 436).

A keyhole saw has a narrow, tapered blade that also can be used to make tight-radius cuts. It won't negotiate curves as sharp as a coping saw, but you can use it on thicker material. Its pistol-grip handle will accommodate compass saw blades, which are slightly broader (more about both on page 436).

A backsaw is a fine-tooth crosscut saw. Use it to cut miters and for other exacting work (see page 436).

A hacksaw cuts almost anything—but its specialty is metals. Its blade mounts with the teeth slanting forward, doing their job on the push stroke (see page 437).

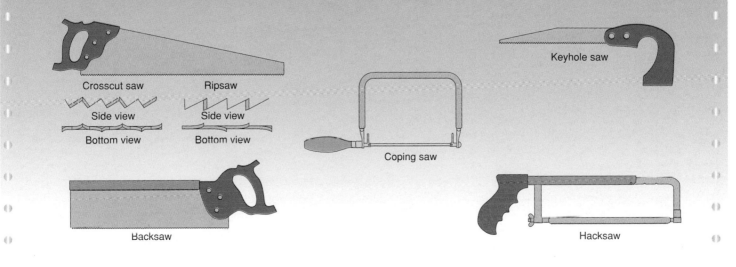

Crosscut saw — Side view — Bottom view
Ripsaw — Side view — Bottom view
Coping saw
Keyhole saw
Backsaw
Hacksaw

Cutting (continued)

USING A CROSSCUT SAW

Whenever you need to cut across the grain of wood or cut plywood or other sheet goods in any direction, a crosscut saw is the right tool to use.

There's a special cutting rhythm in using crosscut saws (and ripsaws). It's a sort of rocking stroke that starts from the shoulder and works down through the arm and hand. Very little pressure need be applied to the saw in this cutting motion. In fact, your main task is to steer the blade while it does its work. If you apply pressure to the saw with your hand and forearm, the saw will bind in its kerf, and often wander off the cutoff line or undercut the wood at a slant so the cut edge is not square. These tips are illustrated below.

When cutting plywood with a handsaw, always make sure that the good side is facing up. In this way, the grain of the plywood will not tear or splinter as much as when the good side faces down. A strip of masking tape positioned over the cut line further reduces the possibility of damage. Cut solid woods with their good face up, too.

When working with wood that has lots of sap in it, the saw may gum up from the wet sawdust. Keep the blade wiped clean with mineral spirits (paint thinner) to prevent the saw from binding in the kerf.

Also, coat a saw blade with light machine oil or paste wax when not in use. This prevents rust damage.

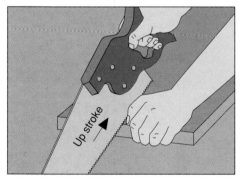

Start a handsaw in a piece of wood at the heel of the saw. The first stroke should be a gentle upstroke.

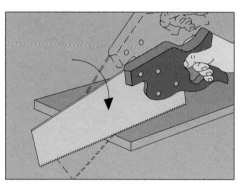

The saw stroke rocks slightly, following an arc as your arm swings from your shoulder. Let the weight of the saw do the work.

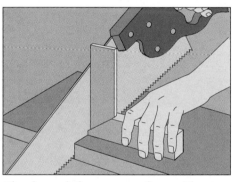

Check work for square often with a try square. Place the square's blade against the saw and slide it along the wood as you cut.

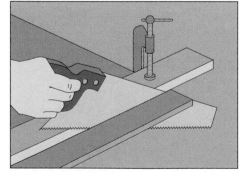

Use a saw guide on long and wide cuts. Clamp a straight board or metal straightedge along the cutoff mark. Let the edge of the guide steer the saw.

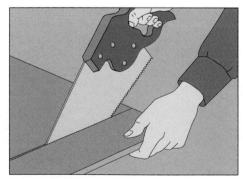

Support the scrap side of the wood as you near the end of the cut. Otherwise, the scrap may splinter the wood as you make your last few saw strokes.

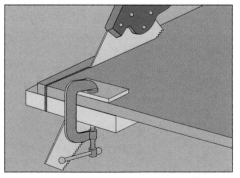

If you are cutting a narrow piece off of a board, clamp a piece of scrap to the underside of the good piece and double-cut through both boards.

USING A RIPSAW

A ripsaw "rips" wood along the length of its grain. This workhorse usually has 5½ points per inch, set about one-third wider than the blade thickness so it slides easily. Ripsaws cut only on the forward stroke.

Use the same techniques with a ripsaw as you would with a crosscut saw: a rocking arm motion that lets the saw do most of the work. But hold a ripsaw at about a 60-degree angle to the work as opposed to the 45-degree angle you'd use with a crosscut saw.

As with any saw, be sure to cut on the scrap side of the cutoff mark—not directly on the mark. "Leave the line," as carpenter's say. This way, the material "fit" you want will not be short; you can remove excess wood with a plane or rasp. Remember, you can always remove wood, but you can't add it.

Start a ripsaw at the heel of the saw with small upstroke. Remember, a ripsaw cuts on the forward stroke.

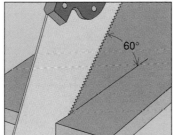

Keep the saw at a 60-degree angle to the work. You'll do this automatically with more experience.

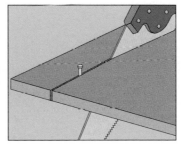

If the saw binds, insert a nail in the kerf to spread it apart. Keep the blade clean of wet sap with mineral spirits.

If the saw veers away from the line, twist the saw blade slightly to steer it back to line. Do not twist too hard.

SHARPENING A SAW

Eventually, the chisel-like teeth of a handsaw become dull, especially if you've been working with hardwoods, such as maple, oak, or walnut. Cutting through stubborn knots speeds the dulling process, too—as does accidentally hitting a nail or bolt while cutting through a board.

If the saw isn't critically dull, some "touching up" is required. You'll need a small triangular file. Secure the saw in a vise with the handle to the right. Starting with the first tooth set toward you, place the file on the front edge of the tooth and make two or three strokes. File every other tooth in this manner using the same number of strokes on each tooth. Then, reverse the saw in the vice and file the teeth you skipped. Sharpening ripsaws and crosscut saws differs only in that you file crosscut teeth at a 45-degree angle and ripsaw teeth at 90 degrees.

Dreadfully dull saws require more complete sharpening. Usually it's best to turn your saw over to a professional for this. The cost is minimal—and the results, miraculous.

Saw teeth also need setting after three or four sharpenings. Setting is best left to a professional because a setting tool is needed to bend the saw's teeth to the correct angle.

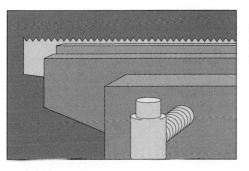

1. Clamp the saw in a vise between strips of wood. Leave about ⅛ inch between the top of the strips and the bottom of the saw teeth.

2. Using a triangular file, sharpen the teeth set toward you. Turn saw around; repeat for remaining teeth.

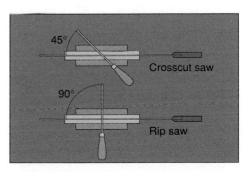

Cutting (continued)

MAKING SPECIALTY CUTS

Trimming, finishing, cabinetmaking, and other special carpentry projects call for special cuts—including miters, bevels, curves, rabbets, circles, slots, grooves, and tongues. Most of these jobs center around the simple miter, bevel, and curve cuts illustrated below.

Miters generally are made at 45-degree angles. Cutting across the grain requires a fine-tooth saw—an 11-point crosscut saw or, better yet, a miter saw. A miter saw usually has 11 points per inch and a stiff spine on its top edge to prevent the blade from bending. It cuts smoothly either with or across the grain.

A backsaw usually is shorter than a miter saw and has 12 to 13 points per inch. When used in a miter box, it produces smooth cuts with or across the grain. It's ideal for cutting special woodworking joints, too.

A dovetail saw cuts such joints as dovetails and mortise-and-tenons. It's smaller and finer than a miter saw, often with a 15-point blade.

Miter boxes are available in a wide range of prices. Inexpensive hardwood or plastic versions suffice for 45- and 90-degree cuts. With the more expensive metal miter boxes, the saw fits into a slotted metal pivot, which then can be pivoted to any angle your project requires.

Other saws you'll need for specialty cuts include a keyhole saw, a coping saw, and a compass saw, which is similar to a keyhole saw but with a somewhat wider saw blade. A drywall saw is also much like a keyhole saw, but has fewer teeth per inch.

For more about making specialty cuts and the joinery techniques that go with them, see pages 495–501.

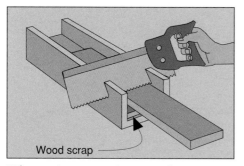

When using a saw in a wooden miter box, place a wood scrap beneath the material to be cut. This prevents damage to the box.

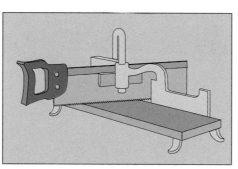

Metal miter boxes provide greater accuracy and let you cut almost any angle. Always use a miter saw or backsaw with this tool.

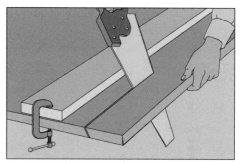

To miter wide stock, mark cut angle on the end, make a few strokes, then clamp a guide at the correct distance away to hold and guide the saw.

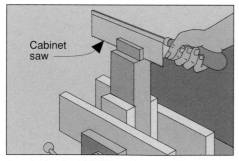

A cabinet saw cuts tenons, rabbets, dadoes, and similar joints. The long blade helps you keep the saw square to the cut.

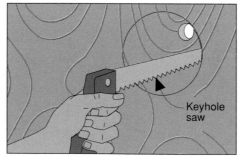

To make inside cuts, drill a hole, then insert keyhole saw blade. A compass saw does the same job on larger circles; a drywall saw, on drywall.

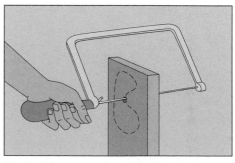

For inside, curved cuts in a narrow board, drill a hole, remove blade from the coping saw frame, insert blade through the hole, and reassemble.

USING A HACKSAW

One of the most efficient tools you'll ever own, a hacksaw is a basic hand tool that, with the proper blade, can cut almost any material. It's easy to use as well as inexpensive to buy.

The blade you need for a given job depends on the type of material you're cutting. Generally, the thicker the material, whether metal, plastic pipe, or something else, the fewer the number of teeth per inch to use. Blade packages usually specify the type of material that the blade is designed to cut.

Mount a hacksaw blade in the frame so the teeth point forward. Blades usually are marked with arrows that indicate the direction that the teeth must point.

The trick to using a hacksaw is to keep as many teeth on the work as possible. Apply pressure on the forward stroke only. Make smooth, even strokes with one hand on the handle of the saw, the other on the front of the frame. This two-handed grip applies even pressure along the length of the blade.

Make sure blades are rigid in the frame by tightening the wing nut, but don't apply too much pressure. If you break a blade while cutting, it's best not to insert a new blade in the old kerf. Instead, turn the work around and start again. A new blade may jam in an old kerf.

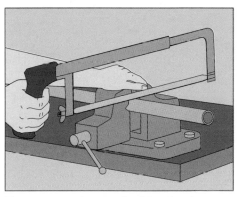

To start cuts in metal with a hacksaw, lock the work in a vise, then make several short forward strokes.

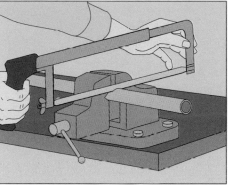

If possible, use two hands on the saw. Don't apply pressure on the backstroke or you'll quickly dull the blade.

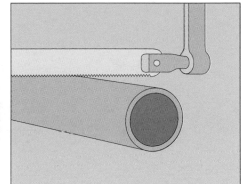

Keep at least two teeth on the work at all times—more if possible. The flatter the angle, the better the saw will cut.

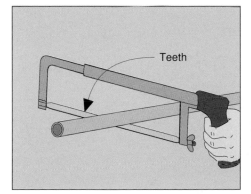

In tight situations, you can turn the blade upside down or reverse the teeth in the frame. For angle cuts, mount the work in a vise at the correct angle so you can hold the saw vertically.

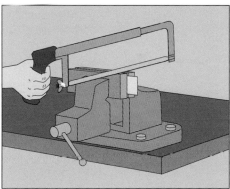

Clamp thin materials that might bend, such as sheet metal, between two pieces of wood. Then, cut through all the layers at the same time, sawing square to the work.

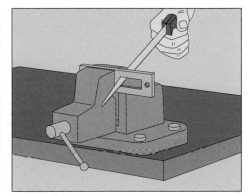

Many multipurpose compass saws have exchangeable blades; a metal-cutting blade made for a compass saw can get into places too cramped for a conventional hacksaw.

Cutting (continued)

TOOL TALK
CHOOSING PORTABLE POWER SAWS

Power saws allow you to get the job done faster and easier—and sometimes more accurately. But don't abandon your handsaws entirely. Rather, view portable power saws as extensions of your handsaws. Situations will arise during home maintenance and improvement projects when a handsaw will be the only tool to use.

When choosing between portable and stationary power saws, consider that portable saws are much less expensive, you can take them to the job site, and they're easy to store. On the other hand, stationary saws are more accurate.

The deciding factor will be the type of work you want to do. If repairs and improvement projects are your prime concern, portable power saws are best. If you enjoy woodworking, stationary saws make more sense.

The first portable saw you buy should be a variable-speed sabersaw. Follow with a circular saw with a blade size that can handle a 45-degree cut in 2-inch material (usually a 6½-inch blade). Reciprocating saws and miter saws, although handy to own, aren't necessary for standard home repair and improvement projects.

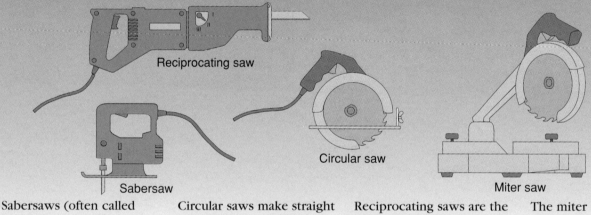

Reciprocating saw

Sabersaw

Circular saw

Miter saw

Sabersaws (often called portable jigsaws) make straight, angle, curve, and hole cuts in boards and sheet materials.

Circular saws make straight and angle cuts and large pocket cuts (see page 440). For most jobs, a 6½-inch blade size is sufficient.

Reciprocating saws are the heavy-duty cousins of sabersaws. A variable-speed model can cut both metal and wood.

The miter saw—or "chop saw"—is the power version of a backsaw in a miter box. Professionals use it for trim and siding work.

HELPFUL HINTS
USING POWER TOOLS SAFELY

Power tools are as safe as you make them. To make your dealings with them as safe as possible, follow these general precautions.
■ Dress appropriately for the job. Don't wear loose clothing, floppy shirt tails, rings, or your watch. Do wear safety glasses for protection.
■ Keep power tools in good repair. If the tool isn't self-lubricating, follow the manufacturer's lubrication schedule.
■ Keep blades sharp—dull ones are dangerous—by filing to original size and shape.
■ Make sure that electric power cables are not frayed. Use the grounding plug sold with the tool or purchase a plug adapter if your outlets are not the three-prong type (see page 237).
■ Hold the power cord in your free hand. This keeps both the cord and your hand away from the blade.
■ Never leave an unattended power tool plugged into the power source.
■ Store power equipment out of the reach of children.

USING A SABERSAW

Crosscut, rip, miter, bevel, and cut holes—a lightweight sabersaw does all of these things to almost any material: wood, paneling, drywall, plastic laminate, hardboard, thin metal, and ceramic.

Of course, you'll need the correct blade for the job: coarse-tooth blades for boards and dimension lumber; fine-tooth blades for paneling and plastic; metal-cutting blades for metal; carbide-tipped blades for ceramic tile and glass; and a knife blade for vinyl tile, leather, rubber, and soft plastic.

Through a gear arrangement, the rotary power from the sabersaw's motor is converted into stroke power. The blade operates in an up-and-down motion, cutting on the upstroke motion.

Only one hand is needed to guide a sabersaw. Most cuts can be made quickly and accurately, especially if you have a rip-guide accessory. Buy a variable-speed sabersaw, a feature that lets you control the strokes per minute and make smooth cuts in almost any material.

Before you use a new a sabersaw for the first time, carefully read the instructions and cutting tips that came with it. Also, keep the following operating tips in mind:
■ Although sabersaws have powerful motors, 2-inch-thick material or heavy-gauge metal is a big bite for the saw blade. Push the blade slowly without forcing it.
■ If the motor gets hot, run it without a load for a while. After the blade cools, check its sharpness—a dull blade taxes the motor heavily.
■ Always start the motor before bringing the blade into contact with the material to be cut. If you don't, you'll break the saw blade, which can fly off and injure someone, and you'll probably damage the material.
■ Because sabersaws cut on the upstroke, make sure the good face of paneling and expensive hardwoods faces down when you make the cuts.

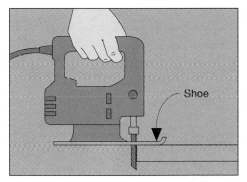

To start a cut, rest the shoe with the blade ¼ inch from the material. Start the saw and move it into the stock.

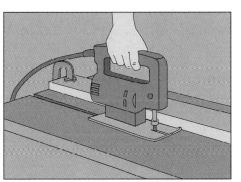

Clamp a straightedge to guide the saw along the cutoff line; be sure that you saw on the line's scrap side.

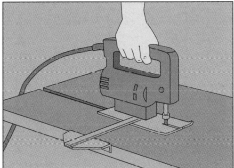

A rip-guide accessory lets you make cuts parallel to the edge of the board. Some guides also let you cut circles.

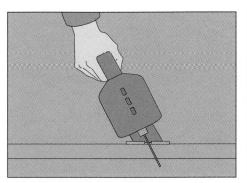

A tilting base makes miter cuts. Ease the blade into the cut, and don't lift the saw until the blade has stopped.

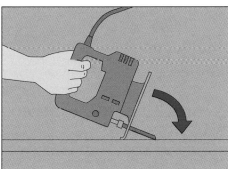

To make a pocket cut without drilling a starter hole, tilt the saw forward, start the motor, and tilt it backward.

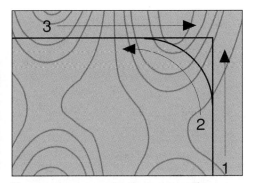

To cut corners, run the saw to the corner, back up, then cut an arc to the other line. Finish as shown.

Cutting (continued)

USING A CIRCULAR SAW

Squeeze the trigger of a portable electric circular saw and you know right away that you've got a handful of powerful cutting machinery. In fact, a circular saw can rip and crosscut materials just about as fast as you can move your arm.

By design, this power equipment won't do the jobs that a sabersaw will. However, the cuts a circular saw makes will trim your working time to a minimum.

Ripping long boards and paneling is the job a circular saw does best. It also zips through crosscuts with accuracy, and you can make miter cuts, bevels, and pocket cuts in paneling and other sheet materials. With special blades, it even can cut metal and such masonry items as bricks, concrete, and cinder blocks.

Circular saws come in several sizes, denoting the largest blade they will accept. The largest is a 10-inch model. The smallest, a 4½-inch version, is called a "trim saw."

For most chores around the house, you're best off buying a 6½- or 7¼-inch model. Be sure the one you buy has an automatic blade guard. This guard slips back as the saw blade enters the wood, then snaps closed after the cut is made.

Other desirable features of a circular saw include a blade depth adjustment that allows you to make shallow cuts such as grooves; a baseplate that can be adjusted for miters and bevels; and a ripping fence accessory, similar to the one shown on page 439 for sabersaws.

When operating a portable circular saw, keep a strong grip on the saw handle as cuts are being made. You don't have to force the saw through the work because the motor is powerful enough to do the cutting job. If you find yourself forcing the cut, stop the saw and check to see if the blade is dull. Also, make sure you start with the correct blade for the material you're cutting.

For safety's sake, never leave an unattended saw connected to power. And, never pick up a plugged-in saw to move it somewhere with your finger on the on/off trigger.

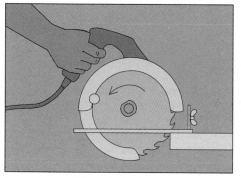

Set the saw blade just deep enough to cut through the material. Make sure the motor is at full power before the blade enters the material.

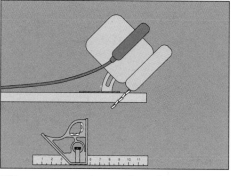

Miters are easy to cut, but always double-check them with a combination square or T-bevel. The gauge on your saw may not be extremely accurate.

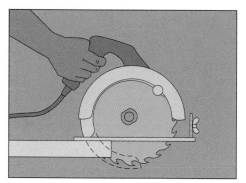

At the end of the cut, be prepared to support the saw's weight. Before you set the tool down, be sure the blade guard is over the blade.

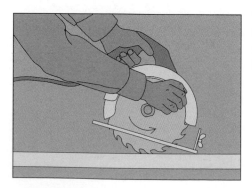

To make a pocket cut, set the saw to the desired depth. Retract the guard, tilt the saw forward, start the saw, and lower the blade.

Purchase several saw blades: a combination blade for ripping and crosscuts; a ripping blade; a plywood blade for paneling and fine cuts; and metal or masonry abrasive blades.

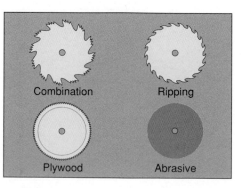

Combination   Ripping

Plywood   Abrasive

TOOL TALK

CHOOSING STATIONARY SAWS

If you're thinking about buying a stationary saw, first determine if you have enough room. Stationary saws require plenty of working room because you need to bring the material to the saw, in contrast to taking a portable saw to the material. Such materials as 4×8-foot sheets of plywood have to be maneuvered around and into the saws. Access to the workshop also is important for getting materials in and out.

A radial arm saw needs less space than a tablesaw because you can place it along a wall. But, you'll need enough space on either side to rip a sheet of plywood or paneling.

The tablesaw, on the other hand, needs space on all four sides because you have to move the material through the stationary blade. Most have locking casters so you can store the saw in an out-of-the-way place,

then roll it into the center of the workshop when needed.

Bandsaws need space on only three sides, as do jigsaws. Like tablesaws, most have locking casters to permit movement.

Your choice of saw type depends on the work you're going to do. The following information provides a basic rundown on each type shown below.

A radial-arm saw is truly flexible. With attachments, you can use it as a shaper, sander, planer, jointer, and drill. What sets it apart from other stationary saws is that, for most cuts, you pull the blade across the work. The exception to this is ripping material, when you lock the head and feed the material into the blade.

A tablesaw can make a variety of cuts, too, including crosscuts, rips, miters, compound miters, grooves, bevels, coves, and moldings. With

special blades, you also can cut metal, plastic, masonry, and stone. You can even convert a tablesaw into a disc sander and grindstone. You always move the material through the blade.

A jigsaw has a reciprocating blade like its portable counterpart. It will handle almost any material—wood, metal, and plastic—with special blades. Use it for straight cuts, curves, keyhole cuts, and tight-radius cuts. For most do-it-yourselfers who do a lot of delicate work, a jigsaw is a better purchase than a bandsaw.

A bandsaw has a continuous blade that loops around two wheels. It is more of a production-type tool for cutting thick material. It will make straight cuts, miters, bevels, and radius cuts. With special blades, the saw will cut metal and plastic. For tight-radius cuts, substitute narrow blades for wider ones.

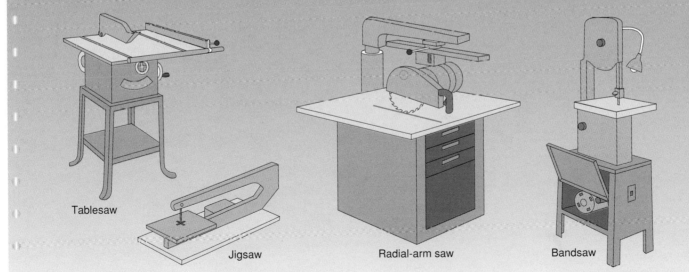

Tablesaw

Jigsaw

Radial-arm saw

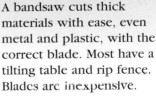

Bandsaw

Tablesaws accommodate blade sizes ranging from 7½ to 12 inches. A variety of blades and accessories are available to increase their flexibility.

A jigsaw, to be used most effectively, should have a spacious distance between the blade and the support post at rear so you can maneuver and cut work.

On radial-arm saws, the entire cutting head, motor and all, is pulled across the material to be cut, except for ripping. It cuts grooves, miters, dadoes, and rabbets.

A bandsaw cuts thick materials with ease, even metal and plastic, with the correct blade. Most have a tilting table and rip fence. Blades are inexpensive.

Cutting (continued)

TOOL TALK

The chisel is an ancient tool, and there are still many tasks that other tools can't do as well. Some of these jobs include shaping mortises; cutting and smoothing wood joints; removing crumbling mortar; and breaking bricks, blocks, and stones.

Don't waste time comparing prices of chisels. These tools are inexpensive enough that your budget can afford top-of-the-line quality and features.

Wood chisels are designed to cut wood. Don't use them as scrapers, screwdrivers, paint paddles, or wire cutters. Most of the wood chisels

CHOOSING CHISELS

made today feature metal-capped handles that you can strike with a hammer or wooden mallet. If the chisels you own don't have this feature, strike them only with a wooden mallet or plastic hammer.

For chisels to cut properly, they must be sharp. Not only do dull chisels ruin expensive materials, they also may slip and injure you. And, keeping chisels sharp is not a hard job (see page 444).

Proper storage is another must. Keep chisels in plastic sleeves hung up on a tool board, or wrap them in

cloth that's been lightly treated with household oil. Don't toss chisels into a drawer or tray with other tools. This dulls and nicks the cutting edges.

Cold and masonry chisels cut or form metal, bricks, concrete, cinder blocks, and stone. Although plenty rugged, their cutting edges eventually become dull; sharpen them with a grinding wheel (see pages 444 and 448). These chisels are designed to be struck with a heavy ball peen hammer or baby sledge—not a carpenter's hammer. When using a cold chisel, always wear gloves and safety glasses.

Selecting Wood Chisels

Butt chisels are designed to remove larger chunks of wood than other types or to work in tight spots.

Pocket chisels—9½ to 10½ inches long—are balanced to be used by hand or struck with a hammer.

Paring chisels have thin blades and are designed for very fine hand work; don't strike them with a hammer.

Gouges, rounded for outside and inside cutting, remove wood fast and may be used for carving.

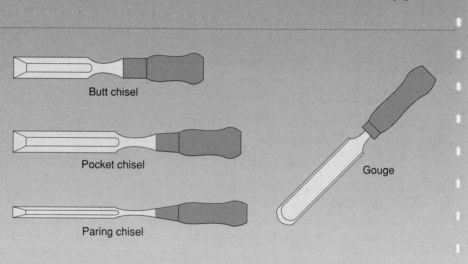

Butt chisel

Pocket chisel

Paring chisel

Gouge

Selecting Cold and Masonry Chisels

Cold chisels cut rusted bolts, rods, and thin bar steel. Masonry chisels cut bricks, cinder blocks, and stone.

A cape chisel is used to gouge metal. A flat chisel may be used to cut bolts and screws; its wedge action shears metal, too. A diamond-point chisel makes V-shaped cuts and grooves in metal.

Use a bricklayer's chisel to cut masonry and stone materials; they're available in a variety of widths.

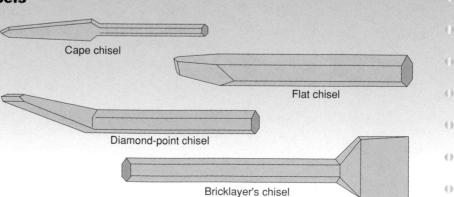

Cape chisel

Flat chisel

Diamond-point chisel

Bricklayer's chisel

USING A CHISEL

Though somewhat of a lost art, wood chiseling is one of those techniques that's not only useful, but fun. With a light hand and some practice, you can learn to use wood chisels to great advantage.

You'll call on these workhorses to remove excess wood from grooves and joints, shape joints, form inside and outside curves in wood, even trim wood to close-fitting tolerances.

Chisel cuts are made much like knife cuts—a paring action that produces shavings. Whenever possible, the work is done by hand without striking the chisel with a hammer or mallet. One hand provides the cutting force; the other hand guides the chisel and provides downward pressure.

What's the secret to using a chisel? Learning to take your time and to make shallow cuts with it! To do this, the chisel must be razor sharp with no nicks or burrs along the finely honed cutting edge (see page 444 for sharpening techniques).

Because you should use both hands, it's important that the work be locked tightly in a vise or clamped so it doesn't move when you apply pressure. If you're mortising a door for hinges, you can butt the top or bottom of the door against a wall to prevent it from moving.

You'll use a chisel quit a bit to cut mortises. Mortises are holes, slots, or other recesses in wood into which another element fits, such as a door hinge. Techniques for making a hinge mortise are shown below.

To make long cross-grain cuts with a chisel, start with the chisel at an angle, then ease the handle downward as it cuts.

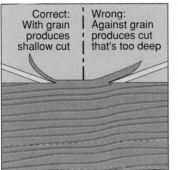

To chisel parallel to wood grain, cut with the grain rather than against it. When you cut against it, you will dig too deep into the work.

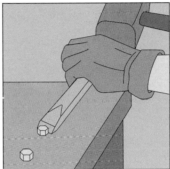

Use a baby sledge, not a claw hammer, to strike cold chisels. Wear a glove to protect the chisel hand against injury.

Start masonry cuts by scoring surface with vertical blows to outline the cut. Then hold chisel at an angle to chip out scrap.

Making a Mortise

1. Score the mortise outline with a knife to keep the grain from splitting at the edge of the cut.

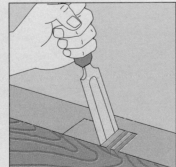

2. Make a series of cuts to the depth of the mortise. Use the chisel with its bevel face going with the grain.

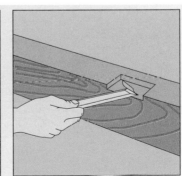

3. If the mortise extends to the edge, pare out chips from the edge with the bevel facing up.

For deep mortises, drill holes within the outline of the mortise, then carefully chip out the remaining wood.

Cutting (continued)

KEEPING CHISELS SHARP

Look down the cutting edge of a wood chisel and you can tell immediately if it needs sharpening. A dull edge reflects light. A sharp edge does not produce this reflection. If you don't trust your eyes, give the chisel the paper test for sharpness, as shown below.

You can sharpen chisels using one of three techniques: whetting, filing, or grinding. Whetting is done with a whetstone. Filing and grinding are done with a single-cut file or a motor-driven grinding wheel. Don't feel compelled to purchase a grinding wheel just for this job. The chisel will sharpen equally well with a whetstone or file.

Bevels on most wood chisels are at 25 degrees. Those on paring chisels, however, are at 15 degrees. But you don't have to be too concerned about the specific angle when you sharpen chisels. Rather, follow the original bevel angle on the whetstone, grinding wheel, or file. The bevel should be a little longer than twice the thickness of the chisel blade.

You can buy a sharpening jig that holds the chisel and maintains the bevel at the proper angle to the whetstone or grinding wheel. With a file, you'll have to rely on a keen eye and a steady hand to maintain the angle.

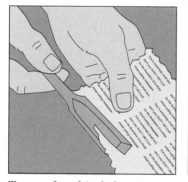

To test for chisel sharpness, shave a piece of paper at a slight angle. A sharp chisel blade will slice right through the paper.

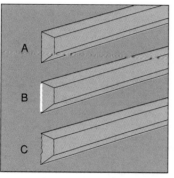

Check sharpness by holding the edge under light. A sharp edge (A) won't reflect light.; a dull edge (B) will. File or grind a nicked edge (C).

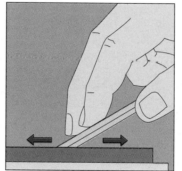

Hone a chisel's cutting edge by rubbing it on whetstone at an angle slightly steeper than the bevel. Keep the whetstone moist with oil.

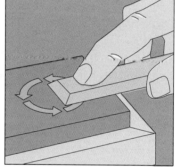

After the cutting edge is sharp, turn the chisel over and hone its flat side to remove burrs. Hone with an elliptical motion.

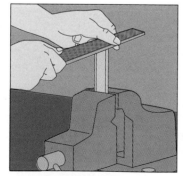

For badly nicked or worn edges, clamp the chisel in a vise. Remove deep nicks by filing at a 90-degree angle, as shown, with a single cut file.

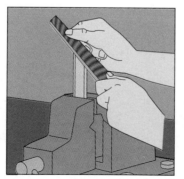

Then, file at the same angle as the bevel. File diagonally, working slowly and evenly. Remove burrs with the whetstone technique above.

To remove nicks with a power grinder, keep the chisel flat against the wheel, moving the chisel from side to side.

To regrind a bevel, set tool rest at proper angle and move chisel along the wheel with light pressure. Cool chisel in water as you work.

CHOOSING AND USING A ROUTER

If not the most versatile tool made, a router certainly comes close. Basically an electric chisel, a router planes, saws, and shapes; makes grooves, mortises, dovetails, and other joints; trims edges off plastic laminate; cuts dadoes for strong shelving; makes pocket cuts in sheet materials; and much more.

A router's immense power is what makes it such an efficient tool. You can get along without one—chisels, saws, files, and planes do the same work—you'll just get it done in a jiffy with a router.

A router's cost depends on its features and accessories. Start with a router and two or three basic bits, along with an edge-cutting guide or (better) a router table. As your budget allows, you can add the specialty bits for fancy joints and moldings (see below).

The more power a router has, the more jobs it will do faster. Routers range from ¼-horsepower to more than 1-horsepower models, running at 25,000 to more than 30,000 rpm. These speeds are achieved because the bit spindle is driven directly by the motor. The baseplate of the unit serves as a guide and a collar near the motor housing lets you adjust the depth that the bit cuts. Edge,

template, and trammel-point guides are available for making special cuts.

In a freestanding model, you operate a router holding onto it with both hands and letting a guide steer the router through the material. However, if you have a router table, the router remains stationary, and you simply feed material into it.

Because a router is so powerful, keep your hands away from the spinning bits; they're razor-sharp and cut fast. When changing a bit, unplug the cord and lock the bit securely to the shaft. As with any power tool, always unplug a router when it's not in use.

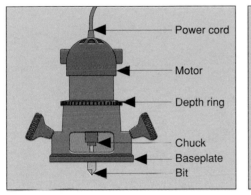

A router is a simple tool. The motor directly drives a chuck that holds the bit. The baseplate keeps the tool square to the cut.

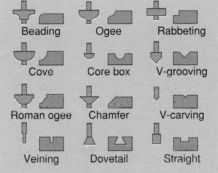

Whatever shape you want to cut, there's a router bit to accommodate you. Intricate cuts sometimes require several passes with two or more bits.

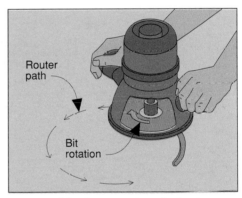

A router bit always spins clockwise (looking from above), and makes the smoothest cuts when the router is fed counterclockwise through the material.

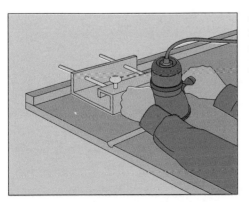

A template guide fastened to the router's base allows you to follow the shape of any template you make. Use plywood for templates.

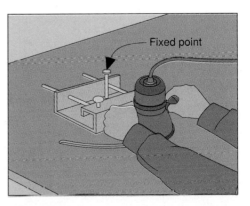

Another accessory, a trammel-point guide, lets you cut perfect circles or curves. Remember to make your cuts in a counterclockwise direction.

Cutting *(continued)*

THREADING WITH TAPS AND DIES

Stripping the threads inside a cast-metal block or on a rod usually leads to one of those "what-do-I-do-now?" panics. A couple of machinists' specialties—a tap for cutting female threads, or a die for making male threads—gets you going again. Just "tap out" the cast block to the next larger size, or "die cut" the rod to the next smaller one.

Although not indispensable in a home tool kit, taps and dies greatly extend your metal-working capabilities, letting you join metals, or join other items to metals, in situations where nuts and bolts wouldn't work.

A close relative to taps and dies is a screw extractor, which offers a quick way to remove a bolt or screw when you've sheared off its head.

Larger dies will cut threads in galvanized steel or iron pipe (see page 306). You can rent these costly devices, along with a large handle to turn the die and a special vise to hold the pipe.

Taps are of three types—taper (the most common), plug, and bottoming. Taper taps are pointed at the end, making them easier to start. Plug taps have less taper; bottoming taps, no taper at all. To thread a blind hole (one that doesn't go all

the way through the metal), you might start out with a taper tap, switch to a plug tap, then finish the job with a bottoming tap. You drive the taps by turning them with a special wrench, as shown below.

For dies, you can choose among solid, adjustable, and hexagonal versions. Solid dies, the least expensive, cut standard-size threads up to ½ inch. Adjustable dies include a screw you turn to make threads slightly larger or smaller than standard. Hexagonal dies can be turned with an ordinary wrench, rather than the die stock necessary for the other types (see below).

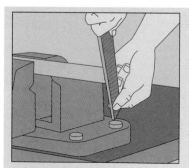

1. To tap a female thread, drill a hole the size specified for the tap. Insert the tap and square it to the metal.

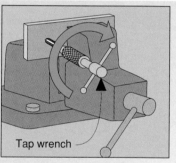

2. Turn the tap slowly with a tap wrench. Keep pressure on the tap. Tap and die sizes are matched.

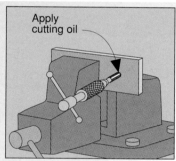

3. Every two turns, back the tap out to clear any chips from the threads. Apply cutting oil to ease cutting.

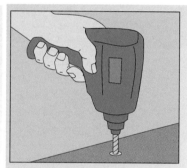

1. Screw extractors tap their own threads. To remove a broken screw, first drill a hole in the screw.

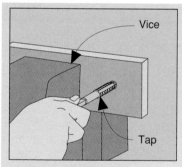

1. File bevel on the end of the item before cutting male threads. Remove enough metal for the die to seat.

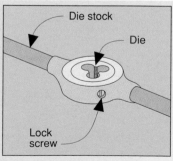

2. Insert proper die in the stock (wrench). Secure die with the locking screw and oil threads with motor oil.

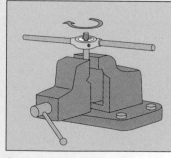

3. Turn the die stock to cut the threads. Back off the die often to clear away metal chips. Use plenty of oil.

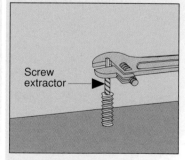

2. Turn extractor into drilled hole counterclockwise. As it seats, the extractor will turn out the broken screw.

TOOL TALK

CHOOSING KNIVES AND SHEARS

There are many, many kinds of knives and shears available. But, the basic ones shown here will handle nearly every job.

A linoleum knife cuts sheet goods and tile. Use a pocketknife for scoring marks. For cutting ceiling tile and general cutting, use a utility knife. Tin snips make straight cuts in sheet materials. Aviation snips are for either straight or curved cuts in ductwork.

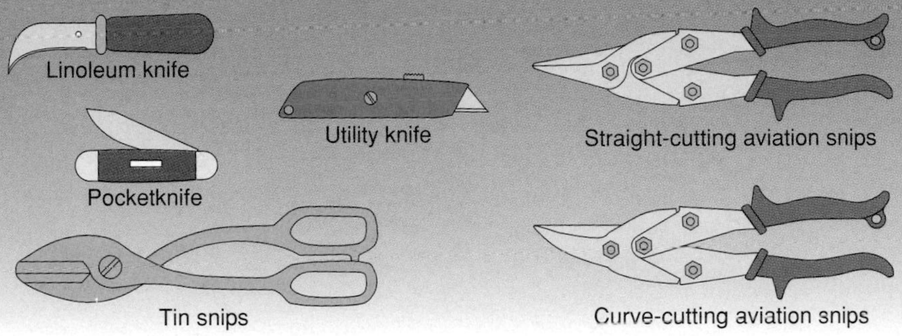

Linoleum knife

Pocketknife

Utility knife

Tin snips

Straight-cutting aviation snips

Curve-cutting aviation snips

KEEPING EDGES SHARP

Cutting something with a dull knife is like roller-skating up a steep hill on a windy day. It's tough, frustrating work—and you risk a dangerous slip. To avoid this uphill battle, all you need to do is keep your tool sharp.

Depending on the type of knife you're sharpening, you'll need a whetstone, sharpening steel, or a silicon-carbide stone. To sharpen a blade with a whetstone, slide the knife along the length of the stone, working away from you. Then, reverse the implement and stroke the opposite side of the blade. Continue to alternate until the blade is sharp. See the sketches below for pointers on how to sharpen other types of knives.

If the cutting edge of the blade you're sharpening is nicked, you'll need to grind it down with a grinding wheel before proceeding. Never try to sharpen knife blades that have sawtooth or serrated edges; you'll ruin them.

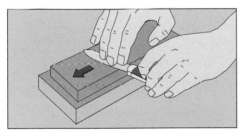

Hone small tools such as knives and scissors on a whetstone. Hold the tool at the correct angle and stroke lightly.

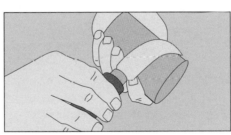

For blades with inside curves, use a "slip" stone. Hold the stone so it conforms to the curve of the blade.

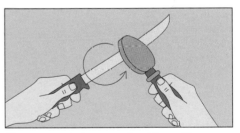

Sharpen stainless steel with a silicon-carbide stone. Whet the blade with a circular motion, alternating sides.

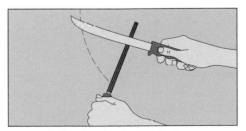

1. For household knives, use a sharpening steel. Pull blade down and across the steel, alternating blade sides.

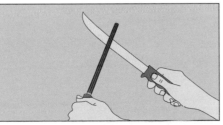

2. Stroke the length of the blade from handle to tip. Several strokes per side usually restores a sharp edge.

Cutting (continued)

USING A GRINDER

If you have a full complement of planes, chisels, bits, drills, knives, and other cutting tools, consider a bench grinder as your next equipment purchase. A grinder not only does a professional job of sharpening tools, it also buffs and polishes a wide variety of materials.

The popular double-wheeled model usually comes packaged with eye shields, adjustable tool rests, quench trays for cooling metals, and rubber supports to reduce vibration. In addition, you can buy special attachments for sharpening drill bits and saw blades and wheels for buffing—fiber and wire brushes and lamb's wool and cloth buffers. You can change the type of wheels with just a flick of a wrench.

For a bench grinder to operate properly, it must be firmly attached to a workbench or grinder stand with bolts. Stability is important because of the high rpm output of the grinder motor. For safety's sake, locate it in a well-lighted spot.

To smooth soft metals, such as brass, aluminum, and copper, use a coarse wheel. For hard materials, a fine wheel is best. Wheel types include "coarse," "medium coarse," "medium fine," and "fine." There's usually a speed limit associated with, and stamped on, each type of wheel. Do not exceed these rpm specifications. Before purchasing a wheel, make sure its holes fit the shaft of your grinder.

Buffing and polishing wheels come in handy for a variety of operations. Wire wheels (coarse or fine) are used for removing rust. Cloth wheels buff and polish metal.

To bring out the best shine in metal items, you'll need to use buffing compound on the wheel. Use red jeweler's rouge for gold and silver items; white rouge is best for chrome, stainless steel, and aluminum; and brown tripoli for copper and brass items. Rub the compound on the buffing wheel, not on the item to be buffed.

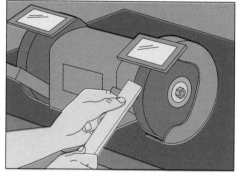

Square up the edges of worn or nicked tools by holding them square to the wheel. Use some pressure, but don't force the tool.

When the edge is square, adjust the tool rest to the proper bevel angle; while the grinder is off, hold the tool on the rest and adjust the rest.

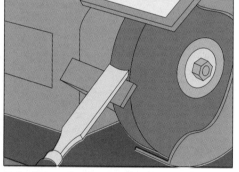

Grinding wheels produce a slightly concave or "hollow" cut. This keeps edges sharp for a longer time and makes for better cutting.

Move the tool back and forth across the wheel. Quench the tool often in water so the metal doesn't lose its "temper," the hardness of the metal.

Hold small tools or other items to be ground with an improvised jig, like the one shown. Use plywood for the jig; it's stronger than solid wood.

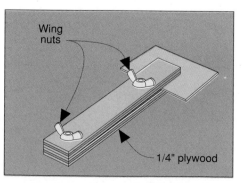

Wing nuts

1/4" plywood

Drilling

In the "You'll need…" boxes throughout this book, a drill is mentioned quite often. The act of drilling, however, requires two items: a drill and a drill bit. A bit is a rotary chisel with two edges. A drill is the drive mechanism that provides the rotary action for that "chisel."

(Because of space considerations in the "You'll need…" items, we only call for a drill, assuming you'll use the required bit.)

Do-it-yourselfers or woodworkers once needed to have several hand-operated drills to get the proper job done. Now, an electric drill will do

all the jobs and more (see pages 451–452). An electric drill should be among your first tool purchases. You may want to add a push drill or a crank-operated hand drill for making small holes quickly or for situations where getting power to the job takes more time than boring the hole.

TOOL TALK

Because of the accessories now available, you can use a power drill for many jobs other than drilling (see page 452). A push drill is excellent for drilling small holes in wood, plastic, and metal. For larger holes, use a ½-inch power drill with a side handle. With a hand drill, you hold with one hand and crank with the other. For large holes, you may still need an old-fashioned brace with auger bits.

You should have a variety of bit styles and sizes in your tool kit. The most common, the twist drill bit, cuts through wood, metal, or plastic. You can buy oversized twist bits with ¼-inch shanks. Spade bits are good for drilling large holes with a power drill. Auger bits are also used for large holes in wood, but are designed for hand braces. For holes over 1 inch in diameter, use an expansive bit, which is adjustable, with a brace or a spade bit in a power drill.

Countersinks let you bore a V-shaped hole to set screw heads flush with or below the surface. Wood drill countersinks predrill screw holes and provide for a countersink in one operation. Reamers are for enlarging holes in metal. Hole saws cut very large holes in wood. For masonry, use a carbide-tipped masonry bit. Awls prepare the way for nails and screws in wood.

CHOOSING DRILLS AND BITS

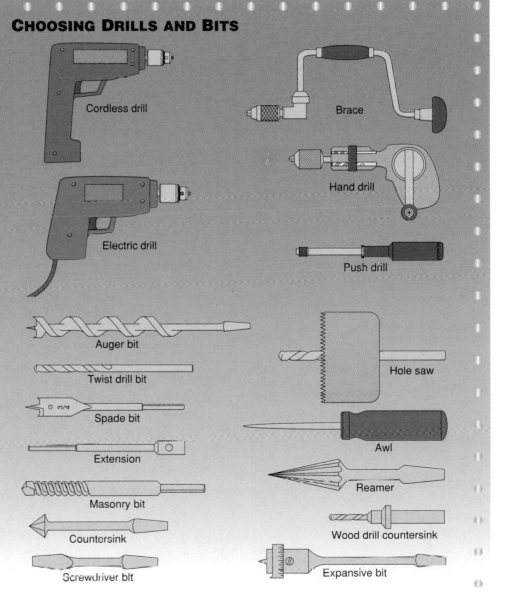

Cordless drill

Electric drill

Auger bit

Twist drill bit

Spade bit

Extension

Masonry bit

Countersink

Screwdriver bit

Brace

Hand drill

Push drill

Hole saw

Awl

Reamer

Wood drill countersink

Expansive bit

Drilling (continued)

USING HAND DRILLS AND BRACES

To use a hand-operated brace or drill with success, always turn the handle or crank slowly and evenly. Don't spin it like an egg beater. If you do, chances are the speed will cause the bit or drill to bind, overheat, or break. Easy does it.

Keep the bit square to the work (see below). Keep your bits sharp (see page 453). Dull cutting edges require more muscle power. Then, you risk breaking the bits or burning their cutting edges beyond use.

For safety reasons, remove bits from their chucks after each use.

On the business end of every drill, there is a round metal housing called a chuck. Inside the chuck are two or three fitted pieces of metal, called jaws. Bits are locked into these jaws, by turning the chuck housing either with your fingers or with a chuck key. Because the chuck is supposed to hold the bit securely, it's important to buy a drill with a quality chuck so the bit doesn't slide, spin, or bend when you apply drilling pressure.

An occasional cleaning and oiling keeps chucks in perfect working order. Deter rust on other metal parts by wiping them with an oil-treated cloth.

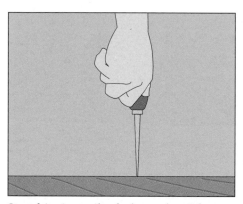

Start bits in a pilot hole made with an awl. Use a center punch for metal. A pilot hole prevents the bit from skating around because of its rotary motion.

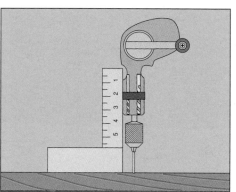

Square the drill with the work before you start. After several turns, check for square again—especially when you are drilling a deep hole.

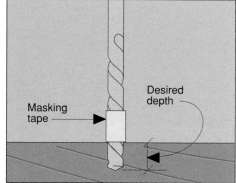

To drill a "blind" hole that does not go through the material, wrap tape around the bit at the desired depth, then drill until the tape touches the material.

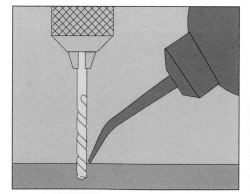

When drilling metals—especially stainless steel—squirt light oil on the bit and the metal. This aids the cutting process and cools the bit.

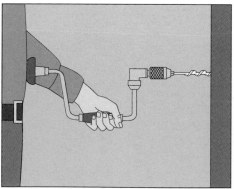

To get more pressure on a brace, hold its head against your body. Level the brace with one hand. This helps keep the bit square.

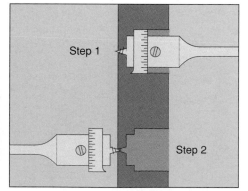

With an auger, expansive, or spade bit, bore until its lead screw breaks through the other side of the material. Then, finish from the other side.

CHOOSING AND USING AN ELECTRIC DRILL

A power drill probably is the most versatile, multipurpose tool you can have in your tool kit. And, because of keen competition in the marketplace, the price of power drills is surprisingly low.

For home use, select a ¼-, ⅜-, or ½-inch drill. These sizes refer to chuck size and, thus, the largest size bit shank you can use in the chuck. Motor horsepowers are matched to fit the different capacities.

Your best choice might be a ¼- or ⅜-inch drill because you can rent a ½-inch drill inexpensively for the few times you might need its low-speed, high-torque action. There isn't much price difference between ¼- and ⅜-inch drills, so the decision usually comes down to the type of work you want it to do.

A ¼-inch drill has plenty of rpms to bore ¼-inch twist bits into metal and wood and ½-inch bits into wood. The drill performs perfectly for most grinding and buffing operations, too. A ¼-inch drill is not a production tool, however, so it won't take a lot of continuous, heavy use or slamming around in the back of your pickup.

For light and heavy work, a ⅜-inch drill has lots of production guts. This comes in handy for working with hardwoods, masonry, and metals in which fairly large holes are needed. You can push on these units without seriously slowing their ⅓- to ⅜- (or more) horsepower buildup. And, the larger ⅜-inch chuck will handle both ¼- and ⅜-inch twist bits and special accessories (see page 452).

Purchase a variable-speed power drill, if possible. With these models, the motor revs up from zero to full capacity rpm, depending on how hard you squeeze the trigger switch.

This lets you start drilling into the material slowly, speed up for the cutting action, then slow down for a nonsplinter finish. You "feel" your way through the material instead of just hanging onto the drill while it chews its way in and out. Variable-speed drills also can be used to drive screws into material, saving lots of hammer-and-nail time.

Some drills have a reversible action, too, which allows you to remove screws and lets you back out sticking or binding bits without breaking them.

Most drills are permanently lubricated, double-insulated against electrical shock, and come with handle and chuck key (wrench).

For special projects, you can buy battery-powered, cordless drills and drills that convert into power hammers for brick, block, and concrete work.

Grip drill with both hands to keep it steady and square to the work. Any wobbling will break a bit quickly.

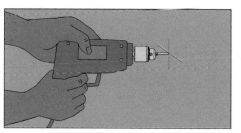

Drill pilot holes using low speed of a variable-speed drill. If the bit starts to skate, use an awl or punch instead.

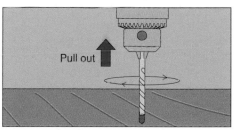

When drilling deep holes, back out the bit often, with motor running, to clear chips. Reinsert bit before starting drill.

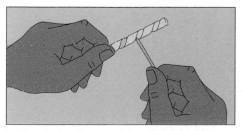

If shavings clog the bit, remove them with the tip of a nail. Clogging results from fast-feeding the drill.

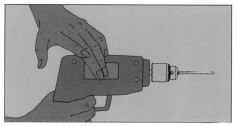

After operating a drill for a long period, touch the motor. If it's very hot, let the drill run with no load to cool it.

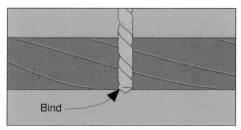

As a drill bit begins to break through the material, especially metal, it may bind. Simply back up and start again.

Drilling (continued)

TOOL TALK
CHOOSING DRILL ACCESSORIES

Portable power drill accessories can magically convert your drill into a shop-full of woodworking and metalworking equipment. Some of these devices are quick changeovers; others take some patience. Overall, the many-tools-in-one concept is good, especially if your workshop space is limited and you are not using your drill constantly for its primary, single-performance purpose.

Keep in mind, however, that drills simply can't be expected to carry the workload of lathes, circular saws, or sanders through mere conversion.

The attachments shown below do not represent the full complement of those available, but they are among the most widely purchased. You can buy such diverse items as circle cutters, hacksaw blade attachments, drilling depth gauges, and many more.

If you plan to buy accessories, invest in a ⅜-inch electric drill. It has the capacity to run the attachments without overloading the motor or damaging accessories.

Discs, brushes, drums, wheels, and stones let you use an electric drill for a wide variety of sanding, cleaning, polishing, and grinding jobs. A lamb's-wool cover (not shown) slips over the sanding disc base and is secured with a drawstring, thus turning a drill into a buffing wheel. These tools often are sold in a packaged kit for less than you would pay for them individually.

A rigid extension turns an ordinary bit into an extension bit, while the flexible power take-off provides even more versatility for getting into hard-to-reach places. With an angle drive, you get gear reduction for slow speed, high-torque jobs. A paint stirrer makes quick work of mixing. A screwdriver/socket set includes standard- and Phillips-blade bits and an assortment of sockets.

Stands adapt a portable electric drill for stationary-tool work. The bench stand converts the drill into a grinder. A drill-press stand gives the drill many of the features of a full-sized drill press. Because it is lightweight, you can set the stand directly on the work when you need to drill holes into large panels. A doweling jig is used to drill holes into smaller materials.

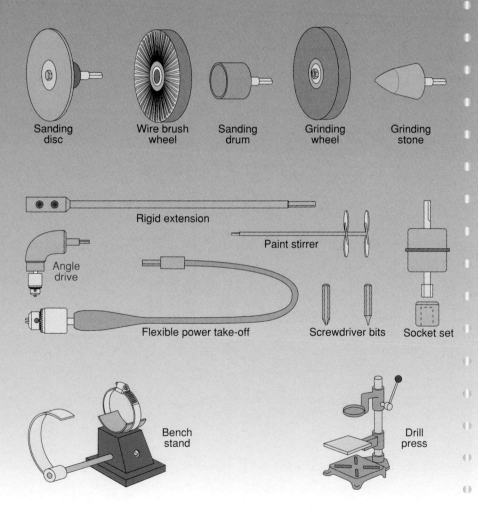

Sanding disc

Wire brush wheel

Sanding drum

Grinding wheel

Grinding stone

Rigid extension

Paint stirrer

Angle drive

Flexible power take-off

Screwdriver bits

Socket set

Bench stand

Drill press

KEEPING DRILLS AND BITS SHARP

You can buy good twist drill bits and keep them sharpened, or you can opt for inexpensive ones and throw them away when they become dull. Cheap bits become dull fast and aren't worth the time it takes to sharpen them.

It's a different story with spade auger bits. It's best to spend your money on quality. Then keep these bits sharpened and free from rust and damage. Spade bits can be sharpened like a chisel with a file or a grinder (see page 448). The cutting edges on countersinks may be "touched up" with a file when they become dull, which is seldom, because they aren't used that much.

Maintaining bits is relatively simple. Twist bits often are packaged in a plastic box that may be closed for safe storage—as long as you use it. Auger and spade bits come in plastic sleeves. Smart professionals use cloth pocket sleeves, which they keep lightly oiled to prevent bits from becoming rusty and dull.

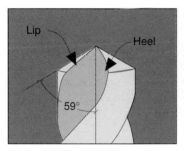

Twist bit lips are the cutting edges; the trailing edge is called a heel. The 59-degree angle is for "standard" work.

You can sharpen twist bits by "eye" if you're really good, but you'll get better results with a grinding jig.

A bench-top sharpener is like an electric pencil sharpener. Some units even fit on and are powered by the drill.

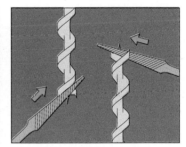

Sharpen auger bits with a file designed for filing the inside of the cutting lips. File burrs off the heels.

CHOOSING A DRILL PRESS

For a serious woodworker, a stationary drill press is a "must-have" tool. Its purpose is to drill holes in any material with precision accuracy. But it can do more than that—use it as a drum or disc sander, a router, a grinder, and a polisher.

Look for these basic features when you shop for a drill press: a tilting table that adjusts up or down its pole support for wide and long materials; a depth gauge setting; a light for close work, and a drill-press vise. As you gain experience, you'll want to add other accessories, such as a fly-cutter for drilling large holes, and specialty drills, such as countersinks and hole saws.

Motor

Quill feed handle

Adjustable lamp

Table lock

Column

Pedestal

Belt and pulley guard

Switch

Quill

Spindle

Chuck

Adjustable table

Choosing Cordless Tools

Imagine walking around a job site without trailing a 100-foot extension cord, working on a boat in the middle of the lake, building a cabin in the woods, scampering around a roof, or standing in water with no danger of shock. All of these scenarios are possible today with cordless, rechargeable tools.

Not to be confused with battery-operated toys, these tools now are used widely throughout the building trades. Potent batteries give these tools surprising power, allowing you to make hundreds of cuts or holes, typically, before recharging.

"Contractor" models feature interchangeable batteries that can be recharged in an hour. With an inexpensive AC/DC inverter, you can even recharge them from your car's cigarette lighter.

Battery sizes and voltages are not universal. If you think you may eventually purchase more than one cordless tool, stick to a single manufacturer and make sure all accept the same battery. Then, you can switch batteries and never have to purchase expensive spares. Many manufacturers offer cost-effective sets of tools—such as a drill and a saw—with a single battery charger.

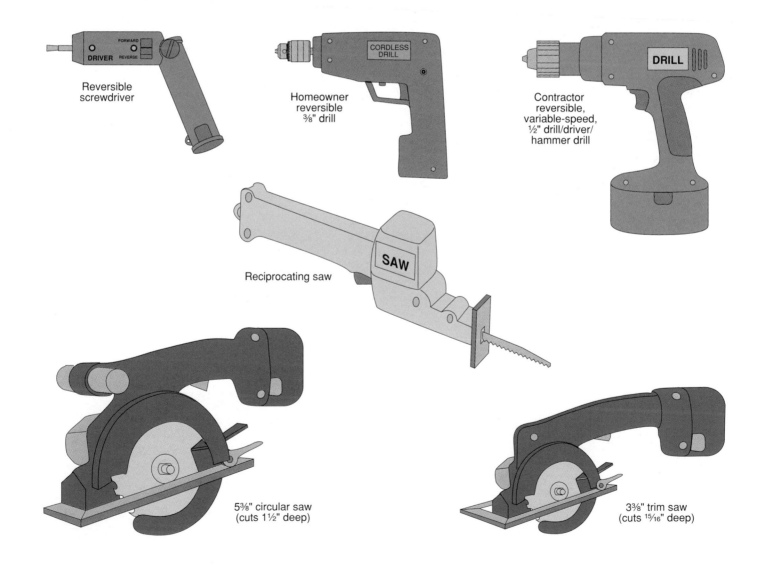

Reversible screwdriver

Homeowner reversible ⅜" drill

Contractor reversible, variable-speed, ½" drill/driver/ hammer drill

Reciprocating saw

5⅜" circular saw (cuts 1½" deep)

3⅜" trim saw (cuts ¹⁵⁄₁₆" deep)

Fastening

"Anyone can pound a nail, drive a screw, or glue one piece of material to another. What's there to learn about fastening, anyway?" You'll find out, in dramatic fashion, the first time you split a perfectly good piece of lumber, break off a screw head, or end up with a project that looks like an orange crate. Actually, you don't "pound" a nail at all—you drive it with a few well-directed blows. You don't drive just any old

nail, either; you must select the proper size and type for the job.

Before you think about what kind of nail to use, you have to decide if a screw would be more appropriate. Screws not only hold more tenaciously than nails, they're also easier to drive in certain situations. Again, you need to know the right size and type to ask for when you venture to the hardware store.

The following pages present a

dozen fastening tools, devices, and techniques. Get to know them, and your projects will go together faster and stay together longer.

You also need to know the right joint for a given situation. For basic joinery techniques, see pages 495–501. Watch out, too, that you don't overengineer a joint with too many fasteners. Often, an extra nail or a screw that's too large actually will weaken a structure.

TOOL TALK

Chances are, you'll never need to buy most of the different types of hammers available. However, if you have a specialized job ahead of you, or if you're going to be using your hammer extensively, it's worth getting the right hammer for the job.

A 16-ounce, curved-claw hammer is the first tool purchase. Besides driving fasteners, a claw hammer also pulls them. Wooden handles, although durable, can break. Tubular steel and solid steel handles are more durable, although tubular steel is lighter. A fiberglass handle delivers less shock to your hand and arm and is nearly unbreakable.

Steel and fiberglass handles feature cushion grips that deter shock. The cushion also prevents damage to fine wood surfaces when you align them by tapping them with the handle.

Use a 20-ounce ripping-claw hammer for rough work, such as removing studs. A 13-ounce claw hammer is easy to swing.

Specialty hammers include ball peen hammers for metalworking, tack hammers for tacks, mallets for driving chisels, and mason's hammers and sledgehammers for masonry projects.

CHOOSING HAMMERS

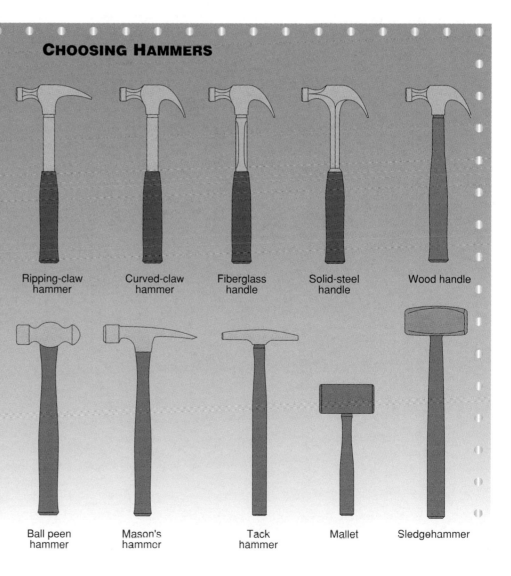

Ripping-claw hammer

Curved-claw hammer

Fiberglass handle

Solid-steel handle

Wood handle

Ball peen hammer

Mason's hammer

Tack hammer

Mallet

Sledgehammer

Fastening *(continued)*

USING HAMMERS

Ask skilled carpenters how to handle a hammer, and they'll show you their hands and tell you, "Carefully." They've found through painful experience that there's a right way and a wrong way to use this most basic of all tools.

For maximum leverage and control, hold onto the hammer at the end of the handle, not up around the neck. If you do this and concentrate on the job at hand, you'll find yourself driving nails without straining (or maiming) your arm, wrist, or hand.

Another important rule to keep in mind for safety and effectiveness is that you should always use a hammer with a face that is slightly larger than the nail or tool you're striking. If you're striking hardened metal, wear safety glasses.

Before using an unfamiliar hammer, always check it for a loose, bent, or split handle. Any of these maladies can turn the hammer into a lethal weapon when you swing it. Make sure, too, that no one is within striking distance should the head and handle—or your hand and the hammer—part company.

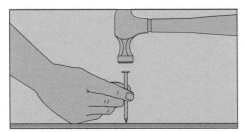

Hold the nail near its head so that if you miss, you'll glance off your fingers rather than crush them.

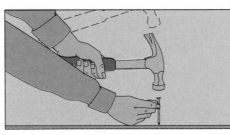

To hit nails dead-on, keep your eye on the nail, not the hammer. Let the hammer do the work.

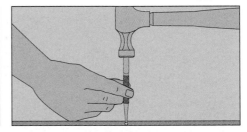

The last blow from the hammer should sink the head flush with the surface. Countersink nailheads with a nail set.

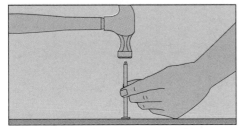

Nailing near the end of a board tends to split the wood. The trick is to blunt the tip of the nail or drill a pilot hole.

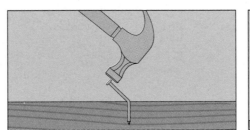

For rough projects, clinching the nails by bending them over gives maximum holding power; clinch with the grain.

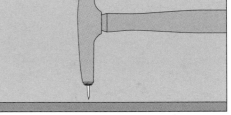

A tack hammer's magnetic head holds and drives tacks. If successive blows are needed, flip the hammer over.

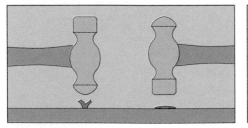

Spread rivets with the rounded side of a ball peen hammer. Then, smack them flat with the face of the hammer.

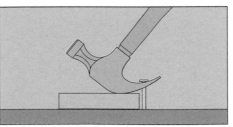

When pulling a nail, slip a scrap of wood under the head for leverage so you're always pulling straight up.

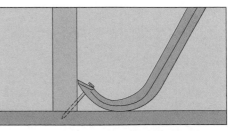

Use a wrecking or pry bar to remove long nails. Add a block of wood under the tool for more pulling leverage.

MATERIAL MATTERS

Once sold for so many pennies per hundred, nails today are sold by the pound. But nails still are described and sized by this old terminology: for example, a 16-penny or a 4-penny nail. To further complicate things, "penny" is signified by the letter "d" (for denarius, Latin for "coin"). So, what you find in a hardware store is a box with a label identifying the type and size nail that's inside—16d common, for example. There's a size of nail for

CHOOSING NAILS

every job. The sketch of the 20d common nail below includes a size scale, cross-referenced to an inch scale.

Just as there are many sizes of nails, there also are many types. For example, if water will come in contact with the nails, choose galvanized or aluminum types. If you're installing plastic or metal roofing, specify roofing nails with a rubber washer under their heads to seal out water. You also can buy brass, copper, stainless steel, and

bronze nails. To get more holding power, select the spiral, threaded, or coated types. Coated nails have a transparent, rosinlike covering that makes them grip the wood fibers better, without making them sticky.

For small jobs, you'll want to stay with 1-pound boxes of nails; some stores still sell them in open, bulk quantities, by the pound. If you're installing flooring or roofing, you can save money by buying cartons of nails.

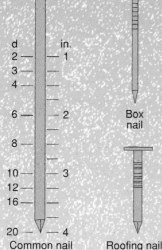

d	in.
2	1
3	
4	
6	2
8	
10	3
12	
16	
20	4

Common nail

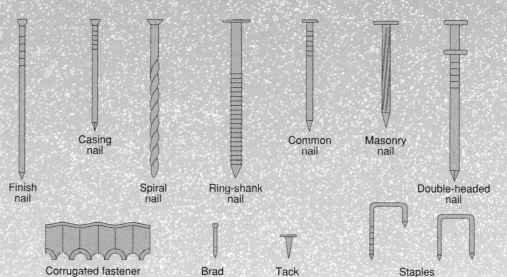

Box nail

Finish nail

Roofing nail

Casing nail

Spiral nail

Ring-shank nail

Common nail

Masonry nail

Double-headed nail

Corrugated fastener

Brad

Tack

Staples

For most fastening jobs, you'll need common, box, finishing, and casing nails. Keep several 1-pound boxes of these nails on hand, as well as an assortment of brads. In shape, brads are junior-sized finishing nails; use them for molding and finishing jobs. For more holding power, spiral and ring-shank nails are tops. Ring-shank nails have barbs on the shanks; spiral nails are "threaded" somewhat like screws and twist into materials. For composition shingles, buy regular roofing nails.

The steel used in masonry nails is specially hardened to withstand the heavy blows needed to drive them. Don't drive masonry nails directly into brick; rather, drive them into the mortar joints. You can buy stud tools and gun-powder-driven stud guns for stud-type masonry fasteners. When driving masonry nails, wear safety glasses to protect your eyes.

Double-headed nails are driven flush with the bottom head and pulled with the top head when the project is

disassembled. Note that some of the nails illustrated have a thicker shank. The diameter of the shank usually increases with the length of the nail. Staples are used to hold wiring, fencing, conduit, ceiling tile, pipe— almost any material or product that is thin and lightweight. The shanks of tacks are cut or round, and lengths vary somewhat. For light fabrication jobs with miter joints, such as picture frames, you can use corrugated fasteners, which lap over the joint.

Fastening (continued)

DRIVING NAILS

It's easy to tell the difference between nails and screws. It's knowing when to use each that takes more perception. Nails hold primarily by friction, which gives them plenty of sheer strength up, down, and sideways. Unfortunately, they're easily popped out by an outward thrust of any type. That's why, for example, you don't see pickets being used to corral livestock or pets—animals could push or pull the slats loose.

Screws, on the other hand, mechanically interlock with wood fibers or other materials, making them more suitable in situations where there's considerable outward pressure on the fastener.

This is why it's important to plan work that will be nailed so that any force that tends to separate the joint is perpendicular—not parallel—to the length of the nail.

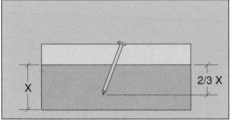

Use nails long enough to penetrate two-thirds of the way through the board into which you're nailing. Nail thin material to thick material.

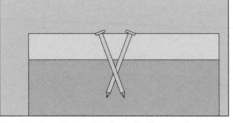

By driving in nails at a slight angle, you increase their holding power. Crossing slightly staggered nails adds more strength to the joint.

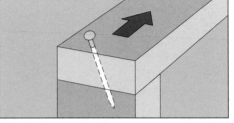

Analyze the direction of the load the nail will carry. Drive it in so the force pushes the nail deeper, instead of pulling it out.

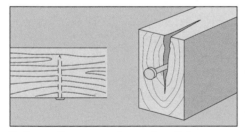

Drive nails across the grain of the wood, not with the grain. Nails in the end grain don't hold well and often split the wood.

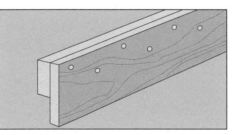

Two nails penetrating the same grain layer also can split wood, so stagger nails along the length of a board, angling them for strength.

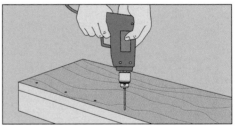

Nailing into hardwood is tough; often, nails bend or the wood splits. Prevent this by drilling pilot holes slightly smaller than the nails.

Drive masonry nails with a baby sledge. Plan the job so the nails go into the mortar joints, not the masonry units.

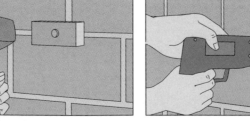

If masonry nails bend or break, drive them into a scrap of wood. Use scrap to hold and guide the nail, then split the scrap as you drive home the nail.

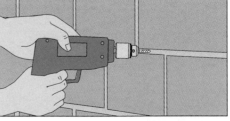

If you have to drive a lot of masonry nails, making pilot holes is faster than using a wood scrap. Use a carbide-tipped drill and wear safety glasses.

TOOL TALK

Yes, you can turn screws with your thumbnail, a dime, a tie clasp, and even a paper clip. But the right tool for the job is a screwdriver.

Although screwdrivers come in a dazzling array of sizes and designs, most have either Phillips or slotted blades—to fit the two basic types of screws. The only screws that these blades won't turn are the so-called specialty screws, most of which are

CHOOSING SCREWDRIVERS

driven or removed with sockets or wrenches tailored especially for them.

Don't be misled into thinking that one Phillips and one slotted screwdriver will satisfy all of your maintenance and repair needs. The slots in screws vary in length and width, and it's important to use a screwdriver that fits the slot.

If the tip is too narrow, it will ride up out of the slot and damage the

screw. If the tip is too wide, it will damage the material around the screw head when the screw is driven flush with the material.

Like any other tool, quality screwdrivers are a bargain in the long run. Their blades have been properly tempered and ground, and they will feel balanced in your hand. Buy a set of them if your budget will allow.

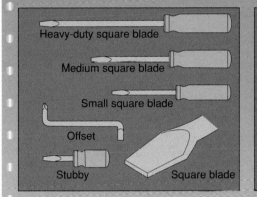

A basic screwdriver assortment includes these standard blade types. Screwdrivers generally are sized based on the length of the blade.

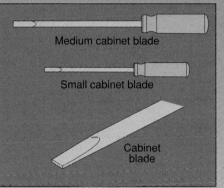

Cabinet screwdrivers have special straight-sided tips so they can drive or remove countersunk screws without marring the material.

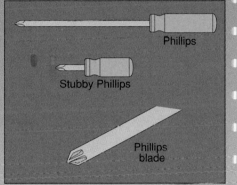

Phillips screwdriver tips have multiple edges for more turning power. They come in three sizes—No. 1, No.2, and No. 3; get one of each.

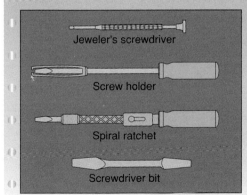

Specialty screwdrivers save time. Spiral ratchets spin screws in and out; bits are used in hand braces. A screw holder attachment aids starting.

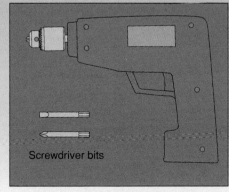

A variable-speed, reversible power drill is excellent for driving in or removing a large number of screws. All standard bits are available.

Fastening (continued)

MATERIAL MATTERS

Screws have a lot going for them. Most important, they're tough and provide all the holding power you could ever need. They're also easy to remove, making them ideal for projects you may want to disassemble later. For projects where fasteners will show, screws add a touch of class that nails can't match.

Screws fall into two types, based on the material into which they will be driven: wood or metal. Threads on a metal screw run the entire length of the shank; threads on a wood screw run about three-quarters up the shank.

Screw heads vary in style and slot type. Styles are flat, oval, round, and hex. Slot types are slotted, Phillips, square, and Torx. Phillips-, square-, and Torx-head screws have only flat heads.

CHOOSING SCREWS

Drywall screws are special wood screws in that their threads run the entire length of the shank. Because of this feature, they have good holding power, and you can use them with great success for projects other than attaching drywall to studs.

To attach heavy objects to wood or masonry, use lag screws. These heavy-duty fasteners are good for such projects as securing together deck framing members. Secure them into masonry using lead expansion shields.

To fasten items into walls, use special plastic wall anchors. Predrill a hole, insert the anchor, then drive the screw into the anchor, which expands in the wall to hold the item in place.

Most screws have a zinc coating that inhibits rust. Because you don't pay much extra for this protection, don't settle for uncoated types. Brass screws are available, too, for both decorative use and their noncorrosiveness.

Use washers with screws to prevent the screwhead from pulling into or marring the material being fastened. Some washers are also decorative.

Screw eyes and hooks are special screws used to hang or hook items together. Another special screw for hanging or attaching heavy items to wood is a screw hanger, which has screw threads on one end and bolt threads on the other. Another item often called a screw, a machine screw, is actually a bolt (see page 464).

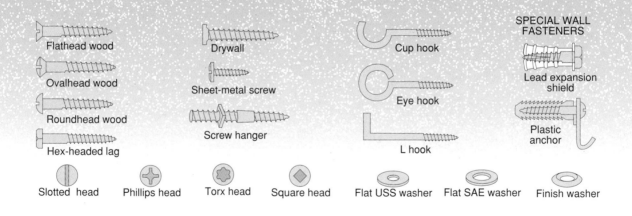

Flathead wood · Ovalhead wood · Roundhead wood · Hex-headed lag · Drywall · Sheet-metal screw · Screw hanger · Cup hook · Eye hook · L hook · SPECIAL WALL FASTENERS · Lead expansion shield · Plastic anchor

Slotted head · Phillips head · Torx head · Square head · Flat USS washer · Flat SAE washer · Finish washer

HELPFUL HINTS

SELECTING THE PROPER-SIZE SCREW

Using the right-size screw is critically important to the success of any fastening job. Screws are sized by their length and gauge (diameter).

■ The length of the screw, designated in inches, should be shorter than the thickness of the material into which it will be driven. The smooth shank of a wood screw should go through the top material being fastened.

■ The gauge of screws you will need for a given project depends on the fastening strength required. Designated by number, gauges range from No. 0, which has a diameter of $\frac{1}{16}$ inch, to No. 20, nearly $\frac{1}{2}$ inch in diameter.

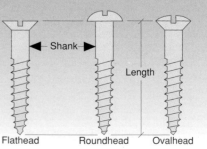

Shank · Length

Flathead · Roundhead · Ovalhead

DRIVING IN SCREWS

If a screw is exceptionally hard to drive, check to make sure the tip of the blade fully fills the screw slot. Try using a longer screwdriver. The longer the blade, the more turning power. Or, predrill pilot holes for screws. Make sure these are deep enough in the stock so you're not driving the screws through solid material. Make the pilot holes slightly smaller than the diameter (gauge) of the screw.

Another trick is to rub wax or bar soap on the threads of the screw as a lubricant.

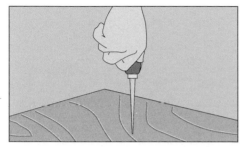

Make pilot holes for No. 8 or smaller screws with an awl. For larger sizes, drill holes with a power or hand drill.

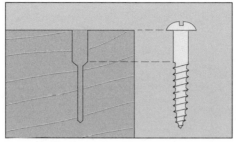

In hardwood, drill a clearance hole to accommodate the shank, then sink a smaller pilot hole for the threads.

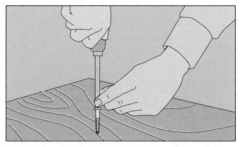

Start screws by holding the screwdriver handle with one hand, the blade with the other. Don't hold the screw.

Put more drive on the screwdriver by turning it with one hand and applying top pressure with the other.

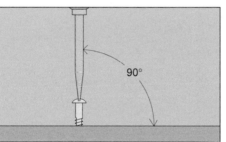

Keep the screwdriver square in the slot. If it's off center or at an angle, it may slip out and badly strip the slot.

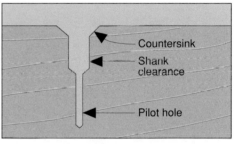

A countersinking bit drills the hole for the threads, the hole for the shaft, and the countersink, all in one operation.

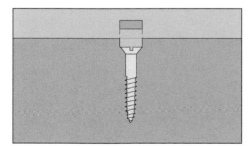

Counterbored screws easily are concealed with wood plugs. Or, fill the holes with wood filler or putty.

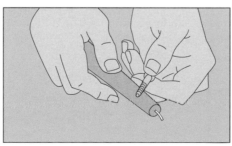

Screws drive easier when threads are lubricated with candle wax. Rub the screw against the candle and rotate.

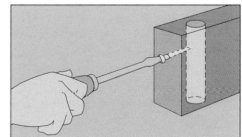

Screws don't hold well in end grain. Dowel the board and use screws long enough to penetrate the dowel.

Fastening (continued)

REMOVING STUBBORN SCREWS

Removing old screws can be a real headache—especially if the screws have rusted in the material, become "frozen" through corrosion, or their slots were stripped when they were driven into the material.

Approach a stubborn screw cautiously. Test it with a screwdriver tip that fits the slot perfectly. If you encounter a lot of resistance when you try to back out the screw, stop immediately. Otherwise, you may damage the screw slot so it can't be used at all. Instead, try the other removal techniques illustrated below.

With work, you often can back them out. If not, you may have to turn to a screw extractor for help (see page 446). As a last resort, you can drill the screw out with a twist drill, but this will enlarge the hole.

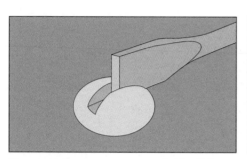

You usually can remove paint buildup from a screw slot by sliding the screwdriver tip in the slot.

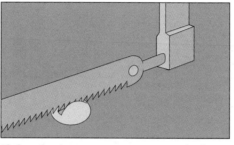

If the slot is too narrow to accept the screwdriver tip, you may be able to widen and deepen it with a hacksaw.

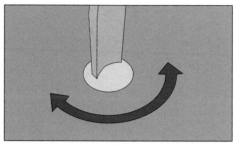

Try tightening the screw a quarter turn, then working it back and forth with the screwdriver.

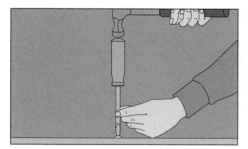

Tap an old screwdriver in the slot to loosen the screw. Make sure you hit the screwdriver squarely.

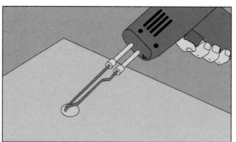

Heat applied to a screwhead with the tip of a soldering iron may break it free. Test the screw often.

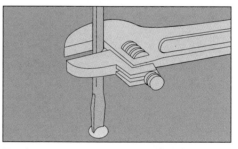

For leverage, use a square-shank screwdriver and wrench. Don't do this with round-shank screwdrivers.

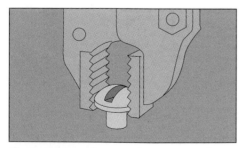

Once a screw is out a few turns, grip it with lock-joint pliers. Pliers will damage the head, but will do the job.

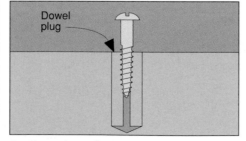

Dowel plug

Don't replace the same screw. Go to a longer or thicker screw, drill out the hole, and fill with a dowel plug.

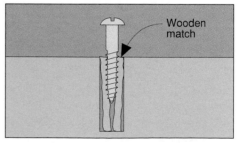

Wooden match

Or, you can fill a hole with wooden match sticks or toothpicks so screw threads have new wood to bite.

TOOL TALK   CHOOSING AND USING WRENCHES

For most home maintenance and improvement projects, the first wrench you should by is an adjustable wrench. Next, come a set of Allen or hex-key wrenches and two pipe wrenches. Other wrenches are specialty items that you can buy or rent as you need them.

Adjustable wrenches range in size from 4 to 16 inches long. If you buy the 6-, 8-, and 10-inchers, you'll be able to tackle almost any fix-it job that requires a wrench.

Allen wrenches tighten setscrews and screws featuring an Allen-type head. They're generally packaged in sets with several sizes.

For assembling pipes and round metal materials, pipe wrenches can't be beat. You'll need to buy two. They can help you solve a host of plumbing problems—from repairs to new plumbing assemblies.

End, box, combination, and socket wrenches are fixed-jaw relatives of adjustable wrenches. They can do anything an adjustable wrench can do, and sometimes better, because they are not as large and can fit into tight spaces. They're essential for working with machinery, especially cars, washers, dryers, and so on.

Socket wrenches have a lever that reverses the turning direction of the wrench. With these wrenches you don't have to remove the "jaws" of the sockets from the work.

Another specialty wrench worth noting is a nut driver. Similar to a screwdriver, a nut driver has a tip that accepts small sockets to fit hex nuts and screws, socket-head cap screws, and metric fasteners.

When using a wrench, pull it toward you. Then, if the wrench slips, you'll run less risk of skinning your knuckles. With adjustable and pipe wrenches, cinch the movable jaw tightly on the work. Pipe wrenches have a movable jaw that tightens automatically on the pipe when you apply pressure.

Select fixed-jaw wrenches to perfectly fit the work they're to turn. If they are even slightly larger, you stand the chance of stripping the metal of the nut or bolt when you turn the wrench.

Never force a wrench by tapping its handle with a hammer. Don't slip a pipe over a wrench handle for more leverage because you may snap the wrench or the material it's tightening.

Quality is important in all wrenches. Because a lot of pressure is applied to tighten and loosen nuts and bolts, wrenches must be able to withstand pressure without breaking.

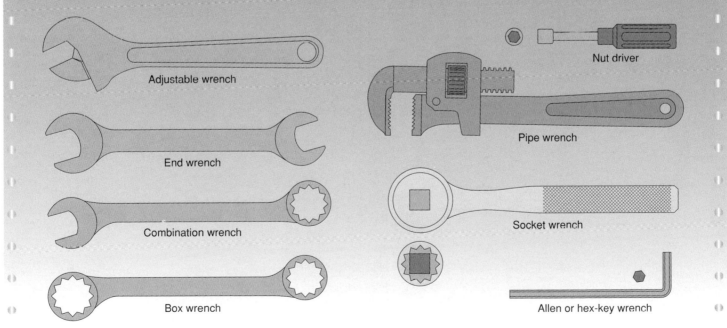

Adjustable wrench

End wrench

Combination wrench

Box wrench

Nut driver

Pipe wrench

Socket wrench

Allen or hex-key wrench

Fastening (continued)

MATERIAL MATTERS

When you need a fastener that can't pull loose yet lets you dismantle and reassemble a joint, you're literally down to nuts and bolts.

In contrast to nails and screws, bolts are not used much in home maintenance and repair work. If you need to fasten two items together securely and have access to both sides of the material, however, a two-sided fastener like a bolt is ideal.

Bolts are also sized by length and diameter (in inches, in contrast to the gauge of a screw). They're also sized by the number of threads per inch. For example, a ½×13×3 bolt is ½ inch in diameter, has 13 threads to the inch, and is 3 inches long.

Machine screws and stove bolts are

CHOOSING NUTS AND BOLTS

identical. They both have threads all the way to the head. Technically, stove bolts should come with nuts; machine screws do not, because they are designed to be screwed into prethreaded holes. Machine bolts have fine or coarse threads. Carriage bolts have coarse threads that extend only partially up the shank.

For many home projects, expandable anchors, toggle bolts, and lag screws (see page 460) are ideal. These "one-sided" fasteners let you work from the facing side of the material.

While wall anchors with screws are easier to use, in many cases you'll need a hollow-wall anchor bolt or toggle bolt, designed to fasten or hang heavy objects. With a hollow-wall anchor, you

slip the anchor into a hole in the wall, then turn the bolt, causing the metal flanges to expand and grip the wall. Then, you can remove the bolt, run it through the object to be hung, and screw the bolt back into the anchor.

A toggle bolt also slips into a hole in the wall. Once through the wall, however, two wings snap open. When the bolt is tightened, the wings grip the back of the wall, holding the assembly in position. To use this fastener, you have to slip it through the object to be hung before pushing the bolt and wing-type anchor through the wall. If you remove the bolt, the wing assembly drops behind the wall.

Both expandable anchors and toggle bolts are made in a range of sizes.

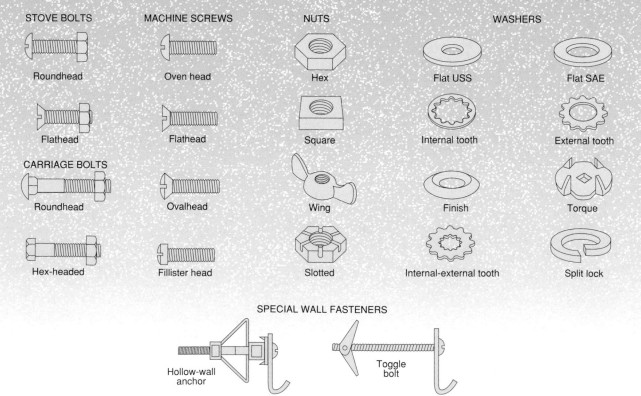

STOVE BOLTS
Roundhead
Flathead

CARRIAGE BOLTS
Roundhead
Hex-headed

MACHINE SCREWS
Oven head
Flathead
Ovalhead
Fillister head

NUTS
Hex
Square
Wing
Slotted

WASHERS
Flat USS
Flat SAE
Internal tooth
External tooth
Finish
Torque
Internal-external tooth
Split lock

SPECIAL WALL FASTENERS
Hollow-wall anchor
Toggle bolt

TOOL TALK — CHOOSING AND USING STAPLE GUNS

For light fabrication jobs, such as installing ceiling tile, replacing window screening, and hanging insulation, no other tool matches a staple gun's ease and efficiency.

Don't confuse this construction tool with lightweight desktop staplers. A staple gun, also called a staple tacker, shoots hefty fasteners into materials as dense as hardwoods.

Just set it down against the material and squeeze the trigger. Your best buy is a double-leverage-action staple gun that handles staples with leg lengths of $\frac{3}{16}$, $\frac{1}{4}$, and $\frac{5}{16}$ inch.

For jobs such as installing roofing felt, carpet padding, and other big-sheet jobs, consider renting a hammer stapler. With one of these handy tools, you swing the stapler onto the

work as you would hit a nail with a hammer. Or, if you really want to go first-class on large projects, rent an electric or pneumatic stapler.

For specialty tasks, there are staplers that can staple wires and cables up to $\frac{1}{2}$ inch in diameter; low-profile staplers for use in tight quarters; and even an outward-clinch tacker for insulating pipes and ducts.

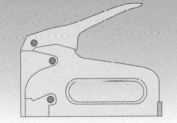

Staple gun

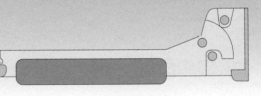

Hammer stapler

TOOL TALK — CHOOSING AND USING A POP RIVETER

Much maligned because they look weak, rivets often are overlooked as a fastener for home use. In fact, they're one of the strongest of all fasteners. A pop riveter can fasten together almost any thin sheet material, including wood, metal, plastic, and leather.

Rivets come in various diameters, $\frac{1}{8}$, $\frac{5}{32}$, and $\frac{3}{16}$ inch, and in short, medium, and long lengths. A kit

usually includes the tool, plus an assortment of rivets and backup plates. The plates hold the rivets securely in soft materials.

The riveting tool operates like a tacker: You squeeze the trigger to set the rivet, which must be hand-inserted into a steel nose guide.

You also can buy solid, tubular, and split rivets for fastening sheet

materials. With these, you need a ball peen hammer, center punch, and a solid piece of steel or a vise to back the material while you're flattening the rivets.

When assembling metal with either pop rivets or hammered rivets, do not mix metals. Use aluminum rivets with aluminum sheet, brass with brass, and so on.

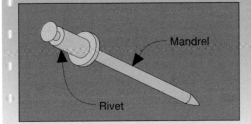

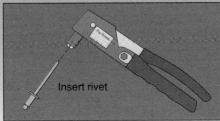

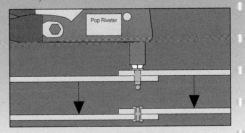

Pop rivets include a stem-like mandrel that breaks off when you squeeze the tool. Little hand pressure is needed.

1. Insert the mandrel into the base of the tool. Squeeze the handle slightly to hold it while you position the tool.

2. Slip rivet into predrilled hole. As you squeeze the trigger, the mandrel withdraws, and the rivet will "pop."

Fastening (continued)

USING SOLDERING TOOLS

By itself, solder doesn't make a strong joint. You have to start with a good mechanical joint, then use solder to complete it. For example, copper pipe needs to be seated snugly into an elbow or other joint; sheet metal has to be crimped or folded; and wire ends have to be pinched tightly to connectors. Once these mechanical joints are sound, solder adds further strength.

Although solder is a soft metal, it requires plenty of heat to fuse it to other metals. For small projects, an electric soldering iron or gun produces sufficient heat. For large projects (copper pipe, gutters, and ducts), you'll need a propane torch.

To solder a joint with a soldering iron or gun, first clean the tip of the iron or gun with steel wool or a file until it's shiny. Heat the iron and "tin" it with solder. When the tip accepts a thin coat of the solder, it's "tinned." Be sure the work to be soldered is absolutely clean and free of paint, grease, and fingerprints.

Apply the proper flux and heat the metal. Hold the solder against the metal joint, not in the flame of the torch or on the soldering gun. When the metal becomes hot enough, the solder will melt and flow into and fuse the joint (see pages 304 and 522). To solder hard materials such as steel, bronze, and

silver, you'll need a propane torch, because a soldering gun won't generate enough heat. Buy wire-flux or solid-core solder for small jobs. Choose bar solder for fabricating sheet materials, such as gutter runs, heating ducts, and so on.

Flux helps fuse the metals by ensuring that the surface is free of corrosion. Use rosin flux for copper, brass, bronze, and silver. Galvanized iron requires an acid flux. Stainless steel needs a special flux.

Warning: For safety reasons, do not solder electrical wiring connections in your house. Most electrical codes prohibit this practice.

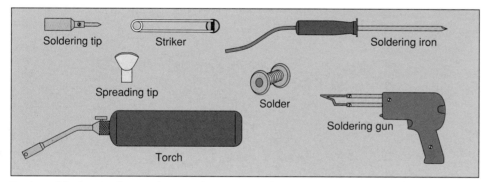

Basic soldering tools are shown above. Both soldering guns and propane torches often are sold in kit form.

Solder, a soft, silver-colored wire, comes in reels. Use 95-5-type solder, which has 95 percent tin and no lead.

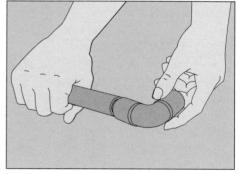

Make sure joints are clean and fit snugly before soldering. Use flux liberally to ensure proper fusion.

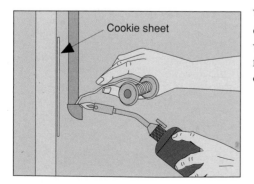

When using a propane torch, or even a soldering iron, near a wood wall or by insulation, always protect flammable objects with sheet metal or another nonflammable item.

Never solder electrical wiring connections. Instead, twist wires together and complete the job with screw-on wire connectors.

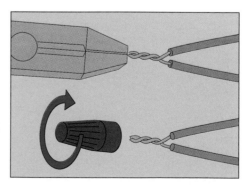

CHOOSING AND USING ADHESIVES

Modern-day adhesives can join together almost any material—often making a joint that's stronger than the original materials themselves. But there now is a mind-boggling array of adhesives from which to choose. The chart on page 468 summarizes the properties of the most useful adhesive types. Product names can be confusing, so read the manufacturer's label—it specifies the material the product is intended for and how to use the product.

Check for the set and cure times. Set refers to an adhesive's initial drying time, which might be a matter of hours, minutes, or even seconds. The bond doesn't reach full strength, however, until the adhesive has cured. Don't apply stress to a glued joint until it has thoroughly cured.

Even very high humidity will destroy the bond of some adhesives. Others can withstand occasional light wetting, and a few remain strong even during prolonged submersion.

Strong glue joints don't just happen. Here are some rules of thumb to help you join and keep materials together better and longer.

■ Always read and follow the label directions for best results.

■ The more surface area you cover with adhesive, the stronger the joint.

■ Avoid fastening weak joints, such as butt joints and end-grain joints, with glue only. (See pages 495–501 for wood joinery techniques and page 506 for tips on fastening plywood.) Acrylic plastic can be butt-glued (see page 516).

■ Unless the manufacturer specifies otherwise, use a clamp or pressure device to hold glued joints until the adhesive cures (see page 475).

■ Make sure the materials to be joined are clean. Also, prefit and assemble pieces to ensure that they will fit together tightly when glued. If either material is uneven, the adhesive will only hold the adhesive next to it, not the material.

■ Unless manufacturer's instructions specify otherwise, apply adhesives at temperatures above 70°F.

■ Make sure your gluing area is well-ventilated when using contact cement, rubber-based adhesive, plastic cement, and most mastic adhesives; fumes from these products can be overpowering.

■ Do not use any of the adhesives listed above near open flames, heat, sparks, or other combustion sources.

■ Don't assemble and glue materials on tables and benches that are sprinkled with sawdust, wood chips, metal filings, dust, dirt, oil, or grease.

■ When regluing materials, be sure to clean off all old dried adhesive before applying new adhesive.

■ Never spread adhesive over a surface that is wet with water.

■ Make sure you have the proper applicators for the adhesive: notched trowels for mastics, caulking guns for cartridge-packaged adhesives, and brushes for fluids.

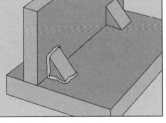

Roughen the surfaces before applying most adhesives. This adds surface area to the joint, strengthening it.

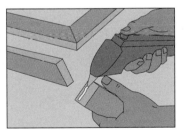

Slip blocks reinforce corner joints, eliminating the need for clamps. Slide blocks back and forth to "set" them.

Hot glue guns have a heating element that melts adhesive cartridges, allowing for quick application of adhesives.

Paneling adhesives, available in cartridges, make quick work of installing bulky sheet material.

Spread floor and wall tile mastics with a notched trowel to control the depth of the mastic. Clean the trowel often during use.

Epoxy putty comes in stick form. To mix it, cut off identical lengths of resin and hardener. Then, knead together like dough.

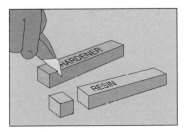

Fastening (continued)

MATERIAL MATTERS · COMPARING ADHESIVES

Type of Adhesive	Primary Use	Holding Power	Water Resistance	Set Time	Cure Time	Adhesive Flex	Type of Applicator
Contact	Plastic laminate, wood veneering, veneer repair	Good	Excellent	Dry, then contact	30 to 48 hours	Soft	Brush, notched trowel, roller
Epoxy	Bonding any material to any material	Excellent	Excellent	5 to 30 minutes	1 to 10 hours	Medium to hard	Cheap brush or frozen dessert stick
Latex-based	Fabric, canvas, carpeting, paper	Fair	Fair	Contact	10 to 60 hours	Soft	Built-in brush or roller
Mastics: latex rosin	ceiling and floor tiles, paneling ceramic, plastic, wood	Good	Good	Contact	2 to 3 days	Soft	Notched trowel or caulking gun
Paste	Wallpaper and other thin paper	Good	Poor	30 minutes	8 to 24 hours	Soft	Brush
Plastic	Wood, glass, plastic, pottery, china, models	Fair	Good	5 minutes to 6 hours	2 days	Medium to hard	Built-in brush
Polyvinyl resin	Wood, plywood, hardboard, paper	Good	Poor	1 to 5 hours	24 to 30 hours	Medium	Built-in brush, frozen dessert stick
Resorcinol, formaldehyde	Wood, plywood, hardboard, paper, chipboard	Excellent	Excellent	7 to 10 hours	24 to 30 hours	Stiff	Cheap brush or frozen dessert stick
Rubber	Wood, concrete, paper, plastic, cork	Fair to Good	Good	Contact	30 to 60 hours	Soft	Brush, notched spreader
Cyanoacrylates (instant bonding)	Rubber, plastic, metal, hardwood, ceramic, glass	Excellent	Fair	Contact to 2 minutes	12 to 24 hours	None	Squeeze tube

REGLUING CHAIRS

Repairing Tight-Fitting Joints

Work the joint apart without further loosening other joints. Scrape off the old glue with a utility knife.

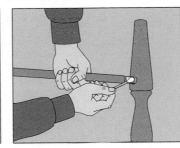

Apply white glue liberally with a cotton swab. Push the joint firmly together and wipe up the excess.

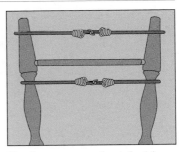

Use bungee cords to hold the joint members firmly together. Don't remove bungee cords for 24 hours.

Repairing Loose-Fitting Joints

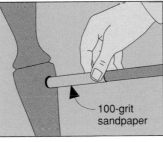

100-grit sandpaper

Remove the loose rung(s). Remove old glue with a utility knife and sandpaper wrapped around a wooden spoon handle.

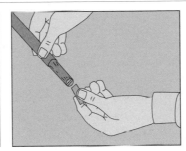

Cut a slot in the end of the rung with a hacksaw. Cut a small wood wedge to the width and length of slot and insert it partway into slot.

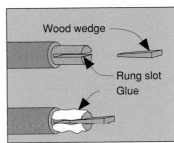

Wood wedge

Rung slot

Glue

Apply white glue to rung and socket. Tap rung in, which drives wedge into and spreads slot to tighten joint. Don't use for 24 hours.

Repairing a Broken Rung

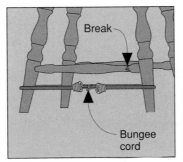

Break

Bungee cord

Clean, then glue both surfaces of the break with white glue. Position carefully and pull together with bungee cords or bar clamp.

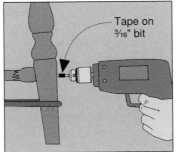

Tape on ³⁄₁₆" bit

Drill a ³⁄₁₆-inch hole through leg into center of rung to ½ inch beyond the break. Use tape on bit to mark the required drilling depth.

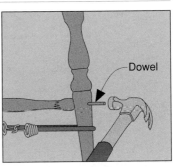

Dowel

Squirt white glue into the hole. Drive a ³⁄₁₆-inch glue-coated dowel all the way into the hole. Cut off excess dowel; let set 24 hours.

Fastening (continued)

MATERIAL MATTERS

What product can clamp, stop leaks, prevent electrical shock and fires, seal, bind, weather-strip, waterproof, trim, insulate—and wrap packages? Tape. Keep a generous supply of electrical, duct, and masking tape on hand. For specialty tasks, choose a tape that's designed to fit the need.

■ Electrical tape can do much more than insulate electrical wires. You can use it to temporarily stop leaks in plumbing pipes, garden hoses, and auto hoses, as well as supply extra gripping power on baseball bats and hammer handles. Because it's so flexible, this tape will conform to almost any irregular surface, except masonry materials.

CHOOSING AND USING TAPE

■ Duct tape, actually a plastic-coated cloth tape, patches plastic, fabric, and metal. But its main job is to seal joints in heating, cooling, and ventilation ducts. It's water- and scuff-resistant, and comes in silver and a number of other colors.

■ Masking tape protects woodwork during painting and wood and metal furniture surfaces while moving.

■ Aluminum foil tape patches metals. Use it, too, as a backup material for auto body repairs and to seal ducts, gutters, and downspouts.

■ Double-faced tape has two sticky sides. Use it for holding light materials together while you saw, drill, nail, or screw. One type is specifically

designed for and exceptionally good at holding down carpet edges.

■ Teflon pipe-joint tape is becoming more popular as a substitute for joint compound to wrap around pipe threads to stop leaks. It also makes nut-and-bolt assembly easier and deters rust, too.

■ Transparent weather-strip tape seals windows, doors, storm windows, and air-conditioners.

■ Plastic decorative tape, in a variety of colors, may be used for minor repair jobs and for decorative accents.

■ Strapping tape, a heavy-duty plastic product, comes in handy for making temporary repairs and sealing and reinforcing packages.

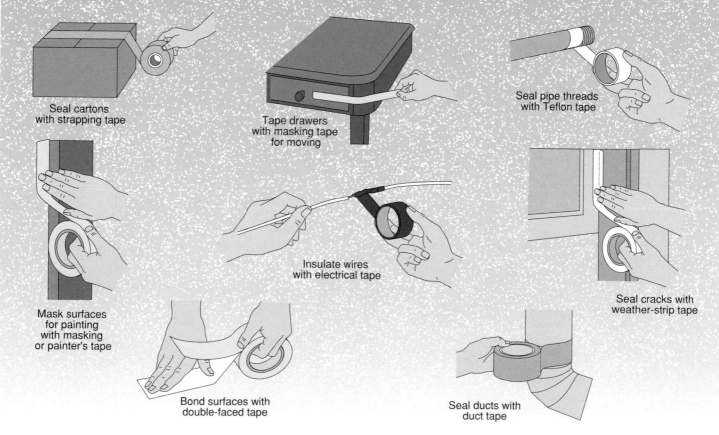

Seal cartons
with strapping tape

Tape drawers
with masking tape
for moving

Seal pipe threads
with Teflon tape

Mask surfaces
for painting
with masking
or painter's tape

Insulate wires
with electrical tape

Seal cracks with
weather-strip tape

Bond surfaces with
double-faced tape

Seal ducts with
duct tape

Holding and Clamping

Pliers, clamps, and vises extend your hands and fingers to let you get a better grip on materials, increase your leverage, or apply pressure. Don't jerry-rig a clamping job rather than using the correct holding or clamping device because you risk injuring yourself or your materials.

Regular slip-joint and needle-nose pliers should be in your basic tool kit. In addition, consider tongue-and-groove pliers, lock-joint pliers, and several different sizes of clamps (see page 475) as the first holding and clamping tools to purchase. Later, you may want to add specialty pliers and clamps, plus a portable or bench-mounted vise.

Workbenches and sawhorses also contribute to holding and clamping needs. Although mechanically different than the tools mentioned, they can help perform the same basic functions.

TOOL TALK

CHOOSING PLIERS

Pliers can be classified as holders, turners, cutters, or a combination of any of those. Holders have smooth jaws or fine serrations. Turners have coarse teeth designed to turn nuts and bolts. Cutters feature smooth jaws with cutting edges to snip wires, nails, and small bolts and screws.

Your tool kit should include at the very least slip-joint pliers and needle-nose pliers. Running a close second are diagonal pliers and tongue-and-groove pliers. After these, your options are almost limitless—lock-joint pliers, lineman's pliers, nippers, and so on. There even are pliers for driving and pulling staples, for forming wire loops, for retrieving small parts that have been dropped in tight quarters, and for precision work.

Quality pliers have machine-milled jaws and are forged from high-carbon steel that has been tempered for durability. When you squeeze the handles together, joints should close smoothly and the jaws should provide a firm, even pressure on the work. Exposed metal parts should be chrome-plated to resist rust and damage. As with other tools, it's best to stay away from the bargain bins when you shop for pliers.

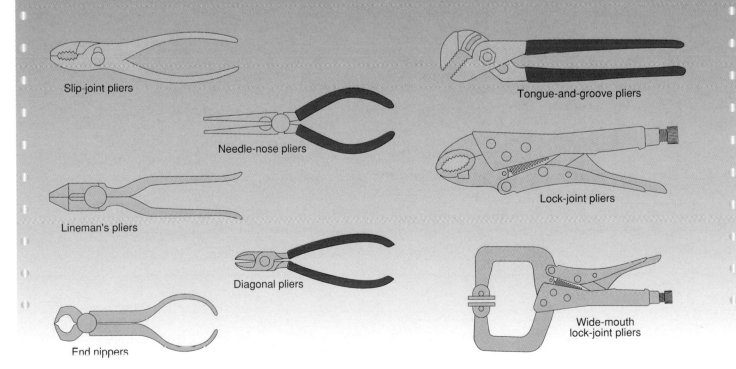

Slip-joint pliers

Needle-nose pliers

Tongue-and-groove pliers

Lineman's pliers

Diagonal pliers

Lock-joint pliers

End nippers

Wide-mouth lock-joint pliers

Holding and Clamping (continued)

USING PLIERS

Matching the tool to the material is the game you play when using pliers. For example, don't use serrated lock-joint pliers to hold wood, because the pressure from the jaws will crush the fibers. Likewise, don't use needle-nose pliers to tighten bolts or to hold a metal rod tightly so it won't rotate.

Pliers are not overachievers, either, so don't expect them to do a holding, turning, or cutting job that rightly belongs to a wrench, vise, or hacksaw. You'll ruin the material, the pliers, or both.

Pliers don't require a lot of maintenance. However, be sure to keep pivot bolts tight, cutters sharp, and jaws and handles free of grease and debris. An occasional buffing with fine steel wool will remove rust and corrosion on metal parts. To avoid rust, wipe pliers occasionally with light oil.

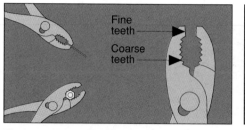

Fine serrations in the jaws of pliers grip small objects. The coarser teeth handle larger jobs. To adjust for bigger bite, move the handle in the slip joint.

Hold pliers with your little finger inside one of the handles, so that as you exert pressure outward with that finger, the jaws open easily.

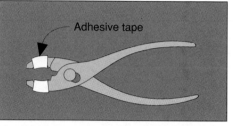

To avoid marring delicate materials, such as softwoods and plastics, use a rag, or wrap jaws with adhesive bandages or tape.

On delicate material, pull small nails with pliers instead of a hammer. For added leverage, use a pulling/rolling-type of motion.

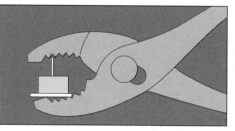

Use pliers to drive brads in small jobs, such as picture frames. Protect the material from the plier jaws with a paper or cardboard pad.

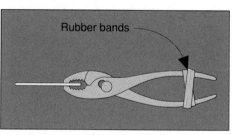

Rubber bands wrapped around the handles transform your pliers into a vise for small projects. Or, better yet, use lock-joint pliers.

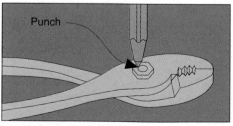

To snug-up a loose pivot bolt, tighten it so it doesn't wobble, then lock the bolt by tapping it with a hammer and a metal punch.

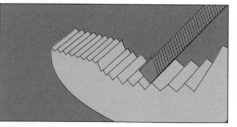

If pliers slip while holding an object, check the jaws to be sure they're clean. If the teeth are stripped, reform them with a triangular file.

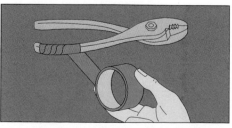

To insulate plier handles for electrical work, wrap them with electrical tape. Tape also adds padding, creating a comfortable grip.

CHOOSING AND USING A VISE

Though not a necessity, a vise is one of those nice-to-have tools you'll eventually want to own. It acts as that extra hand when you need it.

Ideally, it's great to have both a bench vise and a woodworking vise. Unless you're strictly a woodworker, however, spend your money on a bench model. If you don't have a workbench, you can purchase clamp-on vises that you can put on a temporary worktable.

When shopping for a vise, look for one that's made from malleable iron. Inexpensive steel ones will give you trouble.

Mount bench and woodworking vises to workbenches with heavy bolts. If this isn't possible, use lag screws. Never use nails clinched over at the heads.

Because all vises are subjected to sawdust, metal filings, and other material debris, keep the opening/closing screw cleaned and oiled. If the jaws ever wear out or get damaged, install new ones.

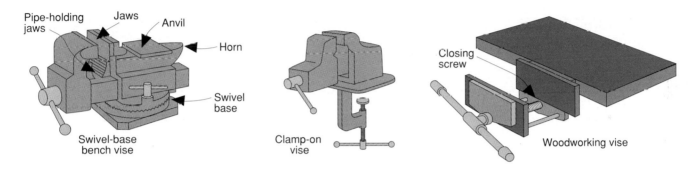

On some bench vises, pipe-holding jaws ride on the screw. Regular jaws hold smooth, flat materials. A swivel base rotates the vise to the desired working position. An anvil serves for peening and smoothing metals; a horn accepts ducts and tubular materials. Jaws on woodworking vises open for capacities from 4 to 7 inches; the 7-inch model is your best buy. Quality woodworking vises have jaw guides and jaws that can be tightened almost with a flip of the handle. Clamp-on vises, which mount on virtually any tabletop, generally have a 2½-inch capacity between their jaws.

MAKING SAWHORSES

Sawhorses are portable workbenches that will save hours of time and pains in your back from bending over material. The sooner you buy or build a pair, the better.

You can buy collapsible sawhorse kits at your hardware store or home center that consist of metal brackets and the required lumber (see drawing below, far right).

But it doesn't take long to construct a set from scratch either. Make the height of your sawhorses 30 inches, setting the legs at a 15-degree angle. Make the length and width of the top rail any size you want, but a 2x8 board 4 feet long makes a stable platform on which to set and work on paneling and sheet goods. You can even add a shelf at the lower leg supports to serve as a tool storage tray.

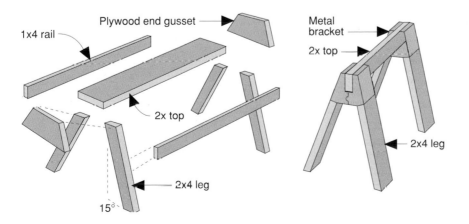

YOU'LL NEED...

SKILLS: Basic carpentry skills.
TIME: 45 to 60 minutes to build sawhorses from scratch.
TOOLS: Tape measure, hammer, saw.

Holding and Clamping (continued)

CHOOSING OR BUILDING A WORKBENCH

If you're just setting up shop, do yourself a big favor and beg, buy, or build a workbench first thing. You can work on projects without one, but having a big, clean work surface makes repair or construction jobs a lot easier.

Commercial benches are worth consideration. They range from simple, steel-and-particleboard arrangements to elaborate versions that would satisfy the most dedicated cabinetmaker or woodworker.

You also can build your own workbench from a kit or from scratch. If you build your own, take a look at what's available in stores. You might pick up design ideas that you can use in a homemade bench.

The workbench shown below is little more than a cut-and-assemble job, yet it's plenty serviceable. Specify your own dimensions to fit available shop space.

The height is important so you won't be bending over more than you need to, and depends on your height. A range of 34 to 40 inches should be in your comfort zone. Width should be 24 to 36 inches. Length will depend on space, although 6 to 8 feet gives you plenty of working area to handle standard-length materials that don't need much cutting.

Fashion the legs from 2×4s or 4×4s; 4×4s are best, with 2×4s to support the top and the shelf. Use 2×6s for the top plank and ¾-inch plywood for the backboard, back, and shelf to supply the necessary strength to stabilize the framing.

For a durable surface, screw a piece of ¼-inch tempered hardboard to the 2×6s. When the surface becomes worn or scratched, turn over the top. When that side outlives its usefulness, replace the sheet.

Assemble the framing with carriage bolts and nail or screw on the shelf and planking.

If you have a clamp-on vise, extend the front of the planking and top so it overhangs the frame by 3 inches to accept the clamp. Bolt a top-mounting vise to the top. Because a woodworking vise attaches to the front rail, provide a proper bearing surface by using a 2×8 there instead of a 2×4.

Cut out and test assemble the parts. Give all the parts, except the hardboard top, two coats of penetrating wood sealer, sanding between coats. Then assemble all the parts.

> ### YOU'LL NEED...
> **SKILLS:** Basic carpentry skills.
> **TIME:** 2 to 3 hours to build a complete bench, excluding drying time for wood sealer.
> **TOOLS:** Tape measure, hammer, saw, drill, screwdriver, adjustable wrench, framing square.

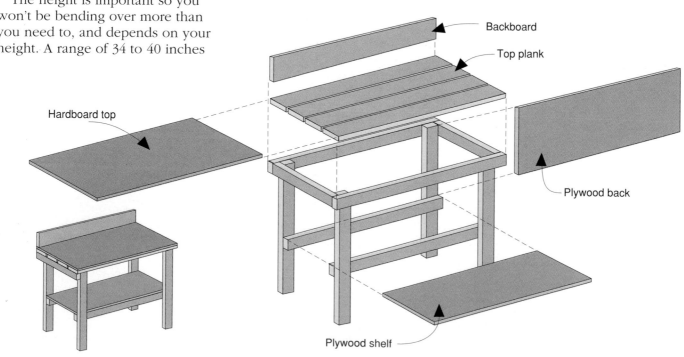

Backboard

Top plank

Hardboard top

Plywood back

Plywood shelf

TOOL TALK

Many adhesives set up quickly, but you still need an assortment of clamps to help with some gluing projects.

For starters, invest in four medium-sized C-clamps and four spring clamps. Add the specialty items—bar, pipe, strap, miter, and handscrew clamps—as you need them. C-clamps, available in aluminum or malleable iron, range in size from 1 to 8 inches, with throat depths ranging from 1 to 3¾ inches. You also can buy special deep-throat clamps.

For light fabrication work, choose spring clamps; they work like big clothespins. Thickness capacities

CHOOSING AND USING CLAMPS

range from 1 to 3 inches, and lengths from 4 to 9 inches.

To glue-assemble wide materials, you'll need pipe clamps. They're sold without pipe, so you'll need to buy galvanized steel pipe in the lengths you want. The clamp parts fit either ½- or ¾-inch pipe.

First cousins to pipe clamps, bar clamps are sold as a unit. To change the capacity of the notched model shown in the sketch, move the back clamp into the different notches, then tighten the screws to exert pressure.

Strap clamps are handy for making furniture, as well as for holding

together objects that are irregular. Miter clamps are used to clamp picture frame corners and for other furniture projects.

Woodworking and cabinetmaking require handscrews. Because the jaws of these clamps are made from maple or selected hardwoods, you never have to add padding to protect the wood you're clamping. You can change the configuration of the handscrews by adjusting the length of one or both of the screws. For most jobs, you'll need at least two handscrews; however, four are ideal if your budget allows.

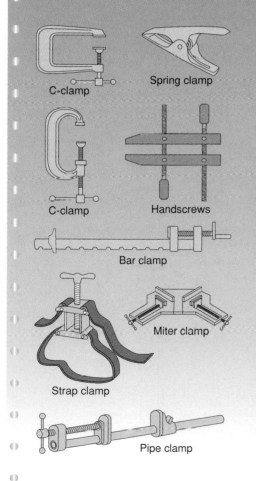

C-clamp

Spring clamp

C-clamp

Handscrews

Bar clamp

Miter clamp

Strap clamp

Pipe clamp

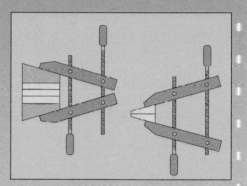
Wood scrap

Work

Protect the material from clamp jaws with thin wood pads. Do not overtighten clamps; finger-tight is tight enough.

Handscrews can hold the work, no matter what the angle. Angle adjustments are made by shortening or lengthening the screws as needed.

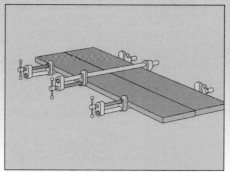

Alternate pipe clamps to equalize pressure and help prevent buckling. Pad the jaws and never overtighten.

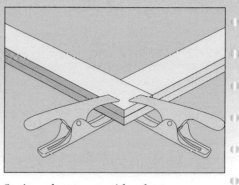

Spring clamps provide plenty of pressure. Use them for holding hanging, cutting, or drilling jobs.

Shaping and Smoothing

Ever wonder why professionally finished work looks that way? Expert drywallers or finish carpenters do their job in much the same way that do-it-yourselfers would. But tradespeople know that it's how you finish a project that counts. That's where smoothing and shaping come in. Most projects benefit from both. The tools to use for these finishing touches are files, rasps, planes, and abrasives.

Knowing what tool to use and where to use it isn't as difficult as it may seem. Choose planes to trim from ¼ to ¾ inch of material from wood. Files and rasps will remove 1/16 to 3/16 inch of material. Abrasives will remove and smooth up to 1/16 inch of material.

TOOL TALK

Files and rasps are basically the same tool, differentiated by their coarseness and the material they're used on. Files remove and smooth wood, metal, and plastic; rasps, on the other hand, finish only wood.

File types take their names from their shapes: flat, round, half-round, triangular, square, diamond, and crossing. Their teeth or "cut" also

CHOOSING FILES AND RASPS

give them away. Rasps feature individually shaped, coarse teeth. File "teeth" are actually a series of grooves cut into the metal. A single-cut file has single teeth or grooves; a double-cut file has crossed rows of teeth; and curved files, not surprisingly, have curved rows of teeth. There also are many gradations of tooth coarseness from which to choose: coarse,

bastard, second cut, smooth cut, and dead smooth.

Specialty items abound in this category. You can buy files for sharpening lawnmower blades; tapered, round files for enlarging and smoothing holes; auger-bit files for sharpening drill bits (see page 453); and even special files for sharpening saw blades (see page 435).

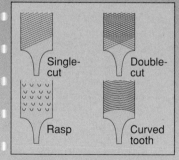

Single- and double-cut files come in degrees of coarseness: coarse and bastard for rough work; second cut for alloys and finish work; and smooth cut for fine finishing. Double-cut files remove more material than single-cut files, which are for smoothing. For removing even more wood, use a rasp for rough shaping, then smooth with an abrasive (see page 480).

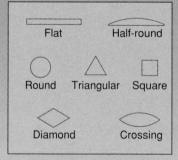

File and rasp shapes often determine which file or rasp to use for what project. For example, a flat file is for general work on metal; a 6-inch triangular file is used for touching up and sharpening saws and other files; a 10-inch round bastard file is used on round openings for metal and some plastics.

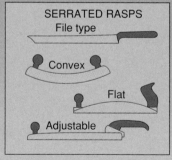

Serrated rasps have a series of tiny cutting blades along a metal strip that looks like a flat file. You can buy them with file-type handles, plane handles, or combination file/plane handles. Serrated rasps cut very quickly for a usable, smooth surface. Their blades last a long time, but when one dulls, throw it away and buy a new one.

A file card has stiff metal bristles on one side for cleaning the teeth of files. The soft metal bristles on the other side are for cleaning wood and plastic debris from the teeth. To deter rust, coat files used on metal with light oil. Don't oil rasps or files used on wood; remove any rust with a wire brush. Keep all tools away from water.

USING FILES AND RASPS

If you furiously saw a file back and forth over your work material, you'll end up with an uneven edge, a dull file, and tired arms. Slow, even strokes are the best technique. If that doesn't do the job, you're using the wrong type of file.

For best results, clamp the work in a vise or clamp it to a firm surface. Keep the work about waist-to-elbow high so you can get the proper leverage on the tool you're using.

Grasp a rasp and all but the smallest files with both hands—one on the handle, the other on the tip. Apply pressure on the forward stroke, and lift it clear or drag it only slightly on the return.

With practice, you'll gain a feel for the right amount of pressure. Too much will jamb the teeth with filings and the file won't cut well; too little won't make any cut. If the pressure exerted is just right, you'll produce a pile of shavings with each stroke.

Because a rasp's job is to remove, not smooth, wood, expect it to leave a rough edge. This tool cuts fast, so check your progress after every few strokes. When you're near your goal, switch to a file or an abrasive for the finishing touches. Files and rasps are rugged tools, but you must store them in such a way that their teeth aren't dulled or damaged by knocking against other tools. Wrap them in cloth or hang them up; don't toss them unprotected into a drawer. When a file finally does dull, replace it—but keep the old one for working softer materials.

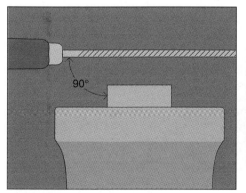

Clamp small work in a vise with the edge to be filed near the jaws. Protect surfaces with wood scraps.

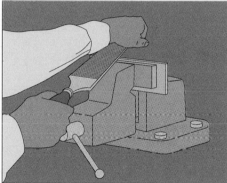

For rough cutting, grip the file on the handle and at the tip to keep the pressure even and guide the file.

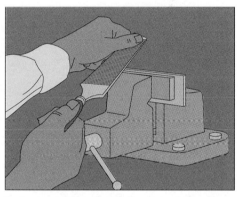

For smoothing, hold the tip of the file between your thumb and forefinger. For best results use lots of light strokes.

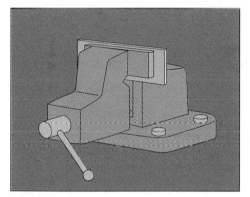

Keep the file perpendicular to the edge you're filing. Don't rock the file, and go completely across the work.

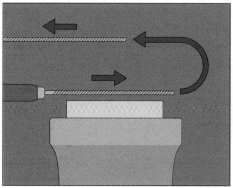

On most jobs, lift the file off the work for the return stroke. On soft metal, drag it back to clear the teeth.

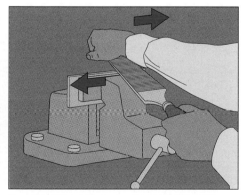

For finishing fine work, push the file across the material at right angles. Use a brush to keep work clean of filings.

Shaping and Smoothing (continued)

TOOL TALK

If you've ever trimmed a binding door or smoothed a rough board or timber, you don't have to be sold on the virtues of a plane.

Obviously, the most important part of a plane is its cutting edge, the blade. Keep it razor sharp so it can produce paper-thin to coarse-thick shavings without much force (see page 479). A dull plane, just like any other dull cutting tool, will drive you to distraction.

For most projects, you need only smoothing and block planes. The other types shown below are required only in woodworking or other specialized projects.

Look for a plane with malleable sides and bottom. Less expensive models won't give you the accuracy and durability required of this tool.

Aside from keeping the blade sharp, a plane requires very little

CHOOSING A PLANE

maintenance. Remove light rust and corrosion from the metal parts with fine steel wool and machine oil. Be sure to clean all oil from the bottom so it doesn't stain wood surfaces.

When you lay down a plane, turn it on its side so the blade can't be dulled accidentally. And when you store one, retract the blade into the body to protect the blade's edge.

Almost every part of a name-brand plane may be replaced; you don't have to buy a brand new one if a part fails. You can even replace handles and knobs by removing a couple of screws that hold them.

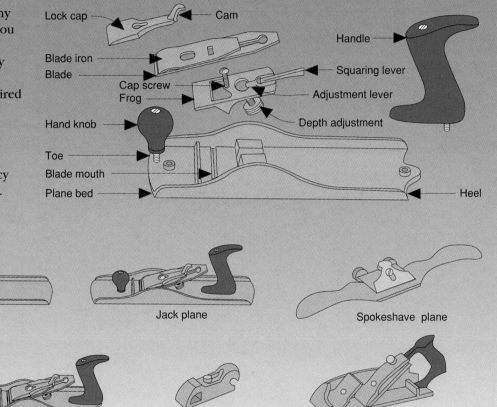

Lock cap · Cam · Handle · Blade iron · Squaring lever · Blade · Cap screw · Adjustment lever · Frog · Hand knob · Depth adjustment · Toe · Blade mouth · Plane bed · Heel

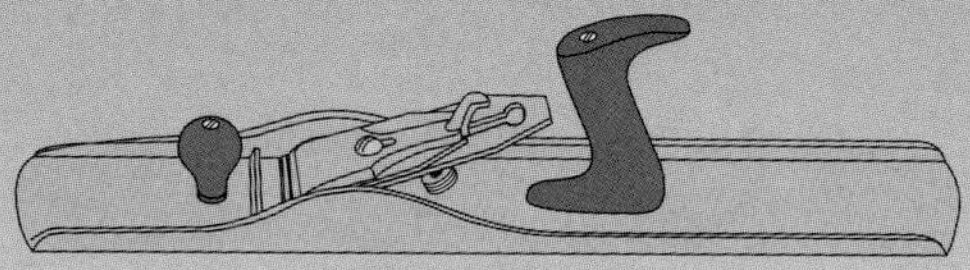

Jointer plane

Jack plane

Spokeshave plane

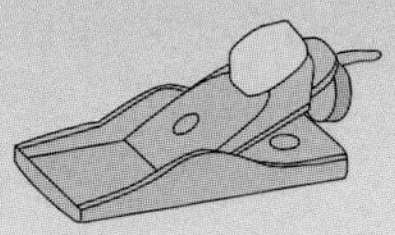

Block plane

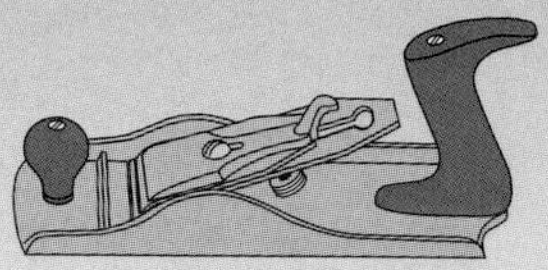

Smoothing plane

Modelmaker's plane

Rabbet plane

A jointer plane squares the edges of materials so they may be joined with adhesive or fasteners. A smoothing plane serves for all-around work and sometimes doubles for both a jointer and jack plane. A jack plane, which is a good general-use plane for both jointing and smoothing, measures from 12 to 15 inches long (compared to 18 and 24 inches for jointers and 7 to 10 inches for smoothers). Use a block plane for end-grain work. A rabbet plane cuts rabbets for joints; a spokeshave planes irregular surfaces and curves. For small planing jobs on wood and soft metal, use a modelmaker's plane.

USING A PLANE

Planes cut best when the work is locked in a vise. If the work is too large for a vise, such as a door, you can wedge one end of it in a corner of the room to help hold it firm.

The trick to using a plane is balance and rhythm. You need both feet firmly planted on the floor to take smooth, even cutting strokes with the plane. The result will be thin, unbroken shavings that are all the same thickness. If the shavings are thick and thin, or if they crumble and break apart, you can bet that the blade is dull or improperly set or that you're off-balance and are jabbing the work.

Planing the edges of soft metals and plastics is similar to planing wood. However, the plane blade must be set to take a very shallow cut, and you must support the material between two pieces of thin wood so the materials won't buckle under the applied pressure.

As a general rule, plane wood just short of the scribed finish line you want to match. Finish the job with an abrasive material stretched over a sandpaper block so you can keep it square to the work (see page 481).

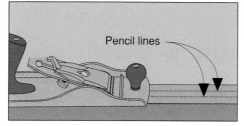

Draw pencil lines on the edge of the piece to be planed. Use them to help locate high spots as you work.

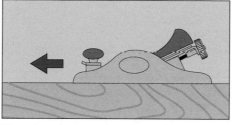

Examine the wood grain to determine its direction. Work with the grain to minimize "snagging."

Begin the stroke by applying most of the pressure to the knob. Complete stroke with pressure on the handle.

Hold the plane at a slight angle to the work. A sharp plane, properly used, will shave off continuous ribbons.

Plane end grain from the sides to the middle to prevent splitting. Then, smooth the hump in the middle.

To bevel an edge, hold the plane at an angle. Mark the depth of the cut first, making a small bevel at the corner.

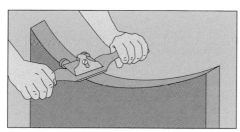

Smooth sharp curves with a spokeshave. Usually, it's best to push a spokeshave along the work rather than pull it.

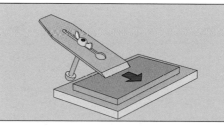

Hone plane blades as you would chisel blades (page 444). You can use the same sharpening jig. Whet burrs.

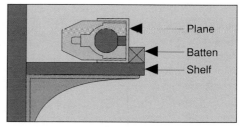

To protect the blade, store the plane on its side. An edge-of-shelf batten keeps it positioned during storage.

Shaping and Smoothing (continued)

CHOOSING ABRASIVES

Funny thing about sandpaper: The sand isn't really sand, but other abrasive granules, and chances are that the paper isn't really paper, but a composition material.

Maybe sandpaper (technically, a coated abrasive) isn't what its name implies, but it's still a smoothing and finishing tool of great importance. A properly selected abrasive saves you plenty of time and effort on many projects around the house. The comparison chart below contains almost everything you might want to know about abrasives—and maybe more than that. Consider it a connoisseur's guide.

For most jobs, selection is relatively easy. Abrasives are classified according to the type of mineral abrasive and its coarseness. Abrasives range from extremely coarse (36 grit or lower) clear up to extremely fine (600 grit). Most manufacturers realize the confusion that surrounds abrasives, so they label packages with information such as "For Metal," "For Plastics," or "For Hardwoods." They also indicate the number and coarseness of the sheets in the package, for example, a package might be labeled, "2 fine, 2 medium, 1 coarse."

MATERIAL MATTERS — COMPARING ABRASIVES

Type	Coarseness Code	Use	Color	Durability	Cost
Aluminum oxide	Extra coarse, 36; coarse, 50–60; medium, 80–100; fine, 120–150; extra fine, 220	Smoothing wood, metal, plastic, fiberglass	Brown	Good to excellent	Moderate
Emery	Fine, medium coarse, extra coarse	Polishing metals	Black	Good	Moderate
Flint	Fine, medium, coarse	Light-duty sanding; sanding tacky surfaces	Yellow-white	Poor	Low
Garnet	Extra coarse, 36; coarse, 50–60; medium, 80–100; fine, 120–150; extra fine, 220	Sanding fine woodworking projects	Red	Good	Moderate
Silicon carbide	Very fine, 180–240; extra fine, 280–320; super fine, 400; ultra fine, 600	Sanding floors, fiberglass, glass, hard plastics, soft metals, and surfaces between coats of finishing liquids	Black	Good to excellent	High
Tungsten carbide	Coarse, medium, fine	Removing stubborn finishes	Red-brown	Excellent	High
Steel wool	coarse, #3; medium coarse, #2; medium, #1; fine, #0; very fine, #00; extra fine, #000; extremely fine, #0000	Removing rust from metal; smoothing surfaces between finishing coats	Black	Fair to good	Moderate
Pumice	Coarse to fine powder	Smoothing finishing coats	White	Excellent	Moderate
Rottenstone	Coarse to fine powder	Smoothing finishing coats	Gray	Excellent	Moderate

USING ABRASIVES

Removing and smoothing material with abrasives is a heavy-light project: You start with a coarse, or heavy, abrasive and finish with a fine, or light, one.

Although not a rule that's etched in stone, you shouldn't skip abrasive sizes. This doesn't mean you should start out with No. 12 aluminum oxide paper and hit every size up to 600. You should, however, go from very coarse to coarse, to medium, to fine, to very fine. You must use your own judgment based on the beginning condition of the material and the final finish desired.

Do not cut abrasive papers with a knife or scissors. Cutting abrasives quickly dulls the edges of your tools. Instead, score the paper or cloth side of the abrasive with an awl or nail, crease it by folding the paper over, then tear it along this creased line on the edge of a hard surface.

Although abrasives can remove a lot of material fast, first determine if another tool will do a better job. Often, you can remove old paint or other finishes faster with paint remover and a scraper than with an abrasive (see pages 571–572).

For general sanding, stock your workshop with very fine to very coarse aluminum oxide abrasives. Include several pads of very fine to medium steel wool. Purchase other abrasives as your projects demand.

Store abrasives flat so the sheets don't curl. Use the sheets until they no longer work; don't throw them away because they're slightly worn.

If you have lots of sanding to do, you can buy abrasives by the box. More about sanding techniques on pages 573–574.

Sand with the grain, holding the abrasive flat with the palm of your hand. Light pressure is adequate.

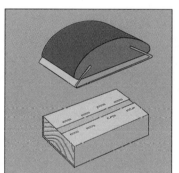

It's best to use a sanding block for more uniform pressure. Buy a block, or staple paper to scrap wood.

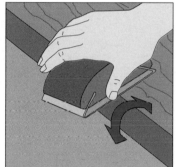

To round the edges of the material you're sanding, rock the sanding block back and forth slightly, as shown.

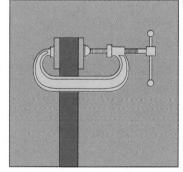

For a perfectly square edge, clamp material between two pieces of scrap. Keep the abrasive square to the edge.

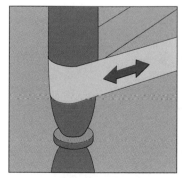

To sand round objects, tear cloth-backed abrasives into long strips; use them as you would a shoeshine cloth.

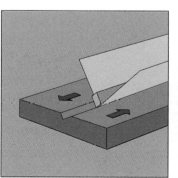

To sand crevices, crease the abrasive, as shown. Use a frozen dessert stick or a thin piece of wood as a block.

Clean clogged paper by slapping it. Or, brush it with a file card. Keep sanding dust off work as you sand.

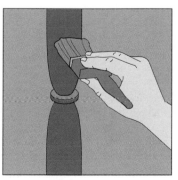

For a super-smooth finish, apply a thin coat of shellac before final sanding. Let dry thoroughly before sanding.

Shaping and Smoothing (continued)

TOOL TALK   CHOOSING AND USING A POWER SANDER

Portable electric sanders supply the continuous back-and-forth muscle power that you need for sanding projects. Just flip the starter switch, press down lightly, and steer. In fact, this equipment does such an efficient job of quickly removing material and smoothing, your biggest problem may be controlling the machine.

An orbital sander has enough spunk to remove excess material quickly. It's designed for smoothing, which it does perfectly. Make an orbital model your first sander purchase; it may satisfy all of your sanding needs.

The sanding pads on orbital sanders "vibrate" in an orbital pattern. They are best suited to flat surfaces on which you don't need to remove a lot of excess material. With special pads, you can use them for buffing and polishing jobs, too.

Straight-line sanders, sometimes called finishing sanders, resemble orbital types, but they vibrate with a simple back-and-forth motion. Many orbital sanders convert to straight-line

action with the flip of a lever, so you can start out in the orbital mode and switch to straight-line sanding for the last few passes.

There are no special tricks to using an orbital sander. Outfit it with a sandpaper pad, then move it with the grain of the material, if possible. Don't apply too much downward pressure; just guide the sander and let it do the work.

A disc sander serves you in several ways. It works for removing excess material and rust from metal. But it's also capable of cutting across wood grain, which makes it an excellent tool for sanding end-grain pieces. Because the disc is flexible, it will go into depressions in wood and metal. If you tilt it, it will sand curves, rounds, and contours. By changing to a wool pad, you can even buff and polish with one.

If you use a disc sander on wood, however, you must hold the disc perfectly square to the work surface. Otherwise, you may mar or cup the

material with the edge of the disc.

Whether you need to buy a disc sander is an iffy question. If you have a ¼- or ⅜-inch drill, you can buy a sanding disc attachment that will function as a disc sander. Such a setup, however, is not well-balanced and doesn't have the same amount of power as a disc sander itself.

If you do a large amount of heavy-duty sanding, a belt sander is the tool to purchase. Or, you can rent this equipment if you're only going to be using it from time to time. If you buy one, make sure it's equipped with a dust bag, an attachment that's worth every penny of the extra cost. It removes a lot of the dust particles from the air and from the material on which you're working. If you use a belt sander to sand floors, panels, and other large surfaces, run it with the grain of the wood, changing belts from medium-grit to fine-grit abrasive.

When you use a power sander, always wear a safety mask to prevent breathing in fine dust particles.

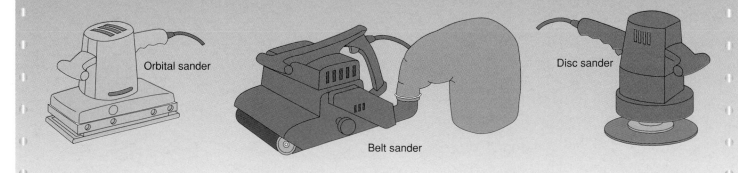

Orbital sander

Belt sander

Disc sander

Electric disc and orbital sanders are comparable in price; belt sanders are more expensive. Because they're lightweight, disc and orbital sanders work well on both horizontal and vertical surfaces. It's difficult to control a belt sander on a vertical surface. Sanding belts for belt sanders often are classified as coarse, medium, and fine, rather than by number.

Features to look for on all three types are locking trigger switches, quick abrasive-paper-changing systems, and dust bag collectors.

TOOL TALK

If it weren't for its relatively high cost, a lathe would be a worthwhile tool just for the fun and enjoyment it provides. Pushing a round-nose lathe chisel into a block of spinning wood and watching the chips fly is exciting. You see the fruits of your labors materialize in a few short moments.

For the serious woodworker or hobbyist who enjoys making furniture, a lathe is much more than

CHOOSING A LATHE

just fun. Not only can you turn squares into rounds with amazing speed and accuracy, but you can create flat, round items, such as dishes, trays, and lamp bases. For these operations, you need a faceplate that fastens onto a lathe's headstock.

A variable-speed motor is an important feature for a lathe. Use high speeds for finishing cuts on small stock, slow speeds on large stock.

Lathe capacity is also important. To handle most woodworking projects, a lathe should have 30 inches between the headstock and tailstock. Of course, this doesn't pertain to small modelmaker's lathes, for which capacity isn't a factor. A lathe also should have sufficient turning diameter capacity for round items. This is the clearance between the headstock and tailstock spindle and the bed of the lathe. The lathe's tool rest should be wide enough (12 inches or more) so you don't have to continually move it along the bed of the lathe to make the necessary cuts.

Basic shaping tools, or turning gouges, include a round-nose chisel for shaping; a gouge for shaping rough work and cutting coves; a skew chisel for smoothing; a parting chisel for straight cuts; and a spear chisel for duplicating contours in the stock.

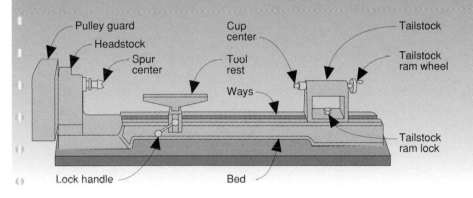

TOOL TALK

A jointer, also called a jointer-planer, is a tool for the serious craftsperson. You wouldn't use a jointer for routine home maintenance.

A jointer's task is to plane the edges of boards perfectly square so they can be joined with other square boards. It cuts rabbets, chamfers, bevels, tapers, and tenons. If the boards are narrow, it even can plane their faces.

A jointer's working part is a steel cylinder containing cutting knives. The jointer's front bed is adjustable, enabling you to set the depth of cut. You can adjust the fence, too, making it possible to cut angles on either the edge or the face of a piece of wood.

CHOOSING A JOINTER

Features to look for include a well-machined table and fence, quick-adjustment levers, and the largest capacity you can afford. Look for high-speed ground steel knives and at

least a ½-horsepower motor for the necessary speed and power. Other nice features are leveling feet for the stand and positive fence stops at 45 and 90 degrees.

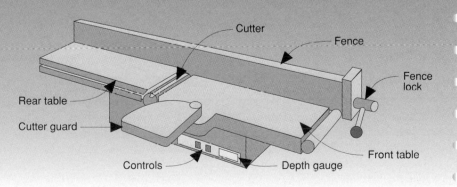

MATERIALS AND HOW TO USE THEM

If you've ever ordered materials for a home improvement project, the first time you did you probably faced unfamiliar terminology and an astounding array of products from which to choose. Getting to know that terminology and learning how to order lumber, plywood, molding, glass, plastic, and other building products efficiently and cost-effectively is the thrust of this chapter. In addition, this section includes tips and techniques for working with the materials after you buy them.

Choosing and Buying Lumber

Learning to be a smart lumber buyer begins with an understanding of some basic things about lumber. First, lumber is boards of solid wood, not paneling or plywood, and is classified as either a softwood or a hardwood (see pages 490–491).

Second, lumber has nominal dimensions and actual dimensions. For example, when you order a 2×4, you get a piece of wood that actually measures 1½ inches thick and 3½ inches wide.

Why the difference? The answer lies in the way lumber is readied for market. Shrinkage is responsible for part of the loss. Air-drying, once the accepted means of reducing the moisture content of lumber, is a thing of the past. Largely due to ever-increasing demand, most lumber now is kiln-dried, a faster method that also introduces more shrinkage. Because of the way lumber is cut out of the tree grain, shrinkage only affects the thickness and width of a board. The length remains nearly the same after drying.

Milling, the process of dressing the wood after sawing to the rough size, accounts for the remainder of the missing material. Most lumber is milled (shaved) on all four surfaces to smooth all the sides.

Third, all lumber is graded. As with most things, the better the quality, the more it costs. This explains the often-bewildering cost differential between two seemingly identical items.

Hardwoods are graded as firsts and seconds (FAS), selects, or No. 1 common. Softwoods, the type you'll buy most often, break down into select lumber and common lumber. Select lumber (B and better, C, and D) has two good faces, making it ideal for "showy" projects. Use common lumber (No. 1, No. 2, No. 3, and No. 4) for all of your other building needs. Your lumber dealer will be able to help you determine the grade of lumber you need for a given project.

UNDERSTANDING LINEAR AND BOARD FEET

Many lumberyards still price lumber by the board foot. One board foot equals a piece of wood 1 inch thick, 12 inches long, and 12 inches wide (see the sketch at right). However, except when ordering hardwoods, you needn't worry about board feet. Simply tell the salesperson the number of linear (actual) feet you need, and he or she will compute the cost.

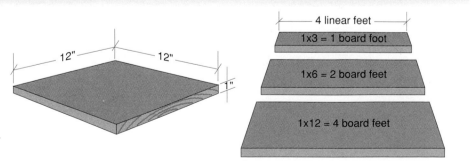

12"   12"   1"

4 linear feet
1x3 = 1 board foot
1x6 = 2 board feet
1x12 = 4 board feet

ORDERING LUMBER

Waiting in line at a lumberyard behind people who don't know quite what they need for their project isn't anyone's idea of fun. Nor is being the person in doubt.

So, before going to place your order, make a list of the items you need.

When jotting down your lumber needs, always put the number of pieces of a particular item first, then list the thickness, width, and length. If you do this, you'll be speaking the salesperson's language and will avoid confusion.

MATERIAL MATTERS   ASKING FOR THE CORRECT MATERIALS

What It's Called	Uses	Size, inches Nominal	Actual
Strips (Furring) Wood less than 2 inches thick and 3 inches wide; some unpatterned molding	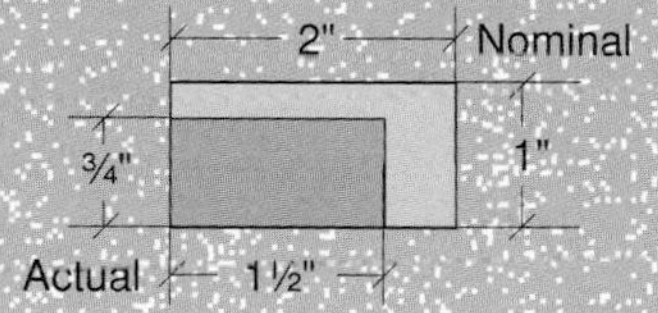 Furring for panels, trim, shims, bridging, stakes, forming, crating, battens, spacers, lattice	1×2 1×3	¾×1½ ¾×2½
Boards Wood less than 2 inches thick and more than 3 inches wide	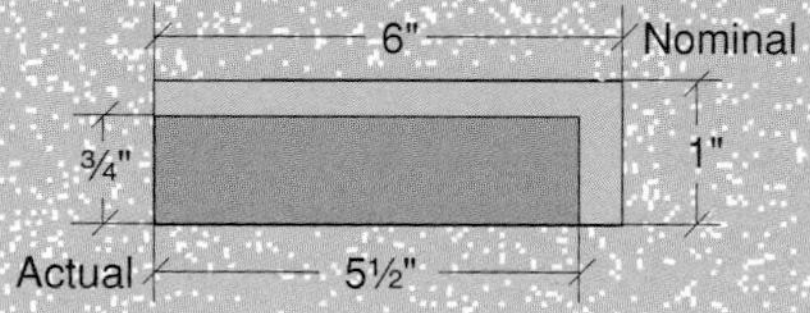 Paneling, trim, shelving, forming, siding, fascias, soffits, flooring, decking, fencing, casing, cabinets, furniture, closet lining, racks, subflooring	1×4 1×6, 1×8 1×10 1×12	¾×3½ ¾×5½ ¾×7½ ¾×9½ ¾×11½
Dimension Lumber Wood 2 inches thick and 2 inches or more wide; studs are 3, 4, or 6 inches wide; planks, 8 inches or more wide	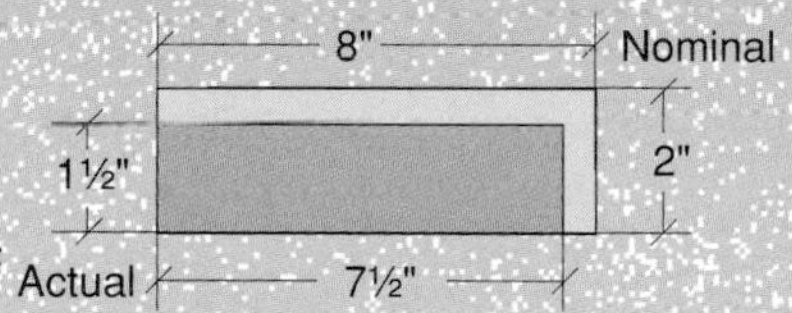 Structural framing and finishing, forming, decking, fencing, walks, benches, screeds, steps, boxed columns	2×3 2×4 2×6 2×8 2×10 2×12	1½×2½ 1½×3½ 1½×5½ 1½×7½ 1½×9½ 1½×11½
Posts Square in cross-section	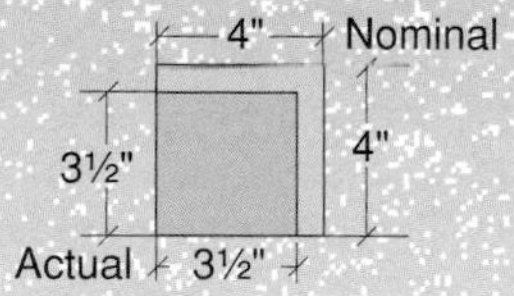 Structural framing and supports, columns, fencing, decking, turnings for wood lathes, decorative items	4×4 6×6	3½×3½ 5½×5½
Timbers 5 inches or larger in the smallest dimension	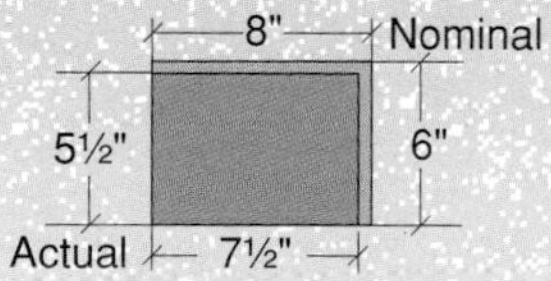 Structural framing, columns, architectural members; decorative items	Varies	Nominal less ½ inch
Matched Lumber Edges and/or ends are tongue-and-grooved	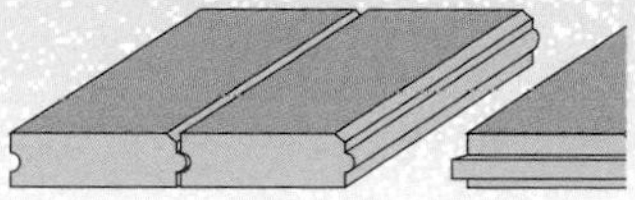 Subflooring, flooring, sheathing	Varies	
Shiplap Edges are rabbeted to form a strong, smooth joint	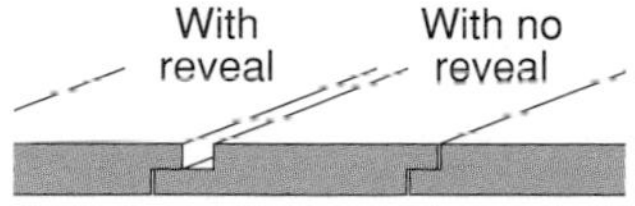 Sheathing, siding, decking, underlayment, finishing; panels with shiplapped edges	1×4 1×6 1×8	¾×3⅛ ¾×5⅛ ¾×6⅛

Choosing and Buying Lumber (continued)

SIZING STRUCTURAL LUMBER

A simple deck illustrates perfectly the concepts of structure from the ground up. The interface with the ground is called the foundation. In the case of a deck, this usually is no more than concrete footings in the ground. Rising from the foundation are vertical posts. Horizontal beams rest on or are bolted to the posts. A series of parallel joists rest on the beams at right angles; they serve to reduce the span. Flat-laid decking boards span the joists and provide a deck upon which to walk.

Continuing from the deck (or floor) up for a building, walls consisting of posts and studs transfer the support upward to a wall top plate. On the top plate may rest a second-story deck, identical to the first. If the building is multistory, the whole sequence will be repeated as

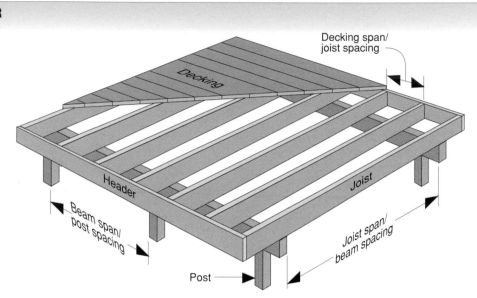

many times as there are stories. At the ceiling level of the topmost story, ceiling joists support the ceiling finish and, if desired, an attic

floor. Finally, a roof—looking very much like a sloping deck—shields the building from weather. For the roof, the "joists" are called rafters.

UNDERSTANDING NOMINAL VERSUS ACTUAL SIZE

When you first measure a 2×4 and discover that it actually measures $1\frac{1}{2}$ inches × $3\frac{1}{2}$ inches, your first thought might be that the lumberyard cheated you. But there is a valid reason for the discrepancy. When a 2×4 is first sawn from the log, its rough-sawn dimensions actually are 2 inches × 4 inches. Because rough-sawn lumber is inexpensive, many rural buildings are still constructed of it. To grade the lumber and guarantee its dimensions, however, the lumber must be dried and planed, both of which reduce its thickness and width.

NOMINAL VERSUS FINISHED SIZES OF LUMBER				
	Nominal Size, inches		**Finished Size, inches**	
Product	**Thickness**	**Width**	**Thickness**	**Width**
Dimension	2	2	$1\frac{1}{2}$	$1\frac{1}{2}$
Lumber	3	3	$2\frac{1}{2}$	$2\frac{1}{2}$
	4	4	$3\frac{1}{2}$	$3\frac{1}{2}$
		5		$4\frac{1}{2}$
		6		$5\frac{1}{2}$
		8		$7\frac{1}{4}$
		10		$9\frac{1}{4}$
		12		$11\frac{1}{4}$
Boards	1	3	$\frac{3}{4}$	$2\frac{1}{2}$
	$1\frac{1}{4}$	4	1	$3\frac{1}{2}$
		5		$4\frac{1}{2}$
		6		$5\frac{1}{2}$

SELECTING AND SIZING STRUCTURAL MEMBERS

Determining the required sizes of structural members is not as difficult as you probably imagine. In the case of a deck, it is a simple five-step process, proceeding from the selection of the deck down to the size of the posts. The procedure and the tables that follow are general, and we use a deck as an illustration. In addition, the last section (see page 489) shows how to size material for roof rafters.

Selecting Wood Species

There are three considerations in selecting a species group for structural lumber: price, strength, and exposure to the elements.

For a deck, exposure is critical. So, select pressure-treated southern yellow pine, group A in the chart, with a fiber stress in bending (Fb) of 1,200 pounds per square inch (psi).

SPECIES GROUPS (#2 OR BETTER GRADE)			
Group	Wood Species	Fb single	Fb repetitive
A	**Southern yellow pine Douglas fir; western larch**	**1,200 psi**	1,400 psi
B	Douglas fir, south; western hemlock; white fir	1,000 psi	1,150 psi
C	Western pines, cedars, redwood, spruces	875 psi	1,000 psi

Selecting Decking Span

Pressure-treated decking usually is available as either ⁵⁄₄ stock or 2×6 dimension lumber. We'll take the more elegant and slightly less expensive ⁵⁄₄-inch decking, which by the chart at right has a maximum span of 24 inches between joists.

MAXIMUM DECKING SPAN BETWEEN JOISTS			
Decking	Species A	Species B	Species C
1-inch boards	16"	Not recommended	Not recommended
⁵⁄₄-inch boards	**24"**	16"	Not recommended
2x3	28"	24"	20"
2x4	32"	24"	16"
2x6	32"	32"	24"

Selecting Joist Span

The ⁵⁄₄ decking we selected will span 24 inches between supports. That means the joists cannot be more than 24 inches apart, on-center.

Now, we have to determine what size joists to use and how much distance they can span between supporting beams. From the chart at right, you can see that if we use joists from species group A set at a 24-inch spacing, we have a choice of four joist sizes, ranging in maximum span from 7 feet, 11 inches to 16 feet 2 inches.

The deck we have in mind is 20 feet wide. If we selected 2×8 joists, they could span the width in two bays of 10 feet each.

MAXIMUM JOIST SPANS BETWEEN BEAMS				
Species Group	Joist Size, inches	Beam Spacing, inches on-center, based on		
		16" joist spacing	24" joist spacing	32" joist spacing
A	2×6	9' 9"	7' 11"	6' 2"
	2×8	12' 10"	**10' 6"**	8' 1"
	2×10	16' 5"	13' 4"	10' 4"
	2×12	19' 11"	16' 2"	12' 7"
B	2×6	8' 7"	7' 0"	5' 8"
	2×8	11' 4"	9' 3"	7' 6"
	2×10	14' 6"	11' 10"	9' 6"
	2×12	17' 6"	14' 5"	11' 6"
C	2×6	7' 9"	6' 2"	5' 0"
	2×8	10' 2"	8' 1"	6' 8"
	2×10	13' 0"	10' 4"	8' 6"
	2×12	15' 9"	12' 7"	10' 2"

Choosing and Buying Lumber (continued)

SELECTING AND SIZING STRUCTURAL MEMBERS (continued)
Selecting Beam Span

We now have to select what size beams we need and how far they can span between supporting posts. Because our beams can be no farther apart than 10 feet, we need either three beams (one at each end, plus one in the middle) or two beams and a ledger against the side of the house.

The next chart shows the possible beam sizes and posts spacings. Assume your deck is 20×24 feet. The beams run the length of the deck, 24 feet. Thus, we need to look in the chart under the 10-foot beam spacing for a post spacing that divides nearly evenly into 24 feet. We find two choices: 3×12 or 4×10, each spanning 8 feet. With a quick call to the lumberyard (or a previous scouting trip), we know that 4×10s are more likely to be in stock, so, that's our choice.

Species Group	Beam Size, inches	5'	6'	7'	8'	9'	10'	11'	12'
MAXIMUM BEAM SPANS BETWEEN POSTS					Post Spacing, Based on Beam Spacing of				
A	3×8	8'	7'	6'	6'	6'	—	—	—
	3×10	10'	9'	8'	8'	7'	7'	6'	6'
	3×12	12'	11'	10'	9'	9'	8'	8'	8'
	4×6	6'	6'	—	—	—	—	—	—
	4×8	9'	8'	7'	7'	6'	6'	6'	—
	4×10	11'	10'	9'	9'	8'	**8'**	7'	7'
	4×12	—	12'	12'	11'	10'	10'	9'	9'
	6×10	—	—	—	12'	11'	10'	10'	10'
B	3×8	7'	6'	6'	—	—	—	—	—
	3×10	9'	8'	7'	7'	6'	6'	6'	—
	3×12	11'	10'	9'	8'	8'	7'	7'	7'
	4×6	6'	—	—	—	—	—	—	—
	4×8	8'	7'	7'	6'	6'	—	—	—
	4×10	10'	9'	8'	8'	7'	7'	7'	6'
	4×12	12'	11'	10'	10'	9'	9'	8'	8'
	6×10	—	12'	11'	10'	10'	9'	9'	9'
C	3×8	6'	—	—	—	—	—	—	—
	3×10	8'	7'	6'	6'	6'	—	—	—
	3×12	10'	9'	8'	7'	7'	7'	6'	6'
	4×8	7'	6'	6'	—	—	—	—	—
	4×10	9'	8'	8'	7'	7'	6'	6'	6'
	4×12	11'	10'	9'	9'	8'	8'	7'	7'
	6×10	12'	11'	10'	9'	9'	8'	8'	8'

Selecting Post Sizes

To determine post size needed to support a certain height deck, we need to calculate the deck area that will be supported by each post. For an intermediate post, this equals the area of a rectangle whose sides are the on-center beam spacing and the on-center post spacing. For our deck, that is 10×8 feet, or 80 square feet. Rounding up to 84 square feet, the chart shows that a group A 4×4 can extend 10 feet in height without being braced from the side.

Species Group	Post Size, inches	36	48	60	72	84	96	108	120
MAXIMUM UNSUPPORTED POST HEIGHTS					Post Height, Based on Deck Area Supported, sq. ft.				
A	4×4	12'	12'	12'	12'	**10'**	10'	10'	8'
	4×6	—	—	—	—	7'	7'	6'	6'
	6×6	—	—	—	—	—	—	—	—
B	4×4	12'	12'	10'	10'	10'	8'	8'	8'
	4×6	—	—	12'	12'	12'	10'	10'	10'
	6×6	—	—	—	—	—	12'	12'	12'
C	4×4	12'	10'	10'	8'	8'	8'	6'	6'
	4×6	—	12'	12'	10'	10'	10'	8'	8'
	6×6	—	—	—	12'	12'	12'	12'	12'

SIZING ROOF RAFTERS

Rafters are similar to floor joists in that they must be designed to carry uniformly distributed loads across horizontal spans. What then are the loads and span? The span is not the length of the rafter. The span is the horizontal distance that the rafter spans from support to support (see drawing). Load is the maximum weight of snow (pounds per square feet) on the horizontal area covered by the roof. Your local building inspector can tell you the snow load in your region of the country.

Example: What size group C ($Fb = 1,000$ psi) rafter will span 10 feet with a snow load of 40 pounds per square foot? Answer: 2×8 rafters spaced 16 inches on center or 2×10s spaced at 24 inches

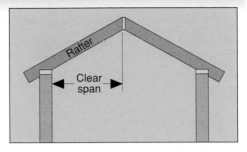

MAXIMUM RAFTER SPANS (ASSUMING ROOF WEIGHS 10 POUNDS PER SQUARE FOOT)

Spacing, inches	Rafter Size	Fiber Stress in Bending, Fb, psi					
		1,000	1,200	1,400	1,600	1,800	2,000
Snow Load 20 psf							
16	2×6	11' 3"	12' 4"	13' 3"	14' 3"	15' 1"	15' 11"
	2×8	14' 9"	16' 2"	17' 6"	18' 8"	19' 9"	20' 10"
	2×10	18' 11"	20' 8"	22' 4"	23' 11"	25' 5"	26' 9"
24	2×6	9' 2"	10' 0"	10' 10"	11' 7"	12' 3"	13' 0"
	2×8	12' 1"	13' 3"	14' 3"	15' 3"	16' 3"	17' 1"
	2×10	15' 5"	16' 11"	18' 3"	19' 6"	20' 8"	21' 10"
Snow Load 30 psf							
16	2×6	9' 9"	10' 8"	11' 6"	12' 4"	13' 1"	13' 9"
	2×8	12' 10"	14' 0"	15' 2"	16' 3"	17' 3"	18' 2"
	2×10	16' 4"	17' 11"	19' 4"	20' 8"	21' 11"	23' 1"
24	2×6	7' 11"	8' 8"	9' 5"	10' 0"	10' 7"	11' 2"
	2×8	10' 5"	11' 5"	12' 4"	13' 2"	14' 0"	14' 9"
	2×10	13' 4"	14' 8"	15' 10"	16' 10"	17' 11"	18' 10"
Snow Load 40 psf							
16	2×6	8' 8"	9' 6"	10' 3"	11' 0"	11' 8"	12' 3"
	2×8	**11' 5"**	12' 6"	13' 7"	14' 5"	15' 4"	16' 2"
	2×10	14' 8"	16' 0"	17' 4"	18' 7"	19' 8"	20' 9"
24	2×6	7' 1"	7' 9"	8' 5"	8' 11"	9' 6"	10' 0"
	2×8	9' 4"	10' 3"	11' 1"	11' 10"	12' 6"	13' 2"
	2×10	**11' 11"**	13' 1"	14' 2"	15' 1"	16' 0"	16' 10"
Snow Load 50 psf							
16	2×6	7' 11"	8' 8"	9' 5"	10' 0"	10' 7"	11' 2"
	2×8	10' 5"	11' 5"	12' 4"	13' 2"	14' 0"	14' 9"
	2×10	13' 4"	14' 8"	15' 10"	16' 10"	17' 11"	18' 10"
24	2×6	6' 6"	7' 1"	7' 8"	8' 3"	8' 9"	9' 2"
	2×8	8' 6"	9' 4"	10' 1"	10' 9"	11' 5"	12' 0"
	2×10	10' 11"	11' 11"	12' 11"	13' 10"	14' 8"	15' 5"

Choosing and Buying Lumber (continued)

SELECTING SOFTWOODS

When ordering softwoods, there's not much selecting to be done. Suppliers save money by stocking just a few varieties. That's not to say that you can't get most any softwood you want, but it may require special ordering and increased cost.

Softwood, which comes from coniferous trees, is less expensive than hardwood. Although redwood is very expensive, its beauty and durability may be worth the price.

Cost also depends on the grade of the wood you purchase. The more knot-free the board, the more it will cost. Any milling of the material, such as grooving or brushing, or if a sealer has been applied, increases the cost even more.

Some lumberyards and home centers frown on customers who pick and choose pieces of lumber. If your home center lets you do so, great. But even with those that discourage it, you should not hesitate to reject any piece that's useless (see page 494).

Most softwoods have rough, splintered, or split ends that should be cut off before use. Be sure to allow for this when you order.

Because of customer preference, many home centers and building material outlets "price-stamp" lumber by the piece. If you're starting a large project that will require lots of lumber, however, ask the retailer for a "contractor's price."

Don't overlook bargains in used lumber. You may find it available at the wrecking site of an old building or advertised in your newspaper classified section. The lumber may look old and dirty, but underneath that grime, often you'll find strong, seasoned wood. You even may find some dirt-disguised lengths of hardwood, such as walnut, oak, hickory, cherry, or maple. Years ago, builders often used these fine materials for structural members.

MATERIAL MATTERS · CHOOSING SOFTWOOD LUMBER

Species	Outstanding Properties	Cost	Common Uses
Cedar	Easy to work; resists shrinking, swelling, and warping; has natural resistance to rot	Moderate close to where it's logged; fairly expensive elsewhere	Trim, paneling, decks, exterior walks, fencing
Redwood	Easy to work; finishes well; has natural resistant to rot; weathers beautifully	Moderate to expensive where logged; very expensive elsewhere; save by using common grades	Trim, paneling, decks, exterior walks, fencing, furniture; use heartwood for posts and near ground.
Fir, spruce, pine	Easy to work; excellent strength; finishes well; pine has some resistance to decay	Moderate; usually inexpensive where logged	House framing, trim, paneling, decking, fencing, furniture, millwork; below-ground, use treated lumber (see page 492).
Cypress	Easy to work with hand and power tools; good strength; finishes well; has excellent natural resistance to decay	Moderate to expensive; limited quantity in some areas	Trim, paneling, fencing, decking, posts, some furniture, hobby use
Hemlock	Easy to work with hand and power tools; uniform grain; natural resistance to decay	Moderate	Framing, paneling, decking, sheathing, subflooring, general utility lumber

SELECTING HARDWOODS

For generations, people have been fascinated by the beauty of hardwood. Hardwood is used for interior trim, fine furniture, door veneer, plywood panels, tabletops, strip and parquet flooring, and a variety of accents.

Hardwoods are expensive and in short supply compared to softwoods. The reason: The deciduous trees that produce hardwoods grow slowly. Demand easily can outstrip the available supply. That's why much more softwood (or hardwood veneers over softwood frames) is used for projects formerly reserved solely for hardwood.

Average home center stores do not stock much hardwood, in the form of either lumber or sheet goods. Some may have a limited supply of selected fast-selling items, but your best bet is a supplier who specializes in hardwoods. Such dealers can get you just about any type of wood you want.

When hardwood is harvested, it's cut into random lengths and widths rather than standardized units to make the best possible use of all the available wood. Thicknesses range from 1 inch to 2 inches.

Hardwood lumber also has both nominal and actual dimensions. When you place an order, realize that a 1-inch piece of stock won't measure quite an inch thick. Likewise, a $\frac{5}{4}$ (1¼-inch-thick) piece will be slightly thinner after milling. The same applies to widths. If you're ordering woodwork trim, don't expect to find all of the pieces cut to the same length. You'll get what's in stock or pay a premium for the lumberyard's cutting trouble.

MATERIAL MATTERS   CHOOSING HARDWOOD LUMBER

Species	Outstanding Properties	Cost	Common Uses
Ash	Easy to work; strong; flexible; holds fasteners well	Medium	Furniture, especially chair parts
Oak	Requires sharp hand and power tools to work; hard, open grain; finishes well; resists water and moisture	Medium	Flooring, furniture, decorative structural supports, trim, barrels, stair railings
Mahogany	Easy to work; fine grain; finishes well; good resistance to warping, swelling, and shrinking	Medium to expensive	Furniture, cabinets, moldings, boats, facings, plywood inlays and veneers
Poplar	Holds paint and stain well	Medium	Furniture, trim, cabinets
Maple, birch	Easy to work; closed grain; finishes well; good resistance to swelling and shrinking; strong and hard	Expensive	Furniture, flooring, moldings, cabinets, inlays, veneers, facings
Walnut	Easy to work; especially strong and durable; finishes well; fine grain; resists warping and swelling	Very expensive	Furniture, cabinets, flooring and paneling veneers, molding, facings
Teak	Requires very sharp tools to work; extremely hard and durable; resistant to rot, swelling, warping	Very expensive	Furniture, cabinets, flooring and paneling veneers, boat construction, trim

Choosing and Buying Lumber (continued)

USING TREATED WOOD FOR OUTDOOR PROJECTS

Pressure-treated lumber is graded structural lumber that has had chemical preservatives forced deep into its fibers under pressure to make it nearly immune to dry rot and insects.

The species you are likely to find depends on where you live. In the East it likely will be southern yellow pine; in the West, ponderosa pine, Douglas fir, or Engleman spruce.

The preservative used on wood is chromated copper arsenic (CCA). While less dangerous than the once-used pentachlorophenol, CCA still can be irritating to human skin; when working with it, abide by the guidelines in the right-hand column.

CCA gives wood a green tinge, but sun and rain will bleach it to a silver gray within about a year. You may want to wait and see before staining. Brown-colored treated wood is now available also.

READING THE AWPB QUALITY STAMP

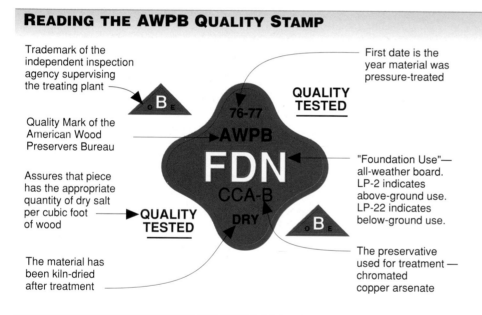

Trademark of the independent inspection agency supervising the treating plant

Quality Mark of the American Wood Preservers Bureau

Assures that piece has the appropriate quantity of dry salt per cubic foot of wood

The material has been kiln-dried after treatment

First date is the year material was pressure-treated

"Foundation Use"— all-weather board. LP-2 indicates above-ground use. LP-22 indicates below-ground use.

The preservative used for treatment — chromated copper arsenate

KNOWING RETENTION LEVELS

Not all pressure-treated wood has been treated equally. The retention level of CCA-treated lumber is the amount of chemical forced into the lumber in pounds per cubic foot.

The chart at right lists the retention levels recommended for different uses. Most of the treated lumber you will find at home centers and lumberyards is LP-22, suitable for decks and ground contact, but not burial. You may have to special-order lumber of other levels.

RETENTION LEVELS	
Retention Level	Recommended Use
0.25 (LP-2)	Above ground
0.40 (LP-22)	Ground contact
0.60 (FDN)	All-weather wood foundations
0.80	Freshwater docks and pilings
2.50	Saltwater docks and pilings

USING PRESSURE-TREATED LUMBER IN APPLICATIONS

The drawings below show some of the many applications in which you should use rot- and insect-resistant pressure-treated wood. Numbers in the text refer to the numbers in the illustrations below.

1. Supporting members in direct contact or embedded in earth.

2. Beams less than 12 inches and joists less than 18 inches above ground level.

3. Plates, sills, and sleepers laid on masonry in contact with earth.

4. Posts and columns on masonry.

5. Girder ends in masonry walls without ½ inch airspace.

6. Permanent wood structures less than 6 inches from the soil.

7. Structural members supporting permeable roofs or floors.

8. Wooden retaining or crib walls.

9. All-weather wood foundations.

10. Structural supports of buildings, decks, balconies, exterior stairs, and porches that are exposed to weather without protection from roof, overhang, or other cover.

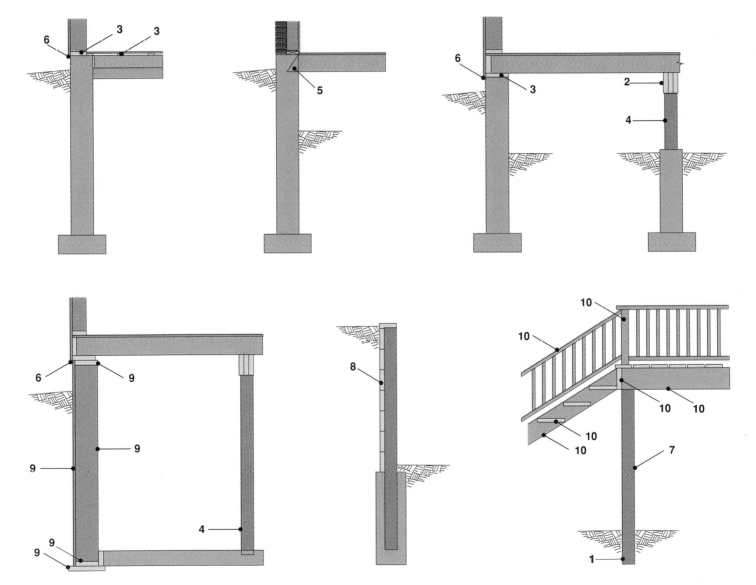

Working with Lumber

Lumber is a wonderfully diverse material. It supports, joins, attaches, frames, and covers like no other material—and at a cost that's not prohibitive. But it's up to you, the woodworker, to make the lumber live up to its full potential.

The previous section briefed you on lumber terminology, how to purchase it, and the properties and uses for each type of wood. This section is devoted to the joinery techniques you need to master as a do-it-yourselfer. One or more of these techniques will come into use whenever you undertake a home improvement or other woodworking project—large or small.

SIZING UP A BOARD

Don't expect perfection in the lumber you buy—you're bound to be disappointed. As shown in the illustrations below, lumber may have any number of ills—knots, splits, cups, twists, checks, warps. Some of these may be serious; others you can live with.

Hopefully, the lumberyard or home center store you deal with won't foist defective material on you. If they do, simply refuse the goods.

Otherwise, you'll have to cope with the wood's problems at home—possibly for years to come. If the lumber you're considering has serious defects, insist on another, better piece.

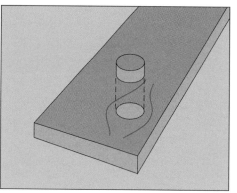

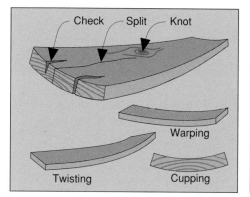

Look for these defects in the lumber. Wood with major problems is best left with the building supply dealer.

Pop loose knots and glue them in place. Plan work so you won't have to cut or nail directly into or near a knot.

Warped lumber sometimes responds to this technique. Don't use too much weight and allow plenty of time.

Cupped boards may respond to water. Wet the concave side and cover it with damp rags. Allow the water to soak in overnight.

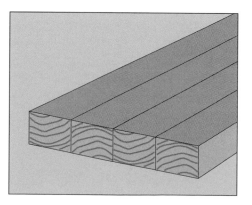

To minimize future movement of edge-joined material, alternate grain direction. This is especially important on outdoor projects.

MAKING BUTT JOINTS

When most people think about joining one material to another, they automatically think of the butt joint, whether or not they know what it is called. This is understandable. Of all wood joinery techniques, the butt joint is the easiest to make. Unfortunately, it's also one of the weakest. If a butt joint will be subjected to lateral stress, be sure to reinforce it in some way.

However, you needn't worry about beefing up butt joints that bear only vertical loads, such as the joints between the studs and plates in a frame wall. For more about framing walls, see pages 50–51.

When making a butt joint, make sure the surfaces you're joining are square. If necessary, trim lumber ends with a saw. Apply glue to both surfaces and nail or screw the materials together. As the glue dries, it creates more of a bond than the fastener you've used.

Wood tends to split when nails or screws are driven into it, especially near the ends of pieces or in end-grains. To prevent splits, drill pilot holes into the material, then drive in the nails or screws.

Generally, butt joints are face-nailed. In certain instances, though, you'll have to toenail materials together. Toenailing involves driving the nails at an angle through one of the materials into the other. For more about toenailing, see page 51.

YOU'LL NEED...

SKILLS: Basic carpentry skills.
TIME: 5 minutes or less.
TOOLS: Saw, hammer.

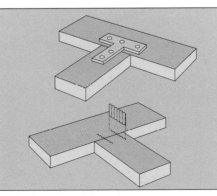

End-nailing creates the weakest butt joint. Nails driven in with the grain may pull out; screws are better.

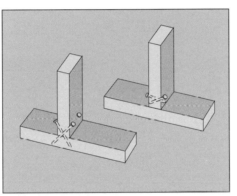

Toenailed butt joints are stronger. It's the only way to make joints when you don't have access to one board face.

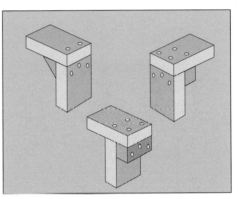

Using wedges and blocks also help strengthen butt joints. Use them with glue and nails or screws.

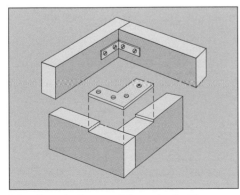

Metal angle irons add strength. For a neat appearance, mortise them flush with the surface, as shown.

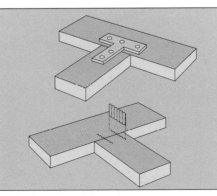

Reinforce T-butt joints with angle irons or T-plates. Or, use corrugated fasteners or wood-joint staples.

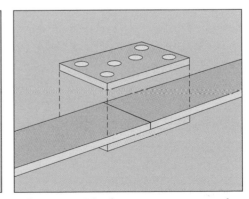

Splices provide the necessary strength to join boards end to end. Use glue and nails or screws to solidify the joint.

Working with Lumber (continued)

MAKING LAP JOINTS

A lap joint joins the face of one material to the face of another or joins a face to an edge. The simplest lap joint is the plain overlap, a good choice for framing projects in which strength is necessary yet appearance isn't critical. To make a lap joint, simply lap the end of one member over another perpendicular or parallel member, then fasten with glue and nails or screws.

Another version, the half-lap joint, is more difficult to make, but stronger. Half-lap joints often are used in furnituremaking and cabinetmaking projects in which both strength and appearance count (see sketch below, top right). You can cut half-lap joints with a saw and chisel. But a tablesaw and a set of dado blades makes the task much easier. Electric routers or radial-arm saws work well.

Full-lapped joints, another handsome furnituremaking standard, are stronger than either their plain or half-lapped cousins. Because you need to make only one cut with a saw and chisel, dado blade, or a router, they're easier to make, too.

If you use adhesive when making lap joints (and you should), clamp the joint to ensure a good, strong bond. Don't use too much adhesive, however, because you may create a situation where the adhesive bonds to itself rather than to the wood. Follow label instructions for the adhesive you're using.

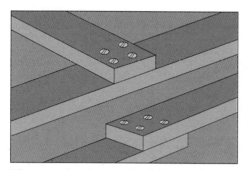

Plain overlap joints should have three or four nails or screws, plus glue. Stagger the fasteners so they don't split the grain.

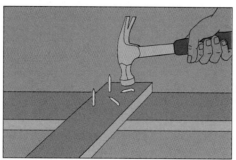

To strengthen a nailed lap joint, use nails that are a ½ inch longer than the joint is thick. Clinch the nails by bending and flattening with the grain.

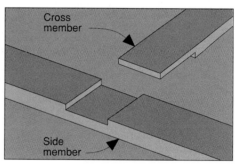

Make a half-lap joint by cutting recesses into each piece of material equal to half the thickness of each piece. This joint takes time to fabricate.

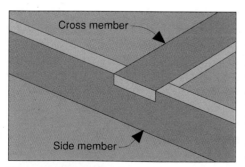

For a neat-looking, stronger joint, make a full lap by cutting a recess into only one member equal to the thickness of the other member.

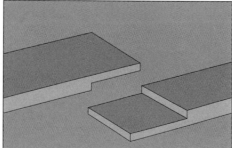

Halved splices are simply half-lap joints used to join two ends. The easiest way to make the cuts is with dado blades. Glue this joint.

MAKING DADO AND RABBET JOINTS

Used in bookcases, cabinets, stair treads, and drawer components, a dado joint is a recessed cut through the face or edge of a piece of lumber. Its popularity stems from the fact that it's both strong and good-looking.

To make a plain dado joint, make two cuts one-third of the way through the material, then chisel away the material left in the slot between the cuts. A tablesaw cuts dadoes more easily than hand tools. And, dado blades for a tablesaw or radial-arm saw make the job even slicker. A router with a straight bit works well also.

If you don't want one edge of the dado slot to show, make a stopped dado, as shown below. While this joint takes longer to make, it looks like a butt joint, but is stronger. Again, power tools will speed the task of making this joint.

Rabbets are recessed cuts along the edge or end of a piece of lumber. A rabbet joint often is used to inset backs for cabinets and bookcases or for drawer assemblies.

With both dado and rabbet joints, accurate measuring, marking, and cutting are critical. If you plan your work carefully, your projects will have that cabinetmaker appearance.

Although you can secure either of these joints with adhesives alone, you'll get a much better joint if you also use screws or nails. Sometimes, screws with decorative washers enhance the appearance of a project—especially if the joint is

being used on a bookcase, shelving, or an open-hutch cabinet.

If possible, clamp both dado and rabbet joints until the adhesive sets.

If you can't clamp the joint, choose a fast-setting adhesive (see page 468). Avoid overfilling the joints with adhesive.

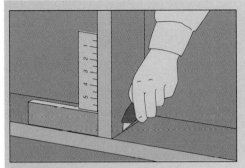

1. Mark a dado cut by holding one piece exactly perpendicular to the other. Scribe the cutting lines with a knife or awl.

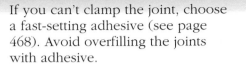

2. Make two saw cuts exactly one-third the thickness of the wood. Chisel away the wood between these cuts. Glue and nail or screw the joint.

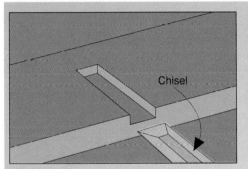

1. For an even neater appearance, make a stopped (or blind) dado by cutting the dado groove only partially through the material.

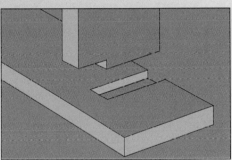

2. On the connecting board, cut away a portion of the edge equal to the depth of the dado and as long as the material left uncut in the other surface.

YOU'LL NEED...

SKILLS: Basic carpentry skills.
TIME: 15 minutes.
TOOLS: Saw, hammer, utility knife, chisel, square, router for long dados or rabbets.

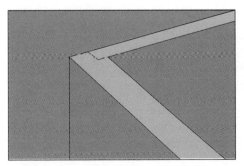

A rabbet is a partial dado. Use it for corners that won't get too much strain and for recessing the backs of cabinets and shelves.

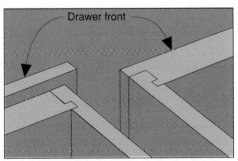

For more strength, you can combine dado and rabbeting techniques in certain projects, such as the drawer construction here.

Working with Lumber (continued)

MAKING MITER JOINTS

Few joinery techniques can outdo the miter when it comes to creating a good-looking joint. That's why miter joints are used for the corners of cabinet cases and picture frames and to join crown, casing, base shoe, and other moldings.

Despite their good looks, miter joints are weak. To make them stronger, you should reinforce the joint with metal angles, gussets, or mending plates. If you feel these add-ons will botch the appearance of the project, use splines or dowels to fortify the joint more discreetly.

Miter joints must be cut accurately. To do so, you need a miter box and backsaw or a power saw that adjusts to a 45-degree cutting angle. Unless you plan to do a great deal of mitering, an inexpensive wooden or plastic miter box will be sufficient.

To make a miter, you have to cut the 45-degree angle in one direction on one piece of stock and in the other direction on the facing piece. Split the cutoff line with the saw. If possible, cut the boards a hair long; you then can use an abrasive to correct any problems. Remember,

you can always take more material off, but you can't add it back on.

When cutting miters on long lengths of stock, support the other end of the material. If you don't, the miter cut will tear from the weight of the material.

> ### YOU'LL NEED...
> **SKILLS:** Intermediate carpentry skills.
> **TIME:** 30 to 60 minutes to make four miters for a frame.
> **TOOLS:** Backsaw, miter box, hammer, clamps.

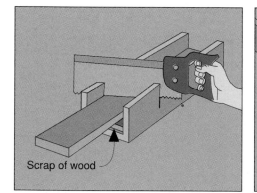

To keep your backsaw from biting into the miter box, place a piece of scrap wood between the work and the box.

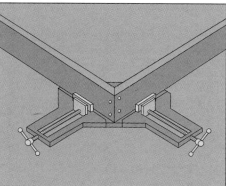

To nail, use wood cleats to hold the stock so you don't knock the pieces out of square. Or, buy miter clamps.

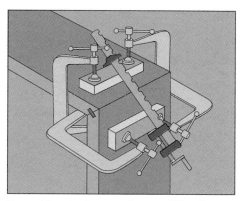

For wide stock, use clamps. Wood blocks protect surfaces and give the clamps something to bite into.

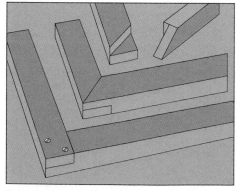

For greater strength, make a half-lap miter. In back, it's a half-lap joint (see page 496); in front, it's a miter.

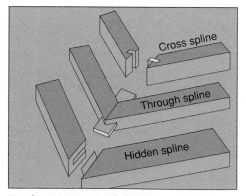

Beef up miters with hidden, through, or cross splines. Cutting these precise grooves is a job for power tools.

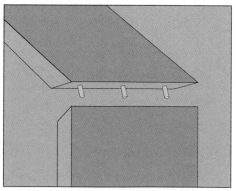

Doweled miters depend on accurate drilling with a power or hand drill and a doweling jig (see page 501).

MAKING MORTISE-AND-TENON JOINTS

If an item has been constructed with mortise-and-tenon joints, you can count on its quality. Normally, you'll find this type of joint used only for fine furniture and some window frames. Unless you're inordinately patient, forget about making these joints with hand tools. Even with the appropriate power tools—a saw with a combination blade, a drill press or drill-press stand for a portable drill, and a chisel set— these joints are difficult for anyone except serious woodworkers.

The mortise is the hole or slot cut in one piece of material; the tenon is the projecting member in the other piece of material that fits into the mortise. Cut the mortise part of the joint first. To be on the safe side when working with hardwoods or the finish piece, cut a test mortise in a piece of scrap wood. This practice can serve as a teaching aid.

Drill the holes at each end of the mortise. Remove the wood between the end holes by drilling more holes, but don't overlap them. Drill individual holes and use a chisel to remove the wood between them. The two end holes must be perfectly square; the others aren't as critical.

After cutting the mortise, use a saw to cut the tenon to match. The easiest way to cut tenons is with a power saw and dado blades. Set the rip fence of the saw to the length of tenon you want, and set the saw depth to the depth you want.

To assemble the joint, sand the tenon so it fits the mortise and spread glue on all surface areas. Strengthen the joint by nailing in brads or adding dowels.

YOU'LL NEED...

SKILLS: Intermediate carpentry skills.
TIME: 45 to 60 minutes per mortise.
TOOLS: Marking gauge, drill, chisel, saw, hammer.

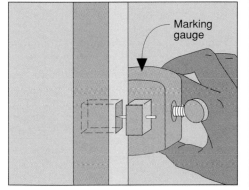

Mark the board for the mortise by carefully dividing it into thirds. Double-check these readings with a good rule.

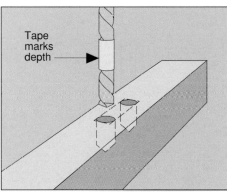

Cut out mortise by drilling a series of holes to depth. Remove scrap wood between the holes with a chisel.

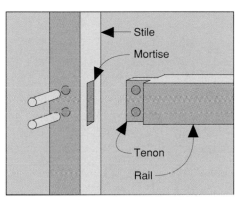

Cut tenon to match mortise. If joint will be assembled with dowels, insert the tenon, then bore dowel holes.

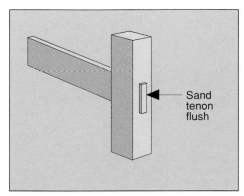

For more strength, cut the mortise through the stock and make the tenon slightly longer. Sand off tenon's end.

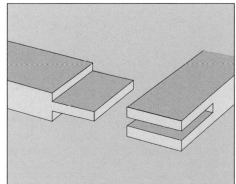

Open mortise-and-tenon joints are less difficult to make. Cut the mortise first, then cut and sand the tenon to fit.

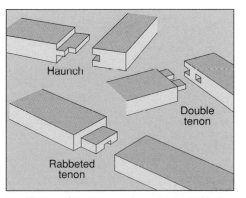

Mortise-and-tenon joint variations include the haunch mortise, the double tenon, and the rabbeted tenon.

Working with Lumber (continued)

MAKING DOVETAIL AND BOX JOINTS

Dovetail and box joints are nifty. They get top grades, too, for strength, durability, and good looks. Making them with a router is the easy way. By hand, the joints involve much tedious work.

If you have a router with a dovetail attachment, the instruction manual will show you how to make the joints. Below, you'll find how to do the job with regular hand tools.

The wood you'll join must be of high quality—no warps or knots. Lay out the project, squaring and matching the corners, then mark the corners that will be matched, for example, A-A, B-B, C-C, and D-D. With a marking gauge, scribe a line on each end of the stock to be joined. Set the gauge to the exact thickness of the wood, plus ⅟₃₂ inch.

With a template, mark the cutting lines for the dovetails. For softwoods, use an angle ratio of 1:6; for hardwoods, a 1:8 ratio (see Step 1 below).

Use a good, sharp backsaw to make the dovetail cuts into the wood. Saw away the excess wood with a coping saw. As you make all saw cuts, leave the scribed line (that is, cut to the line). Smooth the cuts with a chisel.

Use the dovetails on one piece as a template to mark the cuts on the joining piece of wood. Make the cuts and smooth them with a chisel. Fit the pieces together, chiseling one member or the other for a perfect fit. When this is finished, you can use the completed joint as a template for the remaining joints.

A quick technique for making box joints is shown in the bottom two drawings. Clamp several pieces of stock together and make the cuts at one time.

Assemble the joints using a thin coating of adhesive. Position the joint so it's square while the glue dries. Use clamps to ensure good adhesion. For even more strength, drive brads through the dovetails.

YOU'LL NEED...

SKILLS: Intermediate carpentry skills.
TIME: 10 to 20 minutes per dovetail joint and 1 hour for a corner of box joints if done by hand.
TOOLS: Backsaw, coping saw, chisel, clamps, hammer.

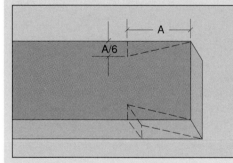

1. Mark the dovetails, making the angle ratio 1:6 for softwoods and 1:8 for hardwoods. Wide dovetails are easier to construct than narrow ones.

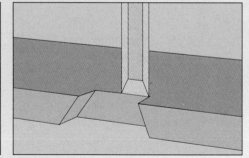

2. Do all work with a backsaw and a coping saw, then smooth the cuts with a chisel. Don't make your initial cuts with a chisel.

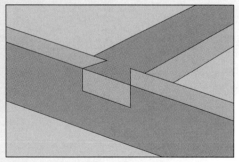

3. Test-fit the joint. At this point, you may have to trim away excess wood with a chisel. Go easy; trim, test, and repeat until fit is perfect.

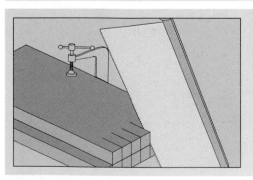

1. To make box joints (also known as finger joints), clamp the two pieces together offset from one another, as shown, and cut both at once.

2. You may have to do some sanding to get the members to fit snugly. Once you're satisfied with the fit, apply glue and brads.

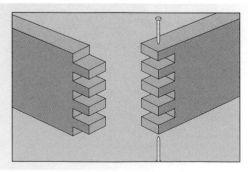

STRENGTHENING JOINTS WITH DOWELS AND SPLINES

To make dowel joints, you should have a doweling jig—a metal clamp-on device that keeps drills and bits square to the stock. You'll also need an assortment of dowels.

You can buy dowels made for use in joints. Or, make your own by beveling the ends of dowel rods with a file or block plane and grooving the length of them with a file so the adhesive can ooze out when you assemble the joint. Cut the dowel pins slightly shorter than the holes they'll fill.

A spline joint consists of two grooves cut in the stock, with a spline fitted between them. This joint

is ideal for joining long lengths of materials. You can make splines from hardwood, softwood, or plywood. Or, you can buy splines, also called biscuits, ready-made.

To end-join narrow material, scribe the groove pattern on both pieces of stock so the grooves will align. Make the parallel cuts with a backsaw, then sand them lightly.

You can cut any width of material for a spline joint with a power saw and dado blades or a router with a groove bit. Make the grooves slightly deeper than the width of the spline. If you want a "blind" spline joint, stop the cut before

you reach the end of the stock.

When you cut a groove, you probably will find that the spline fits very tightly. Don't enlarge the grooves for the spline. Instead, lightly sand the spline and refit it in the grooves. If it is still too tight, take off a little more wood. The trick is to sand and test until you get it pared down for a snug fit.

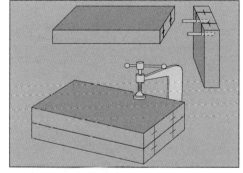

Mark dowel holes by clamping together the pieces of stock you want to join, then locating holes, as shown. Double-check your work.

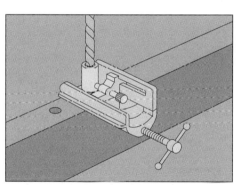

You also can use "dowel centers," which resemble double-headed thumbtacks, for marking. Bore holes using a doweling jig.

You can make your own doweling jig by boring true—absolutely perpendicular—holes in a piece of scrap wood.

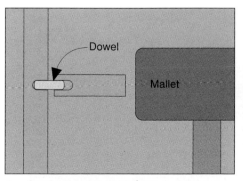

Apply glue and insert dowels into one member, then apply glue to the other and tap the boards together with a wooden mallet.

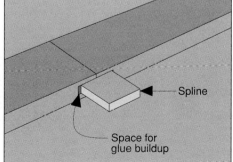

Cut grooves for splines about ¹⁄₁₆ inch deeper than the width of the spline. Lightly coat the spline with adhesive and assemble the joint.

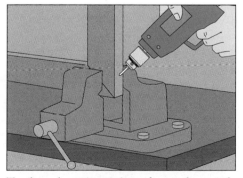

To dowel a miter joint, clamp the work in a vise to secure it. Drill the holes at a 45-degree angle so the dowels will penetrate both members.

Choosing and Buying Moldings

If you've done many do-it-yourself projects, you know by now that mistakes often happen that make your project less than perfect. Maybe your measurements were off slightly, or your saw strayed from the cutting line. That's where moldings help. These strips of wood hide almost any cutting, planing, boring, and fastening mistakes known to woodworking.

You also can use moldings to create decorative effects. Maybe you want to add a chair rail to a dining area, simulate a raised-panel look on a slab door, or personalize a room with crown molding where the ceiling and walls meet. Moldings let you do all of these things, and more.

There are so many shapes and sizes of moldings available that it would be impossible to present all of them here. The sketch below shows common ones. If you don't see that special pattern you want, just stroll through the molding department of any well-stocked building materials outlet. Chances are excellent that you'll find just what you need.

If you need a molding that's no longer stocked, some outlets will mill molding to your order. You'll pay a premium for this service, but it may be the only way to get a molding that matches. If you own a router, you can purchase special bits to create your own molding.

Moldings are sold by the piece or by the linear foot. Those made from exotic woods or with complex patterns cost more than the others.

Depending on your needs, you can purchase moldings unfinished or prefinished. Most manufacturers of paneling also offer prefinished moldings that match the paneling. Many of these moldings are covered with a special plastic coating that resists chemicals, household detergents, water, and moisture.

When you estimate your molding requirements, add 1 linear foot to every 20 feet of material you need. The extra material will allow for miter and trimming cuts.

MATERIAL MATTERS — SELECTING MOLDING

Pattern	Use
Base	Cover joints between flooring and walls; sometimes used on window and door casings
Base cap	Used in older homes to "cap" plain base molding
Brick mold	Used as casings for doors and windows in masonry
Cap	To funnel away water over windows and doors
Casing	Frame windows and doors, covering joints between those units and walls
Corner	Outside corners; edging for shelving and some types of cabinets
Cove	Finish surfaces that adjoin at 90-degree angles
Crown	Trim around ceilings where they meet walls, fireplace mantels, pictures
Glass bead	Hold glass panes in window frames
Half round	Hide material joints; rabbeted types available
Quarter round	Cover and reinforce joints between paneling and framing
Seam	Hide material seams—either paneling or boards
Screen mold	Cover fasteners and edges of screening
Shoe	Nailed to base at floor; often called base shoe
Stool	Used between window frame and apron
Stop	Top and side jambs of doors and windows

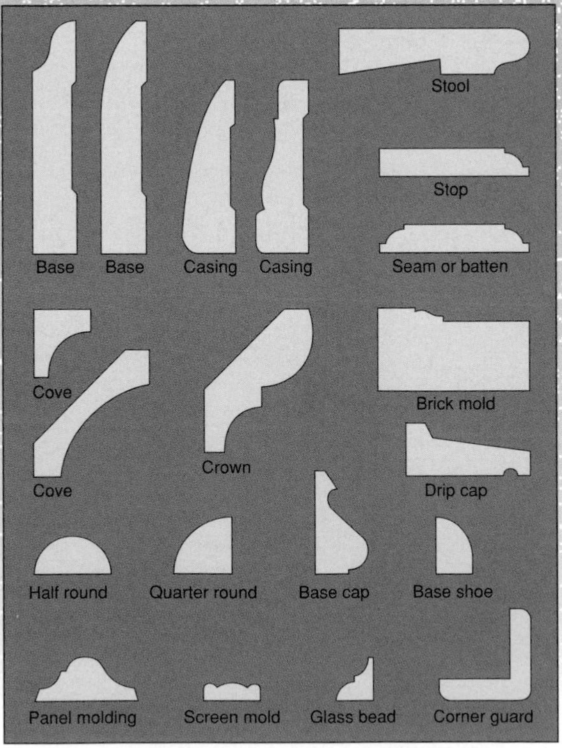

Base Base Casing Casing Stool

Stop

Seam or batten

Cove Crown Brick mold

Cove Drip cap

Half round Quarter round Base cap Base shoe

Panel molding Screen mold Glass bead Corner guard

Working with Moldings

There's no quicker or better way to put the finishing touches on a project than with moldings. Once you get the hang of measuring correctly and cutting miters, it's not difficult, either.

The important thing in cutting miters is to pay attention to the direction of the cuts, so the miters join properly. If you hold the uncut molding in the position in which it will be installed and mark each piece, you'll get most of them right the first time; however, even the pros miscut miters occasionally.

When you're fastening molding along long stretches of parallel surfaces, square the ends and cut one piece 1/16 inch longer than needed. Bow the material, butt the ends, and nail the molding tight, starting in the middle. For a neater appearance, face-miter adjoining pieces (see below, lower left).

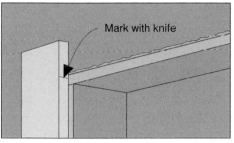

To measure door or window casings, hold the strip in position and mark the inside with a sharp knife. Casing should be set back about 1/4 inch from the jam.

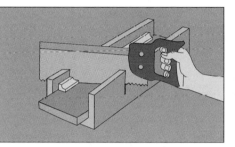

When you cut molding, place the molding against the far side of the miter box. This way, you can hold the molding better while cutting it.

With wide boards, you can be sure you achieve a perfect miter by overlapping the boards and clamping them at 90 degrees. Cut through both pieces.

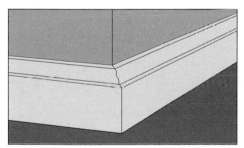

For negotiating outside corners, use 45-degree miter joints. Even with ornately designed moldings, there should be no need to cope this joint.

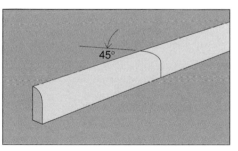

If the molding is wide and won't be painted, you can join two pieces together neatly with a 45-degree face miter.

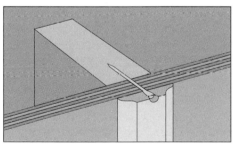

For added strength on paneling seam joints, glue molding to joints, then nail with finishing nails. Countersink and fill nailheads.

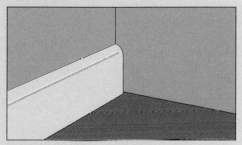

1. To make an inside corner, butt one piece against the wall.

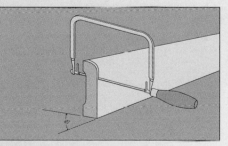

2. On other piece, cut a 45-degree miter, then, trim lower portion off.

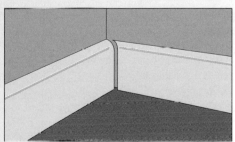

3. Boards then will fit together; if not, use a rasp or abrasive to finalize the fit.

Choosing and Buying Plywood

As its name implies, plywood isn't a solid wood, but a material composed of thin plies of wood laminated together. For strength, the grain of each layer runs perpendicular to those adjacent to it. These layers are held together by a glue bond so strong that the wood will break before the bond comes apart. The resulting product boasts superior split- and puncture-resistance, as well as resistance to warping, swelling, and shrinking. Plywood has good finishing qualities and can be worked easily with hand and power tools.

The two types of plywood you'll be working with most often are softwood- and hardwood-faced plywood. Each is laminated in much the same way; only the materials used differ. Softwood-faced plywood typically has face and back veneers (those that you see) that are cut from Douglas fir or southern pine, with one or more layers in between. Hardwood-faced plywood features a face veneer of hardwood, such as oak, walnut, cherry, birch, and so on; a back veneer of either softwood or hardwood; and one or more plies in between.

There's one other plywood worth knowing about—medium density overlay (MDO) plywood. It has a smooth, resin-impregnated fiber face designed especially for flawless painted finishes. Use MDO wherever you want a really slick surface.

The face and back veneers of softwood plywood vary considerably in quality and are graded and priced accordingly. A-veneer plywood is smooth and ready for finishing. B-veneer has no holes or open defects, but may include tight knots or patched-in repairs. C- and D-veneers may have holes and defects; use them where looks won't matter.

The face and the back veneers can have different grades. For example, if only one of the two sides will be visible in the finished project, ask for an A-D panel.

With hardwood-faced plywood, one surface will always be an A-veneer. The back veneer, however, may have some defects.

Most lumberyards and building products outlets maintain stocks of softwood plywood in several thicknesses—¼, ⅜, ½, ⅝, ¾, and 1 inch. Standard-sized plywood panels measure 4×8 feet, although longer lengths are available on request. Hardwood panels are not readily available but can be obtained from stores specializing in hardwoods.

APA

A-C 15/32 INCH GROUP 1

EXTERIOR

000

PS-1-83

A grade stamp on plywood, based on American Plywood Association (APA) standards, looks like this. Panels also have an edge mark with the same data. Information includes front and back face grade (A-C), thickness (¹⁵⁄₃₂ inch), wood species (Group 1), type of plywood (exterior), mill number (000), and product standard governing manufacture (PS-1-83).

MATERIAL MATTERS SELECTING PLYWOOD

Exterior	Face	Back	Use
A-A	A	A	Exterior where both sides will show
A-B	A	B	Same as A-A, but back may be blemished
A-C	A	C	One good side; siding, soffits, fencing, decks
B-B	B	B	Concrete forms, screening, temporary walks
C-C	C	C	Unsanded; for backing and rough construction
MDO	B	B or C	Applications requiring paint or smooth surface(s)
303 Siding	C or better	C	Siding, interior paneling, fences, storage buildings, where faces with attractive textures are desired

Interior	Face	Back	Use
A-A	A	A	Cabinets, built-ins, furniture, toys, accent panels
A-B	A	B	Same as A-A, except back may be blemished
A-D	A	D	Same as A-B, except back will be rough
B-D	B	D	Utility; rough shelves, cabinetry sides and bottoms
C-D	C	D	Subflooring, utility use, rough construction

Working with Plywood

Most people find that working with plywood is a joy. One reason: The large size of the panels enables you to cover a maximum of area with a minimum of cutting and fitting.

Plywood has almost the same working properties as regular solid wood, plus it has excellent "dimensional stability." This means that it resists warping much better than ordinary lumber.

On the negative side, plywood tends to splinter and split. However, you can overcome these deficiencies, as explained below.

Don't stand plywood panels on edge for long periods. Although highly warp-resistant, plywood isn't totally immune to this problem. That's why you should store sheets laying flat. If you don't have room to do this, set the panels on sleepers on their longest edges and as vertically as possible. Do not store interior-grade plywood in damp areas, because moisture weakens glue and causes delamination.

CUTTING AND DRILLING PLYWOOD

For a project that requires you to cut several pieces out of a sheet of plywood, map out the cuts on a piece of paper. Then, transfer your measurements to the plywood panel, allowing for saw kerfs and any damage that might be present on the panel edges or ends. You can use the same mapping technique to estimate plywood requirements.

To make cuts with a circular saw, use a fine-toothed plywood blade. Otherwise, use the standard woodworking tools and techniques illustrated on pages 449–454.

Outer veneers of plywood tend to splinter where a saw blade or drill bit exits the material. The drawings below show several ways you can minimize splintering problems.

Avoid boring into the edges of standard and particleboard-core plywood. The cores tend to split, and most fasteners won't hold very well in the edges anyway. If you must screw or nail into the edge, be sure to drill small pilot holes first.

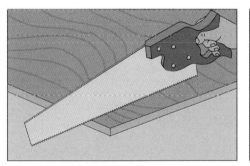

With a handsaw, cut plywood with the good side up. Use a handsaw with 12 to 15 points per inch, and hold it at a low angle.

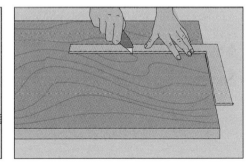

Place the good side down when sawing plywood with a portable circular saw or a sabersaw. With stationary saws, feed the plywood good side up.

To cut across the grain of plywood or to minimize splintering on either side, score the cut first with a sharp knife.

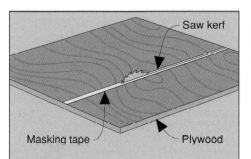

Another effective way to keep the panel from splintering along the cutoff line is to lay down a strip of masking tape on the line.

To minimize splintering when drilling into plywood, bore into a piece of scrap wood on the backside of the panel.

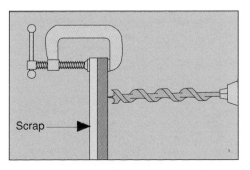

Working with Plywood (continued)

FASTENING PLYWOOD

Despite the obvious physical differences between lumber and plywood (one being solid; the other, laminated stock), you can use most of the same fastening techniques for both materials. Don't be afraid to make miters, rabbets, and dadoes in plywood, also.

However, you should avoid nailing or screwing into the edges of plywood panels. Edge-nailing generally splits the veneer or causes it to "balloon." If you must fasten into the edges of plywood, predrill pilot holes for the fasteners, whether they be screws or nails. Use the smallest-diameter fastener possible.

Using a combination of waterproof glue and a mechanical fastener results in the strongest joints when joining plywood to plywood or plywood to another material. Where appearance isn't important, such as when fastening sheathing and subflooring, fasten down plywood with annular ring nails or spiral nails. These fasteners bite into the plywood laminations and hold them together. For finish work, use finishing or casing nails or small-diameter screws. Countersink and fill the holes with wood putty. For thin plywood, use common brads for assembly. If appearance isn't critical, you can fasten thin plywood with staples. Countersink and fill brad or staple holes, too.

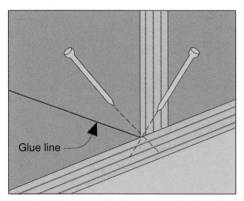

Where the stress is downward, simple butt joints are adequate for most applications that use ¾-inch plywood. Keep joints square.

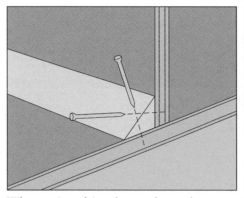

When using thin plywood panels, reinforce joints with square or triangular blocks that are fastened with both glue and nails.

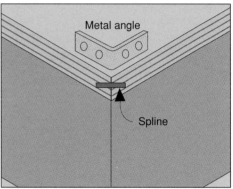

To strengthen mitered joints in ¾-inch plywood panels, use a spline; cut grooves with a power saw. Or, you can use metal angles inconspicuously.

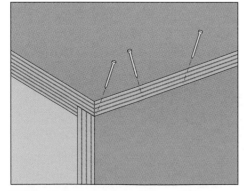

Rabbet joints work well for cabinet and drawer construction. Keep nails away from panel edges and drive them in at angles.

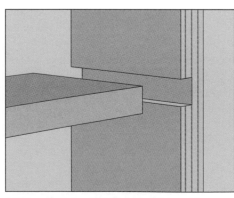

Although you can cut dadoes with a handsaw and chisel, a router or power saw with a dado blade will do a cleaner job in plywood. Glue, nail, and clamp.

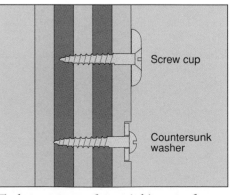

To keep screws from sinking too far into the face of plywood, use screw cups or washers. If desired, you can countersink the washers.

PLANING AND FORMING PLYWOOD

Sometimes, even when you've made smooth, accurate cuts, plywood needs planing or sanding to make it fit. If only a minor adjustment is needed, use a power sander. If it's obvious that you'd have to sand all night long to get it correct, it's time to get out your block plane.

Don't expect to shave a long, thin ribbon like the one you'd get with solid wood. The glue bond between the laminations produces small chips rather than long pieces.

Work the plane from the edges of the material toward the center (see below). Make a series of passes, beveling each end of the plywood across the edge to minimize any splintering of the veneer.

The same procedures apply with a power sander. Make several passes along the plywood edge, starting with a medium-coarse abrasive and working up to a finer grit of paper (see pages 480–481). Keep the power sander square to the edge.

If you ever want to make a decorative or functional curved wood surface, thin plywood panels lend themselves to bending much more than does solid lumber. To bend thin plywood, you need to make a jig with clamps and scrap wood to produce the radius curve you want. Dampen—don't soak—both surfaces of the plywood with water. Bend the plywood and clamp it in position. Let the wood dry overnight. When you unclamp the wood, the curve will be permanent. Simply glue the plywood into the position you want.

To bend thicker plywood, make a series of saw kerfs across or with the grain. Make a jig and clamp the material in the jig. Wet the outside of the material, let it set overnight, and glue it in the desired position.

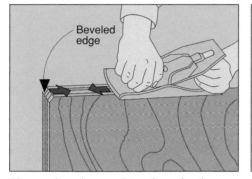

Plane edges by working from both directions. A tiny bevel on each end helps prevent splintering and splits.

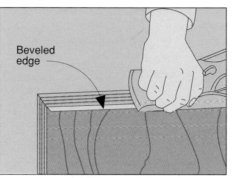

Bevel sharp edges, if you won't be applying an edge treatment. This protects the veneer from splitting.

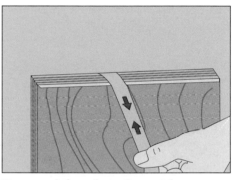

Or, round the edges, first with a surface-forming tool, then sandpaper. Use sandpaper in shoeshine fashion.

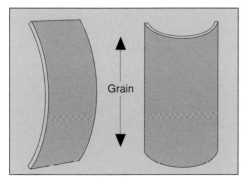

Bend plywood in gradual curves across the grain. For tighter curves, bend the plywood parallel to grain.

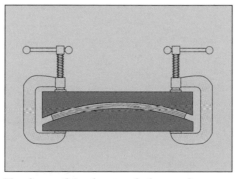

To shape thin sheets of plywood, wet, clamp as shown, and let the panels set overnight. Don't soak the wood.

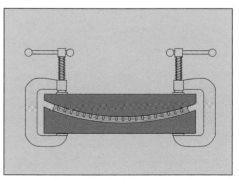

For thicker panels, make a series of saw cuts on the back side. Dampen panel and clamp it tightly, as shown.

Working with Plywood (continued)

BUILDING A PLYWOOD BOX

The average person probably doesn't realize how basic the plain box is to all sorts of home carpentry projects. Once you master the basics of box-building, you can fashion a surprising number of good-looking items for your home—cabinets, bookcases, platform bed frames, end tables, and more—at a cost that's even more surprising.

Pictured below are two simple boxes—essentially the same, except one goes together with simple hand tools; the other, with power tools.

Plywood is an ideal material for a box design for two reasons. First, it comes in 4×8-foot sheets and in a range of thicknesses, which

eliminates the special planing and milling required when using solid wood. Second, it's available in a variety of veneers.

When building a box, determine the dimensions of the sides, bottom, back, front, and special add-ins, such as shelving and drawers. From these dimensions, you can determine how many sheets of plywood you'll need for the job, plus other components, such as adhesive, nails, screws, and finishing materials.

To make sure you have figured your plywood requirements correctly, draw a 4×8-foot sheet to scale on graph paper, then draw in each piece of the box. Pay attention

to the direction of the grain as you lay out the pieces. The grain should run the same direction on all pieces. Label each part "side," "bottom," "back," and so on.

Transfer your layouts to the actual sheets of plywood, marking each part as you go. Be sure to allow room for saw kerfs and special cuts that will require extra material to make. Double-check the layout, then make the cuts, as explained below.

YOU'LL NEED...

SKILLS: Basic carpentry skills.
TIME: 2 to 4 hours.
TOOLS: Circular saw, hammer, drill, screwdriver, bar clamps.

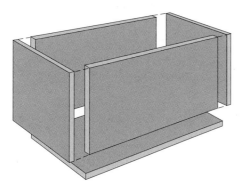

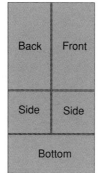

Back	Front
Side	Side
Bottom	

Assemble the plywood box at left with simple butt joints. For strength and appearance, butt-join the ends and sides to the bottom. With ¾-inch material, the ends will be the same width as the bottom; the sides will be 1½ inches shorter than the bottom's length. Use glue and ring-shank nails driven at an angle to assemble the box. To strengthen the corners even more, use the joinery techniques shown on page 495. Assemble the sides and ends first, then attach the bottom.

The box at right is assembled with the more sophisticated rabbet joint, and is considerably stronger than the butted version above. Note that the ends and sides are rabbeted, but not the bottom. Assemble the ends and sides first, using glue and finishing nails driven at an angle. Fit the sides and ends to the bottom. You may have to trim the rabbet cuts slightly here and there to accommodate the bottom. Countersink the nails, fill all nail holes, and apply a finish.

Dadoes

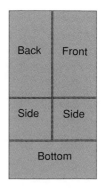

Back	Front
Side	Side
Bottom	

BUILDING DRAWERS

Drawers are simply boxes. They can be constructed quickly and easily.

Determine the measurements of the drawer—sides, back, and front.

Make the drawer slightly smaller than its opening. Take into account that drawer guides will be attached later. Use ¾-inch plywood for the front, sides, and back of the drawer, and ⅛- or ¼-inch hardboard or plywood for the bottom.

If you use hand tools, construct the drawer using butt joints, as in the example at the far left. Cut the sides, back, and front to width and length, and assemble them with glue and ring-shank nails. Check the fit of the unit in its opening. Then, add the bottom and attach guides to the drawer and the cabinet framework.

To make the drawer with dado joints (shown in the right-hand drawing), you need a power saw or router to cut the dadoes.

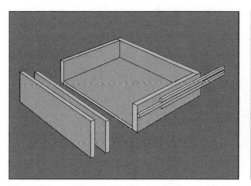

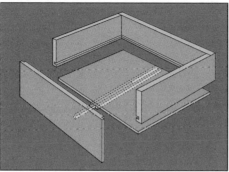

To make a "lipped" drawer front, glue a larger false front to the actual drawer front. Attach wood drawer guides to the sides of the drawer and the cabinet framing, or buy metal drawer guides. Buy the guides beforehand, so you know how much space they need and, thus, how wide the drawer can be.

Flush-fitted drawers fit flush to the cabinet sides and operate on a bottom guide. You can use plywood for the sides, backs, and bottoms of drawers, but solid wood is best for the front. Cut a dado around the sides, back, and front for the bottom. Don't glue the bottom; let it "float" inside the dado.

YOU'LL NEED...

SKILLS: Intermediate carpentry skills.
TIME: 1 hour to build a drawer.
TOOLS: Saw, hammer, screwdriver, drill, router or tablesaw if you use dado joints.

FINISHING PLYWOOD EDGES

There's no one correct way to finish the edges of plywood. Edging tape is probably the quickest way to hide plywood edges. The tape comes in a range of veneers to match the plywood. Glue it on or use the self-adhesive types you iron on with a clothes iron.

Another simple solution is to glue or nail on a molding (see page 502).

Screen molding, which comes in many styles, works well and accepts paint, stain, and other finishes. To increase its holding power on the edge, you can use splines or mitered butt, sandwich butt, or V-groove joints; but these are tricky to cut.

If you plan to paint the plywood, just fill the edges with wood putty or edge filler or a thin mixture of surfacing compound. Let the filler dry a day or so, then sand it. You may need a second application to obtain the smooth edge you want.

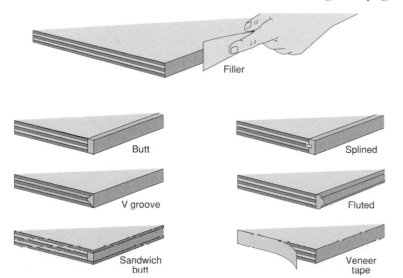

Filler

Butt

V groove

Sandwich butt

Splined

Fluted

Veneer tape

YOU'LL NEED...

SKILLS: Basic carpentry skills.
TIME: 5 to 10 minutes per edge.
TOOLS: Putty knife, hammer, saw, drill, router, clothes iron, depending on which method of edging you use.

Choosing and Working with Composition Board

Composition board includes a range of particulate composite products, from structural framing and sheathing panels—such as oriented strand lumber, waferboard, and oriented strand board (OSB)—to nonstructural panels, including insulation board, hardboard, particleboard, and medium density fiberboard (MDF). Composition products are gaining in popularity among contractors because of their relatively low cost and steadily improving quality.

The low cost results from the raw materials from which the products are made—wood waste from the production of lumber and plywood, including sawdust, chips, and shavings. Recycled wood, such as pallets and packing crates, also can be chipped. A third source is low-strength, fast-growing tree species, such as poplar and aspen.

Boards and panels are made by mixing the wood particles, chips, and shavings with resin and wax and forming the mass into mats, which are cured under heat and extreme pressure. The final products are then cut into standard sizes.

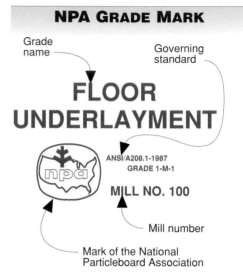

NPA GRADE MARK

Grade name

Governing standard

FLOOR UNDERLAYMENT

ANSI/A208.1-1987
GRADE 1-M-1

MILL NO. 100

Mill number

Mark of the National Particleboard Association

SELECTING COMPOSITION BOARD

■ Hardboard is a dense, smooth product with several desirable characteristics. It accepts paint well, and because it has no grain, the paint won't check or crack. In addition, hardboard won't splinter or crack, yet it's flexible enough to bend for such projects as concrete forms. Hardboard is available in two grades: standard and tempered. Tempered board is stronger and darker brown than the standard version. Either grade comes in several surface textures—grained, embossed, perforated, textured, striated, and filigreed.

■ Particleboard is similar to hardboard in that it is made from wood particles. It's fairly dense, very heavy, and smooth on both sides. It is used primarily for shelving and underlayment and as a core material for plastic-, wood-, and hardboard-veneered products. Particleboard generally must be fastened to some sort of framing material. It also tends to chip and break easily.

■ Medium-density fiberboard (MDF) is a medium-dense, smooth product that is ideal for machining. The small particle size and uniformity result in clean, smooth cuts and tight edges. MDF is rapidly replacing solid wood in cabinets, countertops, desktops, furniture, doors, windows, and moldings. Overlaid with plastic, it can be made to resemble anything from stone to natural-grain wood, and it is used as cabinet fronts and flooring. Sealed for weather resistance, it is used as lap siding.

■ Oriented strand board (OSB) is a medium-dense, long-grained panel product intended for structural applications, such as building sheathing and roofing. Its high strength is achieved by aligning fibers much like those in natural wood, but without the natural uncertainties of knots, cross-grain, pitch pockets, and the like. Fibers can be aligned in the long direction of panel faces and at right angles in the core to produce a panel that is a low-cost replacement for plywood.

■ Insulation board is a low-density, low-strength product used primarily as roofing underlayment and for ceiling tile. Looking at the product, it's hard to imagine that insulation board and hardboard are made with the same equipment; the only difference being the degree of compression. Ceiling tiles can be as light as 10 pounds per cubic foot, while tempered hardboard can weigh up to 65 pounds per cubic foot—heavier than water.

■ High-pressure laminate is a decorative face applied over MDF. The surface can be manufactured to emulate anything from natural wood to polished stone. It is gaining in popularity as a flooring product.

■ Thermally fused laminate is melamine resin-impregnated paper, fused under heat and pressure to a substrate of particleboard or MDF. Factory fusing eliminates one difficult and messy job for do-it-yourselfers—application of plastic laminates to particleboard or plywood cabinets and countertops.

MATERIAL MATTERS   SELECTING COMPOSITION BOARD

Type	Sizes and Thicknesses	Fasteners	Finishes	Uses
Hardboard				
Standard	4×4', 4×7', 4×8', 4×10', 4×12' ⅛", ³⁄₁₆", ¼", ⁵⁄₁₆"	Glue, nails, bolts, screws, clips	Smooth on one or both sides	Interior applications, such as partitions, cabinets, accent panels, work surfaces
Tempered	Same as standard	Same as standard	Same as standard	Interior and exterior use; moisture-resistant; same uses as standard hardboard
Underlayment	4×4', 4×8' ¼"	Glue, nails, screws	Extra smooth and flat	Over subfloors or floors as a base for carpeting, tile, resilient goods, slate
Perforated; standard or tempered	2×4', 4×4', 4×8' ⅛", ¼"	Glue, nails, bolts, screws, rabbeted, dadoed frames	Same as standard	For hanging tools, utensils, etc.; holes drilled on ½- and 1-inch centers; special hanging hardware
Embossed	4×4', 4×8', 4×12', 4×16' ⅛", ¼"	Same as standard	Varied	Furniture, wall paneling, decorative accents, cabinet fronts, drawer fronts
Die-cut filigreed	16"×6', 2×4', 2×6', 4×8' ⅛"	Same as standard	Smooth on both sides	Interior applications, such as room dividers, screens, cabinet fronts, furniture
Siding panels	4×6', 4×7', 4×8', 4×9', 4×10', 4×12', 4×16' ⁷⁄₁₆"	Nails	Unpainted, preprimed	Siding, interior accent panels
lap	9", 12" width ¼" to ⁷⁄₁₆"	Nails	Same as panels	Same as panels
Particleboard				
Grade 1-M-2	¼", ½", ⅝", ¾", 1", 1½"	Nails, screws, bolts, staples	Smooth and flat	Shelving, countertops, cabinets, furniture
Grade1-M-1	¼", ⅜", ½", ⅝", ¾"	Nails, screws, adhesives, staples	Extra smooth and flat	Underlayment
Oriented Strand Board				
Waferboard	¼", ⅜", ⁷⁄₁₆", ½", ⅝", ¾"	Nails, screws, staples	Large wafers on both sides	Wall and roof sheathing
Oriented strand board	¼", ⅜", ⁷⁄₁₆", ½", ⅝", ¾", 1"	Nails, screws, staples	Smoother than waferboard	Wall and roof sheathing, subflooring

Choosing and Working with Composition Board (continued)

WORKING WITH HARDBOARD

Hardboard may appear to be weak when you first look at it. You'll be proven wrong the first time you try to saw or drill it, however. Hardboard is more dense than most softwoods, hardwoods, and plywood. Because of this, you'll find that it dulls the cutting edges of tools quickly, necessitating frequent whetting or sharpening.

Use a 10- to 12-point crosscut saw or a crosscut blade on a power saw to cut hardboard. If you'll be sawing a lot of hardboard, use a longer-lasting carbide-tipped blade.

When drilling through hardboard, work from the smooth side (some hardboard is smooth on both sides). If you don't, the material may tear when the bit penetrates it.

Due to its supple nature, hardboard usually requires backup support. This is particularly true if you're using ⅛-inch-thick material. But even ¼-inch or thicker material needs the reinforcement of studs, joists, or furring strips at intervals not greater than 16 inches.

Tempered hardboard is well-suited for use as paneling. However, if you

apply it to walls that become damp from time to time, you must install a polyethylene vapor barrier on the wall before putting up the panels. Hardboard panels also expand and contract with changes in temperature and humidity. When joining panels that cover large expanses, therefore, leave a ¹⁄₁₆-inch gap at the joints. If this compromises the appearance of the job, cover the joints with moldings. You probably can buy moldings to match the prefinished hardboard panels you're installing.

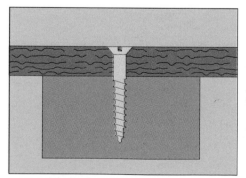

You may have trouble seeing lines on tempered hardboard. Use a pencil with light-colored lead.

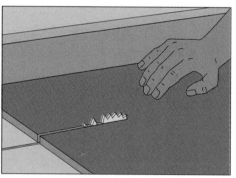

To minimize surface damage when cutting with a power saw, set the blade so that the teeth just barely project.

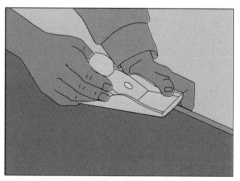

To smooth hardboard edges, use a shallow-set plane; hold it at a slight angle to the edge and use light strokes.

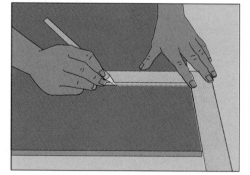

Being "grainless," hardboard doesn't hold fasteners well. Nail, screw, or bolt through hardboard and into the other material, never into the hardboard.

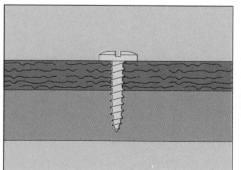

Sheet-metal screws will hold better than wood screws in hardboard. Particleboard holds nails and screws better than hardboard.

When you sand hardboard it tends to get "fuzzy" or "hairy." To minimize this effect, treat it with a coat of shellac before using your abrasive.

DESIGNING A PARTICLEBOARD SHELF

The simplest shelf is a board laying on two supports without its ends or edges attached to anything. Adding intermediate supports or securing the ends or back edge to supports increases stiffness, as the drawing at right shows.

Particleboard cannot span as great a distance or hold as much weight as a solid wood shelf can. Thus, to design a particleboard shelf, you first must determine the uniform load it will carry. Unless you already know the load, use the following guidelines: books, 40 pounds per square foot; closet items, 25 pounds per square foot; kitchen cabinet items, 15 pounds per square foot.

The style and number of supports—simple span, multiple, fixed-end, or back-edge—also affect the weight the shelf can hold over certain spans. Find the style in the drawing at right and divide the uniform load by the factor shown to find the factored load that can be supported.

The type and thickness of the particleboard is the third determining factor of how you design your shelf. Look in the chart below under the material proposed and find the combination(s) of shelf thickness and span between supports that will carry your factored load.

Here's an example. You would like to build an 8-foot bookshelf of ¾-inch unfaced particleboard. The load would be 40 pounds per square foot for the books. You assume you'll need several supports, so start with the four-support version with a load factor of 2; the factored load is 20 pounds per square foot.

In the table below, you find that ¾-inch unfaced particleboard will support only 17 pounds per square foot at a 32-inch span (two supports between 8 feet). So, you'll need to increase the number of supports to three (every 24 inches) to support up to 25 pounds per square foot.

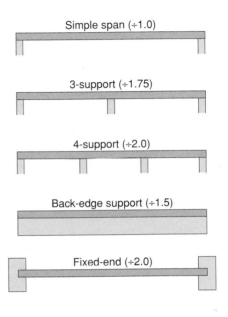

Simple span (÷1.0)

3-support (÷1.75)

4-support (÷2.0)

Back-edge support (÷1.5)

Fixed-end (÷2.0)

DETERMINING SPANS AND LOADS FOR A PARTICLEBOARD SHELF

	Allowed Uniform Load, Pounds per Square Foot (based on type and thickness of particleboard)											
	Unfaced Particleboard Type M–2				High-Pressure Laminated Particleboard				Veneered Particleboard ¹⁄₃₆" Red Oak, Both Faces			
Span, inches	Thickness, inches				Thickness, inches				Thickness, inches			
	½	⅝	¾	1	½	⅝	¾	1	½	⅝	¾	1
16	45	95	165	375	110	190	300	570	135	225	355	675
20	20	45	80	200	55	95	150	325	65	115	180	370
24	12	25	45	115	30	55	85	185	35	65	100	210
28	7	15	25	70	15	30	50	115	20	40	60	130
32	—	10	17	45	10	20	35	75	12	25	40	85
36	—	5	10	30	7	12	20	50	7	15	25	55
40	—	—	7	20	—	7	15	35	5	10	15	40
44	—	—	5	15	—	5	10	25	—	7	12	30
48	—	—	—	10	—	—	7	15	—	5	7	20

Choosing and Buying Plastics

Plastics have proven themselves top-notch materials for a host of tasks and are used quite often for home improvement and repair projects. Three types of plastics are discussed here: high-pressure laminates, acrylics, and fiberglass-reinforced plastics. You'll find all of them in home center stores or lumberyards; laminates generally in the kitchen or countertop section, acrylics in the glass section, and fiberglass-reinforced plastic sheets usually with the roofing materials.

MATERIAL MATTERS

SELECTING PLASTICS

Laminate

A plastic laminate is resin-coated paper that has been formed under high heat and pressure. It's excellent for covering kitchen and bathroom countertops, shower doors, furniture, and cabinets. Although plastic laminate is tough, it can be damaged by heat and household cleaners that contain abrasives, peroxide, or chlorine.

Laminates are available in a wide range of patterns and colors; some of them are even color-keyed to kitchen appliances and bathroom fixtures. You may have to special-order the laminate you want, but delivery usually doesn't take long (a day or two).

Standard sheets are $\frac{1}{32}$ or $\frac{1}{16}$ inch thick and measure from 2×5 feet to 5×12 feet. Buy the thin sheets for vertical applications (for example, cabinet doors) and the thicker ones for horizontal uses, such as countertops.

You can use regular hand and power tools to cut, drill, trim, and form laminate. A router does a great job of trimming edges. You should buy an inexpensive notched trowel to spread on the contact cement. This trowel creates a uniform bed of adhesive that ensures good adhesion.

Acrylic

Although once not widely used for home improvement projects, acrylic plastic is used more often now and has a great deal to offer. You can cut, shape, and form it into insert panels for cabinets, panels for shower doors and stalls, and covers for indirect or recessed panel or strip lighting. You also can use it as a glass substitute in storm doors and as shelving in open cabinets. For specialty and hobby projects, the rigid plastic has nearly unlimited uses.

Except for its tendency to sag in long runs, acrylic's only drawback is that it scratches easily. Follow the advice on page 516, however, and you can work with it without incident.

For most projects, you should fasten acrylic to framing—wood or metal—with screws, clips, bolts, or adhesive. Once supported, acrylic is extremely strong, making it ideal for replacing glass in storm doors and windows.

Most of the acrylic you'll find will be either $\frac{1}{8}$ or $\frac{1}{4}$ inch thick, although thicker sizes are available. Because the material is fairly expensive, you'll usually order a piece cut to size.

Fiberglass

Fiberglass often is used for patio covers and as a patching material for holes, dents, splits, and cracks in cars and boats.

Fiberglass-reinforced plastic sheets for exterior use resemble corrugated sheet metal used to roof many older utility buildings in rural areas. Flat sheets also are available. Panels are available in a range of colors, sizes, and thicknesses.

If you plan to roof with fiberglass, be sure to buy corrugated flashing and moldings so you end up with a professional-looking job. Install the panels with nails or screws that have a rubber gasket just below the head. These seal the panel against moisture.

Polystyrene panels are similar to fiberglass-reinforced plastic panels, except that they're best used indoors. Some are designed to look like leaded stained glass. They make handsome room dividers, cabinet fronts, shower door panels, and window coverings. Flat polystyrene panels generally need to be supported with framing. Fasten them with screws or clips, or glue them into position.

For auto body and boat repair, you can buy fiberglass patching kits. The kits contain fiberglass cloth and a two-part resin (see page 517). Look for the patching kits at home centers and automobile and marine stores.

Working with Plastics

APPLYING LAMINATES

Plastic laminate is one of those materials that becomes more intriguing the more you work with it. With practice, you can learn to lay it down as well as many professionals. Regardless of the project, the techniques remain much the same. So, let's discuss a project you may well encounter: re-covering a countertop.

Remove the old material down to the base material. If the base is badly damaged, tear it out and replace it with at least one layer, if not two, of ¾-inch particleboard or plywood. If the surface is in decent shape, sand it perfectly smooth.

To bond laminates to the base material, you'll need special contact cement. Because laminates adhere on contact, you must carefully cut and prefit the laminate to the base. Once in place, laminate is almost impossible to remove.

The difference between a slapdash and a professional-looking job lies in how you trim the edges. You can smooth them by hand with a file, but a router with a special laminate bit zips through the job.

When applying laminates to cabinet doors, apply a balance sheet to the back side to seal out moisture, which otherwise will cause warping. Or apply laminate to both sides.

> ### YOU'LL NEED...
> **SKILLS:** Intermediate carpentry skills.
> **TIME:** 4 to 6 hours to relaminate a countertop.
> **TOOLS:** Utility knife; tablesaw, circular saw, or backsaw; brush; roller; file; router.

To cut laminate, score its face with a sharp knife, then hold one side flat, grasp the other, and snap it up. Carbide tipped blades work best.

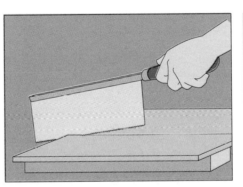

Or, saw the laminate with a fine-tooth backsaw or circular saw. On a tablesaw, cut with the good face up; with a portable saw, cut with face down.

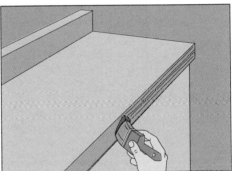

Apply contact cement to both the back of the laminate and the countertop surface. Brush it out evenly. Apply edge strips first.

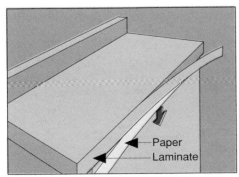

When the cement is dry to the touch, cover the surface with brown wrapping paper, position laminate exactly, then pull out the paper.

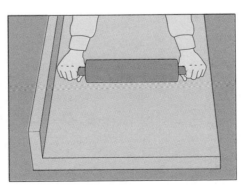

When all of the laminate is down, roll the entire surface with a rolling pin. Tap along the edges with a hammer and wood block.

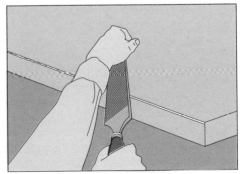

Rout, file, or sand off the excess material. File the edges gently to remove any sharpness. Routing is the easiest for beginners.

Working with Plastics (continued)

WORKING WITH ACRYLIC

When you buy acrylic plastic sheets, there is a paper or plastic-film skin covering both sides. It's there to protect the material while you're cutting it and to provide a surface on which to mark your cut lines.

For straight cuts in thicknesses up to ¼ inch, use the scribe-and-break method shown below. For thicker material and curved cuts, use a saw.

A fine-tooth crosscut saw works best if you're sawing by hand. Power saws equipped with a hollow-ground or plywood blade will do a much smoother job, however. To make the cut, push the material very slowly through the saw—or guide the saw slowly through the plastic. Don't force the acrylic as you would with wood. Also, saw up to, but not directly on, the cutoff line. The cut edge of the plastic will be rough, so you'll need to smooth it with wet/dry sandpaper.

If your project calls for a piece of acrylic bent to a certain shape, first measure, mark, and cut the rigid sheet to the size you want. After peeling off the protective paper, heat the acrylic along the bend line with a "strip heater" specially designed for this purpose. When the plastic softens, bend it a little at a time. Let the plastic cool, then heat and bend again until you get the form you want.

You also can make holes in acrylic. Though most people simply drill through the material, as shown below, in situations where appearance isn't a consideration, you also can heat a pointed metal object and push the tip of it into the plastic. Make sure you keep the point square to the material.

YOU'LL NEED...

SKILLS: Basic carpentry skills.
TIME: 5 minutes to cut acrylic, 15 minutes to smooth an edge.
TOOLS: Utility knife, circular saw or tablesaw, drill, clamp, sanding block, buffing wheel.

To cut thin sheets of acrylic, mark the cutoff line, then score with a scribe, utility knife, or other pointed object, using a straightedge as a guide.

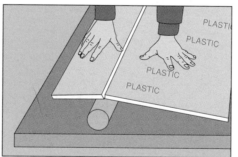

Position a dowel under the sheet along the full length of the scored line. With both hands, snap the sections downward with an even thrust.

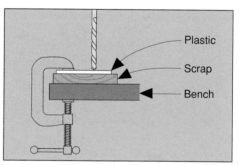

Hand-drill acrylic with twist bits, not auger bits. With a power drill, use bits made for plastics. Clamp the plastic and back it with wood.

Smooth cut edges with medium-grit sandpaper. Finish the job with a wet/dry abrasive on a sanding block.

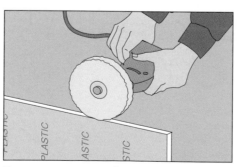

For a transparent edge, continue with very fine abrasive, then buff with a buffing wheel in a power drill.

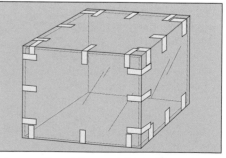

Join acrylic with special acrylic cement. Roughen edges with sandpaper, apply cement, and clamp with masking tape.

WORKING WITH FIBERGLASS

Working with fiberglass-reinforced plastic panels requires no special tools, but there are a few tricks. Cut the panels with a fine-tooth saw blade, and don't force the plastic into the saw or the saw into the plastic. Always drill holes for nails and other fasteners; if you don't, the panel may crack where the fastener penetrates the plastic. To prevent chipping, do not drill closer than ⅜ inch from an edge.

Fasten the panels to framing using nails with neoprene washers or other fasteners suggested by the manufacturer in the instructions.

If you're using fiberglass panels outdoors, be sure to weather-strip the panel joints to prevent leakage. For fencing jobs, toenail the rails to the posts—or dado them in—so the panels fit flush to the posts.

Fiberglass cloth and resin can be used to patch autos, boats, or other items—not necessarily made from fiberglass. These are not the easiest products to use, because if you add too much hardener to the resin, the hardening process begins immediately. Add too little, and the resin won't harden at all. So, always measure out the hardener in drops, according to the instructions.

Fumes from fiberglass resin are extremely toxic, so be sure to work outdoors or in a room that's well-ventilated. Also, the spun-glass fibers in fiberglass mats can damage your lungs, work their way into your skin, and irritate your eyes. Always work with gloves, long sleeves, and a protective respirator.

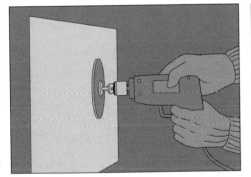

To patch a hole with fiberglass, grind or sand down the surrounding surfaces to bare wood or metal. Keep surfaces clean and dry.

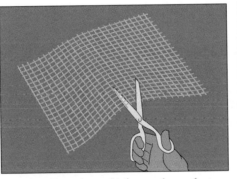

Cut the fiberglass cloth patch so that an inch or two overlaps the edges of the area to be patched. Use regular scissors for cutting.

Carefully mix the hardener with the resin according to the manufacturer's instructions. Stir well in a disposable paper cup or metal tray.

Lay out the cloth on a piece of polyethylene and pour the mixture over it. Spread out the resin mixture with a small brush.

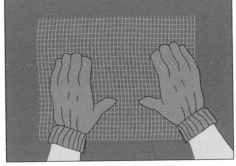

Place the saturated material over the damaged area. Work out wrinkles and air bubbles by lightly stretching the fiberglass material.

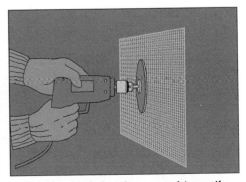

After the patch hardens, sand it until smooth. For an invisible patch, fill low spots with auto-body putty before you paint the patch.

Choosing and Buying Metals

Metal products you'll most likely encounter in your home include aluminum, copper, galvanized steel, mild steel (nails, bolts, and screws), and wrought iron. For specialty projects, you may also need brass and bronze.

Most home centers and building materials outlets stock aluminum and galvanized steel sheets, gutters, and flashing. You may have to special-order copper sheets, gutters, and flashing, although it's worth a call to a metal specialty shop before you do. Check the classified section of your phone directory for help in locating suppliers. For more about repairing flashing and gutters, see pages 130–131 and 134–135.

Because both aluminum and copper are "soft" metals, you can use woodworking tools when you work with those metals. However, heavy steel sheets and bar stock call for special metalworking equipment. Renting these tools makes sense unless you intend to do a lot of metalworking. The tools include metal drills, reamers, countersinks, a ball peen hammer, punches, a tap-and-die set, a sheet-metal fly cutter, a chop (or miter) saw with a metal-cutting blade, tin snips, an electric soldering iron, and a propane torch. Add a welder if you plan to work extensively with steel.

UNDERSTANDING METALWORK TERMINOLOGY

The drawings below and the Material Matters chart on page 519 show and list different metal products you'll encounter in home repair and improvement projects. Here are some metalworking terms you should know so you can speak "metalese" fluently.

■ Alloys are metals made by combining two or more metals. Ferrous metals are made from iron, with traces of other metals. Cast-iron, wrought iron, carbon steel, and mild steel are ferrous metals. Nonferrous metals don't contain iron.

■ Annealing is a process that reduces the brittleness of metal by heating, then cooling it quickly before crystals can form.

■ Etching is the result of the action of acid on metal. The design to be etched is created with an etching tool in a wax substance on the metal. The acid is poured over the wax surface, affecting only the nonwaxed portions.

■ Soldering is the process of joining two pieces of metal with metal—usually tin (see pages 466 and 522).

■ Sweating is a process for joining two pieces of metal by "tinning" each piece—as in sweating copper tubing (see pages 304 and 522).

■ Welding is a technique that uses heat to join two pieces of metal.

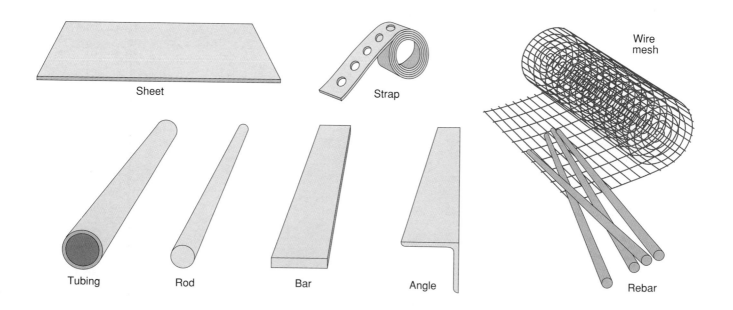

Sheet

Strap

Wire mesh

Tubing

Rod

Bar

Angle

Rebar

MATERIAL MATTERS   SELECTING METALS

Metal	Type	Shapes	Special Tools	Cost	Uses
Aluminum	Nonferrous	Sheet, tube, rod, bar, angle, channel, embossed	Riveter	Moderate	Gutters, downspouts, flashing, patching, furniture, specialty hardware, hobby, crafts, fasteners
Copper	Nonferrous	Sheet, tube, rod	Propane torch	Expensive	Gutters, flashing, patching, specialty hardware, crafts, plumbing, electrical, decorative, fasteners
Galvanized iron/steel	Ferrous	Sheet, tube, rod, bar, angle, channel, ducting	Metal drills, punches	Moderate	Flashing, roofing, ducts, patching, fasteners, braces, pipe, screening, hardware
Mild steel	Ferrous	Sheet, rod, bar	Taps/dies, reamers, welders	Moderate	Tools, fasteners, support columns, framing
Brass	Nonferrous	Sheet, tube, rod	None	Expensive	Decorative, fasteners, crafts
Bronze	Nonferrous	Sheet, tube, rod	None	Expensive	Fasteners, decorative, crafts
Wrought iron	Ferrous	Preformed rod	Welding equipment	Moderate to expensive	Railings, supports, decorative, crafts
Lead	Nonferrous	Bar, cable, sheet, rod	Heater, melting pot	Moderate	Sheet roofing, specialty washers
Silver	Nonferrous	Bar, rod, particles	Melting pot, craft equipment	Expensive	Crafts, furniture and cabinet inlays, jewelry
Gold	Nonferrous	Bar, rod, particles	See silver	Expensive	Crafts, inlays, jewelry
Tin	Nonferrous	Sheet, rod, bar	See lead	Expensive	Used to make solder alloys
Drill rod	Ferrous	Rod	Hacksaw, metal lathe	Moderate to expensive	Cutting tools, punches, taps, chisels, tool bits
Cast-iron	Ferrous	Bar, rod	Hacksaw	Moderate	Lavatories, tubs

Working with Metals

Unless you majored in industrial arts, you're probably a bit leery of working with metals. In fact, many people associate metalworking with something best left to professionals, so they don't tackle even simple metalworking projects themselves.

Dispelling this notion will help you in a couple of ways. When you learn to work with metals, you'll become a more complete do-it-yourselfer. And, if you develop basic metalworking skills, you'll save some money. Suddenly, a leaky pipe or gutter won't be the catastrophe it used to be—and won't be nearly as costly to repair, either. Nor will repairing a chimney flashing or many other common repair jobs.

To be sure, there are some techniques to master. But once you get into metalworking, you'll be surprised to find that many metals are as easy to work with as wood.

Read this and the next five pages to discover just what you can do with metals—you'll be surprised.

CUTTING METALS

What you cut metal with depends on what type of metal it is. For thin and soft metals, you can use a hacksaw, heavy scissors, tin snips, or a cutter designed for the material, such as a tubing cutter. For plate, bar, and rod stock, a hacksaw works best. For thick and hard metals, such as galvanized pipe, reinforcing rod, and girders, a hacksaw will do the job in the end, but a reciprocating saw or a miter (chop) saw with a metal-cutting blade, a pipe cutter, or a gas cutting torch will do a quicker job.

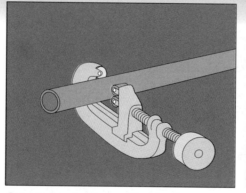

Cut copper tubing with a hacksaw or a tubing cutter (see page 304).

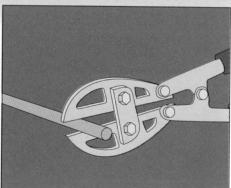

If you have many rods to cut, rent a bolt cutter. This heavy-duty performer makes easy work of it.

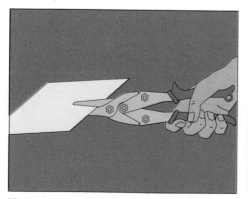

Tin snips, especially the aviation type shown here, make fast work of cutting 20-gauge or lighter sheet metal.

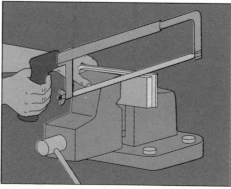

You also can cut sheet metal with a hacksaw. If the metal chatters, sandwich it between boards.

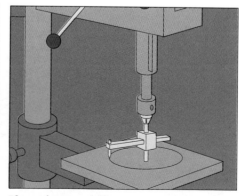

If you have a drill press, you can cut holes up to 8 inches in diameter in thin metal with a fly-cutter rig.

DRILLING METALS

For almost any hole-boring job in metal, you need a twist bit manufactured from high-speed steel. Lesser-quality bits simply can't stand up to the abuse cutting metals involves; they overheat easily, lose their temper or hardness, and dull.

A stationary drill press or a drill-press stand for a portable electric drill is the ideal equipment for drilling metal. You can accomplish the same goal, although more slowly, with a twist bit locked in the chuck of a hand drill or brace.

Before drilling, always lock the metal in a vise or clamp it to a solid base to prevent the drill bit from "catching" the metal and "spinning" it out of your hand. To help you get the hole started and keep the bit from "skating" away from your intended location, use a center punch to mark the hole. Also, be sure to wear safety glasses.

The keys to drilling metal include keeping the drill square to the metal; applying constant, even pressure; and keeping the metal lubricated while drilling. On tough metals, such as iron and steel, use light machine oil as a lubricant. For aluminum, use kerosene. Other soft and thin metals generally don't need lubrication. If the bit gets hot, use light oil.

If the work starts to smoke or the bit binds in the metal, ease up on it. You're either forcing the drill too much or working with a dull bit.

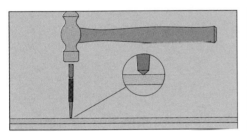

Mark the hole location for drilling with a center punch. This tool has a pointed end that makes a niche for the tip of the drill bit.

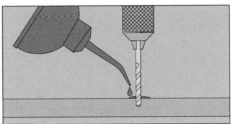

A variable-speed drill works best in metal. Start drilling at a low speed, gradually increasing the rpm. Add lubricant, and keep the pressure even.

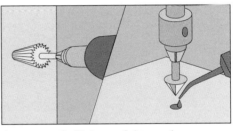

A reamer (left) is useful to enlarge holes in metal. Don't turn backward or you'll nick blade. A countersink (right) makes a flared hole to set screws into.

FASTENING METALS

If you're an average do-it-yourselfer, you probably don't have access to a welding unit. That doesn't mean you can't successfully fasten together metal items. Many mechanical fasteners will do the job—screws, bolts, rivets, and adhesive.

Rivets (see page 465) do the neatest and one of the strongest fastening jobs. You can buy rivets made of different metals to match the metal you're working with— aluminum, copper, iron, and brass. You'll need a ball peen hammer to flatten rivets.

Avoid alignment problems when joining metal by measuring, marking, and drilling the holes for one fastener. Install it, then measure, mark, and drill both pieces of metal for additional fasteners. Stay away from the ends and edges of material.

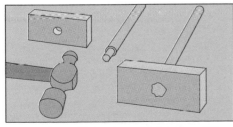

Join rods and bars by self-riveting. File the rod end into a tenon that fits the hole. Insert and peen the end.

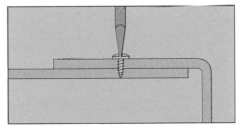

To join pieces of sheet metal, start the hole with center punch, then drive in self-tapping sheet-metal screws.

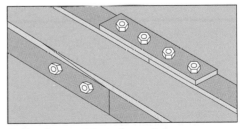

Splice bars with a cleat of the same metal. Make the job neater by grinding a taper on the ends of the splice.

Working with Metals (continued)

SOLDERING METALS

To create a lasting joint when you solder metal, you must adhere to three stringent rules.

First, make sure the material being soldered is clean—shiny clean. Use sandpaper or steel wool to remove all dust, dirt, grease, rust, corrosion, paint, and even your fingerprints.

Second, use enough heat. Don't use a soldering iron or gun to solder pipe, for example. Neither will generate the temperature needed to heat the pipe and melt the solder. Use a blowtorch in this instance.

Heat the metal being joined and the solder sufficiently. If the solder or the metal isn't hot enough, you may get a "cold" joint that looks pitted, like unstirred sugar on the bottom of a coffee cup. The joint must be hot enough for the flux to do its cleaning job and boil away.

Third, use the right solder and flux for the job (see page 466). You can use wire solder with a core that contains flux. Use rosin flux-core solder for copper and acid flux-core solder for metals, such as galvanized iron. Solder containing lead is banned; most today is 95 percent tin.

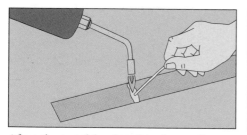

After thoroughly cleaning the surfaces to be joined, "tin" (coat) the surfaces, as shown, with solder. Then, join them.

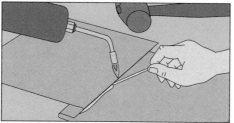

A "stovepipe seam" is the best way to join metal sheets. Fold ends, interlock, and pound flat. Then, solder one edge.

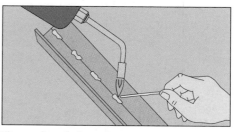

Tin and tack long joints at intervals, then secure the joint by "flowing on" a continuous strip of solder.

BENDING METALS

Adequate support and sometimes heat are the keys to bending metals. They minimize the weakening of the metal that is caused by stretching that occurs during bending.

For most metals, you can improvise a bending jig out of scraps of wood, C-clamps, or a vise. Thick, exceptionally hard metals, such as steel bars, defy bending without applying very high heat. With these, your best bet is to form the bend you want in a piece of thin scrap metal and have a metalworking shop duplicate the bend for you, using the scrap piece as a template.

Thin sheet metals, such as copper and aluminum, are a different story. You must be careful not to overbend them. Thin metals that are bent and creased at right angles tend to tear almost like paper. Simply make the bend and leave it alone; don't wiggle it back and forth.

When measuring the length of a piece that you will have to bend, allow enough length to make up for the bend. A right-angle bend in copper pipe, for example, "absorbs" about half the diameter of the pipe.

Bend a corner in metal by clamping it in a vise and tapping near the jaws. Use a rubber hammer for soft metals.

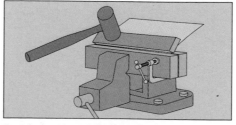

Bend sheet metal the same way, but extend jaws with strips of hardwood and C-clamps. Tap on a scrap block.

For complex curves, slide the metal between bolts. Make the bends in increments, moving the metal.

FILING METALS

Files make quick work of shaping and smoothing metals. Shaping also generally requires a vise to hold the metal so it doesn't slip or vibrate. For soft metals, such as aluminum and copper, use a single-cut file. For harder metals, you'll need a double-cut file.

For more information on file types, see pages 476–477. See page 480 for help with choosing the proper abrasive for smoothing metals.

To file metals, hold the file in both hands and apply the cutting action on the forward stroke only. For a super-smooth finish, draw-file the metal with a single-cut file. Hold the file flat across. Then draw it across the metal in smooth, even strokes.

Using a cloth moistened with light machine oil, keep the surface of the metal free of metal chips and "dust" as you file. Keep the file clean with a file card. Don't tap the file on a hard surface to remove debris. It won't dislodge much, and it may ruin some of the file's teeth.

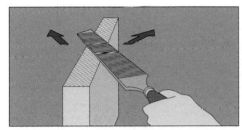

For smooth edges, hold the file at a 30-degree angle. File from left to right, then reverse the angle and cross-file.

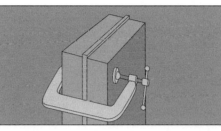

To draw-file a perfectly flat edge, clamp work between boards so you can't rock the file and round the edge.

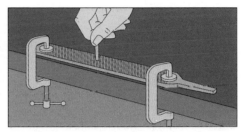

For small pieces, clamp a file to a bench and move the metal along the file. Use a round file for inside curves.

POLISHING METALS

All metals—except gold or those protected with a finish—rust, corrode, and/or oxidize. Silver turns black, iron rusts, aluminum dulls and pits, and brass turns green. To make metals shine again, you need the right abrasive.

■ **Aluminum.** Use a pad of medium to fine steel wool. You also can polish aluminum with a fine wire wheel or a flannel wheel and white rouge polishing compound.

■ **Copper and brass.** Use medium to fine steel wool and emery paper. Polish with a fine wire wheel or a flannel wheel and brown tripoli polishing compound.

■ **Iron and steel.** Use a coarse to medium abrasive, followed with a wire brush and a fine abrasive. If the material is extremely rough, you may have to file it with an abrasive wheel, then polish.

■ **Gold and silver.** Use a liquid polish made for these metals. Buff with red jeweler's rouge.

■ **Stainless steel.** Use extra-fine steel wool and commercial metal cleaners. Buff with white rouge.

Once you've polished a metal, protect the surface to preserve the shine. You can coat aluminum, copper, brass, bronze, iron, and steel with a clear lacquer or polyurethane finish. You also can paint some metal surfaces with a pigmented finish (see pages 564–565).

For a satin finish, buff metal with a wire wheel on an electric drill. Or, rub the surface with a very fine steel wool.

For a higher luster, sand with increasingly finer grades of emery cloth. Reverse direction with each cut.

To highly polish metals, use a buffing wheel with a polishing compound. Seal the surface with a clear finish.

Working with Metals (continued)

WORKING WITH ALUMINUM

Not only is aluminum a versatile material, it's also one of the easiest with which to work. In fact, you can cut aluminum sheeting with scissors or tin snips. However, both tools tend to "buckle" the material around the cut edge. If appearance is an important consideration, use a fine-tooth handsaw or circular-saw blade to make the cuts.

Bar, rod, channel, and track aluminum are too thick to cut with scissors or tin snips; however, a handsaw or a power saw equipped with the appropriate metal-cutting blade will zip right through them.

To mark aluminum for accurate cutting, use a scratch awl. Joining aluminum is almost as easy as cutting it. Screws, bolts, and rivets all work well. You even can use a staple gun to tack aluminum sheeting to wood framing if the sheet is thin enough.

Because aluminum is a soft metal, you can drill, shape, and smooth it easily. Just be sure to use tools designed for fabricating metals.

Sawing, drilling, sanding, and grinding aluminum produce a fine to fairly coarse metal dust or debris; for safety's sake, always wear safety glasses and gloves when you work with this material.

Aluminum won't rust, but it will corrode, leaving the metal white and pitted. To prevent this, coat it with a clear lacquer or polyurethane finish, or paint the surface. Use a zinc-oxide primer before painting (see pages 564–565).

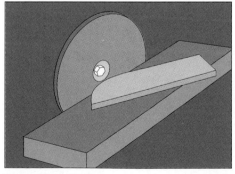

Cut thin sheets of aluminum into various shapes with sharp scissors. Mark the outline you want with an awl or wax-type pencil.

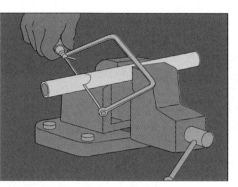

Fine-tooth handsaws work best on thicker aluminum and tubing. Here, a coping saw is used to cut a notch in tubing for a T-connector.

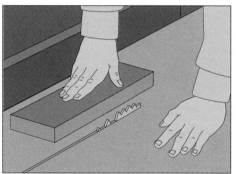

Fine-tooth power-saw blades make accurate, straight cuts. Prevent the sheet from lifting up by pressing down with a piece of scrap.

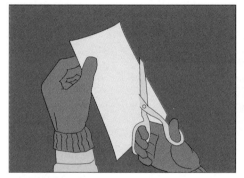

Use a disc sander to round corners and smooth cuts. If you clamp an angled strip to the table, you can grind perfect miter angles.

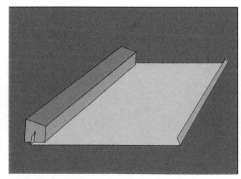

Make an angle jig for aluminum sheeting by sawing a slot in a board. Planing the inside surface of the jig at an angle lets you "shape" bends.

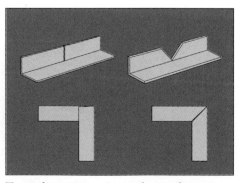

To make corners in angle stock, saw one side at 90 degrees, then bend and overlap it. Or, miter it by making V-shaped cuts.

WORKING WITH TUBING

Although sometimes hidden from view, metal tubing is all around us. Copper tubing carries water throughout our homes. Aluminum tubing is used for furniture legs, shelving spacers, hanger rods, and electrical conduit. Brass and steel tubing have both functional and decorative uses.

You can buy or special-order metals in both rigid and flexible tubing at most building materials outlets. If you can't find them there, check with a plumbing dealer. Tubing ranges from ⅛ to 1¼ inches in diameter and up to 10 feet in length. You can purchase much longer lengths of flexible tubing, which is packaged in long rolls.

By far, the slickest tool for cutting small tubing is a hand-type tube cutter (see page 520). Because the blade burrs the metal, good-quality cutters incorporate an attachment that removes the burrs.

Bending presents special problems—namely, kinking. Once tubing is kinked, it's impossible to re-form it. A spring-type bender (see below) works on thin-wall tubing; a conduit bender works better on pipes with thicker walls. A bending jig or spring is most critical for small-diameter tubing because the tubing kinks very easily when shaped with just your hands.

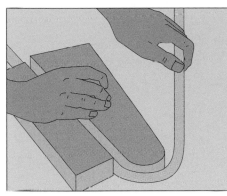

Bend tubing by shaping it around a wooden jig especially cut to duplicate the pattern you want. Make the bend in slow increments.

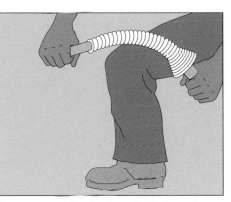

A commercial tube bender is best for forming small-diameter tubing. It's a springlike device into which you insert the tubing.

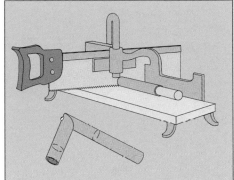

Make mitered corners by driving a wooden plug snugly into the tube, then making a 45-degree cut. A metal screw secures the corners.

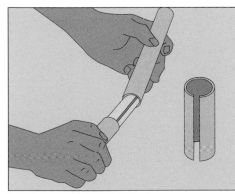

To splice tubing that doesn't carry a fluid, saw a ¼-inch slit in a piece of scrap tubing and slip it into the joint. Tension will hold it in place. Or, insert a wooden dowel that fits snugly.

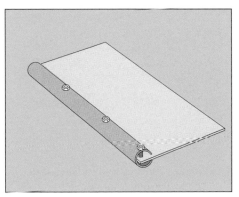

Sawing a slit provides a method to join tubing with wood or metal sheeting. Screws or bolts then can pass through both the tubing and sheeting.

Choosing and Buying Glass

You probably don't live in an all-glass house or throw stones. However, you should know how to buy and install glass for that occasional broken window or storm door that seems to afflict us all.

If you've never shopped for glass before, you'll be surprised at how many different types are available (see chart below). If you're like most homeowners, standard glass will be first on your shopping list, followed by plate glass, which generally is used for shelving and tabletops.

You can purchase replacement glass in several thicknesses. Your best bet is to take a piece of the broken glass with you to the store.

Stores that sell replacement glass stock it precut in standard window and door frame sizes, so you'll need to know the exact size of the space you're fitting. Measure the sash opening, then subtract ⅛ inch from this measurement on all four sides. This lets the glass "float" in the sash and helps prevent it from breaking. If the size you need is not standard, the dealer can cut the exact size for you. Or, you can buy a slightly larger standard size and cut it yourself (see page 160).

When replacing glass in storm doors, use either tempered safety glass or acrylic plastic. Both products help prevent serious injuries from broken glass.

MATERIAL MATTERS   SELECTING GLASS

Type	Strength	Installation	Cost	Uses
Standard SS	Poor	Easy	Low	Windows, doors, storm doors and windows, cabinet fronts, pictures
Standard DD	Fair	Easy	Low	Same as SS
Plate	Good	Easy	Medium	Tabletops, shelves, high-quality mirrors
Tempered	Excellent	Easy	Medium	Windows, doors, patio doors, skylights, shower doors, fireplace doors
Safety	Excellent	Difficult	Medium	Storm doors, patio doors, skylights, tabletops
Wire	Excellent	Difficult	High	Doors, commercial jobs, basement windows, high-crime areas
Insulating	Good	Difficult	High	Windows, patio doors, large glass areas
Tinted	Good	Moderate	High	Windows, doors, large glass areas, commercial windows, skylights
Frosted	Good	Moderate	High	Bathroom windows, shower doors, tub enclosures
Patterned	Fair	Easy	High	Entrance windows, decorative accents, cabinet fronts
Mirror tiles	Poor	Easy	Medium	Accent walls, bathrooms, bedrooms, cabinet liners
Glass block	Excellent	Difficult	High	Basement walls in new construction and remodeling

Working with Glass

The tasks of cutting, smoothing, and shaping glass sound more formidable than they are in reality. If you follow the procedures below and exercise reasonable caution, you should not have many mishaps.

For glasswork, invest in a quality glass cutter and a pair of glass pliers. In addition, you'll need a putty knife, a can of light machine oil, and a thin piece of wood with a straight edge. Also, wear gloves and safety glasses when handling glass.

To cut glass, lay it on a flat surface covered with several layers of newspaper. Clean the glass with glass cleaner before you score and break it.

If you're cutting mirror glass, follow the same procedures, but don't cut or apply oil to the silvered side of the glass. If you're cutting old glass or glass with a pebbled or uneven surface, use a dull glass cutter and apply plenty of pressure to the cutting wheel. Do not attempt to cut tempered or safety glass; leave that job for a professional. Cut wire glass like standard glass, but snip the wire after the break is made. You may be able to bend the glass back and forth until the wire breaks.

To drill holes in glass, use a sharp tungsten-carbide bit and drill at a very slow speed. Keep the tip of the bit lubricated with oil, turpentine, or kerosene.

For information on how to replace a windowpane, see pages 160–161.

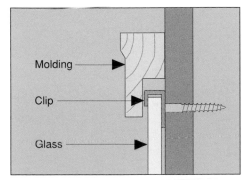

To make straight cuts in glass, score the piece with a glass cutter. Then, snap it by exerting downward pressure with your hand.

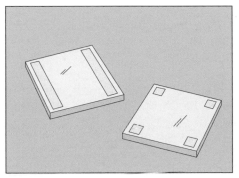

A ruler with a suction cup on one end lets you scribe curves. A glass cutter held at a certain measurement scores the glass.

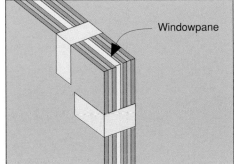

Smooth rough glass edges by rubbing them with an oilstone dipped in water. Use even strokes and keep the stone square to the edge.

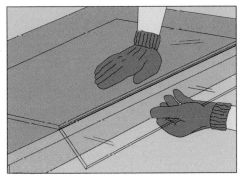

Molding

Clip

Glass

Secure large mirrors with special steel clips sold at glass outlets and home center stores. You can cover the clips with molding.

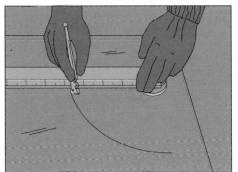

To cover a wall with mirror tiles, square them up as you would ceramic tiles (see page 44). Secure with tape or mastic adhesive.

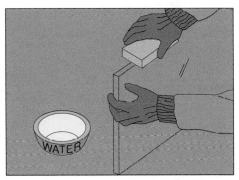

Windowpane

Store extra windowpanes by sandwiching each between two pieces of plywood and taping the package together. Set on edge.

FINISHING

Painting Interior Surfaces

Too many home projects, both interior and exterior, get finished off with little more than a coat of something or other slapped onto a surface that's not properly prepared. The result is a botched job that haunts you for years.

The solution is to learn the correct way to paint or wallpaper a room, revitalize the exterior skin of your house, seal wood grain, or apply special finishing treatments.

We start out this chapter with interior painting, a task that almost everyone faces at sometime. Here, the emphasis is on products and techniques that let you get the job done efficiently and with a minimum of hassle.

Whether interior or exterior, functional or decorative, nearly 90 percent of the work in a successful finishing project happens before you pop open the first lid on a can of paint or other finish. No one enjoys patching, scraping, and sanding chores, and priming seems to add just another product to the list of things you have to buy. It's these no-fun procedures, however, that spell the difference between a so-so result and a professional-looking job.

CHOOSING AND BUYING INTERIOR PAINT

Shopping for paint can be a bewildering experience. Latex, alkyd, acrylic, urethane, epoxy—what do all these mysterious names mean? What kind of preparation do they require, and what sort of results will they produce?

Unfortunately, you can't always rely on the salesperson to straighten you out. Product labels aren't necessarily very helpful, either. But usually a close reading will tell you a few key things. The chart on the next page compares paints you're most likely to use.

Look for the thinner specified by the manufacturer. Today's paints rarely require thinning, but you'll need the proper agent for cleaning up spatters and tools.

Here, there are only two important categories: water-thinned paint and solvent-thinned paint. Water-thinned formulations—latex is the most typical—can be cut with water, which means you can wipe up smears with just a damp rag, wash out brushes and rollers with soap and water, and wash your hands under a faucet. Water-based paints also dry quickly.

Solvent-thinned paints—usually alkyd-based—require a solvent, such as mineral spirits (paint thinner) or special odorless thinners, for cleanup. Solvent-based paints generally are more durable than water-thinned paints.

Interior paints come in different lusters or glosses. Just how shiny a surface you want depends partly on your taste, of course, but the glossier a finish, the harder and more durable it will be. Professional painters generally recommend flat or low-gloss paint—variously called satin, eggshell, or low-luster—for broad expanses of walls and ceilings. They recommend semi- and high-gloss finishes for woodwork, kitchens, baths, and other areas that receive hard wear or in which there is high humidity. Flat and low-gloss paints do a better job of hiding flaws in the surface underneath; you'll pay less for them, too.

After you've decided on a top coat, give careful thought to a primer. Designed to seal raw surfaces, primers have other important uses. If, for example, you want to change colors or apply latex over an existing glossy surface, you should apply a primer first. The right undercoat provides a "tooth" to which the final finish can adhere. You must match the primer to the top coat, so consult the chart on the opposite page and double-check by asking the salesperson or reading labels before making your decision.

Colors present some special problems, too. They react to each other and cast reflections that may change the appearance of everything in a room. Colors look different under different lighting, and large areas may become far more intense than you might imagine while looking at relatively small paint-sample chips. If you're contemplating a drastic color change, consider buying a quart of the hue that catches your eye and trying it out on a wall or sizable area before you invest in several gallons of paint that may not be returnable.

MATERIAL MATTERS — COMPARING INTERIOR PAINTS

Paint	Uses	Features/Characteristics	Thinner/Primer
Latex	Choice for most paint jobs; don't use it over unprimed wood, metal, or wallpaper	Glosses from flat to high; adheres to all but slick surfaces; usually dries fast enough to apply two coats in one day; less durable than alkyd-base paints	Easy to clean up with water and soap; prepare raw surfaces with a latex or alkyd primer.
Alkyd	For tough surface or super hiding; don't apply over unprimed drywall—it will roughen surface	Dry somewhat more slowly than latex; have a slightly stronger odor	For thinning and cleanup, use solvents; coat unfinished surfaces with alkyd primer.
Oil	Natural-resin oil paints have all but disappeared	Dry slowly; give off flammable fumes; don't stand up as well as alkyds	Thin with turpentine or other mineral spirits.
Urethane Polyurethane	Use over almost any porous surface or existing finish	Pigmented versions of polyurethane varnish; resist grease, dirt, abrasion, and alcohol; application is tricky; expensive, so consider whether you need durability	Most are solvent-thinned; check manufacturer's recommendations before you buy material.
Epoxy	Can be applied over nonporous surface, such as tile; won't adhere to previously painted finishes	Strongest and most costly of all paints; most require mixing in a hardening agent just before use—often tricky	Solvent-thinned; check label for recommended primer.
One-Coat	Use only if surface is sealed, is of a similar color, and doesn't have a lot of patchwork that needs to be covered	Ordinary latex or alkyd paints with additional pigment to increase hiding power; more expensive	Thinning lessens paint's ability to hide flaws; clean up with water or solvent, depending on whether latex or alkyd.
Texture	Designed to cover up imperfections and give the look of stucco-finish plaster	Some premixed; with others, you must stir in "sand"; application moderately difficult; usually paint a section at a time and work out desired effect	Thinning defeats purpose; stirring can be arduous; check label for compatible primers.
Acoustic	Coats acoustic tiles without affecting their sound deadening qualities	Apply by spraying or use a special roller; color choice limited	Thin and clean up with water; no primer is necessary.
Dripless	Use on ceilings	Considerably more expensive than ordinary paint	Water- or solvent-thinned; choose appropriate primer.
Metal	Use over primed or bare metal surfaces	Coat previously painted metal with almost any type of paint; self-primers designed to adhere to bare surfaces (see pages 564–565)	Some are thinned with water; others need solvent or mineral spirits; primer depends on the metal being covered.

Painting Interior Surfaces *(continued)*

MATERIAL MATTERS

Spilled and spattered paint always seems to stick to you and your clothes as if it were welded on. But try painting flat latex paint over a gloss oil paint and the new paint peels off as if it were one of those yellow self-stick notes.

SELECTING PAINT

The chart below shows what kinds of paint (top row) will stick to what surfaces (vertical column). If you prime, make sure primer and finish match.

Surface to be painted	Primer Coat									Finish Coat										
	Latex	Alkyd	Aluminum	Rustproofing Metal	Zinc	Cement Paint	Waterproofing Paint	Block Filler	Masonry Sealer	Latex Gloss	Latex Semigloss	Latex Flat	Latex Textured	Latex Acrylic Enamel	Latex Floor Enamel	Alkyd Gloss	Alkyd Semigloss	Alkyd Flat	Alkyd Floor Enamel	Epoxy Paint
Unprimed drywall	●	●								●	●	●	●			●	●	●		
Painted drywall										●	●	●	●			●	●	●		
Unprimed plaster	●	●				●			●	●	●	●	●			●	●	●		
Painted plaster										●	●	●	●			●	●	●		
Acoustic tile												●								
Unpainted wallpaper	●	●										●						●		
Vinyl wallpaper												●						●		
Plywood, wood veneer panels	●	●								●	●	●		●			●	●	●	
Painted plywood										●	●		●			●	●			
Plastic-finish panels											●	●					●	●		
Composition board	●	●								●	●	●		●			●	●	●	
Painted composition board										●	●		●			●	●			
Unprimed wood flooring	●	●								●	●					●	●		●	●
Finished wood flooring										●	●					●	●		●	●
Unprimed wood moldings	●	●								●	●	●		●			●	●	●	
Finished wood moldings										●	●	●		●			●	●	●	
Bare concrete		●				●		●	●	●	●					●	●			
Painted concrete							●			●	●			●		●	●		●	
Bare brick masonry	●	●								●	●					●	●		●	●
Steel				●						●	●			●		●	●			
Galvanized steel, cast-iron				●	●					●	●			●		●	●			
Aluminum			●							●	●			●		●	●			

TOOL TALK   CHOOSING AND BUYING BRUSHES

Selecting the right brush for a paint job isn't difficult. Except for foam types, all brushes fall into one of two categories: natural-bristle brushes and synthetic-bristle brushes. Natural-bristle brushes are made with animal hairs and formerly were considered the finest type available. However, some of today's synthetic versions now perform just as well.

If you're using an oil-based paint, use a natural-bristle or a quality synthetic-bristle brush. Never use a natural-bristle brush with water-thinned finishes. If you do, the bristles will become moplike, resulting in a streaked finish.

Many paintbrush manufacturers label the brush package with the type of finish for which the brush is designed. If the brush you're considering isn't packaged, take a look at its handle; it's probably stamped with the bristle type.

Consider disposable brushes, also. These come in a wide range of widths and sizes and are suitable for many painting projects. Because they're inexpensive, they can just be tossed away when the job's done, saving considerable cleanup time.

Should you spend the extra amount for a quality brush, or are the inexpensive ones the better buy? If you're willing to take the time to clean your brush after using it, buy a quality brush. It will serve you well for years. However, if you paint only occasionally and don't like cleaning up, a less-expensive brush is the wiser investment.

How can you distinguish between a good-quality brush and one of lesser quality? There are several ways. One of the surest is to spread the bristles and inspect their tips. Quality natural-bristle brushes will have little "flags" on the bristle ends—the more the

better. On good-quality synthetic brushes, you'll see fuzzy-looking tips.

Check the ferrule of the brush. This aluminum or stainless steel band near the handle should be wrapped tightly and neatly around the brush and solidly secured to the handle.

Among your first buys should be a 4-inch wall brush, a 2-inch trim brush, and a 2-inch sash-trim brush. Later, you might want to add a 6-inch wall brush for masonry paint jobs and a round brush for delicate work. A brush spinner speeds cleanup jobs.

The four handle styles shown below serve different functions. A beaver-tail handle lets you grip a wider brush in the palm of your hand; pencil and flat handles allow greater fingertip control; the kaiser handle also offers good control, plus a grip that's comfortable to your hand.

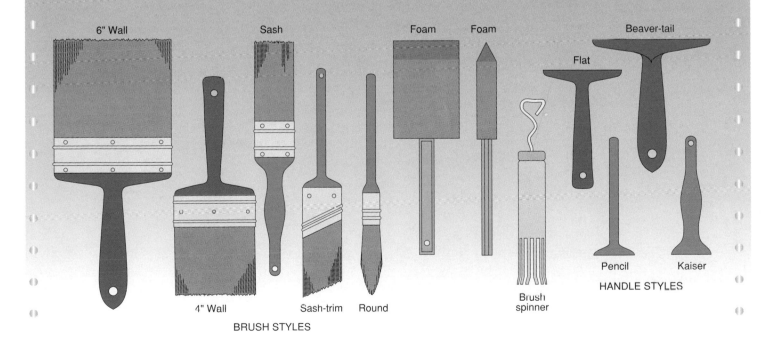

6" Wall Sash Foam Foam Beaver-tail Flat Pencil Kaiser HANDLE STYLES Brush spinner 4" Wall Sash-trim Round BRUSH STYLES

Painting Interior Surfaces (continued)

USING BRUSHES

There's a right way and a wrong way to use and care for paintbrushes. The sketches show the correct basics for loading, holding, and cleaning up brushes.

Before you use a new paintbrush for the first time, spin it by the handle between your hands, then slap it against the edge of a table to remove loose bristles. Work the bristles against a rough surface, such as a concrete wall, to soften the ends of the bristles. If the brush is a natural-bristle brush, soak it 24 hours in linseed oil for conditioning.

When you start painting, you'll notice two things: still more loose bristles and stray bristles that stick out from the sides of the ferrule. Pick up the loose bristles. For stray bristles, sandwich a putty knife between the bristle and the ferrule. Then, snap off the errant bristle.

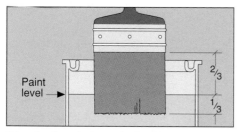

Dip the brush into the paint to one-third the length of its bristles. Go deeper, and you'll waste paint and create a mess.

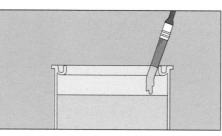

Squeeze the excess paint from the bristles by pressing them lightly against the side of the container as you remove the brush.

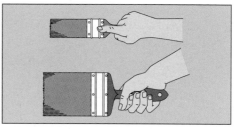

Hold small brushes between your thumb and your index finger. For larger brushes, use a palm grip or lay your fingers on the ferrule.

If your work is interrupted for an hour or less, leave the brush in the paint. Position it so the paint covers the bristle tips.

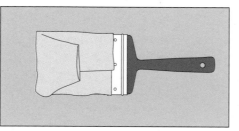

For longer interruptions, wrap the brush in foil or plastic and store it in the freezer. Thaw it out when you're ready to paint again.

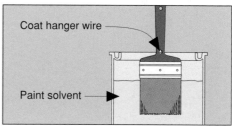

If you'll be using the brush within a day or two, immerse it in solvent or water, depending on the type of paint. Drill a hole in the handle for hanging.

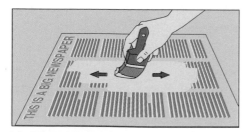

To clean a brush, work out remaining paint by firmly stroking the brush back and forth on newspaper. Work until the brush is dry.

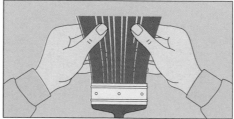

Before storing a brush for an extended period, remove all the paint you can with the appropriate thinner. Work the bristles, as shown.

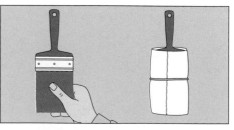

Wash the brush in soap and water, shape the bristles and let them dry. Then, wrap the brush in several layers of paper toweling.

TOOL TALK
CHOOSING AND BUYING ROLLERS

Rollers perform best on large, flat surfaces, but you also can buy trim rollers for small and hard-to-get-at areas. Once you get the knack of using a trim roller, they're as easy to control as a trim brush. Some people prefer to trim with a brush and fill in with a roller. Use the method that works for you.

Rollers range in width from 4 to 18 inches. They have a plastic or wooden handle (often machined to accept an extension handle) and a metal frame on which the roller cover is inserted.

The birdcage type of frame works better if you're using fast-drying paints, because it cleans up more easily than a solid-metal type. For solvent-thinned paints, either type of frame will work.

Trim rollers come in varying widths and configurations. The 3-inch-wide version gets into areas too tight for a full-size roller. Cone-shaped types are used for inside corners, around door and window casings, and almost any point where two planes intersect. Doughnut-style rollers paint moldings and other fine work.

Most roller covers are made from mohair, lamb's wool, acetate, Dynel, or polyurethane foam. They usually are labeled with the type of paint the roller was designed to apply, helping to eliminate guesswork.

Mohair covers are designed for gloss finishes and varnishes; they lay on a smooth finish because the nap is short and tightly woven. Dynel, acetate, and polyurethane foam covers can be used with all paints. Use a lamb's wool roller cover only for solvent-thinned paint.

Roller covers vary in nap length—from $\frac{1}{16}$ to $1\frac{1}{2}$ inches. Use the long naps for rough surfaces, the short ones for smooth surfaces. The nap is fastened to a cardboard or plastic sleeve. If you're using water-thinned paint, buy a cover with a plastic sleeve. For solvent-thinned paint, use a cardboard sleeve.

Pad painters are also handy. The pads may be a carpetlike material or plastic foam inserted in a plastic moplike applicator or a paintbrush handle. Although excellent for applying paint to almost any surface, they really earn their keep when you have to paint shakes, fencing, screening, and shutters.

A paint tray, either metal or plastic, completes the roller painting system. If you'll be working on a stepladder, buy a paint tray that has ladder "hooks" to keep the tray secure. To save on cleanup time, purchase plastic tray inserts, which you simply toss once the painting is done. With these, the paint never touches your tray.

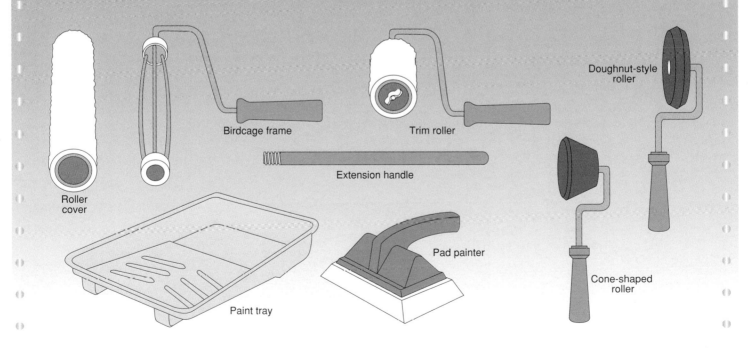

Birdcage frame

Trim roller

Doughnut-style roller

Extension handle

Roller cover

Pad painter

Cone-shaped roller

Paint tray

Painting Interior Surfaces (continued)

USING ROLLERS AND PADS

Anyone who has ever painted with rollers or pads will vouch for the ease with which they lay on paint.

When using a roller, however, keep your eyes peeled for skid marks on the painted surface. Rollers tend to "slide" as they move, causing small tracks in the finish, which will show when the finish has dried.

Most surfaces are irregular to some extent. To achieve the best coverage when using a roller or pad, lay on the paint from several different directions. In this way, you won't miss shallow depressions, such as joints between drywall panels. If you're applying glossy paint, finish an area with vertical strokes to give the surface an even appearance. Don't worry about evening up flat paint, however, because roller marks fade away as the paint dries.

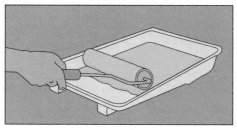

To load a roller cover with paint, turn the roller into the edge of the paint in the tray. Even out the paint on the slant of the tray.

For best paint coverage, apply the paint every which way. Minimize dripping by starting the roller on the upstroke.

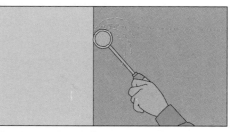

Don't work a roller too quickly, especially when the roller cover is loaded with paint. You'll splatter, which wastes paint and makes a mess.

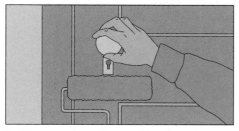

Rollers work well on wide, flat woodwork, such as raised panel doors. Paint the recesses first, then finish the flush surfaces.

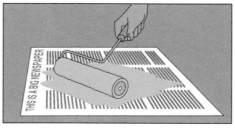

To clean a roller cover, work out all the excess paint you can on newspaper. Keep turning to new pages as you work.

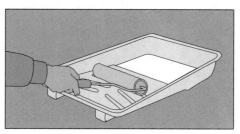

With solvent-thinned paint, pour solvent into the tray and work the roller back and forth. Repeat until the solvent remains clear.

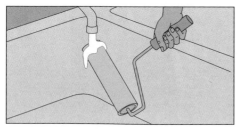

Wash out water-based paints in a sink. Let water run over the roller until clear. Squeezing the roller speeds things.

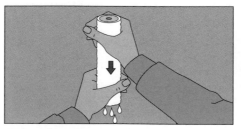

Wring the roller cover dry by squeezing it between your hands. If you're cleaning out solvent-based paint, wear rubber gloves.

Wrap clean, dry roller covers in aluminum foil or plastic bags. Clean pad painters just as you would paint roller covers.

USING POWER ROLLERS AND PADS

If you have ever painted a room with a paint roller, you know that most of your time was spent loading just the right amount of paint onto the roller. After about every 50 to 100 square feet, you had to pour more paint into the paint tray.

Power paint rollers and pads eliminate both of these steps and more than double your speed. The power equipment will pump from a 1-gallon or a 5-gallon can.

Practice your first time out on a large scrap of cardboard. Turn on the paint control for a few seconds at a time until you get a sense of how much on-time is required. Rollers generally require on-times of about 5 seconds; pads require 1 to 2 seconds.

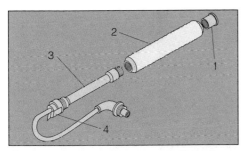

1. After opening the paint container and stirring the paint, put the special paint cover on the paint can.

2. Set the paint can into the base of the paint pumping unit and lock the can securely in place.

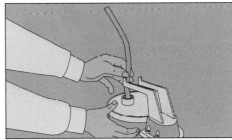

3. Insert the paint suction tube into the hole in the paint can cover. Push it to the bottom, then raise it ½ inch.

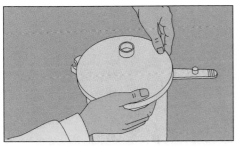

4. Unscrew end cap (1) and slide the roller cover (2) onto the plastic tube (3) until it locks in place with tab (4).

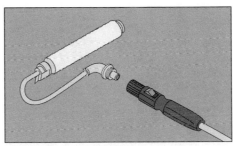

5. Attach the roller arm to the roller handle by inserting the arm into the handle or extension tube.

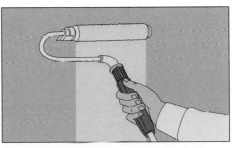

6. Turn the flow on and off with the switch on the handle. Don't overload the roller or it will leak and spatter.

7. When you're finished painting, run the roller or pad dry, remove the arm, and purge the paint from the hose, letting it run into the paint can.

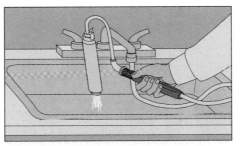

8. Attach the paint hose to a faucet adapter—if there is one—and run water through the roller until clean.

9. Squeeze the excess water from the roller and stand it on end to dry. Clean the seals on the roller arm.

Painting Interior Surfaces (continued)

CHOOSING AND USING STEPLADDERS

If you break into a cold sweat every time you get above the third rung of a stepladder, select a ladder you can trust, then learn a few safety habits.

When buying a stepladder, you'll have a choice of wood or aluminum construction. Aluminum ladders—by far the most popular—weigh only about half as much as wood ladders. Although every bit as strong and safe, metal ladders do flex a little more than wood ladders as you shift your weight around.

Check the ladder's sides. There, you'll usually find a rating that indicates its strength. Type III household-grade ladders are rated at 200 pounds; Type II commercial-grade, 225 pounds; and Type I industrial-grade, 250 pounds. Each type has been tested at four times these loads. For security and durability, buy a Type II ladder.

Lengths range from 2 to 16 feet, 6-footers are the norm for most indoor needs (see page 122 for choosing outdoor extension ladders).

If you follow five simple safety rules, you needn't worry about stepladder accidents.

■ If possible, lean a stepladder against a wall. Make sure that the stepladder sits solidly on the floor.

■ When you open the ladder, double-check that you've opened it fully and you've locked the bucket tray and braces in position.

■ Work from a ladder that is long enough for the job. Don't go higher than one step below the top, and never stand on the bucket tray.

■ Never paint a wooden ladder. Paint hides defects in the wood, preventing you from discovering possible problems.

■ Never climb a stepladder that has loose or broken rungs or a split or broken side rail.

Open the ladder and test it by lifting one side and pulling toward you. Keep the braces fully open and locked.

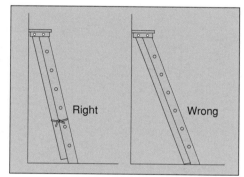

Prop a stepladder against a wall at a steep angle so the back legs don't catch on the floor. Or, tie the legs shut.

Two stepladders and a 2×12 make a convenient scaffold. But for safety, always try to work from the ladder.

If you don't have two stepladders, you can use a sawhorse to support one end of a scaffold plank.

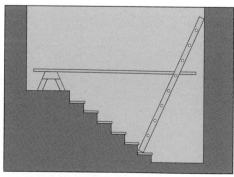

In a high stairwell, use an extension ladder, a sawhorse, and planks. To protect the wall, pad the ladder rails.

Avoid setting a ladder in front of a closed door. If you must do so, face the ladder's steps toward the door.

PREPARING INTERIOR SURFACES

Paint works wonders for a room's appearance, but it can't perform miracles. Paint will not heal cracked walls, smooth rough textures, or fill any but the tiniest nail holes. In fact, you may have trouble even getting paint to stick to some surfaces that haven't been properly prepared.

After you've cleared the room, but before you've opened the first paint can, give every surface careful scrutiny. Start with the walls, checking for cracks, runs, or ridges in the old paint. All of these can be treated easily with a scraper and sandpaper; then, use a primer for bare spots. Use a paint remover (see page 572) to strip cracked or gloppy paint from woodwork. If the old

paint is peeling, suspect moisture or poor preparation. Both require removing the old paint and priming the surface. Of course, any moisture leaks should be solved immediately.

Mend superficial plaster or drywall blemishes with surfacing or joint compound (see page 35–37). Bigger repairs (see pages 36 and 38) require more time, not only for patching, but also for curing and priming. (On textured walls, you may have trouble blending the patched area completely with its surroundings.)

You can paint over clean, sound wallpaper, but in most cases you're better off to strip it off (see page 544). If you do decide to paint over wallpaper, paint a small test spot in

an inconspicuous area and wait for a few days to see if the pattern bleeds through or the paper begins to peel.

After you've made repairs, give the ceiling, walls, and woodwork a thorough bath with household detergent, and rinse well. Prime exposed spots with a compatible primer. At this point, you've completed at least 50 percent of your painting project.

> ### YOU'LL NEED...
> **SKILLS:** Basic skills.
> **TIME:** 2 to 4 hours per room.
> **TOOLS:** Portable light, screwdriver, putty knife, sandpaper, sponge or mop.

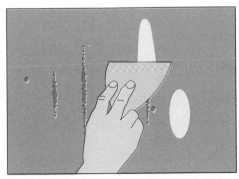

1. Remove all lightweight furniture from the room, group the heavy items, and cover them with drop cloths.

2. Set up strong lights so you can see what you're painting. Aim at angles to highlight minor imperfections.

3. Even if you plan to paint switch and receptacle plates, remove them and paint separately.

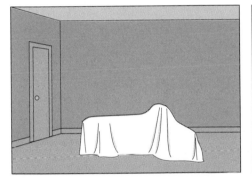

4. Regardless of its size, fill every hole and crack with premixed surfacing compound. Sand dry patches lightly.

5. Sand rough spots smooth, and sand runs from previous paint jobs. Liquid sanders remove gloss from trim.

6. Wash the ceiling and walls with a sponge or mop, paying attention to the tops of baseboards and moldings.

Painting Interior Surfaces (continued)

PAINTING CEILINGS

To be a big success at painting, unlike most other endeavors, you have to start at the top and work your way down. That means the ceiling comes first.

Except for new, unpainted materials, you usually can get by with one coat of paint on a ceiling. Even stubborn stains will disappear if you spot-prime them first.

If you're planning a one-coat application, let the paint lap on the walls. If you opt for two coats on the ceiling, cut in (trim up to the ceiling/wall line) with a trim brush. Otherwise, the paint will build up on the wall and leave a ridge.

Paint across the ceiling in the room's narrow dimension, especially if you're using a fast-drying paint. Otherwise, the paint may lose its wet edge.

You can paint a ceiling with a brush or a roller, but usually a combination of both works best. With a brush, you'll probably need a stepladder. A roller frame with an extension handle does a faster job, although you still will need a trim brush to cut in the ceiling paint where it meets the walls.

Unlike paintbrushes, which sometimes drip, rollers emit a fine spray of paint that settles over the room like dust. It's important, therefore, to cover furniture in the room, as well as the floor, carpeting, and woodwork. Canvas drop cloths work best for this, but plastic drop cloths and newspapers will do the job, too. Secure plastic cloths with tape, because they slip and slide over most surfaces.

> ### YOU'LL NEED...
> **SKILLS:** Basic painting skills.
> **TIME:** 3 to 4 hours.
> **TOOLS:** Drop cloths, brushes, ladder, roller with extension handle.

1. Start a ceiling job by cutting in a strip along the walls, as shown. If you'll be using only one coat, lap the paint onto the walls, as well.

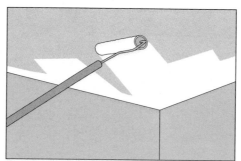

2. Start rolling the paint with a series of diagonal swaths. Don't worry about spreading the paint evenly; just get it on the ceiling.

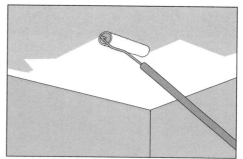

3. Even out the paint and fill in any open areas by cross-rolling. Don't fret about keeping the strokes even. They won't show.

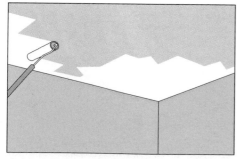

4. Continue working, spreading the paint from dry areas into the wet paint. Rollers "slip" on smooth surfaces, so check for skips.

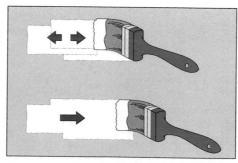

If you use a brush, apply the paint in short strokes, then level it with long, sweeping strokes, with the brush going in one direction only.

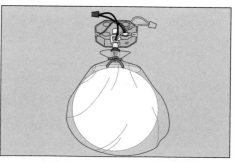

Wrap light fixtures in plastic bags. Drop fixture covers by removing or loosening the screws. (See page 270 for anatomy of a ceiling fixture.)

PAINTING WALLS

Painting walls is a breeze, especially when compared to the gyrations involved in painting ceilings. For one thing, you can stand up straight and reach most spots without much difficulty. Also, because you're working on a vertical surface, you can load both brushes and rollers with plenty of paint to get an initial quantity of the paint on the wall—first spreading it out, then evening it. This doesn't mean you don't have to watch for drips and splatters. Load the brush or roller well, but don't saturate it. It won't take long to get the feel for the right amount.

After the walls have been patched and cleaned thoroughly, the ceiling painted, and all of the switch and receptacle plates removed, you're ready to paint. Do all the edging first. This includes cutting in the ceiling and around moldings and trims. With these details done, you can paint big, flat surfaces quickly.

You don't have to worry about lap marks in the paint, except with gloss and semigloss finishes. With these type of paints, take care to keep painting over the edges to keep them wet and prevent lap marks.

When painting a kitchen, bathroom, or laundry with a semigloss or high-gloss finish, make the final brush strokes away from the light sources in the room, including windows, doors, and the prime lighting fixture. This way, the tiny ridges that a brush leaves won't be as pronounced.

Always give paint a brisk stirring before starting, even if the paint was just shaken at the store. As you work, stir the paint occasionally.

Keep an eye on the paint in the roller tray. As long as you're filling the roller, the paint will remain properly blended. If you leave the tray for an hour or so, cover it with plastic wrap. When you're ready to get back to work, stir the paint lightly with a paint paddle. When left untouched, paint skins over.

1. Begin painting walls by cutting in the corners and around woodwork. Lap the paint only a few inches onto the wall surface.

2. For large surfaces, Load the roller and apply the paint in a large "M" shape. Start the roller going up, then pull it down.

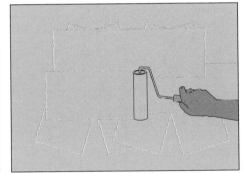

3. Level and fill-in the M by cross-rolling. By working the paint this way, you get an even paint surface. Watch for roller skids.

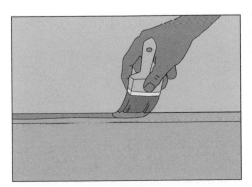

Where two colors meet, use a tapered trim brush lightly loaded with paint. Press it to within 1/16 inch of the adjacent color.

Apply high-gloss or semigloss paint in short, vertical sections that measure a few feet square. Work the paint well so it's even.

Painting Interior Surfaces (continued)

PAINTING WOODWORK

Painting woodwork is hard work. Next to prepping, it's the most time-consuming painting job. If you master the tricks shown here and on page 541, however, you'll minimize the hassle and speed your progress.

If at all possible, learn to paint freehand. With practice, anyone with a fairly steady hand and a good trim or sash brush can master freehand techniques and, in the process, save a tremendous amount of time, compared to applying masking tape.

Before tackling woodwork, check for damage. Patch minor holes with wood filler. Let the material dry overnight and apply a sealer. For major problems, consider replacing the molding (see pages 502–503).

If you'll be using the same paint on the woodwork as on the walls, paint the woodwork as you come to it. Most often, however, you should use a higher gloss on woodwork. In this case, or if it will be another color, do it after painting the walls.

Windows and raised-panel doors are the toughest painting jobs because of the amount of cutting in to be done and the fact that you can't take a full brush stroke as you can on a wall or ceiling. If you can't paint freehand, cover the glass with masking tape or use a painter's shield. Use razor blades and roller scrapers to clean off smeared paint.

If you're using a gloss finish on doors, use a cross-brush technique. Apply paint on the door horizontally. Then, make vertical finishing strokes. Always finish a door once you've started it. If you don't, the lap marks may show after the finish has dried.

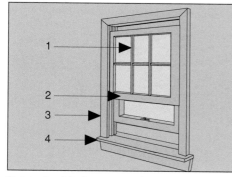

Paint double-hung windows in the sequence shown, starting with the muntins, then working outward.

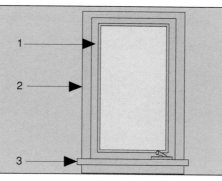

For casement windows, use the same sequence shown at left. Keep them slightly open until the paint is dry.

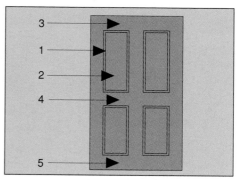

Start panel doors at the molded edges. Then, fill in the panels, the hinge stile, the rails, and the latch stile.

Flush doors are easier and quicker to paint. Either a brush or a roller will give good—though different—results.

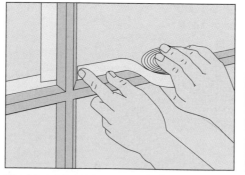

Masking tape protects window panes from paint. Remove the tape immediately after you finish the job.

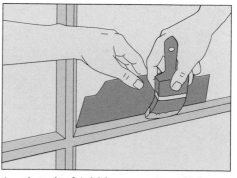

A painter's shield keeps paint off the glass, too. Wipe the paint off its edge as you work around the muntins.

Paint the top edge of a baseboard first. Cut in along the floor, then fill in between. Masking tape helps if you don't have a steady hand.

Clean up overlapping paint smudges as soon as they occur. If you don't, the paint will set up and be much tougher to remove.

A cloth wrapped around a putty knife works well to clean up paint drippings on hardwood and resilient flooring along baseboards.

If a woodwork stain bleeds through the paint, seal the woodwork with the appropriate primer. Remove scuff marks with steel wool.

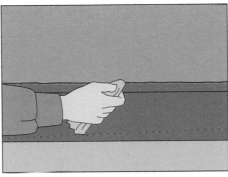

Before painting cabinets, dismantle them as much as possible. Lay out the parts on newspaper and paint all flat surfaces first.

Begin painting cabinets at their least accessible points and work outward. Do the inside edges first, then move to outer surfaces.

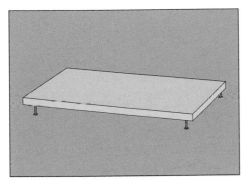

To paint both sides and the edges of a shelf in one session, drive in four small nails to serve as legs. Paint the underside, then the top.

Clean previously painted cabinet, door, or window hardware by soaking it overnight in paint remover. Buff the surfaces lightly with steel wool.

Paint impedes the heating efficiency of radiators. If you must paint them, paint only parts you can see. (More on metal paints on pages 564–565.)

Painting Interior Surfaces (continued)

CLEANING UP AFTER PAINTING

Even professionals painters are messy. But there's one big difference between them and the average do-it-yourselfer: They're more skilled at covering up their mistakes. Their secret is taking care of a spill or splatter immediately.

Even if you've thoroughly covered and masked the surfaces you don't want to paint, you can bet there will be some splatters here and there. For water-thinned finishes, use household dish detergent in warm water and a soft cloth to remove stray paint. If the paint is solvent-thinned, use the proper thinner (usually mineral spirits or turpentine) on a soft cloth. After wiping the areas with the thinner, wash them with water and household detergent.

If you happen to scuff freshly painted walls or woodwork, don't attempt to wash the scuff mark until the paint has had time to cure—at least 30 days. Although paint may feel dry to the touch within hours, it doesn't fully harden until it has cured completely.

After most painting projects, there will be a small amount of paint left over. If you end up with less than a quart, pour the paint into a glass jar that you can seal tightly. The paint will keep better in this small container. If you have more than a quart of material left, however, you can seal it in the original paint can.

Store paint in a cool, dry place where it won't be subjected to freezing and moisture, which can rust metal containers. If you don't use the paint within a two-year period, it's best to throw it away (see disposal chart on page 582).

Take canvas and plastic drop cloths outdoors and thoroughly shake them. Fold them for storing.

> ### YOU'LL NEED...
> **SKILLS:** Basic skills.
> **TIME:** 30 to 60 minutes for a newly painted room.
> **TOOLS:** Rags, razor-blade scraper.

Wipe away splatters with soap and water or the solvent used to thin the paint. It's best to catch these splatters as you work, not hours or days later.

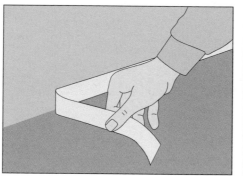

Remove masking tape as soon as you have completed a line. Otherwise, the paint will tear and you'll end up with a ragged and crumbling edge.

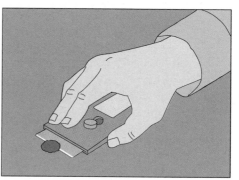

Use a razor-blade scraper to chip off big paint droplets that already have set. A putty knife will work, too.

Use a razor-blade scraper to trim around windowpanes. Try not to break the seal between glass and paint.

Tap container lids with a hammer and block of wood to shut them tightly. Store paint cans upside down to prevent a skin from forming.

Wallpapering

Wallpapering a room—once a messy, tricky task that was best left to professionals—is now little more difficult than painting the same space. Part of the credit goes to improved wall coverings that don't rip, shrink, or wrinkle as easily as the older papers. New, slower acting adhesives help, too, by giving you time to hang the materials correctly.

Here, we'll take you through every step of the job—from removing old paper to the advanced techniques needed for ceiling work. Because vinyl and prepasted coverings make most sense for beginners, there's a page devoted exclusively to hanging these time- and effort-savers.

MATERIAL MATTERS   SELECTING WALL COVERINGS

Type	Use	Application Tips	Cost
Lining paper	A base for foils, murals, burlap, and specialty coverings; excellent over rough or cracked surfaces	Hang with presized wheat paste. If surface has a gloss finish, combine 1 part vinyl adhesive with 3 parts wheat paste, then mix with water. Butt the edges of the liner.	Low
Vinyl-coated	Most any situation, except where there's high humidity	Paste and hang one strip at a time; roll the seams and clean the adhesive from each seam immediately.	Wide range
Paper-backed vinyl	Excellent for high-traffic and high-humidity areas	May be stripped. Hand-printed vinyls must be trimmed. Use abundant adhesive; do not stretch as you hang. If the seams curl, paste them down with vinyl-to-vinyl adhesive; remove excess adhesive immediately.	Wide range
Cloth-backed vinyl	Same as paper-backed vinyl	May be stripped. Stiff and difficult to shape to wall or ceiling surfaces. If the paper is lightweight, use a wheat paste adhesive; if heavy, use a vinyl adhesive.	High
Wet-look vinyl	Kitchens, bathrooms, laundry areas, and mud rooms	Lining paper required; surface imperfections will show.	Medium
Flocked	Especially good in formal areas	Keep adhesive off the face; if adhesive does get on the face, remove it immediately with clear water and blot, don't rub. If flocking mats, gently go over it with a suede brush.	High
Foil	Kitchens, bathrooms, and laundry areas, because it is easy to clean	Use a liner. Don't crease paper as you paste and hang it. Be careful around electrical switches and outlets.	High
Burlap/ grass cloth	Anywhere except in hard-use areas where there's lots of grease, dampness, and dirt	Lining paper required. Butt and roll seams. Mix vinyl adhesive with ½ pint less water than instructed; apply two coats of adhesive with a mohair paint roller cover.	High
Cork-faced	Best for accents; not for hard-use areas	Roll seams quickly. Use wheat paste with 1 part vinyl adhesive to 4 parts paste. Use liner unless wall is new.	High

Wallpapering (continued)

REMOVING OLD WALLPAPER

Ask anyone who has ever stripped old wallpaper and they'll tell you, "Don't." Unless you're working with a strippable-type paper, stripping old paper is a messy, time-consuming task. Before you decide to take on the job, ask yourself if you really need to take the old off before applying the new. If the old wallpaper is on the wall nice and tight, leave it there. You can eradicate a small blemishes by cutting away the damaged section and piecing-in a patch to level the surface. Bubbles can be slit, reglued, and flattened.

But if the old paper is in bad shape, you have no choice but to remove it. In years past the only way to remove old wallpaper was to soak it with water or a chemical solution. This meant continual soaking of the paper and lots of arm-tiring reaching and scraping.

Today, many papers are strippable, meaning they're designed to be peeled off. If you're dealing with a nonstrippable type, you can rent a wallpaper steamer with which you can remove more old paper in an hour than you previously could in a day of soaking and hard work.

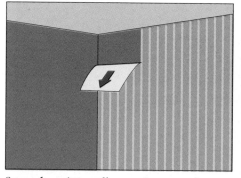

Some heavier wall coverings can be peeled off in strips—especially vinyl papers. Loosen an edge with a knife and pull down.

A wide-bladed wall scraper makes a good paper stripper. Work it under the wallpaper with one hand and peel with the other.

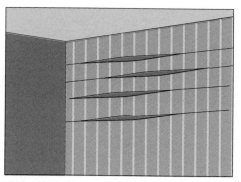

If the paper won't peel off in one continuous strip, make slits just deep enough to cut the paper. The paper may then pop up so you can peel it off.

If removing the paper without a steamer, slit it then soak the slits with a liquid wallpaper remover. Scrape off the old paper.

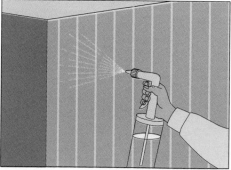

If the wall is plaster, soak the paper with mist from a plant sprayer. When wet enough, use a scraper to remove the paper.

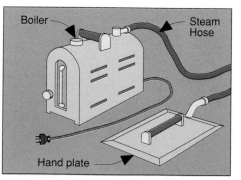

A wallpaper steamer works well for removing lots of paper. A small boiler furnishes steam to a plate that you hold against the wall.

PREPARING WALLS FOR PAPERING

For sheer impact, few interior wall treatments rival wallpaper. Trouble is, some people rush to the paste pot too quickly and botch the job, rather than taking the time to prepare the walls or ceiling. Wall preparation is one thing you just can't hurry. If you do, every nick, hole, and ridge will show.

You're in luck if the wall you want to paper is painted and in good repair. If the paint is glossy, simply dull the gloss with an abrasive so the adhesive will stick properly. Wash down the area with a strong household detergent, let dry, and proceed with wallpapering.

If the paint is peeling from the surface, remove it with a scraper, wash down the walls, then seal the surface with a sealer or wallpaper sizing. For walls with a sand or textured finish, first scrape and lightly sand the surface, then cover it with lining paper.

Lining paper is a plain, lightweight wallpaper without a pattern. You apply it with presized wheat paste, butting the edges and rolling the seams. The edges do not need to be butted tightly. A liner helps in many situations, but is not a cure-all for all surface problems.

Nicked, cracked, and crumbling walls or ceilings call for corrective action. In this case, you have a couple of alternatives. You can repair the surface completely (see pages 34–38) or do as much as you can to the surface and use a liner.

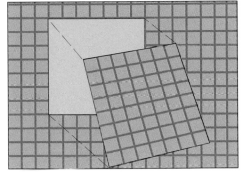

If the old paper is loose in just a few spots and you plan to paper over it, square-off the damaged area and insert a patch.

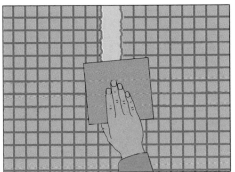

Lightly sand any seam overlaps. If you don't, the seams will show through the new wallpaper. Remove grease and dirt by washing entire surface.

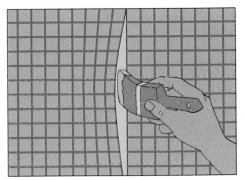

Glue down curled edges with wallpaper adhesive. Vinyl-to-vinyl adhesive is often the best choice; coat both the paper and the wall surface.

Use sizing to seal new walls or walls covered with wallpaper. The sizing keeps the porous surfaces from absorbing the adhesive.

Remove all hardware—and turn off electrical circuits—before you hang paper. If you don't, your trimming task will be more difficult—and dangerous.

Wallpapering (continued)

BUYING WALL COVERINGS AND EQUIPMENT

There are so many types of wall coverings available in so many patterns that selecting the material can become difficult.

First, determine how much material you need. Measure the height of each wall, then measure the distance around the room, including door and window openings. Multiply these two figures and you'll have the area of the wall surface. A wallpaper dealer will translate these figures into the number of rolls of paper you need.

After selecting the type of wallpaper (see page 543), ask the salesperson to recommend the right adhesive and the quantity you need. Foils, paper-backed burlap, vinyls, backed cork, flocks, hand prints, murals, and borders require vinyl adhesive. Prepasted wallpaper requires no adhesive—its major advantage. All that you'll need with prepasted wallpaper is a shallow trough wide enough to soak each rolled-up strip before you hang it.

You'll also need equipment—some special, and some items from your standard tool kit. Specialty items include a paste brush, a water tray for prepasted paper, a seam roller, and a smoothing brush.

Everyday items include a paint roller and tray (if you don't use a paste brush), a utility knife with plenty of sharp blades, a tape measure, an 8-foot straightedge, plumb bob, chalk line, long-bladed scissors, stepladder, drop cloths, wall scraper, and sponges. You'll need a pasting table unless you're using prepasted paper. Rent one or use two card tables covered with a sheet of hardboard.

HANGING WALLPAPER

One key to a visually successful papering job is finding the point in the room where a pattern mismatch will not be noticed. You inevitably can count on a mismatch, because the last strip you put up will have to be trimmed lengthwise to butt up against the first strip.

One such point is adjacent to a door or window frame. This gives only a few inches of discord above or below the opening. A good door is the entry door into a room, because the mismatch is hidden behind you as you enter the room. Other spots are an inconspicuous corner or a location that will be covered by draperies or furniture.

The first strip is very important because it "locks in position" all the strips that follow. Unless the first one is plumb, all other strips will be out of alignment, and the error will compound itself as you apply each successive strip to the walls.

Because wallpapering is a messy job at best, take special pains to "work clean." Wash your hands often. Use clean water and a sponge to wipe away paste after hanging each strip of paper. Keep the pasting table free of adhesive and clean your tools if they have paste on them.

If you're using prepasted paper, disregard Step 3 and simply soak the strip in your water trough.

YOU'LL NEED...
SKILLS: Basic skills.
TIME: 10 hours for a small room.
TOOLS: Tools are listed above.

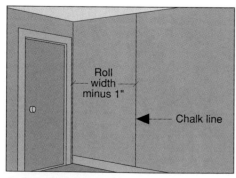

1. Use a plumb bob and pencil to mark a vertical line. Snap a chalk line and double-check the plumb with a level.

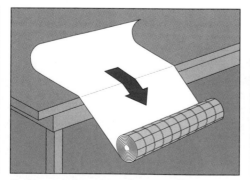

2. Uncurl the paper by unrolling it against the edge of a table. Cut the first strip several inches longer than needed.

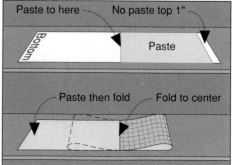

3. Apply paste to half of the strip, leaving an inch at the end to grasp. Fold over and paste the other half.

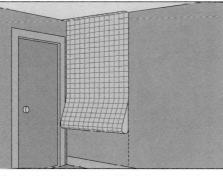

4. "Book" the pasted paper by folding it over twice. Let the pasted paper rest in this fashion for a few minutes, or according to manufacturer's directions.

5. Unfold the top half of the pasted paper. Align the paper with the plumb chalk line you snapped, overlapping the paper onto the ceiling.

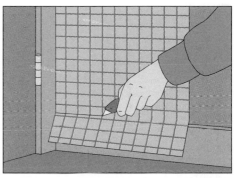

6. Smooth the paper onto the surface with the wall brush or clean sponge. Work from the center to the edges of the paper to remove all air bubbles.

7. Reach behind the strip and unfold the bottom half. Slip it into place against the plumb mark. You can pull and reposition it.

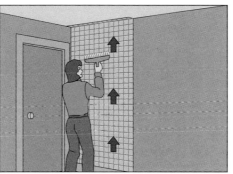

8. Smooth the lower section of paper. With a level, check for plumb. If not plumb, start again. Smooth with vertical strokes.

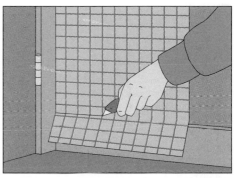

9. Tap the paper into the corners with the brush. Trim with a utility knife. If the paper tears, use a new blade or buy disposable knives with snap-off blades.

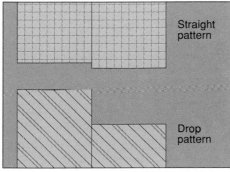

Straight pattern

Drop pattern

10. Cut several strips of paper at a time, allowing extra length for matching the pattern. Before pasting, check the matches, as shown.

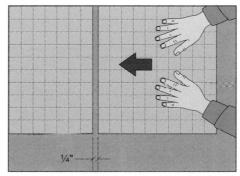

¼"

11. Butt seams by aligning each new strip about ¼ inch from the adjoining one. Slide it over so the edges buckle slightly. Smooth new strip as in Step 8.

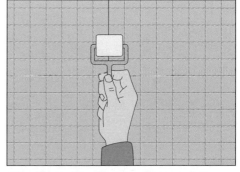

12. About 15 minutes after you've hung each strip, roll the seams with a seam roller to ensure good adhesion. Do not roll flocked papers.

Wallpapering (continued)

PAPERING AROUND CORNERS

Consider yourself lucky if you find a corner in your older house that's plumb. When a house settles, every building component is thrown slightly off level and plumb.

To negotiate problem corners, you need to master "double-cutting." Although it sounds difficult, actually it's fairly simple.

As you hang the adjacent strips, overlap the strips, making sure the pattern matches, and that there is at least a ½-inch overlap. With a very sharp utility knife, cut through both layers of paper. You can do this freehand, but a straightedge will help you make a cleaner cut. Be sure you make the cut while the paste on the paper is still soft.

Carefully pull both selvages from the surface, as shown below in Step 5. With a smoothing brush, smooth the seam created when you removed the selvages.

At either inside or outside corners, be sure you firmly tap the paper against the surface. After you've finished the corner, stick a series of thin straight pins along the edge of the corner—not in it—to "clamp" the paper until the adhesive dries. Arrange the pins in such a way in the pattern so holes won't show after the pins are removed.

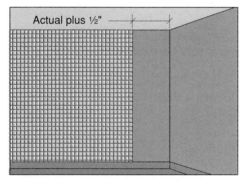

1. Measure the distance from the corner to the near edge of the last strip of paper you applied, top and bottom. Add ½ inch to the measurements.

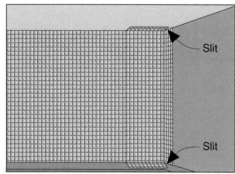

2. Cut, paste, and hang this strip. Tap it firmly into the corner. For a good fit, you will need to trim the margin top and bottom.

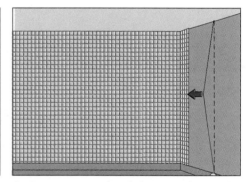

3. Snap a new plumb line on the wall, being sure to allow for a least a 1-inch overlap, or more if the pattern necessitates it, on the previous strip.

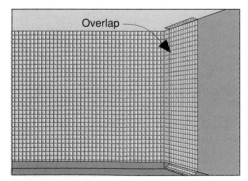

4. Hang the next strip with its edge on the plumb line. Tap the paper into the corner. Double-cut through both thicknesses of wallpaper.

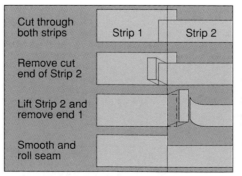

5. Peel off the outer selvage of paper. Lift the edge of the second strip and peel off the inner selvage. Smooth both strips, then roll seam.

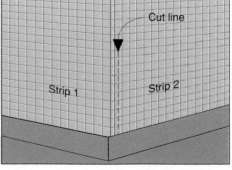

6. On outside corners, wrap the paper 1 inch or so around the corner. Apply the next strip, overlapping it, and double-cut with a sharp knife.

PAPERING AROUND OPENINGS

With the exception of negotiating corners, trimming around woodwork at openings is the most demanding part of a wallpapering project. Mistakes here are embarrassingly noticeable, so take the time necessary to make a good fit.

Always work with a knife that has a sharp blade to avoid pulling or tearing the covering. Before making your cuts around casings, be sure that the covering is snug against it. Otherwise, you may find to your dismay that the line you've cut falls short of covering the wall. If you don't feel comfortable making the cuts freehand, slip a metal straightedge into the joint, then make the cut using it as a guide.

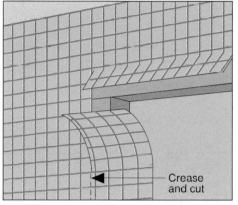

Let the strip adjoining the opening overlap the casings. Crease the covering at the molding's edge and cut it at the crease.

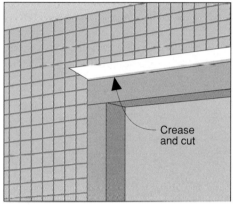

At the top of the casing, crease the paper and cut it where the molding joins the wall. Then, smooth the edge of the wallpaper.

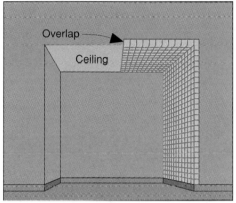

Paper recessed openings first. Lap the paper about 1 inch around the corner. Overlap the strips with the strips applied to the wall.

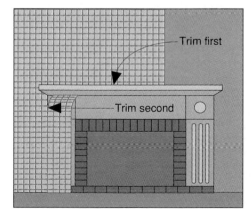

Trim along fireplace mantels or tops of bookcases before you do the sides. This allows you to wrap the paper around the sides and make truer cuts.

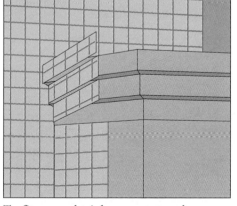

To fit around tricky corners and moldings, you will need to cut diagonal slits so the paper will lie flat. Use plenty of adhesive.

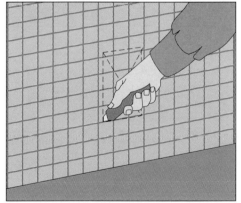

Shut off the electricity to circuits before you work around switches and outlets. Apply paper right over outlet or switch, then trim away the overlap.

Wallpapering (continued)

PAPERING OVER COVER PLATES

To add a professional touch to your wallpapering job, paper over switch and receptacle cover plates. Some fanatics paint the switch handles and receptacles with matching background paint. Before you go that far, however, consider the possibility that anyone with failing eyesight may not be able to find the camouflaged switch or outlet.

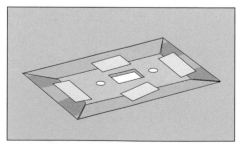

1. Cut a rectangular section of matching wallpaper, line it up over the cover plate so the pattern matches, then tape it to the wall.

2. Gently feel the outline of the cover plate under the paper and prick a tiny hole at each corner of the plate, using a common pin.

3. Remove both the paper and the cover plate. Line up the plate corners with the pin holes and trace the outline on the back side of the paper.

4. Cut the paper so that there is a ½- inch border around the outline of the plate. Trim the corners at 45 degrees down to the outline.

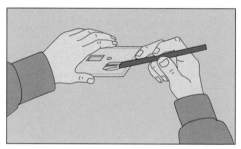

5. Using a small brush, apply vinyl wallpaper adhesive to the front of the plate. If plastic, apply a latex vinyl-to-vinyl adhesive primer first.

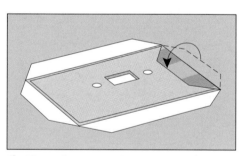

6. Place the paper face-up over the plate and smooth out any bubbles. Then line up the corners and fold the edges of the paper around the plate.

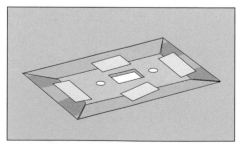

7. Tape the edges of the paper to the back side of the plate with masking tape. Let the adhesive dry before proceeding further.

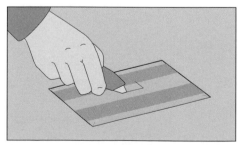

8. Using a sharp utility knife, carefully cut out the openings in the plate. If the cut paper edges are loose, apply more adhesive under the paper.

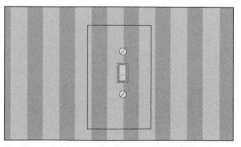

9. Punch through the paper with an awl or nail at the locations of the cover plate screw holes. Fasten the plate with the cover plate screws.

PAPERING CEILINGS

Ever wondered why more ceilings aren't wallpapered? It boils down to logistics. It's physically difficult to maneuver wallpaper strips up onto a ceiling that's 8 feet (or more) high.

If you're bound and determined, there are ways to do it. If you paper both walls and ceiling, paper the ceiling first, then the walls.

Prepare the ceiling as you would the walls (see page 545). Patch all cracks and cover any stains with primer. Drop the cover plates on light fixtures and, after shutting off the power supply, disconnect the fixtures to get them out of the way.

To get up to a workable level, you will need two stepladders and a length of scaffolding. The scaffolding must span the width of the ceiling so you can apply the wall covering without constantly moving the ladders and the scaffolding. A helper will come in handy, too. The long lengths of wall covering are just too awkward for one person.

To start, snap a chalk line across the narrow width of the ceiling, allowing for a slight overlap onto the wall (see below for instructions).

If the paper is especially heavy, as some vinyls are, it's best to pin it in place until the adhesive dries.

YOU'LL NEED...
SKILLS: Advanced skills.
TIME: 2 to 4 hours for a small room.
TOOLS: Smoothing brush; utility knife or razor blade; paste brush and pasting table, unless you're using prepasted paper; roller and extension handle.

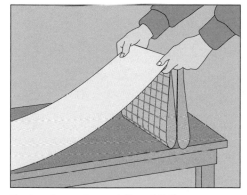

1. Apply paste and "book" the paper accordion-style. Don't crease the paper or touch the pattern side to the paste when you fold it.

2. Align the first strip with the chalk line mark and pat the paper in place with your hand. Overlap the paper onto the adjacent walls.

3. After you've stuck down a portion of the first strip by patting it, brush it smooth. Move on to the next section and apply it.

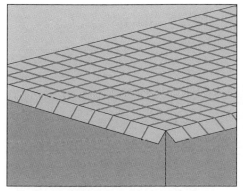

4. At the corner, cut out a V notch to permit the trim edges to lie flat against the walls. Add paste, if needed. If not papering the wall, trim off edges.

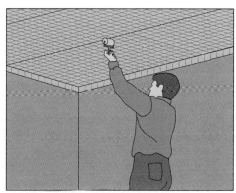

5. After applying each strip, smooth with a smoothing brush, working from the center. Roll the seams, too.

Wallpapering (continued)

HANGING PREPASTED WALL COVERINGS

The reason that prepasted wall coverings are so popular is no secret. They're the no-fuss, little-muss way to a beautifully papered room. There are some secrets, however: wall preparation, adhesive soaking time, and careful attention to smoothing and trimming.

The most critical of these items is the soaking time. Be sure to follow the manufacturer's directions to the letter so the adhesive tackiness will be just right.

Occasionally, depending on the porosity of the wall surface, there won't be enough adhesive on the covering to hold it to the wall. If this occurs, mix a small amount of the proper adhesive for the paper and apply it to the edges and ends of the strips after the strips have been cut to length and soaked. Or, apply the adhesive directly to the wall.

YOU'LL NEED...
SKILLS: Basic skills.
TIME: 10 to 15 minutes per strip.
TOOLS: Water trough plus other wallpapering tools listed earlier.

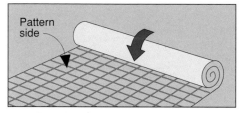

Cut the strips to length. Loosely reroll the paper with the pattern side in. This permits the water to activate the paste.

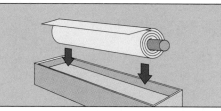

Fill the trough with enough water to cover the roll. Submerge the paper in the water, weighting it with a rod.

After soaking, remove paper by unrolling it as you climb a stepladder. Then smooth, roll, and trim the paper.

HANGING VINYL WALL COVERINGS

A top-quality product, vinyl wall covering is heavier than most standard coverings. You can buy it in wide widths, which reduces the number of seams to fit and roll. Also, the material usually is easy to strip from a wall or ceiling surface.

The heavy vinyls have another important advantage. The strips hides defects in a drywall or plaster wall that is in poor condition.

You can use regular wallpaper adhesive to apply lightweight vinyl papers, but special vinyl adhesive is best. Because vinyl won't stick to itself without special adhesive, all seams that are not butted should be double-cut (see page 548). If you apply untrimmed vinyl with butted seams, be sure the adhesive is soft on both the strips. Lap the seams about 1 inch. Make a freehand cut through both layers of paper, pull loose the selvages, and smooth the seam. If lapping is necessary, you can use vinyl-to-vinyl adhesive. Apply the adhesive just as you would regular wallpaper paste.

YOU'LL NEED...
SKILLS: Basic skills.
TIME: 10 to 15 minutes per strip.
TOOLS: Paint roller, utility knife, wood straightedge, seam roller.

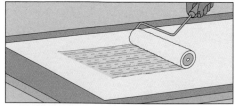

Spread the adhesive with a mohair paint roller. Fold and book the strip as you would a standard covering.

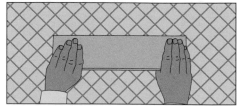

Smooth vinyl strips with a wood straightedge. Don't use steel unless the edges have been rounded.

After 20 minutes, hold a bright light against the wall to check for bubbles. Puncture with a razor and roll flat.

Painting Exterior Surfaces

CHOOSING AND BUYING EXTERIOR PAINTS

Prices for a gallon of exterior house paint begin about where interior wall paints leave off. Why?

First, they contain more resin so that they are more durable and highly moisture-resistant. Second, most also have more pigment, the ingredient that gives paint its color.

Like interior paints, exterior paints come in two basic varieties: water-thinned (latex) or solvent-thinned (oil- or alkyd-based) paint. Those with oil and alkyd bases dry slowly, making them susceptible during application to insects and sudden rainstorms. Once they set up, however, they are exceptionally durable. Latex paints are easier to work with, dry quickly, and have a porous, "breathing" quality that minimizes most moisture problems. They do have a tendency to peel, however, if applied over an improperly prepared oil- or alkyd-based finish, especially if it's a "chalking-type" latex paint.

Chalking refers to a self-cleaning quality formulated into many of today's exterior paints. They shed dirt by gradually eroding with each rainfall. Usually, you can see the "chalk" on foundation walls, shrubbery, and your coat sleeve, if you brush against a painted surface.

Once wood has been covered with a water- or solvent-thinned product, it's best not to change types when you apply subsequent coats. It can be done, of course, but you may run into problems. If you're not sure what type of paint was used before, you'll probably be safest to use an alkyd-based paint.

In addition to deciding what type of paint you want, you also must specify the luster—flat, semigloss, or gloss. (The word enamel often is used instead of semigloss or gloss.) Most people prefer a flat finish for large exterior expanses, and reserve semigloss and gloss for areas subject to hard use or for trim.

What about one-coat house paints? If you plan to match or approximate the present color, any paint will cover in one coat. However, products sold with a one-coat guarantee are thicker, with more resins and pigments. Most guarantees specify that the paint must be applied over sound existing surfaces or primed new wood. You will pay more for a one-coat paint, but the extra money spent might pay off handsomely, especially in terms of time saved.

The chart on the page 554 may look formidable at first, but it will help you deal with the often-confusing array of products that are displayed in paint stores.

These exterior paints fall into two broad categories: house paints—the stuff you'll be buying gallons of—and specialty coatings for a miscellany of smaller outside painting jobs. Organize your shopping list around the information presented, scrutinize labels closely, and you'll find a coating for about every conceivable exterior use.

HELPFUL HINTS

How much paint you need depends upon the type and condition of the surfaces you'll be covering, the method of application, and the paint itself. Conditions vary considerably, so your best bet is to read the manufacturer's coverage figures, then expect to get slightly less.

If your home has narrow lap siding, add another 10 percent to your estimate. For textured materials, such as shingles or shakes, add 20 percent. Masonry and stucco—both porous surfaces that soak up lots of paint—can take up to 50 percent more.

ESTIMATING PAINT NEEDS

To compute surface area, measure from the foundation to the eaves and multiply by the distance around the house. For each gable end, measure the distance from eaves to the peak, measure the width of the wall, and multiply the two. Then, divide the result by two.

If you buy premixed paint, you can always get more, and most stores will let you return unopened cans. Custom colors can be hard to match. So, buy an extra gallon; you can use the overage for various touch-up projects.

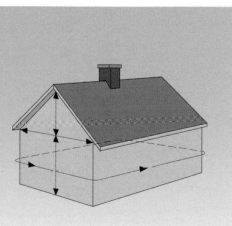

Painting Exterior Surfaces (continued)

MATERIAL MATTERS — COMPARING EXTERIOR PAINTS

Type	Characteristics/Uses	Application
Latex	Easy cleanup, durability, and fast drying make latex the choice for amateurs; can be applied even over damp surfaces; naturally mildew-proof; may be incompatible with a previous oil-based finish	Don't thin; apply with one stroke of the brush or roller; work it out too far and you'll get thin spots.
Acrylic	Actually a type of latex; a water-thinned paint that dries even faster than most and will cover just about any building material, including masonry and properly primed metal	About the same as ordinary latex
Alkyd	Solvent-thinned, synthetic-resin paint; has most of the same properties as oil-based types, but dries more rapidly; good over old oil- or alkyd-based coatings; excellent hiding power	Thicker consistency makes alkyd more tiring to apply, but it levels better than latex.
Oil	Slow drying times (12 to 48 hours), strong odors, and messy cleanup; some professionals still swear by its durability	Lengthy drying time makes bugs and rain real perils.
Primers	Seal new wood and metal with a recommended primer; generally, one coat of primer and one of finish more durable than two finish coats; finish not to be used as primer or vice versa	Priming usually is easier than finishing, but porous surfaces can soak up a lot of paint.
Stains	Solvent- or water-thinned types provide transparent, semi-transparent, and solid finishes for natural wood siding and trim; some include preservatives or offer a weathered look.	Brush, roll, or spray on almost any way you like.
SPECIALTY COATINGS		
Porch and deck	Choices include epoxy, alkyd, latex, polyurethane, and rubber-based; most work on wood or concrete floors and dry quickly; surface preparation varies; colors limited	With most, you just pour on the floor, then work out with a long-handled roller or wax applicator.
Metal	Solvent- or water-thinned types in a wide variety of colors; include rust-resisting priming ingredients so you needn't worry about small bare spots; all-bare metal should be primed separately.	Brush, roll, or spray on for a broad range of finish effects.
Marine	Formulated for boats; provide a super-durable finish on wood and some metal trim; expensive, so not for big areas	A gooey consistency makes them difficult to apply.
Masonry	Include latex, epoxy, Portland cement, rubber, and alkyd; some serve as own primers; seal masonry with clear silicone; for basement waterproofing techniques, see pages 113–115.	Latex is easy to apply; other types can be a lot of work.

IDENTIFYING AND SOLVING PAINT PROBLEMS

Houses typically need repainting every five to eight years. If you wait longer, you'll face a lot more preparation work. If you paint too soon, and thus too often, you may end up with a thick crust.

Analyze the existing finish. Perennial problems—shown in the chart on page 556—will pop right through your new paint job. If your house suffers from any of them, it's best to discover what's causing the problem(s) and correct the condition. Only then is it time to scrape the surface clean and prime it before you put on the final coat.

Most paint problems can be blamed on moisture attacking from underneath the paint. It's interesting that the insulation, weather stripping, and caulking compounds being used in new construction and added to existing structures for energy conservation cause many exterior paint problems. The reason: They seal all the cracks and breaks in the walls and roof of a house, leaving no way for moisture to escape, except through the walls. As this vapor penetrates the walls, it breaks the bond between the siding and paint, resulting in popped or peeling paint on the siding of the house.

The conditions created by energy conservation practices point out more clearly than ever before the importance of adequate ventilation throughout a house. This is particularly true in such areas as the kitchen, bathroom, and laundry, where moisture abounds. Ducted ventilation fans provide the best way to remove excess moisture vapor. Good vapor barriers on inside walls also help control moisture problems.

Lessen the effects of moisture by installing ducted ventilation fans (see page 407). If you don't have fans, opening a window helps.

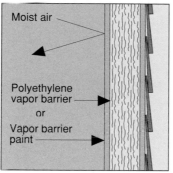

If exterior walls don't have a vapor barrier, painting the interior wall with nonpermeable paint will prevent vapor penetration.

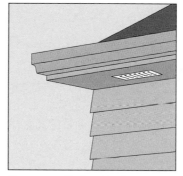

Poor ventilation in the attic may cause soffits to peel. Correct this before you repaint by adding soffit vents (see page 133).

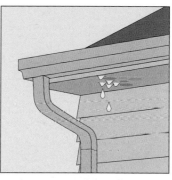

Leaky gutters drip water onto eaves then the house siding, so keep the gutters in good condition (see pages 134-135).

Leaves hold moisture after a rain. Trim trees and shrubs often, especially those along the foundation.

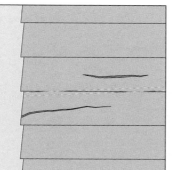

Damaged siding lets in and holds moisture, and must be repaired before you repaint (see page 147).

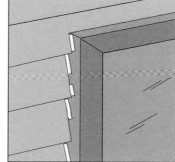

Remove old, cracked caulking material with a putty knife, then apply new caulk (see pages 145-146).

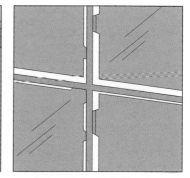

Replace loose and missing glazing compound on windows; let glazing dry a week before you paint it.

Painting Exterior Surfaces *(continued)*

REMEDIES FOR COMMON PAINT PROBLEMS

Problem		Cause(s)	Remedy
Peeling		Moisture from inside or prolonged contact with rain or other moisture; finish coat applied over wet surface	Improve ventilation by installing siding, gable, or soffit vents (see page 133).
Alligatoring		Usually, a finish coat applied over a wet primer, or too much oil in the thinner	Sand down to bare wood, apply primer, and let dry thoroughly.
Checking		Shrinking and swelling of the building material over a period of time	Bare the wood, prime the area, and let dry.
Blistering		Finish coat applied over surfaces that are not completely dry	Same as for checking
Bleeding		Sap and pitch working out of the wood	Apply sealer to all knots and pitch pockets to prepare the surface for a coat of finish.
Nail stains		Using nonrust-resistant nails	Sand the surface and seal with pigmented shellac, then repaint.
Mildew		Usually a combination of moisture, high humidity, and inadequate ventilation	Scrub off the mildew (see page 144), let the wood dry thoroughly, then paint with mildew-resistant paint.
Chalking		Formulation of paint used	Before painting, wash thoroughly; chalking may be intentional (see page 553).

REMOVING OLD PAINT

Many of the problems described on the preceding pages demand that you strip down the defective areas to bare wood and prime them before painting. Unfortunately, there's no easy way to do this tedious job. You'll simply have to experiment with the techniques shown below and use the combination that works best.

Old paint comes off most readily when it's dry. Start in the worst spot, work a scraper underneath, and lift off as much of the old finish as you can. You'll have better luck chipping from the edges of bad spots, rather than trying to wear through an unbroken surface.

Master a pull scraper and it's possible to get down to bare wood with a single stroke. Hold the blade at an angle and apply firm pressure as you drag it along. When a blade stops cutting well, either change it or sharpen it as you would a knife or chisel (see pages 444 and 447).

When you reach tight-sticking paint, feather the edges. Then, spot-prime all bare spots, slightly overlapping the sound paint.

Remove paint from metal surfaces with a wire brush attachment on an electric drill. Don't worry about baring the metal; just remove rust, as well as the loose or caked paint, then prime it (see pages 564–565).

Chemical paint strippers should be your last alternative. Although effective, you risk dripping the remover on sound paint, creating more problems than you're solving.

If you have large areas of masonry to strip, consider hiring a professional contractor to sandblast them. Warn your neighbors first, however, because sandblasting creates lots of noise and dust.

YOU'LL NEED...
SKILLS: Basic skills.
TIME: Several days for an entire house.
TOOLS: Putty knife, scraper, pull scraper, electric paint softener, propane torch or heat gun, power sander.

Remove what paint you can with a putty knife, then go over the area with a wire brush. This combination works well for small areas.

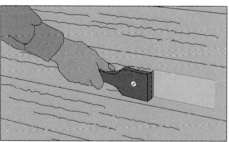

A sharp pull scraper shaves off damaged paint film. Keep the blade sharp and don't dig into the wood.

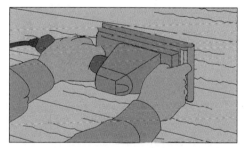

Power-sand large areas with an orbital sander. Don't use a belt or disc sander because both may damage the underlying wood surface.

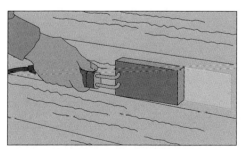

For heavy paint deposits, use an electric paint softener. Hold the tool on the paint until it starts to bubble or wrinkle, then scrape off the paint.

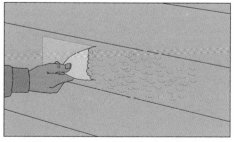

Chemical paint removers are best for heavy paint deposits on small areas. Follow directions to the letter (see page 572).

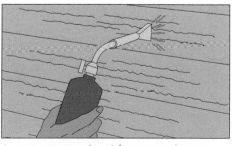

A propane torch with a spreader tip "cooks" paint fast so you can scrape it off. Be careful not to start a fire, and have an extinguisher handy.

Painting Exterior Surfaces (continued)

PREPARING EXTERIOR SURFACES

Consider yourself fortunate if the siding and trim on your house is in good shape when it comes time to paint. If it is, you can happily sidestep the most maddening part of an exterior paint job—removing chipped or peeling paint. But don't get out your paint clothes and brushes quite yet.

Go around the house and remove all screens, storm windows, and hardware that can be removed. Inspect the exterior and replace damaged siding materials (see page 147). Use a nail set to set protruding nails below the surface.

Give your house a bath. For this, you'll need a garden hose and a car-wash brush attachment, a scrub brush or sponge for stubborn dirt, and a mixture of water and trisodium phosphate to remove dirt and reduce the gloss of oil- or alkyd-based paints.

Remove loose and cracked glazing from the windows and reglaze them (see pages 160–161). Glazing should dry a week before painting. Also, caulk all cracks and gaps in the siding; around porch columns; and under, over, and around windows and doors (see pages 145–146).

If you're using an oil- or alkyd-based paint, wait at least a week after its bath before you paint the house. You can paint with latex the next day. When the siding is dry, spot-prime all bare spots. Don't miss exposed metal surfaces on gutters, downspouts, and windows.

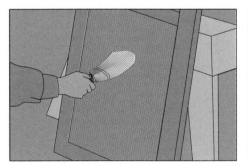

Clean and paint screens, storm windows, shutters, and other removable components separately to speed up the job.

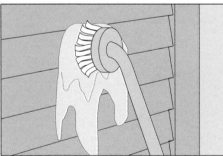

Wash the house from the top down, using a mixture of trisodium phosphate and water. Rinse well and let dry; one day for latex, one week for oil paint.

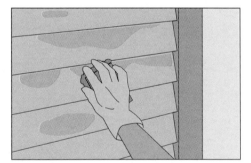

For mildewed areas, scrub with household bleach and water or a commercial cleaner. Repaint with mildew-cide paint.

Set popped nails and spot-prime them. Also, caulk cracks, replace damaged siding, and prime bare metal spots.

With a whisk broom or paintbrush, flick off dust you missed with the hose. Carry this brush as you paint to remove other debris.

Remove fixtures or mask or cover them the day you paint. Don't forget to remove other accessories, such as house numbers and the mailbox.

PREPARING TO PAINT

Don't plan a big evening after your first day of house painting—you'll be tired. If you organize the job properly, however, you can decrease the fatigue factor.

Just as with interior painting, there are some standard operating procedures that you should follow when painting the exterior. Begin when the sun has dried off the surfaces you'll be painting. Follow the sun so you're working in the shade; this gives the paint a chance to cure slowly and adhere better.

Work from the top to the bottom of the house to avoid the mess caused by spilled or splattered paint. Paint the siding first, then go back and paint the windows, doors, railings, steps, and so forth. There's one exception to this. If your house is a two-story structure, paint the trim as you go to avoid having to lean your ladder up against freshly applied paint.

Also, you should paint above the top of the ladder. Don't try to paint under it or you'll have ladder tracks where the rails touch the siding.

Protect shrubs, flowers, patios, and walks with drop cloths. Use rope and canvas or old sheets to tie tall bushes back out of the way.

To avoid variations from can to can, mix enough paint to cover the entire side you intend to paint. Stir the paint thoroughly, even if you just bought it.

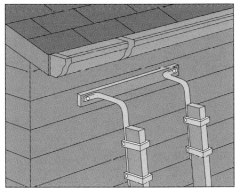

Set ladders on sure footing—never a plastic drop cloth. Use a ladder brace for stability and to hold it away from the sidewall for more painting room.

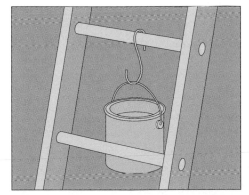

To keep the paint bucket from spilling, hang it from a ladder rung with a bucket hook, which you can buy or make from heavy-gauge wire.

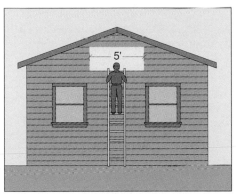

For safety's sake, don't stretch more than an arm's length on either side of the ladder. Instead, move the ladder.

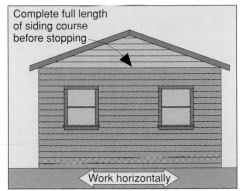

Complete full length of siding course before stopping

Work horizontally

Plan the work so that sundown does not catch you in the middle of several courses of siding. Otherwise, you will get lap marks.

Painting Exterior Surfaces (continued)

PAINTING WOOD SIDING

If any part of a paint job can be deemed fun, it would have to be painting siding. Though siding often comprises the great majority of the total surface area, you'll discover that you can make a surprising amount of progress in equally surprising short periods of time.

Aluminum and vinyl siding shouldn't be repainted, of course. But wood siding will need paint every five to eight years.

To paint siding, coat the undersides of three or four courses, using plenty of paint so the wood seals properly. Level out the paint with the tip of the paintbrush.

After the undersides are covered, fill in the face of the siding courses, flowing the paint onto the surface with fairly short horizontal strokes. You needn't exert too much pressure on the brush; when the surface is covered with paint, just level and smooth it with a horizontal stroke. Make sure tiny cracks are filled.

If you're applying primer to the surface, follow the same brushing procedures you would for the finish paint. You may notice laps with the primer as it sinks into the wood or other material to seal it. Don't worry about these; they won't show after you've applied the finish coat.

As you paint, keep track of the amount of paint required to cover a given area. You then can determine if you'll need to buy more to complete the job. You'll probably use more primer per area covered than finish paint.

YOU'LL NEED...

SKILLS: Basic painting skills.
TIME: 4 to 6 days for a small house.
TOOLS: Brushes, ladder, screwdriver, drop cloths.

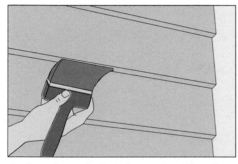

1. Start by painting the underside of the siding course. If you do the faces first, you'll be touching up continually.

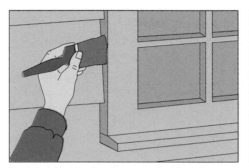

2. When painting next to a casing, paint the corner first, then the underside of the siding. Stab the bristles up into the corner.

3. Apply plenty of paint to the surface of the course and don't worry about lap marks yet. Just cover and seal the surface thoroughly.

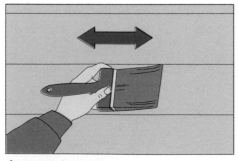

4. Level the paint. Don't try to save money by brushing it thin; just even it out on the surface, using fairly long brushstrokes.

5. Tip the bristles downward as you cut in along the bottom of the last course of siding. This keeps paint off the foundation.

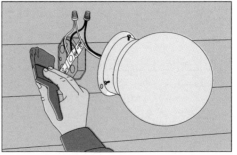

6. Remove lighting fixtures and turn off electricity so you can safely paint behind and below them. Let paint dry well before replacing fixtures.

FINISHING SHINGLES AND SHAKES

If you're about to apply either stain or paint to shingle or shake siding, you've got a couple of surprises in store. First, the job probably will take longer than you think. Second, you'll use more finish than you estimated. The reason: Both shingles and shakes are porous and full of grooves and striations and, therefore, soak up finish like a blotter.

If the wood is new, you can give it a natural look simply by sealing it with a clear penetrating sealer. Because there is no pigment in the sealer, you can slop it onto the wood without worrying about lap marks. If the wood is cedar or redwood, you don't have to finish it if you don't want to. It will weather into a silver-like finish.

Semitransparent and solid stains (see pages 554 and 576) require more care because they contain a pigment that must be smoothed to prevent lap marks. Also, because the pigment in stain settles fairly quickly, you'll need to give the liquid a couple of whips with a paint paddle every so often to keep the finish color consistent.

If you're planning to paint new shingles, test the paint on several shingles that have dark brown stains. If the stains bleed through, switch to a stain finish rather than paint.

Both paint and stain dry quickly. Always work into a wet edge and finish out a course of siding before you leave for any length of time.

Regardless of the finish, a 6-inch-wide brush with short bristles is the best applicator. Keep the ferrule and handle of the brush wiped clean, although this is difficult if you're working with stain. Follow the leveling-out technique described on page 560. If you can, rent a power paint sprayer (see page 568), then touch up with a brush after using the sprayer to apply the paint.

If you use a roller or pad painter for shingles or shakes, use covers with medium to long nap length.

YOU'LL NEED...

SKILLS: Basic painting skills.
TIME: 4 to 6 days for a small house.
TOOLS: Brushes, ladder, screwdriver, drop cloths, rented power sprayer, corner roller, pad applicator.

1. Do the underside of shingles first, as you would with lap siding. Brush out runs down the striations.

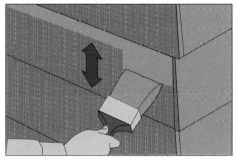

2. Apply paints and stains in the direction of the grain or striations. Check often for missed spots.

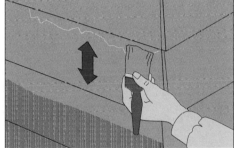

3. Check frequently for drips and runs. Smooth them out with a dry brush while the finish is still tacky.

4. Pad applicators make finishing shingles and shakes easier. Most are designed for edges as well as faces.

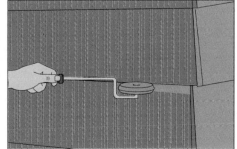

5. Corner rollers work well for undersides; use a medium- or long-nap roller or a wide brush for the faces.

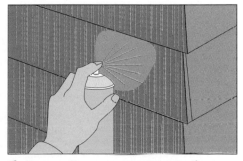

6. For small areas, use an aerosol spray. Use a regular spray outfit for large projects (see pages 567–569).

Painting Exterior Surfaces (continued)

PAINTING TRIM

If someone gives you your choice of painting all of the siding on a house or all of the trim, take the siding. Although it doesn't consume much paint, trimming out a house takes an inordinate amount of time. Using the same paint color for the trim as the siding helps some, but the job is tedious, nonetheless.

> #### YOU'LL NEED...
> **SKILLS:** Intermediate painting skills.
> **TIME:** 45 minutes to an hour for a window.
> **TOOLS:** Sash brush, screwdriver, masking tape.

Before you get out your sash brush and begin work, study the sketches on this page for some of the situations you'll encounter.

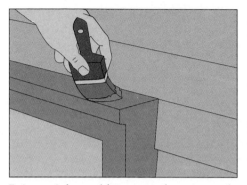

Paint a tight seal between the trim and siding material, especially over the tops of doors and windows.

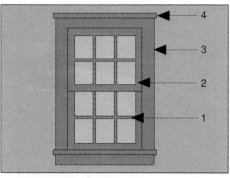

Paint the outside of windows in the order indicated above, starting with the muntins and working outward.

Windowsills take a beating from the elements. If they're weatherworn, give them several coats of paint.

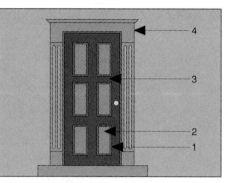

Mask or remove the knob set and other hardware before painting doors. Paint the door in the order shown.

To save time, spray-paint removable hardware, such as house numbers and shutters (see page 569).

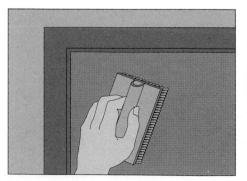

Paint or varnish screening first, then the frame. Use a special applicator pad for the screening.

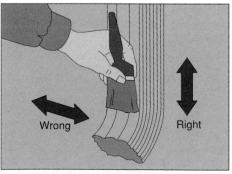

When painting downspouts, be sure to paint parallel to the flutes. If you don't, you risk messy drips and sags.

Do ornamental metal and wood last. Prepare surfaces properly and use the correct primer (see pages 564–565).

STYLING WITH PAINT

If you are going to paint your house, consider changing its appearance. You can do this simply by changing colors. But with some planning, you also can manipulate the siding and trim colors to create a totally different-looking house.

Draw the front of your home on sketch paper as best you can. It doesn't have to be perfect; just include the different elements or components—roof, dormers, siding, porches, windows, doors, and foundation. Or, take a straight-on snapshot of the house and have an enlarged print made to serve as a template. From this, you can use tracing paper to sketch the house. Equipped with one or more sketches and an assortment of colored markers or pencils, you're ready to plan your color-change strategy.

Dark colors make a home look smaller; light colors have the opposite effect. To scale-down a big, older house, for example, paint it a dark color such as brown, red, dark green, or dark gray.

If your house visually looks too tall, you can make it look lower by painting the siding to match the color of the roof shingles. To "raise the roof," paint the house a color that contrasts with the shingles.

If your home's exterior is composed of several different materials and looks somewhat disjointed, unify the elements by using a couple of shades of the same color. Or, if your house has an element that sticks out like a sore thumb, camouflage that element by painting it to blend in with its surrounding elements.

With these guidelines, get out your colored pencils and go to work. Take as much time as you need at the drawing board to come up with a color scheme that works well for you. It's far better to experiment at this stage with colored pencils than later with expensive exterior paint.

If, after all your color scheming, you're still not satisfied that you've found the right treatment, take a drive through your community and try to find some recently painted houses that are architecturally similar to yours. They may suggest some ideas worth adopting.

Outline doors, windows, and even the entire house with a different color to call attention to the more handsome lines of the structure. Use a lighter or darker shade of the same color—or an entirely different hue.

Reverse colors for a change of pace. Paint the siding a darker color and trim it in a lighter hue, or vice-versa. A strong accent calls attention to the front door or other focal point. Don't play up more than one feature, or you'll create visual confusion.

Decide which house components you want to emphasize and which you'd like to "paint out." For example, you may want to paint out a dormer on the roof. To do this, paint it the same color as the roofing material.

Painting Metal

Apply any old paint over metal that is not properly prepared, and you're asking for trouble. All metals oxidize if not properly coated, and paint can't adhere to the oxide coating.

To stop the oxidation process, you need to strip away grease, dirt, or existing rust, then apply a primer that is chemically formulated to neutralize oxidation. This primer provides a surface to which the final finish coat can adhere.

The primer you'll need depends on the metal you're dealing with and its condition. The chart on page 565 compares the major metals and primer needed for each.

You also can buy special metal paints that combine the primer with a finish coating. Use these over surfaces that are still in fairly good condition. Aluminized paint includes aluminum dust as a pigment and also works as a combination primer-finish on metals not exposed to severe weathering.

As essential as a good primer is, you can't expect it to do the entire job. Virtually all primers need a finish coat or coats to protect against weather and abrasion. You can use almost any paint—exterior-grade for outdoors, indoor types for inside jobs. However, don't apply a lacquer over anything but a lacquer-based finish paint or primer.

Even polished decorative metals, such as brass, copper, and bronze, need protection if you want them to keep their shine. Buff tarnished hardware items with fine steel wool, metal polish, or a felt wheel and abrasive compound (see page 523), then coat them with clear lacquer or polyurethane.

PREPARING METAL SURFACES

YOU'LL NEED...

SKILLS: Basic painting skills.
TIME: 4 to 6 hours to prep and paint a metal railing.
TOOLS: Paintbrushes, wire brush, drill with wire-brush attachment, sandpaper, steel wool.

Paint remover works better on metal than on wood. Use it to take off multiple layers (see pages 571–572).

Wash with a commercial degreaser, then wire brush rust. Heat-resistant paints can withstand high temperature.

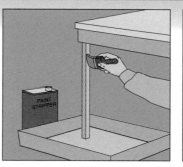
Wire-brush rust or peeling paint. A brush attachment on a power drill makes short work of this task.

Feather the edges of the remaining sound paint. Otherwise, the repaired area will show through.

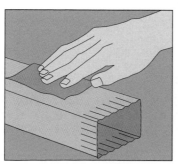
Clean and paint the inside of gutters first. Gutters and downspouts often need only spot-sanding and priming.

Treat sound paint with liquid sander. This product produces a "tooth" to which the new paint can adhere.

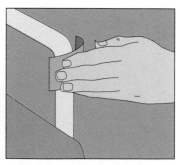
Lightly sand primed surfaces with very fine sandpaper or steel wool. Don't sand through the primer.

MATERIAL MATTERS — CHOOSING THE RIGHT METAL PRIMER

Metal	Condition	Preparation	Primer
Iron and steel	Lightly rusted metal or failing paint	Remove rust and loose paint, then feather edges; for a smoother finish, strip completely	Zinc chromate resists rust; protect bare metal with two coats
	Damp, badly rusted bare metal	Scrape and wire-brush all loose material; wipe away surface moisture	Long-oil primers penetrate to metal underneath
	Heavy rust and scale	Scrape away loose material, but don't try to expose bare metal	Same as badly rusted metal
Galvanized iron and steel	Lightly rusted surfaces	Remove rust and blisters; wash new metal with detergent, let weather, or etch with vinegar	Zinc-oxide or other primers formulated for galvanized metal
Aluminum	Older oxidized surfaces	Remove oxidation, but don't sand under clear finishes; for a shiny finish, use liquid car wax	No primer necessary; if paint will not adhere, use zinc-oxide primer
Copper	Corroded metal or blistered paint	Clean metal with fine steel wool or wire brush; new copper may need acid etch and rinse	No primer necessary; finish with paint or polyurethane
Brass	Tarnished, corroded, or pitted	Soak in paint remover or vinegar-salt solution; buff with polish; may need replating	No primer necessary; coat with lacquer or polyurethane

APPLYING THE TOP COAT

Spray, brush, or roll on metal finishes. Whichever you choose, bear in mind that several thin coats will hold up better than one or two thick layers. Let each coat dry before applying the next coat. Brushed or rolled-on paint should dry at least overnight (36 hours is better) before you apply another coat.

A good job calls for patience and good lighting so you can correct problems before the paint dries. Try to work the paint in one direction and move from dry to wet areas. Don't lap brushstrokes by painting over a dry edge. Smooth corners, too, so they don't dry with large accumulations of paint.

YOU'LL NEED...

SKILLS: Basic painting skills.
TIME: Time will depend on the size of the object, but allow plenty of time for repeated coats with drying time in between.
TOOLS: Brushes and drop cloths.

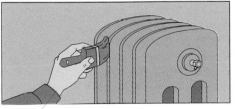

Flow paint on with smooth, even strokes. After a few minutes, check the freshly painted areas for drips, runs, and sags.

To make gutters really last, paint the inside surfaces with an asphalt-based paint. Besides protecting the metal, it seals tiny leaks.

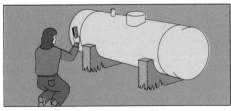

After using the appropriate metal primer, the top coat of paint can be almost any type; exterior for outdoor projects, interior for indoor items.

Painting Masonry

It used to be that painting a masonry foundation or basement floor often doomed a person to all-too-frequent repainting. Most people preferred to accept concrete's dull gray color and go on about their business.

That's not true with today's sophisticated paint products and the understanding that surface preparation is the key to success. There's no reason you can't paint concrete or concrete blocks—and be satisfied with the results.

Several types of paint will adhere to masonry. Epoxy paints, because they dry to a very hard finish, are probably the best all-around choice for floors, walls that are washed frequently, and exterior applications. Portland cement paint is another good choice; it works well on all walls except those that previously have been painted with another type of finish. Latex paint, probably the easiest to apply, adheres to foundation walls, too. Check with your paint dealer for other types suitable for specific applications.

Before painting a masonry surface—especially basement walls and floors—be sure you correct any existing moisture problems (see pages 113–115). If you don't, no paint will adhere. Also, remove peeling paint with a wire brush, and make necessary masonry repairs (see pages 149–150 and 172–173).

The final prep work begins with degreasing the surface with detergent and water. Then, etch the surface with a mixture of one part muriatic acid to three parts water.

This removes and neutralizes alkaline material in the mortar joints. (Be sure to wear rubber gloves and a long-sleeved shirt to protect your skin from acid burns.) Finally, rinse the surface with clear water.

After the surface dries thoroughly, apply the finish with a wide short-bristled brush or a roller cover with a long nap. Because the area you'll be painting probably is large, the wider the brush or roller, the faster the job will go.

YOU'LL NEED...

SKILLS: Basic painting skills.
TIME: 6 to 8 hours to paint a basement.
TOOLS: Scrub brush, paintbrush, roller with extension handle.

Apply a degreasing solution to oily garage or basement floors. Some types are sprayed on; others require a scrub brush.

Smooth rough textures with a 1:1 cement grout mix, scrubbing it into depressions. For light textures, use an abrasive brick.

Apply paint with an old or cheap stiff-bristle brush. You'll have to push hard on the brush and even scrub it into very porous surfaces.

If you want a rough texture, use a long-nap roller to apply the finish. A roller works better than a brush for this type of texture.

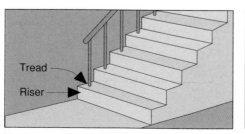

Tread
Riser

To paint steps that are in use daily, paint the risers and every other tread. When the finish is dry, paint the treads you skipped.

To prevent backaches from bending over, paint patios and floors with a roller and extension handle. Paint one section at a time.

Spray-Painting

Spray-painting is by far the fastest means of applying paint, stain, or other finishes. When done carefully and knowingly, spraying yields professional-looking results that are hard to match with brush or roller.

Spray-painting does have its drawbacks. It consumes much more finish than painting with a brush or roller. It's also messy. Overspray makes spraying impractical in many situations, such as in finished rooms or outside where a neighbor's car or house will be affected. Some communities even prohibit spraying.

You'll need plenty of ventilation if you spray-paint inside. Open nearby windows and, if there's an exhaust fan close by, turn it on. Always use a painter's mask to keep from inhaling airborne paint and wear a hat and protective clothing. Painting outside is somewhat less of a problem in terms of ventilation, but wear your mask nonetheless.

The following are some spray-painting pointers to keep in mind:

■ Prepare all surfaces the same way you would for a brush or roller.

■ Tightly cover anything you don't want painted. For smaller areas, use newspaper and masking tape; for large areas, use drop cloths sealed at the edges with masking tape.

■ When spraying solvent-thinned paint indoors, make sure there is no open flame in the workshop area, as the evaporating solvent is flammable.

■ Outside, never spray on a windy day. The air must be fairly calm. You won't get a nice finish and you risk overspraying your neighbor's car. Even on calm days, make sure no valuable items are nearby.

■ Paint mixtures must be specially prepared for a spray gun. If the paint is too thick, it will clog the gun. If it's too thin, the paint will run on the surface. Even a proper mixture requires you to have a brush handy to catch runs and drips.

■ When painting fencing with a spray gun, have a helper hold a wide piece of cardboard in back of the fence to catch the overspray.

■ Don't spray gutters, corner trim, or siding material that joins the foundation of your home unless you have the roof, corner, or foundation covered properly.

■ Don't spray-paint windows; rather, use a sash brush. The same rule applies for other trim—doors, basement sashes, and storm windows. However, a spray gun is excellent for painting screens.

HELPFUL HINTS

If you can't take your work outside, take the time to set up a paint booth. For small projects, your booth need be nothing more than newspapers taped together and positioned behind and below the item to be sprayed. If you're

SETTING UP A SPRAY BOOTH

painting a large piece or have a lot of spraying to do, fabricate a booth from 4-mil polyethylene plastic film and fasten it to the walls and floor in a corner of your workshop.

How large a booth you need depends on the scale of the project being painted, of course. Be sure to give yourself plenty of working room. Overspray carries a surprising distance, and cleaning it off masonry is a chore you want to avoid.

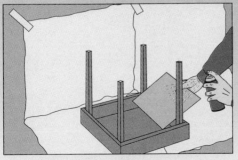

Set up small jobs with newspapers behind and below the object. Use a cardboard shield to absorb overspray.

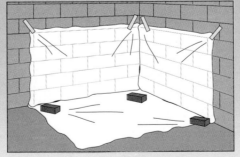

Polyethylene film handles big items. Keep the top of the booth open to allow paint fumes to escape.

For safety reasons and skin protection, wear a spray mask, hat, rubber gloves, and a long-sleeved shirt.

Spray-Painting (continued)

USING A SPRAY GUN

The first rule of spray-painting is to keep your equipment clean. If you don't, you'll spend the majority of your time getting the equipment to run properly and cleaning up spatters and runs, and in the process end up with a shoddy-looking job.

Also crucial is the thickness of paint being sprayed. If too thin, it will not cover and will drip and run. If it's too thick, you'll really have trouble, because it will clog your equipment and result in a rough finish. For best results, read the container label and follow the paint and sprayer manufacturers' advice.

Your spray technique also deserves consideration. When you spray, keep a stiff wrist and hold the spray gun nozzle 8 to 10 inches away from the surface, parallel to the ground. And don't start spraying from a dead-still position. Rather, begin your movement, then pull the trigger and start spraying.

Fan the spray on the surface, using several light coats instead of one heavy coat. The paint will be thick at the center and feathered out at the edges. So, as you paint, overlap your spray pattern by about one third so the thickness of the paint will be uniform.

On gutters, point the gun away from the roof. Along foundations, paint the bottom two courses of siding with a brush, or mask off the foundation to at least a foot below the last siding course.

YOU'LL NEED...

SKILLS: Intermediate painting skills and basic mechanical skills.
TIME: 6 hours to paint the exterior of a small house.
TOOLS: Rented spray gun, filter for paint, brushes, drop cloths.

Before putting paint into the gun's reservoir, run the paint through a strainer to rid the mixture of impurities that may clog the gun.

Experiment on scrap material to gauge the proper distance between the gun and the surface. Also, you can adjust most guns for different spray patterns.

Hold the gun perpendicular to the surface—don't move it in an arc. Keep your wrist stiff to deter this temptation.

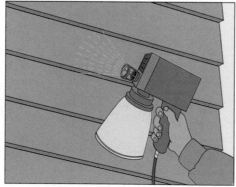

For lap siding, angle the gun to spray the undersides. Apply a thin coating, then let overspray fill it in.

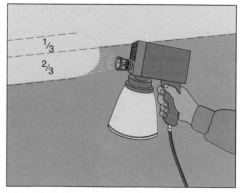

Lap successive strokes by about one third the spray width to achieve even paint coverage.

USING A SPRAY CAN

Shake, rattle, and spray. Shake a spray can to rattle the steel ball inside for about a minute, then push the button. It's that easy.

Painting with spray cans, however, is almost as expensive as it is easy. But the time you save using them usually makes up for added expense. This is especially true when dealing with such hard-to-paint items as wicker furniture, radiators, and small cabinets.

To operate a spray can, first shake the can, as shown below. When you hear the rattle of the metal ball that mixes the paint, shake the can for another minute or so.

The biggest drawback of aerosol painting is that the nozzles on spray cans tend to clog. To prevent this, after each use invert the can and depress the button until only propellant comes out the hole, then wipe the nozzle clean. When the nozzle does clog up, often you can open it again by puncturing the paint seal over the spray hole with a needle. If this doesn't work, buy a low-cost replacement nozzle.

Aerosol paint is flammable, so don't spray-paint near open flames. Likewise, because they are pressurized containers, don't puncture an empty aerosol can or junk it in an incinerator.

With one or two exceptions, the painting problems shown and discussed below apply to both spray cans and spray guns.

Shake the can until you hear the ball rolling freely for at least a minute. Shake the can periodically as you work to keep paint mixed.

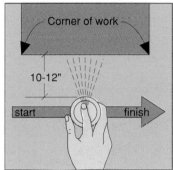

Hold the can 10 to 12 inches from the surface. Apply smooth, even strokes, moving the can horizontally across the surface.

Lap strokes by about one-third. After you've made several passes, stop and check to make sure the surface is covered.

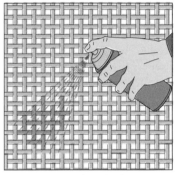

On open work, tilt the can at an angle to minimize the paint flowing through openings. Crisscross spray pattern to catch all edges.

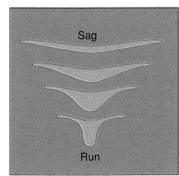

Sags and runs are caused by too much paint. Wipe away the excess, then spot-spray with short bursts to blend in the touch-up.

Holidays occur when there's not enough paint on the surface. Spot-in these areas, as you would a sag or run.

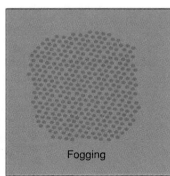

Fogging is the dull, pebbled effect produced when the spray can is held too far away. Spot-spray these areas, as well.

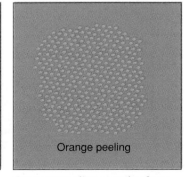

Orange-peeling results from too thick a covering of paint or from too much air pressure. Wipe and spot-paint these.

Antiquing

Antiquing won't produce a clear, shiny surface as a clear wood finish produces, but the technique does have a place in wood finishing. Its forte is making badly outdated or worn furniture look "new" again.

You can achieve many different looks by varying the antiquing technique (see drawings). One of the fun things about antiquing is that you don't have to be careful. In fact, you may want to "distress" the surface even more than it is by smacking it a few times with nails driven into a board or with the claws of a hammer. Before you get carried away, however, make sure that the piece of furniture you're dealing with wouldn't be better refinished in some other manner. Sometimes, hidden under an old finish or a crust of dirt is a real antique that's worth a lot of money.

When antiquing an item, you can either strip it to bare wood or apply the base coat right over the existing surface. Most people choose the latter. Either way, make sure the surface is free of dirt and wax. Remove drawers and hardware if any, and if a mirror is involved, remove it if you can. If not, mask it with newspaper.

Most people buy the materials and tools needed for their project in kit form. Usually included are base and finish coats of antiquing finishes, brushes, and special design applicators. The tools you'll need, if the kit doesn't supply them, include a 3-inch brush, 150-grit sandpaper, a mixing bucket and paddle, thinning solvent, and wiping cloths.

Once you've readied the surface to your satisfaction (be sure to dull a glossy surface), brush on the base coat. You may need two coats to hide dark surfaces. Apply the material in even strokes. If you spot runs or sags, catch them with the tip of the brush stroked across the grain. Look for spots you may have missed; if you find any, coat them now, because the base coat must completely cover the surface. Let the finish dry. Check the can label for drying time—usually 2 to 4 hours.

The next step is to sand the base coat, using a 150-grit open-coat abrasive or fine steel wool. Remove all sanding residue with a vacuum cleaner or tack cloth.

Next comes the glaze. Working in a small area, brush on a thin coating of glaze; don't apply too much.

Wipe the surface or apply the design you want (see sketches and text below for ideas and techniques to create some effects). Then, move on to the next area. The glaze dries fast, so you need to work quickly.

To simulate wear, wipe corners and edges through to the base coat. Wipe gently over carvings and grooves to produce an antique look. On big, flat surfaces, make the edges lighter than the center.

Allow the glaze to dry for 48 hours. Finish the project by applying a clear finish or hard wax to the surface.

Lay on a heavy coat of glaze, then lightly tap the surface with your fingertips.

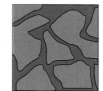

Tortoise-shell

Crumple up a plastic drop cloth, lay it in the wet glaze, then pick it up.

Marbleized

Wipe on glaze; dip small, stiff brush in thinner; shake it out; stroke bristles to spray droplets on glaze.

Splattered

Lightly jab glaze with a wadded-up paper or cloth towel.

Crumpled

With a dry brush, jab straight down into wet glaze. Rotate the brush between jabs.

Stippled

Let the glaze dry, then sand to expose the undercoat.

Distressed paint

Poke glaze with an ice pick, then rub raw umber into scratches and dents.

Distressed wood

Goes on top of other patterns. Do it like the splattered technique, but dip the brush in glaze.

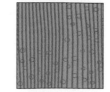

Spattered over

Clear-Finishing Wood

Paint over any properly prepared wood surface and you'll hide, or at least mask, its grain. Clear finishes do exactly the opposite. They emphasize the wood's natural beauty and all of its imperfections.

That's why any clear-finishing job has to start with the wood itself. Before you get into the painstaking preparation that a natural finish demands, take a close look at the wood grain. Wetting the surface slightly lets you see it better and gives you a good idea of what a perfectly transparent coating will do.

If you don't like a wood's color, you can bleach it or tint it with stain—but no amount of staining or sanding will alter a grain's pattern, obliterate knots, or hide surface imperfections or damage.

If you like what you see, prepare for some hard—but ultimately very satisfying—work. Completely bare the wood, then sand it perfectly smooth. Some "open-grain" species, such as oak, walnut, and mahogany, require a filler. You also may need to seal the surface before applying the final finish.

The following pages present the basic products and processes for clear-finishing wood. Master them and you will add another chapter to your repertoire of home improvement techniques.

REMOVING OLD FINISHES

If you're refinishing a major piece of furniture that needs finishes stripped off, the path of least resistance leads to a professional paint stripper. Generally for a modest price, these specialists will dip your piece in a caustic solution and have it back to you in short order, saving you lots of time and a great deal of effort.

If a professional is not available, if the project doesn't warrant sending it to one, or if you're stripping an item such as base or window trim that cannot be removed, there are a potpourri of other paint-removing options (see the chart below).

Before you strip finishes, check a little deeper. Some finishes that appear to need refinishing may only need cleaning. If you're in doubt, wash the item with mineral spirits, then give it three thin coats of wax.

If a white haze appears after you apply the thinner, buff it with extra-fine (000) steel wool before waxing.

> **YOU'LL NEED...**
> **SKILLS:** Basic sanding and paint-stripping skills.
> **TIME:** 4 to 6 hours for a chair.
> **TOOLS:** Brush, sandpaper, electric paint softener, power detail sander.

MATERIAL MATTERS   SELECTING A FINISH REMOVER

Method	Uses	Application Tips
Paint remover	For any finish, thick or thin, on wood or metal	Available in liquid or paste. Paste is best for vertical surfaces. Provide ventilation with paint remover; apply it with a brush; remove it and the old finish with a scraper and steel wool. Wash off water-soluble strippers.
Electric paint softener, propane torch	Both remove old paint from wood; electric softener usually used on flat surfaces such as siding	Use a torch with caution. Provide ventilation. Disadvantage of both is the danger of scorching bare wood, and both methods are tedious.
Abrasives (sandpaper and steel wool)	Remove thin finishes; not for sanding heavy accumulations of paint (a seemingly endless job)	By hand, work is tedious; with a power sander, the finish comes off fast. Use a contour sander in a drill for curved surfaces. Be careful with power sanders not to groove the wood or cut through veneer.
Scrapers	Excellent for removing old, dry paint from wood or glass surfaces	Keep your scraper blade sharp. Maneuver it carefully to be sure you don't dig into the wood as you work.

Clear-Finishing Wood (continued)

USING PAINT REMOVER

Paint removers soften paint and most other brush-on finishes so that you can lift it off with a scraper. They are messy, however, so be sure to cover work surfaces with several layers of newspaper or plastic sheeting. When the removal job has been completed, carefully dispose of the covering.

Apply paint remover with an old or inexpensive brush. Throw away brushes when you're finished.

Fumes from paint removers cause eye irritation and headaches. Ideally, you should work outside. If you can't, ventilate the room in which you're working and take a fresh-air break every 15 minutes or so.

Procedures vary from product to product, so be sure you read the label directions thoroughly before opening the container. Remember, you're dealing with powerful ingredients that deserve respect.

YOU'LL NEED...

SKILLS: Basic paint-stripping skills.
TIME: 3 hours for a chair.
TOOLS: Brush, scraper, steel wool, sandpaper, wire brush.

1. Pour stripper on horizontal surfaces and spread it with a brush. Use plenty of remover; don't overbrush.

2. Brush remover in one direction only. Don't attempt to "rub" it into the old finish—float it over the surface.

3. After several minutes, test the surface by scraping with a putty knife. If you strike bare wood, it's ready.

4. Use a wide scraper or putty knife to lift sludge. Keep the blade at a low angle to avoid scratching bare wood.

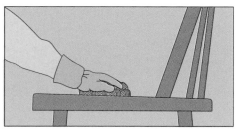

5. Clean off residue with a pad of steel wool. Lift the pad often as you work, and dip it in water to remove sludge.

6. Make a burlap rope to clean round turnings. Dip it in remover and pull it back and forth like a shoe-shine rag.

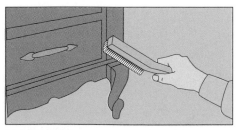

7. For carvings or around moldings, use a wire or fiber brush. Don't use too much pressure because the brush can mar the surface.

8. Remove paint in recesses with a old toothbrush. To strip hardware, soak it in remover, clean with steel wool, then wash it in clean water.

9. If you use a water-soluble stripper, you can wash down the piece with water. Don't use water on veneered surfaces or glued joints.

SANDING A REFINISHING PROJECT

Sanding is the most important phase of every refinishing project. If you're working with old furniture pieces, first make any necessary repairs. Reglue weak joints, glue and clamp loose veneer, patch holes, and repair drawers and guides.

The amount of sanding required depends on the condition of the surface. If it's really banged up, start out by belt-sanding with a coarse- to medium-grit abrasive (see pages 480–482). Be careful, because a belt sander cuts quickly and the edges of the abrasive can groove the wood surface. Dust away sawdust after every step, then wipe the surface with a tack cloth. If the surface is in decent shape, skip this first step.

For the next cut, switch to an orbital sander outfitted with medium- to fine-grit abrasive. Though sanding with the orbital sander should yield a fairly smooth surface, don't stop yet. Unless you plan to bleach or water-stain the wood, dampen the surface of the wood to raise the grain. Use a very fine abrasive on a sanding block to finish. Apply only enough pressure to take off the "tooth" of the grain.

Later, as you're applying the finish, sand lightly between coats with very fine sandpaper. This roughens the surface enough so the next coat can adhere to the previous one.

For final smoothing, substitute very fine steel wool for sandpaper. Even this can quickly cut into sealers and undercoat, so use light, even strokes in the direction of the grain.

YOU'LL NEED...

SKILLS: Basic sanding skills.
TIME: 4 hours for a moderate-size dining room table.
TOOLS: Belt sander, orbital sander, sandpaper, steel wool, drill and counter-sanding attachment, abrasive-coated nylon pads.

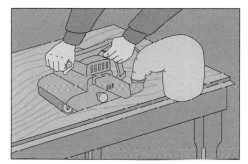

1. Smooth very rough solid wood with a belt sander run with the grain. Don't apply pressure—just guide the sander. Don't use a belt sander on veneers.

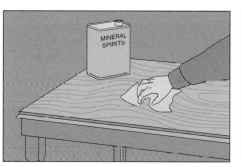

2. Remove all dust and other residue after each sanding. Wipe with a tack cloth or a cheesecloth rag dampened with mineral spirits.

3. Make the second cut with an orbital sander using medium or fine sandpaper. Don't apply much pressure; rather, let the machine do the work.

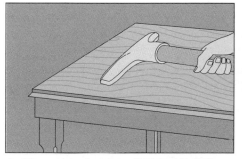

4. If your sander doesn't have a dust pickup and the dust particles become bothersome, vacuum or brush them off, then continue sanding.

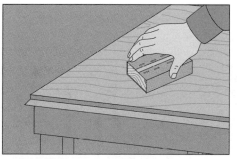

5. Do all final smoothing by hand. Use a fine-grit abrasive-covered sanding block to ensure a smooth, even surface. Sand in one direction only.

6. Extra-fine (000) steel wool does an excellent final smoothing job. Wear gloves when using steel wool, and vacuum up metal particles.

Clear-Finishing Wood (continued)

SANDING A REFINISHING PROJECT (continued)

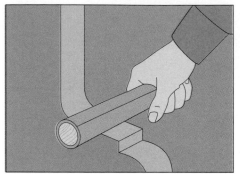

7. Sanding curved surfaces calls for ingenuity. A sanding block fashioned from a dowel rod makes a handy tool.

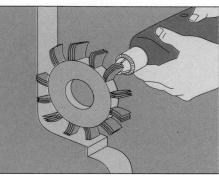

8. A contour sanding attachment for a power drill smooths almost any curve. Use it for removing finishes, too.

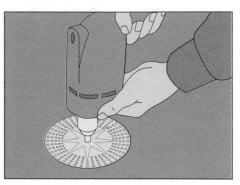

9. A perforated disc takes off lots of wood or old paint quickly. Smooth the surface with an orbital sander.

10. Protect edges of areas that you don't want to sand with strips of masking tape. Make sure the tape is pressed tightly in position.

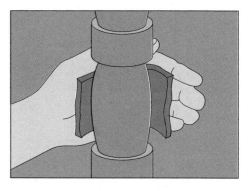

11. Abrasive-coated nylon pads smooth difficult items, such as turnings, legs, and moldings with ease. These pads are washable.

MATERIAL MATTERS   SELECTING WOOD-FINISHING ABRASIVES

Species	Sanding Recommendations
Pine, fir, hemlock, spruce	Rough cut: 60-grit (coarse), open-coat aluminum oxide, silicon carbide, or garnet; second cut: 80-grit, (medium), open-coat; third cut: 120-grit (fine), open-coat
Cedar, redwood	Rough cut: 80-grit (medium), open-coat aluminum oxide, silicon carbide, or garnet; second cut: 100-grit (medium), open-coat; third cut: 120-grit (fine), closed-coat; final: 150-grit (fine), closed-coat
Oak, birch, maple, beech, ash, hickory	Rough cut: 60-grit (coarse), open-coat aluminum oxide, silicon carbide, or garnet; second cut: 80-grit (medium), open-coat; third cut: 120-grit (fine), closed-coat
Walnut, mahogany	Rough cut: 60-grit (coarse), open-coat aluminum oxide, silicon carbide, or garnet; second cut: 80-grit (medium), closed-coat; third cut: 100-grit (medium), closed-coat; finish with 000 steel wool
All veneer woods	First cut: 150-grit (fine) closed-coat aluminum oxide, silicon carbide, or garnet; finish cut: 220-grit (extra-fine), closed-coat; finish with 0000 steel wool

FILLING AND SEALING

Some woods, such as fir and oak, have a prominent grain pattern that no amount of sanding will smooth out. If you want a glassy-smooth finish coat, these surfaces, and those with nail holes or other mars, must be leveled with filler.

After filling a wood surface, you may have to seal it to lock in the filler. Sealers also keep stains from bleeding up through the top coat. Some sealers are applied before stains and slow down the rate at which wood absorbs pigment, giving a lighter, less grainy appearance.

Fillers and sealers differ widely, so read labels carefully before you buy. Some fillers are hole pluggers. These have a doughy consistency that makes it easy to pack them into

depressions. If you want to stain a piece of wood, be warned that many fillers aren't very absorbent, which means the filled areas could show up as whitish spots after you apply the stain. The solution is to buy a filler that has been tinted to match the stain you've selected. Or, you can tint the filler yourself with the stain you'll be using, as long as the filler and stain are compatible.

Other fillers, available in both paste and liquid form, level the pores in open-grain wood. These, also, can be colored.

Sealers amount to nothing more than a clear coating that seals the filler or stain and prevents the finish coats from causing the stain or filler to bleed through or soften. Thinned

shellac makes an excellent sealer, as do some varnishes. Penetrating oils (see page 581) serve as their own sealers. Be sure that the sealer you select won't react adversely with the stain or filler you'll be using underneath, or the final finish you'll be applying over the top.

YOU'LL NEED...

SKILLS: Intermediate sanding and painting skills.
TIME: 3 to 5 hours to fill and seal the surface of a table.
TOOLS: Putty knife, sandpaper, brushes.

Tamp in filler with your finger. Using a putty knife, level it off above the surface to compensate for shrinking.

Once the filler has dried, sand it lightly with a very fine abrasive paper. Be sure to sand with the grain.

Water putty works well with paint. Use on plywood edges or wood end grain, as well as for patching.

To fill end or edge grain, thin water putty to brushing consistency. For other edge techniques, see page 509.

To store leftover water putty, wrap it in plastic or foil. If you don't use it within a few days, toss it.

Apply liquid pore filler with a brush in all directions. Work it into the grain; let it dry 10 to 15 minutes.

Level filler with a piece of cardboard across the grain. When filler is nearly dry, wipe with the grain.

Clear-Finishing Wood (continued)

CHANGING A WOOD'S COLOR

If you're not satisfied with a wood's hue, you can either stain or bleach it. Stain colors wood; bleach lightens it. Except for certain varnish- or sealer-type stains, stains and bleaches do not protect the surface. For that, you need a coat of shellac, varnish, lacquer, or polyurethane.

When you select a stain, make sure it's compatible with the finish you'll be applying. Lacquer and some polyurethanes react adversely to the pigments in a some stains.

Don't let showroom samples determine your final color choice.

They give only a general idea of the finished product. Most dealers offer small samplers so you can make tests (see page 577). Note, too, if the manufacturer recommends sealing the grain before or after you stain it.

Most stains dry a shade or two darker than the color you see. You control the color by the length of time you let the stain penetrate the wood. If it gets too dark, moisten a cloth with the recommended thinner and wipe again to dilute and wash away some of the pigment.

A few stains contain white pigment for a blond or "pickled" look, but a better way to lighten wood is to bleach it. Commercial wood bleaches call for a two-step process that usually involves an overnight wait for the chemicals to do their job.

Laundry bleach or oxalic acid also can be used, but must be neutralized after application with white vinegar or ammonia. Mix one part vinegar or ammonia with 10 parts water. Provide plenty of ventilation; bleach and ammonia give off toxic fumes that can irritate your sinuses and eyes (wear a mask and goggles).

MATERIAL MATTERS   CHOOSING A STAIN

There are many stains from which to choose. Some are designed for ease of use at the expense of control over the result. Others are for the perfectionist who doesn't mind the numerous steps required to achieve the deepest, clearest finish. Consider the end result desired, then decide on the type for the job. Always follow the directions.

Type	Description	Best at	Pros	Cons
Oil-based liquid stains	Traditional stains; concerns now about environmental effects of petroleum vapors	Touching up; restaining	Permanent, doesn't fade; doesn't raise grain; additional coats darken	Hard to find; hard to clean up; unpleasant odor; flammable
Water-based liquid stains	Replacing oil-based stains, because they are easy to use and safe for the environment	Floors and other woodwork; children's toys	Easy to clean up; safe to use; additional coats darken	Raises wood grain; doesn't penetrate deeply; requires finish coat
Penetrating oil stains	Also called Danish oils and rubbing oils; protect wood as well as stain it	High-traffic floors; woods with attractive grain	Doesn't require finish coat; wipes on with a rag; doesn't hide grain	Flammable; limited choice of colors
Gel stains	Simplest for the amateur to use; gel adheres to vertical surfaces and does not run	Complicated or vertical surfaces	Simple to apply; doesn't raise grain; additional coats darken	Expensive; difficult to clean up; limited choice of colors
One-step stain and finish	Quickest way to finish wood if you are not too critical about exact color achieved	Door and window casings	Uniform results; doesn't raise grain; quick to use	Cannot build up color; color not deep or clear

STAINING WOOD

End grain absorbs stain too quickly. Seal end grain with a sanding sealer, then sand lightly before staining.

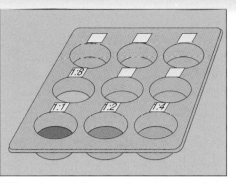

Mix stain and thinner in ratios of 1:0, 1:1, 1:2, 1:4, and 1:8 in a cupcake tin. Label each sample with the ratio.

To evaluate colors, apply test patches of your mixes to an inconspicuous area of the piece to be stained.

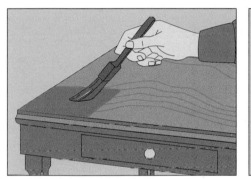

Apply stains by liberally brushing or wiping (as recommended) them on in the direction of the grain.

Let the stain stand for a while, then wipe it off. Darkness of the color depends on how long you wait.

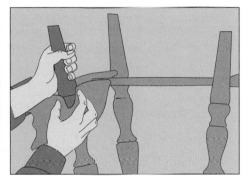

Work gel stains in with a cloth. Apply at least three coats. Let dry, buff with abrasive pad, then apply finish.

BLEACHING WOOD

1. With two-part wood bleaches, flow on the first solution freely. Or, scrub it in with steel wool.

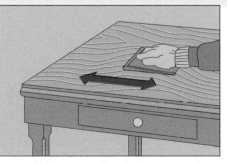

2. Brush the second solution over the first after the required length of time. Let the combination work overnight.

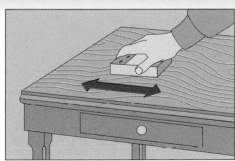

3. Neutralize the bleach as specified in the directions. Wait 24 hours, then sand to remove the grain rise.

Clear-Finishing Wood (continued)

CHOOSING CLEAR FINISHES

There was a time when the choice among natural wood top coatings could provoke hot debate. Should you choose shellac, varnish, oil, or lacquer? Each finish had its partisans and its problems. Then synthetics—chiefly polyurethane, but also epoxies and other plastics—arrived on the scene and settled the issue for most amateur refinishers.

Formulated for easy brushing or spraying, polyurethane dries rapidly; needs no rubbing or polishing, as do oils and lacquers; and makes a surface far more resistant to water, scratching, alcohol, grease, and everyday wear.

The question with polyurethane is deciding when not to use this versatile coating. Why polyurethane a large wall, for example, when you can protect it with shellac for a fraction of the cost?

Synthetic finishes have a few other drawbacks, too. Most build up a thick plastic film that may not enhance a fine old piece of furniture; for a mellow, antique look, apply oil or a quality varnish. Although polyurethane makes an excellent floor coating, you can't smoothly touch-up scuffs and wear marks in heavy traffic areas.

The chart below summarizes the properties and characteristics of today's commonly available finishes.

MATERIAL MATTERS — SELECTING CLEAR FINISHES

Type	Characteristics	Application Tips	Finish	Drying Time	Cost
Natural-resin varnish	Resists scuffs and scratches; available in colors, as well as clear; spar varnish for outdoor applications	Apply with a varnish brush, artist's brush, or cheesecloth; thin with recommended solvent.	From high-gloss to satin to low-gloss	24 to 36 hours; if humid, 36 hours	Low to medium; marine-type, high
Polyurethane varnish	Mar-resistant, durable, remains clear	Use a natural-bristle brush with chisel point, roller, or spray gun; do not apply over shellac.	From high-gloss to dull sheen	1 to 2 hours; 12 hours between coats	Medium to high
Two-part epoxy varnish	Resists scuffs and mars; excellent on floors	Apply with brush; check directions for wood filler usage.	High-gloss	First coat 3 hours; second coat 5 to 8 hours	Medium to high
Shellac	Easily damaged by water; available clear or pigmented; protective coating needed to finish shellac-covered projects	Use small brush with chisel tip; thin with alcohol solvent.	High-gloss; finish may be dulled with steel wool	About $2\frac{1}{2}$ hours to the touch; 3 to 4 hours between coats	Low
Lacquer	Fast-drying; produces a smooth finish; used mostly for furniture	Spray many thin coats; allow last coat to dry 48 to 60 hours; rub with fine steel wool.	Wide variety	Very quickly	Medium
Resin oil finish	Penetrates wood and hardens grain; resists stains, scratches, burns, water, and alcohol	Usually hand-rubbed; most often needs two or three applications.	Deep, rich look	8 to 12 hours	Medium to high

USING NATURAL-RESIN VARNISHES AND SHELLACS

Beautiful, natural-wood results can be yours with varnish, but they're not guaranteed. You have to make them happen. One of the most crucial steps in achieving a beautifully varnished finish is the preparation of the surface to which you plan to apply the finish.

Dust is varnish's mortal enemy. If you're not careful, dust will collect on the newly applied finish and ruin your efforts. To keep this from happening, shut off forced-air heating and cooling ducts in the area and begin thinking dust-free.

Before applying the varnish, thin it according to the instructions on the container label, using the solvent recommended by the manufacturer.

"Float" the varnish onto the surface by spreading it in one direction, then working across the varnish, forming a tic-tac-toe pattern. Fill in the spots you missed.

If while applying varnish you notice air bubbles on the surface of the piece, you are guilty of one of three mistakes: shaking the can, bearing down too hard on the bristles, or wiping the brush's bristles across the rim of the can. To get rid of bubbles after they form, apply more varnish and continue to brush lightly until you work them out.

Applying shellac isn't all that different from laying on varnish, although it usually takes more coats to complete the job. Always use a

new brush when applying shellac. Shellac is available in various cuts or thicknesses. Have your paint dealer advise you on the proper cut for the project at hand.

As a rule, you'll need to apply from five to eight coats of shellac. After letting each coat dry for the time specified, lightly buff the surface with very fine steel wool. Vacuum up all particles and wipe the surface with a tack cloth between coats. Finish the job with hard paste wax, buffing the wax with a cloth to a high-gloss finish. Let the wax dry 24 hours, then wax the surface a second time, buffing it to a brilliant shine.

1. Apply varnish or shellac in several directions, but always finish brushing with the grain. Don't bear down on the brush, or you'll get bubbles.

2. Minimize bubbles, don't shake can, and remove excess varnish from bristles by gently tapping them, rather than wiping, against the can rim.

3. Use very fine sandpaper or steel wool to smooth surface between coats. This roughens the surface enough to allow the next coat to adhere.

4. Level the final coat of varnish or shellac with short, light strokes. Using the tip of the brush results in the smoothest surface.

5. Storing brushes between coats is a breeze. Cut a slot in the plastic lid of a coffee can and insert a nail in the brush handle to suspend bristles in thinner.

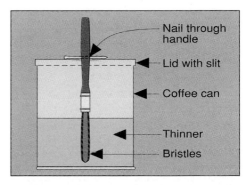

Nail through handle

Lid with slit

Coffee can

Thinner

Bristles

Clear-Finishing Wood (continued)

USING POLYURETHANE VARNISH

When you apply polyurethane varnish to a surface, you're actually sealing it in plastic—a plastic so tough that hardly anything can penetrate it. In addition to this exceptional durability, polyurethane is easy to apply; fairly fast-drying; super-resistant to chemicals and water; and available in low-gloss, satin, and high-gloss finishes.

As with most other finishes, you can apply polyurethane over any surface after completing the preparation steps discussed in this section. If you've applied a stain or wood filler to the surface, make sure the surface is absolutely dry before applying the polyurethane.

Apply polyurethane with a brush, roller, or spray gun. If you plan to spray it, you may have to thin the finish. Be sure to check the thinning recommendations on the container before you start working with it.

All types of wood require at least two coats of polyurethane. The first coat serves as a primer and sealer; the second serves as a finish coat. Sanding is desirable between coats if dust or lint get into the wet finish. It also makes it easier to tell where you applied the following coat.

When you apply the finish—both coats—keep the work between you and a light. In this way, you will see missed spots as the finish is applied. Missed spots are caused by poor penetration into the wood or inadequate application. Missed spots leave little dimples in the finish, and they're almost impossible to spot-in after the material has dried.

Not all polyurethanes are clear. Some are colored to resemble pigmented shellac. With these, you'll usually need to apply several coats of the finish to reach the color tone you want. Each coat of finish will produce a deeper tone, so make a test application on scrap of the same material to determine the number of coats you will need.

If you reach the color tone before achieving the sheen you want, let the surface dry thoroughly, then apply clear polyurethane finish to complete the project. The clear finish will not change the color tone underneath.

If you want to apply a clear polyurethane finish over a colored paint, the first finish should be in perfect condition. Don't expect the polyurethane to hide any defects in the material—it won't.

Low-gloss polyurethanes cost more than high-gloss types and are less durable. Use low-gloss finishes as top coats to cut the shine off high-gloss coatings underneath.

As with other varnish and shellac finishes, dust and dirt control is critical with polyurethane. Work in a still room with no puffs of hot or cold air from heating and cooling ducts. Don't do anything to cause dust to become airborne, especially sweeping the floor just before the finish is applied. Instead, use a tack cloth to remove dust from the work.

USING LACQUER

Lacquer produces a very smooth, quality finish. It dries super-fast, making it a dust-dodger. After it dries, you can rub away dust and brush marks from its surface. It's also inexpensive and available in clear finishes and a variety of colors.

Lacquer's fast drying time also is one of its disadvantages. It dries so quickly that you must correct mistakes immediately. Another disadvantage is that you can't apply lacquer over painted finishes. The lacquer's solvent will lift off the paint finish that lies underneath it.

Again, proper preparation is a key. Prepare the surface as you would for any other clear wood finish (see pages 571–575).

Lacquer may sag and run. It's best to use many thin coats with a spray gun. If you spot a sag or run, let it dry, then remove the defect using wet or dry sandpaper. Or, wipe the run or sag immediately with a soft, lint-free cloth saturated with lacquer thinner. Spot-fill the area you wiped and continue on with the work. The blemish will show after the lacquer has dried, but it won't be noticeable after the surface has been rubbed properly with steel wool or rubbing compound and wax.

Generally, for lacquer to look and perform its best, you'll need to apply at least three coats. Unlike most clear finishes, you don't have to smooth the surface with sandpaper or steel wool between coats because the material "dissolves" and blends into the preceding coats.

After the lacquer has dried for 48 hours, finish by rubbing the surface with very fine steel wool and hard wax or rubbing compound. As you do this, work in a small area. Completely rub out this area before you move on to other areas. Otherwise, the compound will dry and be hard to buff off.

USING OIL FINISHES

That deep, rich patina you see on old gun stocks and some antique furniture probably consists of nothing more than boiled linseed oil and turpentine—coat upon coat, laboriously rubbed into the wood's grain. You can do the same yourself. Just combine two parts oil with one part turpentine, pour it on, rub off the excess, and let it dry completely. Repeat and repeat and repeat until you've totally saturated the grain, a process that may take six to 10 applications and dozens of hours of tiresome rubbing.

Achieving this lustrous effect needn't be that difficult, however. Using a commercial resin-oil finish, sometimes referred to as Danish oil, will ease the workload considerably. Like ordinary oil, these penetrate into the wood for a surface that's more than skin deep. They also contain a synthetic or natural resin that hardens inside the wood grain. The result: a finish that actually toughens the wood, yet doesn't call for nearly as much rubbing.

Usually, you need only two or three applications of resin oil to get a deep, lasting finish. Unlike linseed oil, it dries overnight, doesn't gum up in warm weather, and rarely needs to be renewed. Yet, it's just as resistant to stains, scratches, minor burns, water, and alcohol. If damage does occur, you can just rub it out with sandpaper or steel wool and apply more penetrating oil. Unlike polyurethane varnish, oil lends itself to spot repairs.

Penetrating resin oils vary somewhat. Some include varnish, others plastics, and still others are combined with wax. A few also come in different weights to suit open- or closed-pore woods. Many come in various colors, or you can tint them for staining effects.

Read the manufacturer's instructions before applying a resin oil. Most go on with the easy steps illustrated below.

1. Flood the surface with oil and spread it with a brush or cloth. The first coat will soak in quickly.

2. Wait a few minutes, then test the surface. If dry, apply more oil. Wait a few minutes and wipe off the excess.

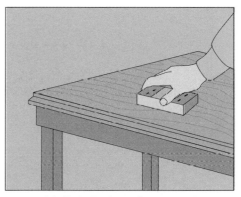

3. Sand lightly before the second coat to remove any raised grain. After this, don't sand again.

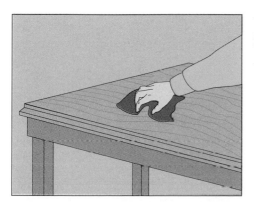

4. Apply subsequent coats with the grain, rubbing hard. Let dry 24 hours between coats. Apply more coats until you're satisfied with the finish.

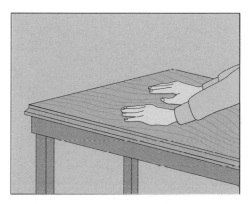

5. Apply the final coat with your palms; your hands supply heat. If desired, finish with a hard wax.

Dealing with Hazardous Materials

We deal with some hazardous wastes almost daily. The chart below lists common waste products and how to dispose of them. If you live in an older home, you may be living with these hazardous substances:

■ Radon is a radioactive gas generated in the bedrock of some regions of the United States. Radon can enter a home through its foundation. Contact your state health department for testing information.

■ Asbestos was once used extensively in siding, floor tiles, joint compound, and pipe insulation. It is dangerous only if disturbed. Do not cut, sand, or handle material that might contain it.

■ Lead was used in paint, water pipes, and pipe solder. Exposed paint predating 1960 should be painted over, and lead pipes should be replaced. Soldered copper joints present little danger.

■ Formaldehyde is a gas emitted by many building products—particularly particleboard. Some people are sensitive to the gas and experience coughing, headaches, dizziness, and nausea. Formaldehyde content is now enforced by federal standards. Fortunately, emissions decrease over time. If you suffer from these symptoms, call your state health department for an air test.

DISPOSING OF HAZARDOUS WASTES

This chart provides general guidelines on how to dispose of common household hazardous wastes. Be aware that waste management guidelines will vary considerably from community to community. Before you dispose of anything that you think might be hazardous, check with a local source, such as your local waste collector or waste management agency, your local or state environmental protection department, or the County Extension Service.

The items checked in the "Special Disposal Problem" column should not be discarded in common trash. Many communities now sponsor annual or semiannual hazardous waste pickup days for these items or have special hazardous waste drop-off facilities where you can take them.

Waste	OK in Trash	Dilute and Flush	Evaporate and Place in Trash	Recycle or Return	Special Disposal Problem
Aerosol cans, empty	●				
Automobile items					
Antifreeze			●		
Battery				●	
Diesel fuel					●
Gasoline					●
Motor oil				●	
Tires					●
Cleaners and solvents					
Brush cleaner					●
Degreaser solvent					●
Drain cleaner		●			
Dry-cleaning fluid			●		
Mildew remover	●				
Oven cleaner		●			
Paints and finishes					
Latex paint			●		
Oil-based paint					●
Mineral spirits			●		
Paint stripper		●			
Paint thinner			●		
Rust remover		●			
Wood preservative					●
Pesticides					
Insecticide					●
Pet pest collar					●
Rat poison					●
Weed killer					●

CONVERTING ENGLISH SYSTEM UNITS TO METRIC SYSTEM UNITS

ENGLISH SYSTEM UNITS TO METRIC EQUIVALENTS			METRIC UNITS TO ENGLISH SYSTEM EQUIVALENTS		
To Convert From	**Multiply By**	**To Get**	**To Convert From**	**Multiply By**	**To Get**
Inches	25.4	Millimetres	Millimetres	0.0394	Inches
Inches	2.54	Centimetres	Centimetres	0.3937	Inches
Feet	30.48	Centimetres	Centimetres	0.0328	Feet
Feet	0.3048	Metres	Metres	3.2808	Feet
Yards	0.9144	Metres	Metres	1.0936	Yards
Miles	1.6093	Kilometres	Kilometres	0.6214	Miles
Square inches	6.4516	Square centimetres	Square centimetres	0.1550	Square inches
Square feet	0.0929	Square metres	Square metres	10.764	Square feet
Square yards	0.8361	Square metres	Square metres	1.1960	Square yards
Acres	0.4047	Hectares	Hectares	2.4711	Acres
Square miles	2.5899	Square kilometres	Square kilometres	0.3861	Square miles
Cubic inches	16.387	Cubic centimetres	Cubic centimetres	0.0610	Cubic inches
Cubic feet	0.0283	Cubic metres	Cubic metres	35.315	Cubic feet
Cubic feet	28.316	Litres	Litres	0.0353	Cubic feet
Cubic yards	0.7646	Cubic metres	Cubic metres	1.3079	Cubic yards
Cubic yards	764.55	Litres	Litres	0.0013	Cubic yards
Fluid ounces	29.574	Millilitres	Millilitres	0.0338	Fluid ounces
Cups	0.2366	Litres	Litres	4.2268	Cups
Pints	0.4732	Litres	Litres	2.1134	Pints
Quarts	0.9464	Litres	Litres	1.0567	Quarts
Gallons	3.7854	Litres	Litres	0.2642	Gallons
Pints	0.5506	Litres	Litres	1.8162	Pints
Quarts	1.1012	Litres	Litres	0.9081	Quarts
Pecks	8.8098	Litres	Litres	0.1135	Pecks
Bushels	35.239	Litres	Litres	0.0284	Bushels
Bushels	3.5239	Dekalitres	Dekalitres	0.2838	Bushels
Drams	1.7718	Grams	Grams	0.5644	Drams
Ounces	28.350	Grams	Grams	0.0353	Ounces
Pounds	0.4536	Kilograms	Kilograms	2.2046	Pounds

To convert from degrees Fahrenheit (°F) to degrees Celsius (°C), first subtract 32, then multiply by ⅝ (0.5555).

To convert from degrees Celsius (°C) to degrees Fahrenheit (°F), first multiply by ⅘ (1.8), then add 32.

Glossary

For words not included here—or for more about those that are—consult the Index on pages 590–600.

Actual dimensions. The exact measurement of a piece of lumber. For instance, a 2×4 is actually 1½ inches thick by 3½ inches wide. *See also* Nominal dimensions.

Ampere (Amp, A). A measure of the amount of electrical current going through a circuit at any given time. *See also* Volt and Watt.

Balusters. Spindles that help support a staircase handrail.

Bat. Half of a brick.

Batt. A section of fiberglass or rock-wool insulation measuring 15 or 23 inches wide by 4 to 8 feet long.

Batten. A narrow strip used to cover joints between boards or panels.

Beam. A horizontal support member. *See also* Post and Post-and-beam.

Bearing wall. An interior or exterior wall that helps support the roof or the floor joists above.

Blanket. Fiberglass or rock-wool insulation in a long roll 15 or 23 inches wide.

Blind-nail. To nail so that the head of the nail is not visible on the surface of the wood.

Bond. The pattern in which bricks or other masonry units are laid. Also, the cementing action of an adhesive.

Box. To mix the same kind and color of paint from small containers together before painting to ensure the paint's color is exactly the same throughout the painting job.

Bridging. Boards nailed between joists to add rigidity and keep the joists from warping. Often used to quiet squeaking floors.

Btu (British thermal unit). The amount of heat needed to raise 1 pound of water 1 degree Fahrenheit. Heating and cooling equipment commonly is rated by the Btu it can deliver or absorb. *See also* Heat gain and Heat loss.

Building codes. Community ordinances governing the manner in which a home may be constructed or modified. Most codes primarily are concerned with fire and health; some have sections relating to electrical, plumbing, and structural work. *See also* Zoning.

Butt. To place materials end-to-end or end-to-edge without overlapping.

Butter. To smear mortar on an edge, face, side, or end of a brick or block prior to placement on a surface.

Butt hinge. The most common type. One leaf attaches to the door's edge, the other to its jamb.

Cantilever. A beam or beams projecting beyond a support member.

Casing. Trim around a door, window, or other opening.

Caulk. Any of a variety of different compounds used to seal seams and joints against infiltration of water and air.

Cement. A powder that serves as the binding element in concrete and mortar. Also, any adhesive.

CFM (cubic feet per minute). A rating that expresses the amount of air a blower or fan can move.

Chalking. The tendency of some exterior paints to gradually erode over a period of time.

Chalk line. An enclosed reel of string coated with colored chalk, used to mark straight lines by pulling the string taut and snapping it, leaving a line of chalk.

Circuit breaker. A protective switch that automatically shuts off current in the event of a short or overload. *See also* Fuse and Short circuit.

Codes. See Building codes.

Compressor. The part of a cooling unit or heat pump that compresses refrigerant gas so it absorbs heat.

Concrete. A basic building and paving material made by mixing water with sand, gravel, and cement. *See also* Mortar and Cement.

Condensing unit. The outdoor segment of a cooling system. It includes a compressor and condensing coil designed to give off heat. *See also* Evaporator coil.

Conduit. Metal pipes used to contain and protect electrical wiring in exposed settings.

Coping. A rounded or beveled cap at the top of a wall so water will run off. Also, a curved cut made so that one contoured molding joins neatly with another.

Corner bead. Lightweight, perforated metal angle used to reinforce outside corners in drywall construction.

Courses. Parallel layers of building materials, such as bricks, shingles, or siding, laid up horizontally.

Cove. A concave curve where vertical and horizontal surfaces join.

Cripple. A short stud above or below a door or window opening.

Crown. Paving that is slightly humped so water will run off. Also, a contoured molding sometimes installed at the junctures of walls and ceilings.

Cupping. A type of warping that causes boards to curl up at their edges.

Dado. A groove cut into a piece of wood, usually to secure a plank or board in place and to give the board added support.

Damper. A valve inside a duct or flue that can be used to slow or stop the flow of air or smoke.

Deadbolt. A locking device activated only with a key or thumb turn. Unlike a latch, which has a beveled tongue, deadbolts have squared-off ends.

Double cylinder. A type of lock that must be operated with a key from inside, as well as outside.

Dry wall. A masonry wall laid up without mortar.

Drywall. An interior building material consisting of sheets of gypsum that are faced with heavy paper on both sides. Also known as gypsum board, plasterboard, and Sheetrock.

DWV (drain-waste-vent). The section of a plumbing system that carries water and sewer gases out of a home.

Easement. A legal right for restricted use of someone's property. Easements often are granted to utility companies so they may service the utility lines running through a property.

Eaves. The lower edge of a roof that projects beyond the wall.

Efflorescence. A whitish powder sometimes exuded by the mortar joints in masonry work. It's caused by salts rising to the surface.

Elbow (L). A plumbing or electrical fitting that lets you change directions in runs of pipe or conduit.

Evaporator coil. The part of a cooling system that absorbs heat from air in your home. *See also* Condensing unit.

Expansion joint. Flexible material between two surfaces that enables joints to ride out differing rates of expansion and contraction.

Fascia board. Horizontal trim attached to the outside ends of rafters or to the top of an exterior wall.

Female. Any part, such as a nut or fitting, into which another (male) part can be inserted. Internal threads are female.

Fire blocking. Short horizontal members sometimes nailed between studs, usually located about halfway up a wall.

Firebrick. Highly heat-resistant brick for lining fireplaces and boilers.

Flashing. Metal or composition strips used to seal junctions between roofing and other surfaces or in the valleys between different slopes.

Floating. The next-to-last stage in concrete work, when you smooth off the job and bring water to the surface.

Flue. A pipe or other channel that carries off smoke and combustion gases to the outside air.

Fluorescent lamp. A light source that uses an ionization process to produce ultraviolet radiation. This radiation is absorbed by the inner coating on a fluorescent tube and re-emitted as visible light.

Footing. The base on which a masonry wall rests. It spreads out the load.

Framing. The skeletal or structural support of a home. Sometimes called framework.

Frost line. The depth to which the ground freezes below the surface. This varies from region to region and determines how deep footings must be.

Furring. Lightweight wood or metal strips that even up a wall or ceiling for paneling. On masonry, furring provides a surface on which to nail.

Fuse. A safety device designed to burn out if a circuit shorts or overloads. This protects against fire. *See also* Circuit breaker and Short circuit.

Gable. The triangular area on the end of a house's external wall located beneath the sloping parts of a roof and the line that runs between the roof's eaves.

Galvanized. Coated with a zinc outer covering to protect against oxidation. Nails and screws used in exterior applications often are galvanized to prevent them from rusting.

Gate valve. A valve that lets you completely stop—but not modulate—the flow of water within a pipe. *See also* Globe valve.

GFCI (ground-fault circuit interrupter). A safety device that almost instantly shuts down a circuit if an electrical leakage occurs. Codes commonly require them on bathroom and outdoor circuits.

Glazing. The process of installing glass, by securing it with glazier's points and glazing compound.

Globe valve. A valve that lets you adjust the flow of water to any rate between fully on and fully off. *See also* Gate valve.

Grade. Ground level. Also, the elevation at any given point.

Graphite. A soft, black carbon powder used to lubricate working metal parts such as those found in a doorknob or lock.

Ground. Refers to electricity's property of seeking the shortest route to earth. Neutral wires have the job of grounding a circuit. An additional grounding wire—or the sheathing on metal-clad cable or conduit—protects against shock if the neutral wire is interrupted.

Grout. Thin mortar that fills the joints between tiles or other masonry.

Gypsum board. See drywall.

Hardboard. A manufactured building material made by pressing wood fibers into sheet goods.

Header. Heavier framing—usually two standard dimension boards sandwiched together and laid on edge—typically above the top of a window, door, or other opening as support. In masonry, a header course of bricks or stones laid on edge provides strength.

Heat gain. Heat coming into a home from sources other than its heating/cooling system. Most gains come from the sun.

Heat loss. Heat escaping from a home. Heat gains and losses are expressed in Btu per hour.

Heat pump. A reversible air-conditioner that extracts heat from outside and inside air.

HID (high-intensity-discharge) lamp. A lamp that operates in the same way as a fluorescent tube, but that has a bulb like an incandescent lamp.

Hip. The outside angle of a roof formed by the intersection of two sloped sides of the roof.

Hot wire. The wire that carries electricity to a receptacle or other device—in contrast to a neutral wire, which carries electricity away. *See also* Ground.

Incandescent lamp. A lamp using a metal filament that glows brightly as electrical current flows through it.

Jack studs. Studs at both sides of a door, window, or other opening that are used to support the header. Sometimes called trimmers.

Jamb. The top and sides of a door, window, or other opening. Includes studs, frame, and trim.

Joint compound. A synthetic-based premixed paste used in combination with paper or fiberglass tape to conceal joints between drywall panels. *See also* Taping.

Joists. Horizontal framing members that support a floor and/or ceiling.

Kilowatt (kw). One-thousand watts. A kilowatt hour is the base unit used to measure electrical consumption. *See also* Watt.

King studs. Studs on both ends of a header that help support the header and run from the wall's sole plate to its top plate.

Laminating. Bonding together two or more layers of materials.

Latch. A beveled metal tongue operated by a spring-loaded knob or lever. The tongue's bevel lets you close the door and engage the locking mechanism, if any, without using a key. Contrasts with dead bolt.

Lath. Strips of wood, expanded metal mesh, or a special drywall that serve as a base for plaster or stucco.

Level. True horizontal. Also a tool used to determine level. *See also* Plumb.

Lintel. A load-bearing beam over an opening, such as a door or fireplace, in masonry.

Low-voltage wiring. Electrical systems that use between 6 and 30 volts to run. A transformer steps down the power from the voltage of the house. Low-voltage systems include phones, doorbells, thermostats, and some lighting.

Male. Any part, such as a bolt, designed to fit into another (female) part. External threads are male.

Mason's line. A heavy string that does not sag or stretch, making it useful for marking the placement of building materials or as a line to indicate level when building a wall. Often brightly colored so it is highly visible.

Miter. A joint formed by beveling the edges or ends of two pieces of material, then fitting them together to make an angle.

Mortar. The bonding agent between bricks, blocks, or other masonry units. Consists of water, sand, and cement—but not gravel. *See also* Concrete.

Mortise. A hole, slot, groove, or other recess into which another element fits. Also the act of making such a hole, slot, or groove.

NEC (National Electrical Code). A set of rules governing safe wiring methods. Local codes—which are backed by law—may partially differ from the NEC.

Neutral wire. Usually color-coded white, a wire that carries electricity from an outlet back to ground. *See also* Hot wire and Ground.

Newel post. A post at the bottom, landing, or top of a staircase to which the handrail is secured.

Nipple. A short length of pipe. Typically threaded and used to connect to runs of pipe for water or gas supply.

No-hub. A clamp-and-sleeve system for joining together cast-iron drainage pipes. (Molten lead was used to join the joints of older hub-type pipes.)

Nominal dimensions. The labels given to a standard piece of lumber. For example, 2×4 is the name for a rough-cut piece of about 2×4 inches. It is then finished by planing and sometimes sanding it down to its actual dimensions. *See also* Actual dimensions.

OC (on center). The distance from the center of one regularly spaced framing member to the center of the next. Studs and joists commonly are 16 or 24 inches OC.

Packing nut. The nut that holds the stem of a valve in place; contains stem packing material to prevent leaks from the stem.

Panel. Wood, glass, plastic, or other material set into a frame, such as in a door. Also, a large, flat, rectangular building material such as plywood, hardboard, or drywall.

Partition. An interior dividing wall. Partitions may or may not be bearing.

Pennyweight. A system of measuring the size of a nail. Originally derived from a unit of weight, pennyweight is represented by the letter "d." For example, a "10 penny" nail would be designated 10d.

Pier. A masonry post. Piers often serve as footings for wood or steel posts.

Pilot hole. A small-diameter hole that guides a nail or screw.

Pilot light. A small, continuous flame that ignites gas or oil burners when needed.

Plenum. The large hot-air supply duct leading from a furnace before branching into ducts.

Plumb. True vertical. *See also* Level.

Point. To finish a masonry wall by filling the cracks with mortar or cement.

Post. Any vertical support member.

Post-and-beam. A basic building method that uses just a few hefty posts and beams to support an entire structure. Contrasts with stud framing.

Pressure-treated wood. Lumber that has been saturated with a preservative.

Primer. A first coating formulated to seal raw surfaces and hold succeeding finish coats.

PVC (polyvinyl chloride). A type of plastic pipe that's suitable for cold water, but not hot.

Radiation. Energy transmitted from a heat source through the air surrounding it. So-called "radiators" actually depend more on convection than radiation.

Rafters. Parallel framing members that support a roof.

Rail. Any relatively lightweight horizontal element, especially those found in fences. Also, the horizontal pieces between panels in a panel door.

Rake. The inclined edge of the roof of a home.

Receptacle box. A small box made to accommodate electrical devices such as switches and plugs.

Retaining wall. A structure that holds back a slope and prevents erosion.

Ridgeboard. Topmost beam at the peak of a roof to which rafters tie.

Rise. The vertical distance from one point to another above it; a measurement you need in planning a stairway or ramp. *See also* Run.

Riser. The upright piece between two stairsteps. *See also* Tread.

Roofing cement. Asphalt- or plastic-based compound used as an adhesive and to seal flashings and minor leaks.

Roughing-in. The initial stage of a plumbing, electrical, carpentry, or other project, when all components that won't be seen after the second finishing phase are assembled.

Run. The horizontal distance a ramp or stairway traverses. *See also* Rise. Also a length of electrical cable or conduit.

R-value. A measure of the resistance to heat transfer that an insulating material offers. The higher the R-value, the more effective the insulation.

Saddle. *See* Threshold.

Sash. The part of a window that can be opened, consisting of a frame and one or more panes of glass.

Screed. A board used to level concrete after it has been poured into a form.

Setback. The distance a home must be built from property lines (dictated by local zoning ordinances). Also, a temporary change in a thermostat's setting.

Settlement. Shifts in a structure, usually caused by freeze-thaw cycles underground.

Shake. A shingle that has been split, rather than cut, from wood.

Consequently, shakes often have a rougher, more natural appearance than standard shingles.

Sheathing. The first covering on a roof or exterior wall, usually fastened directly to rafters or studs.

Shim. Thin material inserted to make adjustments in level or plumb. Tapered wood shingles make excellent shims in carpentry work.

Shoe molding. Strips of molding commonly used where a baseboard meets the floor. Sometimes known as base shoe.

Short circuit. A situation that occurs when hot and neutral wires accidentally come in contact with each other. Fuses and circuit breakers protect against fire that could result from a short circuit.

Siding. Planks, boards, or shingles used as an external covering of the walls of a home. Typically nailed to the sheathing.

Sill. The lowest horizontal piece of a window, door, or wall framework.

Sill cock. The valve of an outdoor faucet. Building codes frequently require sill cocks to be frost-proof so that they are not damaged by ice produced by cold weather.

Sleepers. Boards laid directly over a masonry floor to serve as nailers for plywood, or strip or plank flooring.

Soffit. Covering attached to the underside of eaves or a staircase.

Soil pipe. A large pipe that carries liquid and solid wastes to a sewer or septic tank.

Sole plate. Bottommost horizontal part of a stud partition. When a plate rests on a foundation, it's called a sill plate.

Span. The distance between supports.

Spline. A thin piece of wood fitted into slots on the edges of two joined boards to strengthen the joint.

Stack. The main drain pipe that runs vertically through a house. The stack carries away sewage and waste water to the sewage system and vents gases above the roofline.

Stile. The vertical upright on either side (and sometimes the center) of a panel door.

Story pole. A pole with lines marked on it that indicate the height of courses in a wall or other vertical distances in construction. Used to frequently check the height of building materials rather than using a tape measure each time.

Strike. The plate on a door frame that engages a latch or dead bolt. In masonry, it means to smooth a joint of mortar between bricks, blocks, or stones.

Stringer. A long piece of lumber used to support stairs.

Stud framing. A building method that distributes structural loads to each of a series of relatively lightweight studs. Contrasts with post-and-beam.

Studs. Vertical 2×3, 2×4, or 2×6 framing members spaced at regular intervals within a wall.

Subfloor. The first layer of a floor. Usually made with planks laid across joists. *See also* Underlayment.

Sweep. A flexible strip placed on the bottom edge of a door for insulation and to prevent drafts.

T. A T-shaped plumbing fitting.

Taping. The process of covering drywall joints with paper tape and joint compound.

Thermocouple. An electric device for measuring temperature.

Three-four-five (3-4-5) triangle. A simple mathematical method to check whether a large angle is square (90 degrees). Measure 3 feet along one side, 4 feet along the other; if the corner is square, the diagonal distance between those two points will equal 5 feet.

Threshold. The plate at the bottom of some—usually exterior—door openings. Sometimes called a saddle.

Timber. A structural or framing member that is 5 inches or larger in the smallest dimension.

Toenail. To attach to boards by nailing diagonally through the corner of one board into the other board.

Top plate. The topmost horizontal element of a stud-frame wall.

Trap. A plumbing fitting that holds water to prevent air, gas, and vermin from backing up into a fixture.

Tread. The level part of a staircase. *See also* Riser.

Trimmers. *See* Jack studs.

UL (Underwriters Laboratories). An independent testing agency that checks electrical and other components for safety hazards.

Underlayment. Cement-like product that is used to level floors prior to laying down the surface material. Sometimes used to refer to the subfloor material or material laid on top of the subfloor. Usually some type of plywood installed below the surface material of the floor. *See also* Subfloor.

Union. A plumbing fitting that joins pipes end-to-end so they can be dismantled.

Utility knife. A razor-blade knife with a long handle and retractable blade.

Valley. The intersection of two roof slopes.

Vapor barrier. A waterproof membrane in a floor, wall, or ceiling that blocks the transfer of moisture.

Volt (V). A measure of electrical pressure. Volts × amps = watts.

Warping. Any distortion in a material.

Watt (W). A measure of the power an electrical device consumes. Watt hours (WH) express the quantity of energy consumed. *See also* Volt, Ampere, and Kilowatt.

Y. A Y-shaped plumbing fitting.

Zoning. Ordinances regulating the ways in which a property may be used in any given neighborhood. Zoning laws may limit where you can locate a structure. *See also* Building codes.

INDEX